IBM's Early Computers

Memories That Shaped an Industry, Emerson W. Pugh, 1984
Memoirs of a Computer Pioneer, Maurice V. Wilkes, 1985
IBM's Early Computers, by Charles J. Bashe, Lyle R. Johnson, John H. Palmer, and Emerson W. Pugh, 1986

IBM's Early Computers

*Charles J. Bashe, Lyle R. Johnson,
John H. Palmer, and Emerson W. Pugh*

The MIT Press
Cambridge, Massachusetts
London, England

Second printing, 1986

Photographs for which credit is not given in the captions are from IBM sources.

This book was set in Baskerville by The MIT Press Computergraphics Department and printed and bound by Halliday Lithograph in the United States of America.

Library of Congress Cataloging in Publication Data
Main entry under title:

IBM's early computers.
  Bibliography: p.
  Includes index.
    1. IBM computers—History. I. Bashe, Charles J.
QA76.8.I1015I245   1986   001.64   85-7921
ISBN 0-262-02225-7

Contents

Series Foreword

This book is the third to appear in a new series devoted to all aspects of the history of computers and of information processing. Earlier volumes have been devoted to such topics as technical innovation and the decisions leading to a new computer system or the memoirs of a major pioneer in the area of computer design and operation. It is planned that future volumes will deal with the many aspects of the development of systems, of hardware, and of software. There will be both general works and specialized monographs.

Some books being planned for the series will be of a biographical or autobiographical nature. Others will concentrate on particular aspects of computer history, such as the development and use of a major programming language. It is hoped that there will be technical histories of the industrial companies that have been part of the computer revolution as well as studies of the role of universities and of individuals in this revolution. One goal of the series is to sponsor historically based inquiries into the social, political, and economic aspects of the introduction and use of computers and of information processing.

I. Bernard Cohen
William Aspray

Foreword

All too many histories of technologically based companies prove to be "business histories" rather than records of technical development. *IBM's Early Computers* is devoted primarily to technology; it endeavors to chronicle, understand, and interpret the technical stages of the transformation of IBM from a relatively small manufacturer and supplier of electric accounting machinery into a large and rapidly growing computer company. The time span extends to about 1962, when IBM's revenues from computers began to surpass those from its more traditional accounting machines.

It is difficult today to imagine how small IBM was during the 1920s and early 30s, when the total number of its employees was only a few thousand. In those days product improvement depended for the most part on clever inventors, mechanics, and draftsmen—that is, on men characterized more by their talents for mechanical design than by formal academic training. The most celebrated of these early innovators was James Wares Bryce. Honored in 1936 as one of the ten "greatest living inventors," Bryce was by then holder of more than 400 patents. During the 1930s a few professionals of a new type began to appear on the company's rolls, men with college degrees and in some cases with training in electrical engineering. The latter group contained some figures who emerged to play heroic roles in subsequent expansions of the company's business.

World War II was characterized on the technological plane by tremendous advances and applications in various aspects of electronics, of which the most celebrated example is radar. It has often been remarked (for example, by Maurice Wilkes in another book in this series) how important for the development of the computer was the wartime experience in electronics. In the immediate post-war years IBM moved forward from the 1945 state of electronics and pioneered in new developments and applications of electronics. A significant result was the IBM 604 electronic calculator, introduced in the fall of 1948, a machine important in the transition from calculators to computers. Within the next few years IBM developed its first commercially available computer, the 701, originally called the Defense Calculator.

The company's entry into the computer business required a vigorous upgrading of technical staff and research personnel. In addition to recruitment of scientists and engineers with bachelor's or master's degrees, there was a conscious effort to enlist persons of academic stature. The first doctorate-level employee hired was Wallace J. Eckert, a Columbia University astronomer and pioneer in the use of punched-card equipment for scientific calculation. Eckert (Ph.D., Yale 1931) was a specialist in celestial mechanics; he had directed the Thomas J. Watson Astronomical Computing Bureau at Columbia University and in 1940 had edited the American *Air Almanac*. He joined IBM as director of the Pure Science Department in 1945, in time to participate in the planning of the SSEC and the NORC.

One especially interesting theme of this book is the parallel but independent development, during the 1950s, of machines for scientific (or engineering) and business users. Only after a decade or so did it become widely practical to design and manufacture general-purpose computers that could function well in both domains. Another theme that emerges is the frequent interaction between agencies of the federal government and IBM; as in the case of other computer companies, this took the form of early support for the design, development, and manufacture of computers or computer systems such as SAGE and Stretch. Of most importance in the long run, perhaps, was the opportunity to recruit and to train a cadre of specialist engineers and technicians who subsequently would use their acquired knowledge and expertise to design and build many of the company's computers.

This book is primarily a technical history, but it is not limited to a simple chronicle of events or to a bare exposition of the technical aspects of representative products, functional components, and modes of operation. Rather, the authors have explored the role of management in planning and decision-making at crucial stages. Although a volume of equal size could and probably should be written on the managerial and business aspects of the subject, enough of this important topic has been introduced here to provide some understanding of the kind of interplay that takes place between the internal pressures of technological innovation and the external forces of management and the marketplace. An especially attractive feature of the book is the discussion of the interactions of personalities in the making of decisions that began, altered, or terminated lines of innovation or development.

Although this volume has four authors, its preparation has been from the start a cooperative and nonhierarchical venture. These authors came to their project with credentials that included lengthy participation in the computer industry in a wide variety of roles. The book was conceived and written without any company mandate or directive other than to produce as accurate and complete a technical history as possible.

Those of us who are committed to the historiography of the computer have long expressed the need for technical histories of the many companies that pioneered in the hardware and the software that have produced the computer revolution. We look forward to the appearance of yet additional histories of this type, so that we may attain a thorough evaluation of all the interlocking series of advances that have brought us through mainframes, minicomputers, and microcomputers to the present state of the art and the science.

I. Bernard Cohen

Preface

At the end of World War II, the mainstay of mechanized data processing was still the punched-card accounting machine. The concept of stored-program control was new, and the application of electronics to computation had not yet touched the marketplace. But during a hectic period of about fifteen years thereafter, gears, cams, and relays were largely displaced, first by vacuum tube circuitry and then in turn by transistor circuitry. Before the end of the period, as a result of a drastic turnabout, most of the effort of the IBM laboratories had been redirected from electromechanical accounting machines to electronic computers. During these years the company underwent changes that affected nearly every aspect of its existence.

This book describes the technical work that supported IBM's transformation and moved the company into the emerging computer industry. Except for a first chapter that provides a brief introduction to the company's prior activities, the narrative extends from the war to the early 1960s—from early ventures in electronics to the profusion of computer designs that triggered the development of a unified, modular architecture for IBM System/360. Although we always focused on IBM, we treated external activities when a broader perspective seemed helpful or when such activities were found to have contributed to developments within IBM.

For source material we have relied heavily on IBM publications, internal technical reports, interviews, and correspondence provided by IBM employees or preserved in IBM archival files. Our other primary source was the public literature of the computer industry.

Our emphasis on the fundamentals of technological change has left unchronicled many of the company's experiences outside the laboratories—in manufacturing, field servicing, and marketing, for example. Histories of these deserving subjects, following emphases of their own, would undoubtedly lead to a fuller appreciation of the many dimensions of the company's transformation.

From many concurrent streams of events we have selected those that seemed best to represent the main course of IBM's technical experiences. And because ill-fated projects can be as significant as successful ones in determining the course of history, the former were not arbitrarily excluded. Given the rigorous competition for space, some important events and projects inevitably will be judged to have received too little attention. If such judgments result in additional contributions to the historical literature, our efforts will have been further justified and rewarded.

In our account of the work in the research and development laboratories, we found it practical to mention the names of only a few of the thousands of engineers, programmers, and scientists whose contributions were significant. While these few were important in their own right, the record of their achievements serves also to typify the work of many others whose contributions were essential to IBM's progress.

The support of the IBM Corporation and encouragement from many people both inside and outside the company have helped to make the preparation of this book a pleasant task. We have especially appreciated being given the freedom to develop a technical history in accordance with our own guidelines.

Charles J. Bashe
Lyle R. Johnson
John H. Palmer
Emerson W. Pugh

Yorktown Heights, New York

Acknowledgments

Many people helped in the preparation of this history, either through direct assistance to the authors or through their own history-keeping efforts over the years. Emanuel R. Piore, then IBM vice-president and chief scientist, took an important step in the late 1960s when he commissioned a program of oral-history interviews to preserve the recollections of many scientists, engineers, programmers, and planners of both the punched-card and computer eras. He was also influential in the decision, made during 1979, to prepare a technical history of IBM's computers.

Ralph E. Gomory provided in IBM's Research Divison an environ-ment well suited to the requirements of the task. Hirsh G. Cohen contributed to the earliest plans for the history and has provided helpful counsel throughout the project.

Invited in mid-1980 to initiate the effort, I had the good fortune to be joined by three coauthors with a common interest in the history of computers and computer technology. This interest, along with their professional experiences during the early years of the computer, rep-resented the highest qualifications for the task. Their thoroughness, concern for historical accuracy, and enthusiastic spirit have made the collaboration a most rewarding one for me. And the four of us are thankful to those in the top management of IBM for giving us the opportunity and encouragement to write this book without constraint on content or style.

I. Bernard Cohen, in the dual role of series editor and consultant to the authors, has made valuable suggestions at all stages in the preparation of the book. Bob O. Evans and John U. Barton gave unsparingly of their time to review the preliminary manuscript and provided many helpful comments. Jean F. Brennan's editorial rec-ommendations were of great benefit.

Robert L. Pokorak and Donald P. Kenney of the IBM Archives were ready at all times to assist in locating documents and facts, and they furnished most of the photographs for the book.

To these and to the many others who provided information or directed us to sources, the authors are very grateful. Responsibility for careful evaluation of all such information, and for the accuracy of conclusions drawn therefrom, is of course that of the authors alone.

A special note of appreciation is due Caroline Coppola, whose proficiency in all phases of text processing was an important factor in the timely completion of the book.

Charles J. Bashe

IBM's Early Computers

1

Punched Cards and Plugwires

The Hollerith era. IBM punched-card machine development. Steps toward fully automatic digital calculation.

When Thomas J. Watson (1874–1956) joined the Computing-Tabulating-Recording Company (CTR) in 1914 as general manager, he found himself in three different businesses at once. CTR was the result of a merger in 1911 that had included the Computing Scale Company, the International Time Recording Company, and the Tabulating Machine Company. The first company dealt in commercial scales and meat and cheese slicers, the second in industrial time-recording equipment, and the third in punched cards and tabulators. Since the merger, a need for strong leadership had become increasingly evident; punched-card machine development, for example, had been largely marking time. Herman Hollerith (1860–1929), the inventor of tabulators and still a consulting engineer to CTR, had begun to think of himself as retired.

Watson was at a critical juncture in his career. Recently, at the height of his success as a sales manager at the National Cash Register Company, he had been asked to resign by the firm's brilliant, enigmatic chief executive. Because his capabilities were well known, Watson undoubtedly could have found a secure position with a large corporation. But he was forty years old, and he wanted a challenge that combined managerial freedom and growth potential. In CTR he sensed a growth opportunity: the tabulating machine.[1]

Watson was to lavish a good deal of energy and managerial skill on his tabulator organization before it would truly thrive. But by 1924, when he restyled CTR the International Business Machines Corporation, punched-card products were well on their way toward becoming the firm's main business. Because these products eventually led IBM into the field of electronic digital computing instruments, a summary glimpse of their evolution, starting with Hollerith, serves as a prologue to the electronic machines.

1.1 The Hollerith Era

After graduating in 1879 from the School of Mines at Columbia College, Hollerith left New York to join one of his teachers in work on the U.S. census of 1880. His assignment concerned a steam and water power survey, but during his stay in Washington he became interested in the huge job of processing population data.[2] Social statistics had been attracting congressional attention, and from their respondents, census enumerators gathered data on many attributes, among them, sex, marital status, age, place of birth, education, occupation, and literacy status. To obtain a population count from the enumerators' schedules was a big but relatively easy task. The larger task came in deriving counts for selected combinations of attributes, a laborious process that required several passes over the schedules. These passes inherently involved some duplication, and portions of them had to be repeated whenever inconsistencies were detected.

Census clerks marked off one tally sheet area, called a tally spot, for each attribute combination being addressed during a pass of the schedules. Each tally spot received marks as appropriate, the marks being delineated in patterns of five. At some point, one or more tally spots would overflow, and the number of marks per tally spot would be recorded. The completed tally sheet then went forward for further consolidations. Some thought the process could be mechanized; Hollerith not only agreed but before finishing at the Census Office asked for a special assignment wherein he could study the whole process.

During the 1882–1883 academic year, Hollerith taught mechanical engineering at a struggling new school, the Massachusetts Institute of Technology. In 1883, he returned to Washington as an assistant examiner in the U.S. Patent Office. In 1884, he resigned from the government and first filed for a patent concerning electromechanical tabulation. During the period 1885–1887, he patented a method for actuating brakes by electrical means and tried in vain to convince railroad management of its advantages over compressed-air methods. He had not forgotten tabulation, however, and in 1886 he began trying out punched cards and tabulating machines, first in the Baltimore, Maryland, Department of Health and then in other test locations. In 1889, on the basis of competitive trials, his candidate punched-card system was selected for use in the 1890 U.S. census.[3]

The idea of paper punching did not originate with Hollerith, as witnessed by prior usage of cards or strips for looms, player pianos, railroad tickets, and the like. Charles Babbage (1791–1871), the English mathematician and inventor, had even conceived of uses for punched cards in automatic calculation.[4] Hollerith's contribution was to devise cards and invent machines for a narrow class of data processing tasks. In contrast to Babbage, who had sought to press technology to the very limit and to attain utmost generality of purpose, Hollerith designed within accepted engineering limits and started by tackling a specific application.

Hollerith's census system included three devices: a gang punch, a keyboard punch, and a tabulating machine with an attached sorting box. The gang punch permitted repetitive numerical codes to be punched into several cards at once, thereby saving operator time. In the major punching task, which employed the keyboard punch, cards were dealt with one by one, and only one of many necessary holes was punched at each motion of the punching lever. The operator worked at a display that mapped the card position of each encoded attribute. To punch a desired hole, the operator guided the stylus beneath a levered knob into the indicated hole on the display; the same motion cut a hole in the card. Because the display was larger than the card, the keyboard punch was often called the "pantograph" punch.

In outline, the tabulating machine resembled an undersized upright piano. Its operator looked across a work surface to a panel on which forty dials were arranged in four rows of ten each. Each dial, with a hundred marked positions and two hands analogous to the minute and second hands of a watch, served as a counter with range 0000 to 9999. At the operator's right was the handle of a hinged "pin box," and projecting downward from the box was an array of spring-loaded pins that could be lowered onto a hard rubber card bed containing a matching array of cups. When the operator placed a punched card in the bed and lowered the pin box, a pin descended into a cup at each punched position of the card, other pins being held back by the tensile strength of the card. The cups contained mercury, and each descending pin closed an electrical circuit through connector posts, relays, and wires at the rear of the tabulator and advanced a designated counter by one. At suitable junctures in processing, the operator wrote down dial readings and reset dials to zero.

A sorting box, separately mounted at the far right of the operator, was electrically cabled to the tabulating machine. The box had twenty-six compartments arrayed in two rows. The metal lid of the typical compartment was held open by spring tension until manually closed, whereupon the lid was held shut by a catch; the catch, however, was released whenever the circuit through an associated electromagnet was closed. Hence by suitable wiring, cards being processed could be grouped as appropriate for subsequent processing. Each time the operator tabulated a card, a lid in the sorting box flew open. Then the operator manually disposed of the card in the open compartment and again depressed the lid. The number of compartments, like the number of dials, was a design compromise based on consideration of the application.

The 1890 census was accomplished with unusual dispatch, and Hollerith became known to census officials the world over. During the 1890s, Hollerith equipment was used for censuses in Austria, Canada, Norway, and Russia. But while the system succeeded with the largest census applications of the day, it required cards to be fed manually, and its only arithmetic capability was that of counting (i.e., increasing by one). Work with health statistics had already highlighted this arithmetic deficiency, and Hollerith's first device for adding into dials that represented decimal positions was reported in 1891.[5] The electrical circuit for each dial counter was effectively made and broken as many times as necessary to register the digit represented in a corresponding card column. A supplemental carry mechanism was provided.

Hollerith was to remain heavily preoccupied with U.S. census business and trips to other countries until late 1894, when much of the census work ended, most of his tabulators were returned, and he found himself in financial straits. In 1895 he sold his horse, then closed his shop, and finally sold his house and moved his family into his mother-in-law's quarters. After trying his primitive adding tabulator on a freight accounting task in the offices of the New York Central Railroad and having it rejected, he dispensed with dials and designed a tabulator with several side-by-side accumulators. Each accumulator contained several digit positions, and each position was represented by a ten-position wheel with visible numerals. ("Accumulator," as used here, names a functional unit that during the long era of tabulators was first identified as an integrating device and later as an adding section or counter group.) Hollerith's new system was accepted by the rail company, where it served for years as a rather isolated demonstration of the merits of card equipment.[6]

In 1896, Hollerith incorporated his small business as the Tabulating Machine Company (TMC). Until the U.S. census of 1900, TMC's one big success consisted of a large order for census equipment from the Russian government. At the time, few commercial enterprises seemed ready to give up clerical methods of bookkeeping that were undergoing substantial improvement in response to keyboard-machine inventions. The new desk machines still outclassed Hollerith's products and required fewer changes in methods.

The U.S. census of 1900 involved a census of agriculture, as well as a census of population. For processing of farm and crop data, which were akin to accounting data, Hollerith received orders for tabulators of the type being used by the New York Central Railroad. The railway clerks had manually sorted their cards, but machinery was clearly needed for the huge volume of agricultural cards. Hollerith hurriedly developed an automatic sorter in which card-receiving pockets were arrayed horizontally. He sold twenty of these sorters to the Census Office, a sale he came to regret by 1910, when TMC opened a patent-infringement suit against a census director for having the sorters modified. (The suit, which ended inconclusively, is of no interest here.) The result was to strengthen a rental-only policy.

Although the tabulators used in 1890 again served the 1900 census of population, by 1902 Hollerith was testing a tabulator fitted with an automatic card feed. Spring jacks replaced the mercury cups, and the pin box was vertically rather than horizontally aligned. The trials indicated that such a tabulator should be capable of six times the work of a hand-fed tabulator.[7]

In 1902, a permanent U.S. Bureau of the Census was established. Mindful of ongoing responsibilities, such as censuses of U.S. possessions, the bureau retained a few tabulators on an annual basis. Mutual antagonism between the new director and Hollerith led to a disagreement over rental fees and, in 1905, to cancellation of TMC's annual contract. Since some of Hollerith's early patents were expiring, the irate census director formed a Census Machine Shop, persuaded three TMC men to join the bureau, and announced his intention of developing census equipment.

Hollerith, faced with the stark necessity of tapping the accounting market, redesigned his machines. In this long exercise he was aided by Eugene A. Ford (1866–1948), a former typewriter inventor who, while working for a TMC supplier, had developed a numerical keypunch for Hollerith around 1899. Ford became a TMC employee in 1905.[8] While improving the automatic card feed, Hollerith developed a method of reading each card in motion: stationary, electrically conductive brushes, one per card column, swept the moving card and made contacts through the holes in its columns during the reading cycle. Once the circuit for a given column had been made, the time remaining in the cycle determined the distance that a decimal counter wheel would be moved by an electromagnetically controlled clutch. The advantages in card uniformity led finally to a standard card. It contained forty-five columns and ten rows; a circular hole in a column represented a decimal digit: in the bottom row a 9, in the next row an 8, and so on. The tabulator read the card row by row—the 9 row first. The card's dimensions, 3.250 by 7.375 inches, were sufficiently close to those of the large dollar bills then in circulation to permit the cards to be stored in receptacles designed for the bills.[9] Tabulator operations could be tailored to a specific application by appropriately inserting plugwires into a plugboard at the rear of the machine. Normally, in an application context, card columns were grouped into fields. Each field corresponded to one class of data and contained no fewer columns than were needed to represent the largest datum expected in the class. Also developed was a vertical sorter that economized on floor space. The system as a whole became convincing to the accounting departments of more and more large firms until TMC was serving about a hundred customers.

In 1907, the Census Machine Shop hired James Powers, a prolific inventor, to develop an improved keypunch. The inventor learned rapidly and obtained valuable patents. By 1911, he had incorporated the Powers Accounting Machine Company, which by judiciously expanding on the functional capabilities of Hollerith's machines, soon became a successful competitor to TMC.

In 1911, Hollerith and his fellow directors decided to sell TMC to the Computing-Tabulating-Recording Company. For his shares, Hollerith received over $1 million. He also received a good salary as consulting engineer to the new company and maintained a workshop in Washington, D.C., but his contract essentially said he could do as he pleased. He was not enjoying perfect health and increasingly became content to enjoy retirement.

The three decades that it took Hollerith to become a millionaire were eventful for portents of technological change. During them, for example, the chain-driven safety bicycle made bicycling popular; the early experiments with wireless were performed; the Ford Motor Company was formed; the Wright brothers flew at Kitty Hawk; the vacuum tube triode and the triode amplifier were invented; and General Electric, DuPont, and American Telephone & Telegraph established centralized research laboratories.

1.2 IBM Punched-Card Machine Development

When Watson began to manage CTR in 1914, the company's tabulating machine division offered a manually operated gang punch, a manually operated card punch with numeric keyboard, a vertical sorter, and an adding tabulator—essentially the product line that Hollerith had developed in the previous decade. The tabulator could be ordered with up to five accumulators, each with as many as eight decimal digits of capacity. The counters of each accumulator were mounted side by side, the display digits on the counter wheels being visible to the operator. Hollerith had designed the tabulators to halt whenever they encountered a special card, called a "stop card." Such cards were interspersed in decks of data cards at the points where an operator was expected to copy desired subtotals and clear appropriate accumulators.

Hollerith had taken an early look at the prospects for automatic printing and adopted a conservative, wait-and-see attitude. Watson arrived at CTR only to learn shortly that the Powers Accounting Machine Company was introducing a printing tabulator. Enthusiasm for printing began to grow, as evidenced the following year by a speaker at the annual convention of the National Electric Light Association:

When it is considered that the Powers Tabulator-Printer can be equipped with from one to seven Adding and Designating Units, each of such having a printing or accumulating capacity of nine figures, and that the selection, printing and adding upon all of these is performed simultaneously, it is seen what a decided advantage it offers to the business and statistical world, as compared with a non-listing machine having a capacity of five adding sections.[10]

Fortunately for CTR, the changeover to printing was to be gradual, and some applications did not justify the extra cost of printers (a few nonprinting tabulators were still used in the 1940s). But the long-range future of CTR's tabulating business was clearly at risk, and in 1914 Watson launched a program to invigorate product development by setting up an experimental department in New York City on Sixth Avenue near Pennsylvania Station. This location was selected to make trips from Washington more convenient for Hollerith, who nonetheless continued to withdraw from business activities, pleading health reasons.

Ford's arrangement with CTR had permitted him to work in his shop at Uxbridge, Massachusetts, a location that went back to his early association with a Hollerith supplier. After Watson had brought him to New York to supervise the Sixth Avenue shop, Ford added an electrically powered reset device to the tabulator (previously the operator had reset accumulators by turning a crank) and continued work on a keyboard product, called a "verifier," that was introduced about 1917 as a tool for checking the work of keypunch operators.[11] As the verifier machine fed the cards of a punched deck, its operator repeated the keypunch operator's work (to no effect) until a keying discrepancy occurred, a circumstance the verifier signaled by locking its keyboard.

If inspection revealed the questionable card to be incorrect, the verifier operator prepared a correct card with a key punch.

In 1915, Ford helped Watson recruit Clair D. Lake (1888–1958), an inventor with experience in automotive design. Lake's credentials were based on performance, not on education; after finishing the eighth grade, he had attended a manual training school instead of high school. The following year, Watson hired Fred M. Carroll (1869–1961), an experienced inventor formerly at the National Cash Register Company. Since Watson was pressing them for a printer, the three designers considered various ways of printing and tried out some of their ideas in a limited way. Watson and Ford then agreed that Lake, having become familiar with the existing tabulator, should develop a printing attachment for it while Carroll was developing a novel tabulator-printer. Ford, caught up in a nationwide surge of interest in diesel engines, soon left CTR to pursue engine development. Lake replaced Ford as laboratory supervisor. Following this, in 1917, Watson recruited a well-established inventor and consulting engineer, James Wares Bryce (1880–1949), who had started as a draftsman and designer in 1900 after studying mechanical engineering for three years at New York City College. Bryce was appointed supervisory engineer for the time recording division's plant in Endicott, New York. (One of the consolidations undertaken by CTR in 1912 had been to assign tabulator production to this plant.) Then, to foster ties between the time recording and tabulating divisions, Watson closed the Sixth Avenue shop and moved its personnel the nearly two hundred miles to Endicott.[12]

Printer development proved more time-consuming than expected. As a result, Lake began making product improvements in the tabulator as he went along, giving special attention to changes that would facilitate a printing attachment. U.S. entry into World War I revised many of CTR's priorities and delayed his work. Demand for the CTR tabulator held up well with the armed forces, where the virtues of simplicity, proved reliability, and ease of maintenance compensated for the lack of a printer.

Shortly after the war, Lake simplified the adding mechanisms of the tabulator, a step that eliminated many relays and thereby gave him freedom to bring the plugboard from the back of the machine to a more accessible location at the front.[13] Then Lake, convinced that the stop-card method was too primitive to be teamed with printing, supplanted it in the existing tabulator by mechanisms based on a Hollerith patent for "automatic group control." This technique involved reading each card twice, so that the first reading of a given card would coincide with the second reading of the previous card. Whenever an identification field—the "group indicator"—changed from card to card, the machine would pause, permitting the operator to record subtotals and clear accumulators as desired. This being a fairly complicated development, as a field test Lake sent a nonprinting tabulator with automatic group control to the Cleveland area, where Benjamin M. Durfee (1897–1980) was maintaining CTR tabulators.

Durfee had joined CTR in 1917, attended a training school early the next year, and quickly made a reputation for diligence in servicing tabulators. The service job consisted mainly of checking machine adjustments, oiling and cleaning, and replacing worn parts. With others, Durfee would later recall the standard nonprinting tabulators as highly reliable: "You could go for long periods of time without any service calls." As a result, one person could cover widely scattered installations.

Durfee tended Lake's special machine for six months with the understanding that problems would be reported directly to Lake. Durfee experienced many difficulties and wrote to Lake "practically every day." The grateful Lake, who used the information to improve his design, brought Durfee to Endicott in 1920. By then, Lake's "Type I" printing tabulators were being manufactured, and the task of training repairmen had to be faced. Durfee assisted in assembly and testing and launched some training courses. After the Type I was introduced in 1921, he made "about 300 trips out of Endicott, mostly on sleepers, during the installation of the first fifty machines. . . . we had a great deal of trouble . . . printing hammers broke . . . the type themselves broke off." The foremost problem was grounded circuits, suggesting that insulated wires were being damaged by printer vibration. Again he reported the failures to Lake so that weaknesses could be corrected. The troubles tapered off, and in late 1924 Durfee assembled in Paris the first IBM printing tabulator shipped to Europe. Soon, in a splendid testimonial to Lake's design, the German railway system ordered a large number of the machines.[14]

While developing successful products, Lake was also nurturing talent from within the company. Ralph E. Page, who joined CTR in 1917 as a draftsman and within three years became chief draftsman, found his way into development by working closely with Lake on the printing tabulator. George F. Daly (1903–1983), who joined CTR in 1920 as a draftsman, soon became associated with Lake as an assistant engineer.[15] Once his printing tabulator had succeeded, Lake was made Endicott superintendent of tabulating machine activities.

In 1922, CTR acquired patents from a small firm headed by J. Royden Peirce (1877–1933). Also acquired was the firm's engineering shop at Twenty-fifth Street near Lexington Avenue in New York City.

Peirce joined CTR as an employee (as did at least two of his assistants) and continued working in the same shop as before. A graduate of the Stevens Institute of Technology in Hoboken, New Jersey, Peirce was the first of Watson's main inventors with an engineering degree. Peirce, who had designed and constructed tabulating equipment for life insurance companies, was attuned to the development of exceptional machinery. During his travels, Durfee had examined a Peirce machine. As he recalled, "Technically the one machine included so many features that it would never have been practical for IBM to build such a machine at the time . . . it . . . must have been handmade."[16]

Watson soon enlarged the Twenty-fifth Street shop. While Bryce took an office there as CTR's chief engineer, Lake and Carroll continued to work at Endicott. After his novel printing tabulator had been bested by Lake's machine, Carroll had developed a rotary punched-card press that made printing, cutting, and corner trimming a continuous process. This press opened the way for faster production of cards, which were becoming a profitable business for IBM. Before long, however, Carroll was moved to the New York City shop in an attempt to pool some of CTR's know-how concerning printers. Powers was again taking a technical lead, this time with an accounting machine that printed alphabetic characters as well as decimal digits. Peirce, who had some patent credentials in alphabetic tabulators, was appointed to meet this new challenge.

Ford returned in 1923 with plans for an improved sorter and was rehired.[17] His machine, later called the Type 80 Sorter, was introduced in 1925. It was perhaps best known as the "horizontal sorter," so-named because the card pockets were uniform in height. The new machine was faster, more convenient, and more amenable to continuing improvement than the prior sorter. Both were used in a mode of operation called "column sorting." Card by card, during a sorting pass, the sorter swept a designated column, sensed a digit, and routed the card to the pocket provided for that digit. If no hole appeared, the card went to a "reject" pocket. The operator ended a pass by stacking the contents of the pockets in digit order and, after each pass but the last, placing the deck back into the sorter's hopper. Before the next pass, the sorter was reset to sweep a new column. Sorting a deck on a control field of m columns required m passes through the sorter, starting with the right-most (least-significant) column and working upward column by column.

Sorting was indispensable because desired subtotals could not be obtained unless cards were tabulated in correct order. Subtotals by selected category are as essential to accounting as to census processing.

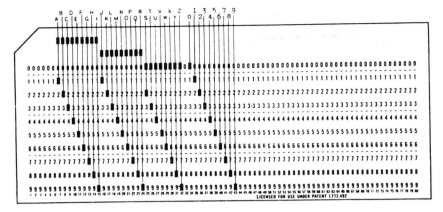

Figure 1.1
IBM eighty-column card. Columns 7 through 32 and 34 through 43 are punched
to show the character code, which with the aid of superimposed vertical lines is
annotated above the card. The card was introduced in 1928 with the numeric
portion of the code. The code shown was adopted in the 1930s. Reading from
the top, the two uppermost rows (not imprinted) were called "12" and "11".
Later the code was expanded to three punches per column to accommodate special characters. The card was often obtained with application-oriented imprinting
that divided the columns into labeled fields. The card imprinted as shown was
called a standard card.

It was partly out of the need for subtotals that tabulators were designed
with several accumulators. In 1927, automatic group control was generalized to permit subtotals within subtotals within subtotals. Subtotals
could be printed or—via the "summary punch," a duplicating keypunch
modified for connection to a tabulator—saved in a punched deck for
further processing. Mechanical bookkeeping systems with keyboards,
accumulators, and ledger sheets could compete rather effectively with
the arithmetic and printing capabilities of the tabulator, but ledger-
style documents could not be rearranged as efficiently as cards.

Increasingly during the 1920s, accountants expressed a need for a
card with greater storage capacity. Lake and Bryce, finding that they
could reduce brush widths and still read cards accurately, recommended
a card with narrower columns and with rectangular (and smaller) holes,
so that more columns could be packed into the card space conventionally allocated to forty-five columns. When a proposed card with
eighty of the rectangular holes proved mechanically stronger than a
card with forty-five of the conventional round holes, the proposed
card became patentable as an engineering advance. IBM introduced
the eighty-column card format in 1928 (see figure 1.1) and began

adapting its product line to the new cards. Both Remington Rand Inc. (which had acquired the Powers Accounting Machine Company) and IBM had long employed the same forty-five-column card, but now card formats were to diverge. Remington Rand opted for a format in which six upper rows could encode forty-five characters, and six lower rows forty-five more.

The eighty-column IBM card preserved the ten rows and the numerical code of the forty-five-column card. Already being considered, however, was an idea for squeezing two more rows into unused space at the top of the card. When the idea met with success, the lower of the two became known as row 11 (or X) and the topmost as row 12. Uses for the new rows will be discussed.

Until 1928, IBM tabulators added unsigned numbers only. Borrowing from accounting terminology, negative data were called "credits" and positive data "debits." To sum a list of numbers that included credits, users could choose between two methods, both involving clerical steps. Under the first method, numbers were appropriately assigned to credit and debit card fields, summed in separate accumulators, and the two sums were printed. The difference in the sums could be obtained by a clerical subtraction. Under the second method, credits were complemented during keypunching, a subterfuge that tricked the unidirectional counter wheels of the accumulator into performing a subtraction. One card field and one accumulator then sufficed, but clerical assistance was still needed if credits outweighed debits—in which case the resulting sum was presented in the form of a complement and had to be clerically recomplemented.

As a hint of how complementation worked, assume a three-position accumulator. The accumulator may hold any integer from 000 to 999. The complement of a nonzero number in this range is derived with respect to 1000, so that the complement of a credit 32 is 1000 minus 032, or 968. If the accumulator happens to be standing at 063 and 968 is added in an attempt to obtain 1031, the upward carry into the implied fourth position is lost (effectively subtracting 1000) and the result is 031, as it should be for the operation 63 + (-32). On the other hand, a problem arises in the operation 23 + (-32), which leads to 023 + 968 = 991. The desired result is -9, but to obtain this answer, 991 must be complemented and labeled as a credit. In dealing with complements, the left-most counter wheel in an accumulator is reserved so that a 9 in that position will always imply a complement. Lacking the left-most 9, the content of the accumulator is said to comprise a "true number."

IBM's Type IV tabulator, introduced in 1928, relieved personnel of the chore of complementing each credit and of having to recomplement negative sums. A credit entry in a card field could be flagged by punching a row 11 hole (an "X punch") in an appropriate column. The tabulator was designed to detect the flag at first reading of the card, form the credit's complement—in a mechanism called an "analyzer"—before second reading, and then add this complement (rather than the punched value) at second reading. This served for summations known to yield a positive result. For the general case, where sums might be either positive or negative, the user could allocate two accumulators: the first plugwired normally, the second plugwired as if debits were credits and vice versa. Then if the first accumulator yielded a debit sum, the sum was printed. But if the first accumulator yielded a complement, the sum in the second accumulator (which in that case could not be a complement) was printed with a special mark identifying it as a credit. This method of balance selection long persisted, although the analyzer was soon replaced by a simpler method that altered clutch behavior at the second reading: instead of engaging a clutch upon reading a hole, the usual procedure, the clutch was initially engaged and then disengaged upon reading the hole, thereby adding the complement of the digit represented by the hole. In 1933, balance selection was supplemented by a functionally equivalent method that required only one (extra cost) accumulator called a "balance counter." A complement in such a counter could be printed as a true number accompanied by a credit symbol.[18]

Once the X punch proved useful for subtraction, Bryce and others saw that the flagging principle could serve other control purposes. They provided for various uses, some of which acquired names. In "field selection," one of two card fields was selected and routed to a given accumulator as indicated by the presence or absence of a flag punch. In "class selection," on the other hand, a card field was selectively routed to one of two accumulators. What the use of card-contained flags meant in practice was that more data processing tasks could be done in one pass of a card file. Versatility was enhanced, moreover, in that field and class selection enabled cards of differing formats to be processed together, as might be convenient when new requirements suggested format changes. Another timesaver consisted of hubs designed to emit control pulses during every card cycle; card counts could be obtained, for example, by selectively connecting such a hub to an accumulator. ("Hub" was the accepted term for a socket into which a plugwire fitted.) Repetitive information, such as a date, also could be routed to the printer.

The eighty-column card was offered with a "reproducer" that punched eighty-column card decks from existing decks of forty-five-column cards. After this had made evident the general utility of copying, reproducers stayed in the product line as a means of copying eighty-column card decks. During reproduction, fields could be rearranged or omitted, fields from various card files could be consolidated by making successive passes, and redundancy in keypunching could be reduced. Another functional advance consisted of a numerical "interpreter," developed by Daly and others, that printed card content along the top edge of a card. After a card deck had been sorted on an interpreted field, the deck acquired some of the convenient, manual-access properties of the card catalogs made familiar by libraries.

In the latter 1920s, IBM's Twenty-fifth Street laboratory moved to larger quarters at 225 Varick Street. Peirce, working there in isolation from the Endicott group, came to favor an alphabetic code and card layout that promised to diverge considerably from those being designed in Endicott. But the successful reception of Endicott's new card finally forced him to adapt his long-awaited alphabetic printing tabulator to eighty columns. Never at ease with relays and electrical circuits, Peirce preferred mechanical methods of control (as did Powers) and was still relying heavily on them in early 1930 when Edward J. Rabenda joined him. Rabenda had been employed by IBM in 1924, trained as a repairman, and recognized for the cogency of his suggested tabulator improvements. After being assigned to the Varick Street laboratory, he introduced Peirce to the merits of relay circuits for control functions and became his circuit designer.[19] Manufactured in Endicott according to specifications written at Varick Street, the first IBM alphabetical accounting machine appeared in 1931. Its card code, which generalized the numerical code to use holes in rows 11 and 12 for alphabetic characters, was insufficient for the full alphabet; some characters were awkwardly simulated by numeric digits, a problem corrected in successor machines by making the zero punching position serve two purposes.

As a result of work by Bryce, Daly, and others, a machine called the multiplying punch was introduced in 1931. (Later it acquired the designation Type 600.) It was designed to read two factors from a card, multiply them, and punch the product into a blank field of the card. The machine was superseded in 1933 by an improved model, first known as the automatic cross-footing multiplying punch and later as the Type 601 electric multiplier. ("Footing" and "cross-footing," at the time, were bookkeeping terms for summing a table of numbers by column and by row, respectively.) If p, q, r, and s denote numbers in card fields, the Type 601 could obtain results of the form pq, or $p + q + r$, or $pq + r + s$. It could subtract as well as add. Designed solely to supplement a tabulator, it was not equipped to print, but it broadened the scope of punched-card calculation at a time when the main machine for digital multiplication was the desk calculator. It could accommodate multiplicands and multipliers of up to eight decimal digits. The multiplication rate decreased as multiplier length increased; for eight-digit multipliers, the rate was 600 per hour.[20] At that rate, each multiplication took 6 seconds. The multiplying punches were not designed to perform division; at the time, accountants made use of reciprocals wherever possible.

Most desk calculators of the era were designed to perform multiplication by over-and-over addition. To multiply 7354 by 87, say, this method requires that an accumulator receive 7354 seven times and again, after a shift, eight more times, for a total of fifteen additions. If their designers had been content with this method, the multiplying punches would have been considerably slower. Instead, with the aid of multiple-contact relays, they endowed the machine with a multiplication table that yielded digit-by-digit products and reduced the number of additions to the number of digits in the multiplier plus one.[21] The final addition combined the two partial products. This method is suggested by the following way of performing a multiplication, using $87 \times 7354 = 639798$ as an example:

		7	3	5	4	
		×		8	7	
L_1			4	2	3	2
	R_1			9	1	5	8
L_2		5	2	4	3	
	R_2		6	4	0	2	
		6	3	9	7	9	8

For 7, the units digit in the multiplier, the table products needed with a multiplicand of 7354 are (from left to right) $7 \times 7 = 49$, $7 \times 3 = 21$, $7 \times 5 = 35$, and $7 \times 4 = 28$. These products are written diagonally, pair by pair, with first digit on line L_1 and second on line R_1. Writing them as two lines postpones the carry problem that would attend adding them into one line. Products for the second multiplier digit are similarly written on lines L_2 and R_2. The 601 followed a method of this sort—summing L_1, and later L_2, in a "left" register and, similarly, R_1, R_2 in a "right" register—using one addition cycle for each pair of lines. Then, in the last addition cycle, it summed the contents of the left and right registers to obtain the final result.[22]

Figure 1.2
North Street laboratory, Endicott, New York.

In 1933, Watson brought most of his engineering activities together in Endicott in a new building (figure 1.2) known as the North Street laboratory.[23] The top-ranking product development title at the time was "engineer." There were seven engineers—among them Carroll, Ford, and Lake—and numerous service groups, such as factory engineering, patent attorney, office manager, special machines, metallurgist, industrial designer, production engineering, methods engineer, electrical engineer, blueprint room, machine shop, traffic department, and tool crib.[24] The engineers, whom Watson typically called inventors, occupied corner areas on the first two floors of the building.

Watson, in directing development, was not reluctant to assign similar missions to more than one engineer. This style of management served him well, but the natural result was to discourage technical communication. Hence, to make the North Street laboratory more effective, perceptive liaison was needed. The liaison role was played increasingly often by W. Wallace McDowell, a graduate of the Massachusetts Institute of Technology. McDowell joined IBM in 1930, attended sales school, and was soon transferred to the laboratory in Endicott. In 1936, when he became an assistant to the laboratory manager, neither manager nor assistant was expected to have much technical influence. McDowell helped to change this, particularly after becoming laboratory manager in 1942.[25]

By the 1930s, neither Watson nor his engineers could stay in close touch with the increasingly diverse requirements of customers. As a result, product planning began to emerge as a distinctive headquarters responsibility. The early career of John C. McPherson reveals the trend. McPherson, who held an electrical engineering degree from Princeton University, joined IBM in 1930. After serving as a special sales representative to the railroads for three years, he was given a headquarters assignment to work on improved methods and machines for the railroads. In 1940, he became manager of a small Future Demands department that grew to play an influential role in product planning. At about the same time, he began to explain in scientific journals how accounting machines might be used for the computations required in scientific studies and engineering design.[26]

The growing diversity in customer requirements called for more responsive methods of machine control. Hollerith, it will be recalled, designed his first tabulator for a huge census application that required only a half-dozen or so different tabulator setups, one every few months. Even though some relay control wires might have to be resoldered at each setup, the proportion of setup time was low. Later, as he moved into accounting areas where applications were smaller and more varied, he provided rudimentary plugboards with hubs that could be interconnected by inserting plugwires, thereby reducing setup time. But as the industry evolved, with plugboards growing larger and users attempting more applications, setup time again became a matter of concern. Removable control panels, the solution introduced about 1933, had two important advantages: (1) they could be wired "off line," that is, away from the punched-card machine and without interfering with its operation, and (2), at the cost of additional panels, a setup could be stored and used again and again.

The 1930s brought other advances of many kinds. In 1933, Lake's tabulators—which had progressed through a long series of improvements—culminated in a long-lived product: the Type 285 numeric printing tabulator (see figure 1.3). The machine could be obtained with up to five accumulators and seven printing sections, one per accumulator and two for printing directly from cards. Meanwhile Carroll provided automatic carriages for controlling printed forms and a special mechanism for automatic posting of individual ledger sheets that helped the new Social Security Administration automate its record keeping.[27] Lake further demonstrated his versatility by developing a smaller

Figure 1.3
IBM Type 285 tabulator. The card feed is at the top left and the card stacker below it at center left. The print unit is at the extreme right. Next above the removable control panel at front center is a row of control switches; above the switches are the visible counter wheels of five accumulators. The 285 printed numeric data only. The fastest version of the 285 tabulated at a rate of 150 cards per minute.

counter, that is, wheel-and-clutch mechanism, than had previously been available; since one counter was needed in each accumulator digit position, size was an important consideration. Lake also developed a smaller and much-improved relay.

The Type 405 alphabetical accounting machine (see figure 1.4) was introduced in 1934. An outstanding success, it remained the flagship of IBM's product line until after World War II. The maximal capacity 405 had sixteen accumulators, evenly divided into lengths of two, four, six, and eight columns. Any two or more accumulators could be coupled to act as a unit, thereby giving the user much freedom in accumulator allocation.[28] The 405 was more versatile and more expensive than the Type 285. Despite official names, both were widely called "tabulators." Names continued to be a problem, for IBM chose "electric accounting machines" as the collective term for its punched-card machines when the division that designed and produced the machines became the Electric Accounting Machine (EAM) division.[29] Later it became convenient for IBMers to speak of EAM products and for customers to refer to their EAM installations or EAM machines. (EAM was pronounced *ee ay em.*)

Figure 1.4
IBM Type 405 Alphabetical Accounting Machine. Covered at the extreme left is
the removable control panel. This panel contained over 1600 functionally significant hubs, which were systematically laid out within a rectangular grid. The machine could tabulate at a rate of 150 cards per minute or tabulate and print from
card fields at a rate of 80 cards per minute. Card reading paused during the
printing of accumulator content, making the rate variable. The print unit contained 88 type bars, the leftmost 43 for alphanumeric characters and the other
45 for digits only.

Based largely on work by Page, a novel machine, the Type 77 collator, was introduced in 1937. It had two card hoppers (for input decks) and four card stackers (for output decks). It was designed to compare two numbers, say b and c, and reach a three-way decision: b less than c, b equals c, or b greater than c. The numbers being compared could come from cards in separate decks or from adjacent cards in one deck. Given a deck purportedly sorted on the contents of a control field, a pass through the collator could segregate any cards not in sequence. One pass could select cards meeting a variety of conditions—for example, all cards with control numbers within a specified range. One pass could match control fields in two decks and yield up to four decks, such as matched and unmatched cards from each of the two decks. One pass could merge two sorted decks into one. The collator was later generalized to handle alphabetic characters as well as decimal digits.[30]

Most accounting applications involved a master card file that contained reasonably fixed information such as name, address, rate, price, customer number, employee number, or the like. Each card in the file comprised one individual record, and the cards were ordered on some numerical identifier. Periodically, decks containing new data were appropriately sorted and matched against the master file to bring together the information needed during processing. Depending on the nature of the application and the capabilities of available equipment, short-lived decks might have to be generated and discarded in the course of producing desired documents, listings, and summary reports. Output card documents—card checks, for example—could be sorted into the order most convenient for distribution.

No summary can suggest the variety of models and options in EAM products, but the trend toward new types was capped by the collator. By the early 1940s, large installations of IBM machines could be expected to have at least one each of the following functional kinds of machines (the reproducer family includes summary punches):

collator
interpreter
keypunch
multiplying punch
reproducer
sorter
tabulator
verifier

Thus the four kinds available in 1914 had expanded to eight. With this added versatility and with removable control panels and card-contained control punches, the punched card had revolutionized many paperwork tasks, among them the processing of sales, purchasing, production, shipping, personnel, and financial transactions. Moreover, large numbers of managers had come to depend on valuable information in the form of printed summaries.

At the close of 1943, IBM had about 10,000 tabulators on rental. Of these, approximately 64 percent were Type 405 alphabetic accounting machines, 30 percent were numeric printing tabulators (mostly Type 285), and 6 percent were nonprinting tabulators. Type 601 multipliers numbered about 2000. The most numerous class of products was the keypunch, the 24,500 on rental being distributed over ten designated subclasses with distinctive features. With 10,200 units on rental, the Type 80 sorter had the largest inventory for a single type of machine.[31]

1.3 Steps toward Fully Automatic Digital Calculation

In the late 1920s, when scientists began to take note of the capabilities of punched-card machines, they had to make addition substitute for multiplication wherever feasible. Some computations can sum a simple series of numbers and take advantage of mathematical properties to obtain a more interesting series. The cumulative sums obtained in the course of summation were called "progressive totals" in punched-card jargon. The progressive totals for the elementary series 1, 1, 1, 1, . . . are the whole numbers 1, 2, 3, 4 . . . , for example. Again, the progressive totals of the series 1, 2, 2, . . . , 2 are the odd numbers 1, 3, 5, 7, ...

To take the idea one more step, the progressive totals of the odd numbers are the squares 1, 4, 9, 16 . . . of the whole numbers. That a table of squares can be generated by two stages of progressive totals begins to hint at the inherent power of additions. Mathematicians, who know the underlying general principle as the "method of differences," have long used summation in producing tables of mathematical functions. The principle is directly applicable to polynomial functions, in which case the number of required stages of progressive totals is equal to the highest exponent appearing in the polynomial, and is further useful in that polynomials often serve as approximations of other mathematical functions. These very considerations, in the nineteenth century, had influenced Charles Babbage in the planning and naming of his mechanical Difference Engine. (Before the machine was finished, he turned to plans for a more versatile calculator, the Analytical Engine, which for various reasons was not completed.)

One noteworthy usage of progressive totaling permitted a sum of products of the general form $x_1y_1 + x_2y_2 + \ldots + x_ny_n$ to be evaluated, without ever obtaining the individual products, by a succession of sorting and accumulating steps.[32] This iterative method, called "progressive digiting" in the technical literature, was helpful in making tabulators attractive to scientists. Even after the advent of the Type 601 electric multiplier, use of the method was often justifiable. In one astronomy computation, about 1.2 million implicit multiplications were performed on a Type 405 accounting machine in 42 hours. Had the multiplications actually been carried out on a Type 601, the computation would have taken about 800 hours.[33]

Among the earliest proponents of accounting machines for scientific computation was Leslie J. Comrie (1893–1950), a British applied mathematician well versed in computing instruments. In 1928, he reported on an application of "Hollerith machines," as IBM machines were known in England. Four years later, in discussing additional applications, he noted, "The mechanical methods that have been applied to certain portions of the work have eliminated much fatigue, increased tenfold the speed with which results can be obtained, and reduced the cost to one-quarter of its former amount."[34]

Wallace J. Eckert (1902–1971), a Columbia University astronomer and, in the 1930s, one of America's leading proponents of punched-card computation, was to recall the era when "computer" meant a clerk skilled in computational procedures:

When I entered the field of scientific calculation in 1925, there were on the market reliable desk calculators, printing adding machines (some with multiple registers) and punched-card sorters and printing tabulators. However, a large part of professional computing was done without these machines. The use of logarithms and other tables in the hands of a professional computer was very effective: many working formulas and tables of functions were arranged for logarithmic computation. . . . My first acquaintance with automatic calculation came in 1929 when I visited the Columbia University Statistical Bureau.[35]

The Statistical Bureau had been conceived and established in 1928–1929 and supplied with standard IBM machines in a pioneering collaboration between Watson and Benjamin D. Wood of Columbia University.

When Wood, who was primarily interested in educational testing, mentioned some special needs, Watson gave the bureau a one-of-a-kind machine, the IBM Difference Tabulator, known to its designers

(Bryce, Daly, and others) as the "Columbia machine." Constructed at Endicott, it was installed at the bureau in December 1929. The machine, endowed with ten accumulators of ten digits each, could be wired to read a card and accumulate card data in the mode typical of any tabulator. But plugwires also permitted accumulators to be paired as desired for two unusual "transfer cycles" that could follow a card cycle. During a transfer cycle, the content of one member of each pair could be summed into its paired accumulator. One of Daly's test problems for the machine calculated the fifth powers of the integers through 99 by progressive totaling.[36]

The Difference Tabulator did not suffice for Eckert, who later wrote,

The machines in the Statistical Bureau were not adequate for astronomical research; however, upon consulting with various people in the company, I learned that a large engineering program had been going on and that a number of new machines with greater flexibility were about to be put on the market. These included the subtraction accounting machine, the summary punch which made it possible to record the results of addition, and the multiplying punch. . . . At that stage there was no provision for division, but that did not worry astronomers who were accustomed to the use of reciprocal tables.[37]

His persistence in using punched-card machines gradually made Eckert an authoritative figure in computing in America. At length he formulated the idea of a "calculation control switch" that should speed up his main computations, which produced numerical solutions to differential equations of planetary motion.

With Watson's support, Eckert obtained a control switch that could step through a dozen different modes of operation in a system consisting of an electric multiplier (Type 601), a printing tabulator (Type 285), and a summary punch. The switch was built at Endicott, Eckert's main contact at that location being newcomer Stephen W. Dunwell, who joined IBM in 1934 after studying electrical engineering for three years at Antioch College.[38] (At the time, job opportunities were scarce; a work program between IBM and Antioch in 1933 led Dunwell to his opportunity.) Under the switch arrangement, individual machines were instructed much as usual, but with the aid of an operator who occasionally changed switch settings and moved cards, it was possible to iterate some of Eckert's main computational sequences without changing control panels. Because nobody in IBM viewed the switch as more than an improvised research tool, the main memorial to it proved to be Eckert's own description:

The calculation control switch contains a row of electric contacts each of which is operated by a rotating cam. The cam is a circular fiber disk which is notched at various points around the circumference. A series of about twenty of these disks are attached to a common shaft to form a sort of player piano roll. When this roll is rotated from one position to the next the various contacts open and close according to the notches in the disks. The circuits from the contacts are used to operate the various control switches on the tabulator and multiplier, and also a number of multicontact relays which effectively change the wiring of the plugboards. Each step in the integration consists of a certain number of distinct machine operations which always come in the same order. Hence in order to have the machines ready for each operation it is only necessary to rotate the roll from one position to the next, one complete revolution corresponding to a complete step in the integration. One roll serves for all equations of a given form, and a new one could be prepared in a few hours.[39]

In 1937, after Eckert's computation center was well underway, its facilities were made available to other astronomers under the auspices of the Thomas J. Watson Astronomical Computing Bureau, a joint enterprise of the American Astronomical Society, Columbia University, and IBM. But despite enthusiasm on the part of a few scientists, technical computation had little economic impact in the 1930s; few universities or industrial laboratories obtained punched-card machines for their scientists.[40] Typically, the interested scientist or graduate student was expected to run his or her computational task on idle machines in the accounting department. IBM machines usually were preferred; as Comrie noted, "For scientific work the flexibility given by easily-changed electrical connections has been in favour of the Hollerith; the Powers, although well established as an accounting machine, has made little inroad into technical computing."[41]

Meanwhile, punched-card machines remained alien to most engineers. Habitually concerned with formulas containing exponential and trigonometric terms, they did many of their computations with handbook tables and the slide rule, a remarkably useful instrument for carrying out multiplication, division, exponentiation, and trigonometric operations to a precision of two or three decimal places. Moreover, impressive computing devices were appearing in their own field. By 1931, for example, they could read about the differential analyzer, a new instrument for obtaining numerical solutions to differential equations, developed at the Massachusetts Institute of Technology.[42] Its many tons of mechanism suggested the descriptive term "large scale," an adjective that was to serve the computing community for over two decades. The differential analyzer came to be viewed as a national resource; subsequently, versions of it were built for the Ballistic Computation Laboratory at the U.S. Army's Aberdeen Proving Ground and for the Moore School of Electrical Engineering, University of Pennsylvania. Kindred machines were built in the research laboratory of the General Electric Company and in England.[43]

The differential analyzer required an elaborate setup prior to obtaining solutions for a given equation. As a result of the setup, it served as a physical model of the equation. Then, as manually guided devices followed traces of input variables, the model would constantly renew its physical equilibrium and trace an output curve. The differential analyzer and the accounting machines provided examples of two contrasting approaches to calculation that came to be described as "analog" and "digital," respectively. In the former, numbers were represented by physical quantities — such as length, angle, or voltage — and the precision of results was governed by the physical limits of instrumentation. In the latter, numbers were represented digit by digit and treated arithmetically, thus making precision a function of register capacity. Each method had its advantages. Eckert, who also dealt with differential equations, was content with punched-card machines, which although slow were readily available and relatively inexpensive. Moreover, they afforded greater precision than attainable with a differential analyzer and provided printing capabilities of considerable utility to him.

In 1937, the digital approach gained a new proponent, Howard H. Aiken (1900–1973), a graduate student in physics at Harvard University. His idea was to couple together all the registers and control mechanisms needed to accommodate long sequences of operations. He found the Monroe Calculating Machine Company, a manufacturer of desk calculators, unwilling to undertake the expensive (and gratis) development he had in mind.[44] His ideas came to the attention of a professor in the Harvard Business School, Theodore H. Brown, who as a consultant to IBM's education department was well acquainted with Bryce and Watson. Following informal inquiries by Brown, Aiken wrote Bryce in early November, asking for an appointment a week later.[45] (A document that Aiken may have prepared for the meeting was published in 1964; it reviews some of the history of computation, discusses scientific needs, dwells on mathematical considerations, and visualizes "a switchboard on which are mounted various pieces of calculating machine apparatus" in terms of desired digital operations.)[46]

The manager of IBM's Boston office wrote to Bryce in mid-December, reporting that at Brown's suggestion he had arranged a training course for Aiken. Bryce responded:

Mr. Aiken called on me some weeks ago and explained to me that Professor Brown had recommended that he come down here and talk over the proposition of putting together some special calculating machinery which they could use in the laboratory for various sorts of computations, involving physics, astronomy, medicine and whatnot.

Of course, these things are very easy to talk about in a general way, but I explained to Mr. Aiken that in order to build anything that would be satisfactory, it would be necessary for us to find out just what computations were to be made on the machine and other facts, such as capacity, and anything that would tend to make a machine of definite dimensions. In order to get together the data for such a machine, I suggested to him that he become more familiar with the general principles of operation of our machines. It is out of that conversation that your contact with him has grown.[47]

Aiken's training in machine functions was completed before Christmas and in machine "workings" during the first week of 1938.[48] At roughly the same time, Watson and his corporate staff were moving uptown to a new corporate headquarters building at Madison Avenue and Fifty-seventh Street.

Bryce chose Lake as Aiken's technical contact point in IBM. Toward the end of January, after four days of discussions among Aiken, Durfee, and Francis E. (Frank) Hamilton (1898–1972), an assistant to Lake who had joined CTR in 1923 as a draftsman, the IBM engineers speculated that Harvard might build a machine with about $15,000 worth of IBM parts. Later, after the growing complexity of the plan had made it evident that IBM should build the machine, the estimate was revised to $100,000.[49] Bryce continued to nourish technical relationships and in January 1939 wrote a memorandum formalizing the project.[50] Late in March, just after the IBM board had approved construction of an "Automatic Computing Plant," a contract was drawn up: IBM would retain patent rights by invention agreements and in return give Harvard "the material and work involved in designing, testing, and completing the plant." The first appropriation for the "Harvard University machine" was approved in May.[51] Subsequently, Aiken spent parts of two summers with Lake's engineers before being called to active duty by the navy. Meanwhile Lake had charged Hamilton with most of the duties of project supervision.

During World War II—while IBM factories were producing carbines, automatic rifles, cannon, bomb sights, gun directors, and fire control mechanisms, as well as punched-card machines of prewar design— IBM engineers undertook about a hundred special development projects for the armed forces.[52] One of Lake's assignments was to develop a faster calculator for Aberdeen Proving Ground, an objective met by making the extensive technological changes required to replace wheels with relay circuits. When the army requested special card reading and punching units for an undisclosed project underway at the University of Pennsylvania, Bryce and his staff coordinated IBM's response.[53] (In 1946, the instrument produced by the project was revealed as ENIAC, the first large-scale electronic digital computing instrument.) Meanwhile, the IBM machine installation at Columbia University served as a model for a number of computing centers concerned with ballistics and atomic physics.

The war slowed progress on the Harvard machine, which first ran a test problem correctly in January 1943. Figure 1.5, a photograph taken at the North Street laboratory, shows the machine at about the time it was demonstrated to members of the Harvard faculty in December 1943. After shipment to the Harvard campus in February 1944, the machine was reassembled, tested, and improved for months under Durfee's supervision. Named the IBM Automatic Sequence Controlled Calculator (ASCC), it was formally presented to Harvard on 7 August 1944.[54] Figure 1.6 shows it at Harvard.

The ASCC was endowed with seventy-two accumulators, each consisting of twenty-four electromechanical counter wheels. An accumulator's high-order counter wheel was reserved for representation of number sign; the other wheels could hold a number of up to twenty-three digits. Sixty nonadding registers, similar in format, provided for the storage of constants; these registers were built of dial switches. The ASCC had two card readers, a card punch, and two electric typewriters. It had four paper-tape readers, one for reading a sequence control tape and three for reading tapes containing mathematical tables.

At the outset of an ASCC multiplication or division, multiples of the multiplicand or divisor were formed for the nine nonzero decimal digits. During multiplication, multiples were iteratively selected as indicated by multiplier digits, shifted as appropriate, and summed to obtain a product. In division, the remainder (initially the dividend) was compared with multiples and the largest multiple ensuring a non-negative remainder was subtracted to obtain the next digit of the quotient. Special sequencing facilities controlled various units of the system during the computation of logarithms, exponentials, and sines.

All ASCC units were gated, by "in" and "out" sets of relays, to a main bus of twenty-four wires. The width of the paper tape was 3.25 inches, the width of a punched card. A "line" across the tape consisted of positions for twenty-four equidistant holes. In a control tape, the positions constituted three fields: the first field designated the location

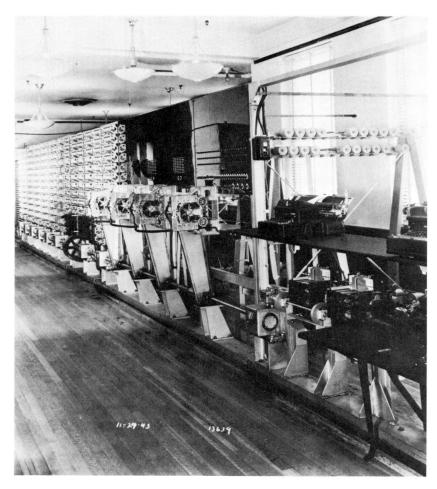

Figure 1.5
Near-complete "Harvard machine" in the North Street laboratory, circa November 1943.

Figure 1.6
IBM Automatic Sequence Controlled Calculator after installation at Harvard University. The dial switches are at the left, followed by the bays of storage counters. Partially obscured by the observers are the multiplying-dividing unit and the counters used in computing logarithmic and trigonometric functions. At the right are the paper-tape units, typewriters, card feeds, and card punch.

of an operand, the second designated a location for the result (typically the location, also, of the second operand), and the third specified the desired operation. In a data tape, four lines represented a number, each digit (and the leading sign) being encoded by the four positions thus made available. In practice, paper-tape ends were pasted together to form loops. The sequence-control tape could be read iteratively or manually reset. The table tapes could be scanned either backward or forward in the course of table-lookup operations.

Containing over 2200 counter wheels for storage and summation and 3300 relay components for control circuitry, the ASCC was 51 feet long and 8 feet high. It weighed about 5 tons. Had not Lake invented improved, space-conserving decimal counters and wire-contact relays before the project started, the machine would have been either much larger in size or much diminished in capacity. With its many wheels and relays, the machine constituted the high tide of the electromechanical tabulator technology introduced by Hollerith.

The machine worked well. In 1946, the staff at Harvard wrote: "Experience has shown that the calculator will operate approximately ninety percent of the time without failure of any kind, and on one occasion has run as long as four weeks without interruption. . . . The calculator is far more nearly infallible than the personnel in charge of its operation."[55] Aiken painstakingly documented the machine, publicized it at gatherings of influential technical people, and made it the centerpiece of a very successful training center in digital computation.

(After operating the ASCC for fifteen years, the Harvard Computation Laboratory retained a section of the machine as an exhibit. Another portion went to the Smithsonian Institution in Washington, D.C.)[56]

Fortunately, in view of the wide exposure given the ASCC, it was photogenic. Thanks to Watson's concerns, the machine had come to be neatly enclosed in stainless steel and glass with the help of an industrial design firm.[57] While making the point that the ultimate purpose of a calculator is to perform useful work in a more economical manner, not to excite admiration, an ASCC programmer wrote, "Large-scale calculators in operation are beautiful instruments to observe."[58]

Recalling the analytical engine in a review headed "Babbage's Dream Come True," Comrie hailed the ASCC as "a realization of Babbage's project in principle, although its physical form has the benefit of twentieth century engineering and mass-production methods."[59] Actually, where Babbage had conceived of a clean separation between his "mill" (arithmetic unit) and "store" (medium for storing operands and intermediate results), the ASCC designers had used counter wheels that served both functions and thereby blurred the distinction in a physical sense.

The ASCC was a novel machine, and novelty can engender problems. One problem was that of finding suitable characterizations. On 7 August 1944, the *New York Herald Tribune* billed the ASCC as a "super-brain," and the *New York Times* called it an "algebra machine." These terms arose from a Harvard University press release that used the phrase "algebraic super-brain."[60]

A second problem concerned the proper allocation of credit among Aiken, Bryce, Durfee, Hamilton, and Lake. Watson assumed that he and Aiken would agree on a press release, this being a courtesy that businessmen, to say nothing of benefactors, confidently expect. Unhappily for all concerned, Aiken was content to have the release approved by the U.S. Navy, which by arrangement had sole use of the ASCC for the duration of the war. The release prompted the following statement by the *New York Sun*, "In charge of the calculator is the inventor, Commander Howard H. Aiken, U.S.N.R., who worked out the theory which made the machine possible." Watson was twice outraged: once for the slight he had suffered and again over the implied insult to his men in the singular use of the term *inventor*. All hope of further collaboration between IBM and Harvard, a hope that must have consoled Bryce and Watson while project costs had mounted, cooled instantly. Watson was barely persuaded to stay for the ceremony that celebrated the ASCC as a technical advance and recognized IBM's gift to Harvard, a gift that by this time included $100,000 toward the operating expenses of the computing laboratory.

No longer could the subject of credit be rationally discussed. Watson personally oversaw the preparation of a carefully worded ASCC brochure that included the paragraph: "The early conversations between Dr. Aiken and IBM's engineers having disclosed that the known requirements could be met by a combination of some of the company's standard and special mechanisms, such as those used at Columbia and other universities, IBM proceeded to build the machine."[61] There followed a long list of the "more-important" ASCC embodiments of components and techniques invented by IBM engineers. Aiken had not invented any of these, as Watson would occasionally remind IBM audiences. In early 1945, when the patent applications concerning the ASCC neared completion, Lake named Aiken on the application that stressed automatic sequencing (the applicants appear in the order Lake, Aiken, Hamilton, and Durfee). Then, presumably as a defensive measure in case Watson heard of this and raised a furor, he signed a memorandum for the record stating that Aiken was being included purely as a matter of courtesy.[62]

That Watson did not soon forget the matter is suggested by a Harvard spokesman's letter in 1948 to the editor of the *Wall Street Journal*. A previous article's mention of Harvard's computation laboratory having given "less than due credit" to IBM, the letter included (straight from Watson's brochure) a list of IBM inventions and inventors germane to the ASCC. Preceding the list was a generous paragraph:

The original IBM automatic sequence controlled calculator, which was formally presented to Harvard University by IBM in August 1944, was invented by engineers of IBM following the basic theory of Professor Howard H. Aikin [sic] of Harvard. Full credit for the invention should go to four engineers of IBM: Clair D. Lake, Frank E. Hamilton, Benjamin M. Durfee and James W. Bryce. The machine was built to their specifications after six years of laboratory work in the IBM plant at Endicott, N.Y., with Mr. Lake in charge of the inventive work.[63]

Although "following the basic theory" may attenuate Aiken's contribution, the phrase was instructive for the time. Fifteen years later, IBM employees would invoke the term "computer architecture" to embrace register formats, storage capacities, machine instructions, and other matters of direct concern to the system user.[64] Then, in retrospect, Aiken could have been described reasonably well as the ASCC architect.

A third quandary concerned how to portray the power of the ASCC compared to other systems. Because calculating systems and their applications are complex, comparisons have to ignore many relevant variables in the interest of practicality. Since multiplications consume more time than other arithmetic operations in many scientific computations, the ratio of multiplication times in two systems provides a rough indication of relative system speeds. This ratio being easy to determine, any analyst can indulge in comparisons. Used with caution, the method has merit. The IBM Type 601 multiplied and punched in 6 seconds, whereas a clerk equipped with a desk calculator of the day might take close to a minute (tenfold longer) to enter a multiplier, wait perhaps 15 seconds for the product, and neatly copy the result. And indeed, experienced observers did tend to think of punched-card machines as about tenfold faster than desk calculators.

The ASCC required from 2.4 seconds (for a zero multiplier) upward to 6 seconds for a multiplication with lengthy factors.[65] For eight-digit factors, the longest permitted in the Type 601, the ASCC multiplied at about twice the 601 rate. Some expert observers thought this rather slow for 1944.[66] Arguing that arithmetic times were not the true measure of a system, Aiken responded:

Obviously, the only way to state the relative speed of the calculator is to solve a problem first by manual methods and then by use of the machine. Such an estimate has been made and apparently the machine is nearly 100 times as fast as a well-equipped manual computer. When it is borne in mind that a computer can work little more than six hours a day before fatigue causes him to produce a prohibitive number of errors, it becomes clear that, in operating on a 24-hour schedule, the calculator may produce as much as six months' work in a single day.[67]

Thus by Aiken's measure the ASCC was about a hundred-fold faster than a clerk with the desk calculator. Although job times are potentially superior to multiplication times for comparative purposes, much depends upon the choice of job or jobs. Since job comparisons are akin to costly experiments, few but machine designers and potential customers are likely to indulge in them. Nobody checked up on Aiken because nobody wanted to buy an ASCC.[68]

In truth, the ASCC constituted a technological dead end. Lake's assistants, for example, were testing an all-relay calculator that dispensed with wheels and relied upon relay circuits for registers and arithmetic control. This "Aberdeen Relay Calculator" could multiply over thirty times faster than an IBM 601, making it about equal to a differential analyzer for computing shell trajectories.[69] Two were delivered to the Aberdeen Proving Ground in December 1944 and during the rest of the war served as America's fastest digital calculators.[70]

A fourth problem that surfaced with the IBM Automatic Sequence Controlled Calculator concerned a suitable name. Convenience demands that every big system have a short name or pronounceable acronym. Aiken opened the way for a series of systems with the suggestive name "Harvard Mark I" (which was indeed followed by Harvard-constructed Marks II, III, and IV). In U.S. computing circles, Harvard's ASCC came to be known as Mark I.

For Watson, there was still another problem: that of surpassing the ASCC. Events had challenged him. In January 1945, his impatience forced McPherson, his engineering director, to begin thinking about the probable nature of a calculating instrument faster than the ASCC.[71] Vacuum tube technology had been advancing as a result of wartime developments, and the designers of such a calculator could be expected to employ it.

2

Electronic Calculation

Flip-flops and counters. The electronic multiplier. The SSEC, a super calculator. The type 604, an electronic workhorse. The Card-Programmed Electronic Calculator.

Until the end of World War II, the top product designers in IBM were, for the most part, self-educated people with a strong bent toward mechanical design. To provide electrical engineering knowledge, a small electrical laboratory had been established as a service department within the main engineering laboratory in Endicott, New York. Its main mission was to help the designers develop better products by carefully testing and analyzing the behavior of relays and other circuit components. One of those assigned to the electrical laboratory was Ralph L. Palmer, an electrical engineering graduate of Union College in Schenectady, New York, who joined IBM in 1932.

Because his training in the dynamic behavior of electrical circuits and in the use of test equipment was superior to that of anyone else in the Endicott laboratory, Palmer derived considerable satisfaction from "straightening out some of the unusual transient conditions in the machines."[1] Before long, Palmer's services became invaluable to Clair Lake, who had turned his attention from machines to components and was designing some new relays and counters. Lake improved on the earlier work of Fred Carroll and others by designing not only a higher-speed and very compact counter but also a fast and space-conserving "wire-contact" relay that could be produced in several sizes with different contact arrangements. Palmer, who became supervisor of the electrical laboratory in 1937, worked with Lake on the magnetic and electrical characteristics of these devices. The first major application of the new components came when they were selected for the ASCC.[2]

The handful of key inventors in Endicott with whom Palmer worked often received project authorizations directly from T. J. Watson in New York City. Palmer's own department received frequent requests from company headquarters, typically from James W. Bryce, the prodigious inventor who had served essentially as chief engineer of the corporation since receiving that appointment from Watson in 1922.[3] Bryce had organized an IBM patent development department at head-quarters in 1926, and over the years he had maintained a small patent development group there, near the patent attorneys, where ideas and models could be turned into patent applications without the distraction of product commitments. The electrical laboratory at Endicott had worked with Bryce on the construction of the IBM Difference Tabulator for Columbia University.[4]

Palmer carried on a number of small exploratory electronics projects, some of which Bryce had suggested. These projects included the pho-toelectric detection of marks on cards and the experimental storage of information by magnetizing spots on card stock impregnated with iron particles. One experiment even involved storage of information on a small magnetic drum. Electron tubes, vacuum or gas filled, were used to amplify signals produced in reading information from the magnetic cards and drum. But those exploratory projects of the 1930s were, as Palmer later characterized them, "toy experiments," and the product line remained electromechanical.[5]

Had Bryce been able to demonstrate a convincing product potential for electron tubes, he might well have proposed that IBM form a research center for electronics. But Bryce's views concerning electronics were undoubtedly tempered by many practical considerations. The business was growing, and, as had long been the case, customers were pressing for incremental improvements, not for radical departures. The electric accounting machine product line was relatively new and still lacked some of the improvements for which he had plans, such as the ability to divide. Moreover, business machine history testified that investments in product-oriented patent development deserved a higher priority than those in non-product-oriented research. Finally, in the 1930s the country was in the throes of a deep depression; fiscal conservatism permeated the thinking of management everywhere.

Bryce knew well the technological limitations of electromechanical products: that speed of operation was limited by physical inertia; product life and reliability by wear; and cost and serviceability by size and complexity. But electronic technology was primitive, and speed was its most apparent advantage. While speed, under the right cir-cumstances, can often be used to reduce cost and complexity, the state of the art had not reached the point where Bryce could confidently formulate such trade-offs. His net conclusion was that while no major expenditure of resources was warranted, electronics should be watched, and that the IBM patent development department in New York City and the electrical laboratory in Endicott should quietly help by performing exploratory chores. Thus, about 1936, A. Halsey Dickinson of Bryce's department began investigating relay and tube switching circuits. At the time, the electron tubes of greatest interest were "thyratrons," which were gas-filled, and vacuum tubes, which were commonly known as "radio tubes" because their main use was in the flourishing radio industry.

Dickinson's early electronics work was based on thyratrons.[6] After about 1931, circuits designed around thyratrons were being used in physics research laboratories for such purposes as counting ionization-current pulses generated by particles emitted from radioactive materials.[7] The original need for electronic counting circuits derived from the inability of electromechanical counting meters to keep up with the repetition rates of the ionization signals. Dickinson's work resulted in a number of patents, including one filed in 1940 that described a system capable of adding and subtracting by means of a circuit combining a thyratron oscillator and a number of vacuum tubes per decimal position.[8] The thyratron generated a sawtooth voltage waveform, and the value of a decimal digit was represented by the phase of oscillation — that is, one of ten allowable moments of conduction of the thyratron within each timing cycle. The operation of gas-filled tubes depended on ionization and deionization of the gas, and the use of such tubes was limited to applications in which their characteristic of being easier to turn on than to turn off was unobjectionable, if not advantageous.

2.1 Flip-Flops and Counters

Vacuum tubes had the advantages of more convenient control and higher operating speeds than gas-filled tubes. Of chief interest was the vacuum triode, an evacuated glass tube containing three elements: a heated cathode, the source of electrons; an anode (or "plate") operated at a positive voltage relative to the cathode in order to collect the electrons; and a control grid placed very close to the cathode. Variations in grid voltage controlled electron flow to the plate, from zero (cutoff) to the maximum current the cathode could provide. The grid voltage had much more influence over plate current than had the plate voltage, and grid current was negligible over most of the control voltage range. Thus the tube provided both current and voltage amplification.

Great strides were made in the 1930s in developing counters based on bistable vacuum tube circuits — circuits in which either of two interconnected triodes, if conducting, could hold the other in the cutoff state. By 1937, investigators at Harvard University and in England were making such a circuit perform as a "binary" counter, one that would cycle through its two triode conduction states once for every two same-polarity voltage shifts, or pulses, applied to its input terminals.[9] A chain of two or more such circuits, each driving the next, could produce an output pulse after four, eight, sixteen, or any number of input pulses, provided that number was a power of two.

Palmer read about binary counters in an article by H. J. Reich of the University of Illinois in August 1939. Reich referred to such bistable circuits as "trigger circuits," a term borrowed from the original description of bistable vacuum tube circuits by their coinventors W. H. Eccles and F. W. Jordan in 1919.[10] Although all such circuits were called trigger circuits (or simply "triggers") in IBM for years thereafter, we shall use the term "flip-flop," which has found much wider use.

Early in 1941, Palmer suggested to Byron E. Phelps, an engineer in his department (and fellow alumnus of Union College, class of 1935) that he build some flip-flop circuits. Phelps did, and the two men were impressed with the reliable manner in which the circuits worked (figure 2.1). They decided to attempt a flip-flop counter for an experimental accounting machine or calculator. In the rotary mechanical counters then in use, a stored digit was represented by one of ten possible wheel positions. If a five-decimal-order counter initially held the number 82741, for example, the hundreds wheel (for example) would have stopped after moving seven positions starting from 0. When an operation called for adding to that number another, say 16503, the hundreds wheel was rotated another five positions, corresponding to the 5 in the hundreds order of the second number. This left it in the 2 position, having gone through 8, 9, 0, and 1 and having generated a carry to the next higher order as it went to 0. The wheels in other orders rotated similarly to accommodate incoming digits, carries being held until late in the cycle and then being added separately to the tentative amount standing in the counter.

To replace a mechanical counting wheel, a circuit would have to store an electronic indication of the total of the digit values fed into each order, including carries from the next lower decimal order, and produce a carry for the next higher order at the count of ten. Interconnected in the most natural manner, with the output voltage shift from each flip-flop used as the driving pulse for the next flip-flop, three flip-flops could serve as a scale-of-eight counter and four as a scale-of-sixteen counter; but neither arrangement would provide scale-of-ten counting.

One way out of the dilemma was to connect ten flip-flops serially in a ring circuit, wherein each flip-flop represented one of the ten

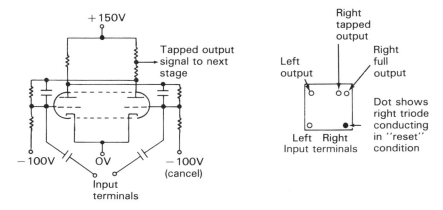

a Flip-flop or "trigger" circuit

b Block diagram of flip-flop

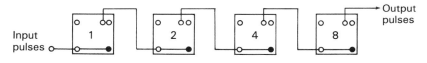

c Scale-of-16 counter

Figure 2.1
Vacuum tube flip-flop and counter. The circuit is reset initially by removing the
"-100 cancel" voltage, so that the right triode is conducting. A sharp negative-
going voltage transition (or negative "pulse") applied to the input terminal associated with the right-hand control grid in a causes the right triode to stop conducting and feeds an amplified positive-going signal to the grid of the left triode,
causing it to conduct. The resulting lower voltage at the plate of the left triode
holds the right triode nonconducting thereafter. Thus cross-coupling, by means
of the resistor-and-capacitor network from the plate of each triode to the control
grid of the other, makes conduction in the two triodes mutually exclusive. Used
as just described, the bistable circuit might store a single fact, such as the occur-
rence of a carry signal from some counter, for as long as desired. If the two input terminals are connected together and if the upper capacitors are sufficiently
large, the "on" or conducting status will pass from one triode to the other for
each negative pulse applied to the common input. The result is that the right
triode goes into conduction, producing a negative pulse at the output, only once
for every two negative input pulses, and the circuit becomes a binary or scale-of-
2 counter. This circuit was used extensively in IBM's electronic calculators of the
1940s. Any desired number n of such binary stages can be connected in sequence, to produce scale-of-2^n counting. Using the block diagram convention illustrated in b, four stages connected as in c produce a scale-of-16 counter, since
$2^4 = 16$. Tapped, or reduced, outputs are used to keep the signal amplitude
small enough to ensure that only negative pulses will cause successive stages to
flip. Full outputs are used for driving switching circuits illustrated in figure 2.3.

digits, and the circuit was preset so that only the 0 flip-flop was "on" (with, for example, its left-hand triode conducting, while in all other flip-flops the right-hand triodes were conducting). With proper connections, such a circuit would respond to an input voltage pulse by turning off the flip-flop that was on and turning on the next one in line. The number of input pulses would thus determine which flip-flop remained on. This arrangement was in fact selected, within a year or two, by the designers of the first large-scale electronic computer, the ENIAC, built at the Moore School of Electrical Engineering of the University of Pennsylvania.[11]

Phelps, who had experimented with ring circuits, was determined to use fewer than ten flip-flops per decimal order, and set about devising a more economical way to convert a scale-of-sixteen counter to scale-of-ten. Available at that time were twin triode tubes in which a single glass envelope contained two independent triode structures, so that a flip-flop could be constructed using only a single tube plus a few associated resistors and capacitors. Phelps discovered a simple but effective circuit arrangement requiring (in addition to the four counting flip-flops) only a single triode to make the conversion to scale-of-ten. The added triode (half a tube) and its connections blocked advancement from 9 to 10, forcing the counter to 0 instead (figure 2.2). Thus, a circuit with four and one-half tubes became the electronic equivalent of a counter wheel. Mounting two such circuits (nine tubes) on a book-sized metal chassis, he could build a twelve-order counter (or accumulator) on six chassis.[12]

Tiny neon lamps connected to individual flip-flops served to indicate that each stage flipped when it was supposed to. The code in which each order of the accumulator registered its contents became known as binary-coded decimal and is much used to this day in small, purely numeric electronic calculators. Initially, Phelps recalls, he viewed it not as a code but simply as a useful sequence of ten states. Only after a number of counters had been tested was it noticed that the decimal value standing in a counter could be read by adding the numeric weights of "on" flip-flops as indicated by glowing lamps. Indeed, a wiring error that appeared in one early group of counters caused the fourth flip-flop to turn on after two, rather than eight, input pulses; and the respective numeric weights (beginning with the input flip-flop) became 1, 2, 4, and 2, rather than 1, 2, 4, and 8. Either form of the circuit was usable, because it was the timing of the decimal carry pulse and not the "on" or "off" status of flip-flops that represented the useful output of this counter. A patent issued to Phelps in 1952 describes both connections.[13]

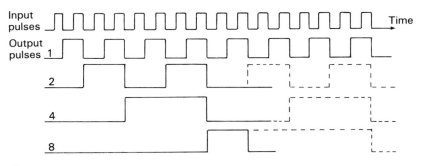

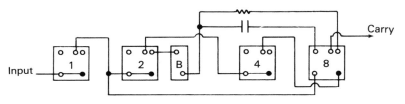

Figure 2.2
Principle of the scale-of-10 counter circuit. The patterns in *a* represent input and output voltage of each flip-flop (FF) of a scale-of-10 (decimal) counter, the upper level of each pattern representing the "on" state and the lower level the "off" state of the corresponding FF. Broken lines show patterns that would exist in an unmodified scale-of-16 (hexadecimal) counter. After ten negative input pulses, in the decimal counter the counting cycle is complete, a carry signal has been generated, and all FFs are off. In the hexadecimal counter, the 2 and 8 FFs would be on, representing a count of 10. The block diagram in *b* represents the circuit of figure 2.1*c* modified to perform as a decimal counter. The rectangle B represents a triode used as a blocking tube. It conducts when its input terminal, in the lower right corner, is at its high voltage level. In that condition, it holds the 2 FF off. The input to its control grid, through a limiting resistor, from the full output of the 8 FF ensures that this blocking action occurs while the latter is on. The input through a capacitor ensures that the blocking action is sustained also during the instant of transition of the 8 FF from on to off. (Circuit described in U.S. Patent 2,584,811, B. E. Phelps, Electronic Counting Circuit.)

The wiring error was soon corrected, because the resulting 1, 2, 4, 2 version of the counter was slowed by the need to effect four binary carries in going from nine (with all flip-flops on) to zero. Using the 1, 2, 4, 8 version, only the first and last flip-flops would be on for a decimal nine, and the number of binary carries was cut to two. (The last of these sequential carries in each case controlled the gating of pulses to other circuits, and its timing was therefore relatively important.) These early electronic arithmetic units, designed to combine counting with digit storing, were in every sense true counterparts of wheel accumulators.

Switching circuits were required for control of flip-flop operations and data transfers from one counter to another. One such circuit used a pair of triodes like those of the flip-flop. The two triodes shared a single plate-circuit resistor, so that conduction of either tube caused a voltage drop at the output (plate) terminal. Since the output voltage could not assume its high (most positive) level while the grid voltage of either the first or the second triode was high, the logical function of this circuit became known some years later as NOR (Not OR). Such terms derive, however, from Boolean algebra, so named for George Boole, the nineteenth-century founder of the mathematical analysis of logic. Lacking the language of that discipline, IBM engineers in the 1940s referred to the circuit simply as a "twin-triode switch" or as "blocking tubes." It performed the blocking function in the scale-of-ten counter just described, but its more general use as a switch appears to have occurred several years later.[14] A single triode with its own plate resistor formed an "inverter," so called because its output level was the inverse of its input (figure 2.3).

Another form of switching circuit employed a pentode: a five-element tube containing two grids that served as input terminals. Because its output voltage could not assume its high level (cutoff condition), if both the first and the second of its input grids were at the high level, its logical function was later commonly labeled NAND (Not AND). In the 1940s the pentode circuit was usually called a "switch." A series of pulses, at the first input for example, would be reproduced (inversely) at the output terminal only if the second input was held at its high level. (See figure 2.3.)

Switching circuits were used in various arrangements to control the transfer of numbers between accumulating counters in true or complement form, thus effecting addition or subtraction (figure 2.4). In a typical circuit, addition was accomplished by the transmission of a train of pulses from each decimal position of a sending counter to the corresponding position of a receiving counter. In this process the sending

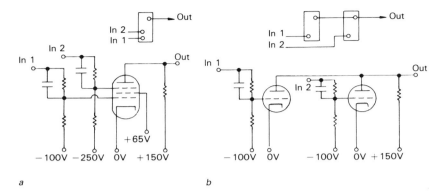

Figure 2.3
Vacuum tube switching circuits. The circuits shown are representative of those used in electronic calculators designed by IBM engineers in the 1940s. In the pentode switch circuit in *a*, the output at the plate is nearly +150 volts when the tube is cut off. The tube conducts, producing a 100 volt drop at the output only when both inputs are at their higher voltage level—near +150 volts. Different bias voltage supplies permit adjustment of the resistor voltage dividers to compensate for different amplification factors of the two grids. In the later machines using this type of switch—such as the 604 calculator—the pentode was replaced by a pentagrid tube whose two control grids had nearly equal control, permitting use of a common bias supply. The pair of blocking tubes at *b* permit the output at their common plate connection to drop to around +50 volts when either input is at the high level. Removal of the common plate connection would permit the right-hand triode, with the load resistor, to function as an inverter, producing high-level output for low-level input, and vice versa. Two such inverters, cross-coupled, form the basic flip-flop of figure 2.1*a*. Circuits *a* and *b*, in later years, would have been called NAND (Not AND) and NOR (Not OR) circuits, respectively, terms describing the combination of high-level inputs required to produce the high-level output. The block diagram symbols were of great value in simplifying engineering, training, and maintenance diagrams, especially for the 1400-tube 604 electronic calculator, introduced in 1948.

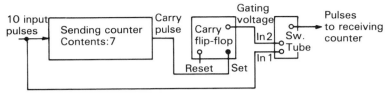

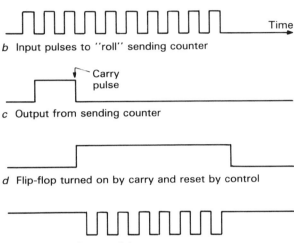

a Method of gating pulses to a receiving counter

b Input pulses to "roll" sending counter

c Output from sending counter

d Flip-flop turned on by carry and reset by control

e Pulses gated to receiving counter

Figure 2.4

Data transfer between counters. The block diagram in *a* illustrates a method used in adding the contents of one counter to another in IBM's electronic calculators of the 1940s. Ten clock (or basic timing) pulses applied to the input of each decimal order of the sending counter "roll" it through each of its ten values, and leaving it in its original state. Clock pulses are permitted to enter the receiving counter only after the sender has emitted a decimal carry. Carries, in the sending counter, are noted only for this timing purpose and do not result in carries between decimal positions of the sender. Only a single decimal position of the sending counter is shown, but in an actual calculator all positions would be transferred simultaneously. A carry from any position of the receiving counter would be stored in a special flip-flop, and time provided just following the accumulation of pulses for each such carry to be added to the next decimal position, propagating over any additional positions that may have held 9s. Thus, for example, a sender initially set at 7 would emit a carry pulse after the first 3 clock pulses, opening the gate (or switch) to permit only the last 7 pulses to reach the receiver.

counter was "rolled," that is, stepped through each of its ten settings, and thus left in its original state. A decimal carry, emitted as the counter passed from 9 to 0, was used to start the train of pulses, which then continued for the remainder of the ten-pulse cycle. The number of pulses transmitted to the receiving counter was therefore equal to the value of the digit to be added. By arranging the circuit so that pulse transmission was stopped rather than started by the carry, a train of pulses representing the complement of the sending counter's contents could be sent to the receiving counter. Subtraction was performed in this manner.

2.2 The Electronic Multiplier

Wallace McDowell, manager of the engineering laboratory at Endicott, urged Palmer and Phelps to demonstrate their new vacuum tube circuits where speed would show to greatest advantage, as in multiplication.[15] Consequently, before the end of 1942 Phelps had constructed a demonstration model of an electronic multiplier. Cabled to a card-reading and -punching machine, it generated the twelve-digit product of two six-digit factors from each card; the result was recorded in the same card at a punching station beyond the reading station. Multiplication was accomplished by repeated addition. The multiplicand was added into a product accumulator under control of successive multiplier digits, starting with the lowest-order digit. As each multiplier digit took control of the process, its value specified the number of additions. And before control passed to the next higher multiplier digit, the multiplicand was shifted left one decimal position relative to the product accumulator, much as a human being shifts successive lines to the left in multiplying by hand.[16] This experimental machine was incapable of division, which involved a somewhat more elaborate process. It was reasonable, however, in the context of punched-card procedures, to consider a machine that was capable only of multiplication. In fact, IBM had not a single product, in 1942, that was able to perform division.

   Meanwhile, because people in the Sales Department had shown interest in some form of rapid addition in a keypunch, Palmer and Phelps also built a cross-footing keypunch. This machine permitted a keyboard operator to enter data and produce a punched card containing not only the keyed information but also the results of "cross-footing" (summing two or more selected fields). The first model of the electronic cross-footing punch became operable in March 1942. After some tuning, it underwent the normal testing process for candidate products. Its performance encouraged the construction and testing of a second, improved model, but sales interest waned and the machine was never marketed.

The electronic multiplier, more complicated than the punch, was capable by December 1942 of running 500 multiplications without error, according to Phelps. The multiplier and cross-footer were, he adds, "to the best of my knowledge, the first complete machines ever to perform digital arithmetic by electronic means." Actually, the multiplier was not fully electronic. In the interest of economy, relays were employed in its column shift unit, which provided columnar alignment of the partial product contributed by each successive multiplier digit. This function was not critical, however, to completion of arithmetic operations within the available fraction of a card cycle.[17]

By mid-1943, Palmer had left for the navy, and the electronic calculator project lost momentum, but Phelps, who continued to study the circuit parameters, made improvements that increased the speed of the counters. In the meantime, the engineering laboratory had been under an increasingly restrictive order from Watson to defer product development and give highest priority to wartime government projects.[18] In retrospect, it may seem strange that the latter category did not include an electronic digital calculator. The explanation is simply that wartime needs urged rapid delivery; as far as IBM was concerned, this urgency plus the lack of operating experience with digital electronic equipment kept vacuum tube machines in the experimental category through World War II.

In fact, aside from specialized electronic equipment designed and used by government agencies in secret work such as code breaking, electronic techniques were not applied to digital computation during the war.[19] Even ENIAC, the pioneering electronic computer built at the University of Pennsylvania for the Army Ballistic Research Laboratory, was not placed in service until after the war.[20] Meanwhile, IBM delivered two high-speed relay calculators to that agency at Aberdeen Proving Ground, Maryland, late in 1944, less than two years after the start of design. (See chapter 1.) Over an order of magnitude faster than IBM's Type 601 electromechanical multipliers, the machines were used extensively during the last eight months of the war.[21]

During 1944, the environment for electronics in IBM changed significantly. Watson had been convinced for some time that "we are not doing enough in electronics" and that to outdistance the ASCC would require the speed of electronics.[22] He expressed these feelings to John C. McPherson, director of engineering, among others. McPherson had been instrumental in the establishment of a punched-card computing facility at the Ballistic Research Laboratory and later in the decision to construct the two high-speed relay calculators. Late in 1944, Watson assigned Halsey Dickinson the task of building an electronic calculator.[23] It was the understanding among Dickinson, McPherson, and McDowell that the unit would serve not only for scientific calculation but for any calculating requirement.[24]

In March 1945, Phelps was transferred to Dickinson's group at corporate headquarters in New York City to work on the project, which was well served by the knowledge gained from work on the experimental multiplier in Endicott several years earlier. The resulting product, an electronic calculating unit with a cable-attached card reader-punch, was essentially a higher-speed version of the Endicott model, with an all-electronic column-shift unit to replace the relay version in the earlier model. Phelps and an engineer from Dickinson's department, with the aid of a technician or two for wiring, assembled the machine by the end of the year.[25]

In April 1946, the electronic multiplier was demonstrated to Watson and to Thomas J. Watson, Jr., the elder of the IBM chief executive's two sons.[26] "Tom" Watson, Jr., had joined IBM as a sales trainee in 1937, shortly after his graduation from Brown University. His IBM career was interrupted by a five-year stint in the U.S. Army Air Corps, in which he acquired the rank of lieutenant colonel by the end of World War II. He returned to IBM in January 1946 as a high-level executive assistant, the position he held at the time he was shown the electronic multiplier.

The younger Watson was deeply impressed to learn that a machine could perform calculations by means of electronics. His interest and support for the project helped to provide an impetus for a first production lot of fifty machines. Designated the IBM 603 Electronic Multiplier (figure 2.5), it was demonstrated at the National Business Show in New York City late in September 1946. It was the first electronic calculator ever placed in production. Probably well over a hundred orders could have been booked, but since a more flexible and powerful calculator, the 604, was already under development, 603 production was limited to one hundred machines. Customer interest in the 603 was encouraging, however, to those in IBM who believed the company should move with increasing determination toward electronic products.[27]

Figure 2.5
IBM 603 Electronic Multiplier

2.3 The SSEC, A Super Calculator

When Watson, Sr., gave Dickinson responsibility for the 603 project, he made it clear to McPherson and Bryce that he also wanted IBM to build a "super calculator" that would eclipse the ASCC (the Harvard Mark I) and with it any expected offspring. (It was understood by then that Harvard's Howard Aiken proposed to build a successor machine, using relays in place of rotary counters, for the Naval Proving Ground at Dahlgren, Virginia.)[28]

In 1944 Watson invited Wallace J. Eckert to join the company. Eckert had left Columbia University in 1940 to become director of the Nautical Almanac at the U.S. Naval Observatory in Washington, D.C. He accepted Watson's invitation on the first day of March 1945, stepping into the new position of director of the Pure Science Department. His many responsibilities could be summed up as helping IBM understand the computational requirements of the scientific community. Eckert understood from the start that Watson expected him to create or endorse the specifications of the planned super calculator.[29]

While awaiting Eckert's arrival, John McPherson as director of engineering felt personally responsible for seeing that the definition of the new machine moved forward. Frank Hamilton, in the Endicott laboratory, had been invited early in 1945 to discussions on the subject with McPherson, Bryce, and Dickinson.[30] He had proved himself while directing the ASCC project and was an obvious choice to supervise the design of the new Super Calculator. He therefore tried persistently during March and April 1945, through correspondence with John McPherson, to obtain Eckert's approval on various proposals for functional components of the new machine. McPherson tried, just as persistently, to get formal replies from Eckert, but Eckert was busy assimilating the many segments of his new responsibility, and such replies were not immediately forthcoming. Although McPherson gave Hamilton his own best counsel over a period of several months, the plans for the Super Calculator during most of 1945 were really only proposals.[31]

Contributing to the difficulty of formulating the new machine was the fact that Endicott engineers were attuned to the requirements of customers for electromechanical machines produced in large quantities. Even were he not still restricted to wartime projects, Wallace McDowell could not have been enthusiastic over the prospect of investing a significant share of his laboratory's resources in another large, one-of-a-kind calculator. Nevertheless, Hamilton continued his attempts to clarify the machine proposal and obtain formal agreement on it. He had expressed his initial proposals for functional elements of the machine in terms of electromechanical components but had suggested that electronics could be substituted in actual computing circuits for the sake of higher speed.

Fortunate for Hamilton was the arrival at IBM, in the summer of 1945, of Robert R. "Rex" Seeber, a Harvard graduate of 1932 long interested in computation. As a civilian in the Navy Department, Seeber had first spent a year and a half in wartime operations research. He had next been assigned, in mid-1944, to the Bureau of Ships computation project at Harvard, to work under Commander Howard Aiken. He had worked long, hard hours as a programmer on the ASCC but had never felt close to Aiken. For one thing, his suggestions about how a computer ought to be designed, which included the storing of instructions and operating on them as data, had been rejected and, he felt, even disparaged by Aiken. For another thing, Seeber had found himself sympathetic toward IBM on matters of disagreement between Aiken and the company. When it had become clear that even Aiken's Mark II was not going to be endowed with the capability of modifying its instructions, Seeber left Harvard for IBM, still determined to see his idea given a fair trial. He went to work under Wallace Eckert in New York City on 1 August 1945.[32]

Eckert made Seeber his representative to the Super Calculator project at Endicott. Hamilton and Seeber hit it off from the start. Their skills and backgrounds were complementary. Hamilton could explain the operation of electrical components and circuits to the young man from Harvard. Delighted to acquire this knowledge, Seeber in turn helped Hamilton and his engineers understand many features of organization and operation that would enhance the usefulness of the new machine.[33]

Hamilton, who had earned the confidence and respect of the old school of inventors in the laboratory, had a clearer understanding than they of the laboratory environment that would be essential to the successful design of a large electronic machine. The inventors had traditionally worked in secrecy, sharing ideas with only their most trusted assistants. By contrast, Hamilton encouraged a cooperative spirit and was careful to recognize the contributions of his subordinates. Phelps recalls, for example, that Hamilton turned down the opportunity to add his own name to a patent disclosure on the basis that two of his engineers deserved the entire credit for the invention. Despite his long years in the laboratory, Hamilton seemed to identify with a new style of engineering management in IBM.[34]

With the end of the war with Japan in August 1945, IBM's engineering organization was again free to turn its energies to peacetime projects. Less than two months after Seeber had joined IBM, a significant meeting was held in Poughkeepsie on the Super Calculator, by then referred to as the "Sequence Calculator." Present, in addition to the headquarters contingent of Eckert, Bryce, McPherson, Dickinson, and Seeber, were McDowell, Hamilton, and several other leading engineers from the laboratories. Seeber described his experiences with the Harvard machine and explained some of its shortcomings: lack of compatible instruction and data formats (and hence inability to operate on its own instructions); inflexibility of subroutine control; inability to *record* in large-scale (paper-tape) storage; and inadequate speed of table look-up. The engineers exchanged views on what was possible and practical in terms of computing and recording devices. It was agreed that the objective was a machine that could be built within twelve months from date of authorization. Hamilton undertook to prepare a design, and for almost two years thereafter, Seeber commuted regularly between Endicott and New York City working constantly to reconcile Eckert's ideas with those of the engineers and to ensure that his own architectural notions received due consideration.[35]

Eckert insisted that the machine was urgently needed and that it should not become a vehicle for technological experimentation.[36] It was to be a transitional machine, carefully tailored to extract from vacuum tubes and electromechanical devices the maximum contribution to performance that each could offer at that moment in history. The arithmetic element and a small amount of storage would be electronic. A next echelon of functional and storage units would employ high-speed relays. The very large storage capacity needed for tables and sequence-control information would be provided in the form of loops and rolls of wide punched paper tape. Eckert's position on technology was consistent with his approach to the computing challenges he had previously encountered. He was neither engineer nor technologist but astronomer and expert computer. He had always delighted in making imaginative use of standard or nearly standard equipment, and a long list of important published tables attested to the success of his methods.

During the fall of 1945 and through the winter, Hamilton and Seeber met frequently with McPherson, Dickinson, and Eckert, working toward a final description of the machine. The ultimate objective was to obtain Eckert's approval. This came in stages, the iterative process being essentially terminated when Eckert wrote McPherson: "The specifications for the calculator contained in Mr. Hamilton's letter of March 14 are in accordance with our previous understanding of the machine. It is anticipated that minor improvements will suggest themselves as the detailed design progresses, and these will be incorporated by mutual consent."[37]

No significant changes occurred. Hamilton's proposed specifications described the machine that was finally constructed. Its storage hierarchy, starting with the highest-capacity devices, included sixty-six paper-tape readers, thirty-six of which were capable of high-speed searching in table-lookup mode, the others capable of sharing tape paths with three tape punches in a variety of arrangements. Next there were 150 high-speed relay storage units of twenty-digit capacity. Finally, eight twenty-digit electronic storage units served both as arithmetic registers and as temporary (or buffer) storage between tape or relay storage and the electronic arithmetic circuits. The twentieth (leftmost) digit position of a storage unit was used to hold the sign, leaving space for nineteen digits to represent the magnitude of a number.

The "paper" tape consisted of IBM card stock 7 3/8 inches wide, the dimension of the standard eighty-column card. Information was represented on tape—as elsewhere in the machine—in the binary-coded-decimal form described in the case of the electronic counter. For highest speed of reading or punching, all holes for each number were punched in a single row across the tape, in what is called parallel recording. Each decimal digit therefore occupied four columns on the tape, for the possible 1, 2, 4, and 8 punches. A twenty-digit number would have required eighty columns, but only seventy-eight were available for information storage—the first and last columns being needed for drive-sprocket holes. The left-most "digit," which had only to represent the sign, was therefore allocated only two columns, and the "twenty-digit" numbers of the Sequence Calculator might be described more precisely as $19\frac{1}{2}$-digit numbers.

The relays in the Sequence Calculator were of the wire-contact type designed by Clair Lake and first used in the ASCC. Available with four, six, or twelve sets of contacts, they could store new information in 4 milliseconds—much less than the time required to position and punch paper tape. When sufficient current was passed through its "pick" coil to actuate a relay, closing its normally open contacts, one such set of contacts could be used to supply a smaller holding current to a separate winding. The relay thus remained energized (storing the fact that it had been activated) until the holding current was interrupted by the opening of another set of contacts. Each digit to be stored required four relays, again representing the weights 1, 2, 4, and 8, respectively.

Similarly, each digit of electronic storage required four flip-flops. Since the storage units were not required to perform arithmetic, they were not wired as electronic counters. Associated with each digit of storage, however, was a good deal of switching circuitry to transfer data between the flip-flops and other units such as relay storage or the electronic arithmetic section. Electronic storage was faster and, digit for digit, more expensive than relay storage; relays, in turn, were not only faster but much more expensive than punched tape.

Late in 1945, after the design of the 603 multiplier had been completed and a model built, Byron Phelps returned to Endicott to assist in the electronic design of the Sequence Calculator. The basic circuits were the flip-flops, switches, and inverters of the multiplier, but the new machine required many thousands of tubes as compared to a few hundred in the 603. While its arithmetic unit performed only the basic operations of addition, subtraction, multiplication, and division, circuit configurations became elaborate as the designers found ways to increase speed. The large numbers to be accommodated and a wide choice of data paths, along with provision for rounding and shifting of results, contributed further to the tube requirements.

Ernest S. Hughes, Jr., formerly a research engineer with the Carnegie Institution of Washington, joined IBM in December 1945. He was a graduate of the University of Tennessee with a degree in electrical engineering and four years' experience in design of equipment, including devices for automatically plotting the paths of army vehicles. He was assigned to the Sequence Calculator, and during the course of the project he assumed a leading position in the overall electronic organization of the evolving machine. James J. Troy joined IBM at Endicott in 1932 as an assembler in the factory. His prewar experience included design engineering in the laboratory and a voluntary two-year stint as a customer engineer. He spent the four years prior to September 1946 as an officer in the army and on returning to the company that month was assigned to Hamilton's project. Troy, who later managed the Endicott laboratory for an unprecedented thirteen years, did a good deal of the detailed design and supervised construction of the electronic panels.[38]

The specifications accepted in March 1946 represented only one step toward the design of a machine. From April to December, Seeber spent many hours each day in a conference room in Hamilton's area of the laboratory in Endicott. There he and Hughes, frequently joined by Hamilton or others in the department, would propose and evaluate a variety of logical designs to arrive at a combination that would provide the desired flexibility of control and speed of data flow. The walls of the conference room were soon papered with huge drawings that detailed the layout and interconnections of the machine.[39] The "calculator," which was in every sense a computer, inherited much in the way of organization and nomenclature from the ASCC. Central to the system was the sequence control, whose special bank of relays held the information and established the interconnections necessary to carry out the operations specified in the current "line of sequence," and to obtain the next such line from "storage." The terms "program," "instruction," or "memory" (as a particular storage application) rarely if ever appear in documents generated in the course of design and construction of the Sequence Calculator. Those terms did, however, gain currency elsewhere during that period and are found in the earliest published descriptions of the machine, all of which appeared after its early 1948 announcement. It will be convenient at times to use both sets of terms interchangeably in describing the organization of the machine.[40]

One of the Sequence Calculator's most novel features was its representation, storage, and transmission of instructions and numerical data in the same storage devices, over the same information channels, and in units of the same fixed length. Any level of storage, from the paper-tape readers to the electronic registers, could hold instructions, ordinary data, or a mixture of the two. An instruction contained six separate fields, typically specifying the locations in storage of two operands, a location at which to store the result, the location of the next instruction to be read, the type of arithmetic operation desired, and the direction and extent of column shifting to be performed upon the result.[41] Because instructions were stored in the same manner as data, the machine could be programmed to perform a wide variety of useful operations on its own instructions. And since every instruction contained a field that determined the location in storage of the next one to be read and executed, one use of instruction modification was to let the results of computation determine the program path selected.[42]

To make efficient use of the fast electronic arithmetic unit, the designers provided many paths for overlapped (concurrent) data transfer to and from the machine's slower storage units. The relays of the sequence control accepted two full instructions at a time. Together they constituted a "line of sequence," and the left and right "half-lines of sequence," or instructions, each called for the transfer of as many as four twenty-digit numbers or instructions between electro-mechanical storage devices and the arithmetic unit. In the left half-line, for example, fields designated P, Q, and R typically called for the movement of two operands and a result, while sequence field S1 indicated the source (such as a tape reader) of the instruction representing the next left half-line of sequence. Similarly, fields T, U, and V in the right half-line might specify two operands and a result, while field S2 indicated the source (for example, a second tape reader) of the next right half-line of sequence. Thus two tape readers were commonly kept busy supplying their respective halves of the successive lines of sequence. The additional two fields in each half-line of sequence, which indicated the type of arithmetic operation and the shifting of the result, did not require additional, concurrent transfer of data.

There were, of course, differences between the inherent operating modes of relay and tape storage. In the relay storage, a number or instruction was transmitted to or from the particular twenty-digit storage unit designated in, for example, the Q field of the instruction being executed. When a tape reader was specified, on the other hand, the choice between two codes assigned to the device determined whether the tape advanced after a row was read. Thus repeated reference to a tape reader could cause transfer of either the same information or successive rows of information, depending on the exact codes used. In a tape punch, however, the tape was always advanced to the next row after punching.[43] (For a more detailed description of sequence control in the SSEC, see appendix A.)

The provision of many paths for overlapped data transfer, which permitted a good speed match between electronic and electromechanical components, also produced a complex machine. No tools, techniques, or conventions existed for the simplification of design record keeping. As the design progressed, the diagrams with which Seeber and Hughes covered the walls of their conference room represented the only complete record of the machine. Even that record was inadequate to display the intricate timing relationships among the separately clocked arithmetic, storage, and control units, and Hughes recalls a period of months during which such details were recorded only in his and Seeber's minds.[44]

Although Eckert's approval came in late March 1946, those concerned understood that the machine was to be completed in a year—and that Watson, Sr., was counting time from the beginning of 1946, when he had personally conferred responsibility for the machine on Hamilton. The deadline turned out to be impossible to meet, but an excellent showing was made. By 31 December 1946, all relay and vacuum tube chassis were in place, and only the interchassis cabling (and, of course, "debugging" and testing) remained to be done.[45]

Cabling and preliminary testing with short programs took until mid-1947, by which time a room in the building on Fifty-seventh Street adjacent to the 590 Madison Avenue headquarters of IBM had been readied for it. When the machine was moved from the Endicott laboratory to New York City, the engineering group moved with it. Then began intensive testing that was to continue until the machine's public presentation. Although dual sequencing—the supplying of left and right half-lines of sequence from separate storage devices—was adopted initially to achieve a higher speed of operation, it was commonly used as a way to facilitate checking of results. Programs were prepared for the concurrent execution of duplicate instructions through separate storage units and data paths. Results of the two concurrent processes were compared at programmed check points and, according to the programmer's choice, lack of agreement either stopped the machine or caused repetition of the preceding sequence of operations until equality was reached.[46]

The machine was dedicated on 27 January 1948 as the Selective Sequence Electronic Calculator (SSEC). The similarity in name to the ASCC (Harvard Mark I) was more than coincidental. The power of a large calculator directed by an ordered stream of instructions from a source of almost unlimited capacity had been demonstrated impressively in the ASCC. Although that machine would now appear slow and inflexible by comparison with the SSEC, the family relationship between them was clear.

Dozens of eminent scientists, astronomers, mathematicians, and leaders of education, government, and business were invited to a luncheon preceding the unveiling.[47] But the probability of a successful demonstration seemed low that morning to the engineers who had lived with the machine for so many months. For one thing, metallic particles from drilling during the installation, as well as particles brushed loose from wall paneling during a last-minute change of decor, had been causing relays to malfunction, and there was the likelihood of at least one failure every few hours among the SSEC's thousands of vacuum tubes. These were standard "radio tubes" of the kind that had been used over the years primarily as amplifiers; service in digital computing circuits required them to operate in modes for which they were not intended.

Nonetheless, after Watson addressed the assembled guests, the SSEC seemed to catch the spirit of the occasion by running all afternoon without apparent malfunction.[48] Watson dedicated the calculator "to the use of science throughout the world." Eckert then described the problem he had selected for the demonstration: the task of computing the position of the moon, for any given time in the past or future. The task involved complicated equations for the evaluation of about 1600 terms. After instructions were inserted and a given date was supplied, the calculator computed and checked the desired position.[49] The demonstration program, prepared under the close supervision of Eckert and Seeber, used the SSEC's ability to modify its own instructions—in this case an instruction for finding the trigonometric sine of an angle.[50]

Designed, built, and placed in operation in only two years, the SSEC contained 21,400 relays and 12,500 vacuum tubes. It could operate indefinitely under control of its modifiable program. On the average, it performed 14-by-14-digit decimal multiplication in one-fiftieth of a second, division in one-thirtieth of a second, and addition or subtraction of nineteen-digit numbers in one-thirty-five-hundreth of a second.[51] With vast banks of tubes and flashing neon indicator lamps that were clearly visible from the street, the SSEC was an impressive sight. Every day hundreds of pedestrians paused in front of the large window on Fifty-seventh Street to gaze with wonder. It inspired a generation of cartoonists to portray a computer as consisting of wall-sized panels covered with lights, meters, dials, switches, and vaguely associated reels of tape (figure 2.6).

The SSEC was more novel in its design than in its technology. Its electronic nucleus consisted primarily of an arithmetic unit, 160 digits of storage, and the switching circuits necessary to control the flow of

Figure 2.6
IBM Selective Sequence Electronic Calculator (SSEC). Visible along the end wall, in the background, are the three paper-tape punches and the thirty paper-tape readers that form the paper-tape storage. A large supply roll of tape is positioned above each punch. Behind these units, and not visible in the photograph, are the relay storage and various power distribution and control units. Along the left wall are located panels of vacuum tube circuits for card reading and sequence control and thirty-six paper-tape readers comprising the table-lookup section. These readers, like those in the tape storage, could be used to read program instructions as well as data. Most of the panels along the right wall are occupied by the electronic arithmetic unit and electronic storage. Units in the center of the room include card readers, card punches, printers, and (obscured by the pillars) an operator's console.

data in a highly overlapped mode of operation. While the SSEC was much more flexible than the ASCC and possessed approximately 250 times more productive capacity, its designers had not extended the frontiers of electronic technology. The ENIAC, completed by J. Presper Eckert, Jr. (no relative of Wallace J. Eckert), and John W. Mauchly at the University of Pennsylvania in 1946, was faster at the level of individual operations than the SSEC. The SSEC, however, was capable of solving a wider range of problems—including, for example, simultaneous equations and partial differential equations requiring more addressable storage capacity than was available in the ENIAC.[52]

For more than four years, the SSEC fulfilled the wish Watson had expressed at its dedication: that it would serve humanity by solving important problems of science. It enabled Wallace Eckert to publish a lunar ephemeris (table of positions of the moon at regular intervals) of greater accuracy than previously available. This ephemeris was the source of data used in man's first landing on the moon. The SSEC, in keeping with its dedication, was operated on a nonprofit basis. For problems of pure science, there was no charge at all; for problems of government and industry, charges covered only operating expenses.[53] A programming staff set up and directed by Seeber included a number of people destined to become influential in IBM and well known in the computer field.[54]

The SSEC was used on more than thirty problems involving planetary orbits, fluid flow, atomic fields, optics, ordnance, and hydrodynamics. Among the problems beyond the reach of any other computing instrument at the time was Hippo, a classified project for the Los Alamos Laboratory of the Atomic Energy Commission and the largest problem ever placed on the machine. And John von Neumann, the renowned mathematician from the Institute for Advanced Study who made important contributions to the early development of computer concepts, brought in a problem concerning the origin of turbulence in high-speed fluid flow that had puzzled scientists for over sixty years. This problem failed to run successfully because of the accumulated rounding errors in the approach suggested by von Neumann, and it was abandoned. Later Llewwellyn H. Thomas of Wallace Eckert's staff reprogrammed and ran it successfully, proving in the process that fluids of low viscosity, when moving rapidly, become unstable without any outside influence.[55] The SSEC was shut down in July 1952 and dismantled to make room for the fully electronic IBM 701, the first computer IBM placed in production (see chapter 5).

It is natural to ask whether the SSEC was influenced by ideas that grew out of the computer projects at the University of Pennsylvania.

No such influence was recalled by Seeber or the SSEC engineers. They have stated that, to the best of their knowledge, the SSEC architecture originated with the project.[56] That architecture, like the terminology used to describe it, was sufficiently distinctive to cast doubt on any external influence. It is, in any case, implausible that a computer of the size and complexity of the SSEC could have been produced in the short time that it was, using the new machine organization ideas of a separate and remote group.[57]

Furthermore, although the SSEC was the first operational computer known to have been able to modify its program, it had little influence on the design of subsequent machines. Not surprisingly, the next project of Hamilton and his SSEC group—the 650 Magnetic Drum Calculator (see chapter 3)—showed traces of its SSEC ancestry. These appeared mainly in the form of a table-lookup instruction and the manner of indicating the source of each next instruction. But the SSEC, complicated by features designed to offset the lack of a single large electronic-speed storage, and consequently somewhat awkward to program, was not an appealing model for later computers.[58] In IBM as elsewhere, these tended to follow architectural concepts that arose from early work at the Moore School of the University of Pennsylvania and at the Institute for Advanced Study (IAS) in Princeton, N.J.

J. P. Eckert, Jr., and J. W. Mauchly at the Moore School were aware of limitations imposed on the ENIAC's versatility by the small capacity of its electronic flip-flop storage (200 digits) and by its plugwired program and manual function-table switches. These limitations and proposed methods of overcoming them were discussed with John von Neumann of IAS, a consultant, and Captain Herman H. Goldstine, the representative of the Ballistic Research Laboratory (BRL) who had been instrumental in establishing the ENIAC project.[59]

The first documented description of the machine planned to correct the deficiencies of the ENIAC was the mid-1945 "First Draft of a Report on the EDVAC," by von Neumann. Important concepts that became accepted as essential to computer systems were set forth in that report, which was distributed initially to only two dozen people closely connected with the project.[60] But the EDVAC itself was neither the first nor, apparently, the most important computer that was built incorporating these ideas.

Two important families of computers came into existence following the Moore School planning discussions. One family of machines employed acoustic (mercury tank) delay lines in a circulating form of serial memory: a memory in which all the binary digits (bits) of an instruction or an operand were transmitted over a single path, one at a time. Included in this family were the EDVAC, built at the Moore School for BRL, where it became operational in 1951; the EDSAC, built under the direction of Maurice V. Wilkes at Cambridge University in England (operational in 1949, first of the class); and the BINAC (1949) and UNIVAC (1951), ventures of Eckert and Mauchly after their departure from the University of Pennsylvania.[61] A second family of machines had as its prototype the machine built at IAS under the direction of von Neumann during the years 1946 to 1951.[62] They all shared its principal feature of parallel memory, in which all the bits of an instruction or an operand were transmitted simultaneously, on separate wires. It is not our purpose to describe the machines of either family in detail here; as the early computers of IBM are introduced, the pioneering machines that influenced them will be identified.

2.4 The Type 604, an Electronic Workhorse

Ralph Palmer had left the Endicott laboratory for military service in 1943. When the war ended, he was serving as an officer in the Naval Computing Machine Laboratory on the premises of the National Cash Register Company in Dayton, Ohio. He had also spent a good deal of his time shuttling between that laboratory and the Naval Communications Annex in Washington, D.C., to which machines developed in Dayton were shipped.[63] The navy assignment had exposed him to some of the most advanced electronic circuit developments in the highly classified projects of an organization that later became part of the National Security Agency.[64]

When he returned to IBM from the navy early in 1946, Palmer faced the dubious prospect of influencing the company toward exploitation of electronics, the technology that had served the country so effectively during the war. He was surprised to learn that during his absence a distinct interest in electronics had arisen at company headquarters, as evidenced by Phelps's transfer to New York City and the new multiplier that had been modeled there. Within weeks of returning to the Endicott laboratory, Palmer was asked to form an electronics group in Poughkeepsie, New York.[65]

Arriving in Poughkeepsie, Palmer found that the "laboratory" there consisted of unrelated groups under several "development engineers," and no real manager over all. Ralph E. Page, H. S. Beattie, Edward J. Rabenda, and others who had moved there from the East Orange Laboratory when it closed in 1944 were working to complete an accounting machine incorporating a new wheel printer on which work had started in the late 1930s.[66] The resulting 407 accounting machine,

Figure 2.7
IBM laboratory at the former Kenyon Estate, Poughkeepsie, N.Y.

introduced in 1949, was an innovative and highly successful product, destined for a place in history as IBM's last major new electromechanical accounting machine. Meanwhile, the 407 group was housed at the Kenyon Estate, a mansion on 217 acres the company had purchased in 1944 for use by development engineers until postwar availability of materials should permit the construction of a modern laboratory (figure 2.7).

Another group there consisted of engineers from the Rochester, N.Y., laboratory. Rochester had been the development and manufacturing location for the electric typewriter, which IBM had added to its product line in 1933 through purchase of Electromatic Typewriters, Inc.[67] In 1944, that engineering group transferred to Poughkeepsie, along with typewriter manufacturing, and was housed in one of the buildings on the Kenyon Estate.

Realizing that his was to be just another group, Palmer moved into an office at the head of the central stairway on the top floor of the Kenyon House and began to recruit (mainly from within IBM) a few engineers with backgrounds in electronics. Jerrier A. Haddad, who had come to IBM in Endicott from Cornell University during the previous summer, joined Palmer early in 1946. Max E. Femmer, a University of Missouri graduate who had acquired wartime electronics experience in the army, was hired later in the year.[68] And Byron

Phelps, who completed his work on the SSEC before year end, moved to Poughkeepsie in December as Palmer's assistant.

Palmer believed in involving his laboratory in experimental work on all devices and technologies that showed real promise for the electronic approach to calculation. As a result, this small nucleus of an electronics group began to experiment with a variety of techniques for electronic switching, counting, and storage. The group's first major assignment was one that would occupy most of its attention for several years and constitute an intensive experience in electronic product development. It had become evident months before announcement of the 603 Electronic Multiplier in September that a device able to calculate at electronic speeds was used to little advantage in a product of such limited function. All the machine was required to do was multiply one number from a card by another and present a result to be punched in the same card; it was capable of neither division nor cross-footing. Clearly, the electronic box in such a configuration ought to be able to do a great deal more than it was doing in the time available—the "card cycle" that corresponded to a feeding rate of one hundred cards per minute.

Reporting on the laboratory's September 1946 activities, McPherson said, "Mr. Palmer is redesigning the machine to include crossfooting and dividing on a larger-capacity basis to replace the present machine within eight months after production begins."[69] The result of this effort was the IBM 604 Electronic Calculating Punch, a machine on which considerable expectations for the future of the business were pinned and in which a corresponding amount of planning talent was invested. Assigned to the project from IBM world headquarters was Stephen W. Dunwell, who had returned from military service to IBM's Future Demands department in mid-1946.[70] Dunwell had taken part in highly secret projects of the Army Signal Corps. Recalling those projects years later, he said, "I think they are forever classified." He also said of his and Palmer's closely related wartime work, "I feel sure that [Palmer] felt the same dismay and astonishment when he walked in and saw some of the things that had been done. . . . They often involved vast numbers of vacuum tubes . . . vast numbers of relays."[71] Clearly, it had been a sobering experience to become suddenly immersed in secret data processing developments involving electronics, a technology to which IBM had not yet made a commitment. Partly, no doubt, because of their shared but never-to-be disclosed wartime experience, Palmer and Dunwell made a strong engineering and planning team. Dunwell contributed a great deal to the understanding of the new calculator's requirements and to evaluation of alternative solutions.

Plans for the new machine progressed so rapidly that the decision was made to accept orders for no more than one hundred 603 multipliers. The 603 had provided a set of basic circuit designs, which, with some improvements, could be used in the 604. The "clock" or basic timing signal frequency was increased from 35,000 to 50,000 cycles per second, so that more operations could be squeezed into a card-feeding cycle. And although additional versions of the flip-flop and the switching circuits were required in the more complex new machine, these were basically the circuits invented in 1941 and 1942 for the Endicott model cross-footer and multiplier and used in both the 603 and the SSEC.

When the 604 was first delivered in fall 1948, no other calculator of comparable size or cost could match its capability. It could execute at least twenty, and optionally as many as forty (soon increased to sixty), plugboard-controlled program steps each time a card was read by the accompanying reader-punch and could suppress specified steps under control of input data or results of calculations. Division was included in its set of arithmetic operations, and the 604 was only the second product IBM offered with that capability. (The first was the 602, an electromechanical calculating punch introduced about two years earlier.) The 604 could hold thirty-two digits in "general" and "factor" storage units consisting of flip-flops, and was able to perform any sequence of arithmetic and data-moving operations that did not exceed program-step capacity or the time allocated within a card cycle.[72] The 604 was not, however, a *computer* in the sense that word has acquired. It lacked the essential characteristic of a stored program; its program was bound to the reader-punch, operating within the time provided by that unit rather than directing input-output along with internal operations. In short, it was a punched-card calculator in the EAM tradition, with impressive new capabilities derived from the speed and flexibility of electronics.

In the 604, IBM had to face for the first time a number of problems whose solutions would be important to the computer industry as a whole: the problems of manufacturing, testing, maintaining, and repairing an electronic machine to be produced by the thousands and installed wherever punched-card machines were used for calculating. Ralph Palmer had wisely exerted great pressure on his engineers to hold the number of circuit types to the minimum that would permit an efficient system design. It is usually desirable to maintain "standard circuit" control (i.e., avoid the unnecessary proliferation of circuit types) in an electronic system in order to ensure predictable operation and minimize the time required for testing and servicing. And Palmer had hit on an idea that greatly increased the benefits to be gained from this element of design control: he theorized that if every vacuum tube and its closely associated resistors and capacitors were packaged separately in a "pluggable unit," each such circuit could be tested before insertion into the machine, and the manufacturing-test process could be greatly simplified.

The 604 pluggable circuit unit was a fundamental contribution to the art of digital electronic equipment design, not only because it improved manufacturing efficiency but also because it increased the ease of problem diagnosis and repair of machines in the field.[73] For customer engineers who had been trained and provided with tools to maintain electromechanical accounting machines, it was important to minimize the new requirements suddenly imposed by the arrival of the 604, with its all-electronic calculating unit that contained more than 1400 vacuum tubes. It became a common servicing technique to "swap" pluggable units as a simple and effective means of locating defective components. If the trouble moved to a new location along with the pluggable unit, then that unit was likely to be defective. If the trouble remained—for example, in a particular order of a counter—when pluggable units were switched between columns, then something in the back-panel wiring or elsewhere in the machine was suspected of being faulty.

A noteworthy feature of the pluggable-unit mode of construction is that, for the first time, electronic machines were built to occupy space efficiently in three dimensions instead of two (figure 2.8). Such familiar products as television sets continued for fifteen years or more to be designed so that the vacuum tubes and other components were spread out over the two-dimensional surface of a metal chassis, occupying no more of the third dimension than was required by the height of a vacuum tube. The 604 pluggable unit greatly increased the packing density of electronic equipment; the idea was adopted, with appropriate evolutionary changes, for all subsequent calculators and computers developed by the company.

The 604 used so-called "miniature" vacuum tubes, which were much smaller than the standard radio tubes of the 603 and the SSEC. Because they had the advantage of compactness, which was especially important in mobile equipment, miniature tubes had undergone great development and rapid improvement during World War II. Both vacuum tubes and the so-called "passive" class of components—mainly resistors and capacitors, which did not amplify signals—required a great deal of further improvement in order to make the 604 a practical, successful product. The history of these improvements is extensive,

a

b

c

Figure 2.8
Packaging of electronic circuits in the IBM 604. A pluggable circuit unit is shown
in *a*. A panel containing such units is seen in *b* from the pluggable unit insertion
side. The same panel is seen in *c* from the opposite side, showing the wires that
interconnect the sockets of the pluggable units.

but a few examples suffice to show the relationship between the newly emerging field of digital electronics and the well-established "radio electronics" industry of the late 1940s.

Consider the vacuum triode, the three-element electron tube invented by Lee de Forest in 1906. From the day of its first application through years of improvement in design, materials, and fabrication, its main purpose had been to amplify—that is, turn weak signals into strong ones. To preserve the "shape" of the signal—maintain the proportionality of output to input signal as a function of time—it was necessary to operate the tube in a moderately conductive mode: neither cut off nor fully conducting. It could then be used as a linear amplifier, in which a small negative signal on its control grid decreased anode (or plate) current by an amount equal to the increase that a positive signal of the same magnitude would produce. Many types of tubes were designed, tested, and improved over the years with this operating mode as an important consideration.

In the case of vacuum tube flip-flops and switching circuits, on the other hand, the tubes had to be driven beyond their linear response range—driven, that is, by signals so large as to force the tubes into either the fully conducting or the cutoff condition—in order to produce unmistakable output voltages representing either 0 or 1. Early digital circuit designers and tube manufacturers alike were surprised to find that tubes often exhibited a degradation in their ability to conduct current after being held in a cutoff condition for long periods of time with their cathodes heated as for normal conduction. This problem, which was alluded to in the description of the SSEC operation, was known as "cathode interface resistance."[74] Its solution required careful analysis and improvement in cathode material, and it provides an example of setbacks engineers encountered in their attempts to turn radio tubes into computing elements. It was neither the first nor the most urgent problem that arose during the 604 project; indeed, until certain less subtle effects had been discovered and corrected, the one involving interface resistance went unnoticed.

Some of the earliest problems—and some that demanded the most urgent attention—revealed themselves through intermittent failures. A component in which an undesired open or short circuit occurs occasionally, for perhaps a fraction of a millionth of a second each time, might easily pass the tests required for use in radio or television circuits. The human eye, ear, and brain are insensitive to interruptions of such short duration. In a digital circuit, however, a single such mishap could cause a miscount of voltage pulses somewhere and an erroneous result. Again, the vacuum tube, a complex component to make, provides a good example. For years tubes had been manufactured under conditions of cleanliness and quality control adequate for radio or television components but quite unacceptable for the production of digital devices. As the quantities of vacuum tubes used in digital circuits increased, tube manufacturers came to recognize the need to revise their production methods, installing "clean rooms" for assembly and establishing a clean room mentality among employees.

Miniature tubes had been chosen in order to minimize size, power consumption, and heat dissipation in the 604, which was to be used in an ordinary office environment. But the new tubes introduced some problems of their own. For example, the spacing between cathode and grid of one of the miniature types—the 6J6 twin triode—was so small that particles of conducting dust or other loose material too small to be visible could bridge it, causing intermittent operation or outright failure. It became obvious to Palmer that the available tubes were neither satisfactory for digital calculator use nor likely to be improved by the manufacturers for a market as small as that for calculators. After a number of 6J6 tube failures, Palmer asked Haddad to explore the problem. Haddad built an elaborate tester in which the vacuum tubes were rotated on a wheel and turned on their own axes in such a way as to test them in every possible spatial orientation, while being tapped regularly by metal studs on rubber mountings outside the circumference of the wheel. The tubes were connected to test circuits during this grueling process, and as Haddad recalled many years later, "every single tube we put on that machine failed." Palmer asked him to design a tube that would not fail.[75]

Tube design was a specialty not included among the academic experiences of the typical electrical engineer, even one trained in electronic circuits. Haddad recalls that he went out and bought a copy of a new book on the design and construction of vacuum tubes and with the help of that textbook designed a 6J6 replacement. A good deal of the solution lay in reshaping the grid and plate structures and providing separate cathodes for the two triodes in each tube. (The 6J6 used a single cathode shared by both triodes.) The new tube was sufficiently better than the old one that General Electric was eventually persuaded to build it.

A comparable story can be told about the pentagrid switch tube, a miniature tube known as the 6BE6 used in the 604 in place of the pentode switch of the 603. The 6BE6 had been designed for mixing radio-frequency signals in a superheterodyne receiver. As the tube was used in the 604, secondary emission from certain of the grids, due apparently to their contamination during manufacture, caused loss of control of the voltage on those grids. Gold plating the offending grids was found to be the solution, and RCA finally agreed to manufacture the corrected tube. While these and other tubes were being analyzed and eventually replaced by improved types, Haddad, Phelps, and several other IBM engineers spent many days each month at the factories of the tube manufacturers.[76]

Considering the critical importance of tube quality to the reliable operation of digital circuits, it would seem that IBM might have decided to manufacture its own vacuum tubes, just as it had manufactured most of the components of its electromechanical machines. Indeed, at an early stage in production of the 604, Palmer set up a tube-making laboratory in a building known as the "pickle factory," located on the east bank of the Hudson River just below the Poughkeepsie IBM factory. (This building was one of those on a parcel of land purchased by IBM in 1941 from the R. U. Delapenha Company, food packers.) In view of the difficulty of obtaining usable tubes from manufacturers of radio tubes, Palmer thought it important at least to demonstrate that they could be produced, given proper attention to design details and proper care in manufacture.

IBM management was not inclined, however, to go into full-scale production of tubes. The electronics industry was already well populated with manufacturers of radio tubes. RCA, Sylvania, CBS Hytron, General Electric, and Tungsol—to name only a few—each produced many millions of tubes every year. It was questionable that IBM had anything to offer in the manufacture of vacuum tubes that would make such a venture profitable. But the facility for turning out even small quantities of tubes permitted laboratory representatives to approach the regular tube manufacturers with convincing samples, rather than mere designs on paper, of the higher-quality tubes IBM was asking for. Directly or indirectly, the tube laboratory seems to have had the desired effect. One manager of that facility recalled that, when "word leaked out that we were doing something mystical in vacuum tubes," several of the large tube manufacturers became much more responsive.[77] As it turned out, other benefits were derived from the tube laboratory. At about the time it had served its original purpose in ensuring a supply of good triodes and switch tubes, it was found to be a valuable facility in which to experiment with special counting and storage tubes, and in particular to improve the cathode-ray tube for use as a large-capacity storage device (discussed in chapter 4).

The 604 (figure 2.9) was manufactured in quantities of over a thousand per year in some years, and more than 5600 were built over a ten-year period.[78] There is no question that its development and success

Figure 2.9
IBM 604 Electronic Calculating Punch

in the marketplace enhanced the ability of IBM engineers to cope with the demands of the dawning age of computers. It introduced a remarkably useful pluggable circuit package, along with a set of standard circuits whose simplicity and versatility would help to promote design standardization in later projects, and broke the ice for acceptance by the marketing and service departments of widely distributed electronic calculating machines. Finally, by encouraging manufacturers to develop computer-grade tubes, the 604 program made a significant contribution to computer development in IBM and elsewhere.

2.5 The Card-Programmed Electronic Calculator

The 604 was to play a part, too, in a system that helped IBM and its customers significantly in the transition from calculating machines to computers. The background of ideas that culminated in the machine's use in such a system may be traced back to at least two years before the introduction of the 604.

At an IBM-sponsored computation forum in August 1946, W. J. Eckert described the facilities of the Watson Scientific Computing Laboratory at Columbia University (more commonly known as Watson Laboratory, see chapter 13). Installed there, he pointed out, in addition to a complete line of IBM accounting machines, were two relay calculators. The first of the two was simply an experiment in producing a calculator with a minimum of relays. The second, he said, "has two principal functions: it multiplies and divides. It cannot read cards, it cannot punch cards, and its storage capacity is limited. . . . Many of you may make suggestions which will cause us to change this program for a more useful one, but at the present time we propose attaching the . . . machine to the 405 Accounting Machine with a summary punch and to use it as a small flexible machine sequence calculator."[79]

A year later, at a similar forum under similar circumstances, Eckert mentioned that the Watson Laboratory had acquired two large relay calculators of the kind developed by IBM for Aberdeen Proving Ground. Then he went on to say, "We have two small relay calculators which are experimental; one is being tied in with an accounting machine and a special control box to operate as a baby sequence calculator with instructions on punched cards."[80]

Eckert was on the right track, but his "baby" was not destined to stimulate the introduction of a new product. It remained for an IBM customer, Northrop Aircraft, Inc., of Hawthorne, California, to spark the first commercially marketed sequence calculator. Northrop had been calculating guided-missile trajectories with the 601 electric multiplier and the 405 accounting machine. Northrop's tabulating supervisor, G. J. Toben, would later recall of the trajectory computation: "We did it by a batch process at first, and since each calculation was dependent on the one ahead of it, you really had a batch of one, which was awkward. So this led at once to the thought of connecting machines together . . . we were able to . . . make cables connecting them which ran across the floor and accomplish the interconnection of all the machines without actually passing any cards through them."[81]

The Northrop people interconnected the machines without bothering to get IBM's approval and were pleased with the way they had bypassed card-handling steps. But their 601 was not the fast calculator they yearned for. Then, during the winter of 1947–1948, to quote from a paper presented by Toben at an IBM computation seminar in 1949,

we were presented with a problem involving the step-by-step solution of a set of 14 simultaneous nonlinear differential equations. No analytical solution was possible because of step functions. The two large-scale digital machines capable of doing the problem were busy on higher priority work, and the problem was not suited for analogue computers such as the differential analyzer because of a large spread in the size of the numbers. Shifts of 10^4 sometimes meant that a gear would have to turn for years to effect the result. Moreover, it was a design problem, and the whole course of the investigation depended upon the early results. The solution was important to the guided missile program, and we were able to persuade IBM to convert our IBM Type 405 Alphabetical Accounting Machine into something suitable for the job. They made available an IBM Type 603 Calculating Punch, which was then out of production, and connected it, via cable to the 405. Forty class selectors and 40 x distributors were added to complete the job. The elapsed time from preliminary design to delivery of the machine was only six weeks . . . the sequence of operation is controlled by a set of program cards fed through the 405. These cards contain x or digit punchings to pickup selectors to call for the required transfers, etc. These cards may also contain factors to be used in computations.[82]

These words reflect the frustrations of the design engineers in the aircraft industry, who were generating day-to-day computational requirements that could not wait for the advent of stored-program computers.

Northrop made no secret of their 405-603 combination, which they named "Betsy" and billed as a "poor man's ENIAC."[83] By December 1948, IBM had logged nearly a dozen requests for "combinations," and Dunwell, in the Future Demands department, was hurriedly completing specifications for a product system. A viable system, he thought, should improve on "Betsy" by utilizing IBM's newest machines, by including additional storage capacity, and by making some concessions to user convenience.

In January 1949, Jonas E. Dayger, manager of a special engineering department in the Endicott laboratory, undertook the urgent task of developing the combination that would satisfy Dunwell's general specifications. Announced in May as the IBM Card-Programmed Electronic Calculator, the new system included a Type 604 calculator with its Type 521 card punch, a Type 402 accounting machine, and an optional Type 941 auxiliary storage unit. The 402, which had been announced in July 1948 along with the 604, was an improved and modernized successor to the 405 accounting machine, the choice of type number notwithstanding. The 941, constructed of components used in an electromechanical calculator, stored sixteen signed numbers of ten decimal digits each.[84] An optional version of the 402, without alphabetic printing, was also provided; it was given the designation Type 417. The 402 and 417 read 150 cards per minute. The 417 matched this speed by printing numbers at 150 lines per minute, whereas the alphabetic 402 could print only 100 lines per minute.

The Card-Programmed Electronic Calculator, almost always referred to as the "CPC," was designed to be particularly useful for evaluating long engineering formulas requiring storage of no more than twenty numbers or so. In the CPC configuration, the 604 operated as a slave to the 402, the principle being that in each card cycle two numbers would be moved to the 604 and operated upon and the result returned to storage. Two channels were provided for routing data to the 604 from storage locations or input reading brushes. One channel was provided for routing results from the 604 to storage, punch, or printer. Storage locations were designated by a two-digit code. The desired operations—addition, subtraction, multiplication, division, and even iterative procedures such as square root—could be wired on the 604 plugboard and called for by instructions in cards read in the 402. As the CPC's operation was described at another of the computation seminars, late in 1949, the instruction format occupied eight card columns: two columns each to specify the locations of the two operands and the result; one column to designate an operation; and one to specify a result shift. Instructions, one per card, were interpreted by class and digit selection methods.[85]

CPC deliveries started late in 1949, and it soon became clear that while most customers agreed with Dunwell's scheme, others emphatically did not. The Northrop group, exceptionally skilled in plugboard techniques, felt that their hands had been tied; they wanted to be able to move more than two operands and perform more than one operation per card cycle. To satisfy such users, the CPC was modified the following year to provide a user with the option of more control over the system; additional storage was made available as another option. These changes contributed much to the success of the CPC, of which nearly 700 were built during the first half of the 1950s. Although the system had been designed for engineering computations, it soon came to be used for large accounting applications as well.

For IBM, the CPC constituted an extremely valuable learning experience. In 1948, after the dedication of the SSEC, Watson, Sr., had asked for studies of the possibility of marketing a small SSEC (a matter further discussed in chapter 3). His staff saw little in the ponderous machine that was immediately relevant to the marketplace. But stimulated by a resourceful customer, within a year IBM was designing not a small SSEC but a "poor man's ENIAC" with a reasonably clear view of product objectives. CPC experience raised IBM's expectations concerning what people could afford to pay for computational capacity, and when CPC customers expressed the desire to exchange information, IBM established an influential series of technical newsletters to meet the need. The CPC also gave IBM a solid reason for acquiring and training a substantial number of technically qualified people. In this respect it was unquestionably more influential in the development of IBM's product line than the SSEC.

Finally, the CPC, an interim system, held the line while the United States was girding itself for its technological leap into the age of stored-program computers. It introduced many engineers and scientists to the merits of automatic digital calculation and thereby helped to divert attention from analog computers. In so doing, it went a long way toward solving the pressing design problems that were proliferating in aircraft and nuclear engineering.

3

A Machine for Ordinary Businesses

The choice of drum storage. The drum-augmented 604. The influence of mathematical computation. The Magnetic Drum Calculator. The squeeze on resources. The president's decision.

Enjoying a change of climate in Florida two weeks after the January 1948 dedication of the Selective Sequence Electronic Calculator, Thomas J. Watson, Sr., reflected on the event and its implications for his company. In developing the ASCC and SSEC, IBM had built two notable but not profitable machines. Now Watson sensed that the SSEC heralded a new direction for his product line. Accordingly he sent a directive to IBM headquarters to begin planning "a machine of the same type, with reduced capacity, to meet the requirements of the ordinary businesses we serve." The SSEC, said Watson, must be viewed "only as the prologue."[1]

Watson assigned James Bryce, Wallace Eckert, Frank Hamilton, John McPherson, and Rex Seeber to plan the new machine, thus giving the experienced SSEC team the job of creating a commercial version. Seeber, however, was fully occupied in managing the SSEC programming and operating staff, and Bryce, who had been too ill even to attend the SSEC dedication, was unable to take part. Having advised Watson for over thirty years and helped him to the threshold of a new technological age, Bryce was now unable to step across it with him. He died the following year.

Thus it was that only McPherson, Eckert, and Hamilton met on 17 March 1948 to begin planning the new product. They had in hand the recommendation of Gordon A. Roberts, head of Future Demands, the department with responsibility for representing product requirements to IBM's development engineers. Roberts, a veteran IBM salesman who for over fifteen years had headed up IBM's marketing activity in the public utility industry, believed the IBM 604, due to be delivered late in the year, offered those features of the SSEC that seemed most useful for business and accounting applications. He observed that it differed from the SSEC mainly in having a more limited storage capacity and a different programming method but that these features seemed "not too significant in considering commercial applications as we now know them." He saw further development of the 604 as the correct response to Watson's directive.[2] Roberts was probably not the only IBM executive who saw the SSEC as an unworldly laboratory device. By grandly dedicating the SSEC to science, Watson had inadvertently discouraged any association of it with business data processing.

After weighing Roberts's recommendation, McPherson, Eckert, and Hamilton elected instead to plan a product aimed at meeting the requirements of engineering and scientific applications—not at all what Roberts seemed to understand by "the requirements of the ordinary businesses we serve." For their part, McPherson and Eckert had broader visions; their interpretation of Watson's directive was colored by their keen interests and personal stakes in scientific computing. The two had been nervously watching the upward trend in federal grants to large-scale digital computer projects. Such grants were a new, postwar phenomenon and one that conceivably could upset IBM's expectations in some unpleasant way. To help ensure against such surprises, they felt a responsibility to nudge IBM in the direction of more funding for scientific requirements. As for Hamilton, his selection as the engineer to build the new machine was based not on his long service as a punched-card machine designer but on his successes in developing science-oriented machines, such as the ASCC and SSEC.[3]

Having shaped the project to their own tastes, the three men felt more comfortable with their assignment. It suited their professional interests and strengths while offering the satisfaction of contributing to the product line—a refreshing contrast to the singularity of the SSEC. Moreover, events indicated that a significant degree of interest in scientific computing was beginning to emerge. For example, the special request for help from Northrop Aircraft at the beginning of the year had revealed Northrop's sustained efforts to adapt punched-card equipment to the computational needs of engineers. And Northrop was only one firm in the rapidly growing postwar airframe industry.

In addition, IBM representatives were reporting with increasing frequency examples of engineering applications for the IBM 602 and 603 calculators. (The 602 was an electromechanical machine, capable of division as well as multiplication, introduced at about the same time as the 603 Electronic Multiplier.) In January 1948, for example, two representatives of the education department in Endicott had journeyed to Fort Worth to teach operation of the IBM 602 to a class consisting mainly of employees of Consolidated Vultee Aircraft Corporation. The students not only proposed several engineering problems but in informal discussions told the instructors that IBM should be actively promoting use of the 602 and 603 in the engineering field. They added that aeronautical engineering, where the potential for computing was just beginning to be tapped, was itself only a vanguard; there were plenty of other opportunities in fields such as bridge, dam, and building construction. The instructors' report on all this had gone to IBM's director of education and from him to McPherson.[4] Not long after, one of the instructors began a new session of the course in Los Angeles, and after eight days with students from fifteen EAM installations, he sent back this reaction: "IBM . . . is not doing nearly enough in the way of helping those of our customers who are . . . solving complicated mathematical problems on our machines. Only by brute strength, long hours, extraordinary talent and sheer bull headedness, have they accomplished what they have."[5]

Eckert, meanwhile, at the Watson Laboratory in New York — a kind of crossroads for computation — had already sensed the new surge of interest in computing. To provide an opportunity for workers in the field to exchange ideas and for IBM people to learn more about progress in the area, he planned a summer Scientific Computation Forum at the department of education building in Endicott. At the meeting held in August, his sixty guests included scientists, engineers, and mathematicians. Topics of the two dozen papers ranged from "Integration of Second Order Linear Differential Equations on the Type 602 Calculating Punch" to "Computation of Shock Wave Refraction on the Selective Sequence Electronic Calculator."[6]

3.1 The Choice of Drum Storage

Following the meeting with McPherson and Eckert in March, Frank Hamilton returned to IBM's North Street Laboratory in Endicott with a modest objective for a new machine. Basically he was to interconnect a 604, a printer, a table-lookup unit of electromechanical design, a reduced complement of SSEC-like paper-tape devices for program and table storage, and perhaps 200 digits of vacuum tube storage.

Hamilton's group included seasoned engineers from the SSEC project, among them E. S. Hughes, Jr., and J. J. Troy, for whom Hamilton's objective was scarcely a challenge. But vacuum tube storage in the amount projected was judged too bulky and costly, and Hamilton soon ruled out electromechanical relay storage for the same reasons. By early May, he had tentatively decided to use magnetic-drum storage, an emerging technology. The basic idea was that an electromagnetic recording head could mark a small portion of the drum surface with one or the other of two distinct magnetic states. A binary-coded decimal digit could be represented by four such marks. As the drum rotated, a sequence of such markings would produce a pattern of magnetization representing the several digits of a number on a portion of a circular drum "track." A number so stored would erase the number previously stored on that portion of the track. When later read, the magnetic recording would produce electrical signals in the head representing the number most recently stored. With each track subdivided into m positions for numbers, a drum with n tracks would have mn storage locations for numbers mapped on its surface. A machine so equipped could calculate a result, store it on the drum at a location not then in use, and later read it as a factor in a new calculation.[7] (See chapter 6 for a more detailed description of magnetic recording and reading.)

Hamilton calculated that, by using four tracks together to achieve 8-4-2-1 decimal digit encoding, he could store 500 digits (about fifty numbers) on a four-track band of a drum of about $1\frac{1}{2}$ inch diameter. The advantages in cost and space over SSEC-type vacuum tube storage were evident, but the concomitant disadvantage was greatly increased access time; the calculator would have to wait for the first digit of a desired number to reach a reading head. An average delay of a few thousandths of a second in operand access could slow an arithmetic unit to a fraction of its top potential speed.

Despite the shortcomings of drum storage, its choice was agreeable to Hamilton because of his close association with magnetic recording experiments at the Endicott laboratory. Stimulated by Bryce, who filed a patent application in 1938 (issued in 1943) covering magnetic recording and reading on magnetically treated cards, a number of Endicott engineers had worked on digital magnetic recording. In 1941, they had made a comprehensive study of ways to apply magnetic recording to accounting processes and compiled design data on elements of the technology: recording media, recording and reading heads, and amplifiers. In 1943, Hamilton built an experimental ledger posting carriage, for attachment to the 405 Accounting Machine, in which the magnetically coated border of a ledger sheet was used to record binary-coded account balances and carriage-positioning control signals.

Four years later, Hamilton and Hughes attended a Harvard University symposium at which a representative of The Brush Development Company, manufacturers of sound recorders and reproducers, surveyed recording technology and gave a brief appraisal of its potential for computing machines.[8] And at the 1947 National Electronics Conference, a speaker divulged advances in drum development that had been attained at Engineering Research Associates, Inc. (ERA), where drum tracks with suitable magnetic properties were obtained by bonding magnetically coated paper-tape strips to the drum surface.[9] In March 1948, just a week after Hamilton had begun planning the new machine, an ERA engineer described a substantial refinement of that company's drum work at a professional society meeting in New York.[10] All of these events prompted a renewed interest in magnetic recording at the Endicott laboratory.

During the summer of 1948, the design of the "Magnetic Storage Calculator" evolved from that of an SSEC descendant into a markedly different kind of machine. The principal physical units remained the magnetic drum and the 604 calculating-storage unit. But the method of control underwent a fundamental change. The paper-tape equipment with its "lines of sequence" was abandoned once drum storage of a thousand ten-digit words was deemed feasible. It became clear that instructions could be read from the drum, one by one, and executed as systematically as if read sequentially from paper tape. To facilitate this scheme, a special instruction counter would hold the three-digit location number (the address) of the instruction being executed and, when automatically augmented by one, point to the location of the next instruction. A special *branch instruction* could load that counter with a new address and thereby interrupt normal sequencing whenever, for instance, a just-completed string of instructions was required to be reexecuted from the beginning. Given compatible formats for instructions and numbers, as in the SSEC, the drum could hold both instructions and data and readily permit arithmetic operations to apply to instructions. A just-executed instruction could be altered in its address field and, at next execution, operate on a number at a different location. Such alterations, appropriately arranged, permitted strings of instructions to operate iteratively upon successions of data elements systematically arrayed in storage.[11] Thus, in mid-1948 the idea of instruction modification became, for the first time, central to the plan for a regular IBM product.

The advantages of dynamically modifying instructions had been concisely put at a January 1947 Harvard symposium by J. W. Mauchly:

Instructions are stored in the internal memory in the same manner as are numerical quantities, and one set of instructions can be used to modify another set of instructions. . . .

. . . An unlimited number of different instructions may be generated within the machine by this process. One can, therefore, modify not only the numbers which are substituted into a process, but the process itself, in any desired systematic way. By use of this facility, an EDVAC-type machine can, with surprisingly few instructions, automatically carry out processes which would otherwise require an instruction sequence greatly exceeding its internal memory capacity.[12]

In the audience as Mauchly spoke were IBM's Eckert, Hamilton, and Hughes—all absorbed at that time in construction of the SSEC and in planning for its use. That machine did not have an internal memory that was both large and fast, a property necessary to full exploitation of the flexibility Mauchly described. The capability seemed again beyond reach when McPherson, Eckert, and Hamilton in 1948 set down the first specification for an SSEC-descendant that would have a storage capacity of only 200 digits. Presumably they considered large memory relevant solely to large-scale machines. Only after Hamilton calculated in mid-1948 that he could fit 10,000 decimal digits on a drum of practical size did he and Hughes realize that their modest machine could equal an EDVAC in storage capacity and in flexibility.

By autumn 1948, W. W. McDowell, the Endicott laboratory manager, was fretting over the lack of carefully stated market requirements for the Magnetic Storage Calculator. Judging that the project could not long survive without the help of Future Demands, he asked Roberts to cooperate with Hamilton in writing specifications.[13] Roberts assigned S. W. Dunwell, coming off his 604 planning assignment, to the project, but any further response was delayed by a diversionary study of the machine, ordered by T. J. Watson, Sr., as a candidate to meet the Swedish Navy's requirements for trajectory calculations.[14] That plan failed when Sweden balked at the two-year development period projected. Early in 1949, McDowell renewed his request, and Dunwell began working regularly with Hamilton.[15]

By March, the Magnetic Storage Calculator design was beginning to show the clean and simple characteristics of EDVAC-like machines. Nevertheless, its SSEC lineage was still evident. It was a decimal machine with 2000 ten-digit words of drum storage. (For a machine that stores numbers and instructions together, a *word* is the unit in which data are stored, transmitted, and processed. A particular word in storage is identified by an address.) The instruction consisted of a two-digit operation code and two four-digit "P" and "Q" operand or result addresses (notation and function both carried over from the SSEC). There was a "transfer" register to reconcile data transfers between the drum (8-4-2-1 encoding, parallel by bit, serial by digit) and the computer, a 604 calculating-storage unit with its SSEC-like, parallel-by-digit counter. The 604 plugwired "program unit" had been replaced by the stored-program capability. Moreover, Hamilton had broken with EAM tradition. His machine was not "driven" by the card reader, in the manner of punched-card machines all the way from Hollerith's first tabulator up through the IBM 604. Instead, operation codes were provided to initiate card reading, punching, and printing. In brief, his machine was designed to feed cards while computing rather than to compute while feeding cards.[16]

On 19 April, Hamilton presented his specifications to a group that included McPherson, Eckert, Roberts, and Dunwell. No objection of any consequence resulted, but a promising suggestion was put forward: the machine deserved an arithmetic unit designed to its own requirements rather than one simply carried over from another product. The idea of a truly new IBM product, tentatively called the "Intermediate Electronic Calculator," was conceived that day.[17] But it would be four years before it entered the IBM product line as the Type 650 Magnetic Drum Calculator.

3.2 The Drum-Augmented 604

A month later, in mid-May, IBM sales manager Charles E. Love told McPherson to stop work immediately on the sequence calculator. Instead, he was to exploit drum storage as a new table-lookup capability for the IBM 604. The need for such a feature had been established by visits to some forty customers using 604s. Table lookup was fundamental, for example, to rate-table applications, such as utility billing based on customer meter readings.[18] (Table lookup was simulated in EAM installations by costly card collating and reproducing machine runs.) The idea was that, in operation, number pairs would first be loaded onto the drum, each pair consisting of an "argument" and its related "function value." During computation, whenever an argument was read or calculated, the desired table-lookup operation would search the drum for the matching argument and bring the corresponding function value to the arithmetic unit for processing.

McPherson first set his engineers working with Roberts and Dunwell to learn exactly what was required. Then he responded with a memorandum to Love—sending a copy to T. J. Watson, Jr., vice-president—listing all outside organizations known to have ordered, to be planning to order, or to be building electronic computers for either scientific or accounting applications. He noted that with cessation of work on the Intermediate Electronic Calculator, IBM had no program to offset the competition implicit in his list.[19]

Watson, Jr., read the memorandum one week after holding a meeting of IBM engineering and sales people to formulate a response to Prudential Insurance Company's order of a UNIVAC from Eckert-Mauchly Computer Corporation. At that time, he had asked that the sales and engineering departments act to determine, by actual test, whether magnetic-tape equipment was truly practical for accounting and had inherent advantages compared to punched-card equipment. When the Intermediate Electronic Calculator was mentioned during the meeting, he declared that it had been halted because no such determination of its commercial utility had been made.

Now, McPherson's memorandum provoked Watson, Jr., to reiterate the point. He invited McPherson to make a complete analysis of customer requirements for a computer, surveying at least half of the organizations known to be interested, before undertaking to revive Hamilton's project—which, he acknowledged, he had acted to stop. He implied that Hamilton's work relied too heavily on published specifications of machines being developed by others and pointed to the lack of any novel provisions for "the accounting field." In Watson, Jr.'s, view, Hamilton's project had strayed in motivation and definition from IBM's traditional strengths: accounting applications and new-product requirements gleaned from customers.[20]

When Hamilton began meeting with Roberts and Dunwell to settle specifications for table lookup, his engineers had nearly completed a magnetic drum to demonstrate their mastery of the art. For the crucial problem of producing a suitable magnetic surface, they had found a method less elaborate than those ERA and Brush Development Co. were known to be using. From among available wires with good magnetic recording properties, they selected one made of a copper-nickle-iron alloy called cunife (from a combination of the chemical symbols for the three elements) and wrapped it tightly on the drum until the surface was covered by a single layer. Then, turning the drum on a lathe, they ground off half the material and worked the resulting surface smooth. This simple and inexpensive process gave excellent results. In June, their drum system became available for test, observation, and refinement.[21]

Roberts and Dunwell, on behalf of Future Demands, set tough goals for the drum-augmented 604: monthly rental was not to exceed $1000; there was to be drum capacity for 10,000 table digits; and the table-lookup operation was to be "checked and proven automatically." The last requirement was readily accepted at Endicott, where the engineers evaluating early SSEC operating experience had found that programmers were building checking procedures into their programs to over-come the effects of intermittent machine errors.[22]

In the ensuing weeks of negotiations, however, the engineers and planners failed to reach agreement on a balance between cost and function. Despite a series of revisions to his first proposal, including a change in drum encoding, Hamilton could not, using the 604 as a base, arrive at a design meeting Dunwell's objectives: preserve 604 function; add versatile, self-checked, drum-based table lookup; and satisfy the cost ceiling. In August, Love wrote to Watson, Jr., that three months had been wasted since the redirection of the project in May and that despite objections from McPherson and Ralph Palmer he contemplated entering into a contract with ERA for development of the needed drum.[23]

Love had believed, as a result of his experience with electrome-chanical technology, that the table-lookup feature could be provided in a "reasonably short" period, as had usually been the case with improvements to the product line. He was stunned, therefore, when McPherson told him that development of the magnetic drum was as substantial an undertaking as development of the 604 itself. Now that planners and engineers had been unable to agree on its design, he began to see that the urgently needed table-lookup feature was many months away. Perhaps, given Endicott's strengths and weaknesses, it would not be done at all. Pained at his first jolt from the new technology and unwilling to admit that well-tested company guidelines could be wrong, he proposed to go outside IBM and deal with the drum spe-cialists of the day.

The plan to turn to ERA was supported by Dunwell. While in the army, he had acquired some knowledge of the wartime accomplish-ments of the navy personnel who founded the company. Another influential supporter was James W. Birkenstock, who, after joining IBM in 1935, had come up through sales ranks to precede both Love and Roberts in their posts. Now an assistant to headquarters executives, Birkenstock became IBM's representative in contract negotiations with ERA while Dunwell handled the technical details.[24] Clearly, the view at IBM headquarters was that Hamilton's drum development work was not moving fast enough.

The following week, however, just when the future of Hamilton's project was most in doubt, events took a new turn. At a meeting of engineers and planners attended by Birkenstock, McPherson, and Rob-erts, Hamilton presented his most recent 604-based design, including some new cost-cutting features. Then Dunwell proposed that a new magnetic-drum calculator be built, doing away with the 604 and getting back to drum-contained programs. His detailed plan included ingenious uses of special "revolver" tracks on the drum as inexpensive replacements for the 604 vacuum tube registers of previous designs. The plan looked promising, and Hamilton agreed to evaluate it as an alternative approach.[25]

To McPherson and Hamilton it might have seemed that their Intermediate Electronic Calculator, which they had been forced to abandon, was now being offered to them as the answer to a 604 improvement problem they had failed to solve. But the new departure was too exciting to be derailed by rancor. It was, after all, an improvement over the design set aside in May. Hamilton began detailed studies of the two alternatives. Meanwhile, the ERA contract for a drum was changed to encompass design of a magnetic-drum computer whose sole purpose was to serve as a yardstick against which to measure Hamilton's design.[26]

By October, Hamilton had obtained wide agreement to a plan based on Dunwell's proposal. The project was free at last of 604 influence. On 17 November 1949, he signed and sent to McPherson, Watson, Jr., Birkenstock, and others a description of the plan, said to be a "final draft . . . the result of many discussions with Mr. Roberts and his staff as well as members of the Sales Department."[27] However, Hamilton had barely dispatched this "final draft" when Dunwell visited Endicott and reopened a number of basic questions Hamilton had believed were settled, including the number of addresses in an instruction and the code to be used on the drum.

Since a cost study of such fundamental changes in specifications can approximate the work of a new design, Hamilton was dismayed. The project had suffered two major changes in direction in the preceding six months; he felt that the time for new proposals was past. Moreover, he was unwilling to engage ERA in a design competition while Dunwell was free, on one hand, to involve him in diversionary studies and, on the other, to guide ERA toward a fixed and presumably well-chosen objective. He announced that in order to evaluate Dunwell's suggestions, he was halting all development work.

But McPherson, after meeting with other headquarters executives, sent Dunwell's new proposal, by now documented, to McDowell and told him, "We should investigate this suggestion as quickly as possible. However, this suggestion should not interfere in any way with the present work being performed."[28] There the matter rested. A formal evaluation of Dunwell's suggestions was deferred until it was lost in the welter of questions later raised by the arrival of ERA's proposal.

However, Dunwell's proposals themselves were not lost; some were subsequently incorporated into Hamilton's design.

Tension at Endicott was dissipated somewhat late in 1949 when Watson, Sr., accompanied by a small retinue, visited the North Street Laboratory to see a demonstration of the magnetic drum. On a control panel, up-down switches and neon lamps were used to set up and indicate half a dozen bits. The system transferred these to the drum at the touch of a button, a fact that could be demonstrated by clearing the lights and—at the touch of another button—reading the bits back and restoring the original light pattern. The technician (later an engineer) who gave the demonstration was preparing to leave the room when one of the secretaries in Watson's party detained him and said, "Don't leave until Mr. Watson leaves." To Hamilton's department of some fifteen members, Watson remarked how impressed he was with everything he had seen and spoke of the importance of their work. He added that IBM would show its appreciation "in the usual way," a reference to the selective pay raises that on occasion followed soon after Watson's laboratory visits.[29]

3.3 The Influence of Mathematical Computation

Despite the 1949 redefinition of the Magnetic Storage Calculator project in Endicott, the need for marketing and product support of scientific computing was a growing influence in the company's affairs. Shortly after Hamilton began his work on a reduced-capacity SSEC in the spring of 1948, John McPherson and Wallace Eckert began recruiting employees with mathematical training. Their objective was to help the sales force communicate with people interested in doing technical calculations on IBM machines. They estimated that eight or ten mathematicians could respond to needs reported by branch offices and IBM service bureaus.[30]

At the Endicott Scientific Computation Forum in the summer of 1948, when a Beech Aircraft Corporation engineer from Wichita gave a paper describing three-dimensional flutter analyses of aircraft structures and other engineering applications that he had accomplished principally with a 601 multiplier and a 405 accounting machine, he recommended that "local IBM offices be provided with up-to-date information on the full computing capabilities of the machines in their region." In response, Eckert underscored the local IBM manager's difficulty "when you ask him for methods of doing things that he has never heard of." Clearly, airframe designers using IBM equipment needed access to IBMers who understood some of the mathematics underlying the problems to be solved.[31]

By the spring of 1949, however, only four men had been hired or reassigned to the "Scientific Sales Program." The first of these, Walter H. Johnson, joined IBM in September 1948. During 1949, he established IBM's Technical Computing Bureau in New York City, a contract service for performing scientific and engineering computations, whose centerpiece was a 604. Concern over the slow progress of the recruiting program increased after the May announcement of the Card-Programmed Electronic Calculator (CPC), conceived by engineers for use by engineers. With first deliveries only six months off, the machine clearly demanded customer assistance of the type discussed at the 1948 Scientific Computation Forum. By midsummer, McPherson concluded that success in the new scientific sales endeavor would require creation of a new post with promotion of technical computation as a principal responsibility. In August, he recommended that such a position be established, and a recently hired headquarters employee, Cuthbert C. Hurd, was assigned to the new job.[32]

Hurd, who had given a paper at the Scientific Computation Forum, had been stimulated by the interest in faster computing instruments he encountered there. For instance, a Northrop engineer had described "Betsy," the CPC prototype recently flown from IBM Endicott to Hawthorne, California (see chapter 2), as "a machine comparable in programming technique to current large computer designs."[33] A mathematician from the Naval Ordnance Laboratory at White Oak, Maryland, described the solution on the SSEC of a gaseous shock wave problem "which otherwise probably would never have been solved."[34] Hurd had seen punched-card machines doing statistical computing work when he was a graduate student at Iowa State College in the early 1930s. Ten years later as a mathematics professor, he established a similar service at the U. S. Coast Guard Academy. In 1947, he was hired to set up a technical computing service at the Oak Ridge National Laboratory, where a gaseous diffusion process for the production of a uranium isotope was being designed. While at Oak Ridge, he engaged John von Neumann as a consultant on modeling the diffusion process. He also heard about the IBM 604 in time to apply for, and get, one of the first production models for Oak Ridge. And he obtained for Oak Ridge an early position in the queue of jobs being scheduled for the SSEC. After long exposure to tediously slow computations, Hurd sensed that computing machinery was on the brink of developments that would make it a significant element in society. Soon after the forum he wrote to Watson, Sr., asking for a job; he was at work at IBM on 1 March 1949.[35]

Hurd was pleased to find that Frank Hamilton in Endicott had been working for a year on the Intermediate Sequence Calculator for technical applications. But Watson, Jr.'s, redefinition of the machine in May 1949 as an improved 604 for business applications was a pointed reminder that the bulk of IBM's business derived from applications outside the scientific field. When the CPC was announced, therefore, Hurd decided to make it the focus of his activities. He began a description of the CPC for the 1949 Scientific Computation Seminar, which he had been asked to organize, and supervised the writing of the CPC instruction manual.[36] In this period Hurd established a one-week session in Endicott during which customer personnel could program and run problems on the CPC prior to delivery of their own machine.[37]

The 1949 Scientific Computation Seminar attracted so much advance interest that two sessions were scheduled, one of three days in November and a second of five days in December. Watson, Jr., by now executive vice-president, was pleased by CPC orders, which reached over two dozen by year end, and by the customer list, which was a who's who of the airframe industry and of important government agencies and laboratories.[38] Soon after the November meeting, Watson, Sr., made Hurd the director of a new department, Applied Science, with responsibility for the Technical Computing Bureau and instructions to hire and train as many "Applied Science Representatives" as were needed to demonstrate and promote the technical computing capabilities of IBM machines. Thus the Scientific Sales Program was reborn, this time with support from the top.[39]

Hurd recruited actively on college campuses in 1950, participated in making the CPC modifications demanded by some users, and sought ways to extend the benefits of information exchange — so apparent at the 1948 and 1949 Scientific Computation forums he had attended — to more users. He acted on a suggestion of Dunwell, who after visiting ten prospective CPC customers in the spring of 1949,[40] had proposed a "national department in a position to visit this type of customer regularly and to prepare special bulletins" from which customers could learn of "methods developed by others with similar problems."[41] In June 1950, the first issue of the IBM Applied Science Department Technical Newsletter appeared. An informal publication, it contained four papers describing useful IBM 604 general-purpose, control-panel wiring arrangements. In effect, these were 604 "programs" for calculating frequently used sets of mathematical functions, which, in the form of wired control panels, could be used for the solution of a variety of specific problems on the 604 and the CPC. One of the papers was by an IBMer, the other three by CPC customers.[42]

3.4 The Magnetic Drum Calculator

Early in 1950, Hamilton began to build an engineering model of his machine, now known as the "Magnetic Drum Calculator" (MDC), incorporating a 10-inch diameter drum, to prove his design and to substantiate component counts and cost estimates (figure 3.1). He scheduled its completion for early summer. Meanwhile, relations between the marketing and engineering organizations remained chilly. Future Demands found its comparison of the Hamilton and ERA specifications under criticism for using stale information from Endicott. Since Hamilton had turned off the flow of information, the criticisms were entirely valid. Roberts therefore asked McPherson to take remedial steps. McPherson assigned the job to McDowell, who attempted a reconciliation, helped along in March 1950 by the arrival of ERA's calculator design, an expensive but valuable current of fresh thinking.[43]

To evaluate ERA's design and review Hamilton's plans in its light, McPherson convened a meeting of over a dozen engineers from the Endicott, Poughkeepsie, and Watson laboratories in Poughkeepsie on 13 and 14 March. Ralph Palmer led the delegation from Poughkeepsie, where a large-scale magnetic-tape computer (see chapter 4) was being considered, and Dunwell attended for Future Demands. McPherson's objective was to review the two drum-machine proposals, hear Dunwell's observations, and "arrive at conclusions that would provide a machine to meet the field requirements in the shortest possible time." Since ERA's design was very different from Hamilton's, the meeting served primarily as an intensive workshop on engineering trade-offs. ERA's drum-encoding scheme of seven parallel bits for each decimal digit, for instance, had the advantage in storage economy and speed over Hamilton's serial one-out-of-twelve plan (modeled after a punched-card column), but the gains had to be balanced against extra expense in card input-output circuits and arithmetic units. The costs of the two machines appeared roughly comparable. The IBM machine was clearly superior in checking capabilities; the ERA machine seemed to have an edge in speed.

For Hamilton's people, the meeting also served to ease tensions. It showed that, with their SSEC experience, they had acquitted themselves well against an innovative engineering organization with roots in advanced wartime electronics. And they received a new spur to their

Figure 3.1
Magnetic Drum Calculator engineering model. The first engineering model of the
Type 650 Magnetic Drum Calculator was built at the North Street Laboratory in
Endicott in 1950. Here it is at an early construction stage. The drum is 10 inches
in diameter, belt driven at 4280 revolutions per minute, with a cunife wire-
wound surface. The special magnetic-head assembly (shown separated from the
drum surface) served one of the drum revolver tracks used for storage registers.
Two later preproduction models, each of substantially different design, were built
in 1952 and 1953. The production model drum was 4 inches in diameter, 16
inches long, had a plated surface, and turned at 12,500 revolutions per minute.

efforts when a report on the meeting stated: "It is evident that ERA engineers are capable of planning and designing a computing machine in the class of IBM's commercial market." For McPherson, however, the meeting was a failure because no formula for a successful product emerged. The key reason was reported in one laconic line, "Neither machine can be built for a $400/mo. rental." Clearly, Future Demands' cost objectives were becoming ever more stringent. In his opening presentation at the meeting, Dunwell had called for a modular system within which the smallest model would rent for less than an IBM 604. Nevertheless, the ERA design and the March meeting had turned up some good ideas and provoked an intensive review by Hamilton's engineers of their entire design.[44]

On 3 April 1950, a top-level meeting was convened at corporate headquarters to evaluate all IBM product development programs. Although such assessments were not unusual, a sense of urgency was evident in this meeting's statement of purpose: "With the advent of electronics, developments which can affect our business are moving faster than ever before since the inception of the Company." Watson, Sr., did not attend; his long association with development decisions had begun to decline after Bryce died. Watson, Jr., chaired the meeting. The only attendee from either product development laboratory was McDowell from Endicott.

Most of the day was devoted to determining the future course of each of the company's thirty-nine development projects ranging from an improved summary punch to cathode-ray-tube storage. When its turn came, the Magnetic Drum Calculator project at Endicott—to McDowell's chagrin—was adjudged "controversial," and the decision was made to move all but the mechanical units of the project to the Poughkeepsie laboratory. Clearly, the sales people and planners present were dissatisfied with the MDC project, and Watson, Jr., leaned to their view of Hamilton as too conservative, too encumbered by the spirit of the electromechanical era, to be entrusted with the MDC. Better, Watson reasoned, to shift the project to the heady, new-era atmosphere that Palmer had created—in effect, to concentrate all electronics work in Poughkeepsie.[45]

As it turned out, the plan to move the MDC project out of Endicott ran afoul of another decision made in the wake of the April meeting. Since project-by-project direction of the laboratories was clearly an inappropriate task for a collection of corporate executives, Watson, Jr., decided that headquarters needed a man with laboratory management experience to coordinate all IBM development programs and to manage expansions of the engineering work force. McDowell had managed the Endicott laboratory for eight years and had earned the confidence of both young electronics engineers and self-made EAM "inventors." Therefore Watson, Jr., journeyed to Endicott to offer him the job.

McDowell's promotion to the post of IBM director of engineering, vacant since McPherson had held it during the war years, was announced by Watson, Sr., at IBM's annual Hundred Per Cent Club sales meeting in May 1950.[46] But for at least two reasons it was important to McDowell to delay the transfer of the MDC project to Poughkeepsie. First, he had a high opinion of Hamilton's qualities as a development manager and believed that they easily outweighed his lack of formal electronics training. Second, it would not be helpful to McDowell's standing in Endicott if his first act as a headquarters executive was to strip the laboratory of its technologically most-advanced project. The transfer never came to pass.[47]

Meanwhile McPherson, who had hoped that dramatic cost-performance improvements might emerge from the MDC-ERA comparison, saw his hopes frustrated. Roberts had informed him that, even with Hamilton's latest improvements stemming from the March meeting, sales would be limited because "present competition for the projected machine is our own sort and gangpunch techniques. Obviously in contemplating production of a machine of this character, we should be able to visualize being in a position to offer a substantial percentage of our customers an improved result, and this does not seem likely."[48] To buttress that appraisal, a committee was formed by the sales department to assess MDC performance on jobs known to stretch the capabilities of existing equipment. From McDowell, the committee obtained a projected monthly rental of $1500, an estimate that assumed the low manufacturing volumes indicated by Roberts's preliminary appraisal. One of the committee's typical studies, done for mortgage loan accounting, showed the MDC finishing the work in one-quarter the time taken by the IBM 602A calculator (successor to the 602). But the 602A produced a thousand result cards for $3.70, compared with $4.28 for the MDC. The committee concluded that many customers might consider the MDC "a step backward."

Nonetheless, the committee found much to admire in the MDC. It liked the simplicity of the new single-address instructions and the increased storage capacity (one hundred words compared with fifty digits in the 604). Committee members recognized, some for the first time, that punching a program on cards might be less tedious than wiring one on a control panel. Consequently, the tone of the committee's report was encouraging. By the time the report had been reformulated into a new sales department specification and forwarded to McPherson, its message was, in effect: Reduce the cost of the machine to permit a monthly rental of $1000, make the thousand words of table capacity usable for programs and data (a provision eliminated earlier in an economy move), and we will sell between 200 and 300 units. Hurd was the committee member who demanded flexibility in the use of storage; assuming such flexibility, he estimated sales of 50 to 75 machines for scientific computing applications—harking back to the machine's original intended application area but now in combination with, rather than instead of, commercial applications.[49] In May 1950, Hurd and others suggested further that the machine be given broader appeal by endowing it with optional storage. For instance, some 604 users (rental $550) ready to try more applications would probably balk at paying $1000 per month for a 1000-word MDC but might move up to a 100-word MDC at a rental of $750.[50]

On 1 July 1950, at the conclusion of his design review, Hamilton issued a new MDC description spelling out four significant changes. First, he contemplated a system with three models having 200, 1000, and 2000 words of storage, respectively. (Provision for table lookup was omitted in the smallest model.) Second, table storage was made usable as "general" storage. The extra equipment needed for restoring generality to storage was partially compensated for by curtailing the variety of allowed table entry formats. Third, a substantial redesign of the card punch provided greater distance (hence more processing time) between the reading and punching stations. This, together with additional buffer storage in the form of drum tracks, allowed processing, reading, and punching tasks to overlap. Previously, processing and input-output activities could not proceed simultaneously, and buffering increased the allowable processing time per input card from about 100 to 500 milliseconds (thousandths of a second) for applications planned to run at the top card reading speed of 100 cards per minute.

The fourth change revised the instruction format again, this time dramatically, in recognition of the dynamic nature of drum storage. In the one-address scheme, adopted in April, program steps (two to a word) were obtained from the drum two at a time. Except when a branch occurred, they were executed in the strict numeric sequence of drum locations. Most instructions—all arithmetic instructions and the store instruction, for instance—included a memory address. Hence a typical pair of instructions implied three memory accesses: one to get the pair and two to move operands. But at 4280 revolutions per minute, the drum revolved once every 14 milliseconds. With ten words stored serially by digit around a drum track, each word access could take from 1.4 milliseconds, at best, to 14 milliseconds, at worst, depending on the angular position of the desired word location relative to the stationary head when search began. Taking half a complete rotation as the average, 7 milliseconds fetch had been assumed in reckoning MDC speeds. Since there were many instructions that could be processed within a single word time (1.4 milliseconds), execution times were clearly being dominated by waits.[51] Hamilton and Dunwell concluded that execution times could be improved, perhaps halved, if program step positions were "advantageously chosen" instead of "following each other sequentially."[52] The idea was that, if successively executed program steps could be stored, say, diametrically opposite one another on a track instead of in adjacent positions, speeds could be improved with no cost penalty. Of course, for this to work, the location of the operand needed by a given instruction would have to fall about midway between the locations of the given instruction and the next instruction. Variety in instruction timings made it unlikely that a fixed rule for spacing successive instructions would achieve much improvement.

For this and other reasons, Hamilton, in his July specification, exploited the principle in another way. He reverted to an instruction format with two addresses, now labeled P and S, but with this new twist: the sole purpose of the second (S) address was to identify a next-to-be-executed instruction. P and S addresses could be chosen by the programmer so as to reduce waits, perhaps even to minimize them. With 200 tracks available, there would be, for each instruction or data word, 200 equally suitable candidates having a most-favorable angular position. At the same time, speed expectations were enhanced by overlapping the execution of a given instruction with the fetch of the next-to-be-executed instruction. Thus, once the P-address of an instruction had been used in obtaining a desired data word, the S-address could be dispatched to the drum-addressing circuits and search for the next instruction begun. For extended-execution-time instructions such as multiply, divide, and table lookup, the next instruction could in many instances be obtained before an execution had ended.[53]

Although the new instruction format permitted Hamilton to claim a faster MDC, the burden of realizing that increased performance had been placed on the application programmer. Storage allocation, the process whereby instructions and data are assigned to storage locations, had seemed a tedious clerical task even when it could be done arbitrarily or by rote. Now that the MDC's programming "flexibility" (Hamilton's word) would permit heightened machine performance at the programmer's expense, storage allocation loomed as a very substantial and complicated task.

The problem of "waiting time" had come to the attention of the earliest computer designers, largely in the context of mercury-delay-line storage. In 1944, that technology was perceived by Eckert and Mauchly of the Moore School as a means whereby the idea of storing programs could reasonably be exploited.[54] In England, M. V. Wilkes, builder of Cambridge University's EDSAC (which was equipped with mercury-delay-line storage) chose a straightforward one-address instruction even though he estimated that two-thirds of EDSAC operating time would consist of waiting. He characterized "optimum programming"—as English programmers called placement of data and instructions to reduce waiting time—as an "exercise of cunning." Expecting random-access memories to be forthcoming "sooner or later," he felt that optimum programming "was misplaced as a long term investment."[55]

A far different view prevailed at England's National Physical Laboratory where, in late 1945, logician Alan M. Turing completed his proposal for the Automatic Computing Engine (ACE). To reduce waits for data words, Turing provided some fifty "quick reference temporary storage units" (each a one-word delay line) that helped to reduce the number of required main-memory accesses. He considered instruction-fetch delays intolerable, and his design avoided them in most cases. By the time a pilot model ACE was completed in late 1950, that aspect of its design was similar to the MDC scheme: a "timing number" field in the instruction allowed the programmer to specify the location of the next instruction relative to the location of the present instruction.[56]

The notion of somehow avoiding the waiting time penalty may have been suggested to Dunwell and Hamilton in September 1949 when they attended a Harvard University symposium and heard an English speaker outline developments in his country. He briefly contrasted the EDSAC and ACE designs, noting that in the latter there would be "facilities for putting instructions in nonserially and in such a way that when one is obeyed the next instruction is immediately available."[57]

The new MDC design issued on 1 July 1950 was accompanied by revised manufacturing cost estimates, based on quantities as high as 750 machines. This was a response to the sales department committee's suggestions in May that an entry-level model priced near $750 might permit that volume of sales. Economies of scale, applied to the engineers' tightened design, thus resulted in the lowest cost estimates that had yet been achieved. The headquarters financial staff, however, in converting cost estimates to rentals, arrived at a rental range of $1000 to $1250 for the three MDC models. Hurd and others, feeling that the engineers had accomplished in the new design everything requested by the committee, protested that the rentals should be 20 percent lower, in the $750–$1025 range. The higher range, they pointed out, would reduce the market by a factor of three. While eager to see IBM introduce a stored-program product aimed at IBM's traditional customers, they insisted that pegging the minimum at $1000, nearly twice the 604 rental, would be "a serious error," so serious that it justified dropping the whole project.[58]

Thus the persistence of the headquarters view that the MDC must be a "growth machine" for 604 customers had come to threaten MDC development, despite the fact that neither by constantly pressing the engineers, as Dunwell did, nor by demanding bolder pricing, as Hurd did on this occasion, could it be made to fill that role. Nevertheless, Hurd's interest in the MDC continued throughout 1950 and provided a welcome boost to the project at a time when Future Demands was becoming particularly dubious about it.

In September 1950, it was decided at headquarters that continuation of the MDC project, by now relocated from the North Street laboratory to a drab building on Broad Street in downtown Endicott, should hinge on a technical audit by engineers from the Poughkeepsie laboratory, where the experimental stored-program "Test Assembly" (see chapter 4) had run test problems for the first time on 12 September. Consequently, two engineers from the Test Assembly project spent most of the first two weeks of October with a group from Endicott. Anticipation of the event gave rise to strong feelings among the Endicott engineers. They, after all, had built the SSEC and had it running well over two years before Poughkeepsie's experimental machine had even made its first calculation. Even Poughkeepsie's 604, a solid achievement in engineering design, had borrowed heavily from SSEC circuits. The Test Assembly magnetic drum and heads had been developed at Endicott, and the first model used Endicott circuits for reading and writing data on the drum. To deepen Endicott's feelings of ignominy, the audit meetings were held at Poughkeepsie. Fortunately, the Poughkeepsie engineers proved skillful in neutralizing hostility by turning the meetings into a vigorous study of MDC circuits, of alternative circuits, and of the circuit-cost implications of differing codes. At the conclusion, their report took a highly favorable view of the MDC design. The machine was deemed "very well thought out," the circuit techniques "excellent" and "as inexpensive as they could possibly be." A by-product of the study was a roughed-out design of an alphabetic model of the MDC envisioned by Hamilton, which was found to require some 12 percent more vacuum tubes and germanium semiconductor diodes than the numeric model.[59]

On the final day of the Poughkeepsie conference, after the MDC engineers had returned to Endicott, the audit committee's conclusions were presented to Future Demands, with Palmer attending. It was his responsibility to report the outcome of the study to McDowell and to estimate the likelihood of the project's leading to a marketable product. Like his engineers, he was impressed with the MDC design and told McDowell it would be a good choice for a product if the effort to make it one were mounted immediately. But, given any delay, he said, there would be pressure to augment the design, based on a profusion of new ideas spawned by Future Demands in its continuing studies of potential applications.[60]

Palmer had aptly portrayed the situation. On 27 November, less than two weeks after a meeting that had settled a number of questions raised by Future Demands and Applied Science during the summer,[61] Dunwell journeyed to Endicott with a proposal for further elaboration of the punch unit specifications. Hamilton's reaction was less mercurial than it had been a year earlier in similar circumstances. But he informed the Endicott laboratory manager and McDowell that he was "proceeding on the basis of agreements reached in New York," alluded to the impossibility of making substantial changes in his working model then under construction, and voiced his concern that Future Demands, while asserting that the MDC was too expensive, continued to press costly revisions upon him.[62]

Dunwell seemed to understand that the way he performed his planning job made life difficult for the engineers, for he told Roberts that the basic problem in integrating electronic technology into the product line was that "our plans became obsolete more rapidly than the machines embodying them can be produced." But he felt that his demanding pace was justified by the circumstances. He believed Hamilton should cope with fast-changing requirements by shedding the conservatism of the old technological era and agreeing to incorporate new functions suggested by the planners despite contrary arguments based on complexity and initial design cost. Dunwell held that rapid and unforeseen improvements in engineering design could be expected to appear routinely, justifying bold engineering that would be considered reckless in a more mature technological environment. Cost reduction and simplification were sound objectives but should not be pursued too early in the development process, thereby depriving customers of useful capabilities. The MDC, he said, was a victim of an outdated engineering philosophy. Out of a series of compromises had emerged a machine both too expensive for 604 users to grow into and with too many functional deficiencies to attract users who could spend more.[63] The emergence of this philosophy signaled a perception by Future Demands that the MDC was a dead-end project, salvageable only by changes too drastic for the conservative engineering team to consider. The first hint of the new attitude had come at the audit committee presentation in Poughkeepsie when Dunwell unexpectedly gave Palmer an outline of the capabilities of a quite different drum calculator, one less powerful than the MDC, with perhaps 50 words of data storage and 300 program steps.

What Hamilton, in Endicott, had not divined was that Future Demands, shaken by seemingly endless, unquantifiable pressures, was no longer confident it could control IBM's product destiny. Since the onset of the Korean conflict in mid-1950, the defense industries had begun to clamor for additional computing capacity. Moreover, Hurd's Applied Science department no longer had the time to continue fencing with Future Demands over the prospects for the MDC; its members were too busy introducing IBM's Card-Programmed Calculator to eager engineers and scientists. Hurd himself was busy traveling, meeting with defense industry customers in an attempt to crystallize the essential elements of the new demands. Although Hamilton would continue to receive suggestions and criticisms from Future Demands, the record gave him no reason to expect much encouragement or support. Hamilton's only strength at headquarters was McDowell, but behind that bulwark, Hamilton felt assured of the MDC's future.

In early January 1951 (see chapter 5), Tom Watson, Jr., decided that IBM Poughkeepsie should undertake a crash program to design a large-scale "Defense Calculator," slanted toward the needs of design engineers, and to manufacture copies for selected defense industry customers. Endicott did not figure in the undertaking.

3.5 The Squeeze on Resources

During the fall of 1950 the MDC was redesigned to reflect results of the summer negotiations and to incorporate a new code for decimal digits on the drum and in the processing circuits. The seven-bit "biquinary" code, suggested for the processing circuits by Dunwell a year earlier, was deemed by Hamilton to be the best compromise among cost, speed, and checking capability. It was the third code specified for the MDC, preceded by the original 8-4-2-1 code and by the one-out-of-twelve code that emerged during the drum-enhanced 604 era in mid-1949. In January 1951, the new design was complete.[64] To Hamilton, Troy, and Hughes, engineers marking their third anniversary on the project, this seemed an auspicious time to press their case for the machine as a product, but for that effort a fully operating model would be needed. Hamilton was so confident of the design that he proposed to build three models simultaneously: one for tuning by the engineers, one for application testing by Future Demands and Applied Science, and one for the product-testing department.

The plan was to build the electronic portions of the models at the Poughkeepsie plant, where workers by now had over two years experience building 604s. Endicott would build the card punches. By the time the necessary cost estimates had been assembled, it was May 1951. With a go-ahead from McDowell, the Endicott laboratory drafted a Development Work Order for $430,000, a substantial commitment for a project that had already accumulated engineering expenses of about $250,000.[65]

McDowell received the work order in late May, and, on the same day, a memorandum from sales confirmed that there were about twenty customer orders for the Defense Calculator.[66] Soon, there was evidence that the manufacturing cost for the Defense Calculator would be well above that underlying the rental charge on which orders ("letters of intent") had been based. Although McDowell got a tentative cost estimate from Palmer, in July he told IBM's treasurer that because of the complexity of the Defense Calculator, he was "not in a position to submit an estimate that means a great deal at this time."[67] Thus, with Defense Calculator development demanding a large and growing rate of expenditure and with the manufacturing cost of twenty large machines still uncertain, it was clear that Hamilton's expensive model-building plans for a machine with a zero market forecast had no chance for approval. In July, he reverted to a plan for a single model to be built at the Endicott laboratory.[68] If the model looked promising, he would presumably be authorized to build one or two more for reliability testing. In the hope that a more favorable climate might evolve, even the reduced work order was held back until mid-October.[69]

During 1951, Future Demands pressed more or less continually for refinement of and changes to Hamilton's January specifications, the basis of the reduced, single-model building program.[70] The engineers on the MDC project continued to feel that their product was being scuttled by accusations that its definition was always incomplete. In their frustration, they turned to the Applied Science department for counsel on applications, thereby appearing to grow indifferent to the MDC's potential in the commercial accounting field. This attitude simply intensified the estrangement from Future Demands without building comparable marketing support, for Applied Science was increasingly preoccupied with the Defense Calculator.

During a concentrated period of effort in June, however, Future Demands and Applied Science wrote a number of programs to obtain precise projected performance figures for key MDC applications, such as public utility rate extension and mathematical subroutines. The results, significant only in combination with projected rentals, were construed by Dunwell to demonstrate the need for two major functions on which Engineering and Future Demands had taken firm and opposing positions: alphabetic processing capability and higher speed (the latter to be achieved by more quick-access registers for data or program steps and/or a higher-speed drum). In July a member of Roberts's staff recommended that Future Demands "transfer our attention temporarily to a smaller, cheaper, and if possible faster machine, which would be satisfactory for perhaps ten times as many customers."[71] Such a machine had been first outlined by Dunwell at the September 1950 audit committee meeting. He had begun then to work with two Poughkeepsie laboratory engineers, James E. Fernekees and L. Roy Harper, who were building a model of it.[72] In February he wrote a three-page specification, formalizing a Future Demands view that the correct entry into commercial applications below the large-scale level of UNIVAC was a machine with a price "within the range of present calculators and accounting machines."[73]

In September, a Future Demands memorandum on the MDC to a member of McDowell's staff was uncompromising. It asserted that "alphabetic storage, faster programming, and lower cost" were considered "essential for general sale of this machine" and that the issue of including those features would have to be "faced again if and when we reconsider general sale of this machine."[74]

Viewed in retrospect, the failure of the three-model plan to gain approval eliminated once and for all any chance that the MDC would be IBM's first computer. The Defense Calculator was now destined for that role. A later starter by almost three years, it sailed by the MDC in 1951 on the wings of Tom Watson, Jr.'s, sponsorship and with the support of a list of users who had been told about it and wanted it. Struggling in the wake of the Defense Calculator, the MDC seemed to have no future. It lacked two vital elements: a consistent set of figures on manufacturing costs, projected rentals, and market forecasts that spelled profit; and the genuine interest of a corporate or marketing executive of the company.

3.6 The President's Decision

In the face of waning interest from the Future Demands and Sales departments at headquarters and cramped by a decreasing budget, the MDC team late in 1951 doggedly pursued completion of a single model to Hamilton's January 1951 specifications. The central processing unit had already been started in Poughkeepsie in anticipation of approval of the three-model plan. But the shipment of a single, partially wired unit to Endicott in October marked the end of the Poughkeepsie location's association with the out-of-favor project. In January 1952, initial tests of the MDC model were begun. Tests and design refinements continued through the year; final tests were conducted in October. By then only a half-dozen members of the laboratory staff were still assigned to the MDC project.[75]

The MDC electronic circuits were supported in single-tube, pluggable units similar to those of the 604 calculator. The packaging of tubes and diodes in separate units, a practice made tolerable by the modest switching speeds of the MDC, facilitated pluggable unit circuit standardization and avoided undesirable concentrations of back-panel wiring. The circuits used in the MDC included sense amplifiers for reading the small signals from the drum; power amplifiers to handle the current required for recording on the drum; and the inverters, cathode followers, and diode circuits required for logic and switching. The conventional flip-flop of the preceding model was not employed; where single-element storage was required, a novel "latch" circuit, invented by Hughes, served instead.

This latch circuit consisted of a pair of inverters (occupying one pluggable unit), a cathode follower power amplifier (half of another unit), and four or so diodes (one-third of a special diode unit). The latch differed from a flip-flop in that the output voltage of the second inverter was coupled to the input circuit of the first inverter not directly, but through a cathode follower and diode circuits (figure 3.2). This arrangement, while favored by MDC designers as more reliable in some respects than the conventional flip-flop, had a more obvious appeal in the variety of control combinations afforded by the diode switching in its input circuits.[76]

By late 1952, the 604 was four years old, the CPC three. The MDC project, seen at various times as a successor to both machines and to which great urgency had been attached back in mid-1949, had slowed to a near halt. Small stored-program computers were being offered by competitors as replacements for IBM CPCs. Hurd's Applied Science representatives had begun hearing of such proposals the previous

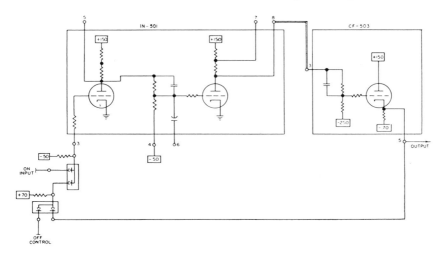

Figure 3.2
Magnetic Drum Calculator latch circuit. Large rectangular outlines show the confines of single-tube pluggable units used to construct the circuit. IN-501 is a double inverter unit; CF-503 is one-half of a cathode follower unit. Four diodes are used for on-off control in this form of the latch circuit. The small rectangles indicate that the diodes are on a separate pluggable unit consisting exclusively of twelve diodes in a standard wiring configuration that could be adapted to a variety of circuits by choosing (1) the orientation of individual diodes in their plug-in clips, (2) the set of pluggable unit base pins wired to adjoining circuits, and (3) the resistors connected, at the back of the mounting panel, between pluggable unit base pins and power distribution buses.

summer. Some IBM customers called McPherson and Hurd directly at headquarters, inviting some kind of response from the company. To make matters worse, the 604 was being threatened by a new low-cost Remington Rand machine, the 409. By mid-November, McPherson was able to list seven competitive small, stored-program drum computers threatening "complete obsolescence" of IBM's 604 and CPC. These included Consolidated Engineering Corporation's Model 30-201, Computer Research Corporation's Model 102-A, and Underwood Corporation's Elecom 100.[77]

In the early fall of 1952, IBM planners and engineers had sought a joint solution to the competitive situation. But there was disagreement in both camps, and a chaotic period ensued. Sales management supported an engineering plan to counter the Remington Rand 409 with an enhanced 604; members of the Future Demands staff railed against that decision, arguing that the 604 technology was a dead end and that IBM must now either switch its customers to newer technology or lose them (see chapter 12). Dunwell advanced his concept of a low-cost, magnetic-drum calculating and card read-punch combination that could be incrementally enhanced to offer a spectrum of cost, capacity, and input-output functions—with provision for card-controlled programming for users with occasional scientific computing needs. To replace the CPC, he proposed a reduced version of the large-scale magnetic-tape-oriented machine being developed at Poughkeepsie, an idea that had been brewing for six months and on which John von Neumann had been brought in to consult in March.[78] Dunwell's proposals left the MDC out completely (except that he found value in the multifeed card input-output unit being developed). His proposals also exacerbated the natural rivalry between the Poughkeepsie and Endicott laboratories.

Hurd, disappointed by the indecisiveness he had observed as a guest at a mid-October engineering conference held by McDowell in Harriman, N.Y., needed a machine soon to counter the competitive threats to the CPC. In view of the urgency of the problem, Hamilton's machine, complete and running programs at the Endicott laboratory, had to be considered a potential solution. Hurd had worked with an earlier model of the MDC in July 1950 and at headquarters had unsuccessfully sought a formula to bring it to market. By competitive standards, the current model was too slow, but Hurd believed he could persuade Hamilton to increase the speed in return for Applied Science's support of the beleaguered machine—a belief that became the basis of an agreement with Hamilton on 6 November 1952. The speed-enhancement feature was to consist of new drum tracks housing thirty 5-word "revolvers" in which programs would store frequently accessed data and instructions. Since general storage was deployed at 20 words per track, each of 150 words in the new storage units would be available once every quarter of a drum revolution, thus requiring only one-fourth the "waiting time" of general storage numbers. There was no new technology involved; the MDC had been using drum revolvers for its accumulator register and distributor register ever since Dunwell had suggested them in the summer of 1949.[79] The engineers thought a production prototype of the enhanced MDC could be running by February 1954.

Following the meeting with Hamilton, Hurd assigned a small mathematical planning group of Applied Science staff members he had previously established at the Poughkeepsie laboratory to work with Hamilton's engineers on incremental improvements to the MDC. He added Elmer C. Kubie, a senior member of the New York Technical Computing Bureau staff, to the group.

A week later McDowell, armed with cost data on the enhanced MDC, met with Louis H. LaMotte, vice-president for sales, but could not persuade him to endorse the project.[80] Thus, the stage was set for Tom Watson, Jr., IBM president since January, to resolve the stand-off. He discussed the situation with Hurd and on 18 November convened a small meeting at which he asked who or what was holding up establishment of the MDC as a full-scale product program. On being told that the sales department had some reservations about it, he asked that these be cleared up the next day at the latest, adding that if sales could give McDowell its approval of the program promptly, he would not have to renew his personal involvement. McDowell got the go-ahead from LaMotte at noon the next day.[81]

Watson, Jr.'s, November 1952 action restored vitality to a project that had never fully recovered from his rejection of its premise in May 1949. Not surprisingly, Hamilton's month-end report for November dropped the tentative language of prior reports and stated, "The organization of a group of personnel is under way to redesign portions of the Calculator and prepare drawings for production release." He confidently projected group size at fifty, up from only four the previous month.[82]

Although substantial obstacles, not yet perceived, remained (see chapter 5), the president's decision set the stage for announcement of the MDC as the IBM Type 650 Magnetic Drum Calculator in mid-1953.

4

The Tape Processing Machine

The CRT memory project. The Data Processing Test Assembly. Plans for the Tape Processing Machine. TPM engineering. A time for waiting.

In 1947, while Frank Hamilton and Ralph Palmer were occupied with the SSEC and the 604 electronic calculator, respectively, John Mc-Pherson paid careful attention to news of the EDVAC. This project at the University of Pennsylvania, given publicity early in March, was known to have attracted the interest of the Prudential Insurance Company.[1] In April McPherson reviewed this development with key IBM engineers and executives, noting especially the planned use of magnetic tape for input, output, and large-capacity storage in the EDVAC system. It was decided that the company should establish a laboratory project to explore magnetic tape as a storage medium.[2] In May, the project was assigned to Endicott and placed under Hamilton's supervision. (See chapter 6.)

Nearly a year later, largely because of the heavy workload imposed by the SSEC, the new project was still dealing only with the basics of recording phenomena. This delay was to prove embarrassing in March 1948 when members of the sales department, discussing IBM's SSEC with a group of actuaries from the insurance industry, found themselves trying to answer searching questions about magnetic tape—questions perhaps prompted by the actuaries' discussions with the Eckert-Mauchly Computer Corporation.[3] The latter had begun publicizing a prospective UNIVAC system in which card files were replaced by reels of magnetic tape.[4]

Prominent among IBM executives who recognized the growing professional and governmental interest in EDVAC-like machines was Louis H. LaMotte, head of IBM's Washington office, who had assigned a member of his staff to track the considerable developments in large-scale computers. In August 1948, this assistant returned from the Symposium on Modern Calculating Machinery and Numerical Methods at the University of California in Los Angeles[5] and promptly recommended that IBM construct an "intermediate-type" calculator. LaMotte forwarded the recommendation to corporate headquarters, observing that "there must be some very fundamental reason why so many outside agencies are intensely interested and active." He posed the question: "Inasmuch as IBM is the leader in the field of calculating equipment, does it not seem reasonable that it too should be kept abreast of all developments by active participation in this field, either to an equal or greater extent than any of the listed organizations?" The nineteen "listed organizations" included the National Bureau of Standards (with its planned SEAC), Harvard University (Mark II and Mark III), the University of Pennsylvania (EDVAC), and the Institute for Advanced Study (von Neumann's machine), among other government and educational institutions in the United States and abroad. But it also included half a dozen commercial companies in this country, "notably Eckert-Mauchly [Computer] Company, Raytheon, and the Reeves Instrument Company." LaMotte's main plea was that IBM ready itself "to entertain invitations to construct modern calculators for any legitimate purpose on a cost-plus basis." He sent his memorandum to several headquarters executives, including Tom Watson, Jr., and Gordon Roberts, head of the Future Demands department.[6]

By December, Watson, Jr., was asking McDowell for a review of the Endicott engineering laboratory's postwar headcounts and hiring policies. McDowell's reply indicated the following population numbers: 408 (September 1945), 440 (January 1946), 457 (January 1947), 407 (January 1948), and 418 (3 December 1948). The rise in late 1945 and 1946 had consisted mainly of "builders and model makers" assembled for the SSEC project and subsequently assigned to the Endicott and Poughkeepsie factories. The slight rise in 1948 was authorized after "it became evident that we were not doing adequate engineering work from a factory and service point of view." As for the future, Endicott was planning that during 1949 its engineering training program "cover the training of 20 men, half of whom will have specialized in Electronics."[7]

Watson, Jr., was evidently dissatisfied with this report, for within three days McDowell was writing: "Based on a review with Mr. McPherson with respect to hiring young Electronic Engineers, we expect to hire 25 men during 1949. Roughly, 7 will be assigned at Endicott, 5 at the Watson Laboratory in New York, and 13 to Mr. Palmer at Poughkeepsie. Every effort is being made to have 10 of the 25 hired by the end of January, 1949." LaMotte was beginning to see at least some of the action he desired.[8]

4.1 The CRT Memory Project

By the late 1940s, the need for large-capacity data storage was widely recognized, particularly with the advent of the stored-program concept. An IBM engineer who was especially interested in this problem was Philip E. Fox, who joined IBM in Endicott in October 1946. An MIT graduate, he had acquired experience in electronic circuit design while serving in the Army Security Agency during the war. He worked briefly on the SSEC until it was shipped to New York City, then requested a transfer to Poughkeepsie where, as a member of Palmer's electronics group, he worked initially on engineering changes in IBM 604 circuits and on problems related to tube life and reliability. Then in 1948, as he later recalled, it was becoming quite clear that "one of the big problems in going anywhere with electronic computers, beyond what the 604 could do, was that we needed lots of storage, and we had the feeling that it was going to be some sort of special vacuum tube."[9]

Indeed, special vacuum tubes were being investigated as potential devices in a number of laboratories at that time. In February 1946, a conference held at the Naval Research Laboratory discussed the use of electrostatic storage tubes for digital information. J. W. Forrester of MIT attended this conference and was influenced by it in his early decision to use electrostatic storage tube memories for Whirlwind, a large electronic digital computer that MIT was building under military sponsorship.[10] (See chapter 7.) This conference dealt with "classified" technical developments to which IBM engineers were not privy, but by September 1947 an article in *Electronics* on work at the Naval Research Laboratory described how a special cathode-ray tube could be used to store for protracted periods television pictures, radar indicator patterns, oscilloscope traces, or other information.[11] Believing the special tubes described in the literature were too complicated, Fox and others obtained a vacuum system (intended as an evaporator) and installed it in the Kenyon House basement where they began making experimental tubes.

Around the end of 1948, Fox received from Palmer a preprint of a paper by F. C. Williams and T. Kilburn of the University of Manchester in England,[12] describing what came to be widely known as "Williams storage." It made use of a cathode-ray tube (CRT) of a type by then in ordinary use as the display device in instruments such as the oscilloscope. In such a CRT, a beam of electrons is emitted by a heated cathode at the small end of a glass tube of tapering diameter. After passing through an intensity-control grid, the beam is shaped and focused by the voltages on a set of anodes, and it attains its final velocity through the attractive force of around 2000 volts at an accelerating anode. The inside surface of the large end of the tube— the tube's face—is coated with a phosphor, a material that emits visible light from any spot struck by electrons of sufficient velocity. Before striking the phosphor coating, the accelerated beam passes between two plates, one for horizontal and one for vertical deflection, that can direct the beam to any desired spot on the CRT face, which is typically 3 to 5 inches in diameter.

With the standard CRT as a point of departure, Williams turned to the use of secondary emission, a phenomenon unrelated to luminescence, for information storage. The phosphor, when struck by a beam of electrons of sufficient energy, emits more than one secondary electron per impinging electron. It is thus possible to create a "well," a very small region of positive charge (due to loss of secondary electrons) at a selected spot on the tube face by directing the beam to that spot. It is possible to "fill" the well by directing the beam to a second spot nearby—typically just over one beam diameter away. Secondary electrons released from the second spot are attracted to the first by its positive potential and fill the well. The first spot of a pair is either charged positively (and may arbitrarily be said to store a 0) or discharged (storing a 1) depending on whether its companion spot is also struck by the beam. The beam is directed to the second spot only if a 1 is to be stored (figure 4.1.). A display of, say, 500 spot pairs on a tube face can store 500 bits of information, each pair serving as a storage cell for one bit.

The sudden changes in potential that occur at the face of the tube when the beam strikes the phosphor are of opposite sign, depending on whether the beam is "digging" a well or landing in one. These changes can be detected by an electronic amplifier connected to a conducting plate placed close to the exterior surface of the tube face. The value of a bit previously stored can be sensed by detecting the positive or negative signal (a stored 1 or 0, respectively) that results when the beam is directed to the first spot of a pair. If the signal-pickup plate consists of a piece of wire screen or conducting glass fastened to the face of the CRT, the stored information can be read visually by interpreting a single spot of light as 0 and a pair of spots as 1. Williams, as well as others who experimented with his system, tried numerous variations on the pair of spots.[13] In one version (the one Fox ultimately selected), the beam was merely deflected to the second spot, while still turned on, if a 1 was to be stored. The result was a dot or dash display for each stored 0 or 1, respectively.

Jan. 15, 1957   F. C. WILLIAMS ET AL   2,777,971
INFORMATION STORAGE MEANS

Filed May 16, 1949   5 Sheets—Sheet 2

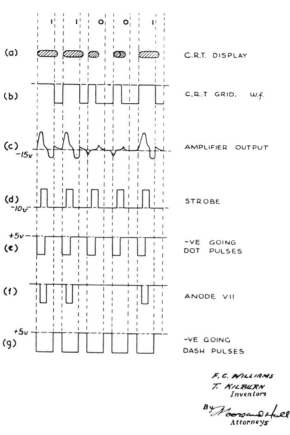

Figure 4.1
Voltage waveforms illustrating the principle of Williams storage. At *a*, shading indicates bright spots on the CRT face corresponding to stored bit values of 1, 1, 0, 0, 1. This display results from application of the voltage sequence at *b* to the intensity control grid of the CRT. The output waveform at *c* shows in amplified form the voltage detected at the pickup plate. The large positive pulses occur at "strobe" pulse times *d* if the beam strikes the phosphor coating where a dash has been stored, releasing secondary electrons. Where a dot has been stored, secondary emission is negligible, and the detected signal consists only of slight negative and positive pulses due to turning the beam on and off, respectively. The negative-going pulses at *e* and *g* are used in switching circuits to produce dot and dash voltages on the control grid. The final output of the sense amplifier, after shaping, is as shown at *f*. (Figure from U.S. Patent 2,777,971 of F. C. Williams and T. Kilburn.)

Because deflection of the beam to any desired location required a short time relative to the whole read-and-write-back cycle, usually termed the memory cycle, the time required for access to a stored bit was essentially independent of the bit's location. (Years later, this useful quality became known in the context of computer memory as "random access.") Typically, designers of Williams-tube memories chose a memory cycle in the range between 10 and 20 microseconds. Since CRTs could be operated in parallel, an instruction or operand could be called from a CRT memory in a few microseconds by reading all the bits of a word simultaneously, each from a different CRT.

A troublesome characteristic of Williams storage was that the charge at every bit cell had to be regenerated every few milliseconds. Memory regeneration periods had therefore to be interspersed among use periods. The need for regeneration stemmed mainly from two effects. First, without regeneration, the natural leakage of electrical charge due to imperfect insulating characteristics of the phosphor would, within a few tenths of a second, change all bits to 1s. Second, each access tended to cause partial filling of neighboring wells. This latter effect, known as "spill," made it necessary to complete a full cycle of the regeneration process, refreshing each bit cell once, not merely within a given time but within the time some maximum number of references could be made to adjacent bit cells. This maximum, called the "read-around ratio," was approximately 200.[14] It was up to the computer designer to ensure that regeneration would proceed rapidly enough to avoid spill at the most frequently used spots. Moreover, every CRT had to be subjected to a "spill test" to ensure its suitability for a particular machine.

When Fox heard about the Williams technique, he began immediately to experiment with CRT storage. Assisted by a technician, he carried on his initial experiments in the Delapenha House, a Mediterranean-style dwelling on a hill overlooking the Hudson River, to which Palmer and some of his electronics engineers moved in the spring of 1949.[15] In July, he was joined by Nathen P. Edwards, a graduate of Stanford University with a master's degree in electronics and radar experience from wartime service in the navy. Fox and his associates corroborated Williams's findings and soon became convinced that the method possessed advantages that far outweighed its disadvantages. Use of a standard CRT presumably made device development unnecessary. Furthermore, this method nicely combined large-capacity storage with short access time.[16]

Any notion that the Williams storage method would be easy to apply was soon dispelled. Sophisticated electronic design was required because the small, usable signal—only a thousandth of a volt or so—was critically dependent upon the proper positioning of an electron beam subject to thousands of volts during acceleration and to deflection-voltage changes measured in hundreds of volts per microsecond. Amplifiers and their power supplies had to be designed and constructed with exceptional care just to keep the ratio of signal to "noise" voltage acceptably high. The whole storage system, comprising many charged points in a high-resistance complex, was sensitive to small static electric discharges and other sources of electromagnetic radiation. Between the first seemingly successful experiments and a working CRT memory there lay, as will become evident, a long and difficult series of engineering improvements in both the tube and the manner of its application.

4.2 The Data Processing Test Assembly

Nathaniel Rochester, who joined IBM in November 1948, was an MIT graduate and wartime employee of MIT's Radiation Laboratory, the locus of a government-sponsored program for radar research and development. Just before joining IBM he had been an engineering manager at Sylvania Electric Products Company where, in 1947, his department had obtained a contract to construct the arithmetic portion of the Whirlwind computer. Because of this contract, Rochester was permitted to attend the engineering meetings and seminars in which the computer's organization and operation were described. Fascinated with the logical power implicit in that description and convinced that Whirlwind represented a class of machines with an uncommonly bright future, Rochester resolved to be part of that future. After carrying through the Sylvania contract, he applied for positions in General Electric and IBM, accepting the better offer, which came from IBM.[17]

Arriving in Palmer's laboratory in the fall of 1948, Rochester was taken aback by its lack of any stored-program computer development project. With the SSEC, IBM had shown it could design, build, and operate a large electronic calculator. But large-scale computing instruments were still not viewed as potential products at IBM. Gordon Roberts, who typified executives experienced in electric accounting machine (EAM) applications, could see no practical relationships between giant electronic installations and punched-card accounting. As head of the Future Demands department, he argued that the new IBM 604, with improvements that would follow, was the right product for bringing the benefits of electronic technology to EAM customers.

Rochester spent a few months becoming acquainted with IBM products, most notably the 604. He visited the SSEC at its showroom in New York City and was not impressed. For one thing, the small capacity of its relay memory suggested that "it was designed with the expectation that most of its instructions would be read from paper tape and then executed."[18] Rochester was interested in the possibility that the 604, if given much larger storage capacity and modified to utilize a stored program, would be able to handle a much wider range of business and scientific problems. He believed that such a machine, if only modestly more expensive than the 604, would constitute a marketable computer. Between January and May 1949, he wrote several technical reports—one of them with Fox—describing a 604 enhanced with stored-program capabilities, using acoustic (mercury) delay line or CRT memories.[19] But aware of the likely difficulty of obtaining approval to devote product-development resources to a computer project, Palmer asked Rochester to study magnetic tape, "how it would stack up compared to punched cards; what sort of thing was this that was coming over the horizon."[20]

Magnetic tape was by then generally regarded as the medium that would serve, in electronic computer systems, most of the file storage requirements to which the punched card had been applied in IBM's product line. By any reasonable estimate, tape could be expected to occupy less than 1 percent of the volume of punched cards for a given data-storage capacity. And being erasable and reusable, it had potential for large savings in cost of the recording medium relative to cards. Furthermore, both by reason of its relative compactness and because the recording method was nonmechanical, tape could be expected to permit information recording and reading at many times the speed of the fastest card machines. Rochester's assignment came during a period of extensive evaluation by Future Demands and Engineering of the potential of magnetic tape and just after the responsibility for tape development had been reassigned from Endicott to Poughkeepsie. (The background for this move is described in chapter 6.)

Werner Buchholz joined IBM in August 1949 and became Rochester's first associate in what would become an engineering planning group. Buchholz had a Ph.D. degree from California Institute of Technology, where he had become acquainted with analog computers. In partnership with Stephen Dunwell of Future Demands, a frequent visitor who was already persuaded of the importance of magnetic tape, Rochester and Buchholz generalized the magnetic-tape studies to embrace those aspects of computers of wide concern to users, including the means by which machine capabilities and capacities were to be organized and invoked. Their work as engineering planners complemented that of the dozen engineers, headed by Byron Phelps, assigned to study the mechanical and electronic technologies involved in tape reading and recording. While Rochester's assignment seemed originally to have been concerned with magnetic tape per se and while magnetic tape could far outperform cards, he soon concluded that the superiority of tape would be realizable only in a system with the high degree of automaticity and the great flexibility of control provided by a stored program.[21]

Indeed, during the fall of 1949, it became evident that the exploratory technology and planning efforts were converging toward some kind of stored-program system wherein magnetic tape could play the dominant role in storing large files. Aware of deficiencies in IBM's technological inventory, Rochester proposed, and Palmer agreed, that an experimental machine, a "data processing test assembly," should be constructed prior to undertaking the design of a complete system.[22] Topping the list of deficiencies was memory, a memory fast enough to be compatible with the envisaged arithmetic unit and cheap enough to be viable for the capacities needed.

The idea of using a mercury tank acoustic delay line for storage in computers had originated about five years earlier at the University of Pennsylvania, where J. P. Eckert, Jr., and J. W. Mauchly were in need of an economical memory for the EDVAC, the machine they proposed as a successor to the ENIAC. (See chapter 2.) Eckert had invented the mercury delay line, prior to the ENIAC project, for the storage of signals in radar applications.[23] He recognized in the delay line a device capable of storing a large number of binary digits (bits) while requiring relatively few vacuum tubes. His idea was to introduce a train of electrical pulses and gaps representing 1s and 0s, respectively, to a quartz-crystal piezoelectric transducer at the front of a mercury tube or tank and allow the acoustical waves generated by the transducer to propagate through the mercury. At the far end of the tank the train of electrical signals was reconstructed by another piezoelectric transducer, amplified and reshaped by electronic circuits, and reintroduced at the front of the tank. Because of the time required for acoustic transmission of the pulses through the mercury, each delay line could store hundreds of bits at the cost of a few vacuum tube circuits and a temperature-controlled tank.

The advantages of the mercury delay line were impressive; if the EDVAC had been constructed using flip-flops instead of delay lines for its 1024 words of 44 bits each, memory alone would have accounted for more than 45,000 vacuum tubes—about ten times the number actually used in the entire system.[24] But there were disadvantages, too. Assume that each delay line held 8 words. The arithmetic unit, having called for a desired 44-bit word (by specifying an address that identified both a tank and a word therein), would have to wait an average of 4 word periods for the designated word to arrive. This is a significant price to pay, in the form of idle time, for an arithmetic unit that must be capable of adding 4 words during that same interval. Similar idle periods occurred in the fetching of the instructions themselves. Furthermore, the memory lacked the random-access characteristic; the delay preceding arrival of the first bit of an instruction or operand depended upon the sequential position of that information in the mercury tank. Since a delay line is analogous to a single track on a drum, this problem has already been discussed in the context of Hamilton's MDC. (See chapter 3.)

John von Neumann, who was interested in solving large problems, and therefore in very fast machines, favored a memory technology that permitted random access—and one that also made practical the simultaneous storage or retrieval of all bits of a word. Such a memory was one of the objectives of the computer project he initiated late in 1945 at the Institute for Advanced Study (IAS).[25] After consideration of other technologies, the one ultimately chosen was the Williams (cathode-ray-tube) storage. Later around the country, a number of other large-scale computer projects were heavily influenced by the "IAS Machine" design, among them the Whirlwind project at MIT. All of these projects were troubled from the start by technical difficulties inherent in their CRT memories.

Still, at IBM's Poughkeepsie laboratory in 1949, Palmer and Rochester regarded CRT storage as the most promising contender—indeed the only realistic choice—for fast electronic memory. It was still unproved technically, but the economics looked right, and it could keep up with the fastest arithmetic units envisaged. They realized, however, that the total experience of the laboratory with CRT storage lay in Fox's few months of experimentation. They believed that if they were to propose a computer, they would need the assurance that comes with a working model. Consequently, Rochester wrote a technical report in October describing the proposed Data Processing Test Assembly, soon known simply as the Test Assembly. The primary objective was to test the CRT and other memory technologies. A secondary objective was to investigate the use of magnetic tape, which was expected to become the principal input-output medium for any computer developed as a product. The plan was to put together an arithmetic unit as quickly as possible, devoting the major efforts in design, experimentation, and construction to CRT memory for the Test Assembly. A magnetic drum was to be attached as larger-capacity, although slower, memory.[26]

The Test Assembly, which was constructed in the former dining room of the Kenyon mansion, included an IBM 604 electronic calculating unit with its separate reader-punch and an additional frame comparable in size to the 604 itself. This frame contained the circuits that adapted the 604 to the CRT memory, magnetic-tape recorder, and magnetic drum—the drum mounted atop the frame. The appended unit was designed and constructed largely by two former customer engineers, Clarence E. Frizzell and Howard A. Mussell, both of whom Palmer had brought into the laboratory during 1949 for their unusual combination of electronics and IBM product knowledge. Frizzell had acquired training in radar electronics during World War II. Mussell was among the few who had maintained 603 electronic multipliers, and he had just completed a customer engineering course on the 604.[27] They received general direction from Buchholz, who formulated the logical organization, and Louis D. Stevens, who had joined IBM in August. While a graduate student at the University of California in Berkeley, Stevens had acquainted himself with an experimental drum-memory computer being built there. By December, project members began checking out the magnetic-drum unit—the alternate main memory with which the configuration of calculator and input-output devices could be tested long before the Williams storage was operational. Stevens, who was responsible for the design of the drum circuits and their integration with the 604, received technical advice and the drum itself from Hamilton's project in Endicott.[28]

Fox's memory for the Test Assembly was housed in special frames. Its capacity was 250 words, each of five decimal digits and sign, stored in six pairs of CRTs—one pair per amplifier circuit. The first pair held lowest-order digits, the second pair next digits, and so forth, to the sixth pair, which held signs. Each digit was represented by five bits in a modified biquinary code. Four of the bits represented decimal values 1, 2, 3, and 4; all of them could be 0, or one and only one could be 1. The fifth bit, representing decimal 5, could be 0 or 1. While the five decimal digits and sign of a word were treated in parallel for the sake of compatibility with the 604, the five bits of each digit were treated serially in order to minimize the number of CRTs required. With its serial and parallel data-handling aspects, the Test Assembly provided a good demonstration of the flexibility of application that had made CRT storage attractive to Palmer and his engineers in the first place.

During the winter of 1949–1950, while the CRT memory was being designed and constructed, a large part of Palmer's electronics group moved from the Delapenha House and the Kenyon Estate to the third and top floor of a necktie factory located on High Street in Poughkeepsie. Spring and summer were devoted to debugging and adjusting the memory. In September 1950, the main objective—an operating CRT memory—was achieved when Rochester found the machine "in good working order and available for the running of long test problems from 11 a.m. until 4 p.m." In the longest type of test problem—the generation of random numbers by a center-squaring technique—two errors were found to have occurred in 44 minutes of running time. Seven shorter programs were run, including a square root calculation and a Lagrangian interpolation. Encouraged at the production of useful results even on such an insignificant sample, Rochester allowed himself the speculation that "100 or 1000 times fewer errors might represent an acceptable performance. . . . the random errors will probably be a less frequent source of trouble than tube failures."[29] Had he foreseen the agonizingly slow process by which engineering problems in the memory would be identified and corrected, it is unlikely that Rochester would have mentioned such large factors of improvement so casually.

While in principle Williams storage employed ordinary cathode-ray tubes available from most suppliers of electronic components, in practice only careful selection was found to yield tubes sufficiently defect free to work reliably. "Defects," for storage purposes, were not limited to discrete bad spots on the CRT. A whole host of phenomena having adverse effects on storage operation came to light, and each ultimately required either the use of better tubes or some compensating adjustment in the system. Edwards, who had spent a good deal of 1950 attempting to put the memory into working order, later remembered many more months in which he could expect calls for assistance at almost any time of day or night from someone trying to operate the Test Assembly.[30] Still, CRT was the most attractive memory scheme available for consideration, and the laboratory's plans for computer development would continue to center on it. Experiments were also conducted with RCA's Selectron tube, a device von Neumann had initially chosen for the IAS computer; but because a Selectron memory proved too expensive, the plan to attach it to the Test Assembly was never carried out.[31]

In normal operation the Test Assembly relied, 604 fashion, on punched cards for input and output. Magnetic tape was attached, in a primitive way, for the sole purpose of establishing the reliability of transfer of data between an electronic memory and reels of tape. The

Poughkeepsie group under Byron Phelps, which was experimenting with alternative circuits and magnetic heads for recording, had purchased a thirteen-channel magnetic-tape recorder, designed for the U.S. Air Force by the Cook Electric Company for recording temperatures from an array of thermocouples.[32] Although this device was less than adequate for exploring the problems of handling tape at large-scale computer speeds, it served the purposes of the Test Assembly project. Robert P. Crago took responsibility for modifying the Cook recorder and for designing circuits to attach it to the Test Assembly. Crago, like Buchholz, had come to IBM in the summer of 1949 after graduate work at the California Institute of Technology. In his attachment scheme, the simplest that could be contrived, the tape was made to run continuously in either the recording or the reading mode. Data were written or read at intervals timed to simulate the punched cards for which the 604 had been designed. For the most straightforward adaptation to the 604, the eight-digit (maximum) field of the 604 was matched to eight tape channels. Timed pulses on individual channels were used to represent digits in the punched-card (one-of-ten) numeric code.[33]

Despite its small memory of 250 five-digit words, the Test Assembly gave Poughkeepsie engineers valuable first-hand experience with the preparation of programs for a fully electronic stored-program computer. Rochester programmed it in March 1951 to solve second-order differential equations using ten-digit ("double-precision") arithmetic.[34] More important, by year-end 1950, the Test Assembly had given Palmer's planner and engineers confidence that the basic technologies for a complete, large-scale computer system were at hand.

4.3 Plans for the Tape Processing Machine

In spring 1949, well over a year after dedication of the SSEC, that machine and the ENIAC were still the only large-scale electronic computing instruments. But reports of the progress of competitive projects were received with increasing frequency. Of these, the UNIVAC, which Eckert-Mauchly Computer Corporation (EMCC) had been publicizing since 1947, was receiving particular attention in IBM. UNIVAC, the commercial venture that had grown out of the EDVAC project, was of considerable interest to IBM sales executives because EMCC claimed that it was designing the system to include many features of special importance to business applications. The machine's mercury-delay-line memory was to store 1000 twelve-digit words, and provision would be made for storing alphabetic and other nonnumeric characters.

Magnetic tape would be the primary file storage medium for the computer, and the system was to control a dozen or so tape units.[35] Instructions and data were to be recorded on tape by means of keyboard-to-tape devices separate from the computer and analogous to keypunch machines for cards. Similarly, results would be printed by tape-fed electric typewriters. EMCC stressed that UNIVAC would not only serve as a scientific computer but also provide the storage capacities and operational versatilities needed in accounting applications.

Those in IBM who paid attention to reports of progress on the UNIVAC were given additional cause for unease briefly in August 1949 when EMCC demonstrated the BINAC, its one-of-a-kind computer for Northrop Aircraft Company. The BINAC had an attached magnetic-tape reader and recorder, albeit a rather primitive arrangement requiring manual control of tape starting and stopping. But Phelps attended the demonstration with Dunwell and recorded the observation, based on "haywire and components hung on the outside," that the machine did not appear ready for delivery.[36] The UNIVAC, for which IBM understood EMCC had garnered seven orders, still loomed as the major competitive entry among computer projects.[37]

Thus by mid-1949 the UNIVAC was regarded as a potential threat to the large-application end of the EAM market. But important questions lingered: Would such a system be reliable enough for business use? How would price and processing speed of a tape system compare with those of the well-established punched-card system? Such questions brought into focus fundamental differences perceived to exist between mathematical computation and business data processing. Scientists and engineers tended to think of their computations as personal, transitory jobs—the user enjoying privacy with regard to methods and data and being free to adjust schedules to changing circumstances. Prompt access to arbitrarily selected data was usually a convenience, at most, in mathematical computation. Accountants, on the other hand, typically dealt with extensive files; with periodic, tightly scheduled runs that updated files and generated voluminous outputs, and with a variety of chores ranging from the selection and processing of portions of files to answering a request by telephone for information in an individual record of a file. And business files had to be archived periodically for possible auditing or reconstruction at a later date, whereas any analogous need in scientific computation was usually short-lived.

Along with Palmer and Rochester, Dunwell felt that the company should design and build in the laboratory a large-scale, tape-oriented machine with special utility for accounting applications. In this way the answers to the specific question of reliability, along with a broader assessment of the benefits of tape compared with cards, could be obtained first-hand. An obvious advantage of cards was that they could be clerically selected and individually inspected. Another, more difficult to assess, was the ease with which files of cards could be arranged in any desired order with the economical punched-card sorter. But tape, too, had its appealing features, one being that it readily accommodated unit records of more than eighty characters. The eighty-character limitation of the card was irksome to customers because it often necessitated multicard records, complicating procedures and slowing operations. Many proposals for increased-capacity cards had been considered in Endicott over the years, each ultimately dropped when product-cost consequences were duly weighed. Magnetic tape promised not only higher data-handling speeds and more compact storage but, given the capacity for longer records, the opportunity in many instances to consolidate partially redundant files. An experimental system seemed the best instrument with which to measure the benefits offered by tape, along with its shortcomings.

In October 1949, Dunwell set forth his first requirements for a tape-based system. The explicit functions he addressed were manual recording and verifying; processing, including sorting, collating, reproducing, calculating, and summarizing; printing; reference to individual records; and card-to-tape conversion, a matter of prime interest if EAM installations were ever to be converted to tape operation.[38] In general configuration, Dunwell's requirements suggested a system akin to that of UNIVAC—although many of the devices and capabilities he specified left room for significant differences. The one sharp conceptual departure came in his requirements for "complete flexibility" in the lengths of fields and records—fields to be demarked by special end-of-field characters and records by end-of-record characters. Freedom in field and record lengths meant that the programmer could treat any given file as if provided with a punched-card record of exactly the number of characters desired.

Reflecting on this requirement many years later, Rochester recalled that "Steve Dunwell was sure that if we offered our customers a fixed-word-length machine, they wouldn't accept it."[39] The UNIVAC user, after all, would be confronted with a fixed twelve-character word as the basic operand and a sixty-word "block" as the basic unit in memory-to-tape and tape-to-memory operations; given a file, the programmer had to map records into blocks and fields into words. To provide utmost compatibility with EAM practice, Dunwell wished to avoid the inconveniences and inefficiencies that attended such mappings. He wanted EAM specialists to feel liberated by computers rather than to feel that they were trading one set of restrictions for another. (Detailed features of the machine were of great importance to the user in the early years of computers; lacking higher-level languages and compilers, the programmer was forced to deal with machine-language instruction sets and with actual addresses and data lengths.)

Interrupting his work on the Test Assembly, Rochester quickly promulgated Dunwell's requirements within the Poughkeepsie laboratory and, with Palmer's encouragement, began responding to them. By March 1950, Rochester and Buchholz had prepared a technical report, "Preliminary Outline of the Tape Processing Machine," that began: "The planning of the data processing machine has now reached the stage where the general outline is clear enough to divide the machine into sections so that the sections can be worked on by separate groups."[40] Their preliminary plan envisioned a CRT memory of 2000 (augmentable to 10,000) characters, an optional drum for faster-than-tape storage, an unspecified number of magnetic-tape units, and a stored-program system with a repertoire of about forty single-address instructions. Additional CRT storage of 200 characters (the capacity assumed for a single tube) was termed "accumulator storage." The maxima for operand and result field lengths in the various types of instructions were defined to accord with efficient use of the accumulator. The logic of add-like instructions worked character by character, taking one character from memory, another simultaneously from accumulator storage, and yielding a result character to replace the operand character from accumulator storage (or the one from memory, depending on the instruction). Provision was to be made for reading from one tape and recording on another concurrently, with adequate buffer storage to compensate for speed differences in the two tapes.

The Tape Processing Machine (TPM) as designed, built and tested during the subsequent two years departed from the original (March 1950) plan only in a few details. The accumulator, for example, finally accommodated only 100 characters, that having been found to be the capacity of a single storage tube. The concurrent reading and writing of tape was dropped, as will be explained, the multiple-address counters for reading, writing, and processing being adjudged too expensive. (For a description of the internal organization and operation of the TPM, see appendix B.)

4.4 TPM Engineering

For Palmer, the TPM offered a project around which he could organize the activity of essentially all of his electronics group, including fifteen to twenty engineers hired during 1949. Rochester and Buchholz, the main planners, remained in close touch with Dunwell. J. A. Haddad assumed leadership in the design of arithmetic and logical circuits. The CRT and Test Assembly projects continued with renewed purpose. Phelps's group, working on tape recording and feeding, was given more specific objectives.

The newly hired engineers, along with a smaller number of technicians hired or transferred from the factory, had more than doubled the population of Palmer's electronics group during 1949.[41] The atmosphere in the Poughkeepsie laboratory—staffed largely with electronics-trained engineers, many with experience in such World War II developments as radar—bore few traces of that which had prevailed in Endicott during the heyday of the card machine engineers.

The typical engineer in Palmer's small organization was entirely unaware of the tradition of secrecy that had characterized life among the "inventors" in the Endicott laboratory for so many years. New technologies, often stemming from developments outside the company and usually requiring the efforts of substantial groups to carry them forward, replaced the jealously guarded inventions of the previous era. Furthermore, the planning and design of a system as complex as the TPM demanded the close cooperation of many people. Thus patents, for example, tended to receive secondary consideration, at least until some years later, when a program of invention awards was created in order to restore some of the desired emphasis to the company's patent position.

Among the significant developments in electronics since the design of the 604 was the use of the germanium diode as an adjunct to the vacuum tube.[42] The germanium diode was a two-terminal semiconductor device whose resistance depended on the polarity of voltage applied to it. In the forward direction of applied voltage, its resistance was low, and it conducted easily. In the reverse direction, its resistance was typically at least one thousand times higher, and little current flowed through it. Its usefulness in switching depended on arranging circuit voltages so that the diode presented its "forward" or "back" resistance, permitting or blocking the flow of current as desired. Prior to the availability of suitable diodes, vacuum tubes had performed all electronic switching functions, as in the circuits of the SSEC and the ENIAC. A switching circuit with two inputs, for example, required at least one vacuum tube. This placed the vacuum tube at a disadvantage compared to a device such as the relay, in which multiple contacts could be actuated by a single coil, with the design of the relay often permitting expansion of a switching circuit merely by wiring in unused contacts.

The "crystal diode," as the germanium diode was called, lent some of the same flexibility to vacuum tube circuits: with the vacuum tube relegated to the role of a power amplifier and diodes performing combinatorial logic, a given signal line could serve as input to multiple logic circuits. The anticipated result was a reduction in cost, space, and power consumption. At the time, vacuum tubes purchased in large quantities cost around sixty-five cents (equivalent in buying power to about three dollars in 1985). They consumed power not only to heat their cathodes but as a result of their inability to behave as low-resistance closed switches. The crystal diode, because of its simplicity, was foreseeably (although not initially) lower in cost. It was smaller, it required no cathode heating, and it behaved as a nearly ideal switch—dissipating little power in either the "closed" or the "open" condition. All of these qualities were of interest to those working on circuits for the TPM. (Crystal diodes were already in use elsewhere, in the BINAC and in several computers under development, including the UNIVAC, EDVAC and Whirlwind.)

When a representative of General Electric estimated that computer-grade GE diodes would soon be selling for fourteen cents each, Haddad decided to use crystal diodes.[43] There ensued a long and somewhat discouraging effort to obtain diodes fulfilling the early promises. The devices exhibited wide variations from sample to sample, in values of back resistance, recovery time (time to recover back resistance after conducting in the forward direction), and other characteristics important to computer design. They cost about two dollars apiece initially, and the price declined much more slowly than expected. Nevertheless, diodes were accepted for the reasons described and because diode circuits switched faster than 604-type circuits. In the latter, delays resulted from the need to drive control-grid voltages from negative values beyond cutoff, into the region of full conduction; diodes, as normally used, switched with less delay. Where diodes were used in "logic" (or switching) circuits, the multigrid switch tube of the 604 and earlier machines was no longer needed. Another type of circuit was regularly used: the cathode follower, which was especially suitable for driving the diode circuits. Cathode followers ordinarily used the same dual-triode tubes that served in inverters and flip-flops (figure 4.2).

One of the first panels of the TPM to be wired, in mid-1950 at the High Street laboratory, contained the arithmetic unit. The first plan had been to package tubes, diodes, and other components in the single-tube pluggable unit Palmer had invented for the 604. Circuit

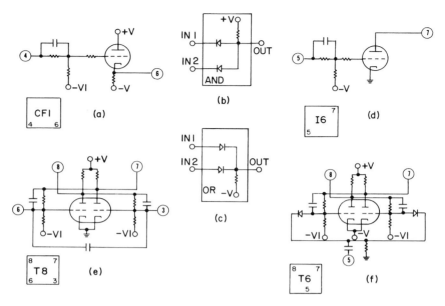

Figure 4.2
Representative circuits used in the TPM. In the CF1 type cathode follower circuit at *a*, the input voltage divider reduces the plate-level voltage swing of nearly 100 volts, from a circuit such as a flip-flop, to a 40 volt swing with nominal limits of $+10$ and -30 volts. The output, at almost the same levels, is powered sufficiently to drive many diode circuits, such as the AND and OR circuits at *b* and *c*. In the AND circuit, the output voltage cannot rise appreciably above the lower of the two input levels because of the low forward resistance of the diodes, and the output is therefore "up" (or logical "1") only if both inputs are up. In the OR circuit, either input being up can force the output up. The inverter shown at *d* is one of many types used in the TPM to repower signal lines or reestablish signal swings at the output of cascaded diode logic circuits. The "trigger" circuit at *e* is a flip-flop quite similar to those used in the 604 calculator. The trigger circuit at *f* contains diode steering or switching of input signals so that only the grid that is at roughly ground potential (the grid of the conducting triode) will receive a negative pulse when a negative voltage shift is applied at the common input terminal (5). The circuit is internally wired as a scale-of-2 counter. (Diagrams from U.S. Patent 3,245,039, "Electronic Data Processing Machine," N. Rochester et al.)

units were to be inserted into 604 panels, on the other side of which was the yellow signal wiring as well as DC power and AC heater wiring. But halfway through the wiring job, the yellow wires became so dense that a wireman could no longer see the sockets. Having made feasible an increase in the number of decision circuits per pluggable unit, diodes had caused the number of signal wires to become impractically large. To solve this problem, the designers developed an early form of multiple-tube pluggable unit within which signal wires from circuits associated with one tube could connect to those of another tube without involving back-panel wiring. The resulting rather crude eight-tube unit, widely used in the TPM, was considerably improved later for machines designed to be produced in quantity. (See chapter 5.)

The process of fixing specifications for the TPM often caused tension between engineers and product planners. By mid-1950 Haddad and Phelps had made it clear that they planned to record in serial-bit fashion on tape; they would rely on a relatively high tape speed for a data rate compatible with that of the arithmetic unit. They had decided that concurrent reading from one tape and recording on another, which had been part of the original plan for the TPM and in which Dunwell had at times expressed great interest, would lead to unjustified cost and complexity.[44] Future Demands brooded over these decisions and then, in a large September meeting, struck back. As Phelps reported the discussion, Dunwell seemed to argue that the tape needed to be speeded up by a factor of ten, while Roberts pressed for a basic version of the system that could rent for $1000 a month.[45]

Roberts's demand seems largely to have been ignored, but perhaps partly in answer to Dunwell, Phelps's group decided at about that time to double the tape width to half an inch and to record all bits of each character simultaneously across the tape. Seven separate channels were thus required, each character being represented by seven "data" bits plus a "parity check" bit. The check bit of a character was 0 or 1, whichever was needed to make the total count of 1 bits for the character odd. It was thus possible, by counting the bits each time a character was transmitted, to detect a "single-bit" error—an error resulting in the substitution of a 0 for a 1, or vice versa. In principle, parallel-bit recording permitted an entire character to be recorded across the tape in the linear space previously occupied by a bit. In practice, an increase of only about two to one in characters per linear inch was achieved for tape as applied to the TPM, the remainder of the theoretical improvement being deferred pending solution of timing problems caused by channel-to-channel variations and tape "skew." The parallel-bit recording mode did, however, permit a long series of recording density improvements thereafter. (See chapter 6.)

During 1950, Palmer and a few others, including his planners, were housed in the Kenyon building south of Poughkeepsie, while engineering design of the TPM was conducted at High Street. Palmer kept in touch with the project, routinely receiving copies of TPM-related memoranda of import and, when he felt it appropriate, participating in engineering decisions, often through a mere suggestion to Phelps or Rochester.

Then in June came the outbreak of the Korean war. There was a surge of interest in computing power and a quickening tempo in IBM and all other defense-related companies. In August, Palmer was appointed manager of the Poughkeepsie laboratory and immediately fell heir to the war-related pressures.[46] Cuthbert Hurd, director of the Applied Science department, began urging Palmer and Rochester to increase the arithmetic capabilities of the TPM. In early November, Palmer named Phelps to head the entire TPM effort. On his first day in command, Phelps received a memorandum from Dunwell urging that in the face of "insatiable demands for speed," the TPM specifications be overhauled to provide one-bit access to seven CRTs in parallel—that is, to a character at a time—and thereby to provide for faster arithmetic. Dunwell expected that this could be accomplished with "little, if any, increase in the amount of circuitry."[47] Phelps expressed to Palmer his concern that the emphasis seemed to have shifted from low cost to high speed but reported at the same time that he had commissioned an engineering study of the consequences of a change to the parallel-bit mode of CRT operation.[48]

The investigation revealed that the character cycle could be reduced from 128 to 35 microseconds but only by adding some 750 vacuum tubes, 500 crystal diodes, and 40 CRTs. This represented roughly a 30 percent increase in the number of those components in the main frame and memory of the TPM.[49] Of greater concern was the likelihood that the change would delay the project, detracting from its value as a timely learning exercise. For that reason Phelps and Haddad continued to argue successfully against any major changes to the TPM, which was already largely designed and portions of which would soon be ready for initial testing. It was still their contention that the project, which had started out of the need for exploration, should not be expected to bring forth a prototype for the production line.[50]

Meanwhile, Rochester sent Hurd a report describing a method of improving the speed of multiplication in the TPM. Observing that variable field length would have to be at least partially sacrificed,

Rochester suggested, "The next step in determining the value of such a device would be to work out programs for the most important kinds of scientific calculations. Such programs would be very valuable to have for they might reveal other changes which should be made in the Tape Processing Machine in order to adapt it to scientific work." Noting that he had discussed the matter with Palmer, Rochester invited Hurd to have some of his people become familiar with the TPM. In developing the machine for commercial applications, Rochester wrote, "We have always followed the policy of working closely with the Future Demands Department" and would like, with Applied Science, "to follow a similar policy with regard to the scientific application of the machine."[51]

Hurd welcomed the invitation to become better acquainted with the objectives of the main project in Poughkeepsie. There is no indication, however, that the TPM impressed him as likely to make a meaningful contribution to computing in the realms of science or engineering, with whose requirements he was most familiar. Within six weeks, he and Palmer were instrumental in persuading the company to lengthen the schedule for TPM completion and divert most of Palmer's engineering force into a project for developing a computer that would far outdistance the TPM in computational capacity.

During much of 1951, progress toward completion of the TPM was slowed by Palmer's reassignment of engineers—among them Haddad, Rochester, and Buchholz—to the "Defense Calculator." (See chapter 5.) TPM construction and initial testing proceeded slowly under a small group of engineers retained by Phelps. The slow pace eventually worried Palmer, who in September began invigorating the project by scheduling the return of some engineers from the Defense Calculator project. The TPM project went on a three-shift schedule in October 1951, and the machine was completely assembled by year end.[52]

The largest unit in the system was the main frame, often called the "ALU" for Arithmetic and Logical Unit (figure 4.3). Each of its four main "gates," or subframes, supported three panels of circuits, and to save on mechanical design, panels of the type developed for the 604 electronic calculator were used. Inserted into each panel was a mixture of single-tube circuits using the 604 pluggable unit and multiple-tube pluggable units designed for the TPM. The ALU was more than twice the size of the 604; its four gates held about 2500 vacuum tubes and a somewhat larger number of crystal diodes. The ALU comprised the basic timing and control circuits, the arithmetic unit, registers and control circuits for input-output, and power supplies for

Figure 4.3
TPM main frame and electrostatic storage (left)

converting AC power to DC at various voltage levels required by the many types of circuits in the machine.

A second and narrower frame held the CRT memory. There were ten drawer-like chassis of 200-character capacity each for the memory, one drawer for the accumulator, and a spare drawer. Within each memory drawer, two CRTs shared a video amplifier for output signals. Each CRT stored 100 characters—that is, 700 bits.

The magnetic-tape units comprised the most important input-output subsystem of the TPM (figure 4.4). These incorporated vacuum-column control of tape and a method of recording wherein a 1 bit could be represented by a change of magnetization of either polarity and a 0 was represented by no change. (See chapter 6.) Recording was in the parallel-bit mode at a density of 100 characters per inch. The speed of the tape, and therefore the data rate, differed among tape units tested at various times during 1951. The highest-speed units—those used in the system for application testing in 1952—operated at approximately 70 inches per second and a corresponding data rate of 7000 characters per second, this being the highest rate the TPM could accommodate.[53]

Figure 4.4
TPM tape units and typewriter

Other units of the system in their separate frames included a magnetic drum, a card reader-punch, a printer, and an electric typewriter. The drum served both as auxiliary storage and as a buffer for the conversion of data passing between the ALU and the slower input-output devices. Information was recorded in serial-bit form on the drum, and (like tape) the drum furnished data at a rate only slightly below the maximal data rate of the ALU, the latter interspersing regeneration cycles among full character cycles as required for synchronization. Drum capacity was fifty-eight tracks of 100 characters each. Exactly 5000 characters (fifty tracks) were used as auxiliary storage. The remaining eight tracks were reserved as I/O buffers for the card machine as well as the printer. The reader-punch was a modified Type 519 reproducer with its reading and punching feeds separately addressable. Either feed could operate at 100 cards per minute. The printer, which operated at 150 lines per minute, was the wheel-type printing unit of a Type 407 accounting machine, which operated at 150 lines per minute.[54]

In the early planning of the TPM, it had been assumed that the system would include a separate tape sorter for rearranging records according to the values appearing in a specified field. This machine was conceived as a remedy for one of the most serious shortcomings of magnetic tape as a medium for business files: its linear nature and the sequential access to data that its use imposed. Phelps carried on a tape sorter development project for several years, concurrently with the TPM, but tape sorters never became part of IBM's product line.

For Ralph Palmer's engineers, the TPM represented a first opportunity to study CRT storage and its peculiar problems in the context of a complete, large-scale computer. Until completion of the TPM memory unit, however, Fox and his colleagues had continued to use the Test Assembly as an instrument for observing the effects of variations from tube to tube in, for example, the phosphor coating. To help solve these problems, Fox had enlisted the capabilities of the tube laboratory, originally established in the "pickle factory," to develop tubes for the 604 electronic calculator. The key person in the design and development of improved CRTs for IBM was Walter E. Mutter, who joined IBM immediately after receiving his doctorate in physics at MIT in October 1949. He had a bachelor's degree in chemistry and had worked at RCA on cathode-ray tube development for about three years before returning to school for his Ph.D. At IBM, he was assigned initially to the exploration of special vacuum tubes for use in computing. After constructing a multiple-anode, magnetically controlled CRT intended to replace several conventional tubes as a decade counter and finding it umpromising, he turned his attention to the problems of the conventional CRT used in Williams storage.

The primary objective was to improve the reliability and uniformity of the tubes. It was recognized quite early that changes would have to be made in the CRTs and that it might be necessary for IBM to manufacture its own storage tubes. It was not clear initially whether a tube with face diameter of 3, 5, or 7 inches (these being standard tube sizes) would represent the best choice. More bits could be stored on the larger surface, but the electronics required to drive a large tube would be more expensive. Furthermore, to achieve the same reliability, the bits stored in the 7 inch tube had to be more widely spaced. In terms of number of bits per tube volume—the measure Mutter finally concluded was most important for commercial machines—the 3-inch tube was actually 2.5 times more efficient than the 7 inch tube.[55] The 3 inch tube had already been selected for use in the Test Assembly and the TPM, and Mutter's work confirmed it as the preferred tube for commercial computers that followed.

Mutter asserts that he made no fundamental changes in the CRT design. Instead he made a number of minor changes to improve the spot size and the deflection mechanism.[56] According to a status report of May 1951, "Smaller spot size has been achieved by means of improved gun and deflection plate design. Two tubes, the IBM 77 and the IBM 79, are now being tested." The report concluded optimistically that it might be possible to store around a thousand bits per tube.[57] Increased care was also taken in achieving a uniform phosphor coating on the tube face. It cost IBM more per tube to make them than to buy them from RCA, but the quality and yield of the IBM tubes for the Williams storage application more than justified this higher cost.[58]

Development of CRT storage was being carried out in Wallace Eckert's group in New York City, concurrently with the work in Poughkeepsie. Engineers developing the Naval Ordnance Research Calculator (see chapter 5) at Watson Laboratory had chosen the Williams storage technology for that machine's memory. Although it is not well documented, there was interaction between the two projects, and the Watson Laboratory investigators were credited with discovering at least one phenomenon in CRTs that produced errors under certain operating conditions.[59]

The improvements achieved in CRT performance and reliability, combined with the lack of a suitable alternative technology, caused IBM engineers to be quite optimistic, perhaps overly so, about Williams storage. As it turned out, the memory was one of the most troublesome components of the TPM system, if not the most troublesome. Its erratic behavior was masked to a considerable degree, however, by a variety of problems throughout the system that stemmed from the experimental nature of many of its vital parts.

Intended, in fact, as an experiment, the TPM project encouraged a multiplicity of circuit designs for meeting the diverse switching and storage requirements. One reason for the potpourri of circuits has been mentioned: the emergence of the semiconductor diode, leading to the development of new circuits that combined tubes and crystal diodes for most switching functions. As it turned out, nothing could more effectively have impressed the Poughkeepsie engineers with the importance of circuit standardization than the experience of living with the TPM. That it was operational at all was due to the presence of an engineering staff that included some of its designers.

By the end of 1951, when the machine was essentially completed, many ideas had been accumulated toward a "TPM II" that Engineering could offer in the event the TPM won acceptance as a product. In October, for example, Buchholz proposed that the arithmetic unit be simplified by substituting binary-coded-decimal for the excess-three code (see appendix B) and by accepting the time penalty of recomplementing all accumulator-held negative numbers to true form.[60] Furthermore, additional studies of parallel-bit transmission, processing, and storing of characters had begun to reveal that the "saving" in circuits achieved by the serial-by-bit organization of the TPM was small at best—largely because an increase in control circuitry had offset the decrease in data-path circuitry obtained by handling bits sequentially.

One mistake the designers of the TPM vowed never to repeat in an IBM computer was the overabundance of automatic stops. These could result from any of a wide variety of machine-detected inconsistencies or errors, among them a parity failure, a field mark where none should be, and the absence of a field mark where one should be. During early efforts to program and operate the machine, Rochester wryly noted that the true objective ought to be to keep a computer running, not to stop it. The experience suggested making the checking circuits interrogable through some "transfer (branch) on condition" instruction, so that the programmer might devise alternate program paths for handling exceptional conditions. Subsequent machines were designed to provide that capability.

4.5 A Time for Waiting

In September 1951, prior to completion of the TPM, Palmer met with McDowell, Roberts, and others and urged that a substantial group of people be assigned to programming actual applications and assessing the viability of the TPM versus established accounting methods.[61] It was decided that a group of three would be assigned initially to study IBM's accounting applications in its Poughkeepsie plant. Future Demands and Engineering agreed to supply one man each, and it was expected that the factory would provide a third. Similar arrangements would be pursued for other applications—those of customers with large punched-card installations representing a wide variety of requirements. A minimum of four applications was to be programmed and ready for testing on the TPM by March 1952.

Application studies became the order of the day. Rochester's group was enlarged for the purpose through the hiring of engineering graduates and acquisition of customer engineers from the field. The studies included specific government agencies, insurance companies, public utilities, and manufacturers. There were fifteen units in the "survey team," each typically consisting of a young engineer trained by Rochester and a member from Future Demands or Sales—the latter usually selected for knowledge of the customer's in-place procedures. The original plan, like almost all other programming activities of the era, proved optimistic in its schedule; the effort required in recasting EAM applications for the novel TPM proved to be greater than anyone had expected.

In early 1952, the still-shaky TPM was demonstrated to representatives of the armed forces and other selected government agencies as evidence of IBM's exploratory work on tape-based systems. At the time, the machine was being readied for use in the application studies; engineers were replacing unreliable components and in a few cases redesigning circuits deemed insufficiently reliable under test conditions. It was not until the middle of the year, when the survey team began getting long periods of machine time for program trials, that Future Demands was willing to speak of the TPM as "in operation."[62]

The final report of the TPM Survey Team, issued in February 1953 over the signature of Roberts, was reserved in its support of the TPM as a replacement for EAM in accounting applications.[63] Perhaps too much had been expected of the team; at least one member from Engineering had argued that the applications were not being reformulated to the extent required for full usage of the TPM's advantages; the TPM, in other words, was being forced to compete on EAM grounds. Despite all the survey team learned, its conclusions were somewhat academic; by 1953 the TPM was outdated in its circuit and device parameters and its overall design. A thorough-going redesign, for which planning had begun in late 1952, was promising a several-fold gain in speed.[64]

Although their project had been sidetracked by the Defense Calculator, the engineers of the TPM had good reason to be optimistic. Even in the absence of announcement plans for the TPM, there was no question about the need for a business-oriented large-scale computer with the TPM's general capabilities. The acquisition of Eckert-Mauchly Computer Corporation by Remington Rand early in 1950 would ensure against IBM's overlooking the much-publicized UNIVAC as a competitive challenge in the business data processing arena.[65] Furthermore, the Defense Calculator would make use of the key technologies— electrostatic storage, magnetic recording, and tube-diode logic circuits— in which the TPM had provided valuable early experience. The TPM engineers could take advantage of the interruption as an opportunity to consolidate plans for an improved machine, confident that a successful Defense Calculator could only help to pave the way for a commercially viable TPM II.

First-Generation IBM Computers

The need for fast computers. Planning for the Defense Calculator. Engineering considerations. The Type 701 computer. The Type 650 Magnetic Drum Calculator. The Type 702 Electronic Data Processing Machine. Later vacuum tube computers.

After North Korea attacked South Korea in late June 1950, the United Nations decided to dispatch a fighting force to oppose the incursion. Thus the United States, playing a leading role, was faced with a substantial military engagement. Less than five years had elapsed since the end of World War II, but aircraft and missiles had been undergoing brisk development. Suddenly new armaments that worked at higher speeds and temperatures were desired on urgent schedules; one result was a bulge in the requirements for engineering calculations.

As he had in previous emergencies, T. J. Watson, Sr., sent a telegram to the White House placing IBM's resources at the disposal of the federal government. At the same time he charged J. W. Birkenstock, who had recently been promoted to the position of executive assistant to Executive Vice-President T. J. Watson, Jr., with finding ways of implementing his message.

On arriving in Washington, Birkenstock quickly learned that IBM already figured in the government's plans. The U. S. Air Force wanted the company's assistance in the development of an electromechanical bombing and navigation instrument system for the B47 bomber. Birkenstock lost no time in working out the details for IBM participation, and a substantial program emerged.[1]

Watson, Jr., however, was not satisfied. A year earlier, while speaking to over a thousand of the company's salesmen, he had predicted that in ten years most of the moving parts in IBM machines would be replaced by electronics. In his view, too little of that had happened. Another spur to his thinking was that six UNIVACs had been reported ordered when Remington Rand Inc. acquired Eckert-Mauchly Computer Corporation in early 1950. He knew that Ralph Palmer and Nat Rochester in Poughkeepsie and Stephen Dunwell in Future Demands believed that the TPM represented a likely next step beyond the 604; instinctively, he felt that they were right. But product visions were blocked by financial, sales, and planning considerations of the "show-me-a-market" type, which he respected and indeed nourished.[2]

Sensing Birkenstock's assignment as an opportunity to break IBM's product stalemate, Watson, Jr., told Birkenstock that he favored contracting to build some electronic computers for the government. Birkenstock divulged this to W. W. McDowell and Palmer, who advised him that three or four large-scale machines were all the Poughkeepsie laboratory could undertake on parallel schedules. His next step was to identify possible contract partners.

Realizing that he was not equipped to discuss large-scale computing applications with experts in technical fields such as missiles and atomic energy, Birkenstock proposed to Cuthbert Hurd that they visit prospective customers together. By this time, Hurd's Applied Science department had compiled a list of some sixty installations at which IBM punched-card equipment, including the CPC, was being used in defense-related engineering and research applications.[3] It was a made-to-order itinerary for Birkenstock. Together at first and then separately with other colleagues, the two men called on over twenty government installations during the late summer and fall, ranging from the Army's Aberdeen Proving Ground in the East to the Los Alamos Scientific Laboratory in the West. They found people not only anxious to talk about their growing computation needs but also knowledgeable about the expected capabilities of the computers nearing completion at a dozen or more government-aided institutions.[4]

5.1 The Need for Fast Computers

At Poughkeepsie, meanwhile, where the Test Assembly had just begun to run short programs and TPM units were in various stages of construction, Palmer thought the TPM might serve as a prototype for contract machines. But Hurd knew that for the applications he had been hearing about, a faster machine would be needed. When RAND Corporation, an early CPC customer, wanted to add substantially to its computing capacity, Hurd invited RAND executives to visit the TPM being constructed at Poughkeepsie. They were politely but openly contemptuous, deeming the still-unfinished machine far too slow for their needs.[5] Hurd then invited Palmer to accompany him on a trip, during which they made several calls, including one at the Banana River center for guided missile development at Cape Canaveral and another at the U.S. Weather Bureau in Washington. Palmer became amply convinced that "the fastest machines which can be made today are not approaching the maximum speed which could be profitably employed," as a later report noted.[6] Palmer knew, too, that W. Buchholz had compared anticipated TPM speeds with those given in a current UNIVAC brochure; at multiplication, UNIVAC was several times faster.

Once convinced of the need for a computer faster than the TPM, Palmer knew that his engineers would probably have to revert from the serial organization of the TPM to the parallel-by-digit organization of IBM's 604 and electromechanical tabulators. The parallel methods were familiar enough, but they had been shunned in the cost-sensitive TPM project on the grounds that extra circuits would be needed to process all digits of a number simultaneously. Fortunately, CRT memory afforded freedom of choice between serial and parallel methods. Palmer now had reason to be thankful that, a year or so earlier, he had decided to follow the lead of F. C. Williams and concentrate on CRT memory.[7]

Palmer's interest in scientific computation was further whetted by events in Wallace Eckert's Watson Laboratory in New York City. "Supercalculators," of which the SSEC was an example, were part of Eckert's mission from Watson, Sr., and had led Eckert to hire Byron L. Havens, a wartime member of MIT's Radiation Laboratory, in January 1946. While assembling a small group of engineers, Havens had been patiently developing and testing the components he considered suitable for construction of an ultrafast, all-electronic, modernized successor to the SSEC. By July 1950, he was ready to propose a large stored-program machine with at least ten times the computing power of other one-of-a-kind computers reported already under construction. In August, Havens's plans were discussed with representatives of the U.S. Naval Ordnance Laboratory, who had expressed interest.

By September, the tentative specifications for the new machine called for a sixteen-digit-word, floating-decimal-point system with 2000 words of Williams-tube memory, several magnetic-tape units, and auxiliary devices for transcribing from cards to tape and vice versa. The number format accommodated a thirteen-digit value, a one-digit sign, and a two-digit "index" (power-of-ten representation). Each number thereby carried an indication of decimal point position relative to its digits. The "floating-point" arithmetic unit took account of the indexes in its operations, thereby relieving the programmer of knowing the decimal point position of every number developed during a computation and of programming shift operations to align decimal points prior to add and subtract operations.[8] Other basic parameters included a million-cycle-per-second electronic clock, a memory cycle of 8 mi-

croseconds, a thirteen-digit addition in 15 microseconds, and a multiplication (of thirteen digits times thirteen digits to obtain a twenty-
six-digit product) in 35 microseconds. Because the instruction format
called for three addresses, execution of a typical instruction required
four memory-access cycles—to fetch instruction, fetch operand 1, fetch
operand 2, and store result—plus time for arithmetic and memory
regeneration. As planned, the number of regeneration cycles was expected to equal or exceed the number of access cycles, but because
the count could be averaged over several milliseconds, many of the
regeneration cycles could overlap arithmetic processes. The planned
machine would be capable of executing well over 10,000 instructions
per second—and do this, moreover, for powerful floating-point instructions on unusually long operands and with automatic checking
of the arithmetic operations. The system was expected to require about
6000 vacuum tubes and 15,000 crystal diodes. In estimated computing
power, the planned machine was rated at over 200 SSECs.[9]

On 19 September, an IBM committee including McDowell and Palmer recommended to Watson, Jr., that IBM proceed as rapidly as
possible with detailed development of Havens's plan. A week later,
the Naval Ordnance Laboratory wrote of its interest in procuring the
machine; J. C. McPherson replied that IBM would "be pleased to
undertake the development and construction of such a machine for
you on a research and development basis, under which we would be
reimbursed for our costs plus a fixed fee"; soon after, the fixed fee
was set at $1. The principal incentive for IBM was experience in design,
construction, and maintenance—for a customer with demanding computing requirements—of a machine that would embody the latest and
most promising technologies. Other incentives were potential patents,
customer goodwill, and favorable publicity.[10]

The navy's interest in a 200-times-SSEC computing instrument
served as a very tangible signal to IBM management of the burgeoning
need for technical computations, although it was to be several months
before a contract was signed for the machine, which became known
as the IBM Naval Ordnance Research Calculator (NORC). To Palmer,
now manager of the Poughkeepsie laboratory, the recognized center
of electronics within IBM, Havens's admirable work had to be viewed
as a stimulating challenge. If the demand for high-speed computers
persisted, Palmer's laboratory would have to contribute to IBM's
response.

Upon Hurd's return in late November from Banana River, Birkenstock asked him to categorize by importance the development activities
encountered on their various trips to government installations.

Hurd named atomic energy, guided missile control, strategic planning (cryptanalysis, weather, and theory of games), and jet engines, adding that IBM might make its maximum contribution by building computers useful to the guided missile program. On 30 November, a joint Birkenstock-Hurd recommendation to that effect went to Watson, Jr. With specific reference to the missile program, it named six substantial government centers of effort and nine participating private contractors, most of them airframe companies. The recommendation noted that a successful contract-solicitation program in the missile area could well serve as a marketing model for other application areas.[11]

Two weeks later, Birkenstock sent a second, action-oriented recommendation to Watson Jr.; this one included Palmer's analysis and opinion as well as Hurd's and his own. It began, "IBM has the 'know-how,' developments and brains to put together a machine . . . vital to the war effort," and went on to assert that "the machine should be general purpose in concept to permit our duplicating the prototype in the order of 25 to 30 times." Hurd had come to believe that one design could serve all the diverse applications encountered during his trips. In the light of the one-of-a-kind practices being followed by most computer designers at the time, the plan was technically bold. It was financially bold in eschewing the safe-in-concept practice of negotiating each sale as a special contract. Birkenstock's memorandum further recommended that Watson, Jr., appoint a committee with representatives from Engineering, Future Demands, Applied Science, and the Watson Laboratory to draw up some broad specifications for a machine. The committee held its first meeting the day after Christmas.[12]

Early in January 1951 Watson, Jr., held a meeting in his office to hear additional recommendations. Birkenstock reviewed the 15 December proposal and recommendation; Rochester spoke for the appointed committee. Up to 20,000 digits of CRT memory and a 1-millisecond multiplication time (defined to include factor access and result storage) were specified; attached devices—card reader, card punch, printer, magnetic tapes, and magnetic drum—with their access times, capacities, and speeds, made up a major portion of the specifications. The specifications of such devices were significant in that most computers then completed or near completion were severely handicapped by lack of sufficient variety in their input-output and auxiliary-storage capabilities. Further elaboration of plans was hardly necessary because the decision that Watson, Jr., faced turned not on technical details but on whether the Poughkeepsie laboratory could build a manufacturable machine at a price that Applied Science could sell in sufficient numbers to justify the program.

Declaring that the machine would well serve the needs of the prospective customers with whom he had spoken, Hurd asserted he could sell six or more. McDowell and Palmer reported that all necessary technologies were being tested at Poughkeepsie or Endicott. These included stored-program design, CRT storage, diode logic, magnetic tape, and magnetic-drum devices. Palmer assured Watson that the contemplated product would be easy to ship—it comprised separate physical units that could be accommodated by ordinary doorways and elevators—even though no other computer builder had yet set that objective. Not every problem relating to design, construction, customer preparation, and installation could be foreseen, Hurd and Palmer conceded, but neither expected any insoluble problems.

Gordon Roberts of Future Demands thought the program premature at best. He foresaw a product that would serve only a few special customers, after absorbing a great deal of engineering effort that might better be spent improving IBM's commercial product line. At the least, he argued, further study should precede any commitment to an all-out development program or to customers.[13]

Watson, Jr., decided to go ahead with the plan. As a product venture, it was riskier than his original idea of building contract machines for the government. It meant IBM would have to invest heavily in product development before any contracts could be signed. But in return for incurring such risk, IBM would own, rather than share with contract partners, any inventions and patents that might result. That could be important if and when the technologies Palmer had named found their way into IBM's commercial product line. To Watson, Sr., however, and to skeptics in the Sales and Future Demands organizations, the decision was best explained as a special undertaking in support of the war effort, an interpretation artfully emphasized in the name chosen soon afterward for the machine: the Defense Calculator.[14]

McDowell was told to refine the description of the machine and establish a development program. Hurd was told to take the machine description back to prospective customers and determine whether they would acquire it; Birkenstock was to help. In the event that the two turned up little or no interest, Watson, Jr., knew he could quickly terminate the project; if there was keen interest, on the other hand, there would be no turning back.

As it turned out, Hurd was delayed until the rental to be charged ($8000 per month) and the date of first delivery (spring 1952) could be estimated from projected costs and schedules; these figures were reached without the customary staff studies because Watson, Jr., was determined to insulate his still-fragile project from the scrutiny of all except partisans. It was February 1951 before Hurd and Birkenstock set out on their trips.[15]

5.2 *Planning for the Defense Calculator*

Palmer returned to Poughkeepsie from the meeting in Watson, Jr.'s, office realizing that the assignment to develop a large-scale computer for the product line had been attained at a substantial price. To be useful in the war effort, the machine was needed on an unprecedentedly tight schedule—by spring 1952, judging from the sentiment at the meeting.[16] But all Palmer had were three pages of description and a block diagram. Only by severely telescoping the conventional project phases—specification, design, model assembly, model test, and manufacture—could he succeed. Consequently, he decided to assign day-to-day engineering responsibility to two men instead of one. He made Rochester responsible for defining the functional structure of the machine and for working with Hurd. He picked Jerrier Haddad to manage engineering design, build the engineering model, and set up manufacturing and servicing plans.[17]

Rochester knew from the start that the organization of the machine had to be sufficiently straightforward to permit Haddad to proceed without delay and to hold testing requirements near a minimum. He knew also that simplicity of design would improve the chances of achieving adequate reliability. The parallel-by-digit organization, already chosen for the sake of speed, aided simplicity: an entire level of control—that which orchestrates the digit-by-digit progression of individual numbers through machine circuits—could be omitted.

A functional plan for the parallel computer being developed at the Institute for Advanced Study was available; it had been circulated in 1946 and again in a second edition of September 1947.[18] The report reasoned out a number of design choices made for the IAS machine. Rochester had studied the IAS papers, and his Test Assembly design had been influenced by them. Whereas the serial, variable-word-length Tape Processing Machine, intended to be economically viable for accounting applications, represented a substantial departure from IAS concepts, the Defense Calculator—a machine for scientific work—could make good use of them. Upon this knowledge rested Palmer's confidence that the job could be completed the following year.

Early on, an important decision was made: the Defense Calculator, like the IAS machine, would use the binary number system to represent numbers in electrostatic storage and in arithmetic circuits. This decision, which ran counter to a sixty-year tradition of decimal representation in census and accounting machines, acknowledged the nature of electronic components. The vacuum tube flip-flop and electrostatic storage using the dot-dash method are examples of binary components. The 8-4-2-1 digit encoding in the counter circuits of the SSEC and 604 (see chapter 2) illustrate the ingenuity required to force "base 2" components into a "base 10" representational system.

It was understood that users required decimal representation in devices or displays with which they work directly, such as typewriters, card punch keyboards, printed reports, and data sheets, but there was no intrinsic requirement that internal representation be decimal. Binary representation was more economical in the amount of equipment required both to represent numbers and to process them arithmetically. (Four binary digits, which represent only ten different values in binary-coded decimal, can represent sixteen values in binary.) That gain might have to be paid back, however, by making provision for the conversion of internal binary numbers from and to their external user-oriented decimal representations. The internal (binary) and external (decimal) representations of a number are not related on a simple digit-by-digit basis, and the translation is a nontrivial arithmetical process.

The binary versus decimal question was examined by John von Neumann in the context of the Moore School's EDVAC planning in 1945.[19] A year later, the subject was further developed by von Neumann and his colleagues at the Institute for Advanced Study. Both the EDVAC and the IAS machine were to be binary, with the binary-decimal number conversions performed as executions by the computer of suitable programs in conjunction with input and output operations. This scheme, one of many novel elements of the EDVAC design, is practical for machines and applications for which "the time consumed in the decimal to binary conversion is only a trivial percent of the total computing time," or where computing speed so far exceeds the speed of decimal I/O devices that number conversion may be completed during the time in which the device executes a reading or writing operation.[20]

By January 1951, when Defense Calculator planning began, *Digital Computer Newsletter* (a quarterly publication of the Office of Naval Research) had reported some twenty stored-program electronic digital computer projects worldwide. All but three were building binary machines. In contrast, decimal had been chosen for each of IBM's unreported projects: the Magnetic Drum Calculator, Test Assembly, TPM, and NORC.

Rochester and Hurd, each for his own reasons, concluded that the Defense Calculator should be a binary machine. Hurd saw in the elegance of binary a boon to reliability and rapid development. In conversion programming he foresaw the beginning of a role for Applied Science in development and marketing. Finally, the prospective users to whom Hurd had talked were not daunted by the prospect of binary arithmetic; indeed, some had read the IAS papers and wanted an IAS-like machine.[21]

Rochester favored a binary Defense Calculator not only for the sake of efficiency but also because binary had been chosen by most designers of machines for scientific applications. A decimal machine, Rochester feared, would provoke a perception by other workers, particularly those in academia, of IBM as technologically inflexible—unable to break with its past. Finally, Rochester felt that in its initial stored-program products IBM should seek experience with a variety of design choices. If and when the TPM entered the product line, it would certainly enter as a serial, alphanumeric, variable-field-length machine. The Defense Calculator would, in any case, deal in parallel with all bits of a fixed-length word; were it to be based on the binary number system as well, the range of design choices would be more fully explored.[22]

On 8 January 1951, Rochester and Haddad met with some of the engineers chosen to work on the Defense Calculator. They characterized their goal as a machine "like IAS but with good input-output." One participant, finding the discussion unrewarding, recorded in his diary, "Trouble is, no one knows what IAS machine is," indicating that von Neumann's precepts were far from familiar to many of IBM's electronics engineers.[23] Rochester, of course, knew very well what the IAS machine was; he had visited the Institute for Advanced Study in February 1949 and seen it in construction. His four-page report, handed out at the meeting, included details concerning logical design, circuit types, and input-output devices. Since his visit, reports in the *Digital Computer Newsletter* had mentioned only one major change at IAS: a switch from RCA Selectrons to Williams-type cathode-ray tubes as elements for the memory.[24]

By early February, Rochester and others had described a system that, while similar to the IAS computer, departed from it in a number of fundamental respects.[25] First of all, word length would be thirty-six bits instead of forty. One reason was that the tape development group had already chosen to record six parallel tracks, exclusive of the parity-bit track, on half-inch-wide tape; a thirty-six-bit word could be neatly recorded as six subwords. A second reason derived from needed numerical precision. In the word format for operands, one bit was reserved for sign indication (0 for positive, 1 for negative). Since a survey of proposed applications had suggested the need for some 2000 words having a numerical precision of ten to twelve decimal digits, which corresponded to a binary precision of thirty-four to forty bits, the other thirty-five bits of the word satisfied the precision range. A thirty-six-bit word could hold two eighteen-bit instructions, just as the IAS word held two twenty-bit instructions. Each Defense Calculator instruction embraced a five-bit operation field (capable of representing up to thirty-two instructions), a twelve-bit address field (capable of representing 4096 addresses), and a sign bit.

In a second departure from IAS conventions, wherein an address always referred to a full forty-bit word, each Defense Calculator address referred to a single eighteen-bit half-word. Normal thirty-six-bit-word processing was designated by a negative sign bit in the instruction. Two half-words associated with two successive addresses were then processed as one word; by convention only even-numbered addresses were used in such instructions, which thereby could address 2048 full words. The Defense Calculator addressing arrangement facilitated the use of half-words where seventeen-bit precision sufficed. Moreover, branch instructions, whereby an instruction-contained address points to the location of another instruction, fell naturally into the addressing scheme; the Defense Calculator did not require, as did the IAS machine, two unconditional branch instructions—one to transfer to a left-hand instruction and another to transfer to a right-hand instruction. Similarly, the IAS scheme required two conditional branch-on-accumulator-sign instructions and two instructions for storing a computed address in a memory-held instruction.[26] These complications for the programmer were avoided in the Defense Calculator at the apparent cost of two bits per instruction: one to double the address range and another (the "sign" bit) to indicate whether half-word or full-word operations were intended. As it turned out, once the requirements for thirty-two instructions (five bits) and about 2000 full words of memory (eleven-bit address) were met, exactly two bits were still available within the eighteen-bit half-word.[27]

A third step away from the IAS design was that "in memory and in the arithmetic circuits the numbers are represented by their absolute values with a separate sign indication."[28] In a decimal context, this magnitude-and-sign representation is the familiar one used in printing positive and negative numbers, by contrast with the arcane complement form described in chapter 1. The complement principle, described there for base 10 (decimal) numbers, applies to any number base; base

2 (binary) is the relevant one here. Complement representation of negative numbers, together with reservation of high-order positions for sign indication, serves to unify algebraic addition and subtraction. Thus an arithmetic unit equipped with a complementing mechanism for subtrahends makes a complete add-subtract unit in which the sign digit is processed in the same manner as other digits; that is, algebraic sign control is accomplished without need for additional circuits. This convenient property does not extend to the operations of multiply and divide, however. The complement representation used throughout the IAS machine necessitated correction rules for sign control in the multiply and divide circuits. In the Defense Calculator, any complement developed in the accumulator was immediately recomplemented to magnitude-and-sign format; this choice simplified multiply-divide sign control and a number of other logical processes at the cost of some add-subtract sign control circuits. The basic execution-time unit, a memory cycle, was long enough to accommodate an addition or subtraction and, if necessary, subsequent recomplementation.

One very evident advantage of magnitude-and-sign representation was convenience for the operator. Neon lamps on the operator's panel were connected to each of the machine's internal storage registers, one lamp per bit. A panel button enabled the machine to be operated in a "manual" mode; one depression of the button brought the next instruction into the instruction register, and the next depression caused the instruction to be executed. In manual mode, the instruction-by-instruction progress of a program could be monitored by watching the neon lights as a check for correct operation of program and machine. Initially, at least, operators found base 2 representation something of a challenge, but they were spared the additional burden of learning to cope with complements.[29]

In view of his computer's kinship with the IAS machine in arithmetic and control features, Rochester found the greatest freedom for innovation in the input-output area. Most early electronic digital computers lacked adequate input and output devices. For the customers Hurd had in mind, better devices were needed; these could be borrowed from IBM's EAM line and the magnetic devices maturing in Endicott and Poughkeepsie. Defined in rudimentary form in the early February specification, input-output capabilities were settled by June 1951.[30]

Input-output control was an obvious area for application of a design principle that omitted circuit components wherever a programmed substitute would suffice. This was because of the disparity in speed between the mechanical units and the central processing unit. For instance, the Defense Calculator could execute hundreds of instructions between the moment it sent a "start" signal to the card reader and the moment when the reading brushes encountered the first row of the card to be read. It could execute over 200 instructions between one row and the next. It could execute a dozen instructions between consecutive words coming from magnetic tape (built-in circuits automatically arrayed six six-bit groups into a word). During these intervals, the user's program was required to intervene between words and determine which memory locations the input (output) word should go to (come from) and how many words should be transferred. The programmer's tool was a single instruction, termed "COPY," used to direct the movement of one word between a given memory location and the thirty-six-bit MQ (multiplier-quotient) register, which served as a way station for every word en route to any I/O device. Multiple executions of COPY via a programmed loop would transfer the whole string of words desired of a requested I/O operation.

To be able to use input and output instructions, the programmer had to understand not only how to write a "COPY loop" but also how thirty-six-bit binary words were recorded, or mapped, on the various recording media. The mapping of a sequence of thirty-six-bit words onto magnetic tape was a sequence of six-line groups, each line having six bits, beginning wherever the tape was positioned when the operation began. For the magnetic drum the mapping was simpler: a sequence of thirty-six-bit lines, each line being thirty-six bits recorded simultaneously by thirty-six magnetic recording heads, beginning at any one (programmer-specified) of an ordered group of 2048 drum locations—four groups being provided. On a punched card, up to twenty-four words could be recorded or read. The first was punched in columns 1–36 of the nines row, the second in columns 37–72 of the same row, the third in columns 1–36 of the eights row, and the last in columns 37–72 of the twelve row. Twenty-four words of data, or forty-eight instructions, could thus be punched on a single card.

In an era when each programmer was expected to catalog and retain his or her own programs, the card was a convenient medium for programs. Instructions sufficient to load the entire memory could be stored in a deck little more than 1/2 inch thick. Such decks were to be punched by the computer itself. A programmer preparing a program initially on a card punch might punch one instruction per card: a two-digit operation code, a four-digit address, and the sign in the first seven columns. Then columns 8 to 72 could contain an alphabetic comment on the purpose of the instruction. A program would read each card in turn, by a 24-COPY loop, into the same programmer-specified twenty-four-word memory area. The resulting twenty-four-word array in storage was termed a "card image," a phrase coined to describe the result of the simple card-to-storage mapping operation. The program could be printed with its comments by simply dispatching each card image to the printer by another 24-COPY loop. If the program was to be punched in compact forty-eight-instruction-per-card format, for subsequent loading and execution, the portions of the card image taken from the seven-column instruction field of each card would be isolated and converted to the appropriate binary numbers: a five-bit operation code, a twelve-bit address, and a single-bit sign. The conversion would thereby compress the information from twelve thirty-six-bit words into a single eighteen-bit half-word instruction. For each forty-eight cards read, forty-eight instructions would be assembled into a twenty-four-word memory area, and a single card would be punched by a 24-COPY loop.

The COPY instruction and the first such program-loading program were devised by Morton M. Astrahan. He joined IBM at the Endicott laboratory in June 1949 after obtaining a Ph.D. at Northwestern University. Werner Buchholz and he were Rochester's principal colleagues in Defense Calculator system planning.[31]

Another input program, similar in principle, was devised for data. Given, for example, seven ten-digit decimal numbers punched in seventy card columns, the speed discrepancy between calculator and card reader was such that the seven decimal-to-binary conversions for each card could be performed row by row while the card image was being built up. Not only could such cards be read at the full card-reader speed of 150 cards per minute, but there remained time "between cards" to check the process by comparing the result of a reverse (binary-to-decimal) conversion for each number to its decimal image and scanning all seventy columns of the card image for errors of the double punch and blank column types.[32]

The speed at which decimally punched data could be entered into the machine was in doubt until several decimal-to-binary loading programs had been formulated and written, a substantial task completed in March 1951. From Test Assembly experience, Rochester knew that it was not safe to predict system performance for particular applications solely from system-organization plans and circuit and device specifications. As a result, he and his small planning group undertook programming exercises as soon as their first description of the Defense Calculator was completed in early February. Before the construction schedule forced him to "freeze" his plans, he wanted to have a basis for evaluating alternatives that might make the machine more cost-efficient in use.[33]

Hurd and Rochester agreed that the numerical solution of partial differential equations would provide a realistic test of Defense Calculator performance. Rochester's Test Assembly program to integrate a particular ordinary second-order differential equation had just been completed.[34] But that 150-step Test Assembly program and a few lesser programs constituted the entire programming experience of the engineering planners. Many of Hurd's Applied Science people, on the other hand, had acquired months of experience on the CPC; some had SSEC experience as well. In March 1951, to supplement the engineers' efforts, Hurd named a five-man "mathematical committee" from these sources to assist the planners. Wallace Eckert contributed an experienced member of his Watson Laboratory staff.[35]

At a management meeting in New York, Hurd and Birkenstock reported that their calls of the preceding four weeks on potential customers had yielded gratifying results; they had eight orders in hand and another dozen "possibilities." T. V. Learson, EAM sales manager, then proposed to coordinate marketing activities, marking the end of Birkenstock's special assignment. This was readily agreed to, but McDowell hesitated before agreeing that Sales, which usually worked closely with Future Demands, should regain its usual prerogative of approving specifications. Hurd and Birkenstock had talked to prospective customers of possible deliveries in the spring of 1952, and McDowell knew there was little time for haggling over what to build. He wanted specifications frozen within six weeks. Besides, his engineers were already working with Applied Science, IBM's center of expertise in scientific computation. Nevertheless, two weeks later, at a meeting with Watson, Jr., McDowell agreed that "the specifications would be completely reviewed and agreed to by the Sales Department and Future Demands Department before they were frozen for the construction of the first model." Thus the tradition of strong leadership by the sales function was resumed. Watson Jr., having shown his sales staff that he did not regard them as infallible, may have felt that after three months their role as onlookers could be replaced by a more active one.[36]

By that time, however, the joint Engineering–Applied Science mathematical programming study was fortified with results. Early in April, just as Future Demands began its evaluation of Defense Calculator specifications "from the point of view of utility to the customer," Hurd reported that the study group had completed its initial phase, which included programs for floating-point, complex and double precision arithmetic, and the extraction of roots. Moreover, changes rendering these programs more economical had already been proposed, tried, and agreed upon.[37]

The group went on to work on complete application programs and in about two weeks completed a program for solution of Laplace's equation, a partial differential equation applicable to determining the distribution of temperature in a nuclear reactor. For this problem, the computer would provide a solution in less than a day and for less than $500, far below the cost of performing such prodigious amounts of arithmetic by any other means.[38] Similar mathematical procedures and economics could be applied to other fields, such as the aerodynamics of high-speed aircraft and missiles. This first Defense Calculator application program explains why Hurd and Birkenstock had enjoyed so favorable a reception when calling on defense agencies and contractors: the electronic computer was seen by imaginative prospective users as a catalyst to advance technological undertakings from the realm of scientific experiment to the realm of engineering design and practical realization. It would accomplish this not by doing what had not been done before but by making economical what had not been economical before.

Fourteen basic changes resulted from the joint Engineering–Applied Science study, among them new instructions, such as "add absolute value," and a revised treatment of zero, which, alone of all numbers that could be represented in the machine, could appear with either the "plus" or "minus" sign bit.[39]

By April 1951, although conceding that the Defense Calculator's speed and storage capacity were impressive, Future Demands questioned whether customers would fully benefit. The department's main reservations concerned the lack of attention to reliability, to program preparation and testing, and to finding and repairing machine faults. Actually there were no specifications in these areas because the engineers had little relevant experience on which to rely. A consensus was reached, however, that the processing unit should provide error-free runs averaging 2 hours. This implied error-free execution, on the average, of 100 million program steps. Mechanical devices running at speeds of ten cycles per second would execute that many cycles in perhaps a year of normal use, during which several failures could be expected.[40]

Rochester remembered that in the previous September, when the Test Assembly first ran well enough to execute nontrivial programs, a 44 minute run of over a million program steps produced two known errors. On the basis of that and subsequent Test Assembly runs, Palmer agreed to the reliability goal set by Future Demands. But the validity of such an extrapolation from the Test Assembly to a much larger machine was arguable, and during April concern mounted in Engineering that Sales might choose to keep Rochester's specifications open to negotiation. At a meeting late in April, Sales and Future Demands termed the specifications "indefinite" with respect to reliability, usability, and cost. But they did not formally disapprove, and so a confrontation was avoided.[41] Subsequently, Learson wrote, "Neither the Sales Department nor the Future Demands Department wish in any way to slow down the building of the model, but only to bring to light those elements of the machine about which we do not have sufficient information to be sure of its complete acceptability." The message seemed to be that the marketing executives were unenthusiastic over the risky project and did not share with Watson, Jr., Engineering, and the Applied Science staff a sense of commensurately high reward.[42]

There was also encouraging news. At that same meeting it was reported that eleven prospective customers for the Defense Calculator had signaled their intention to order, in documents styled "letters of intent" by IBM, and ten more letters were expected. Although everybody was heartened by this, Learson punctured the euphoria by questioning whether Engineering was prepared to build as many as twentyone machines. As Learson well knew, most computers under construction in the United States or abroad were being assembled by their designers in a laboratory environment. The hard questions concerning computer reliability were as yet unanswered, even in the case of computers put together under the most supportive conditions. Late in 1948, J. W. Forrester, Project Whirlwind head at MIT, had spoken for the engineering community when he said, "I believe that, barring an all-out emergency effort such as went into the development of radar, large-scale computers will for several years need the sympathetic care of a laboratory crew."[43] Now, in 1951, early reports on the reliability of completed machines like BINAC and the National Bureau of Standards SEAC were not very encouraging, and the Defense Calculator planners had decided that each machine would be assembled in the laboratory under the supervision of the engineering department rather than in the manufacturing plant. Consequently, McDowell parried Learson's question by agreeing to recommend after study the maximum number of machines that would make most effective use of his development engineering resources.

Learson's question, of course, also forced the engineers to face one consequence of rigorous design simplicity: possible early obsolescence. They decided that the first few machines would teach them much about the relationships among simplicity, reliability, and serviceability. In mid-May, McDowell let it be known that he would like to build just five machines and then evaluate the design based on user experience with them. "It seems probable," he wrote, "that soon after the first machines are installed we will learn how to build a better and more flexible machine."[44] Learson, with fourteen letters of intent in hand and six more "expected shortly," responded by recommending that McDowell add factory manufacture of the sixth through twentieth machines to his objectives. He shared McDowell's concern about early obsolescence and decided to solicit no more orders.[45] As a result of selling efforts already in process, however, the number of machines ordered by letters of intent drifted up to twenty-seven over the next several months.[46]

In early June, with fifty engineers at work on the project in Poughkeepsie, Roberts again questioned whether so substantial a commitment was justified. At a management meeting, proposals for separate engineering and even sales organizations for scientific-oriented products were aired. The possibility of competition from builders of less expensive special-purpose computing instruments came up, and Hurd found himself in the frustrating position of trying to explain and defend the concept of a "general-purpose" machine. McDowell tried to counter the uneasiness at the meeting with a vague promise that the factory-assembled machines would be even more flexible and effective than the first five built at the laboratory. This was hardly convincing, since it was evident that knowledge required to build a better model had to be based on user experience and prospective users could not be expected to sustain their orders through two design-build cycles separated by a vendor education period. The plan that was ultimately made and carried out had all the machines except the engineering model built by the Poughkeepsie plant, with no hiatus for evaluation. McDowell also divulged preliminary estimates of the cost of the Defense Calculator. It appeared that the $8000 monthly rental discussed by Hurd and Birkenstock with prospective customers was low; a $12,000–15,000 range was more likely.

All in all, it was a divisive meeting. The decision to seek no more sales, although made for good reason, tempered emerging Sales Department enthusiasm; Applied Science would have the leading role in working with customers. Learson himself, however, had begun to value the project and was planning a dramatic public introduction of the engineering model Haddad proposed to complete by 1 September. Allowing a few weeks for testing and getting loose ends together,

McDowell thought that customer demonstrations could start in October.[47]

5.3 *Engineering Considerations*

Haddad had divided the project into six sections and named engineers with experience on the Test Assembly, TPM, or NORC to head each. Four of them had been with IBM for over four years: M. E. Femmer (tape/drum input-output, maintenance planning), P. E. Fox (electrostatic storage), C. E. Frizzell (timing circuits and control panel), and H. A. Mussell (card and printer input-output). The other two, Harold D. Ross (arithmetic circuits) and L. D. Stevens (general control and input-output control circuits), had been hired as electrical engineering graduates in the summer of 1949, Ross coming with Astrahan from Northwestern University. Because space was limited at High Street, four of them were assigned desks in the same office. One result was a "constant conversation on design tradeoffs," a form of communication so evidently beneficial that the four-man office was continued when the Laboratory Annex (also called "South Road Lab") was occupied in June 1951.[48]

In the 604 each single-tube pluggable unit was one of some forty distinct circuits in five functional classes. As the engineers had learned from the TPM project, the Defense Calculator could not enjoy that degree of circuit standardization. The principal reason was that the crystal diode had emerged as a component for performing switching functions formerly implemented by vacuum tubes.[49] To achieve required circuit speeds, the diodes could not be physically isolated; they would have to share space on the pluggable units with other components. Further, efficient design demanded that they be used in a variety of configurations and with a variety of resistance values. Another reason was that the range of circuit speeds and loads was much broader than the 604 range, and so circuit component values would both cover a broader range and be chosen more selectively in each instance of use. In these circumstances, circuit types could easily proliferate and lead to unwelcome complexity in a design task with more than enough novel features already. Proliferation, in turn, could magnify the costs of manufacturing, personnel training, and service.

The design team observed, however, that most processing and control functions could still be implemented with a few fundamental circuit classes including the trigger, inverter, multivibrator, cathode follower, and diode circuits. The decision was therefore to standardize methods of circuit design instead of circuits themselves. The standards were embodied in a circuit design manual. It set out standard circuit configurations, as well as design procedures for determining tube types, diode types, and values of passive circuit elements based on circuit speeds and loads.[50] This degree of standardization produced several benefits: standard signal and power supply levels, a uniform approach to reliability and serviceability, and opportunity for section heads to communicate at the level of "logical design." In short, engineering plans for machine units could be expressed in terms of diagrams with symbolic circuit representations from which less experienced engineers, using the design manual, could make detailed circuit designs and drawings of physical layouts.[51] To complete the hierarchical approach to design, Haddad established a wiring room where pluggable units were assembled by technicians.

The circuit design manual, which appeared in the spring of 1951 as a series of handwritten procedures, was finished in June. It was largely the responsibility of David J. Crawford, a 1944 MIT graduate with both digital and analog circuit design experience. Following work in military electronics, he participated in the Whirlwind project during 1947, both as a graduate student and after obtaining his master's degree. Later he worked on precision radar-ranging equipment before joining IBM in September 1950, where his manager, Haddad, was soon to be given the engineering design responsibility for the Defense Calculator.

Increased circuit packaging density and speed facilitated by crystal diodes provoked, in turn, a requirement for pluggable circuit assemblies accommodating more than one vacuum tube; an initial version of such an assembly was already being used in the construction of the TPM. However, a unit with eight tubes strung out along the top and with eight clusters of nine pins each in its base was not really "pluggable." The number of contacts and the flexibility of the structure were such that it could not be inserted into its socket by hand pressure alone; threaded rods were needed at intervals along the unit to draw the base pins into their sockets. Initially, the Defense Calculator laboratory model also used these primitive threaded-rod units, but replacement was found to be more exacting and to require more time than would be tolerable in subsequent service operations. What was needed was a strong, rigid unit with several dozen contact pins distributed along a base 10 inches long (the length of a string of eight miniature vacuum tubes) that could be plugged into a matching socket as readily as the one-tube, nine-pin unit Palmer had developed for the 604.

The solution was a greatly improved pluggable unit (figure 5.1), in which the insertion of the assembly and making of electrical contact

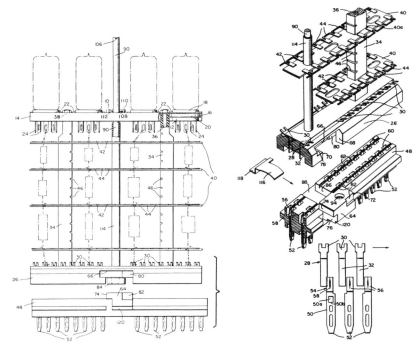

Figure 5.1
Pluggable unit design of the Defense Calculator, with socket and connector detail.
These patent drawings show a four-tube unit; the machine as manufactured used
eight-tube units. Metal connector strips (44) could be severed with a wireman's
cutter to isolate groups of connected lugs, as on the single-tube pluggable unit of
the 604. A novel feature is the means by which the base pins (32) were pre-
aligned with and then made to engage and connect to the socket connectors (52).
The "plug-in" process began with the fitting of the base (26) to the socket (48)
with a displacement to the left relative to its final position established by the registration of a guide block (64) on the socket with a guide slot (66) in the base. The
base pins entered the socket slots but because of the displacement made no contact with the pin sockets (54). Lateral movement of the pluggable unit to the right
would now seat the unit, causing connection of each base pin to its corresponding pin socket. The lateral force that seated the pluggable unit had to be substantial to overcome the frictional force of sixty-four base pins engaging their
respective pin sockets. That force was developed by turning a slotted shaft (90)
with a cam (84) mounted on its bottom end. The cam, as it turned a half revolution, drove the unit base into its clamped, seated position. There were two possible orientations of a pin socket in its recess. Thus a selected group of electrical
connections could be established before all others when the unit was being
mounted to prevent electrical surges that could damage fragile components. (Illustrations from U.S. Patent 2,754,454 of R. D. McNutt and E. J. Garvey.)

Figure 5.2
Electronic panel of the Defense Calculator, with eight-tube pluggable units

occurred in two separate motions. The eight-tube pluggable unit was almost 10 inches long, 5 inches high from base to tube deck, and a bit more than an inch wide; figure 5.2 shows a typical array of them in a production machine. The unit, the basic building block for IBM computers throughout the vacuum tube era, simplified manufacturing by isolating circuit assembly from framing and cabling. Its component density enhanced circuit speeds by allowing related circuits to be connected by short leads. Serviceability was not sacrificed: a pluggable unit could be removed or replaced with a twist of the wrist.[52]

Haddad encountered many problems to which no previous experience was applicable. Bold steps were often necessary in order to keep the project on an even keel. For example, he learned from Hurd that prospective customers were questioning the ability of IBM's field organization to service computers, and, given the sharp upward jump in complexity from IBM 604 to Defense Calculator, the concern was a reasonable one.[53] Consequently, when some twenty raw engineering school graduates were hired for the project in June 1951 to assist in circuit design and layout, Haddad made sure they expected to be called upon for some installation and service work in the field, not normally the province of design engineers. He foresaw that design experience would fit them ideally for helping members of the regular "customer engineering" service staff meet the challenge of Defense Calculator installations.[54] Likewise, when the decision was made for Manufacturing to build the later machines, Haddad eased the shock for his colleagues in that area by promising to have his engineering staff assist on the plant floor. He suggested that each of the June recruits participate in the construction and testing of the same machine he was later to install and maintain at a customer location, thereby settling any doubts about Engineering's attentiveness to Manufacturing.[55]

So many of the new men arrived on one day, 18 June, that Haddad interviewed them two at a time before assigning them to experienced engineers. Each was given work space consisting of a table measuring 2 by 3 feet and half a file drawer.[56] With their help in design, layout, and testing, over half of the projected pluggable units had been built and tested by the end of September.[57]

But in other areas, the problems proved harder to solve. Haddad and Palmer both retained vivid memories of their difficulties with vacuum tube quality during 604 development. That experience had impressed them with the importance of knowing as much as possible about components that, in computer circuits, might reveal erratic behavior not evident in more usual applications. Now they worried about the crystal diode. There would be over 12,000 of them in each Defense Calculator. They speculated that an encapsulated chip of germanium with a small wire "whisker" welded to one face could easily be a source of maintenance problems. Byron Havens had already reported finding their performance unpredictable in his work at the Watson Laboratory. The TPM project had not progressed far enough to provide sufficient data before it was slowed by diversion of engineers to Defense Calculator development.

Consequently, even as pluggable units incorporating diodes were being built, Haddad instituted a diode study program, in which Crawford and others participated. A dynamic tester, capable of displaying diode voltage and current characteristics on an oscilloscope, was built. Observed instabilities in electrical characteristics were classified as "hysteresis," "flutter," and "drift." Some diodes seemed to develop instability as they aged, an effect that if widespread could defeat attempts to select "good" diodes from production lots. Moreover, diodes from single production lots were sometimes found to vary considerably in their ability to carry current in the forward direction and block current in the reverse direction.[58]

In an attempt to accelerate the effects of aging as a part of the diode study, a number of environmental tests were devised. Diodes were cycled in and out of high humidity chambers, boiled in water, and cycled through a household-type pressure cooker. Statistical studies were made of the correlations between diode performance and physical properties. Some of the diodes had glass bodies, permitting use of a microscope to search for debris or moisture in the neighborhood of the contact and to check the wire whisker for distortion.[59]

As late as June 1951, with the Defense Calculator scheduled for completion in the fall, one or two of Haddad's fifty engineers could still be seen peering through microscopes at diode structures. Their concern was not misplaced, for diode manufacturers themselves were still trying to understand the basic physics of their products. Notes from a meeting with one manufacturer (evidently based on the manufacturer's own comments) mentioned that "the diode at its present stage of development is erratic in its resistance stability." And in describing a particular aspect of diode aging, "There is no information at the present time how this transformation takes place or in which direction it will go."[60] The persistence of Haddad's engineers in seeking cooperation from the component makers is suggested in the report of a September meeting: "[the manufacturer] emphasized the fact that there are many other applications for diodes . . . and that they could always sell their diodes without trying to meet IBM specifications." Nonetheless, the manufacturer agreed to try to deliver one thousand diodes a week to the Poughkeepsie laboratory and to establish production tests using procedures developed by IBM.[61]

Eventually, the diode study program of 1951 was undoubtedly of some help to the manufacturers in achieving more uniform products. For the Defense Calculator, however, the costly but effective answer was to establish stringent manufacturing testing procedures for every diode stockpiled for use. With equipment developed by the laboratory, these tests segregated diodes into five categories of use based on forward and back resistances measured dynamically. Since both resistances were known to decrease with increasing temperature, the forward resistance was measured at the lowest operating temperature expected (25°C), and the back resistance at the highest (55°C). Instability, or inability to meet resistance specifications, eliminated a candidate diode. Another test series, for evaluating diode make-and-model prior to ordering, made use of daily high-to-low temperature cycling in a saturated water vapor atmosphere to show up faulty construction.[62] Had the aim of the Defense Calculator project been simply to build a one-of-a-kind machine in a laboratory, the diode problem would have been merely vexatious. But concern over having several thousand mysterious devices in each of some twenty IBM machines scattered around the country had driven Haddad to set up the study that led to the manufacturing tests.

Despite the deliberate pace of early projects like the Circuit Design Manual and the diode study, Haddad managed to imbue his engineers with a sense of urgency. The objective, he would recall years later, "was not to do anything particularly new . . . it was to get out a computer to help the defense effort in the shortest possible time."[63] This pragmatic attitude extended from the use of magnetic-drum technology developed at Endicott, and adoption of the printer mechanism of the 407 Accounting Machine, to the employment of a new circuit that competed with the flip-flop as a means of storing a single bit of information. Byron Havens had developed the circuit at the Watson Laboratory soon after arriving there.[64] Although the Havens delay unit, as the circuit was termed, was intended for use in the Watson Laboratory supercalculator, the Defense Calculator engineers recognized its merit and adopted it.

Havens's circuit was a particularly attractive choice for the Defense Calculator because its output voltage level, during each time interval defined by the applied synchronizing and clamping "clock" pulse trains, was the same as its input voltage level during the preceding period. This property substantiated Havens's original concept of the circuit's purpose: since voltage pulses typically exhibit both delayed and degraded rises and falls and also reduced amplitudes after transiting one or more "levels" of logical circuits, the circuit could be used to reshape and "retime" pulses at the output of logic-performing circuits.[65] (See appendix C for explanation of the circuit's operation.)

The second purpose of the delay unit Havens envisaged was storage of information. A number of delay units could be configured with the output of each connected to the input of the next. Assuming an n-bit word, a string of n delay units could store one word in the form of a recirculating pulse train until needed. Since the principle applied to a single delay unit ($n = 1$) as well as to a longer string, one unit could store a single bit much in the manner of a flip-flop, a point crucial to usage in the Defense Calculator. Figure 5.3 is a block diagram of a single delay unit circuit configured to receive information and store it, by gating output back to input, until new information is received.

In operation, the memory register of the Defense Calculator—thirty-six delay units (each with essentially the input controls of figure 5.3)—received each word read from electrostatic storage. Bits were read simultaneously (one from each of thirty-six cathode-ray tubes) into their respective delay units during a 1-microsecond interval, after which the output of each unit was gated back to the unit's input once every microsecond, thus preserving the word until arrival of another word from memory. While so stored, the contents of the memory register could be gated to other registers as required. The accumulator register also consisted of delay units with input switching controls. The instruction ADD, for instance, called for the word at the memory location designated by the address part of the instruction to be summed into the accumulator register. The execution phase of ADD began by bringing the word from memory to the memory register. Next the outputs of the corresponding stages 1–35 of the two registers were connected by pairs (by switching circuits) to thirty-five adder stages (of diode matrix type). Each stage received three binary inputs (addend, augend, and carry from the preceding stage) and produced two binary outputs (sum and carry).

Since a carry output of "1" acted to change the tentative sum bit and sometimes the carry bit of the succeeding adder and since inherent circuit delays caused output levels to change a fraction of a microsecond after input changes, 5 microseconds had to be set aside for propagating a carry through the maximum of thirty-seven adder stages.[66] To move the sum to the accumulator, the thirty-seven adder sum lines were then connected for 1 microsecond to the thirty-seven inputs of the accumulator delay units, following which the connection of the thirty-seven inputs to their respective outputs was restored, thus preserving the sum and completing the execution of ADD.[67]

ADD illustrates how well suited the Havens delay unit was for use in the Defense Calculator registers. Where sum digits are obtained

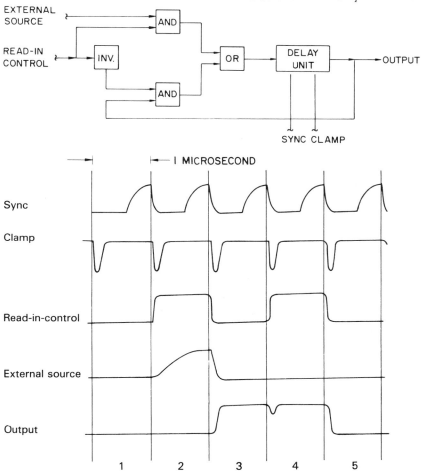

Figure 5.3

Havens delay unit configured for storing binary information. The output of the unit is connected to the input (by the lower AND circuit and the OR circuit) at all times except when a line called "read-in control" is at its upper level. With "read-in control" up, the circuit simply sharpens, retimes, and delays by 1 microsecond the pulses appearing on the input line labeled "external source." With "read-in control" down, the input to the unit is its own output, that is, its input delayed by 1 microsecond. In this configuration the circuit may be viewed as a storage unit that will exhibit, in a particular 1 microsecond period, information read into it in the previous period and will retain that information until new information is read in. The waveforms illustrate this capability. A 1 is read into the unit in time period 2 and a 0 in period 4. Thus in periods 3 and 4 the output is 1, and in period 5 and thereafter the output is 0. (Block diagram at top from H. D. Ross, Jr., "The Arithmetic Element of the IBM Type 701 Computer," *Proceedings of the Institute of Radio Engineers*, Vol. 41, pp. 1287–1294. © 1953 IRE [now IEEE].)

not by counting pulses, as in electromechanical equipment and in the 604, but by a process of logic (embodied here in the diode matrix adder networks) in which the initial content of the accumulator register necessarily plays an input role, there is a trap for the designer. The connection of adder output to register input is actually a connection of register output, by the adder diode network, back to its own input, and will not work for a storage device such as a flip-flop, where output begins to change as soon as its input changes. In those circumstances a "race" develops: Can the storage device achieve its changed output before that very change, being connected to its input, reverses it? Usually such races have unpredictable outcomes. Since the Delay Unit output persists until the input time interval has ended, it does not even introduce the problem. A contemporary paper put it concisely: "The delay feature . . . enables the unit to read-in and read-out simultaneously."[68]

Early on, the race problem had been recognized by the builders of the IAS machine, who used flip-flops for their accumulator. To get around it, they had considered introducing a fixed delay into the addition process, thereby ensuring that the race would always have the intended outcome, but deciding that the extra delay was intolerable, they established instead a double row of flip-flops. During operation, the lower row would be connected to the adder input to form the sum, and the sum would be transferred from the adder to the upper row. The sum in the upper row would then be transferred to the lower row to complete the operation.[69]

Shifting operations in the Defense Calculator accumulator register— whether invoked automatically during multiplication or division or by programmers to align binary points prior to addition and subtraction— were easily provided for. Since the output of a delay unit could be gated to the input of another, a shift of all bits in the register by one position in either direction could be accomplished in 1 microsecond. Thus a typical accumulator stage had four sources of information connected to the diode switching circuit at its input: the output of the corresponding adder stage, the delay unit to the left, the delay unit to the right, and its own output.[70] In all, the Havens circuit represented a combination of economy, speed, and versatility that accorded well with the objectives for the Defense Calculator.

In September 1951, with construction of parts for the engineering model and its assembly proceeding at maximum rates, the number of people assigned to development of the Defense Calculator peaked at 155. While the principal objective was to complete and test the engineering model, preparations for the construction and installation of eighteen production machines could not be ignored. An instruction program was begun for the group hired in June who would be responsible for installation of customers' machines. These young engineers had worked for four months on a variety of design tasks without any formal orientation in such fundamentals as the stored program and binary arithmetic. Haddad's section heads and other key engineers served as instructors. Convened for part of each day, the courses continued for nearly a year and covered a spectrum of technologies, ranging from card readers and punches to electrostatic cathode-ray-tube-storage. In May 1952, before the first class was completed, a new class was started for fifteen students, most of them customer engineers with 604 experience who would have permanent maintenance assignments. The students in these first two classes were to use their training in important ways when production began toward the end of 1952. For example, they wrote diagnostic programs to be used for testing in both manufacturing and the field. Such programs capitalized on the virtuosity of the computer by indicating, even while running, whether the results were correct, and if not, which unit of the machine was most likely at fault.[71]

In December 1951 Haddad established three shifts of engineers to put the Defense Calculator's unit and system testing on a twenty-four-hour basis. By the end of the year the CRT memory and processing unit frames, cabled together, had limped through a few short test programs keyed in at the operator's panel. Unfortunately, these could be run only with CRT memory operating at half-density (512 bits per tube) because the memory was proving to be the most intractable of the machine's components. By mid-March all units except the drum were connected. All-out efforts were directed to obtaining system-type operation reliable enough for a scheduled demonstration at a board of directors meeting in Poughkeepsie. On 27 March 1952, the model (figure 5.4) was demonstrated at a meeting of the boards of directors of IBM and the IBM World Trade Corp. A program of 350 program steps, using twenty-eight of the thirty-two operations, was used (the drum was still not working). It multiplied a 300 by 25 matrix times a 25 by 6 matrix. A single execution of the program required 1.5 million program step executions and took about five minutes. This was very nearly the first substantially error-free run of a useful program using most of the machine's facilities. Without knowing the boards' reactions, the engineers deemed the demonstration a successful culmination of months of around-the-clock work. A celebration of the event that evening at a local restaurant relieved some of the built-up tensions.[72]

Figure 5.4
Defense Calculator, shown in the Laboratory Annex ("South Road Lab"), Poughkeepsie, March 1952. Clockwise from the left: two tape units (each had two tape
drives), magnetic-drum unit, cathode-ray-tube storage unit, L-shaped arithmetic
and control unit with operator's panel, card reader, printer, card punch. Three
power units are in back.

The twenty-four-hour test schedule continued. Now, however, only
thirteen hours were devoted to engineering tests and design refinement.
Eleven nighttime hours were devoted to running programs of increasing
length and complexity, work carried out by Rochester's planning group
and by members of Applied Science. On 21 June, exactly fourteen
months after it was written for a nonexistent machine, the program
to solve Laplace's equation was successfully run.[73]

A comprehensive view of the design and engineering features of
the Defense Calculator was given by Poughkeepsie laboratory engineers
in three papers published in 1953.[74] Two exhibits used by Buchholz
in the paper on system design provide a concise summary of machine
components, capacities, speed, and instruction repertoire; they are
reprinted in appendix D.

5.4 The Type 701 Computer

On 29 April 1952, Watson, Sr., told the stockholders at IBM's annual
meeting that the company was building a general-purpose electronic
machine expected to occupy less than one fourth the space of the
SSEC and operate twenty-five times faster. It would, he said, be rented

and serviced along with the company's regular line of products.[75] In the first week of May, Rochester and Astrahan presented a paper on the machine design at two computer conferences.[76] On 21 May, L. H. LaMotte, vice-president for sales, wrote to his branch office managers of a "new Calculator, tentatively referred to as the IBM Electronic Data Processing Machine."[77] This letter was meant to help sales people in the field to answer questions about the machine provoked by Watson, Sr.'s, April announcement and the conference paper. But LaMotte, citing manufacturing limitations, cautioned that sales were to be handled only by the sales department at headquarters. He added that during the month preceding the date of his letter, prospective customers for the new machine who had signed letters of intent in 1951 had been advised that the rental for it would range from $11,900 to $17,600 per month.[78]

Obviously, the hasty cost estimate of early 1951, resulting in a tentative rental of $8000, had proved much too low. Prospective users, facing a rental increase of almost 100 percent, reacted variously. Although original "orders" had totaled twenty-seven machines, by the time of LaMotte's letter only ten were confirmed. By early August, orders for thirteen machines had been confirmed; the remainder were classified in three groups as "orders in process," "being considered," and "possible cancellations" (two, three, and nine machines, respectively). Since the first production machine, already under construction at Poughkeepsie, was to replace the SSEC at corporate headquarters, there were fourteen machines with known destinations, and places for fourteen more might be found.[79] But parts for only six machines were on hand, the result of a carefully conservative order placed in February. The question was, How many sets of parts should be ordered? On 18 August LaMotte wrote a two-line memorandum approving a production lot of eighteen machines.[80]

No group in IBM learned more from the Defense Calculator effort than the Poughkeepsie manufacturing plant, which was known as Plant No. 2 (the Endicott plant being No. 1). Since close cooperation between the development and manufacturing departments was obviously required for the Defense Calculator, Plant No. 2 management acted long before product release—formal passage of engineering drawings and other specifications from laboratory to factory—by attaching Richard J. Whalen, one of their young project managers, to the laboratory. Notified in October 1951 that he would be responsible for production of the new machine, Whalen had ample incentive to become familiar with the computer and the skills needed for producing it. By January 1952, general manufacturing plans and schedules had been prepared, parts involving special tooling were being released in advance, and procurement of test instruments had started. Soon after the production program was approved in February 1952, about 4000 drawings of new parts and subassemblies were released.[81]

By April 1952, the laboratory model was fully assembled, and by June it was performing computations that exercised all units of the system. Nevertheless, development engineers were still discovering flaws that, from the standpoint of reliability and maintainability, demanded correction. Later in the year, C. E. Frizzell, one of Haddad's original six managers and the oldest in terms of IBM service, assumed responsibility for all engineering changes to the model, including relations with the factory. The Test Assembly project had marked his transition from a skilled technician to a design engineer. Just before the Defense Calculator project began, he had participated in a field study of the applicability of the TPM to the Social Security Administration.

Since it fell to Frizzell to attend weekly meetings with the plant superintendent and managers concerned with production, he soon found himself faced with a barrage of complaints about the frequency of engineering changes. Despite their experience with the IBM 604, the managers in the factory were still attuned to the lengthy tooling and procurement cycles associated with electromechanical products. Although the 604 production program had introduced them to electronic circuit components, they continued to view that machine as an improved successor to the electromechanical multiplying punch. Naturally, so long as they considered electronics as a special-purpose box subservient to a slow card-feeding cycle, they saw no reason to make major revisions in their production methods. Thus Frizzell's requirement for rapid engineering changes struck the factory managers as naive.

To dramatize the new circumstances, Frizzell prepared himself for one meeting at the plant by carefully studying every engineering change for the week. The changes, he learned, involved only a handful of small components, for example, resistors and diodes, within pluggable units. Picking the needed parts from the laboratory stockroom, he placed each in a small envelope marked with the change number and other information. Then he pocketed the envelopes before going to the meeting at the plant. After again being exposed to the familiar complaints about engineering changes, he produced his envelopes and suggested that the managers walk upstairs to a machine assembly area on the plant floor, where the meeting might constructively close by installing the week's engineering changes, which required neither special tooling nor new procurement.[82]

Frizzell's point was not lost on the resourceful managers at the plant, who quickly saw that a new era was dawning and went about modifying manufacturing procedures accordingly. By assiduously applying their skills to the challenges posed in the course of producing nineteen machines—challenges that demanded the development of more flexible production methods—they opened the way for computer assembly lines.

The first production machine was shipped from Poughkeepsie to New York late in December 1952. It was set up in the headquarters building on Madison Avenue in the space formerly occupied by the SSEC. There were eleven separate physical units to be uncrated, arranged, cable connected together, and made to operate as planned. Before then, a CPC installation of four units, each using well-established technologies, had been the most complex installation of an IBM product. The electrostatic storage unit held seventy-two cathode-ray tubes, sufficient to provide the specified 2048 thirty-six-bit words *if* each tube held 1024 bits. But the engineers had not yet established reliable operation at that density. Consequently, a second storage unit was required, edging the total number of units up to twelve. In addition to three units for power supply and distribution, these were:

Type 701 electronic analytical control unit
Type 706 electrostatic storage unit (two)
Type 711 punched-card reader
Type 716 alphabetical printer
Type 721 punched-card recorder
Type 726 magnetic-tape reader and recorder (two)
Type 731 magnetic-drum reader and recorder

The first type number in the sequence gave the system the informal name by which it was widely known beginning in June 1952: the 701.

Early in 1953, intensive cathode-ray-tube testing at 1024 spots per tube was initiated at the factory using the second 706 production unit. The unit was soon connected to the second production main frame, destined for delivery to the Los Alamos Scientific Laboratory, and the tests continued. At the same time, similar tests began on the third memory frame. After a final series of tests on Sunday, 1 March, Fox sent Palmer a recommendation endorsed by the senior engineers on the project: "make 1024 bits/tube standard on the 701 as soon as possible."[83] The decision to do so was divulged three weeks later in a paper, describing the 701 storage circuits and their development, presented at the Institute of Radio Engineers National Convention in

New York.[84] By that time, Hurd had informed customers that, since one memory unit would suffice to store 2048 words, the monthly rent for the full machine would be $15,000 instead of $17,600.

The Defense Calculator was unveiled to the public on 7 April 1953 as the "IBM Electronic Data Processing Machines, known also as the '701.' " At a gathering reminiscent of the SSEC dedication five years earlier, over 150 guests selected by Wallace Eckert, Hurd, and IBM sales executives sat down to a lunch catered by a midtown hotel. Some forty IBM people attended, including a contingent from the Poughkeepsie laboratory. Thomas J. Watson, Sr., presided; the guest speaker was J. Robert Oppenheimer, director of the Institute for Advanced Study. After lunch, Hurd hosted a demonstration. The machine performed "a test calculation on neutron scattering, an unclassified check problem furnished by Los Alamos Scientific Laboratory of the University of California." Hurd took pains to point out that the various machine units could be easily disconnected and shipped. He illustrated by noting that the second production machine had begun doing useful work at Los Alamos on 3 April, just three days after arrival of the shipping crates on the site. Since the Los Alamos Laboratory began paying rent on 17 April, the installation and shakedown period for the first IBM computer shipped to a customer lasted only seventeen days.[85]

Production of the 701 continued at the Poughkeepsie plant at an average rate of one machine a month through June 1954, when the eighteenth machine was completed and shipped to Lockheed Aircraft in Burbank, California. There were enough spare parts on hand, it appeared, to assemble a nineteenth machine and a motive to do so, although some production facilities already shut down would have to be reestablished, had emerged earlier in the year. At the Institute for Advanced Study a group of meteorologists had spearheaded some dramatic advances in the science of "numerical weather forecasting" that required prodigious computing power for timely results. Their evolving methods had been proved on the ENIAC, beginning in early 1950, and again on the IAS machine when it began running in 1952. As a result, a joint group was formed by the Weather Bureau, air force, and navy to begin operational forecasting. The government committee planning for the operation determined that the choice of a computer came down to the IBM 701 and the Remington Rand ERA 1103. A key meteorological calculation that had been run on the IAS machine was reprogrammed and run on the two machines. The 701 program was prepared jointly by IBM, the air force, and the navy; it was run and the 701 performance measured in January 1954 on the machine at IBM headquarters. The results led to a government request that IBM produce a 701 to be applied to the rapidly evolving science of weather prediction. Thus it was that in April 1955 the nineteenth and last IBM 701 to be built began preparing daily weather forecasts for the Joint Numerical Weather Prediction Unit operated by the U.S. Weather Bureau at Suitland, Maryland.[86]

Late in 1952, Haddad had modified somewhat his plan to have his engineers supervise each installation and stay on site as long as needed. He asked four of the group originally destined for those assignments to stay at the laboratory instead. He reasoned that, while helping to plan improvements, they would have an opportunity to enhance their expertise and thus be better prepared for their principal assignment: to visit on short notice any installation afflicted with persistent operating difficulties and cure them.

One of the four who stayed at the laboratory was Bob O. Evans, a 1949 electrical engineering graduate of Iowa State College. While working for a utility company in 1951, he had heard about the Defense Calculator, and he wrote to IBM asking for an interview. In September, he joined the project as a late but somewhat more experienced member of the group of engineers who had joined in June. As it turned out, installations of the 701 did not always proceed as smoothly as the first one at Los Alamos. For example, in August 1953 at the Consolidated Vultee Aircraft (later Convair) plant in Fort Worth, troubles with the new 701 had been multiplying ever since a power supply mixup had ruined a number of components in the power units. The local customer engineering group called East for help and, according to a later recollection, "Evans . . . came down on a night flight and steamed into the plant at dawn on a Saturday." With a colleague from Poughkeepsie and the local group assisting, Evans had the machine running and ready for customer testing by Sunday evening. Evans had earlier been helpful at Douglas Aircraft in Santa Monica, where an IBM salesman remembered supplying him with coffee while he worked around the clock to fix a problem with the tape units.[87] The roving troubleshooter job was as educational as it was demanding, a stimulating melange of laboratory and field experience at a critical juncture in the development of IBM's computer business. Evans subsequently advanced to engineering management positions in which he made a number of crucial recommendations and decisions. (See chapters 12 and 14.)

While manufacturing was learning to cope with the new technology and engineering was acquiring an accelerated education in field maintenance, corporate headquarters and sales were learning how to deal with a highly expensive product—a computer system. They found that because of inventory costs and attendant business risks, negotiations with customers must occur early in the product cycle: computers were too expensive to be permitted to remain idle after being built, whether in the customer's or IBM's possession. At the same time, for a customer to make productive use of a delivered computer, a year or more of advance preparation was required, both to obtain and train candidate programmers and to prepare and test a set of programs for initial applications. The customer also had to prepare a suitable physical environment for the computer system. As J. W. Forrester, speaking at a 1948 symposium, had said, "if a high-speed computer . . . were sitting here today, it would be nearly two years before the machine were in effective and efficient operation."[88]

These lessons had been learned on a small scale with IBM 604s and CPCs, but the 701 experience drove them home and led to stricter notions of "announcement" as a formal way of crystallizing relationships between IBM and its customers. Only after the logical organization of a computer system had been defined to the point of a principles-of-operation manual and tested with the aid of a laboratory model; after the technologies necessary to construction of the system had been carefully tested; and after parts requirements had been worked out to the point where the products of a system could be objectively priced—only then might a system become a candidate for announcement. In brief, announcement meant that the design was frozen, that IBM's reputation was reasonably safe with the product, and that the sales organization could act on IBM's intent to field the system in a certain number of months, typically twelve to twenty-four—that is, in roughly the time a typical customer would need to prepare to use it.

The 701 experience was uniquely important in the history of IBM's transition from punched-card machines to electronic computers. Prior to that experience, planning and marketing executives could speculate endlessly on whether data could safely be entrusted to invisible tape recording or control entrusted to the ethereal stored program. But when it had been demonstrated that 701s could be manufactured, programmed, maintained, and relied upon for useful results as promised, the speculation subsided. The question thereafter was not *whether* to build new computers but *which* machines to introduce and *when*; and by March 1955 when the nineteenth 701 was installed, the company had announced a variety of new computers.

5.5 *The Type 650 Magnetic Drum Calculator*

While large-scale machine development work was being pressed at Poughkeepsie in 1951 and 1952, the Magnetic Drum Calculator (MDC) project at the Endicott laboratory had been nearly dormant. Rejuvenated by Tom Watson, Jr.'s, November 1952 decision, as related in chapter 3, it was further strengthened by scientific application studies. Hurd's Poughkeepsie mathematical planning group worked intensively with the MDC for the next three months, to considerable effect. Its members wrote and ran on Frank Hamilton's model many programs, such as floating-point subroutines, expected to find heavy use by customers. They formulated additional instructions to make such programs more efficient and were able to demonstrate the results to Frank Hamilton and E. S. Hughes, Jr., who had become Hamilton's principal assistant on the project. For example, Store Address and Shift-Left-and-Count were added to the MDC during this period.[89] They made a variety of user-oriented suggestions, ranging from better arrangement of console lights to cost-saving refinements of the plan for implementing high-speed revolver storage. They wrote two alternative proposals for adding three index registers to the machine (devices to facilitate address modification and control of iterative calculations, see chapter 9) but bowed to Hamilton's decision not to use any because of the resulting delay (three months) in the production schedule.[90]

Finally, the mathematical planning group found much to admire in the MDC. An excerpt from a December report:

Very impressed with this machine. There are features about it which are not apparent until one actually uses the machine. The checking facilities are excellent. When an error did occur, it was usually a programmer's error. Ease of programming impressed us considerably. The I-address is an extremely important aid in programming. The methods of balance testing and zero testing are good. The ability to address the distributor, both accumulators, and the dial switches increased the ease of programming. In regards to ease of use of the machine, the console is extremely useful, especially in checking out programs, changing programs, monitoring problem solutions.[91]

Early in 1953, Hurd established a new mathematical planning group, at the Endicott laboratory. Elmer Kubie was its first member.

In mid-March 1953, Kubie completed a report describing a technique for selection of instruction and data locations in programs so as to minimize "waiting time." With 100 drum storage tracks of twenty words each, there were initially 100 locations to choose from once an "optimum" angular position had been determined for a particular word. The new, fast-access storage complicated the problem somewhat beyond what Dunwell and Hamilton had foreseen when they settled on the "modified one-address" instruction format for the MDC. To answer the problem, Kubie designed a nomograph device consisting of two concentric disks pinned together. Starting with a particular instruction located at a particular address, the programmer would set a mark on the top disk corresponding to the operation type opposite one of twenty marks on the bottom disk representing the location. Four windows in the top disk then revealed codes for optimum data and next-instruction locations for each of the four cases in which both data and next instruction could be in either "fast" or general storage.[92]

Just as things seemed to be going fine technically and otherwise, however, the MDC project received a blow that threatened a substantial setback. On 20 March two lawyers in IBM's patent department at headquarters completed an analysis of a patent issued on 24 February to J. P. Eckert, Jr., and J. W. Mauchly, originators of Remington Rand's UNIVAC. One of some thirty-six claims read as follows:

In combination, a delay device having an input and an output and arranged to deliver through the output, after a predetermined delay interval, signals entering the input, and electrical devices joining the output and the input to reintroduce through the input signals emitted from the output to provide recirculation of a predetermined pattern of signals through the delay device, said delay device comprising a cyclically moving carrier on which said signals are sequentially impressed as magnetic patterns.

The lawyers opined that this "covers any 'revolver' using a cyclically moving carrier, magnetic or otherwise."[93]

Eckert and Mauchly had built BINAC and UNIVAC using mercury delay lines for storage. Each such line required the continuous service of electronic reading and recording amplifers to reintroduce information from the output back at the input. The feedback path could be broken for all or part of a cycle for the purpose of storing—that is, substituting new data for old. The magnetic drum was a less expensive, if slower, storage device not only because it was mechanically simpler to construct and control but also because data recorded on its surface could remain, without need for continuous recycling, until needed. Thus a single pair of amplifiers could be shared by all drum tracks, switched from track to track as needed to access instructions and data in turn.

The Eckert-Mauchly patent did not enjoin use of a drum in this arrangement, which differed conceptually as well as physically from the use of mercury delay lines and which was used for the bulk of the MDC storage. But the drum was also used in a manner analogous to the recirculating mode of the delay lines. On a separate drum track, data in the form of recorded spots moved from a recording head to a reading head, where they were read and copied back at the recording head. Depending on the spacing between the heads, dedicated amplifiers thus facilitated storage of data for which the waiting time could be as little as one "word time" rather than a full drum revolution. Such revolvers were basic to the MDC plan. They were used for the accumulator, distributor, and program registers (the accumulator was double length), as well as for the 150 fast-access words that had been added to the design for speed-enhancing purposes the previous winter. Now IBM's principal rival, Remington Rand, had acquired the exclusive right to this principle by virtue of original work done years earlier by the two inventors whose financially troubled company it had acquired in 1950.

The signal from IBM headquarters to the Endicott laboratory engineers was that there would be no licensing arrangement with Remington Rand to bail them out. The principal problem raised by the patent situation was the machine registers, which would have to be moved from the convenient drum revolver tracks to an alternative technology. This meant finding a way to store some forty decimal digits without causing the projected machine cost to skyrocket. A principal candidate was magnetic-core storage (see chapter 7). By early April, Hamilton had sketched out five machine designs using cores, with corresponding cost increases and schedule delay estimates. Kubie worked out the performance increments and decrements associated with each. His summary of all the data concisely expressed the dilemma: "Delaying production of the MDC and increasing its cost predicate improvements in the machine's power. If these improvements are not commensurate with the increased cost and later delivery, the effect will be detrimental to the machine's sales value. . . . [N]one of the plans proposed . . . meet this requirement."[94] That result, coupled with the fact that rights to critical patents covering ferrite-core memory had not yet been obtained (see chapter 7), ruled out cores.[95]

In early May, Hamilton settled on capacitor storage, an option open to him only because a few Endicott engineers had been working with it since mid-1952. During the period when the MDC project was close to extinction, it had been kept alive by moving personnel—and therefore cost—to other projects that could be construed to support laboratory objectives, such as the investigation of new memory technologies. Now, in an unexpected turn of events, a capacitor storage model was in operation on a laboratory bench, and there was no question that the substitution was technically feasible.[96]

The capacitor has been a central element in a variety of electronic digital storage systems. Because the electrical charge on a capacitor, and the voltage proportional to it, remain for a time after the source is removed, a later "reading" by a device able to discriminate between two levels of voltage can determine whether a charge has been stored earlier; hence the memory capability. Since the charge tends to dissipate over time, some means of regeneration is necessary. As with a CRT storage spot, a convenient scheme is periodically to "read" the stored information (a process that typically discharges the capacitor) and, based on the result, reestablish the initial level of charge.

Circuits embodying these principles had been built at Endicott in 1945–1946, at the Watson Laboratory in about 1947, and at Poughkeepsie in 1948–1949 but had never found their way into full IBM models or products.[97] The minimum equipment per stored bit of information included the capacitor itself and two diodes to isolate one terminal of the capacitor from the storing and reading circuits. To minimize leakage, and thus the frequency of regeneration, vacuum tube diodes were used, accounting for a minimum cost of one tube per bit exclusive of any provision for reading and storing. The various ways of providing those functions, and of sharing the required circuits across an array of diode-capacitor pairs, accounted for the wide variety of storage schemes that arose.

During 1952, researchers at the National Bureau of Standards reported promising results with capacitor storage circuits using germanium diodes and very low level signals of about 2–4 volts in amplitude.[98] The interest at Endicott in capacitor storage, thereby rekindled,[99] favored higher signal levels for compatibility with already established levels in the MDC and other development projects, and vacuum tube diodes. Circuits were developed, tested, and found to operate reliably. Two double-diode tubes (one above the other) and two capacitors, all of the elements associated with two bits of capacitor storage, fit neatly on a "single-tube" MDC pluggable unit. Indeed, Hamilton chose capacitor storage over core storage as much for its component availability and easy integration into his electronic packaging plan as for its cost and performance.[100] Management would be impatient enough with the delay the redesign would provoke; any suggestion of contingent further delay would not be welcome.

Because of its substantially higher cost per digit, Hamilton had substituted capacitor storage for revolvers only in the machine registers mentioned previously. A perplexing problem remained: how to restore performance lost through the ruling out of inexpensive drum revolvers providing 150 words of fast-access storage. The performance issue was critical because the six week struggle with the patent problem had spawned new doubts at headquarters about the entire project's future. Once again, the MDC found itself in competition with a host of other laboratory projects for the role of successor to the CPC. These included the Harper-Fernekees small drum machine at Poughkeepsie, a "modified 701," a "stripped TPM," and the so-called Wooden Wheel. The last of these designations was concocted from the names of three engineers—W. W. Woodbury, G. J. Toben, and L. T. Wheelock—who had built a computer at the Poughkeepsie laboratory during the previous year, around the old Test Assembly. Woodbury and Toben, who conceived of the ancestor of the CPC while at Northrop Aircraft (see chapter 2), had later joined IBM and teamed up with Wheelock, who had a part in the construction and maintenance of the Test Assembly. The Wooden Wheel (also referred to as the "WTW") had a modest amount of cathode-ray-tube storage, but its unique feature was its method of programming. The "plugged program" technology of the 604 and CPC, disdained by the Test Assembly builders, had been thoroughly modernized (for example, by substituting vacuum tube flip-flops for wire-contact relays as selectors), thus providing switching speeds adequate for control of individual program steps.[101]

An eight-member evaluation committee including engineers, Applied Science representatives, and planners from J. W. Birkenstock's Product Planning and Market Analysis Department (successor to Future Demands) ruled out the Harper-Fernekees machine as too far from announceable state. The modified 701 and TPM machines were conceptual projects with high cost implications; the MDC and Wooden Wheel were running in their respective laboratories with more attractive cost data. The study therefore came down to consideration of the latter machines. (MDC data were taken from a specification prepared before the patent problem came up.)

On 30 April, Hamilton presented to the committee his plan to restore performance to the revolverless MDC (so recently formulated that a description had not yet been prepared): he would equip each of the 100 MDC storage tracks with four equally spaced heads instead of just one; with appropriate head switching, every word in storage would be accessible in the same time as the fast-access words of the prior design. The waiting time for any word in storage could never exceed a quarter of a drum revolution. By 8 May, the Endicott plant had arrived at augmented manufacturing and tool costs for the committee to consider.[102]

The evaluation committee's final report, after a preliminary report favoring the Wooden Wheel[103], concluded that "both machines are superior to any present competitive machine" and that each machine bested the other in some respects. The Wooden Wheel had the edge in lower cost, faster memory access, and "superior logic"; the MDC excelled in ease of use and checking facilities. To these two lists of several features each the committee added only, "No course of action can be recommended beyond that indicated by the above conclusions."[104]

Hurd's recollection is that Watson, Jr., this time urged him and McDowell to stop "fiddling around"—to "decide on a machine and announce it."[105] They did; it was the MDC, announced 2 July 1953 as the Type 650 Magnetic Drum Calculator. Hurd believes the deciding factor was ease of use, observing that the Wooden Wheel could out-perform the MDC only when programmed by very talented people and that the simple terms in which the MDC could be programmed would attract more customers.[106] It had not been an easy decision; ease of use is an extremely subjective concept. In mid-June, a group of five programmers and planners, including members of Hurd's Poughkeepsie mathematical planning group, avowed admirers of the MDC, had completed a programming study and sent him their blunt conclusion: "the WTW is an easier machine to use than the MDC."[107]

By the date of announcement, the 650's drum plan had once more been revised. Recording would be parallel-by-bit in a new five-bit self-checking code applicable just to the drum. This would permit fifty words per five-track band on a drum of reduced diameter (4 inches, compared with the prior 10 inches). With only one set of five heads per band, access-time improvement would be retained by speeding the drum up to the rather remarkable speed of 12,500 revolutions per minute. Drum rotation period would be 4.8 milliseconds and average access time 2.4 milliseconds. Word time, also a factor in performance, was substantially reduced in this scheme to $1/50$ of 4.8 milliseconds, i.e., approximately 100 microseconds. It had previously been $1/20$ of 14 milliseconds, or 700 microseconds. All of these revisions left recording density and circuit frequencies unchanged. A substantial new challenge, met in the end, was to engineer a new and truly high-speed drum.

The announced rental was substantial: $3250 and $3750 per month, respectively, for a 1000-word and a 2000-word machine, without a printer (the accounting machine attachment feature was one of the items left unspecified and unplanned in the hectic first half of 1953). Just before announcement, only Hurd's Applied Science representatives and some salesmen to government agencies in Washington would predict they could sell any 650s, their combined estimate coming to 250.[108] But orders began to come, some for accounting and commercial applications, and by late August, forecasters monitoring the order rate predicted there would be 550 sales in five years, including 200 for commercial use.[109]

Frank Hamilton and his engineers finally had the commitment that had been their objective from the start but in terms they could hardly have predicted. The machine IBM had announced and was successfully selling was different in almost every respect, excluding basic electronic technology, from the model that had been running on the floor of the laboratory. Hamilton had told the evaluation committee that the first production model would come off the plant line eighteen months after his new plan was approved. There was much to be done and no time to lose. But with orders on the books, there was at last little likelihood that the project would again be canceled or redirected.

As it turned out, the redesigned engineering model first ran programs in February 1954.[110] A month later it ran a comprehensive series of diagnostic programs. The first delivery of the Type 650 was to the John Hancock Mutual Life Insurance Company in Boston in December 1954. By that time IBM had orders for over 450 650s.[111] Despite all the impediments the project had encountered, the 650 had emerged as the right machine at the right time. It was very competitive, not only in performance and price, but also in its concept as a small, reliable machine offering the versatility of a stored-program computer in a punched-card environment. This last consideration was important to prospective customers whose data processing requirements were not large enough to justify trading the convenience of the familiar punched card for the vagaries of magnetic tape. So successful was the 650 that it is worthwhile to examine the competitive environment in which the machine was introduced.

In the early 1950s any small computer was, almost of necessity, a drum machine; no other main-memory technology afforded comparable economy. By 1954, when the first 650 was installed, a number of drum computers were available. "It was almost too easy," observed one early computer historian, "to design and build a prototype computer. It was not quite as easy to develop a production facility, a marketable product, and adequate support."[112]

In an industry conference paper presented in December 1954, a university speaker compared the IBM 650 with eight other small digital computers. Of the eight, only two offered punched-card I/O comparable to that of the 650: the 30-203 (later called the "Datatron") of

ElectroData Corporation, and the Elecom 120 of Underwood Corporation. The National Cash Register 102-D was described as having punched-card output but paper-tape input; all three manufacturers purchased their card input-output units from IBM. These three machines were among the very few small computers to which magnetic tape could be attached; but magnetic tape was not of high priority to small-computer users at that time. The unusually high speed of its drum placed the 650 in a very good competitive position. None of the eight computers offered anything comparable to the 650's average access time to main memory of 2.4 milliseconds; and for the three machines with card input-output, average access time was at least 3.5 times that of the 650. This advantage was enhanced by the modified one-address instruction format, which helped optimum programming. The single-instruction table lookup was especially attractive to such businesses as public utilities and insurance companies, whose applications required frequent reference to rate tables.[113]

Engineering emphasis on reliability was rewarded. Equipped with a substantial number of control-circuit and data-validity checking circuits, the machine earned a high reputation among users for reliable operation.

The 650 was supported throughout its long life (the last unit was manufactured in 1962) by a steady stream of product enhancements. With the machine's early and unexpected acceptance for business data processing, it became obvious that alphabetic-character capability should be added. This need was met in mid-1954 by the announcement of a feature that permitted alphanumeric information to be read and punched. An alphabetic character was represented inside the machine as a pair of digits. There were also frequent improvements in the speed and flexibility of attachable card input-output machines, most notably the provision in 1955 for attachment of the popular 407 accounting machine, which made the excellent print quality of that machine available for reports printed on-line.

Primarily, however, the success of the 650 was attributable to its initial design. In mid-1956, there were 300 machines installed—many times more than all of the IBM 700 series machines combined—and 650s were coming off the production line at a rate of one every day, most of them destined for business data processing applications.[114] Frank Hamilton, whose name had been linked for fifteen years to the one-of-a-kind ASCC and SSEC computers, was released from his bondage to exotic systems by the 650, which became, as Thomas J. Watson, Sr., had hoped in 1948, a machine for ordinary businesses.

5.6 The Type 702 Electronic Data Processing Machine

TPM planners had been afforded a breathing spell in 1952 by management's concern over the higher-priority 701 project, a project that was taking significantly longer than expected. IBM felt its reputation was at stake in the 701, and until the 701 succeeded, a commercial future for the TPM was considered somewhat academic. When tested diodes were in short supply for a time, the needs of the TPM project had been made to defer to those of 701 production. Buchholz took advantage of the period of relative inactivity to explore ideas that might significantly improve the TPM system. In April 1952, he proposed a common information trunk to which independent system units might attach, regardless of trunk position, unit complexity, or numbers of units already attached.[115] Although input-output units were his main concern, he anticipated the feasibility of communication among separately attached arithmetic and logical units (ALUs). Since each ALU or input-output device was to have its own power supply, the number of attachable units was—within reason—unrestricted. Then in August, Buchholz made a second major proposal—a method whereby tape reading, tape writing, and ALU processing could overlap one another; this, he wrote, would speed up tape sorting and file maintenance by a factor of three.[116] As we shall see, the first of these two input-ouput proposals was acted on; the second was not.

By this time it was obvious that the TPM laboratory model, with its serial-serial mode of operation and its 128 microsecond character cycle, was much too slow. A parallel-by-bit, serial-by-character mode was therefore chosen as a major objective. Although simple enough technologically, the change in mode involved a thorough redesign of the ALU. The resulting machine, called the TPM II, had a character cycle of 23 microseconds. To increase effective data rates further and also to save memory space, field marks were eliminated as separate characters; instead, numeric fields were to be demarked by "zone" bits on least-significant digits and nonnumeric fields by accumulator settings. As suggested by Buchholz, the excess-three code was dropped in favor of straightforward binary-coded-decimal coding of the digits 1 through 9.

Meanwhile, L. H. LaMotte had moved from the Washington office to IBM corporate headquarters to become vice-president for sales. In September 1952, F. J. Wesley, one of the more careful observers of computer trends among LaMotte's former staff assistants, rejoined him at headquarters as his technical assistant.[117] Wesley's tendency to recommend action by IBM added to a growing tension between

LaMotte's office and Future Demands, still headed by the conservative Roberts. The well-publicized UNIVAC had been in use by the Census Bureau for over a year; Remington Rand had completed three other UNIVAC installations in 1952, and customer excitement over electronic machines was mounting. Future Demands' studies showed punched-card systems to be more economical and less risky than tape-based electronic systems. But cool empiricism is rarely the farsighted measure of market tastes; the tide of general opinion was with electronics, as IBM salesmen were beginning to sense. In February 1953, the month in which the TPM Survey Team delivered its final report, Roberts was made an administrative assistant to LaMotte, and the Future Demands department was replaced by the new Product Planning and Market Analysis function, headed by Birkenstock.

The survey report provided scant reason for optimism on the part of TPM engineers. The team had examined the data processing requirements of nineteen organizations, among them insurance companies, manufacturers, utilities, and government agencies including the U.S. Census Bureau. While customers seemed receptive to new technologies and while TPM capabilities sufficed for all customers but one (that one requiring immediate file reference), the team reported the machine did not have the performance to provide "an economic profit both to the customer and IBM." The comments applied solely to the original TPM. Assumed monthly rentals included: main frame, $6200; drum (60,000 characters), $4800; CRT memory (10,000 characters), $7050; tape units, $700 each; and other peripheral units, such as printer (150 lines per minute), $2500. (Later these assumed rentals were judged to have been much higher than necessary.) Although price for performance was the major concern, the team also faulted the lack of instantaneous proof of accurate recording on tape. It reiterated that the inherent inefficiency in sorting would necessitate an auxiliary machine for the purpose.[118] (Such a machine, part of the TPM program all along, was later shown to be uneconomical. A special tape sorter-collator was eventually constructed in a project headed by Femmer, but it never became part of the regular product line.[119])

Despite the less-than-enthusiastic tone of the Future Demands report, the TPM II engineers and planners proceeded with redesign plans, confident that the enhancements being planned would produce a machine that would win market acceptance. The first major Buchholz proposal, for a common trunk, was studied by R. P. Crago, H. A. Mussell, W. D. Winger, and others who shared engineering responsibility for the TPM improvement program. With regard to Buchholz's proposal for a common input-output trunk, Winger suggested putting the power supply for each type of device in a control unit serving a group of similar units.[120] This suggestion was followed in the case of tape drives, but otherwise the Buchholz plan was adopted essentially as written. The two modes of operation proposed for input-output units — the "on-line" mode (connected to the main trunk) and the "off-line" mode (coupled in independently useful subsystems) — provided important benefits. An off-line card-to-tape conversion subsystem, for example, could be fashioned out of any free card reader and a tape drive.

Furthermore, while connected to the common input-output trunk, each control unit decoded the combination of voltages representing the address of any device attached to it when that combination was transmitted (by the address wires of the trunk) during execution of the SELECT instruction. The sixteen address wires of the input-output cable, representing four binary-coded decimal digits, provided for 10,000 addresses. While 90 percent of these were reserved for individually addressable 200-character drum sections, 1000 addresses remained for allocation among tape units, card machines, printers, addressable check indicators and console switches, and any other devices that might be introduced. Such an addressing scheme was extremely ambitious, considering the much more limited configuration foreseen for actual installations. But in combination with the independent power supplies, this arrangement preserved the generality intended in the original common-trunk proposal.

Buchholz's second major input-output proposal, which involved overlapping of tape reading and writing with ALU processing, was less successful. The TPM II engineering team was unable to justify the additional development time, expense, and product complexity involved. However, magnetic-core storage units called "core buffers" were developed by E. Bloch and others to match the relatively slow card readers, card punches, and printers to the higher-speed ALU (see chapter 7). These took the place of the special drum tracks that had served the purpose in the original TPM with its slower ALU. A core buffer stored a card image of 960 bits (twelve rows of eighty bits each) for a card reader or punch; for the printer half again that many bits were stored to accommodate the line length of 120 characters by then established for tabulators. The content of a card or line of information to be printed could be transferred from or to a buffer at memory speed without waiting for a mechanical cycle.

Within a few weeks after the 7 April 1953 public showing of the IBM 701, IBM executives were coming under extreme pressure to unveil the TPM II. Although their product-planning studies still indicated that tape-based electronic technologies were not ready to compete profitably and safely with punched-card accounting systems, customers with voluminous files were impatiently clamoring for an announcement. Well over a year had elapsed since the TPM demonstrations. Now customers wanted to see what IBM had to offer before deciding whether to order a UNIVAC. During the summer of 1953, Wesley, on LaMotte's staff, argued for announcing the TPM II "with price and firmness but without fanfare" and for letting the customers decide the economic questions for themselves.[121] Roberts, as LaMotte's administrative assistant, characteristically argued that IBM should make a positive case for waiting until the technology could be profitably exploited. In September, LaMotte and Watson, Jr., came to a decision. The TPM II was announced "without fanfare" in September 1953 as the IBM 702 Electronic Data Processing Machine, for delivery beginning early in 1955.[122]

Nearly all of the prospective 702 customers were large enterprises heavily dependent on punched-card accounting equipment. Their sorters, collators, tabulators, and electronic calculators performed limited tasks that allowed for manual checking processes and for inspection of the cards at the beginning and end of every pass. The 702, by contrast, a system in which operating records had to be entrusted to an erasable medium that held records in an invisible form, offered neither convenient random access nor especially efficient sorting procedures; it relied on sequential processing of ordered files while providing no very economical way of marshaling records into desired order. Against these disadvantages the potential customer had to weigh the advantages of longer records, more compact files, faster sequential operations, and greater automaticity, advantages that could lead to savings in many important applications.

For IBM, one of the attractive features of its 701 program had been the opportunity it offered the company to plunge into electronic data processing without facing the central problem of the magnetic-tape file. The typical 701 user was more interested in magnetic tape as an extension of computer memory than as a medium for the processing of large files. It was with its 702 customers that IBM first confronted the file problems head-on. Most customer executives were amazed at the amount of work required to train personnel, revise procedures, and program applications.

The mixed emotions toward computers that prevailed in 1954 were illustrated by the cautious-but-determined attitudes in the insurance industry. Insurance companies were among the largest and most sophisticated business users of punched-card machines in the late 1940s and 1950s. Publicity about wartime developments, and later about the plans of Eckert and Mauchly for their UNIVAC, alerted the companies to the possibility of combining electronic computers with magnetic-tape storage. Given the high costs of nonreusable cards and of finding and keeping qualified accounting machine and clerical personnel, no promising alternative to punched-card systems could be overlooked. Thus in 1948, the Society of Actuaries had appointed a committee whose objective was to evaluate the applicability of computers to the insurance field. By 1952, it was clear to the committee that effective use of computers required extensive reorganization of insurance operations: procedures would have to become more centralized and some files consolidated.[123] The committee also concluded that a high percentage of the potential savings gained through an automatic tape-based system would result initially from the procedural reorganization, a sound investment whether a company opted for magnetic tape or chose to stay with cards.

Despite all the pros and cons of conversion, the insurance industry provided more than its share of tape pioneers, albeit with a certain degree of foreboding. At a late 1953 computer conference, the committee's chairman, a vice-president of the Metropolitan Life Insurance Company, still expressed concern for the integrity of tape files: "Perhaps the most radical idea which business is being asked to accept is the idea that a reel of tape can safely be used to carry information now being entrusted to visual card files. . . . The adequacy of tape for this purpose has not yet been sufficiently demonstrated. . . . We are not quite sure that [tapes] are sufficiently safe from accidental erasure, loss of information through breakage, kinks, dimensional instability, flaking, and other such occurrences. Nor have we been satisfied that the devices currently being employed to read and write on magnetic tape can be relied on to do so with accuracy."[124] Many of the insurance companies that led in the use of magnetic-tape data processing systems continued to maintain some of their files in punched-card form for many years, primarily because of the effectiveness of cards as a source of answers to random inquiries regarding the status of individual policies.[125]

Early IBM experience with the 702 revealed that because it lacked capabilities for reading one tape and writing another simultaneously or for overlapping either activity with ALU operations, too much of the system's time was devoted solely to tape operations. A few magnetic-core storage units of 1000 characters each were built on a special-engineering basis and furnished as tape-data buffering devices for customers particularly desirous of increasing the efficiency of their systems in that respect. While the overlapping of tape operations provided considerable improvement in cases where input and output record lengths could be closely balanced, buffers for tape were not nearly so effective as those included in the card machines and the printer, devices in which mechanical motion occupied a much larger fraction of input-output execution time. The ALU still had to deal with input and output records in sequence and was unable to execute internal instructions while so doing.

Moreover, the 702 became technologically obsolescent within a year of its announcement. The magnetic cores used for buffer storage had been considered for memory but, for reasons of cost·and schedule, cathode-ray tubes were chosen instead. In June 1954, by which time about fifty 702s were on order, IBM management decided to limit 702 shipments to the scheduled 1955 and early 1956 deliveries. Remaining orders would be satisfied with a faster and functionally improved successor machine that, as it turned out, would have magnetic-core memory.[126] This decision was a fortunate one; the CRT memories delivered in 1955 created maintenance difficulties in the field, and teams of laboratory-trained specialists had to be sent to customer premises to adjust them. By the time the CRT problems were isolated in autumn of 1955, the decision had been made to replace the CRTs in the installed 702s with magnetic cores.[127]

Fourteen 702s were delivered, including the first built, which was used in IBM's Poughkeepsie plant.[128] The fourteenth received a core memory in the factory prior to delivery; in the rest, the new memories were installed later in the field. The machine's novel system organization, formulated in the early phases of the TPM project, endured; the value of variable-length fields and records and of flexible input-output unit configurations was confirmed in the 702. The system was convincing and congenial to users of punched-card machines, and the problems of training and familiarization were minimized. The people who programmed 702s and descendant machines were typically not mathematicians but former EAM operators, and this circumstance unquestionably contributed to the early growth of the computer industry.

5.7 Later Vacuum Tube Computers

IBM's first three computer systems—the large-scale 701, the less powerful 650, and the large-scale 702—proved sufficiently responsive to customer requirements to justify continued development. The first of the three systems to be improved was the 701. In late 1953, Gene M. Amdahl, one of the IBM engineers reporting to Nathaniel Rochester, began spending some of his own time thinking about feasible improvements to the 701. While earning his Ph.D. degree at the University of Wisconsin, Amdahl had designed a practical computer capable of executing arithmetic in a floating-point mode of operation. Following graduation in the summer of 1952, he had joined IBM and had been assigned by Rochester to a character-recognition project. The reawakening of his interest in computer design was timely; various customers wanted faster machines, and Product Planning was assessing alternatives. About year-end 1953, Rochester made Amdahl responsible for a 701 improvement project and assigned some 701-experienced engineers to him. The first objective was to develop features that could be installed in the field, but mounting pressures for faster computers soon led to consideration of a 701 follow-on product. The simple organization of the 701 lent itself readily to improvement, and Amdahl's group exploited the opportunity. They designed circuits for new automatic floating-point operations, provided three index registers and their associated circuits, and essentially doubled the speed of multiplication and division by providing for two of the constituent add (or subtract) operations in the time formerly allocated to one. To control the enhanced 701, the programmer was provided with forty additional instructions, enough to more than double the repertoire. Drum-to-memory transmission rates were increased more than tenfold.

On 1 April 1954, Tom Watson, Jr., announced the appointment of T. Vincent Learson as director of electronic data processing machines (EDPM) in order, Watson said, "to coordinate the various aspects of this complicated work."[129] Learson, a fast-rising young executive, had been a member of the sales organization since joining IBM in 1935. He had come to WHQ in 1946 as head of a special sales department. Branch and district managerships followed in rapid succession, and in 1949 he had been given the post of EAM sales manager. For the year preceding his appointment to the EDPM directorship, he had been general sales manager. In his announcement, Watson explained that departments associated with EDPM would continue to function as before, with Learson acting as liaison among them.

Thus without altering the organization to reflect IBM's new and vital computer business, Watson, Jr., ensured that it would have the daily attention of an executive with the training and instincts to detect and solve business problems. Learson, an incisive decision maker, was the ideal choice to focus attention on EDPM matters requiring prompt action and close cooperation among the product planning, engineering, manufacturing, and sales departments. In November he was elected IBM vice-president in charge of sales and was succeeded in the EDPM position by Hurd. As we shall see, however, Learson made good use of his eight months as EDPM director.

The redesigned 701 was announced with CRT memory on 7 May 1954 as the IBM Type 704 Electronic Data Processing Machine. An October announcement made the 704 even more attractive to customers by offering magnetic-core memory (4096 words) and by doubling the former speed of tape. Magnetic-core memory obviated the need for regeneration cycles and thereby increased substantially the speed of internal operations. For instance, the two 12 microsecond regeneration cycles were eliminated from the ADD operation, reducing its execution time from 60 microseconds to 36 (see appendix D). In job-processing capability the 704 was rated two to twenty times faster than the 701, depending on the job mixture. Naturally the high end of the range applied only in jobs dominated by floating-point arithmetic operations. Such an operation was executed by 704 circuitry at the behest of a single instruction, whereas in the 701 it required the execution of a subroutine. Instruction-modification efficiency was enhanced by provision of three index registers.[130]

Deliveries of the 704 began in late 1955. Aided by the new instructions and faster tapes and drums, by new programming tools and an organization of users (see chapter 9), and by a dramatic increase in maximum memory capacity (deliveries of 32,768 word core memory units began in the spring of 1957), the system economically satisfied a wide variety of user requirements. Customer acceptance made it a resounding success, and 123 704s were produced in the period 1955–1960.

The IBM Type 705 Electronic Data Processing Machine was announced in October 1954 as a successor to the 702. Its 20,000 character magnetic-core memory, with double the capacity of the 702's CRT memory, was closely akin to the 4096 word memory of the 704 in capacity and speed. In the 705, however, the 704's thirty-six-bit word was reduced to thirty-five bits (representing five 705 characters) and the 12 microsecond memory cycle was "split" by a 5 microsecond processing interval between read and restore. Hence the character cycle during processing was 17 microseconds, compared to 23 microseconds for the 702. Moreover, by observing a convention that instructions be aligned with words, a whole five-character instruction could be obtained in one character cycle of the 705. The two improvements roughly halved the time needed for ALU operations. In addition, the 705 was equipped to read one record while writing another, which meant that the tape operations in typical file maintenance and sorting tasks could be completed in about half the former time.[131] Tape buffering similar to that provided in a special device for the 702 was available with the 705 system in a regular product, the 775 Record Storage Unit. Its use permitted overlapping of processing with tape reading and writing.

As in the case of the 704, the 705's improved performance could be provided at less than twice the former rental; at the same time, the price-performance gain increased the number of punched-card applications that could justifiably be converted to tape. Other improvements followed. In June 1955, IBM announced the Type 777 Tape Record Coordinator, which combined in a single unit the functions of tape control and tape buffer. Using it, a file maintenance application could be executed so that only active records were read into 705 memory. Inactive records (those with no matching transaction records) were bypassed. Several "TRCs" used in this way made possible an early form of multiprogramming since the tape files being interrogated could belong to entirely different applications. In September, the 705 II was announced, with memory capacity doubled again, to 40,000 characters.

The IBM Naval Ordnance Research Calculator (NORC) was demonstrated to the public in a formal ceremony on 2 December 1954 at the Watson Laboratory. Byron Havens's machine, started in October 1950 and supported soon after by navy funds of approximately $2.5 million,[132] was recognized for several years as the fastest computer anywhere (figure 5.5). Designed for Naval Ordnance on a research and development basis, NORC was characterized by high-speed, high-precision, floating-point operations, automatic address modification, and automatic checking of arithmetic accuracy. The system contained two word-length central registers for general use and three address-length index registers for use in automatic address modification. The instruction format provided memory-address fields for two operands and a result, but the program could elide memory references wherever register reference sufficed.

The NORC was endowed, as planned, with a 1-microsecond clock period and a CRT memory of 8-microsecond read-restore cycle. Adder circuits were fed decimal digits at a rate of one per microsecond from each operand register. Elaborate circuits for multiplication generated all nine multiples of the multiplicand, each digit by digit, and at appropriate times fed those multiples corresponding to the multiplier digits to a combining circuit which included twelve serial decimal adders. The twenty-six-digit product of two thirteen-digit factors appeared in 31 microseconds—twenty-six cycles plus five control cycles. The twelve adders simply hastened the familiar long-hand process of

Figure 5.5
IBM Naval Ordnance Research Calculator (NORC), designed and built at the
Watson Laboratory and demonstrated in December 1954. The special card-tape-
card machine and magnetic-tape units came from the Poughkeepsie laboratory
and the printers from the Endicott laboratory. NORC had the following
characteristics:

General - Decimal notation and operation; automatic floating-point and specified
    decimal-point operation.
Word Size – 16 digits plus check digit (64 bits plus 2 check bits) represent a 13-
    digit number with algebraic sign and a 2-digit decimal index, or one
    instruction.
Instructions – Three-address including automatic modification; 64 operations; one
    instruction controls the process of reading or writing a block of words
    on tape (including checking).
Computing Speed – 15,000 operations a second with automatic checking.
Arithmetical Unit – Two universal registers; 1,000,000 digits per second; addition
    time: 15 microseconds, multiplication time: 31 microseconds, division
    time: 227 microseconds, (excluding storage access, checking, etc.); serial
    multiple-generator.
Random-Access Storage – 3,600-word capacity; 8 microsecond access time.
Magnetic Tapes – 8 units; 71,500 characters read or written per second; recording
    in four parallel channels, 510 characters to the inch; capacity of one
    reel: 350,000–450,000 words, depending on the average block length;
    1.25 inches between blocks; time of acceleration to reading or writing
    speed: 0.008 second; reading in either direction, writing in forward di-
    rection; reading may include searching for a specified block; with cer-
    tain limitations, blocks can be rewritten between other blocks on a tape.

writing out all the multiplier-digit-times-multiplicand subproducts and then summing to complete a multiplication.[133] The NORC went to the Naval Proving Ground at Dahlgren, Virginia, in the summer of 1955.

In May 1956, a few weeks before his father died of a heart attack, Tom Watson, Jr., became chief executive officer of the company; he had been IBM president since January 1952. During the intervening years the product line had broadened and increased in complexity at a remarkable rate. Electronic data processing systems had become established alongside, not in place of, electromechanical products. Revenues had doubled, but electronics had brought new, strong competitors into the business machinery field. Throughout the period Thomas J. Watson, Sr., chairman of the board and chief executive officer, had maintained the monolithic management structure of IBM's preelectronic years. In the last week of November 1956 over 100 company

---

Figure 5.5 cont.

Printers - Two printers, only one operating at a given time; 150 lines printed per minute, with 120 characters (7 words plus 8 characters) on a line; printing interrupts computing (other than tape operations) for only 0.010 seconds of the 0.400-second print cycle; printing is checked by verification of check digit accompanying each word via the echo contacts of the printer.

Card-Tape-Card Machine - Separate machine operates at a rate of 100 cards a minute with four words per card; for card-to-tape operation, the check digit for each word on the input tape is evaluated by an independent reading of the card; for tape-to-card operation, each check digit is verified after the word has been punched into the card.

Control Console - Decimal display of contents of registers; controls for manual operation; indicator lights showing problem and calculator status.

Checking - Tape reading is checked by an x-bit count (modulo 4) accompanying each word, and by end-of-word and end-of-block characters; storage is checked by x-count verification whenever a word is read in, read out, or regenerated; number and instruction transmission is checked by the x-count; arithmetical operations are checked by an auxiliary computer operating on the basis of casting-out-9's; the registers are checked by the x-count and serve as a transition between the x-count and the arithmetic check.

Characteristics are reprinted from W. J. Eckert and R. Jones, *Faster, Faster: A Simple Description of a Giant Electronic Calculator and the Problems it Solves*, McGraw-Hill Book Company, Inc., 1955. The indicated 3600-word capacity was not normally used. A 2000-word mode, yielding wider spacing between storage spots on the cathode-ray-tube storage faces, was preferred.

executives met in Williamsburg, Virginia, to hear Watson, Jr., announce a reorganization emphasizing decentralization of responsibility. One of the new product divisions, the Data Processing Division, brought together all nonmilitary data processing product development and domestic sales of such products under Executive Vice-President LaMotte. R. L. Palmer was DPD manager of product development. A corporate staff with eight functions was established; W. W. McDowell, vice-president, headed the research and engineering function.[134]

The reorganization of November 1956 was a timely one, for the industry was on the brink of a new period of expansion fueled by the transistor (see chapter 10). The last of IBM's vacuum tube computers were announced the following year. In January 1957, the Type 709 Electronic Data Processing System superseded the 704. The 709, one of the most versatile vacuum tube computers ever built, included new table-lookup instructions that not only simplified conversions between differing codes and differing number bases but also facilitated decimal summation (something an accountant, under some circumstances, might prefer to a binary summation followed by conversion to a decimal result). Also with the 709 came an effective solution—in the form of a special-purpose computer called a Data Synchronizer—to the long-standing problem of how best to overlap input, output, and processing operations. (It will be recalled that Buchholz tackled the problem in 1952). The following is from the 709 announcement letter:

Up to three Data Synchronizers can be used, each containing two input-output channels. . . . Eight tape units can be attached to each of the possible six channels for a total of 48 tape units. A card reader, card punch and printer can be attached to one channel of each Data Synchronizer for a total of nine additional input-output units. Any combination of six input-output units, one per channel, can operate simultaneously. For example, a tape and and card reader may be reading while two tapes, a printer and a card punch are writing. During the transmission of information, the arithmetic unit is completely free for any arithmetical or logical processing.[135]

The orders directing a channel—called "commands" to distinguish them from 709 instructions—were provided by the main program when it meted out a task to a Data Synchronizer. In operation, the channels had a higher priority for memory cycles than the 709's main frame, which occasionally had to wait its turn and hence was forced to idle a fraction (typically small) of the time; in the idiom of the day, the channels were said to operate in a "cycle-stealing" mode.[136]

Among other innovations in the 709 was indirect addressing, a mode of operation whereby an instruction-contained address pointed to a memory word whose content was interpreted not as an operand but as the address of a desired operand. With the aid of indirect addressing, a programmer could use a table of stored addresses to systematize the program changes involved in the identical processing of records stored in two or more memory areas; such problems naturally arise where records are simultaneously being read, processed, and written— for example, the program may have to process record n in area A, record $n + 1$ in area B, and record $n + 2$ in area A.

The product life of the 709 was foreshortened by the sudden advent of the transistor era (see chapter 11). Thus its product history vividly illustrates one of the difficulties facing the developers of complex systems: various technologies, by their separate and unpredictable abrupt advances, make a hostage of every system and expose it to an uncertain future.

IBM's last-designed large-scale computer using vacuum tubes was the IBM 705 III Electronic Data Processing System, announced in September 1957. Compared to the 705 II, the memory was again twice as large (80,000 characters) and the magnetic-tape character rate increased more than fourfold. The 705 III also offered channels and indirect addressing, capabilities previously announced for the 709.[137] Among IBM's smaller vacuum tube systems were the disk-based 305 RAMAC, a small system announced in July 1956 (discussed in chapter 8), and the very small 610 Auto-Point Computer announced in September 1957 (discussed in chapter 12). While IBM's computers of the vacuum tube era were generally successful in meeting the expectations of the company and its customers, few went very far beyond the applications envisioned by their designers. Members of the first generation of computers, they helped found an industry based on the stored-program principle, but the limitations of vacuum tube technology tended to hold them back from widespread acceptance.

The one runaway success, the one stunning surprise to its designers, was the IBM 650. A series of enhancements, beginning with the alphabetic and printer capabilities, sustained its initial popularity. In May 1955, magnetic tape was offered to 650 users in the form of the 727 tape drive first used in the 702 system. A modest ten words of magnetic-core storage was provided, in a separate frame, to allow the necessary speed buffering between tape and drum; addressable by individual word, the core unit could also be used as additional, higher-speed main memory for improved computing performance. By July, the number of attachable tape units was increased from four to six and the capacity of the core unit from ten to sixty words. Still later in the year, this "high-speed storage unit" became the "auxiliary unit," housing the important additional features of index registers and automatic floating-point arithmetic.

An important enhancement to the 650 system, announced in September 1956, was the attachment of disk storage. Introduced at the same time as the 305 RAMAC system (see chapter 8), this 650 version had the additional capability of multiple-access stations, being equipped with three such mechanisms rather than the single-access device of the 305. Four disk storage units could be attached, each storing up to 6 million digits (3 million alphanumeric characters) in the 650 coding scheme. But improvements continued to 1959, at which time disk units of twice that capacity were made available; the same year, the available drum memory was doubled to 4000 words. In all, about 1800 650 systems were produced. As the first computer having a production run of more than a few dozen machines, it afforded thousands of people their first "hands-on" experience with a stored-program computer.[138]

6

Magnetic Tape

Magnetic tape studies in IBM. Magnetic recording in Poughkeepsie. Tape-handling devices. The need for better tape. First-generation tape machines. More and faster. Excursions from the beaten path.

Electromagnetism, first demonstrated in the early nineteenth century, underlies technologies of great importance to the computer industry. The use of magnetic materials to store information dates back to the start of this century when Valdemar Poulsen, a Danish physicist, invented a magnetic-wire speech recorder called the telegraphone.[1] In its September 1900 issue, *Scientific American* reported that Poulsen's device had been demonstrated at the Paris Exposition in that year. The apparatus shown there employed several hundred feet of fine steel piano wire wrapped spirally around a brass drum of 5-inch diameter. The magazine commented, "With this instrument, the sound as heard in the receiver is very distinct and is entirely free from the disagreeable scratching noises generally heard in the phonograph."[2]

The article explained that, for best results, the wire had to move at about 1.6 feet per second. For conversations lasting more than a few minutes, the drum and its single layer of wire could be replaced by a thin steel ribbon fed from one reel past the recording and reading station and wound layer after layer upon a second reel. The magnetic recording on one layer of tape was said to have no effect on that of adjacent layers. Also, "a conversation once magnetically recorded can be repeated indefinitely. Experiments which have been made show that a conversation can be reproduced from one to two thousand times without any perceptible diminution in clearness."[3]

One application mentioned in Poulsen's patent was remarkably accurate in its forecast of devices that appeared over half a century later: "The invention is of great importance for telephonic purposes, as by providing a suitable apparatus in combination with a telephone, communications can be received by the apparatus when the subscriber is absent, whereas upon his return he can cause the communications to be repeated by the apparatus."[4] Elsewhere, Poulsen described the quality of sound reproduction as excellent, asserting that "The later apparatuses not only reproduce in an extraordinarily correct manner what was spoken and sung, but also what was whispered into the microphone; even the slight sound of taking a breath can be reproduced."

In addition to high-quality reproduction, magnetic recording offered a combination of features that was unavailable through any other method: immediate replay, convenient editing, and apparently unlimited reusability of the recording medium. These features were in wide demand by the rapidly growing radio broadcasting and motion picture industries. But in the years before the advent of the vacuum-triode electronic amplifier, the relatively weak signals from Poulsen's wire and tape had tipped the scales in favor of Thomas Edison's phonograph. In addition, the bulkiness of the magnetic recordings, resulting from the need to move the wire at relatively high speed to obtain good speech quality, militated against its wide acceptance. It was reported in 1937 in the *Journal of the Society of Motion Picture Engineers* that "of the three known methods of recording sound, only the mechanical and photographic methods have come into wide use, while the magnetic method has been hardly touched."[6] Prior to World War II, magnetic recording was used primarily in dictating machines employing steel wire or tape. It was not generally considered adequate for the range of sounds required in radio broadcasting,[7] where the use of wax records containing mechanically formed sound tracks persisted, or in the "talkies" of the motion picture industry, which made exclusive use of photographic sound tracks on celluloid film.

A most significant development during the war was the introduction in Germany of plastic recording tape coated with iron oxide. A machine using such tape was reported to have a much wider frequency response than previous magnetic recorders, and the tape was far less expensive than steel wire or steel tape. Ease of editing, ease of splicing, and low noise level all added to the attractiveness of this tape. It was reported, furthermore, that recordings on the tape had apparently unlimited life, some having been used at Radio Luxembourg from 1941 to 1945 (during the German occupation of that country) with no sign of deterioration.[8]

The slow development of magnetic recording up to the mid-1940s is explained in large part by problems inherent in the behavior of magnetic fields in and around metals and other magnetic materials. Chief among these is the problem of controlling the size and shape of magnetized regions in the wire or tape in order to achieve the range of amplitudes and frequencies desired in the recording without objectionable distortion or background noise. Magnetic fields tend to "fringe," or spread out. This fringing seriously limits the minimum dimensions of regions that can be magnetized in a given polarity. It places corresponding upper limits on the highest frequencies obtainable at any given speed of the wire or tape. These limitations will be examined more closely in connection with digital recording.

The idea of recording digital information magnetically for accounting purposes had occurred some years earlier to inventive people concerned with the cost of cards, which, once punched, were not reusable for new information. One such person was IBM's most renowned inventor, James Bryce. In 1937 and 1938 he investigated the use of both magnetic surface coatings and laminated internal layers of magnetic materials for cards, to permit the recording of data.[9] He was assisted in this work by Ralph Palmer and several others in the Endicott laboratory. By 1941, considerable information on the usability of magnetic recording for accounting-related purposes had been collected. Some of the experiments, including a National Cash Register machine fitted with magnetic tape by Bryce, involved sensing information on a recording medium not in motion. In the case of the cash register, the magnetized spots on a tape "consisting of a sandwich of iron powder and glue between the strips of paper" were sensed by means of magnetic heads in a revolving drum.[10]

In a project initiated in the Endicott laboratory in 1941 at Palmer's request, considerable progress was made in the design of recording and sensing heads, amplifiers, magnetic media, and recording techniques. In 1943, Frank Hamilton designed a "balance pick-up carriage" for a ledger-posting machine on which the magnetically recorded balance was read from the stationary ledger sheet by means of a rotating head.[11] This experience would prove helpful, first in magnetic drum development (see chapter 3) and then in magnetic tape development.

6.1 Magnetic Tape Studies in IBM

In September 1945, a progress report was issued on the government-contract EDVAC project at the Moore School of Electrical Engineering of the University of Pennsylvania. In the report, which remained classified until March 1947, J. Presper Eckert and John W. Mauchly found it reasonable to expect "that the EDVAC will read from a steel wire or tape . . . and . . . output will be automatically recorded on steel wire."[12] Magnetic recording possessed at least three characteristics of great importance to the automatic computing system they envisioned.

First, it would make possible the recording and reading of data at speeds well matched to those of an electronic computer. Second, because the tape was reusable, it would minimize the need for manual operations corresponding to the loading and unloading of hoppers and stackers in punched-card systems; a high degree of automaticity could be achieved in the input-output subsystem. Finally, both the high recording density and the reusability of tape promised substantial cost savings in the storage medium and the space required to house it.

Wallace Eckert and John McPherson were generally aware, during the latter part of 1946, of the progress of the EDVAC project as well as of computer projects at MIT (Whirlwind), the Institute for Advanced Study at Princeton, and elsewhere.[13] In April 1947, a few weeks after the EDVAC was announced in the press, Eckert and McPherson attended an "electronics meeting" at IBM headquarters.[14] Also present were Ralph Palmer and Frank Hamilton from the Poughkeepsie and Endicott laboratories, respectively, Byron L. Havens from Watson Laboratory at Columbia University, and Halsey Dickinson of the Patent Development department at headquarters. According to information made available at the meeting, the EDVAC was to handle data to and from magnetic tape at a rate of 5000 binary pulses per second. McPherson noted in his record of the meeting that this rate compared with "the equivalent of eight hundred binary digits per second" for standard punched-card reading. Also considered were comments attributed to Edmund C. Berkeley, a senior methods analyst with the Prudential Insurance Company, that a million binary digits could be stored in a cubic inch on magnetic tape.[15] This amount of information, McPherson observed, would require 3000 punched cards (about 500 cubic inches). None of the figures mentioned was justified or further clarified in the record, but they reveal an appreciation of the impressive potential of magnetic tape.

Early reports of progress in electronic computers, starting with the ENIAC, had met with interest but nothing resembling trepidation on the part of IBM executives concerned with the development and marketing of punched-card machines. They were well aware that accounting-machine procedures centered on cards and that simply to convert the computing operations from electromechanical to electronic devices would have little effect on the amount or nature of equipment required. But the possibility of an alternative to the punched card itself, especially one with the capacities and data rates attributed to magnetic tape, had a far more sobering effect. The mood of the 17 April meeting suggested action. It was agreed that a project on magnetic recording should be established immediately and be made "the undivided responsibility of the people to whom it is assigned."[16]

The project was assigned to Hamilton in Endicott during May 1947. McPherson made it clear that he wanted the work directed toward demonstrating the practical use of tape in the specific environment of the "Super Calculator" (the SSEC, then still being completed in Endicott) and at perhaps ten times the speed of that machine's paper-tape punches.[17] Magnetic tape, of course, formed no part of the SSEC as planned; McPherson had merely seized on the SSEC as a convenient system in which to investigate the possibilities of magnetic tape. Furthermore, he wanted attention given to certain problems that appeared to be characteristic of magnetic tape as a file storage medium. The first of these was that an individual record on tape could not simply be replaced with a corrected record in order to update the file, as in the case of punched cards. With tape, the need to provide space for the insertion of additional records meant it would be necessary to read a file from one reel of tape and record it on another, appropriately modified by the insertion or deletion of records or the updating of fields in existing records. The need for frequent reproduction of entire files in this manner made it important to be able to verify the accuracy of recording "at the earliest possible point."[18]

Another problem was that access to the records of a magnetic-tape file was fundamentally a sequential, or serial, process. If the records were not in the order required for efficient execution of a particular job, the tape had to be "sorted"—that is, put into that order. This involved not only the problem of verification (because the tape had to be rewritten in the sorting process) but also the discovery of a suitably efficient procedure for accomplishing the sort. McPherson recognized the fundamental nature of the sorting and verification problems and wanted them to be considered from the start.[19]

There was, moreover, the need to develop a fast way to start and stop magnetic tape between reading or recording operations in order to take advantage of the high speeds of tape data transfer. If too much time were spent in acceleration and deceleration, the average speed would be unacceptably low; in addition, too much tape would be wasted between records, and the information capacity of a reel of tape would also be unacceptably low. This problem in particular was one McPherson believed should be confronted in a program that included the commitment to construct a working tape unit for attachment to the SSEC on the best possible schedule. He felt that such matters as highest achievable density of recording and data rate could be addressed after feasibility had been proved.[20]

As it turned out, the program in Endicott did not go as McPherson had requested. Well-designed experiments were performed and analyses made of alternative recording techniques. The project represented a high technical level of investigation. What was lacking was the recognition of the practical mechanism design and system problems that were highest on McPherson's priority list. He pleaded for recognition of these problems, in correspondence with both Hamilton and Endicott laboratory manager W. W. McDowell,[21] but for nearly two years the program in Endicott remained more exploratory than practical.

According to a December 1948 report from Hamilton's department, "The background of information obtained to the present time has been from drum recording [although] data obtained from drum will apply equally well to tape recording." The report went on to acknowledge that "tape recording presents additional problems such as rapid acceleration and deceleration, wear on the heads, and maintenance of small tape to head gap without chatter." The next report, prepared in August 1949, showed little change in emphasis, and the recording surface of chief interest was that of the cunife-wire-wound drum of the Magnetic Drum Calculator project. (See chapter 3.) Only one paragraph described experiments with tape-clutching methods, and no mention was made of tape-takeup or reel-clutching mechanisms.[22]

Several factors entered into the Endicott engineering organization's treatment of the tape project. At the time Hamilton was given the assignment, he was still testing the SSEC, an enormous project then involving more than fifty people in the laboratory. The SSEC was complex mechanically, and such mechanisms as its high-speed paper-tape punches challenged the best designers in the laboratory. Engineers who could have made a significant contribution to the solution of magnetic-tape problems were occupied with the SSEC and not readily available for such a project. By early 1948, Hamilton had been caught up in plans for the Magnetic Drum Calculator, and there continued to be little to motivate him on the magnetic-tape project.

In addition, the Endicott laboratory was not the most advantageous spot in IBM from which to view and evaluate magnetic tape as a threat to punched cards. At least as early as 1944, studies had been made there of an "increased-capacity card." Such an enhancement of the card product line was thought to have considerable competitive value. Many punched-card applications were based on files of records that used all eighty columns of the standard IBM card and really needed more. The additional fact that IBM's archcompetitor Remington Rand had a card with a capacity of ninety characters helped to sustain interest in the increased-capacity card program.

Furthermore, in a meeting at the Endicott laboratory in June 1946, T. J. Watson, Sr., had practically demanded a card "large" enough (in information-storing capacity) to permit its use as an original document rather than one into which only selected information from an original document could be squeezed.[23] The increased-capacity issue became so important that, late in the summer of 1946, McDowell informed the IBM executive vice-president that Engineering had decided "we should, for the most part, stop all development and tooling on all 80 column machines." At that time, a three-deck-high, 180-column card had been chosen—a card, that is, with its rows subdivided into three tiers (or zones) each containing 180 columns.[24] The choice failed to stick, and new configurations would continue to be considered for another five years. But by January 1947, the increased-capacity program was second only to the SSEC project in size and apparently second to none in importance.[25] Thus, in plans at least, the Endicott laboratory already had its new record-storage medium, which possessed all the advantages of the unit record then in use and presented none of the system problems associated with tape.

McPherson was not alone in his frustration with Endicott over the lack of a product-oriented tape program. In the summer of 1948, a memorandum from the Future Demands department pressed Hamilton for answers to the question of the practicality of magnetic-tape equipment for sorting, compared to corresponding punched-card machines. A report attached to the memorandum described in considerable detail a method for sorting by successive merging and rewriting of tape records from two reels—a method that was later used widely in magnetic-tape computer systems—and asked for estimates of the speed at which sorting could be done for realistic record and file sizes.[26] Answers were not forthcoming, in spite of repeated inquiries from the Future Demands department.

The urgency of planning for magnetic-tape devices was becoming increasingly evident to such engineers as Palmer and Rochester in Poughkeepsie, as well as to Dunwell and others in Future Demands. Early in 1949, however, Gordon Roberts, manager of Future Demands, was still protesting that without some information about the operating characteristics of tape equipment, he would be unable to proceed with his evaluation of tape versus cards. McPherson, meanwhile, found himself trying to explain to Tom Watson, Jr., a magnetic recording study in Endicott that lacked realism with respect to tape handling.[27]

By spring, it was becoming clear that Watson regarded the program as inadequate. He said as much in a meeting in May with McPherson, C. E. Love, Roberts, and other members of their respective Engineering, Sales, and Future Demands departments. The subject of the meeting, which went on for two days, was the competitive threat to IBM punched-card installations, specifically in the insurance accounting field, posed by the increasingly active computer-development groups. Chief of these was the Eckert-Mauchly Computer Corporation, which according to IBM's information had a contract to build UNIVACs for the Prudential Insurance Company, along with half a dozen other customers. Metropolitan Life Insurance Company was also known to be negotiating with other developers of special equipment, including magnetic-card and punched-tape machines designed especially for insurance accounting. It was a thoughtful meeting in which the special needs of the insurance application were well described and the advantages and limitations of both new and established media recognized. Watson, however, laid down a challenge by saying that the willingness of the insurance companies to underwrite the developments of relatively unknown promoters indicated that IBM was not doing a proper job for their industry.[28]

Meanwhile, the Endicott engineers had begun to respond to requests from Roberts and others at corporate headquarters for information on such matters as the amount of time required to start or stop a tape.[29] Shortly after the May meeting, McDowell submitted to McPherson a statement of the manpower needed to mount a program for the development of a variety of tape machines.[30] But it was too late; before the end of June 1949, the responsibility for magnetic tape had been assigned to the Poughkeepsie laboratory.[31]

Palmer and his engineers, who had been working closely with the Poughkeepsie factory on early 604 production problems, had been relieved of the day-to-day burden of that successful project and were receptive to new computer-related assignments. An intensive program of hiring engineers with advanced degrees, initiated early in 1949, had approximately doubled the number of electronics engineers in Palmer's group by the end of summer. While the total figure was still only about twenty-five, it was a significant start. By September, Byron Phelps had established a magnetic-tape engineering project that included James A. Weidenhammer from Endicott and a group of five or six mechanical engineers under him, plus another seven electronics engineers. The latter included J. A. Haddad, M. E. Femmer, R. P. Crago, and several others, most of whom, like Crago, had joined IBM during the summer of 1949. Weidenhammer's group was concerned with mechanisms for the physical handling of the tape (described in section 6.3), while the electronics people turned to the studies of magnetic recording and reading of information in digital form, and the associated electronic amplifiers and control circuits.

During August 1949, the BINAC—the first machine of the Eckert-Mauchly Computer Corporation—was demonstrated to visitors from many organizations.[32] Phelps, attending one of the demonstrations with Dunwell, noted that plastic magnetic tape was used in the system.[33] The tape machine was a rather uncomplicated device, manually controlled and similar in appearance to an ordinary sound recorder of the reel-to-reel type then coming into use for home recording. Parallel-bit recording was used, however, and Phelps thought there were five "channels" (or tracks) on the tape. The attendees were also given some information about plans for the UNIVAC, and it was revealed that thin metallic tape would be used on that machine. The reason, as reported later by UNIVAC engineers, was the greater uniformity and durability of metal tape (including resistance to fire) compared to the plastic tape then available. The tape actually consisted of a nonmagnetic metal, plated with a thin film of magnetic material. It was of half-inch width, and recording was in parallel-bit mode, all bits of each character being recorded or read simultaneously, on seven separate tracks. (There were eight tracks in all, one of the two innermost being used to record synchronizing pulses.) The recording density was 120 bits per inch, and the tape moved at 108 inches per second.[34]

In a symposium at Harvard in September 1949, Richard M. Bloch of Raytheon Manufacturing Company described the Raytheon electronic digital computer (later named Raydac) then being designed. He reported that the system employed four tape units with plastic, iron-oxide-coated tape 0.003 inch thick and approximately 0.05 inch wide. Information was recorded on six parallel tracks, at 100 pulses (bits) to the linear inch in each track.[35]

6.2 Magnetic Recording in Poughkeepsie

Phelps and his associates in engineering and planning in Poughkeepsie believed that IBM, too, should base its plans on oxide-coated plastic tape rather than plated metal tape. Their reasons are not well documented, but they included plastic's lower cost and lighter weight (for convenient handling); its increasing use in sound recording (hence commercial availability); and the ease with which it could be repaired by splicing. Safety apparently was also a consideration, the assumption being that an operator was more likely to be injured by the sharp edge of a metal tape than that of a plastic one.[36]

Before the end of September 1949, Phelps's group had begun to explore the electronic, magnetic, and mechanical problems that needed to be solved in order to use tape in a computer system as the counterpart of punched cards in an EAM installation. The main elements of tape recording and reading they had to understand have remained important considerations in the design of magnetic storage devices over the years.[37] There must be a magnetizable medium, and in the case of plastic tape this is usually a paintlike coating consisting of finely powdered iron oxide in an organic binder. The tape is passed at uniform speed over a magnetic "write head." This head is an electromagnet, consisting of a core of magnetic material on which is wound a coil of wire and which contains a very small gap in just the region where the tape comes in contact with the head. Without the gap, called an "air gap," the core of the head would form a closed magnetic circuit, and no magnetizing force would be applied to the tape. Because of the air gap, the magnetic field passes through the coating of the tape, and the oxide in the coating has the characteristic that it retains a part of the magnetization that has most recently been induced in it. When the tape is subsequently passed over a similarly positioned "read head," a signal voltage is induced in the winding of the head as each region of magnetic transition on the tape passes the air gap of the head (figure 6.1). Reading and writing may also be accomplished with the same head, referred to in that case as a "read-write" head.

The head is usually so oriented that the direction of the magnetic field at its air gap, and therefore the direction of magnetization of the tape, is parallel to the length of the tape; it is longitudinal. Recording could be and has been done also in the transverse direction (parallel to the width of the tape) or perpendicularly (with the poles of the head on opposite surfaces of the tape). Both of these geometric arrangements, however, presented requirements on head design, thickness of medium, and control of all dimensions that made them relatively unattractive for several decades. Some projects for which perpendicular recording was attempted in the initial stages will be described in chapter 8. The products we will consider here were all based on longitudinal recording.

The challenges of adapting a sound recording system to the recording of digital information were somewhat like those of adapting radio tubes to the job of counting pulses, a problem described earlier in connection with the 604 calculator. (See chapter 2.) In sound recording, it was desirable to be able to control the degree of magnetization of the tape to correspond to the "amplitude," or intensity, of sound being

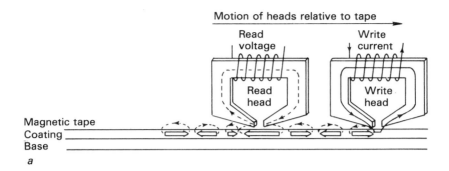

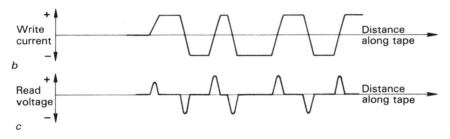

Figure 6.1
Digital magnetic recording and reading process. For convenience, the magnetic heads in *a* are shown as moving along a stationary tape, whereas in most tape-storage devices the heads are fixed and the tape moves. The solid loop with arrows, through the core of the write head, shows how the magnetic field due to the write current is diverted from the air gap to the magnetic coating of the tape, which offers an easier path. The wide arrows show the direction of residual magnetization in the coating after recording. The broken lines represent the residual magnetic fields, which during reading are diverted to a path through the read head. Each change in the residual magnetization along the tape, resulting from a write-current pattern such as that shown in *b*, produces in the read head a voltage of corresponding amplitude and polarity, as in *c*.

recorded. Small variations in the amplitude of the original sound should result in small variations in magnetization of the tape, and as the intensity of the sound increases, the extent of magnetization should increase in a smooth and continuous manner. It was undesirable to "saturate" the tape with magnetization at any time—that is, to magnetize it with such intensity that an additional increment of input current to the recording head would produce little or no additional magnetization.

Essentially the opposite requirements applied to magnetic recording of digital information, where it was desirable to record the largest possible change in magnetization wherever the bit coding of the data indicated that a signal was to be recorded and no change at all in response to ambient electrical "noise" or stray signals unrelated to the data. Magnetic saturation of the tape was sought because it would help to make the system less sensitive to such unwanted signals; and the recorded transitions should be abrupt rather than gradual—more like square waves than sine waves—in order to produce the sharpest and most accurately timed signals in the reading process.

Certain physical dimensions are critically important in magnetic recording, especially if it is desired to achieve a high recording density in bits per inch along the tape. In general, a computer system will demand a high data rate. For a given data rate, the distance between magnetic reversals can be increased by moving the tape faster. There are upper limits, however, on the speed at which the tape can be moved and controlled with sufficient precision, and there is a persistent demand for higher recording density. An early assumption of Phelps's group was that it would be important to record at a density of about 500 bits per linear inch.[38] The basis for this assumption will be discussed further on (p. 203). It was understood that in order to record at this high a density, both the head-to-tape spacing and the effective thickness of the magnetic coating on the tape would have to be considerably less than two-thousandths of an inch (2 mils). They observed that small head-to-tape spacing, in particular, was difficult to maintain in the presence of particles of dust or loose oxide. Furthermore, in order to read the information during a subsequent pass of the tape, the effective air gap in the head had to be small compared with 2 mils; otherwise, the reading head would "see" more than one magnetic reversal at a time, and the signals might cancel each other.

Designing and constructing heads of suitably small dimensions presented a serious challenge. Phelps's group not only undertook the design of experimental heads but also evaluated existing heads, such as those available from Cook Electric Company in Dayton and Brush

Development Company in Cleveland, Ohio. Femmer, Crago, and others concerned themselves at the same time with the design of writing circuits, sense amplifiers, and the associated logic and control circuits. Wayne D. Winger, who joined the project in February 1950, began investigating methods of erasing the tape prior to recording.[39] Much valuable information was also gained, especially by Phelps in visits to Endicott, from the recording work that had been done there in previous years and continued in support of the drum calculator project.

The difficulty of head design and fabrication, along with the apparently high cost of both heads and associated electronic circuits per track, dictated using as few tracks as possible and keeping the head configuration uncomplicated. Thus, in spite of their awareness that parallel-bit recording was employed in at least the Eckert-Mauchly and Raytheon computer systems, the IBM engineers continued for the first year or so to plan on serial-bit recording. This, they assumed, would require one or at most two tracks, depending on the recording system chosen.[40] Tape of quarter-inch width was used, this being a common size in sound recording and wide enough to accommodate at least two tracks.

A wide variety of recording techniques was considered.[41] One of the earliest to be studied was known in IBM as "discrete pulse" (DP) recording. Current pulses of short duration in either direction through the read-write head would produce magnetized spots of corresponding polarity in a tape previously demagnetized by an "erase" head. Since the current returned to zero between pulses, any desired sequence of 1's and 0's could be recorded by applying current pulses of the appropriate polarity. DP recording had the advantage of being self-synchronizing (not requiring a separate timing track) since the data track could be depended on to provide either a positive or a negative pulse of voltage in the read head at every possible bit time.

Attractive in its implications of low product cost, DP recording was pursued as one of the more reasonable alternatives until about mid-1950. It had, however, the undesirable characteristic that at higher densities of recording, adjacent bits interfered with each other; the amplitude, shape, and precise timing of a reading signal varied, depending on the pattern of 1s and 0s in which it occurred. As of May 1950, Phelps estimated the maximum density for DP recording to be 200 bits per inch, allowing a 100 percent margin of safety for reliable operation.[42]

A second technique given serious consideration from the beginning was known as "non-return-to-zero" (NRZ) recording. With this method, the current in the head was held constant in one direction for any bit period in which a 1 was to be recorded and in the opposite direction when a 0 was to be recorded. The current in each case was sufficiently large to saturate the tape magnetically. This method resulted in the minimum density of changes in magnetization along the tape for any combination of bits to be recorded. Lacking any semblance of self-synchronization, however, NRZ required a separate timing track. This requirement raised the possibility of introducing a long sequence of errors during reading, simply through failure to recognize a single signal from the timing track. Then, near Christmas 1949, according to notes he kept of the project, Phelps conceived of a way to combine the advantages of DP and NRZ recording.[43] His idea was to permit the current in the write head always to remain at tape-saturating value in the direction that had last been set until a 1 was to be recorded and then switch it to saturation level in the opposite direction. In this way, a change in magnetization—and hence in voltage, upon reading— would occur for each 1, and none would occur for a 0. Phelps named this unique version of NRZ recording NRZI, for "non-return-to-zero-IBM."[44]

Since a succession of 0s would produce a corresponding length of tape without changes in magnetization, NRZI still required a second track to ensure synchronization. But in the case of NRZI, the second track could be recorded by simply reversing the rule for the first— that is, letting a change in magnetization stand for 0 and no change for 1. This could be regarded merely as recording 1s and 0s on separate tracks. Since a signal would be present on one track or the other at every bit time, synchronizing pulses were available at the output terminal of an OR circuit for which the signals from both tracks were used as inputs (figure 6.2). The most serious problem of NRZ recording—the loss of synchronization for indefinite periods—was avoided.

Although the DP and NRZI methods were both contenders until mid-1950, the latter was rapidly gaining favor. By May it was estimated that a density of 500 bits per linear inch (bpi) could be achieved with this method, about as reliably as 200 bpi with DP recording.[45] The effective advantage of NRZI was reduced to 25 percent by the requirement for a second track, but the reading signals obtained using this method were much less affected by adjacent bit patterns than those from DP recording, at the respective densities mentioned.[46] Thus NRZI seemed to offer a greater opportunity for future increases in density of recording.

The NRZI method became even more attractive early in the autumn of 1950 when, partly to leave room for future improvements in tape capacity and data rate, the change was made to parallel-bit recording

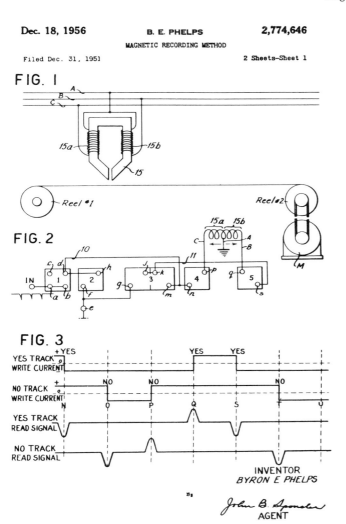

Dec. 18, 1956   B. E. PHELPS   2,774,646
MAGNETIC RECORDING METHOD

Filed Dec. 31, 1951   2 Sheets—Sheet 1

FIG. I

FIG. 2

FIG. 3

INVENTOR
BYRON E PHELPS

John B. Spenser
AGENT

Figure 6.2
NRZI method of recording. Writing current and reading voltage waveforms are
shown for a two-track system. Changes of magnetic polarity in the "yes" and
"no" tracks represent the 1s and 0s, respectively, of a serial stream of bits.

of seven-bit characters on tape. At the same time, tape of half-inch width was substituted for the quarter-inch tape that had been used for serial recording. Six of the seven tracks were used for the six-bit character code and the seventh for a parity-check bit. It was a simple matter to arrange the coding and the parity-check rule so that there would always be a 1 bit in one or more of the tracks. Since each character was thus assured of a synchronizing signal, it was unnecessary to provide a duplicate set of tracks for recording 0s.[47]

The NRZI method was employed, at a density of 100 bpi in parallel-bit recording, in the tape units of the experimental Tape Processing Machine described in chapter 4. The magnetic-tape project had been closely associated with the TPM ever since planning for that machine began in late 1949. Indeed, by November 1950, Phelps had engineering responsibility for the TPM as well as magnetic-tape devices. NRZI recording was also used in the early magnetic-tape computer systems IBM began delivering to customers in 1953. It was thereafter widely adopted by other manufacturers and was for many years the "work-horse" of tape-recording methods in the computer industry.[48]

6.3 Tape-Handling Devices

In the spring of 1949, before the responsibility for magnetic tape was shifted from Endicott to Poughkeepsie, W. W. McDowell asked James Weidenhammer (then still in the Endicott laboratory) to study the problems of handling magnetic tape: starting and stopping it rapidly, maintaining constant speed during recording or reading, controlling the supply and takeup reels — in short, providing all the physical conditions required to make the tape useful as a recording medium. Weidenhammer had joined IBM in 1938 after receiving the bachelor of science degree in mechanical engineering at Lehigh University and was assigned to Clair Lake's department. One of his earliest projects was designing the control-tape stepping mechanism for the ASCC, which Lake was building for Howard Aiken at Harvard. He remained in Lake's department during most of the time that machine was under construction but took leave of IBM for military service in 1943. Returning after the war, he joined a department headed by George Daly, another prolific inventor of punched-card machines.[49]

To carry out the magnetic-tape-handling assignment, Weidenhammer was removed from Daly's group and told to report directly to McDowell. He and two engineers assigned to help him had hardly begun to test experimental designs — the foremost being a hydraulically powered tape drive — when Ralph Palmer asked him to move to the

Poughkeepsie laboratory, which by then had been given responsibility for the tape program. Weidenhammer made the move to Poughkeepsie and by September had assembled a group of half a dozen engineers. Among them was Walter S. Buslik, who had been chief mechanical engineer at Avion Instrument Corporation, and who had experience in high-speed mechanisms with rapid starting and stopping requirements.[50]

In early plans based on serial-bit recording, each character was to occupy ten bit spaces along the tape: seven for the parity-checked character itself and three to allow switching time between characters.[51] A data rate of 7000 characters per second (cps) was considered adequate, being nearly as high as the internal data rate of the TPM with its 128 microsecond character cycle. It was assumed that recording at 500 bpi (corresponding to 50 characters per inch) was feasible; that the 140 inch per second (ips) tape speed required to produce the desired data rate at that density would pose no major problem; and that the tape could be accelerated from standstill to the desired speed in about 5 milliseconds (ms). Rapid, accurately controlled acceleration was necessary to minimize both the amount of magnetic-tape surface wasted in the interrecord gaps and the time spent in passing them by the read-write head. The assumption of 500 bpi density was apparently regarded as achievable for serial-by-bit recording until at least April 1950.[52] The speed of 140 ips, however, combined with the requirement to start or stop the tape within a period of 5 ms, was quickly found to present many problems to the designers of tape-handling devices. These difficulties are readily appreciated if one considers, for example, that the tape was to be brought up to the desired speed in the brief time specified, without significantly overshooting that speed even momentarily; that acceleration or deceleration was to occur without the tape's breaking because of its own inertia or that of any part of the handling mechanism; and that contact with the accelerating and decelerating device must not damage the tape or its magnetic coating.

Initially the group's tape-handling investigations employed both plastic and paper quarter-inch-wide audio recording tape. Paper-based tape, although less desirable than plastic because of its tendency to break under rapid acceleration, seems to have remained under consideration for a year or so, primarily because it was the only tape with which the "electrostatic clutch" would work.[53] This clutch depended on a phenomenon known as the Johnsen-Rahbek effect, after two Danish engineers who contributed much to its early development.[54] Theoretically, it represented a solution to the central problem of tape handling: getting the section of tape closest to the read-write head up to speed quickly. It had the further advantage of requiring no moving parts, its operation deriving from the electrostatic attraction that resulted when voltage was applied to a capstan, or driving wheel, over which the tape was passed.

The electrostatic clutch had been tried at IBM on a number of earlier developmental projects, but without success. One problem, apparently the main one, was that of controlling the rate of charge dissipation, which depended on variable conditions such as the relative humidity of the atmosphere. However, because Ralph Palmer had expressed a great desire to see this type of clutch incorporated in the tape unit, Weidenhammer gave it his best effort. The cause turned out to be hopeless. "I can still remember," he says, "over at High Street, we used to open the pipe on the steam radiator in order to get some steam into the room and make the thing work."[55]

As an alternative to the balky electrostatic clutch, Weidenhammer and Buslik began to experiment with a tape-driving device that became known as the "pinch roller."[56] In this device the tape was wrapped around roughly half the circumference of an idler pulley on each side of the read-write head. By displacing the axis of the right-hand idler pulley to bring it into contact with either a constantly rotating "forward capstan" or a nonrotating "stop capstan," the tape could be pulled toward the right side of the drive. Corresponding displacement of the left idler pulley would drive the tape to the left. Each idler was set to an intermediate position, contacting neither the drive nor the stop capstan, while the tape was being driven past the head or stopped by the action of the opposite idler. The device was driven by a "voice-coil" actuator, so named because of its similarity to the element used to vibrate a loudspeaker diaphragm. A complex linkage system was used in order to move each idler to the desired one of its three positions and to synchronize the actions of the idlers on both sides of the tape unit (figure 6.3). Clearances were small, tolerances were tight, and careful adjustment was essential. The pinch-roller system was adopted, however, and used first in a few experimental tape units and eventually in a series of tape machines that served IBM computers for nearly two decades.

At least as challenging a problem as the rapid starting and stopping of the tape near the head was the control of supply and takeup reels. Furthermore, since the tape was to be accelerated from standstill to its full speed of 140 ips in 5 ms, or decelerated in an equally short time, it was necessary to make provision for taking up the slack in the tape between the capstans and the reels. The tape would otherwise be broken because of the inertia of the loaded reels and the impossibility

Oct. 9, 1962   J. A. WEIDENHAMMER ET AL   3,057,568
                              TAPE FEED MECHANISM

Original Filed May 28, 1952   13 Sheets–Sheet 5

FIG. 10

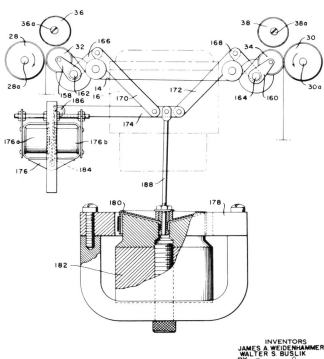

INVENTORS
JAMES A WEIDENHAMMER
WALTER S. BUSLIK
BY
ATTORNEY

Figure 6.3
Pinch-roller system for driving tape. The lightweight winding 180 is in the radial magnetic field of permanent magnet 182. When the coil is energized to impart an upward thrust to operating lever 174, one of two actions will result, depending on the position of armature 184, which is controlled by electromagnets 176a and 176b: (1) If the armature and lever 174 are in their right-most position, as shown, roller 34 presses the tape against forward-drive capstan 30, while roller 32 is free to turn, allowing the tape to move to the right. (2) If the armature and lever are in their left-most position, roller 32 presses the tape against reverse-drive capstan 28, while roller 34 is free to pass the tape leftward. If, in case 1, voice coil 180 is energized with current of opposite polarity, imparting a downward thrust to rod 188, roller 32 presses the tape against fixed capstan 36, called the forward-stop capstan, while roller 34 assumes its intermediate position and thereby removes the forward-driving force from the tape. Stopping in the reverse direction works in a similar manner, with armature 184 in the opposite position.

of starting or stopping them in the time provided for the corresponding acceleration or deceleration of the tape itself.

Other companies working with magnetic tape, including Raytheon and Eckert-Mauchly, were planning to use systems of multiple spring-mounted pulleys over which the tape was stretched back and forth, allowing tension to be maintained and providing a reasonably low-inertia combination of tape and pulleys so that acceleration could be achieved without breaking the tape. The tape reels were controlled in response to the positions of the pulleys, which could be sensed by a variety of methods.[57]

Because paper tape was still under consideration in spite of its relative fragility and because even cellulose acetate plastic tape was easily broken, Weidenhammer next sought a method that would provide a lower-inertia tape reservoir than that afforded by loops of tape wrapped around spring-mounted pulleys. Phelps had suggested blowing tape into suitably positioned loops by means of air jets, and a good deal of experimentation was done using this principle. It yielded poor results until, at Weidenhammer's request, one of his engineers fashioned a column of rectangular cross-section, adequate in its smallest internal dimension to accommodate the quarter-inch tape. Covered by a glass front plate, the column was roughly 2 inches in width and 2 or 3 feet long. By connecting the positive-pressure or exhaust side of a vacuum cleaner to the top of the column, a loop of tape was forced down into the column. The tape failed to descend very far, however, because the pressure inside the loop forced it against the sides of the column, where it tended to stick.

"We were missing one subtle point yet," said Weidenhammer of the experience many years later. When everyone else left for lunch, and things quieted down so that he could "think straight," he recalled, ". . . for some reason or other I just switched things around. I put the hose on the suction end of the vacuum cleaner . . . and fastened it to the bottom of this rectangular tube, and it worked much better. Because I found that if I held the sides of the loop a little bit away from the sides of the column at the top, then the suction at the bottom drew air down between the tape and the sides of the column so that there was no contact at all."[58]

It was indeed a subtle point. A pressure differential between the portions of the rectangular column above and below the loop might have been expected to have equal effect however it was created, but this was not the case. With higher-than-atmospheric pressure above the loop, multiple and complex additional jets of air would have been required to separate the tape from the side of the column, whereas with less-than-atmospheric pressure below the loop, inward leakage producing the effect of multiple jets at the upper edges of the column could be obtained merely by adjusting the angle at which the tape entered the column.

Vacuum columns were used in pairs: one associated with the tape supply reel and one with the takeup reel. This method of tape loop control worked very well from the start and even provided an additional benefit over springs and pulleys: The tape on either side of the driving capstan was held in essentially constant tension because, in principle, the force on the tape was not affected by its position in the column. Disregarding friction between the tape and the sides of the column, the total force (in pounds) on the tape at rest, regardless of its position, was simply the pressure difference (in pounds per square inch) multiplied by the cross-sectional area of the column (in square inches).

In order to start and stop the tape reels when the tape loop approached either limit of the vacuum column, two things were needed: a rapid means of applying turning or braking force to each reel and a means of sensing the position of the tape in the column. The first of these requirements had been met even before the invention of the vacuum column by means of electrically controlled magnetic clutches. Filled with a mixture of magnetic iron powder and graphite, which stiffened in the presence of a magnetic field, the clutches provided the smooth buildup of torque required to get the reels moving without causing tape damage through the slippage between layers that might result from too abrupt a start or stop. Buslik's earlier experience at Avionics had included work with magnetic clutches, and his knowledge of their characteristics was of great benefit in the design of the early tape machines.

To sense the position in its vacuum column of the tape loop on either side of the read-write head, a method using pressure-sensitive switches was devised. Since the air pressure above the loop would always be atmospheric and the pressure below the loop less than atmospheric, a pressure-sensitive switch recessed in the wall of the column would provide a signal as the loop passed it. The switches were improvised by drilling holes at appropriate positions in the rear walls of the columns and covering them with flexible diaphragms. Each change of pressure caused a diaphragm to flex, actuating electrical contact in the circuit controlling the reel clutches. Two very early experimental machines incorporating the vacuum columns are shown in figure 6.4. The tape-handling mechanism actually used in the TPM and in the first tape units IBM delivered to customers is illustrated in figure 6.5.

Figure 6.4
Two early laboratory-model tape units incorporating the vacuum-column tape-handling device

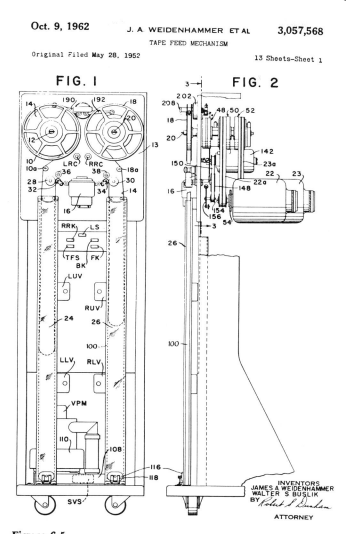

Oct. 9, 1962   J. A. WEIDENHAMMER ET AL   3,057,568

TAPE FEED MECHANISM

Original Filed May 28, 1952   13 Sheets-Sheet 1

Figure 6.5
Mechanical portion of an early tape unit. The tape-handling mechanism is similar to those used in the TPM, NORC, and 701 computer systems.

Only a few experimental tape drives were built for quarter-inch tape. After September 1950, IBM's tape drives were all designed for tape of half-inch width, or greater, in the case of special machines to be described. The change to half-inch tape was partly to provide for future increases in recording density and data rate. At least as important a consideration was the desire to reduce the required tape speed in the earliest tape units—those for the TPM—to less than the 140 ips originally specified.[59] Indeed, the use of parallel-bit recording essentially required a reduction in tape speed because of the greater sensitivity of that recording mode to the effects of uneven tape motion. The highest-speed tape drives used on the TPM operated at 70 ips, and those first put into production (for the 701 computer) operated at 75 ips. Interest in paper-based tape had declined after the electrostatic clutch was abandoned, and the first tape drives IBM produced commercially were supplied with tape having the cellulose acetate base previously mentioned.

The vacuum-column system of tape control became one of the most widely used inventions in the history of the modern computer. It was adopted for use in high-performance tape drives by all, or most, of the large-scale computer manufacturers, and many thousands of copies of the vacuum-column tape machine were in use by the early 1960s, a time when the number of all installed computers was still in the low thousands.

6.4 The Need for Better Tape

The early problems with tape went beyond its tendency to break under tension. The sound-recording tapes available in 1950 and 1951, when the TPM and Defense Calculator were under development, had never been required to pass the kinds of quality tests essential for digital recording. Even at the recording density of 100 bits per linear inch— very low by the standards of later decades—a spot from which the oxide was missing or a nonmagnetic foreign particle extending for as little as 5 mils along the tape could result in failure to record and subsequently read a bit correctly. Such defects did occur frequently in the tapes of the very early 1950s, and they presented a severe problem. By contrast, the same defect in sound recording would likely pass undetected, its effect lasting less than 1 percent of a single cycle of a tone at 1000 hertz. Clearly, there was a need to concentrate on improving the quality of tape for digital recording.

Victor R. Witt joined IBM in March 1951 after ten years' experience at Western Electric and Sperry Gyroscope companies. His first assignment was to evaluate all the magnetic tape then available and determine which kinds were best, especially for the Defense Calculator (701), a project rapidly becoming a commitment on IBM's part. Witt designed and constructed a test device whereby the tape could be scanned for small defects. Armed with information obtained through the use of this instrument, he would visit tape manufacturers and point out to them tape quality problems they had never suspected. Many of his visits were to IBM's main tape supplier, Minnesota Mining and Manufacturing Company (3M, makers of "Scotch" Tape). Other vendors included Audio Devices, Inc., and Reeves Soundcraft.[60]

A long period of cooperation with tape manufacturers, especially 3M, ensued. A wide variety of defects or potential defects were of concern, and these might occur in either the coating or the acetate base, which 3M obtained from du Pont. Witt remembers meeting with representatives from both companies at the IBM laboratory in Pough-keepsie to discuss the situation. At the time, the tape requirements of the computer business were small indeed compared with the total production of 3M or du Pont, and it is a testament to the spirit of enterprise and cooperation of those companies, as well as to the patience and diplomacy of IBM and other computer manufacturers, that high-quality magnetic tape became available approximately as it was needed by the data processing industry. As plans for additional computers beyond the 701 became firm, IBM established a tape testing facility in Minneapolis. Known as the IBM Tape Center, it turned out its first reels of tested tape in March 1955. Many improvements were made, both in the plastic tape itself and in the magnetic coating. In 1956, Mylar (du Pont trademark) was substituted for the original cellulose acetate base, to provide greater strength and dimensional stability. Improved binders were introduced, in 1959 and subsequently, to pro-vide the greater durability of magnetic coating required as the speed and acceleration of tape increased with higher-performance new tape units.[61]

6.5 First-Generation Tape Machines

The NRZI recording method, and the pinch-roller tape drive with its vacuum columns, served IBM computer systems through a long series of improvements in overall tape machine performance. The first IBM tape units produced in quantity and made available commercially were the Type 726 tape units used in the 701 computer system, produced in 1953. They operated at 75 ips, with a tape-recording density of 100 bpi.[62] Weidenhammer's group had substantially exceeded both of these figures, not only in experimental models but also in eight high-performance tape units constructed for the Naval Ordnance Research Calculator (NORC), which was under construction at the Watson Laboratory in New York City concurrently with the TPM and the engineering model of the 701. (See chapter 5.) Each NORC tape machine operated at 140 inches per second and just over 500 bits per inch.[63] As Byron L. Havens, the manager of the NORC project, later explained, "This gave it the speed of about 70,000 decimal digits per second, which at that time was far faster than any other operation of which we knew. The tape drive itself was developed at Poughkeepsie, and Ralph Palmer was the fellow who recommended that we try to make them work at that speed and density."[64]

The high data rate of the NORC tapes was achievable partly because the purely numeric data format of the system minimized the effects of character skew, a factor limiting the recording density and tape speed of the commercial machines. Character skew in a machine such as the TPM—or in the 701, which also recorded data in seven-bit groups—resulted from minor misalignment or distortion of the tape that might occur when it was accelerated rapidly. If the tape stretched while being brought up to speed, the bit at one end of a character or bit group (one edge track) would arrive at the read head too early relative to the arrival of a bit at the opposite edge of the tape. Since parallel recording relied on the sensing of all the bits of a character within a specified time interval in order to avoid their being mistaken for bits from adjacent characters, skew could result in confustion of timing and thus cause errors in reading (figure 6.6).

Because the NORC was a purely numeric, decimal machine, only four tracks were required for representation of its binary-coded-decimal digits. (No parity-bit track was used; a check digit was provided at the end, or seventeenth-digit position, of each word.) The width of tape occupied by the recording was therefore much less than that for alphanumeric characters, and skew was much reduced for that reason. Furthermore, by judicious encoding and allocation of tracks to the individual bits of the decimal digits, it was possible to ensure that a reversal of magnetization occurred in one of the two innermost tracks for each character.[65] All of these characteristics helped make it possible for NORC to achieve reliable operation at 70,000 digits per second.

There were other important tape requirements besides higher data rates to be met in the design of tape machines. For one thing, the capability of rewinding the tape at high speed was becoming very important. This was especially true in the case of the TPM, or its successor the 702, and the experimental sorter. These machines were

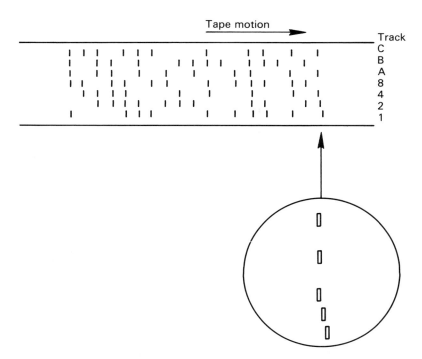

Figure 6.6
Illustration of NRZI recording on seven-track magnetic tape. Each mark represents a change in magnetized state and signifies a recorded 1 bit. The horizontal spacing of bits is shown disproportionately large. Each vertical column of bits represents a code group, or character, and the parity-check bit in this example is chosen so that the total count of 1 bits is odd. The first bit of each character to be sensed by the read head produces the timing pulse for that character. The effect of character skew is exaggerated in the enlarged view of the first character, at right. In this case, the bit in the bottom track would initiate a character gate, a voltage of fixed duration long enough to admit the remaining bits of the character but short enough to exclude the first bit of the next character. Excessive skew could prevent proper character separation and cause errors to be indicated in reading.

designed to deal with files of data somewhat like those of a punched-card installation, where cards were placed in a hopper, read or punched in sequence, removed from the stacker, and again placed in a hopper for the next operation. The high-speed rewind feature for tape was basic to its gaining a competitive edge over the card system in business applications. In the engineering or scientific problems to which the 701 computer was typically applied, by contrast, tape was often used as auxiliary storage (that is, as an extension of main memory). Shorter lengths of tape were provided, the maximum being 1400 feet per reel as against a standard 2400 foot reel for the 702, and it was more important to be able to read backward (to recover and further process intermediate results) than to rewind at high speed. The 701 tape units therefore were designed to read in either direction but lacked the high-speed rewind.

From the start, Dunwell had been adamant about the need for high-speed rewind on the TPM tape units. While praising the general design and performance of one of Weidenhammer's early experimental tape drives, he took the opportunity to tell Palmer, "The demonstration was a reminder that net tape handling speed must take into account the time required to rewind. This is true because the operation of the processing machine will usually be followed by some other operation on the same tape for which it must be rewound."[66]

High-speed rewind was by no means an incidental capability of the tape-handling mechanisms developed for the TPM and the 702. In order to achieve a rewind speed of 500 inches per second in the tape drives of the 702, the tape was automatically withdrawn from the vacuum columns and stretched almost directly from reel to reel. The driving capstans were retracted, the read-write head was moved out of the way, and only a pair of idler pulleys remained in the tape path. The rewind problem was essentially that of accelerating the file reel to high velocity while the machine reel followed with just enough damping to prevent its overshooting when the driving reel slowed down. It seems straightforward enough, but the tapes of the time were easily broken. More than one engineer associated with magnetic tape projects in those days recalls the jarring sequence that followed a sudden breakage of tape during rewinding: a loud flapping sound, the air suddenly filled with short pieces of tape, and these ultimately coming to rest in a random distribution on the floor. A potential customer observing the results would undoubtedly have given second thought to committing important business files to tape without assurance that such disasters rarely, if ever, occurred.

Many techniques were explored and a good deal of effort applied to solving the problems one by one before the rewinding process was considered ready for use in a product. But by September 1953, when the 702 was announced, the high-speed rewind was included among the features described to customers. It had also been possible, through other improvements in the tape drives, to increase recording density to 200 bpi—and hence 200 characters per inch. Tape length was increased to 2400 feet, a figure generally adopted and retained thereafter throughout the industry. The doubled data rate (15,000 cps), more than trebled reel capacity (around 5 million characters), and high rewinding speed made the Type 727 tape units of the 702 very attractive. Along with the retracting tape-drive capstans, essential for the high-speed rewind, came significant improvements in the ease with which an operator could install new reels, attach the tape, and remove the reels from the machine. Because of its desirable features, this tape unit was soon made available for use in the 701 computer system and was the standard tape machine for the 650 and for other 700 series machines introduced over the next several years.

The tape subsystem, comprising the Type 727 tape units and an electronic control unit through which as many as eight of the tape devices could be attached to the computer, had a number of features designed to increase the reliability of magnetic-tape storage operation. These and subsequent innovations contributed importantly to the popularity of IBM's tape subsystems for many years. One such feature, introduced with the Type 727 tape units, made it possible to correct single-bit errors and detect certain multiple-bit errors that occurred in reading information from tape. It had been discovered that by "resetting" the current in each track of the seven-track head to a given polarity after writing a record (a related group, usually of 200 or more characters), a "longitudinal" check character for that record would be recorded. This came about because, in NRZI recording, the head for any track in which an odd number of 1s had been recorded would be carrying current in the "on" direction prior to resetting. Only in those tracks, therefore, would an additional change of magnetic polarity signifying a 1 occur in resetting the heads. The longitudinal check character therefore contained 1 bits in just those track positions necessary to make the total count of 1s in each track—including the check character—even. This meant further that upon reading the character, an even number of 1 bits should be detected in every track. Since each character included a check bit (that being the purpose of the seventh track) that would indicate any character in which an error was detected on reading, and since the logitudinal check provided an indication of any track containing an error, an operator had sufficient information to correct a single-bit error by inverting the 1 or 0 value of the bit (in memory) corresponding to the track and character positions thus exposed.

Since this error-correcting scheme was manual and could be employed only by programming the computer to stop and permit the operator to intervene, it was not likely to be widely used. Programmers were aware, or rapidly becoming so, that the all-important objective was to keep the machine running rather than allowing every untoward event to hold up the entire process while manual remedies were applied. For this reason, the cross-checking feature of the 727 tape system was more often used for additional error detection than for error correction. The longitudinal check made it possible, for example, to detect an error involving any number of the bits of a single character. Far more automatic than manual intervention, and therefore more efficient, was the recommended practice of programming the computer to cause rereading of any record for which a tape-reading error had been detected. It had been found in the laboratory, prior to introduction of the 702 system, that an error detected in reading tape was correctable in a very large percentage of cases by one or more repetitions of the reading of the record involved. Largely for this reason, the 727 tape unit was designed with the ability to execute a "backspace" command, which involved moving the tape backward to the preceding interrecord space in preparation for another reading attempt.

Backspacing, in fact, was a feature sometimes used in writing on tape as well. Errors could not always be counted on to disappear upon rereading or to limit themselves to the single-bit size correctable with the cross-checking feature. Therefore, it was highly desirable to know at the time of writing a record that all the information had been correctly recorded on the tape. Limited checking was afforded by circuits, which indicated whether the writing current in the heads conformed to the even-count parity check required of each character, and the recording of a record would be repeated under program control if this check indicated an error. In some applications, the importance of ensuring accurate recording on the tape itself, at the time of writing, was sufficient to justify using the sequence write, backspace, read-check, for every record transferred to tape. However, since this procedure consumed at least triple the time required for the fundamental process of recording, it was not considered a permanent solution to the problem of checking tape writing.

A much better solution to the problem was provided by the invention of a read-write head containing separate recording and reading gaps placed sufficiently close together to permit the reading for parity checking of every record as it was written. Commonly called the "two-gap head," it was designed so that both gaps could fit within the interrecord space at the same time and still provide enough shielding to prevent the powerful magnetic field due to recording from interfering with the much lower-level signals being read (figure 6.7). This head represented a significant improvement in tape unit design. It was first incorporated in the 729 tape unit, which was a prominent feature of the 709 computer, introduced in January 1957. Thereafter it became a standard feature of all tape machines introduced by IBM.[67]

The two-gap head permitted improvement in the reliability of recording in more ways than one. Besides providing assurance that each character recorded could be read once correctly, the use of separate air gaps for reading and writing allowed the recording of a track whose width exceeded that of the reading head. The use of the "write wide, read narrow" technique avoided the introduction of certain unwanted signals, such as those resulting from incomplete erasure, that might be introduced through imperfect tape alignment when the reading width was exactly equal to the recording width in each track.

Even more significant was the opportunity the two-gap head provided to detect marginally reliable recording at the time it occurred. This detection was accomplished by the invention of an electronic system employing two-level sensing of signals during reading—whether reading to check recording or reading a previously recorded tape to retrieve the information. By comparing the signals detected at two levels of reading sensitivity during recording, a bit recorded with only marginal signal strength could be identified: It would pass correctly through the low-level detector but fail to pass through the high-level detector. Such marginal recordings could be corrected by backspacing and recording an entire record one or more times, as required, until the test was passed. Two-level sensing was also used, in slightly different ways, by various computer systems to provide useful information about the reliability of the signals from the tape during a reading pass.[68]

Some IBM computer systems employed an unrecorded area several inches in length along the tape as an indication of the end of file or end of tape. Other systems, principally those operating in the binary-coded decimal mode, used a special recorded character called a "tape mark." Still other systems used both. With few exceptions, coding problems were worked out to provide reasonable compatibility among the systems. One of the strangest exceptions was the use of odd-count and even-count parity checks, respectively, in the 701 and 702 and thereafter in the successor systems of each. This peculiarity had its

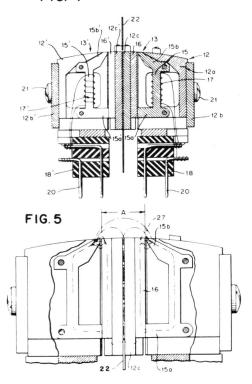

Jan. 26, 1960   V. R. WITT ET AL   2,922,231
MAGNETIC TRANSDUCER

Filed April 26, 1956   2 Sheets—Sheet 2

Figure 6.7
Two-gap magnetic-tape head, as illustrated in a patent of V. R. Witt and R. C.
Bradford. The actual distance between the writing and reading gaps in this head,
corresponding to dimension A in figure 5 of the patent, was 0.3 inch.

origins in the inability of Phelps, Rochester and Buchholz to agree on a code for the 702. Phelps wanted to use an even-count check. By excluding the all-zeros character, he could then depend upon the presence of at least two 1 bits in every character on tape. Since changes of magnetization (which represented 1 bits on tape) were the source of character-synchronizing signals, he had achieved a more reliable means of synchronization than was obtainable using a code that included several characters of a single 1 bit each.

It would be easy enough in the 702, in which fewer than sixty-four distinct characters were needed, to exclude a single six-bit combination. The character "zero" had only to be moved to the position in the code table that would have been occupied by "ten" had such a single character existed; appropriate circuit modifications in the arithmetic and logical unit would cause the ten to behave like a zero. Both Rochester and Buchholz, however, felt strongly that to exclude even the single all-zeros combination would be to sacrifice desired generality in the tape-storage subsystem. In fact, in the 701 computer it was important that all six-bit "characters" be usable because six such characters were combined to form each binary word on tape. That logic notwithstanding, the engineers of the 702 program supported Phelps's proposal, and the 702 had even-count checks both transversely and longitudinally on tape, while the 701 used only a transverse odd count.

6.6 More and Faster

By 1957 many improvements in reliability and in convenience of use had been made in IBM tape drives, but the increase in raw performance was not spectacular. Density had doubled to 200 bpi since the introduction of the 701; the speed of the tape remained at 75 ips, and the resulting data rate was 15,000 cps. Competitive pressure had been moderate. Rivalry among computer companies during the early 1950s had emphasized central processing capability and the speed, capacity, and reliability of main memory; tape performance had only to be good enough to keep the overall system in reasonable balance.

A significant competitive threat to IBM's tape subsystems was felt at the end of 1956, however, when the Datamatic Corporation revealed plans for its Datamatic 1000 computer with tape drives reported to handle information at a rate of 60,000 decimal digits per second. This was four times the rate of IBM's commercially available tape machines, at least for purely numeric information. The Datamatic Corporation had been established in 1954, jointly by Raytheon Manufacturing Company and Minneapolis-Honeywell Regulator Company, Raytheon having lost interest in the computer business after building Raydac and Honeywell having developed a new and growing interest. According to computer historian Saul Rosen:

Built on a grand and expensive scale, the Datamatic 1000 had enough air conditioning to cool not only the computer but also the room in which it would be installed. Its most interesting feature was its tape system, which used three-inch-wide magnetic tape and fixed-length blocks such that the interblock gap equalled the block length. When reading in one direction, the interblock gap was the recording area that was used when reading in the reverse direction. The use of three-inch-wide tapes and the existence of no waste space in the interblock gaps combined to permit the storage of very large files of information on relatively few tapes.[69]

Instead of spreading a character across the tape on seven tracks as had been the practice with half-inch tape, Datamatic recorded a pair of words in serial-by-bit fashion on each of thirty-one tracks simultaneously; the recording of a "block" was completed when the sixty-two words had been written in this way. The high data rate, compared to that of the IBM 727, was obtained entirely through the use of wider tape and more tracks. "By the end of 1957, when the first Datamatic 1000 was delivered, IBM had been delivering 705s for two years, and the 1000s were too late and too high priced for the market at that time," adds Rosen.

Although the Datamatic tape subsystem did not represent a technological threat (IBM's NORC tapes had a higher data rate), it seemed to require a response in the commercial product line. IBM, of course, had a considerable commitment to half-inch tape; by December 1956 the company had installed roughly a hundred 700 series machines and was beginning to deliver 650s that had been enhanced by the attachment of magnetic-tape units. Both the IBM marketing and engineering teams favored upgrading the performance of half-inch tape— upon which the files of many customers were now recorded—rather than pursuing higher performance through the medium of wider, and therefore incompatible, tape.

This preference was not based on a belief that IBM could afford to ignore either the opportunities that might lurk in wider tape or the competitive pressure that might come from another company's introduction of a product in that area. In fact, a project code-named Tractor was started early in 1957, under contract with the government, to study the technological requirements of a tape system to record and read data at 1.5 million cps—one hundred times the rate of the

727 tape units. (That development will be described later in this chapter.) In such a program, there were no restrictions on tape width or compatibility with existing files. However, since the challenge posed by the Datamatic 1000 represented less than a fourfold improvement in average (alphanumeric) data rate, it seemed entirely reasonable for IBM to respond by upgrading the performance of its half-inch tape.

There already existed a plan to increase the speed of the 729 tape unit by 50 percent, to 112.5 ips, and the data rate correspondingly to 22,500 cps. This would serve two purposes: to provide the soon-to-be-announced IBM 705 Model III with a tape subsystem more in balance with its internal performance and to offer competition to a new UNIVAC tape drive, which, according to rumor, would operate at 20,000 cps or faster. After the Datamatic announcement, this plan was extended. It was decided to retain the objective of 112.5 ips, but to leapfrog the tape unit that was to have been the 729 Model II, and introduce a 729 Model III with data rate of 62,500 cps achieved by increasing density to 556 bpi.

This turned out to be an overly ambitious plan, for a number of reasons. At the outset of the original 729 improvement program, it became clear that to increase the tape speed by 50 percent would require a faster and more powerful actuator than the voice-coil linkage that has been described to operate the pinch rollers. An intensive study of alternatives by the tape-devices group resulted in a device known as the "prolay," a configuration of electromagnets with their poles arranged in such a way that any of three stable positions of a common armature bar could be selected according to the combination of coils energized (figure 6.8). Each of the two pinch rollers had its own prolay, from which it derived its "go," "stop," or "neutral" positioning.[70] It was a deceptively simple, high-speed, high-precision mechanism of the type that required extensive testing to ensure that problems such as sticking and corrosion were discovered in time to solve them. Unfortunately, the 729 III had been committed to announcement on a schedule that did not adequately allow for such problems.

The tape unit had other important new design features. One was the "air head," so called because its surface was carefully shaped to permit a thin film of air to be drawn between it and the moving tape. The purpose of this design was both to reduce wear of the head due to abrasion by the tape's oxide coating and to provide greater uniformity of head-to-tape spacing, an improvement found to be important in increasing the density of recording by the desired factor of more than two.[71] Another new design feature was the complete change to

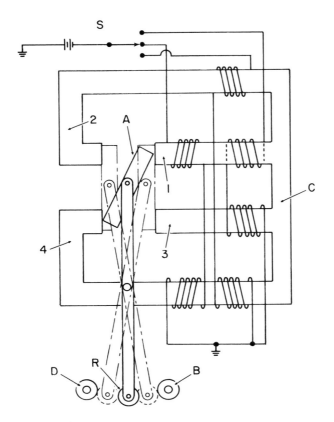

Figure 6.8
The "prolay," an improved actuator for the pinch roller. This schematic diagram
illustrates the principle of operation only and is not representative of the physical
configuration of the device. The core C is of metal which provides a good magnetic path, and the coils of wire wound on it can be energized with current in
several combinations. With switch S in its center position, legs 1 and 4 become
south and north magnetic poles, respectively, holding armature A in a diagonal
position and roller R in the neutral position. Tape passing over the roller will
then be in contact with neither drive capstan D nor brake capstan B. Each of the
other positions of switch S will result in a north-south pole pair on the right or
left, forcing the tape into contact with one of the capstans. Each tape drive required two prolays: one on the right and the other on the left side of the read-
write head. (Figure adapted from U.S. Patent 3,007,086 of H. K. Baumeister.)

transistor circuits from the vacuum tube circuits used in all previous tape units. While the change did not present a special technical problem, it was time-consuming. But the day of the transistor was at hand, and Ralph Palmer was anxious to get transistors into the computer product line. The tape drive, with a relatively small number of electronic circuits, was a logical proving ground for transistors, which were still hard to obtain in quantity with the desired uniformity of electrical characteristics.[72]

In a normal new-product program, with a year or two of design and model testing prior to announcement and production scheduling, it is unlikely that any single problem caused by these new design features would have been a "show stopper." In combination, however, the problems were serious indeed, and the 729 III project was to be a traumatic experience for all who took part in it. Palmer had wanted the fast new tape unit to be introduced with the 705 III, a powerful new version of the 705 (and a 702 descendant) for which a September 1957 announcement date had been established. In August, N. P. Edwards, then on Palmer's staff at Data Processing Division headquarters, led a committee to evaluate the risk that announcement of the 62,500 character per second tape unit the following month would entail. In mid-August, Edwards reported to McDowell that a data rate of 45,000 cps was as high as could be safely promised by that time and that skew was the factor that would limit reliable operation at the planned higher rate. In spite of that warning, the 62,500 cps specification and the September announcement schedule were maintained.[73]

By early spring 1958, during the testing of early production models of the 729 III, a number of significant problems had been uncovered. The tape was becoming wrinkled in places due to the high-speed operation of the pinch rollers. For this reason and because of loose oxide particles on the tape, more than the allowable number of reading errors were occurring. The prolays were not operating reliably. Sensitive to adjustment, they were showing effects of wear, and their speed of response appeared to vary with such operating conditions as frequency of start-stop. Power supplies (the circuits involving transformers, rectifiers and voltage regulators, that produced DC voltage and current from the AC power lines) were becoming overloaded and failing to hold their intended voltage levels.

These and a number of other problems continued to plague the 729 III for over a year, threatening to delay shipment of the entire 705 III system, which was being evaluated by the product-testing department. Projected maintenance—both scheduled (preventive) and unscheduled (fixing problems)—was exceeding the maximum number of hours per month agreed upon in advance as part of IBM's new-product introduction procedures. Furthermore, by mid-1959, several new IBM systems using transistors in place of tubes were being tested. These were to use close relatives of the 729 Model III tape unit—a Model II, operating at the old speed of 75 ips but using the new prolay and the new recording density of 556 bpi, and a Model IV, which operated at the speed and density of the Model III but included some changes to adapt it to the new 7000 series computers. Both of these models used solid-state (transistor) circuits, and some months after their first announcement late in 1958, both were provided with the capability to read or record at either 200 bpi (for compatibility with existing tapes) or 556 bpi.

Each of these new tape units shared some or all of the problems of the 729 III, which was struggling to pass its "ship" tests. While no one remedy could be credited with solving all or even most of the problems, the recommendations of a high-level manufacturing and engineering task force, established in May 1960 and led by C. E. Frizzell, finally turned the tide.[74] Modifications in the prolay design, a key element in the new tape units, and in the lubricant used were responsible for substantial improvements in its operation. The struggle had been long, but in the 729 III IBM now had a half-inch tape drive operating at 62,500 characters per second, the fastest in the industry.

Although only a few hundred of the 729 Model III drives were delivered, limited as they were to the single density of 556 bpi, the combination of Model II and Model IV units shipped numbered well over 8000 machines and represented a very successful pair of products. Moreover, by "sharpening" the write-current pulse and using skillfully designed circuits to sharpen further the signal obtained in reading, it was found possible to increase the density of recording to 800 bpi. The 729 Models V and VI, announced in September 1961, were capable of operating at 200 or 556 bpi for compatibility with existing systems and data files, as well as at the new density of 800 bpi. In great demand for the 7000 series computers of the early 1960s and available through field conversion of 729 Models II and IV, respectively, these triple-density drives with their maximum data rate of 90,000 cps became the standard tape units of IBM's product line.

6.7 Excursions from the Beaten Path

On occasion, the frontiers of recording technology were explored through projects in which the well-established medium of half-inch tape was momentarily abandoned in the interest of attaining the highest possible performance. Outstanding among such projects was the Tractor development, which began in January 1957. Tractor, designed and built under contract for the National Security Agency (NSA), was to have one hundred times the data rate of the 727 drive (1.5 million cps compared to 15,000 cps), and this performance was achieved through the use of wider tape, increased speed, and increased density. Initiated as a study program in Research, it was soon taken over by the Data Processing Division engineering laboratory in Poughkeepsie, where it was managed by Carl L. Christiansen.

Christiansen had been in the group of some twenty new engineering graduates, hired in 1951, who first worked on the 701 in the laboratory and then maintained the various installations in the field. Returning to the laboratory in 1953, he designed arithmetic circuits for the 704. He was one of the planners of the 709 and a coinventor of the data synchronizer that incorporated the "channels" introduced with that system. He remained manager of the Tractor program from spring 1957 until he assumed responsibility for the entire magnetic-tape devices area in mid-1958.[75]

The Tractor tape subsystem was part of a contract package for NSA that included also the Harvest system, a special model of an advanced computer known as Stretch. (See chapter 11.) Each reel of Tractor tape, together with its companion take-up reel, was enclosed in a dust-proof cartridge designed to be stored, retrieved, mounted on a tape drive, and dismounted automatically by a mechanical "tape library." The system included three such automatic-library complexes, each capable of providing access to a maximum of 160 cartridges for two of the six tape drives. Each cartridge had a data-storage capacity equivalent to about 120 million characters; the combined capacity of the cartridges available to each pair of tape units was therefore over 19 billion characters, making Tractor a most impressive storage system for its time. Equally impressive were its physical size and the dynamics of its operation (figure 6.9). Each of its three automatic cartridge handlers could change the 15 pound cartridges on either of two associated tape units in 18 seconds and be prepared within another 30 seconds to effect the next such exchange.

The high data rate was achieved by the combination of a tape speed of 235 ips, recording density of 3000 bpi, and tape 1 3/4 inches wide with recording in twenty-two tracks. The arrangement of information was such that two eight-bit characters (or "bytes") were recorded simultaneously in sixteen of the twenty-two tracks. Automatic checking, which included a Hamming code (named after its inventor, Richard W. Hamming of Bell Telephone Laboratories), used an additional six

Figure 6.9
Tractor tape units and tape cartridge library. The automatic tape library delivered to the National Security Agency early in 1962 consisted of three such complexes, each serving two Tractor tape units (the cabinets at extreme left and right, with vacuum-column tape-handling components visible). The central unit is an automatic cartridge handler. The storage racks on each side of it can handle up to eighty cartridges each and also provide staging for cartridges to be mounted upon or withdrawn from the tape drives.

tracks. This checking method was capable of correcting all single-bit errors and detecting any error that involved two bits, in any row across the tape, during reading.[76] There was yet another track, recorded during initial testing of the tape and used thereafter to signal regions in which satisfactory recording could not be achieved. By means of this "demarcation" track, as it was called, such areas of tape could be avoided during the recording of data.

The Tractor tape unit was the first in which IBM used another tape-clutching mechanism in place of the pinch rollers that served its half-inch tape product line. In the Tractor machines, the tape passed around a capstan at each side of the head, oppositely rotating so that each could pull the tape in its own direction if sufficient friction was maintained between the tape and only that capstan. The peripheral surface of each capstan contained holes through which air was fed outward under pressure when it was desired to counteract the effect of friction between the tape and that particular capstan. The tape moved in the direction of the capstan through which no air was being fed at a given instant. While these tape units performed well at NSA, their tape-clutching principle was not advantageous enough to justify its application to the regular tape product line.

Skew had limited the half-inch tape to 800 bpi (announced but not yet delivered). Meanwhile, the Tractor machines, with their 1 3/4 inch tape and 3000 bpi, were scheduled to be shipped to NSA with the Harvest system delivered early in 1962. Skew was dealt with in these much-higher-performance Tractor machines by means of electronic "deskewing buffers." During reading, the information from each track was considered independently of other tracks and transferred, bit by bit, into an electronic register, or "buffer," for that track alone. Only after several bits had been read from each track and stored in this way were the bits combined to reconstruct the twenty-two-bit groups that had been recorded across the tape. Because the recording along an individual track might consist of a string of many 0s, a separate oscillator provided timing signals for each track, and a synchronizing pulse was recorded at every fifth bit position along the track in order to control the frequency of the oscillator. Although the effective data-recording density was thereby reduced to four-fifths of 3000 bpi, the equivalent data rate if expressed in six-bit characters was still over 1.5 million cps, and the objective of one hundred times 727 performance had been met.

The Tractor tape machines did their job very well. According to a 1977 report by Samuel S. Snyder of NSA, "HARVEST was used for 14 years with emphasis on jobs not even conceivable for any other computer. It functioned very well throughout, and to the surprise of many, even the TRACTOR tape transports turned out to be quite reliable. . . . The TRACTOR Tape System was the first completely automated tape library. This sytem also pioneered the use of error-correcting codes and deskewing buffers."[77]

Commercial efforts by IBM to produce a superpowerful tape subsystem met with considerably less success. During 1958, the second year of the Tractor development, a small tape project had been set up in the Poughkeepsie laboratory with the objective of converting to commercial use some of the technological accomplishments of the Tractor program. Progress had been slow, and Weidenhammer was asked to participate in a technical audit in April 1960. The report resulting from this audit stated that the proposed design was unsatisfactory in a number of important respects, most of them simply reflecting that the project had not been staffed by people who had worked on the 700 series tape units. Before the end of May 1960, Weidenhammer had been given responsibility for the project.

The density objective for the new tape unit—called Hypertape, or Hyper for short—was around 1500 bpi. The tape speed was to be the same as that of the then-current 729 Model VI—112.5 ips—and the tape was to be 1 inch wide, with eight tracks for data and several additional tracks for checking. While the data rate was to be less than one-eighth that of the Tractor tape unit, it would be almost twice that provided by the 729. The number of tracks required for checking would depend on the method of recording. Engineers responsible for magnetic head and amplifier design suggested to Weidenhammer that consideration be given to a form of recording known as phase encoding, or phase modulation, in place of NRZI.[78] In phase encoding, both possible values of a recorded bit were represented by magnetic changes—but changes of a given magnetic polarity for a 1 and of the opposite polarity for a 0. The technique was self-clocking, partially self-checking, and more easily adapted to error correction than was NRZI (figure 6.10).

Phase encoding also possessed other, subtler properties that were becoming interesting as recording densities increased above 800 bpi. When NRZI was used, the entire magnetic and electronic system for each track, including recorded signals, read-write heads, amplifiers, and detection circuits, was subjected to a wide range of local recording densities and instantaneous data rates. This occurred because, in any track, one or more 1s (pulses) could follow or be followed by a widely varying number of 0s (no pulses). Such local differences in pulse crowding produced complex timing irregularities in the reading signals. By contrast, with phase encoding, local densities and instantaneous data rates could never vary by more than two to one. Continued testing of phase encoding showed it in an increasingly favorable light, and by March 1961 Weidenhammer had made the decision to use it. It was also decided at that time to use a total of ten tracks on the tape: eight to handle the eight-bit characters (bytes) introduced by the Stretch computer and two for checking and error correction.

The Hypertape mechanism was unique among the IBM tape units of its time in that it employed only a single capstan for driving the tape. The tape was always in frictional contact with the capstan, which in turn could be rotated in either direction or held stationary by high-speed mechanical clutching. This, incidentally, was the first IBM tape unit since the 726 that was capable of reading tapes both forward and backward. Like Tractor, the Hyper drive used two-reel cartridges for ease of loading and for protection of the tape against contamination.

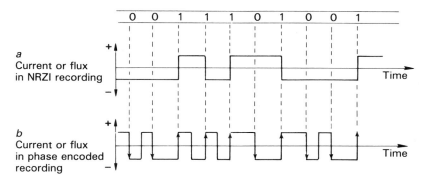

Figure 6.10

Recording current waveforms for NRZI and phase encoding. For NRZI at *a*, changes of current (and thus of tape magnetization) occur only when 1 bits are recorded; and therefore, upon reading, voltage signals are produced only for 1s. (There is no significance to the polarity of the voltage signals.) Using phase encoding at *b*, a current change occurs at every bit time, and its direction depends upon whether the bit recorded is a 1 or a 0. This rule requires changing the direction of current between bit times whenever the bit to be recorded is the same as the preceding bit. The arrows drawn at the current transitions indicate the polarity of voltage produced in a read head upon a subsequent pass of the tape—a 1 producing a positive signal and a 0 a negative signal. Clocking circuits responding to the read signals are capable of discriminating between the data signals (transitions with arrows) and the half-time signals that must occur incidentally in order to set the current for the desired transition at data times. Phase encoding results in a two-to-one variation in data rate or in the number of changes in magnetization per inch. This is advantageous in the design of sensing amplifiers. NRZI, for example, can produce a much wider range of data rates or densities of magnetic changes.

The Hyper cartridges, however, were smaller and were loaded and unloaded manually rather than by means of an automatic tape library.

When announced in August 1961 as the 7340, Hyper with its 1-inch tape was the highest-performance tape unit commercially available. It was able to transfer data at a rate of 170,000 cps and was expected to represent a considerable enhancement of the higher-performance computers in the 7000 series—the 7070, 7074, 7080, and 7090. More important, it was designed to afford high-performance auxiliary storage for future systems envisioned in the early 1960s, systems that would be able to make efficient use of its eight-bit byte and high data rate. (In 1964 the rate was doubled, to 340,000 cps.)

Technologically, Hyper was an outstanding success. Commercially, it failed; there were very few customers for it. Half-inch-wide plastic computer tape had existed at least since the days of Raytheon's Raydac computer, and by 1961 it had grown in popularity as the principal on-line auxiliary storage and off-line data-file storage for systems provided by Univac, IBM, National Cash Register, Honeywell, General Electric, Burroughs, RCA, Control Data, and a number of other computer makers. The customers' business records were on those half-inch tapes, as were their libraries of programs. The ability to read them on any available computer, from the smallest to the largest, was not only a convenience but a major economic consideration, and it could be a vitally important element of safety in case of failure of any one computer system. The increased speed of Hyper represented inadequate compensation for the inability to handle existing tape files. Good inventions, however, tend to survive, and Hyper had introduced recording and tape-handling techniques that were to be incorporated in machines of later generations.

Following the developments described here, there was relatively little improvement in the physical characteristics and performance of magnetic-tape devices in IBM for two years or more. The proximate cause of this hiatus was apparently a well-considered and high-level decision to allocate the major share of development resources to a new line of processor products, leaving correspondingly less support for new input-output products.[79] But that decision, as it affected tape devices in particular, was rationalized to some extent by the level to which expectations for disk storage had risen by about 1960. System planners were encouraged to emphasize the future role of disk storage, which contained inherent solutions to many of the vexing problems stemming from the purely sequential nature of tape. As will be evident in several subsequent portions of this account, disk storage did not come along rapidly enough, either technologically or in terms of market acceptance, to justify the prevailing expectations.[80]

It soon became clear that magnetic tape would continue to be an important storage and input-output medium. Its performance had kept reasonable pace with that of the computers of two generations, from the 701 in 1952 to the 7000 series systems of the early 1960s. The density of recording on half-inch tape had increased by a factor of 8, from 100 to 800 bpi; data rates had increased by a factor of 12, from 7500 to 90,000 cps; and the capacity of a reel of tape had increased by a factor of more than 11, from about 1.5 million to 17 million characters. There was no reason to believe the rate of improvement would be diminished in the foreseeable future. Meanwhile, IBM had established itself as a leader in many aspects of tape-product technology, introducing methods of recording, tape handling, checking, and control that were widely adopted in the computer industry.

7

Ferrite-Core Memories

Getting started in cores. Project SAGE. Commercial memories. Pushing the limits. Fabrication. Patents and innovation.

"The problem of electronic storage of numbers during the calculation is of fundamental importance, and we have no adequate solution of the problem. This development should be pushed with all possible vigor."[1] So wrote Wallace Eckert and John McPherson to Watson, Sr., in November 1946, over a year before the IBM Selective Sequence Electronic Calculator (SSEC) was dedicated. Their statements expressed a growing conviction of many engineers that storage—cheap and reliable yet fast enough to keep up with vacuum tube arithmetic circuits—was urgently needed for data processing equipment. The need they identified related only to numbers because they had not fully grasped the implications of operating with programs stored in memory. Certainly no one at the time anticipated that stored-program operation would lead to a nearly insatiable demand for high-speed computer memory capacity for decades to come.

Numerous ideas for high-speed memory were considered at IBM during 1946 and 1947. These included electrical delay lines, acoustic and supersonic delay lines, capacitive storage, magnetic drums, magnetic cores (then called rings), and a variety of specialized electronic vacuum tubes.[2] By mid-1949, however, the primary emphasis was on the cathode-ray storage tube, named the "Williams tube" after its British inventor.[3]

Successfully tested on the experimental Test Assembly in Poughkeepsie in September 1950, the Williams-tube memory developed at IBM was first shipped as the Type 706 Electrostatic Storage Unit on the IBM 701 computer in 1953. Williams-tube memory was later built into the IBM 702 computer shipped in 1955. With a read-write cycle time of 12 microseconds, the Williams-tube memory met the high-speed requirements of the electronic logic circuits. Its cost of about $1 per bit was less than that of vacuum tube flip-flop storage and was consistent with the overall costs of the machines on which it was used. Moreover, a concerted research, development, and manufacturing program had so improved the reliability of Williams tubes in a relatively short time that many believed improvements in reliability and cost would continue for years to come. (See chapter 4.)

Ralph Palmer was among those who held this view, but consistent with his policy of looking for better ways to satisfy all product requirements, he supported experimental work on alternative memory technologies. One of the more promising of these was magnetic cores.

7.1 Getting Started in Cores

During the mid-1940s a number of apparently independent proposals were made to use ferromagnetic rings to store information. The first reference to magnetic-ring (core) storage in IBM is contained in a memorandum of November 1946 and apparently refers to a proposal by IBM scientist Llewellyn H. Thomas, which was subsequently described in greater detail in the minutes of a two-day meeting at the IBM Watson Laboratory in June 1948. Attended by McPherson, Eckert, Palmer, and others, the meeting had been convened soon after the SSEC dedication in order to discuss IBM's next large-scale calculator. At the meeting, Thomas and an engineering colleague described experiments with information storage in ring-shaped cores made by wrapping many turns of ferromagnetic wire or ribbon around a 1.5 inch diameter spool. Thin ribbons, less than 0.002 inch thick, were preferred because eddy current losses were smaller, permitting more rapid switching than in cores made with thicker material. But none of the cores switched more rapidly than about 0.5 millisecond—even when driven by currents of 1 ampere in wires wound as many as 100 times around the core.[4] Learning of the "far more advanced work" of An Wang at Harvard during a technical symposium in September 1949, Thomas terminated his work with magnetic-ring storage believing Wang had demonstrated all of the important concepts.[5]

Wang, who soon founded Wang Laboratories, had in 1948 just obtained his Ph.D. at Harvard, only a few years after immigrating to the United States from China. As described by Wang, "Magnetic cores with a rectangular hysteresis loop are used in a storage system which requires no mechanical motion and is permanent. The binary digit 1 is stored as a positive residual flux and the binary digit 0 as a residual flux in the opposite direction." These two information states (clockwise or counterclockwise magnetization directions) were created by sending current of appropriate polarity through a wire wound about the magnetic core. To detect the information stored in a core, Wang sent current through the wire to switch the core to the 0 state. If the core was already in the 0 state, it did not switch, whereas a core in the 1 state did switch to the 0 state. A second wire was wound about the core, much like a secondary winding of a transformer, and was used to detect the induced voltage, which was up to thirty times higher for cores switching from 1 to 0 than for cores already in the 0 state.[6] Wang at first believed the loss of information in the core during reading was a serious problem. He soon realized, however, that the output signal from one core could be used to switch an adjacent core to the 1 state, thus preserving the information and providing a satisfactory memory system.[7]

An important aspect of Wang's work was the use of a ferromagnetic nickel-iron alloy developed by the Germans during World War II for magnetic amplifiers used in gun control systems. Commercially produced in the United States after the war under the name Deltamax, this material had a very sharp applied-field threshold for magnetization reversal (switching) between its two stable states. Magnetic materials that possess this characteristic are referred to as rectangular or square loop materials because a plot of magnetization on the vertical axis and applied magnetic field on the horizontal axis has the shape of a rectangle or square. The word *hysteresis* is often inserted before the word *loop* to emphasize that the magnetization reversal lags behind the applied current.

Although Wang's results had discouraged Llewellyn Thomas, they inspired Munro K. (Mike) Haynes, a graduate student in electrical engineering at the University of Illinois. Learning of the results soon after the 1949 Harvard symposium, Haynes obtained Deltamax material and began studying its switching characteristics. In short order, he not only verified the results, but by Christmas he had observed another interesting property associated with the sharp switching threshold of Deltamax cores. The clockwise or counterclockwise direction of magnetization in doughnut-shaped cores could be reversed completely by a current less than twice as large as one that did not reverse the direction of magnetization at all. This property, Haynes recalls, caused him to conceive the idea that cores could be wired for individual selection in a two-dimensional array in which each core had two wires passing through its hole perpendicular to each other — an X wire parallel to one edge of the array and a Y wire parallel to the other edge. A current in either of the two wires could be made small enough not to switch the core, whereas a simultaneous current in both wires would switch it. Thus the magnetization state of any core in the array could be reversed by the coincidence of current through appropriate X and Y wires, without altering the magnetization state of any other cores through which these wires passed (figure 7.1).

From fellow graduate students at Illinois, Haynes knew of the technical problems inherent in the Williams-tube memories being developed for the university's computer, the ILLIAC. But when he tried to devise a substitute memory using *coincident-current selection* of magnetic cores, he found the cores would not switch fast enough. The problem resulted from his coincident-current selection scheme, whereby the current in each drive line had to be small enough so that current in one wire alone would not switch a core. Unfortunately, this coincident-current constraint required the sum of the two to be too small to switch a core in less than a few milliseconds—too slow to be practical.[8]

Haynes therefore quit working on coincident-current magnetic-core memory arrays and turned his attention to nondestructive readout and magnetic logic. Magnetic logic appeared to be particularly attractive because larger drive currents could be used, thus permitting relatively fast switching. Ironically, however, magnetic logic never achieved significant commercial success whereas coincident-current magnetic memory arrays became one of the most important technologies for the computer industry.

Haynes's Ph.D. thesis, dated August 1950, was devoted primarily to magnetic logic, but it also contained a five-page section called "Static Magnetic Memory Proposal." This is the only written record of his work at the University of Illinois. The proposed memory, which he did not attempt to build, was expanded beyond his original ideas by using a form of diode matrix selection to reduce the number of vacuum tube drivers.[9]

Haynes's decision to join IBM was influenced by Arthur L. Samuel, whom he had known at the University of Illinois before Samuel left to join IBM. Samuel, who had worked on electronic vacuum tube design at Bell Laboratories for more than fifteen years before coming to Illinois in 1946, was hired by IBM in September 1949 to provide technical guidance for the development and manufacture of vacuum tubes for computers. As IBM's technical requirements shifted during the 1950s, Samuel's areas of interest also shifted from standard vacuum tubes to Williams tubes, then to ferrite cores and transistors, and finally to studies of artificial intelligence using computers.[10] Together with Ralph Palmer and Nathaniel Rochester of IBM, Samuel had attended the 1949 Harvard Symposium at which Wang described his magnetic-core shift register.[11] After this, Samuel diligently followed Haynes's

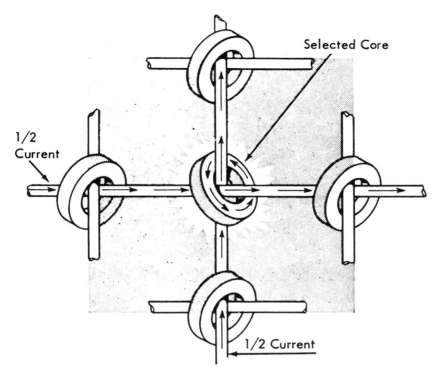

Figure 7.1
Coincident-current selection. The half-select currents applied through the indicated vertical and horizontal lines are each too small to switch the cores through which they pass. The one core in the center of the figure is switched, however, by the coincidence of the two currents. (Illustration from the *IBM News*, 10 November 1967.)

work on magnetic cores at the University of Illinois and urged him to come to IBM when he finished.

In October 1950, Haynes joined IBM in Poughkeepsie, where he continued his work on magnetic-core logic and memory devices. Not long after, he began seeing advertisements for ferromagnetic ferrite materials with sufficiently sharp switching thresholds to suggest their use in digital circuits. Ferrites, being poor conductors of electricity, exhibited much faster magnetization reversal than ferromagnetic metals, such as Deltamax, originally used by Wang and Haynes. The particular ferrites of interest had a complex cubic (spinel) crystalline structure and consisted of an iron oxide (Fe_3O_4) in which some of the iron was replaced by such metals as aluminum, magnesium, manganese, or zinc. Small additions of these metals critically affected the magnetic properties of the ferrites in ways that were not well understood.

Haynes ordered samples of every kind of ferrite in toroidal form made by the General Ceramics Corporation in New Jersey. Typical cores were about an inch in diameter and cost several dollars. All of them failed to exhibit magnetization switching thresholds sharp enough for magnetic-core logic or memory devices. Nevertheless, Haynes enjoyed carrying around one of the smaller cores, telling his colleagues that it would soon replace the devices in the machines they were making.[12]

During the fall of 1951, a small group of engineers and technicians working with Haynes on magnetic-core devices learned that General Ceramics had developed a magnesium-manganese ferrite material with superior properties for digital circuits. They ordered samples, built some very small prototype memories, and began looking for possible applications. Their most enthusiastic contact was Edward J. Rabenda, who had begun his IBM career twenty-five years earlier servicing unit record equipment. With many years as a successful engineer and inventor, Rabenda had considerable freedom to choose his own assignments. He proposed using a small magnetic-core buffer memory as part of a device for translating the IBM punched-card code to a binary-coded decimal form. This buffer memory was to have one storage location for each hole in the punched card: 960 bits arranged in an 80 × 12 bit array.[13]

In order to get enough good cores, several orders of one thousand cores were placed with General Ceramics. The size of these cores was specified as 150 mil inside diameter, 240 mil outside diameter, and 45 mil in height, using the English units notation of 1 mil = 0.001 inch. A heavy-duty wire was threaded straight through each of the twelve rows of cores in the long (eighty core) direction. A current of about 2 amperes was used to drive these lines. Each of the eighty columns was threaded by a fine, number 32 (8 mil diameter) wire, which made fifty turns through the twelve cores in the column. With fifty turns through each core, the 2.5 ampere turns required to drive the cores was achieved with only 50 milliamperes, a current small enough to be supplied by the card-reading brushes of the Type 405 accounting machine. The data in the core array were read from the eighty columns in parallel by sending a drive current through each of the long straight wires, one at a time. The output signals, from cores being switched from the 1 to the 0 states, were used to control a Type 517 card punch (figure 7.2).

The ferrite-core array was assembled and tested, and on 22 May 1952, Rabenda conducted the first test of the entire system. Forty-three of the eighty columns of ferrite cores successfully accepted data from the card reader and then transmitted them to the card punch in what is believed to be the first test of a ferrite-core memory in an application. But because of poor reliability and lack of uniformity of the available ferrite cores, the buffer was not implemented as a product.[14]

News of the experimental core buffer spread quickly, with a number of alternative applications being proposed. One of these was for buffers for the card reader, card punch, and printer for the IBM 702 computer. A rotating magnetic drum had served as a buffer on the experimental TPM, but a better scheme—free of the timing constraints of mechanical motion—was desired for the 702. One solution was to use a Williams-tube memory, such had been demonstrated on the TPM and was planned for the 702 main memory, but this appeared to be too expensive for a small buffer. As a result, Erich Bloch, who had recently been assigned to the card buffer project, was asked to look into the possibility of designing a ferrite-core buffer to perform this function.[15]

Bloch had joined IBM in January 1952 after receiving the bachelor's degree in electrical engineering at the University of Buffalo, where he had taken one of the few courses on computer technology offered anywhere in the country. A careful, methodical person in planning and getting things done, he quickly acquired a reputation for hard work and long hours. His heavy accent, the result of a boyhood in Germany, precollege education in Switzerland, and two years study of electrical engineering at the Swiss Federal Institute of Technology before emigrating to the United States in 1947, seemed to enhance the precision with which he spoke. After spending considerable time with Rabenda and Haynes learning about ferrite-core technology, Bloch

Figure 7.2
Ferrite-core buffer application. A ferrite-core array is shown installed (top) in the
IBM Type 405 alphabetical accounting machine. Its output was used to drive the
Type 517 summary punch. A close-up of a 10 × 12 section of the 80 × 12 bit
ferrite-core array (bottom) shows the single drive lines through the cores in the
long direction and fifty turns in the short direction. The cores are 150 mil inside
diameter, 240 mil outside diameter, and 45 mil high. This experimental system
was tested in April 1952, making it the first ferrite-core memory known to have
functioned in a system application.

became convinced that a reliable buffer could be made using improved cores and core-test procedures then available.[16]

Crucial to Bloch's planning was a smaller-sized core specified by Haynes with a 60 mil inside diameter, making the hole through the core smaller than the letter "o" printed on this page. With a 90 mil outside diameter and 30 mil height, this core was difficult to handle and wire, but it required much smaller drive currents than cores previously available. The IBM engineers believed the smaller core size was an advantage because current in a single turn of wire would be sufficient to switch the magnetization of the core from a 1 to a 0. The use of wires straight through the core, without multiple turns, would make core wiring easier. General Ceramics agreed to fabricate the cores using dies ordered by Haynes in March 1952. Later known as 60-90 mil cores (the dimensions of the inner and outer diameters), cores of this size were soon supplied by General Ceramics to engineers at MIT and Engineering Research Associates (ERA) as well as to IBM.[17]

The circuits selected by Bloch to drive the ferrite cores in the buffer employed magnetic switch cores driven by small thyratron (gas-filled) tubes. The magnetic switch cores consisted of ferromagnetic metal ribbon wrapped around ceramic bobbins and were similar to the cores Wang and Haynes had first used for storing information, except that the switching threshold was smaller and perhaps less sharp. Bloch used switch cores in his memory drive circuit in much the way a transformer is used. Primary windings, driven by the thyratron, supplied the current needed to reverse the magnetization of the switch core, and voltage induced in the secondary winding was used to drive current through the ferrite cores in the memory array.[18]

The engineering work on the two-dimensional (2D) buffer memories proceeded in a highly empirical way. Little was known about magnetic-core characteristics such as speed of magnetization reversal and sensitivity to changes in drive current or temperature. By February 1953, an eighty-by-twelve (80 × 12) bit buffer was operating reliably on a printer attached to the TPM.[19] The following summer, the 2D buffers were reworked by Bloch during the final design effort for the IBM 702. Used in the card reader, card punch, printer, and control units, with the IBM 702 and 705 data processing systems, these buffers were first shipped with the IBM 702 in February 1955 and are believed to be the first production use of ferrite-core storage in computing systems.[20]

7.2 Project SAGE

One might assume, from the preceding account of IBM's early work on magnetic cores, that these efforts led to larger and larger core memories until arrays capable of replacing Williams tubes evolved. But ferrite-core memory products did not evolve in this manner because of a seemingly unrelated event: the explosion of the Soviet Union's first nuclear weapon.

The August 1949 disclosure by U.S. intelligence (made public late in September) that the Russians had exploded a nuclear bomb and had developed bombers capable of reaching the United States jolted the Truman administration into action. At the recommendation of George E. Valley, an MIT professor and member of the Air Force Scientific Advisory Board, a committee was formed to address the issue of air defense. In a few months, the Valley committee concluded that the U.S. air-defense network was wholly inadequate. The committee recommended that the existing system be upgraded as quickly as possible while a longer-range solution was developed.[21] By March 1950 it was agreed that such a long-range solution should make extensive use of computers to handle surveillance, control, and bookkeeping functions. This air-defense system was to have numerous large computers distributed about the country and connected to radar-monitoring stations, as well as to the other computers, so that flight paths of all planes over, or near, the United States could be calculated and monitored continuously.[22] Back even before the first UNIVAC was delivered, the proposed air-defense system was to be a nationwide, on-line, real-time computing system—a grandiose scheme, well suited to the skills and self-confidence of a group at MIT then working on a project known as Whirlwind.

Under the leadership of Jay W. Forrester, a young engineer who had spent the wartime years in the MIT Servomechanisms Laboratory, Project Whirlwind had its origins in a program, begun late in 1944, to develop an analog system to simulate airplane-flight characteristics. In January 1946, following a suggestion first made in 1942 by Perry O. Crawford, a fellow graduate student at MIT, Forrester proposed to use *digital* computer technology instead of *analog* techniques to accomplish the flight simulation functions. Crawford, who joined IBM some years later (1952), had begun promoting the use of digital computers for combat information and control long before any reliable, high-speed digital computers had been demonstrated.[23]

As it developed, Forrester's decision to act on Crawford's proposal and shift from analog to digital techniques proved to be crucial to the future of his project; it may also have been the first time digital techniques were chosen to implement a major control function. Thus it became the first task of project Whirlwind to design a digital computer; the second task was to adapt the computer to the analyzer problem.

Whirlwind was a large effort. During 1947, the project employed fifty people, half of them professional engineers or MIT graduate students. By the fall of 1949, when the Russians exploded their first nuclear weapon, Forrester and his group had won the respect of technical leaders for their competence; but they had also created deep concern in government funding agencies for their extravagance. However, just when Forrester's propensity for spending money and expanding his project was bringing him into serious conflict with his funding agencies, U.S. air-defense needs demanded a massive development of digital computer systems. Instead of being subjected to severe funding constraints, Forrester found himself thrust into the leadership of the largest and most significant computer development in the country.[24]

Because of the size of the air-defense system and the urgency attendant to it, the requirement for high-speed main memories was more pressing than that of any other system then being considered. The importance of memory, however, had been recognized by Forrester for some time. As early as 1947, he had identified main memory as a critical computer requirement and had proposed replacing an MIT-designed, electrostatic storage-tube memory in the Whirlwind computer with a three-dimensional array of memory elements. But the gas-glow tubes he attempted to use as memory elements were neither reliable nor uniform enough. Then in April 1949, he saw an advertisement for Deltamax, the same nickel-iron alloy used by Wang at Harvard and by Haynes at the University of Illinois. Forrester says the unusually sharp switching threshold of Deltamax inspired him to reconstruct his proposal for a three-dimensional selection memory array—this time using magnetic cores. By June he began spending time alone in the laboratory working on his ideas.[25] His engineering notebook entries of 13 and 14 June include the following statements:

A method for using magnetic cores for data storage in three dimensions appears possible. The magnetic core material would be the non-linear type such as now being sold under the trade name Deltamax. . . . In practice it may be possible to use a single conductor running straight through the core of the magnetic material instead of a coil around the core. Also it should be possible to make a three-dimensional array where one choice takes all cores in a given plane and the other two axes are selected to choose a single conductor running in perpendicular to all planes. Circular magnetic cores can be set in at an angle such that straight runs of wires could be used in both directions.[26]

By the end of June, Forrester had studied the characteristics of a number of magnetic cores. The cores were made with ceramic bobbins around which thin strips of Deltamax were wrapped. The cores were about 1 inch inside diameter, 1.25 inch outside diameter, and 0.125 inch high. His experimental results were not as good as he had hoped. Among other problems, the cores switched too slowly to be practical, and they exhibited peculiar magnetization reversal characteristics that he noted were not consistent with simple theory.[27]

Three months before Haynes even began working with magnetic cores, Forrester had thus proposed not only a two-dimensional but also a three-dimensional (3D) coincident-current selection scheme for magnetic cores. He had also encountered the same problem observed by Haynes: Deltamax cores switched too slowly to be practical in the coincident-current mode. To solve this problem, he initiated a project under William N. Papian, an MIT graduate student, to measure the properties of magnetic cores of different types in an effort to find one that would be suitable for his proposed 3D memory array. By the fall of 1950, Papian had constructed a 2 × 2 array of magnetic cores in which he demonstrated the "successful storing and cycling of information throughout the array" using coincident-current selection. Each of the four magnetic cores in the array consisted of ten turns of 1 mil thick silicon-steel ribbon wrapped around a ceramic bobbin. These cores, while apparently superior to Deltamax, nevertheless switched too slowly and required too much drive current to be practical.[28]

Immediately following these somewhat discouraging results with magnetic cores, Forrester initiated an effort to develop ferrite materials capable of satisfying the requirements of his proposed memory. This activity involved materials research at MIT and at General Ceramics, where E. Albers-Schönberg had already developed ferrite materials possessing the rectangular hysteresis loop associated with sharp switching thresholds.[29] The development effort at General Ceramics, partially funded by Forrester, produced ferrite cores that were used almost simultaneously at MIT and IBM. In May 1952 Forrester demonstrated the operation of a 16 × 16 (256) bit array of ferrite cores of 140 mil outside diameter.[30] This was just one month after Haynes and Rabenda at IBM had demonstrated the use of a larger, 80 × 12 (960) bit ferrite-core array as a buffer on the Type 405 accounting machine. While the cores used in the IBM array had nearly twice the diameter of those used at MIT, it was Haynes who first ordered the very much smaller 90 mil diameter dies of the size soon used to make cores for both IBM and MIT.

As early as 1951, the Whirlwind computer had been coupled with prototype radar-tracking equipment for the proposed air-defense system and had successfully performed several computer-controlled collision-course interceptions.[31] The electrostatic storage-tube memory and other parts of the equipment functioned sufficiently well that Forrester concluded it was time to select a company capable of completing the development of the computer for quantity production.

In the summer of 1952, Forrester and others from MIT toured IBM's research, development, and manufacturing facilities in Endicott, Poughkeepsie, and New York City as part of their effort to evaluate the company's ability to develop and manufacture the air-defense computer.[32] Forrester must have been surprised to see an 80 × 12 bit ferrite-core array attached to an accounting machine when he visited Rabenda's laboratory that July. His decision to select IBM, however, appears to have been influenced primarily by other factors. According to Forrester, the MIT representatives were unanimous in their ranking of the three top contenders: first, IBM; second, Remington Rand; and third, Raytheon. The MIT representatives were particularly impressed by the "degree of purposefulness, integration, and esprit de corps" in IBM. Other factors cited by Forrester were IBM's greater experience in transferring electronic equipment from development to the factory, superior technical ability among key staff members, superior field service force, closer proximity to MIT, and the fact that over 3 million vacuum tubes were already operating in IBM equipment at customer locations.[33]

In anticipation of receiving the contract for the air-defense computer, IBM rented office space on the third floor of a necktie factory on High Street in Poughkeepsie, New York, where work on the TPM and the Defense Calculator previously had been concentrated. The company's part of the effort got its first name, Project High, from this location, and the overall project continued to be known by the MIT designation, Whirlwind II. But as IBM became more deeply involved, a name less closely identified with MIT was needed. The name SAGE (Semi-Automatic Ground Environment) was adopted and remained the designation to the end of the project. The large SAGE computers received the service designation AN/FSQ-7 (Army-Navy Fixed Special eQuipment); the first prototype computers were designated XD-1 and XD-2.

By the end of November 1952, fourteen IBM staff-level employees had begun work on the project. Within a year, the planned level of about 300 total employees had been reached, consisting of 17 supervisory and administrative, 162 professional-level technical, 65 technical support, and 52 clerical persons. Technical information exchange between MIT and IBM was crucial to the success of the effort. During the first nine months of Project High, IBM personnel spent nearly one thousand man-days at MIT learning about the Whirlwind computer and the proposed air-defense system, and MIT personnel spent 34 man-days at IBM learning about the design and structure of commercial electronic calculators and computers, standard pluggable units, and manufacturing methods. Literally hundreds of technical reports were exchanged. A series of monthly meetings was established midway between IBM and MIT in Hartford, Connecticut, to facilitate information exchange and rapid decision making.[34]

In 1953 Robert Crago, who had worked on the TPM and the 702 computer, was assigned to Project SAGE. He was subsequently appointed assistant manager in 1955 and manager in 1956 of the Kingston plant and laboratory, where Project SAGE was by then located. Of the project Crago says, "It was probably the first experience most of us in IBM had in working with an outside group and taking the leadership from them. . . . It took us a while to realize that we were dealing with some very professional people who knew what they were doing. . . . I think the kind of technical camaraderie that grew out of this project made it the most exciting thing that I've ever been involved in."[35]

Project SAGE became a pioneering technical effort in many areas: ferrite-core memories, marginal testing of circuits and components, worst-case systems design for high reliability, duplexed computer operation, large-scale use of telephone lines for digital data, cathode-ray-tube displays with light guns (now called light pens), real-time on-line operation, and many more.[36] When fully deployed in 1963, the system consisted of twenty-three direction centers distributed throughout North America, three combat centers, and one programming center—each with a duplexed AN/FSQ-7 computer system.[37] Each central processor was capable of driving 100 display consoles, accepting data from 100 on-line operators and 12 remote sites, and providing data to these same sites and more. Each duplexed system contained over 50,000 vacuum tubes, weighed 250 tons, occupied an acre of floor space, and used electrical power sufficient for a town of several thousand people. Project SAGE was truly exciting because it was embraced and successfully developed as the primary air-defense system for the country in spite of the improbability that so much could be accomplished in a few years. Its reliability and serviceability when completed was excellent, with an operational availability far in excess of 99 percent. To achieve these objectives, IBM alone, at its peak involvement, had over 7000 people assigned to SAGE in development, manufacturing, maintenance, and other support functions.[38]

An early recruit to the SAGE program was N. P. Edwards, whose first assignment at IBM had been to work with P. E. Fox developing Williams-tube storage for the TPM and the IBM 701. Edwards joined Project High in December 1952 and was soon placed in charge of memory systems. He immediately recruited two engineers from Haynes's group and, nine months later, a third one.[39] Haynes himself continued to work on magnetic-core logic and small buffer memories for commercial products, and he hired and educated more people in magnetic-core technology. Edwards and those he recruited for Project SAGE spent considerable time discussing the relative merits of Williams-tube storage, the MIT storage tube, and various drive and sensing schemes for ferrite-core arrays. A 2D selection scheme of the type proposed by Haynes in his thesis was considered, as an alternative to Forrester's approach, by the IBM and MIT engineers.[40]

Serious consideration of alternative memory approaches for SAGE ended, however, in the summer of 1953 following the successful test at MIT of a 3D selection, $32 \times 32 \times 17$ bit ferrite-core memory containing 60-90 mil cores. On 8 August it was placed in operation in the Whirlwind computer side by side with an electrostatic storage tube memory of the same capacity. The superior reliability of the ferrite-core memory was immediately evident, making it possible for the first time to check out systems programs. The following month, a second memory array was inserted into Whirlwind with equal success. A satisfactory solution to main memory had finally been found.[41]

The ferrite-core memories on the Whirlwind computer served as models for memories jointly designed by MIT and IBM for SAGE. The SAGE memories had eight times the capacity of the Whirlwind memory, containing thirty-three planes of 64×64 cores each plus three spare planes that could be wired in if a failure occurred in service. The cores were 50-80 mil in diameter, judged to be the smallest cores that could be wired by hand without breaking the wires. Four wires were threaded through the tiny 50 mil diameter hole in each core. Drive currents of 0.4 ampere and 2 microseconds in duration were supplied by large push-pull cathode follower vacuum tubes through a transformer. The output signals from the cores were 0.15 volt. The selection plane equipment contained 673 vacuum tubes and 1071 diodes, and the control circuits and digit plane circuits contained another 103 tubes and 292 diodes. Ferrite cores were so reliable that the 776 vacuum tubes in each memory were a greater reliability and service problem than the approximately 150,000 cores.[42]

To facilitate service, all SAGE memory drive circuits were contained in pluggable units that could be replaced quickly when a malfunction occurred. These pluggable units were huge by today's standards: about 1.5 feet long, 1 foot high, and 2.5 inches wide. Each unit had eight to ten vacuum tubes plus ten to fifteen printed-circuit cards. Large vacuum tubes, rather than the newer miniature tubes, were selected because the large glass surface area facilitated cooling and because it was easier to achieve the required internal grid tolerances. Forced-air cooling with a laminar flow of air about each tube, plus a temperature monitoring system, made it possible to maintain a temperature of 24°C to within plus or minus 1°C.[43]

The agreed-to read-write cycle of the memory was 7.5 microseconds, but in July 1954 there was increasing pressure from the systems designers to shorten the memory cycle.[44] The time required to get information out of the memory (read time) was, of course, much less than the time required to read information and then restore the information back into the cores (read-write cycle). The read-write cycle was frequently the more critical parameter because new requests to memory could not be accepted until after information read out of the cores had been restored.

That October the first memory bank was completed and operating with a faster-than-projected cycle of 6 microseconds. This was the speed MIT had originally requested but which the more conservative IBM engineers had thought too ambitious. In January 1955 the first SAGE prototype computer (XD-1) was shipped to MIT's Lincoln Laboratory where it soon replaced Whirlwind in the prototype air-defense system known as the Cape Cod System. A second prototype computer (XD-2) was retained by IBM.[45] (The SAGE ferrite-core memory is shown in figure 7.3.)

In spite of these significant achievements, IBM management was concerned by competitive accomplishments. Remington Rand had shipped a ferrite-core memory to the National Security Agency for its ERA 1103 computer in November 1954, and International Telemeter had shipped a ferrite-core memory to the RAND Corporation for its Johnniac computer in February 1955. (The RAND Corporation, unrelated to Remington Rand, was a California-based, nonprofit corporation that specialized in operations research for the air force.) These events occurred, respectively, about two months before and one month

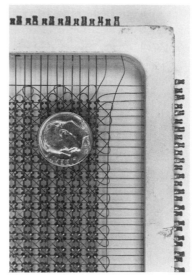

Figure 7.3
SAGE memory. The glassed-in space of the SAGE memory unit (top left) holds
thirty-six ferrite-core planes, three of which are spares. Vacuum tube drivers are
positioned above and below the core array. One memory plane containing
64 × 64 (4096) ferrite cores is shown (bottom) ready for insertion in the glassed-
in space. Each core is 50 mil inside diameter, 80 mil outside diameter, and has
four wires passing through its center as revealed (top right) in the close-up photograph of the corner of a core plane. A U.S. dime on the cores helps indicate size.

after IBM had shipped the XD-1 computer to the MIT Lincoln Laboratory. The Remington Rand and International Telemeter memories, like those designed for SAGE, made use of Project Whirlwind designs and research results. IBM management derived some comfort from the fact that the memory for Johnniac was less than half as fast as the SAGE memories and the one for the ERA 1103 was only one-fourth as large and still not as fast. Less evident, but perhaps more significant in the long run, these memories had not been as thoroughly engineered for reliability, mass production, and easy maintenance as the SAGE memories, nor had extensive production capability been developed.[46]

7.3 Commercial Memories

The expertise in ferrite-core memory design and manufacture acquired by IBM through its participation in Project SAGE was not immediately applied to commercial products, for two main reasons. First, the people and resources committed to SAGE could not be applied to commercial products. Second, and perhaps more important, the needs of the air-defense system were perceived to be different from those of commercial customers. In particular, Project SAGE placed major emphasis on system reliability, whereas commercial customers were more concerned with costs; the high cost of early ferrite-core memories made cost-competitive applications difficult to define.

During the summer of 1953, as Erich Bloch was completing the small ferrite-core buffers for the card reader, card punch, and printer for the IBM 702 computer, an application for a somewhat larger ferrite-core buffer memory surfaced. Because the 702 lacked any ability to overlap tape operations with processing, its performance was not adequate in applications involving heavy use of magnetic-tape storage. Wayne Winger, who was now responsible for tape subsystem attachment, believed the problem could be solved by a buffer memory, designed to receive data from magnetic tape at tape speed and transmit it to main memory at memory speed. The use of such buffers would permit considerable overlapping of tape reading, data processing, and tape writing functions. By the end of the year, Bloch was assigned the job of designing a ferrite-core buffer to perform this function.[47]

The buffer size finally selected was 800 characters of seven bits each and was achieved in an array of seven planes of 40 × 20 cores each.[48] The large size of the buffer made Forrester's 3D wiring scheme more attractive than the 2D scheme Bloch had used on the earlier buffers. Using 3D selection, each core in a cubic array could be selected by the coincidence of three currents passing through it instead of two. To improve the margins of operation, Forrester had proposed that coincident-drive currents in the X and Y lines be large enough to switch all the cores on the Z line intersected by the two planes containing the driven X and Y lines. Currents of opposite polarity, known as *inhibit currents*, were then used in selected Z planes to prevent certain cores from switching. Thus, cores were selected by the coincidence of X and Y currents and the absence of a Z inhibit current. However, even if Bloch had wired the buffer in Forrester's 3D manner, sixty vacuum tube drivers would have been required for the X and Y lines plus seven more for the inhibit lines. Believing this was too many vacuum tube circuits for such a small memory, Bloch became interested in matrix selection schemes proposed by Haynes and others as a means of reducing the number of drivers.

Haynes and his group had been experimenting with diode matrix selection of the X and Y drive lines, an extension of ideas he had proposed in his thesis at the University of Illinois. At the same time, Kenneth H. Olsen, a graduate student at MIT, who later founded Digital Equipment Corporation, and Jan A. Rajchman of RCA were experimenting with magnetic switch-core matrices to perform the same function.[49] The matrix selection schemes external to the core memory array were conceptually similar to the core array in operation. Each diode or switch core in a 2D matrix was addressed by electrical signals applied simultaneously to the two orthogonal lines passing through it. The output signal from the selected diode or switch core was then used to drive one of the X or Y lines of the memory array. For large memory arrays, a substantial reduction in drive circuits was achieved.

Switch-core matrices not only reduced the number of drive circuits, but they also provided impedance matching between the vacuum tube drivers and the memory lines. The successes reported for these experimental efforts encouraged Bloch to use the same techniques in his buffer memory product. Using switch cores wired in 4 × 5 matrices, he was able to drive twenty memory lines with only nine vacuum tube drivers. Thus, in contrast to the sixty drivers that would have been required using the simple 3D drive scheme employed in the SAGE memories, only twenty-seven drivers were required to drive the 20 X and 40 Y lines of the new memory.[50]

The ferrite-core size, wire size, and wiring configuration in the memory array were to be the same as those in SAGE, thus reducing costs substantially. No new core type had to be developed, and many of the same procedures and fixtures for core testing and wiring could be used. To cut costs further, grade B cores (rejects from core batches intended for SAGE) were used.[51] The large variability in characteristics of these cheaper cores caused undesirable electrical noise in the memory, which was overcome by two innovations. The first was staggered read, proposed independently by Haynes and Forrester and patented by Haynes.[52] In this scheme, a time delay between initiation of read pulses permitted the noise induced by the first pulse to decay before the second pulse switched the core. The second innovation was disturbance cancellation, whereby an additional core of the same material as the memory cores was driven by the X and Y lines and coupled to the sense amplifier so as to counterbalance the disturb noise of the nonselected memory cores.[53]

In February 1954, development of circuit and array technologies for the 3D ferrite-core array tape buffer was initiated in Haynes's group in support of Bloch.[54] Assembled and debugged during May and shipped to Commonwealth Edison in Chicago in June 1955, the resulting IBM 776 tape buffer was the first 3D ferrite-core memory produced by IBM for a commercial customer.[55] The basic design was modified during the ensuing years, resulting in several products. The Type 775 record storage unit, for example, was announced in October 1954 for use on the new IBM 705 computer. This buffer provided one thousand seven-bit characters, physically organized in a $25 \times 40 \times 7$ bit ferrite-core array permitting, according to the announcement letter, "almost complete overlapping of tape reading, data processing, and tape writing functions."[56]

Thus, by the end of 1953, IBM had programs underway to develop commercial products using 2D ferrite-core arrays of approximately 1000 bits and 3D arrays of 5000 to 7000 bits, but it was not clear that ferrite cores provided the best solution for main memories, requiring something like 100,000 bits. Good cores alone cost thirty-three cents each, and the cost per core of a fully wired and tested array with support circuitry was estimated to be many times that much. Unlike the SAGE air-defense application, in which reliability was far more important than cost, commercial applications were very cost-sensitive.

There was increasing interest among those working with ferrite cores to develop large main memories in time for use on the IBM 702 computer. Although announced in 1953, the 702 was not shipped until one month after the company had successfully tested large ferrite-core memories on the SAGE prototype computer. The effort to shift from the planned use of Williams tubes to ferrite cores was defeated in 1953 when Philip Fox proposed using an improved version of the storage tube that was more reliable and could store ten times as many bits per tube as the earlier version. Called the barrier-grid tube, it had a conducting wire mesh over the storage surface that increased the storage retention and resolution. This tube was more complicated than those used on the IBM 701, but the tenfold increase in storage capacity was expected to result in major cost savings. Because the barrier grid was similar to the Williams tube, it provided a seemingly low-risk path to improved memories for commercial computers. Accordingly, a plan evolved to ship the first IBM 702s with Williams-tube main memories similar to those on the 701, while developing the more reliable, higher-density barrier-grid tube for use on future 702s. In words that convey the competitive spirit that exists when more than one technological approach is under consideration, Fox recalls how pleased he was when his barrier-grid proposal finally "pulled the rug out from under cores for the 702."[57]

This decision was reassessed almost continually during the following year for several reasons: first, there were severe service problems with Williams tubes installed on the 701 computer; second, there was growing confidence in the feasibility of making ferrite-core memories at a reasonable cost; and third, the success of the UNIVAC in the commercial market made IBM corporate management more sensitive to the reliability of electronic computers. Following a visit to MIT in April 1954, Watson, Jr., wrote to Palmer urging greater use of cores, saying: "I recognize that the use of cores in IBM as a commercial end product has been limited by patent problems, problems of uniformity of quality, etc. Nevertheless, if the problem of stringing the cores can be licked, it seems to me, as a layman, that the cost of storage using these cores would be far less than using anything else. . . . I think a tremendous amount of thought should be put into the decision as to how many cores will be used in the 702 in the first models and how quickly we can get them into use on a very broad basis in this machine."[58]

It was at this time that Watson appointed T. Vincent Learson director of Electronic Data Processing Machines (EDPM) to improve IBM's position in electronic computers. Two months later, David Crawford was transferred from Project High to the commercial development area of IBM to develop magnetic-core memories for commercial computer systems.[59] Crawford had not been involved with memory work in Project High, but he had directed the work of fifty engineers in developing vacuum tube circuits, including some of those used in memory. Previously, he had worked for Jerrier Haddad on the IBM 701 computer.

Crawford recalls that one segment of engineering management believed that an experimental ferrite-core memory system should be built in order to develop techniques for reducing costs. Another group argued that there was not enough time for an experimental approach; by the time the results were determined, they reasoned, the 704 and 705 computers would be fully committed to using electrostatic memories. Furthermore, they believed the feasibility of memory cost reduction had already been established by the success of the 776 tape buffer and that the price of critical components, such as cores, would come down as large-scale production was achieved.[60]

This latter view was held by three engineers, assigned to Crawford, who had previously helped design the Type 776 ferrite-core buffer while in Haynes's group.[61] They believed a low-cost main memory could be achieved if ferrite-core specifications were set loose enough that grade B (SAGE reject) cores could be used and if a switch-core matrix—similar to that used in the Type 776 buffer—could be used to drive the much longer lines of the proposed memory.[62]

Preliminary tests of grade B cores from General Ceramics indicated that about 70 percent would be acceptable, but driving long lines using a matrix of switch cores appeared to be more difficult.[63] The engineers at International Telemeter, for example, had reported that small currents induced throughout the memory array from partially selected switch cores resulted in too much electrical noise. A discussion with MIT engineers revealed that they also believed this was a very difficult problem. However, bench tests conducted in the summer of 1954 demonstrated that it was possible to use a switch-core matrix to drive the long lines required for the proposed memory. Critical to this accomplishment were the noise-control techniques implemented earlier on the tape buffer.[64]

Additional cost reduction was to be achieved in a variety of ways. Molded frames were designed with grooves into which core plane wires could be placed, eliminating the need to thread wires through holes in the frame as was done for SAGE. Circuits were designed to minimize the use of vacuum tubes and to be tolerant of changes resulting from tube aging.[65] This feature reduced the frequency with which tubes needed to be replaced and was especially important to IBM because maintenance was included in the rental price.

In July 1954 the new director of EDPM, T. V. Learson, and IBM's director of engineering, W. W. McDowell, toured the Poughkeepsie laboratory and learned about the new engineering results and the lower projected costs of ferrite-core memories. Learson, already convinced that more reliable memories were needed, was quick to act.

That same month, a product program was initiated to put ferrite-core memories on the IBM 704 computer, and in the following month, a similar decision was made for the IBM 705. It was also decided that ferrite-core memories would be made available for replacement of Williams-tube memories on the 701 and 702 computers.[66]

In October 1954, one month before Remington Rand delivered to the National Security Agency its first ferrite-core memory on the ERA 1103 computer, IBM announced that ferrite-core memories would be available on its 701 and 704 computers beginning early in 1956. As first announced only a few months earlier, the 704 had 2048 words of electrostatic memory at a monthly rental of $2600 and an optional second memory of the same capacity for an additional rental of $3500. The new Type 737 magnetic-core storage unit, with 4096 words of memory, was announced at a price of $6100 per month—identical to the price previously announced for the same total amount of electrostatic memory. The announcement did not mention the anticipated, but unverified, improvement in reliability with ferrite-core memories. Instead it cited an improvement in processing speed: "An advantage of Magnetic Core Memory is that regeneration time is not required. Consequently . . . customers who elect to order Magnetic Core Memory will obtain advantages in processing speed. For example, addition time including access is reduced from 60 microseconds to 36 microseconds."[67]

Designs for the just-announced ferrite-core memories were completed in short order, with final memory testing undertaken by mid-1955.[68] These memories used 50-80 mil cores and the array wiring pattern of SAGE. The lower performance required of the memory made it possible to use half-select current pulses of 0.37 ampere—about 10 percent less than in SAGE.

The Type 737 memory used in the IBM 704 computer was housed in its own cabinet, which was 98 inches long, 29 inches wide, and 64 inches high and weighed 1620 pounds.[69] It contained thirty-six planes, each holding 64 × 64 cores plus two spare lines of cores to facilitate repair in the field. Each plane therefore had 64 × 66 (4224) cores. The memory was capable of achieving a 9 microsecond cycle, although only 12 microseconds was required by the computer. By contrast, the memory used in the IBM 705 computer, announced for use in business applications, was built into the computer and consisted of thirty-five planes of 50 × 80 (4000) cores each. Its 9 microsecond cycle was used to handle input-output devices of the system and also to transfer data between locations in memory. The memory was used at a cycle time of 17 microseconds during operations involving the arithmetic section of the processing unit.[70]

Both of these memories employed switch-core drive matrices similar to those Bloch had used in the Type 776 tape buffer. The switch cores were molybdenum-Permalloy tape cores with two primary windings driven by Type 5998 vacuum tube drivers.[71] A secondary winding from a selected switch core transmitted the induced current to the corresponding drive line in the memory array. In the case of the IBM 705 computer, for example, 80 switch cores in an 8 × 10 matrix switch drove the 80 X lines of the memory array and 50 switch cores in a 5 × 10 matrix switch drove the 50 Y lines. Only thirty-three current drivers were thus required to operate the two matrix switches, about a quarter as many as would have been required using direct drive as employed in SAGE.[72]

Shipments of the IBM 704 and 705 to outside customers began in January 1956. That same month, the fourteenth and last IBM 702 was retrofitted with a ferrite-core memory before it was shipped to the Ford Motor Company in Dearborn, Michigan.[73] Customers who appreciated ferrite-core memory the most were those who had previously worked with an IBM 701 or 702. Computing jobs on the 701 were frequently run twice because, without parity check, there was no other way to know if an error had occurred. On the 702, which had parity check, errors detected in the Williams-tube memory occurred with annoying frequency. On one occasion, when an IBM 702 was retrofitted with ferrite-core memory, a programmer at the Bank of America in San Francisco recalls how impressive it was to see the "banks upon banks of electrostatic storage tubes replaced by a small metallic box with a glass window, revealing the compact ferrite core memory with twice the storage capacity of the previous memory."[74]

7.4 Pushing the Limits

The July 1954 decision to develop ferrite-core memories for commercial computers was made none too soon. From the first installations of IBM 702 computers in 1955, it was clear that business users were not as tolerant of poor memory reliability as had been the scientific users of the IBM 701. The resulting customer dissatisfaction was unacceptable to Tom Watson, Jr. At a meeting of engineering managers in August 1955, he vented his displeasure with the decision to use Williams-tube memories on the 702 because they were cheaper than ferrite cores, saying, "If they made this decision to buy something that *didn't work* for X dollars against something that *did work* for 5X dollars, that's the damnedest decision I ever heard of." On a more conciliatory note, Watson acknowledged that engineering had done a remarkable job of catching up with Sperry Rand—especially since a market study conducted three years earlier, to which he had been a party, had "shown conclusively" that no commercial customer could use computers in the 702 class.[75]

Inability to anticipate customer requirements continued to be a major problem. For example, no sooner had the Type 737 ferrite-core memory with twice the capacity of the standard electrostatic memory been announced than customers involved in cryptography, nuclear weapons simulation, and weather forecasting requested yet larger memories. Even for typical data processing applications, large, reliable main memories made programming easier and helped the programs run faster. When programmers learned how reliable ferrite-core memories were, they requested larger ones. It was the beginning of a long-term trend in which user requirements for main memory seemed to increase without limit.

In mid-1955 McDowell asked Bloch to build a memory with over 1 million bits as requested by the RAND Corporation for its 704 computer. As part of the initial assignment, Palmer urged Bloch to use transistors instead of vacuum tubes in all memory-support circuits. This was believed to be possible because of reports written by Kenneth Olsen at MIT and because of IBM's own success nine months earlier in building an experimental 604 electronic calculator with transistors instead of vacuum tubes. But replacing vacuum tubes with transistors in memory circuits was found to be very difficult because of the large currents needed to switch ferrite cores. Within a few months, it was concluded that—MIT reports notwithstanding—transistors with sufficient power to drive ferrite-core memories economically were not yet available. Furthermore, the logic circuits of the 704 computer, to which the megabit memory was to be attached, were built with vacuum tubes. This led to a decision to use vacuum tube logic in the memory as well in order to make the manufacture and service of the total computer easier. Transistors were used in the memory sense amplifiers, however, making the Type 738 memory the company's first product containing transistors to be shipped to a commercial customer.[76]

The megabit memory array was organized with 128 address lines in the X direction, 256 address lines in the Y direction, and 36 bits per word in the Z direction. Once again switch-core matrix drive was used to reduce the number of drive circuits. The switch cores were arranged in 8 × 8 matrices, two matrices being used to drive the 128 X lines and four to drive the 256 Y lines. The large size of the memory array caused a delay of about 0.3 microsecond between the establishment of a half-select current in the first and last cores in a string of 8192 cores. To minimize this effect, the inhibit winding was divided into four independently driven sections, and the sense windings were similarly divided.[77]

The Type 738 memory was shipped to the RAND Corporation in April 1957. Its 32,768 word, 36 bit per word, memory array had 1,179,648 bits—eight times as many ferrite cores as were used in the Type 737 memory originally shipped on the 704 computer. Yet the Type 738 memory occupied a volume only about two and a half times larger and weighed only about two and a half times as much. The sale price of the megabit memory, first set at $1,040,000, was soon reduced to $940,000 or 80 cents per bit—expensive compared to today's prices but cheap compared to $1.31 per bit then charged for the smaller Type 737 memory.[78]

At about the same time that Bloch began work on the Type 738 memory, Crawford's group was assigned the task of designing small memories for the proposed Modular Accounting Calculator (MAC) system. An important technical objective was to use all solid-state circuitry—no vacuum tubes. The Type 608 calculator with a 40 bit by 38 word, 10 microsecond cycle memory was to be the first unit of the MAC system. Larger, compatible calculators were to be designed later. To meet these objectives, three transistor drivers were used in parallel to drive each line in the memory array. This memory, containing the same 50-80 mil ferrite cores that were used in the 737 and 738 memories, was completed in 1955 and first shipped on the IBM 608 calculator in December 1957.[79]

The main memory was very small, but it was IBM's first commercial ferrite-core memory to be built using transistors for all the support circuitry. Thus, Palmer achieved his objective of producing what is believed to be the world's first fully transistorized commercial calculator to be placed into production. But because of changing market requirements and new system designs, the 608 calculator was the only member of the MAC series ever produced (see chapter 12).

Beginning early in the spring of 1955, Palmer sought funds to pursue advanced solid-state technologies needed for future products. The company's development resources appeared to be inadequate for the major thrust he believed was essential. But in seeking government contract money, Palmer was concerned lest he be trapped into committing vast resources to projects that might not provide the significant technological advances he was seeking. Finally in September, a contract opportunity appeared to be right. The National Security Agency (NSA) indicated its interest in funding two advanced-memory development projects proposed by IBM. One was to develop a 2 microsecond cycle megabit memory using small ferrite cores. The second was a smaller, 0.5 microsecond cycle memory using ferrite cores with three holes instead of one. Both memories were to have all-transistor support circuits designed with high-performance transistors being developed at IBM. The contract, signed in January 1956, called for NSA to contribute $1 million to a memory development program called Silo. Project Silo, led by David Crawford in Philip Fox's area, was later incorporated into Project Stretch—a project intended to "stretch" all computer technologies.[80] (See chapter 11.)

The difficult problem of devising semiconductor circuits with sufficient speed and power to switch ferrite cores in the memory array became the primary responsibility of Gregory Constantine, Jr., who joined IBM and Project Silo in March 1956, immediately after receiving the master's degree in electrical engineering from MIT.[81] The magnitude of the problem was not fully appreciated at the time, nor were the limitations of semiconductor devices well understood. The very long drive lines, threading through 4096 cores of the Z line or through 9216 cores of the X and Y planes, experienced heavy inductive loads, creating large back voltages.[82]

By December, Constantine was considering "some crazy ways of adding currents and cancelling currents with transformers." He says, "I suggested it might be possible to use these concepts to drive the memory even with the available transistors. I remember being laughed at. Several of the managers who laughed at my idea had to go to a conference immediately following that meeting. By the time they came back, we had such a device wired and working."[83]

By January 1957, Constantine had written a report describing a new matrix switch that combined the input power from many transistors into one larger output pulse; by the end of the summer, he had designed and fabricated a matrix switch similar to the ones ultimately used in the Type 7302 Stretch memory. He called it a load-sharing matrix switch. It consisted of sixteen magnetic switch cores used as transformers. The output from thirty-two separate transistor drivers drove thirty-two primary windings, which were coupled positively and negatively to the sixteen switch cores in such a way that only one core experienced the positive input from all sixteen drivers when an appropriate sixteen drivers were activated. The positive and negative orientations of the selected primary windings were such that each of the other fifteen cores experienced exactly eight negative and eight positive input pulses. Proper selection of sixteen out of thirty-two drivers permitted any one of the sixteen cores to be activated. In this way, the output power of sixteen transistor drivers could be combined to drive any one selected line in the memory array.[84]

For the planned 2 microsecond main memory of Stretch, 125-250 mil diameter ferrite switch cores, 1.8 inches long, were used. Drive line currents of 0.58 ampere at 100 volts—58 watts of power—were required from these switch cores. Assuming a 90 percent efficiency in the load-sharing matrix switch, the sixteen input transistors had to supply a total of 65 watts or only about 4 watts each, well within the state of the art. The most difficult problem of all—providing the required large currents and high voltages with transistors—had been solved.[85]

The remaining problems were not trivial. For example, to stabilize the core temperatures, many things were tried: talcum powder, grease, oil, and Freon. Only complete immersion in a liquid was satisfactory. Ultimately the entire core array was immersed in transformer oil. The oil was cooled or heated under thermostatic control to maintain the temperature of the cores to within a few degrees of the nominal temperature at which they were designed to operate.[86]

The problems of the 2 microsecond memory were small compared to those encountered in the effort to develop a 0.5 microsecond cycle memory using three-hole cores. Lloyd P. Hunter, hired in 1951 to manage IBM's growing effort in solid-state technologies (see chapter 10), had originally proposed this novel concept at a brainstorming session in July 1955, only one month before it became a critical element in the project proposals presented to NSA. The anticipated advantages of three-hole cores were described by Hunter as follows: "A coincident summation of magnetic flux causes the element to switch, and the magnitudes of the currents inducing the flux are not critical. This allows the switching time to be freed of the current-selection-ratio limitation typical of the coincident-current selection systems. In the coincident-flux system, one may use selecting flux densities representing fields very much greater than the coercive field, giving very fast switching times."[87]

Enthusiasm for three-hole cores gradually faded as an increasing number of technical problems was discovered. One was the large back voltage induced in the drive lines by the large amount of magnetic material that was partially switched with each current pulse. This was reduced somewhat by use of an extra bias winding through the core that reduced flux switching in partially selected cores. However, the need for more than one wire per hole continued to be a deterrent to improvements in packaging. Cores with five and six holes (using fewer wires per hole) were developed and tested, but these presented even more difficulties.[88] So severe were the problems that by July 1959 the 0.5 microsecond memory was eliminated as a requirement on the Stretch computer so that schedules could be estimated more realistically. However, it remained a requirement of Harvest, the special-purpose computer for NSA.[89]

Technical problems with the high-speed memory and its three-hole cores persisted. The project seemed doomed to failure in the fall of 1959, when David Crawford and another engineer first learned of an experimental two-core-per-bit memory during a visit to Mullard, an English subsidiary of the Philips Corporation. This memory was wired in a 2D manner, permitting large drive currents to be used for fast switching; the difference in output signal between the two cores of each bit was sensed, resulting in good noise rejection. A partial-switching mode, in which cores were not switched to full saturation, further enhanced the memory speed. An information-exchange agreement with Philips (to be discussed later) permitted the IBM engineers to learn about these concepts and to use them. Modifications of the Philips scheme were made primarily to permit use of support circuits already developed by Crawford's group for the three-hole core memory.[90]

The two-core-per-bit memory proposal adopted for Harvest in May 1960 provided 73,728 bits, organized in a 2D array of 1024 words of 72 bits each. The memory cycle was to be as close to 0.5 microsecond as possible. Each bit consisted of a pair of ferrite cores, 30-50 mil in diameter and 11 mil high. The information in all 72 bits on a word line was read simultaneously by sending a large current pulse through the selected word line. Thus, the readout current could be made as large as needed to switch the cores rapidly because it was not limited by half-select requirements of coincident-current selection. There were separate write and read lines, the readout line being wired twice through the cores so that twice the ampere turns could be achieved with the given current. In this way the same load-sharing matrix switch could be used to drive both the read and write lines.[91]

One of the last problems to be overcome was magnetostrictive ringing—a mechanical oscillation of the ferrite cores that occurred when the electrical drive pulse was applied. The oscillation, in turn, induced undesirable electrical noise (or ringing), and there was concern that the cores would wear out mechanically. Caused by the well-known phenomenon of magnetostriction, the core oscillation problem was first observed in this memory because of its high speed.

There was no time for basic studies or analyses. The engineers placed a large tub out on the lawn, held the wired core arrays over it, and poured over them a polyurethane material, hoping the liquid would dry into a soft coating and damp out the mechanical vibration. "It was kind of a gamble," one of the engineers recalled. "We were afraid it might change their switching characteristics, and we had no solvent to remove the material from the cores." But the technique worked and was used in later core memories as well.[92]

Two of these memories were completed and supplied to the Harvest system in December 1960.[93] The cycle time was 0.7 microsecond instead of the targeted 0.5 microsecond, but they were still the fastest full-sized memories built to that time.[94] The memories were actually used at a cycle of only 0.9 microsecond in Harvest, which was able to make effective use of a memory cycle of 0.6 or 0.9 but not 0.7 microsecond. The Harvest system itself, including these memories, was finally shipped to NSA and accepted in February 1962 (see chapter 11).

Meanwhile, numerous changes had occurred in the objectives of Project Stretch. Most significantly, in 1958 IBM had obtained a contract to provide a transistorized version of the 709 computer, later known as the 7090, for the Ballistic Missile Early Warning System (BMEWS). Subsequently, the company decided to market a transistorized version of the business-oriented IBM 705 computer, designated the IBM 7080. To help keep manufacturing and service costs of these systems low, the 2 microsecond memory was designed so that it could be reconfigured for use on the different systems with only minor changes in its support circuitry.[95]

The first shipment of the 2 microsecond memory, called the Type 7302, was on an IBM 7090 computer in November 1959 to Sylvania in Needham, Massachusetts, for use in BMEWS. Its actual cycle time was 2.18 microseconds as compared to 12 microseconds for the earlier Type 738 memory. It used all semiconductor circuits, smaller 30-50 mil ferrite cores, and was housed in one box, 30 inches wide, 56 inches long, and 69 inches high..[96] Its vacuum tube-driven predecessor, the 738, had been housed in a T-shaped structure three times longer and wider.[97]

The technical difficulties encountered in developing the ferrite-core memories for Stretch and Harvest created considerable pessimism that significant additional improvements could be achieved. But in fact these memories were followed by a rapid succession of improvements that made core memories very cost-effective, thwarting all efforts to introduce alternative technologies. The inconvenient oil-immersion cooling of cores was replaced by air cooling. This was accomplished by reducing the core size from 30-50 mil to 19-32 mil, thus creating a larger area-to-volume ratio of the cores, which automatically made them easier to cool. The smaller cores also facilitated a small reduction in the read-write cycle time from 2.18 to 2.0 microseconds. The air-cooled, 2.0 microsecond cycle memories were first announced for the IBM 7094 in January 1962, and shipments began during that year on the 7094 as well as on systems previously using the oil-cooled version. Further improvements reduced the memory cycle time to 1.4 microseconds as announced with the 7094 II in May 1963.[98]

7.5 Fabrication

The ferrite cores used in the experimental buffer built by Haynes and Rabenda on the Type 405 accounting machine in 1952 were 150-240 mil inside-outside diameter; cores used in SAGE and the first commercial memories were 50-80 mil; and cores used in the oil-cooled Type 7302 were 30-50 mil and those used in the air-cooled 2.0 microsecond memories in 1962 were 19-32 mil—about eight times smaller in diameter and several hundred times smaller in volume than the cores used by Haynes and Rabenda only ten years earlier. Core-size reduction was particularly significant because the energy dissipated during magnetization switching in a core is proportional to its volume. Small cores could therefore be switched faster, even with lower power circuits. The company's ability to produce, test, and wire the smaller cores was therefore critical to its success with ferrite core memories.

The unavailability of ferrite cores with sufficient uniformity to permit manufacture of the buffer proposed by Rabenda in April 1952 prompted Palmer to establish an exploratory process development effort under Lloyd Hunter in Arthur Samuel's area. Furnaces, ball mills, and presses were ordered and the recruitment of key people begun.[99]

The first recruits to arrive that summer were M. Clayton Andrews and Andrew H. Eschenfelder, with Ph.D. degrees from the University of Illinois and Rutgers, respectively. Andrews had worked on semiconductors for his thesis, and Eschenfelder had worked on paramagnetic resonance for his, but at IBM both were assigned to work on ferrite cores. They bought cores from General Ceramics, analyzed and tested them, and then attempted to duplicate them. In November, they pressed and fired their first manganese-magnesium ferrite cores, and by December they had achieved cores with reasonably good hysteresis loops. But they were not as good as those obtained from General

Ceramics. Eschenfelder therefore began to study the effects of sintering and annealing of cores under various conditions. In February, he was rewarded by a report from Haynes that one of his cores had performed well under pulse-test conditions used to simulate operation in a coincident-current memory.[100]

The rate of progress was increased substantially after James M. Brownlow joined the effort in March 1953. In addition to a bachelor's degree in 1943 from Alfred University, an upstate New York school that offered one of the few courses in ceramics in the country, Brownlow had a master's degree in ceramics from MIT in 1948. He also had five years' experience at the Glenco Gulton Company before joining IBM.[101] His extensive practical knowledge and experience in working with ceramic materials soon led to his being placed in charge of ferrite-core fabrication. Meanwhile, Eschenfelder and Andrews turned their attention to more fundamental studies of ferrite materials and processes.

In May 1953, Forrester, who had supported ferrite-core development work at General Ceramics since 1950, agreed to fund a ferrite-core development effort at IBM to create a second source of cores for SAGE. Ralph Palmer's plan was to establish a ferrite-core production line, which would be supported by basic studies in Hunter's Physical Research Department.[102] That June, John W. Gibson, who had just obtained the Ph.D. degree from Johns Hopkins University, was hired "to develop the materials, techniques, and equipment for production and testing of ferrite cores for Project High."[103] Before earning his doctorate, Gibson had served in the navy, worked at the Naval Research Laboratory, and had obtained a master's degree from Johns Hopkins.   To learn about core fabrication, Gibson and Brownlow made numerous trips to MIT, which, unlike General Ceramics, did not regard its processes as proprietary. The MIT procedure achieved uniformity among cores by processing enough in one batch to populate an entire array. Gibson and Brownlow, however, noted that a manufacturing facility would have to be able to make identical successive batches. They therefore chose to make many small batches under well-controlled conditions. Cores were pressed to the desired shape, placed in small platinum boats for insertion into a 2-inch diameter furnace, where they were heated to about 1300°C, and then withdrawn at a carefully controlled rate. After much experimentation, it became possible to make cores with properties superior to cores produced by General Ceramics.[104]

The MIT quarterly progress report of September 1954 describes MIT's evaluation of cores from three potential suppliers. Cores from Ferroxcube were said to "require considerable alteration in properties in order to meet the present memory specification." RCA core production was reported to be "not stabilized and that insufficient control of processing variables is the underlying cause." Concerning IBM, the report said the pilot line "has produced three lots of 740 cores each. . . . the yield of acceptable cores for the three lots averaged about 95 percent. . . . On the basis of these preliminary lots, IBM appears a very probable second source of supply of ferrite memory cores."[105]

Consistent with these early findings of the SAGE group at MIT was the selection of IBM as a second source of cores. The company had been careful to develop its process independent of General Ceramics because it planned to produce cores for commercial products as well. However, General Ceramics held a basic patent on the magnesium-manganese (MgMn) ferrite composition for which it was reluctant to negotiate either a simple royalty-bearing license or a paid-up license as IBM preferred. In addition to receiving royalties, General Ceramics also insisted on supplying a guaranteed percentage of IBM's core requirements, a condition the company was not willing to accept.[106]

When a meeting in July 1955 failed to break the impasse, IBM initiated a program to develop an alternative composition. Studies were undertaken by Brownlow in Physical Research and by Gibson in Component Research. The most promising material appeared to be a copper-manganese (CuMn) ferrite composition developed by the Philips corporation in the Netherlands. Rights to use this material were easily and quickly acquired because Philips was eager to obtain automatic core-handling and core-testing knowledge possessed by IBM. In May 1956 the companies signed an agreement "to facilitate the interchange of technical information on such circuitry and elements . . . with the objective to expedite progress with respect to their activities, by eliminating duplication of efforts, exchanging information on accomplishments and pooling resources to solve particular problems."[107]

Later that month, Philips supplied IBM with samples of the CuMn ferrite cores, which they were producing—with only about 10 percent yields—to the IBM core specification. Gibson's group initiated an effort to improve the processing procedures. Various adjustments to the Philips process were made, including the use of a unique two-stage quenching process invented by Brownlow. He cooled the cores from an initial high temperature, such as 1300°C, to about 950°C, where they remained for 5 to 15 minutes depending on core size and composition before they were quenched to room temperature. This caused the formation on the core surface of small inclusions of a nonmagnetic ferrous oxide (Fe_2O_3) which raised the coercive force at the inner surface of the cores and improved the switching characteristics.[108]

By October 1956, IBM was able to produce CuMn ferrite cores for the Type 738 memory with a 60 percent yield. Cores tailored for small buffer memories were also developed, and in January 1957 the ferrite-core development and product engineering activities were transferred to the Poughkeepsie Product Development Laboratory. The company now had a fully operating ferrite-core development and manufacturing facility and had acquired the freedom to manufacture the CuMn ferrite cores in return for reasonable royalty payments to Philips.

The Philips agreement made negotiations with General Ceramics easier. In April 1957, IBM signed agreements with General Ceramics to purchase 49.5 million cores during 1957–1958 for an average price of 3.4 cents each and an additional 30 million cores (or half of the SAGE requirements, whichever was smaller) for an average price of 2.7 cents each. The company also agreed to pay $250,000 for the right to manufacture 50 million MgMn cores.[109] One month later, the company agreed to buy 90 million CuMn ferrite cores for commercial machines from Ferroxcube, a U.S. subsidiary of Philips, during a three-year period, at an average price of 1.5 cents each. Although this price seemed low at the time, IBM's own cost of manufacturing cores averaged only about 0.8 cent per core during the same three-year period.[110]

The MgMn ferrite cores covered by the General Ceramics patent continued to be used for SAGE, but after 1958 IBM never again manufactured or purchased MgMn ferrite cores for commercial machines. Refusal to negotiate more flexibly had cost General Ceramics its position as the primary supplier of ferrite cores.

Critical to IBM's success with ferrite-core memories was its automation of the fabrication process, beginning in Gibson's group with the development of high-speed core pressing equipment. A rotary press, of the type used in the pharmaceutical industry to produce aspirin tablets, was purchased and modified to produce the doughnut-shaped cores.[111] The ferrite material was so abrasive, however, that it quickly wore out the metal dies. After several attempts, Colton rotary presses were purchased and modified with tungsten carbide dies. The modified Colton press had eight sets of pressing tools with upper and lower punches that moved around the periphery of the circular press table. The ferrite powder was inserted in the dies in the periphery of the press table and then compacted by the punches to form a toroidal core. Completed in 1954, the eight-station press was capable of pressing the newly defined 50-80 mil cores for SAGE at a rate of 30 cores per minute.

This basic design was improved many times. By 1957 eight-station rotary presses were producing 320 cores per minute. By then, most of the cores were 30-50 mil in diameter, small enough to fit inside the cores used in SAGE. Four years later, sixteen-station presses were introduced to produce 19-30 mil cores, small enough to fit inside the 30-50 mil cores. By 1963 core production exceeded several million per day.[112]

Each core, after pressing and firing, was tested electronically before it was wired into a memory array. Semiautomatic and fully automatic testers, developed for Project SAGE, were capable of testing up to one core per second. The electronic design was based on that of MIT, but the core-handling equipment was developed at IBM. By the end of 1953, the company had built ten automatic handlers for use at IBM, MIT, and General Ceramics to test cores required for SAGE prototype memories.[113] When a rotary "corn-planter" mechanism, used in the early testers, proved slow and broke cores, it was replaced by a vibratory bowl that fed the cores smoothly into the tester mechanism.

In 1958, the reciprocating motion of the solenoid-operated test probe was replaced with a rotating drum equipped with electrical probes sticking out radially from the surface. Cores were fed into a vibratory bowl that spiraled them to the outside edge, where they were picked up one at a time by the electrical probes as the rotating drum was stepped past the pick-up position. A vacuum system in the rotating drum helped to pull each core onto the probe and hold it. As the drum rotated, the core came to a test station where electrical contact was made to the end of the probe, and a series of electrical tests were made. The results of these tests determined whether the vacuum mechanism should release the core into the accept or reject bin.[114] By 1960, these core handlers were operating at speeds of 12 cores per second, and there were two core handlers per tester.

The wiring of the core planes for Project SAGE had been a particularly laborious task requiring great patience and skill. A long hypodermic needle was probed by hand into a glass dish containing the cores until sixty-four cores were loaded onto the needle. Then a copper wire was inserted through the hypodermic needle and the needle withdrawn to cause the sixty-four cores to be strung on the copper wire. The wire was attached to the terminals of the memory array. A total of sixty-four wires, with sixty-four cores each, were so attached. These were the X wires. The sixty-four orthogonal Y wires then had to be threaded through each of the cores at 90 degrees to the X wire. As each core was approached by the needle, it was hand manipulated to ensure a proper orientation in the array.

When all wires were threaded in this manner, a core mat of 4096 cores having an X wire and a Y wire through each core was ready for insertion of the third and fourth (inhibit and sense) wires. Before this was done, the array was tested to be sure that all cores were good. A bad core was removed by cutting the X and Y wire through it. Then new X and Y wires were restrung through the cores in the row and column containing the removed core, and a new core was inserted during the restringing operation. The inhibit and sense lines were then strung through each core in the plane.

Assembly time for the X and Y wires of a single core plane was about 25 hours for skilled operators. Stringing the third and fourth lines required another 15 hours.[115] The high cost of this tedious work was a major contributor to IBM's reluctance to become committed to the manufacture of ferrite-core memories for commercial systems and resulted in a search for ways to automate the process.

One who responded was Hans Peter Luhn, a prolific inventor who had been hired by T. J. Watson, Sr. Luhn devised a number of ways to wire core arrays. A simple device was a large takeup spool to facilitate wiring of the long, thin, continuous-sense wire that ran diagonally through all cores in a core plane. The takeup spool helped to keep the wire from twisting or breaking. An even more innovative idea was the use of a comb-shaped structure that not only held the cores for wiring but also became an integral part of the memory structure.[116] This method was used in the small memory of the Type 608 calculator, completed in 1955 and first shipped in 1957. Even more attractive methods were soon developed by others.

The most successful core plane wiring method was based on an MIT proposal that a flat plate with cavities regularly spaced on its surface be used to hold the cores in the desired position for wiring. As implemented by IBM, this matrix was a plastic plate with cavities in which individual cores were held by a vacuum applied through a small orifice in the bottom of each cavity. The matrix was mounted on a vacuum manifold affixed to a vibrator. Loose cores were dumped on the surface of the matrix and vibrated until they came near empty cavities, where the vacuum drew the cores into the cavities. Because of the high cost of the plastic matrix and vacuum system, a technique was developed in which a sheet of sticky tape was placed on the array of cores once they were oriented in the plastic matrix. The vacuum system was then turned off, and the array of cores, held in place on the sticky tape, was ready for wiring.

To wire the array, insulated wire was inserted approximately 1 or 2 inches into a long piece of hypodermic tubing that was used as a needle to thread a line of cores. Friction between the wire and the interior of the tubing held the wire as it was being pulled through the cores. Once through the cores, the end of the wire was attached to a terminal on the edge of the array. The needle was then withdrawn, automatically rethreading itself as it was drawn back along the continuous length of wire from the large spool.[117]

An important IBM invention resulted from the observation that manual guidance of the needle through the cores was not required because the cores acted as guides. Needles could therefore be propelled through the cores in gangs, instead of individually. A machine was devised, capable of impelling up to eighty hypodermic needles through cores at one time, using typewriter rollers mounted like old-time washing machine wringers, to drive the needles.[118] The time required to thread the X and Y wires in a 64 × 64 plane was reduced dramatically, from 25 hours to 12 minutes.[119] The core threading machine, conceived late in 1955 and first implemented in production in 1956, was replicated and improved innumerable times during the 1960s. (See figure 7.4.)

7.6 Patents and Innovation

At an August 1955 meeting with key engineers in Poughkeepsie, Watson, Jr., chided them for hesitating to use ferrite cores in commercial products because of Wang's patent. He quoted his father as saying, "That's the most ridiculous reason for not moving into a new area that I've ever heard of because, one way or another, we can negotiate with Wang."[120]

Indeed the company was able to obtain rights to Wang's patent for the reasonable fee of several hundred thousand dollars. Learning of a related patent filed by Frederick W. Viehe, two years before Wang's, IBM obtained rights to that patent as well.[121] When negotiations with General Ceramics for use of its MnMg ferrite patent reached an impasse in mid-1955, an effort to find an alternative ferrite material was launched. One year later, an agreement was signed that provided IBM with rights to use a CuMn ferrite composition developed by the Philips Corporation.

Watson's confidence that rights to any patent could be obtained at a reasonable fee, or the patent circumvented, appeared to be justified by these cases. But by the end of the decade, his confidence was

Figure 7.4
Core threading machine. The vacuum matrix and covers (top) hold an array of
128 × 128 cores in place ready for wiring. The sixty-four needles to the right
have been withdrawn, leaving the sixty-four wires threaded through the cores.
After these wires are attached to the terminals on the edge of the core plane, the
needle feeder is indexed to the left to insert the adjacent group of sixty-four
wires. The array is then rotated 90 degrees to permit the orthogonal wires to be
similarly threaded. Needles of the wiring machine are shown (bottom) passing
through the cores and over orthogonal wires previously inserted. The cores have
an inside diameter of 30 mil and outside diameter of 50 mil. When first introduced in 1959, this core threading machine reduced the time to thread X and Y
wires in a 64 × 64 plane from 25 hours to 12 minutes.

deeply shaken. Forrester had filed a patent application under which MIT (through its patent management firm, Research Corporation) was demanding royalties of 2 cents for every magnetic core used in a coincident-current memory. This demand, made in November 1959, was quickly rejected for IBM by James Birkenstock who noted that "in our core storage units we employ seven of our own patents, as well as having acquired licenses under five patents from outsiders, which were necessary to make the Forrester patent usable." If a royalty of 2 cents per bit were demanded under each of these patents, the cost per bit for royalties alone would be 26 cents, making core storage economically infeasible. Based on this analysis, Birkenstock concluded that a royalty of 2 cents per bit was ten to twenty times too much. But Research Corporation indicated it had already rejected an offer of 1 cent per bit, so an impasse resulted.[122]

Three years earlier, in September 1956, an interference had been declared between Forrester's patent and one filed by Jan Rajchman of RCA. Rajchman, like Forrester, used coincident-current selection of magnetic cores in an array. Admitting that Forrester had conceived the idea first, Rajchman asserted that Forrester had failed to show feasibility and had failed to pursue the idea diligently as required by U.S. patent law. The Board of Patent Interference agreed, and in October 1960 it awarded to Rajchman what many believed to be the ten broadest claims of the Forrester patent.[123] It was a happy result for IBM, because three years earlier, a cross-license with RCA had been negotiated that provided IBM, among other things, with rights to Rajchman's patent.[124]

The jubilation was short-lived, however, as Research Corporation continued to demand royalties of 2 cents per core and initiated a civil action to regain the lost patent claims. Thus while IBM engineers were developing cost-effective memory designs and improving manufacturing techniques, litigation between RCA and MIT plodded slowly in the courts toward a settlement that would have profound ramifications on IBM and the entire data processing industry.

To help break the deadlock, IBM put together a presentation of prior art showing that Forrester's patent claims were subordinate to claims in the earlier patents of Wang and Viehe, and the company also initiated a study of alternative memory technologies not covered by the Forrester patent.[125] The most promising of these alternatives in 1960 appeared to be two cores per bit as developed for Harvest and which IBM patent attorneys believed was covered by an RCA patent under which IBM was licensed.[126] However, experimental work on other memory devices was also supported both because the devices were believed to circumvent Forrester's patent and because they were expected to be faster than ferrite cores. These alternatives included tunnel diode devices based on discoveries of Leo Esaki, who joined IBM in 1960; superconducting memory cells that operated at liquid helium temperatures of −269°C; and a variety of structures employing metallic ferromagnetic films plated on conductors or sandwiched between conducting lines.

When in late 1962 IBM Research engineers observed a fast rotational switching in ferrite memory structures that they believed were not covered by Forrester's patent, their embryonic idea was escalated rapidly into a major project. Known as the Flute because of its appearance, the proposed memory array consisted of many parallel hollow ferrite tubes, on a single substrate, with a wire running the length of the hollow center of each of the tubes. Other wires were laid over the tubes, perpendicular to their length. Information was stored by the clockwise or counterclockwise direction of magnetization of the ferrite tubes, each bit being defined by the intersection of the internal and external wires. Within a few months, more than twenty-five people were assigned to the project, but in vain. Heavy electrical attenuation on the sense lines made the approach unattractive, if not inoperable.[127]

The experience with the Flute helped to emphasize that there was no attractive alternative to coincident-current 3D selection ferrite-core memories. IBM had obtained rights to use all relevant patents except Forrester's—and the validity of that patent was still being argued in the courts.

Meanwhile, IBM engineers continued to develop improved ferrite-core memory designs and manufacturing methods as customers ordered more and larger memories. By the end of 1963, the company's annual production of ferrite cores exceeded 1 billion; a royalty of 2 cents per core would alone have cost more than $20 million per year. With the IBM System/360 slated for announcement early in 1964, the situation was intolerable. In February 1964, an agreement was finally reached in which the company agreed to pay a one-time fee of $13 million for the use of Forrester's patent if at least one of the claims was upheld in the litigation between MIT and RCA.[128] The following month RCA and MIT reached an agreement in which the validity of Forrester's patent was affirmed, and IBM made its payment to MIT.[129] Larger than any previous payment on record for a patent, it was nevertheless dramatically cheaper than the requested royalty of 2 cents per bit.

The trauma of the Forrester patent case is legend. It made engineers and managers keenly aware of the importance of patents. Somewhat surprisingly, however, the case appears to have had very little impact on the company's patent policy, which had been formulated following the settlement in January 1956 of a federal antitrust suit. The consent decree in that suit required that the company license certain data processing patents at reasonable royalties and certain card machinery patents without charge. To minimize the chance of future antitrust action, the company chose to adopt an open patent license policy for all patents pertaining to the manufacture, sale, and use of data processing equipment. By this policy, anyone could obtain a license to use IBM patents at a reasonable fee. The company's patent portfolio was to be used only to ensure its own freedom of action. Product superiority was to be achieved by effective use of all existing knowledge rather than by excluding competitors from IBM patents.[130] With technological advances occurring all over the world, it was a wise policy. It helped to facilitate a rapid rate of product development through sharing of inventions.

Responding to the number of invention disclosures submitted by a rapidly growing technical staff, the company established a Technical Disclosure Bulletin (TDB) in June 1958, in which disclosures judged to have limited value could be published to ensure freedom of use for all. This avoided the time-consuming process of filing and processing patents. Although the percentage of invention disclosures filed (instead of published or dropped) was cut in half, the number of patents issued per year to IBM employees increased over fourfold from the early 1950s to the early 1960s.[131] A patent-awards program established in 1961 stimulated even more invention disclosures. It offered "inaugural" awards to 225 employees for patent activity prior to 1961 and $1000 for patents issued or applied for after January 1961 and judged to be outstanding by a local IBM board. An award of $5000 was available for any patent rated special by a corporate special-awards committee. Finally, the plan established a schedule of awards based on the total number of inventions published or patents issued or pending.[132]

The large sum of money paid for the Forrester patent has tended to obscure the fact that there were many other inventors of magnetic-core memories. Indeed, IBM's patent attorneys believed the patents of Wang and Viehe dominated Forrester's. Of even greater historical significance is a proposal of J. Presper Eckert and Chuan Chu of the Moore School of Electrical Engineering at the University of Pennsylvania, which was made before Forrester, Haynes, Rajchman, Thomas, or Wang (and probably before Viehe) even began working with magnetic cores. They proposed the storage of information in a 2D array of toroidal ferromagnetic cores. Each core in the array was wound by a wire (in series with an oxide rectifier), which was connected between an X and a Y drive line. Separate drive circuits for each X line and each Y line made it possible to pass current through any one selected core in the array. The nonlinear properties of the oxide rectifier provided the switching threshold for the coincident-voltage selection. These ideas were documented in the June 1946 report on the EDVAC submitted by the group at the Moore School.[133] Although the EDVAC report was classified, it was distributed widely enough to cast doubt on the independence of magnetic-core memory proposals made by others at a later time.[134]

Forrester's role as a technology champion and promoter was far more important than his role as an inventor. By promoting and building Whirlwind, he created the most pressing need for a large, fast, reliable, random-access memory. Moreover, he had the resources to develop the first large memory using magnetic cores, and he chose to do that. Forrester also had a clear vision of the ultimate form of core memories: a simple 3D array of toroidal-shaped magnetic cores with three drive wires strung straight through each core. His observation that nonmetallic ferrite cores might be more suitable than metallic cores was particularly significant. Unlike Haynes, Forrester spent little time considering alternative selection schemes for memories or studying magnetic-core devices for logic. He had a single purpose, and he had faith that magnetic cores with the required properties could be achieved.

Without Project SAGE, large ferrite-core memories would certainly have been developed, although somewhat later. IBM, with its early start, would surely have produced one of the first commercial ferrite-core memories and would have achieved a leadership position in electronic computers. But this gradual process did not occur. Instead, IBM management seized the opportunity to participate in SAGE, the successful execution of which helped provide the company with technical leadership in the design and manufacture of main memories. This leadership was enhanced by Project Stretch and even more so by emphasis on manufacturing. Electromechanical skills, previously used to design punched-card equipment, were pressed into service to design equipment to produce, test, and wire ferrite cores; and ferrite-core memories were themselves specifically designed to facilitate mass production. As a result, ferrite-core memories were among the most profitable items in IBM's product line.

8

Disk Storage

A separate group. The source recording project. Disk-array feasibility and early development. Record addressing and RAMAC. Slider development in San Jose. IBM's first slider product. Collateral storage development. The removable disk pack.

In 1952, IBM opened a small laboratory in California and gave its newly assembled staff a measure of freedom for advanced development. Within a few years, the members of the laboratory had distinguished themselves by creating a novel storage product, the magnetic disk file. On the strength of this initial success, they went on to develop disk file technologies that revolutionized the whole field of data processing. This chapter starts with the inception of the laboratory and traces the main events during the first decade of operation.

8.1 A Separate Group

In early January 1950, as if resolved to start the new decade by facing up to an old problem, W. Wallace McDowell, Endicott laboratory manager, wrote John McPherson, now vice-president handling engineering matters, that responses to the need for advanced development had too often been frustrated by "the ever-insistent demands of the sales department." As a solution, he suggested "a separate group or groups whose sole function is to work on long-range component development."[1] The components on his mind were card feeds, card punches, decimal counters, alphanumeric comparators, and storage mechanisms. Aside from a study of xerographic printing methods, the projects he nominated for the separate group were aimed at reducing production costs or increasing machine speeds and capacities. He recommended a headcount of about fifteen as a start.

McDowell, who had given the matter "much consideration," was probably encouraged to make his unusual request by an expansionary mood that had begun to pervade headquarters (see chapter 4) and was already pointing toward more dramatic actions. Three months later, McPherson circulated a memorandum for discussion to other executives, among them Tom Watson (T. J. Watson, Jr., executive vice-president). The document proposed a vigorous expansion of IBM's whole engineering program. McPherson based his case on several considerations, foremost among them "the advent of electronics" in the business machine field.[2] Because his main thrust was toward more research in electronics and physics, and he gave mechanical components little emphasis, the effect was to sidestep McDowell's request for advanced development of card-machine components.

In May, Tom Watson signaled his approval of expansion by formalizing a corporate engineering staff and appointing McDowell as director of engineering. Thus it fell to McDowell to guide the expansion, a task soon magnified by the outbreak of the Korean conflict. When the defense industries and the federal government began projecting increased requirements for data processing, IBM was quick to respond with development programs for the Defense Calculator and NORC (see chapter 5), as well as for bombing and navigational equipment.

During 1951, despite the overriding need for additional manpower in the defense-related programs, McDowell continued to nourish the thought of having the Endicott laboratory do more card-related advanced development. To his list of deserving subject areas he added "automatic data reduction," a project aimed at developing better methods of converting instrument readings into numbers and thence into punched cards. Because the cards thus generated would lead into various computations, the area seemed likely to generate more business for IBM equipment. One obvious application area was the booming airframe industry, where wind tunnels were generating increasing quantities of data. The major technical problems lay in analog-to-digital conversion, a specialized discipline for electrical engineers. Such engineers, unfortunately, were in short supply; IBM personnel managers were advertising for them from New York to Los Angeles and Seattle.

The Endicott laboratory manager's staff tried in vain to subcontract work on analog-to-digital conversion.[3] Then, because engineers seemed reluctant to move away from the Pacific Coast, the idea of forming a western laboratory was considered. Not only would this ease the recruiting task, but long-range projects could be sheltered by geography from the deadline pressures assailing the older laboratories. In late 1951, McDowell asked his staff to investigate suitable sites for such a laboratory. Soon the search closed upon San Jose, California, where IBM already had a plant for making cards.

McDowell, as an experienced laboratory manager, well appreciated the challenges involved in opening a new and distant applied-research laboratory: after a reasonable period of accommodation, the laboratory would be expected to develop new products, a difficult endeavor under the best circumstances and a risky one with newcomers to the business. Knowing this, he carefully planned to shield the new laboratory from any unnecessary risks. First, he envisioned a facility with about 50 people, a modest number when Poughkeepsie, the younger of IBM's two main laboratories, had already passed 700 employees.[4] Second, the automatic data reduction project, which was already approved, could support half of the 50. The other half would avoid exploring areas being covered by Endicott and Poughkeepsie. McDowell explained his plan to Reynold B. Johnson, an Endicott engineer, and astonished him by asking him to head the new endeavor.

The background of the new laboratory manager merits a flashback. Johnson was a University of Minnesota alumnus with a degree in education. About 1932, while teaching high school science in Michigan, he developed an electrical device for scoring multiple-choice tests by effectively counting answer-sheet pencil marks. His initial efforts to generate commercial interest in the device were unsuccessful. But in early 1934, by which time the depression was reaching its low point and he was unemployed, IBM informed him of its interest in his device. As he would later learn, the Endicott laboratory had encountered difficulties in trying to develop an ambitiously conceived scoring machine for Benjamin D. Wood, a professor at Columbia University, a leader in the field of educational testing, and one of T. J. Watson's consultants. That summer, after a panel of IBM executives decided that Johnson's design assumed an impractical degree of student cooperation in the formation of pencil marks, Wood interceded with Watson. Johnson was promptly hired as an engineer and assigned to Endicott.[5] A prototype test-scoring machine based on his design was field tested in 1935 and 1936.[6] The product system was announced as the IBM 805 Test Scoring Machine in 1937.[7] Subsequently, Johnson helped develop an IBM mark-sensing reproducer that could read pencil marks on decimally formated cards and appropriately punch the cards. During World War II, he directed a variety of IBM developments for the armed forces. Following the war, he became interested in wire-matrix printing and other ideas, among them a notched-card mechanism for locating and extracting any specified card from a deck. This card-retrieval idea lapsed into obscurity after McDowell, in April 1949, advised the Future Demands department in corporate headquarters that the approach was sound but that short-range projects of higher priority precluded its further development.[8] Presumably it was the

Figure 8.1
IBM laboratory building, 99 Notre Dame Avenue, San Jose. After R. B. Johnson leased it in early 1952, it remained an IBM location until 1968. This photograph was taken in 1953.

loss of projects such as Johnson's that prompted McDowell, some months later, to propose establishment of a separate group for advanced development.

Named laboratory manager on 15 January 1952, Johnson soon signed a five-year lease on a stuccoed cement-block building at 99 Notre Dame Avenue, San Jose (figure 8.1). Previously the building had housed a printing establishment. In early February, with building renovation underway, Johnson and his staff of two placed notices in several West Coast newspapers, announcing the new laboratory and soliciting applications from scientists and engineers.[9]

After receiving a sizable response to his advertisement, Johnson decided he needed someone with a strong electronics background to help in assessing applicants. Ralph Palmer, Poughkeepsie laboratory manager, came to his aid with L. D. Stevens, who in his three years with Palmer had contributed to magnetic tape and drum devices and to the design of the input-ouput system for the Defense Calculator. In May, Stevens moved permanently to San Jose as Johnson's technical assistant. The laboratory numbered eight employees by the end of March and about thirty by the end of June.[10]

At Endicott, Johnson had been indoctrinated in a long tradition of secret fiefdoms for inventors. But in 1952, faced with a big educational problem, the teacher in him vanquished the inventor: he not only dropped the old ways but took explicit measures to contravene them. To facilitate assimilation of new arrivals, he announced that every engineer should be conversant with all projects and that requests for consultation deserved top priority. Such guidelines are unworkable, for the most part, in the development milieu; engineers normally have to live with deadlines, disciplining their attentions and curbing their curiosities accordingly. But the organization was still just a collection of talent, not a development laboratory, and Johnson's objective was to hasten the desired evolution.

Most of the first recruits were assigned to projects related to data reduction. In June, a qualified manager for some of the data reduction work arrived in the person of John W. Haanstra, who had received his master's degree in electrical engineering from the University of California at Berkeley in 1950, joined the IBM Poughkeepsie laboratory, and subsequently worked on projects with Stevens. Now, finishing a short tour of duty with the navy, Haanstra elected to return to IBM at San Jose rather than at Poughkeepsie.

With the data reduction program largely on its feet, Johnson turned to other matters. Most of his recruits were new to punched-card machines and knew little of digital computers. To hasten indoctrination, engineers were encouraged to write surveys of recent engineering developments and summaries of relevant presentations at meetings of professional societies. And to reveal individual strengths, Johnson began assigning people to small projects of his own choosing.

8.2 The Source Recording Project

When asked to head a "Source Recording" project in September 1952, Arthur J. Critchlow wrote in part, "I am to study the form in which information is now being made available to key punch operators and endeavor to determine means of supplying information in better form."[11] Critchlow was a 1947 graduate of the California Institute of Technology. Before joining IBM in 1952 he had worked in a missile project at an aircraft corporation. Now, for an intensive briefing on business data processing, he turned to a special representative in IBM's San Francisco branch office. Critchlow's tutor was well acquainted with many applications, among them inventory control, which he felt was sorely in need of more suitable equipment and methods.[12]

The archetype of punched-card applications was payroll accounting, a job that deals with matters familiar to almost everyone. A payroll master file might consist of one punched card per employee, each record containing long-lived data such as name, employee number, location, pay rate, and so on. Typically, this file was kept in employee-number order. After weekly time cards, suitably punched, were sorted into masterfile order, processing runs brought together the data needed during preparation of pay checks and stubs, payroll registers, and accounting summaries. Payroll processing ran smoothly and efficiently because most of the work could be done weekly.

Not all applications were so tractable. In accounting practice, the term "transaction" connotes an event or input that triggers some processing steps and necessitates access to one or a few records. So viewed, time cards were transactions that could be processed weekly in batches; at worst, a few had to be handled by clerical intervention — as when an employee quit during a week and needed to be paid at once. On the other hand, as Critchlow observed during some customer visits arranged by the branch-office specialist, the haphazardly arriving transactions characteristic of warehouse operations led to a great deal of clerical intervention. Every time an order came in, one or more files had to be entered, data had to be assembled, and appropriate documents had to be generated for activities such as picking, shipping, and billing. Typically a clerk removed relevant cards, used them in generating other documents, and then refiled cards as necessary. The part number punched in each inventory card was printed across the top of the card; the cards were filed in part-number order. Clerks consulted such files, searching for the card with a given part number in much the way they would have searched a card-index file in a public library. For the convenience and safety of side-by-side clerks, drawers of cards were set out on work tables, the whole inelegant layout being known as a "tub file." These files were tedious to use and conducive to clerical mistakes.

Critchlow began thinking of ways of mechanizing tub-file operations. In this, he was encouraged by Johnson, who knew that Poughkeepsie and Endicott were neglecting the area to concentrate on the Defense Calculator and the Magnetic Drum Calculator. After McDowell had halted Johnson's storage-related work in 1949, there had been sporadic interest in an "automatic file," which by 1951 had advanced in concept beyond the punched card to a magnetically recorded plate capable of storing the equivalent of many cards. But the plate idea, still not grounded in convincing requirements and estimated to require a million-dollar development and tooling effort, was lying dormant for lack of a suitably high priority.[13] Thus, in 1952, the field was open for San Jose. Moreover, Johnson knew that the president of the fledgling Telecomputing Corporation had recently caught McDowell's attention with an idea for a slow but capacious storage device. Telecomputing's main product was a device that could plot points on a plane as instructed by numbers that represented x (east-west) and y (north-south) coordinates, as in a chart or map. The scheme that interested McDowell would suspend strips of magnetic tape at points in the plane and provide a mechanism to select, read or write, and reposition any designated tape strip. McDowell had supported the idea with a contract for additional investigation and, because the firm was located in California, he had asked Johnson to monitor the work.

After considering various possibilities, Critchlow ended up with an idea for a belt that would loop around to move the cards of a tub file past the clerks, a turnabout of conventional practice.[14] He was elaborating a belt proposal when, in November, Johnson made his first visit to Telecomputing and encountered the notion of a bin of tape strips. Johnson immediately thought of the bin as a tub-file substitute but was not persuaded that magnetic-tape strips were suitable; after further discussion, he advocated a bin of plastic-encased magnetic wires. (At the time, magnetic-wire recorders were a consumer product.) As a result of this burst of activity, Critchlow's proposal came to include a magnetic-wire storage device instead of an endless belt.[15]

Then, abruptly, circumstances jolted the source recording project into a larger arena. Stevens flew East in early December to attend an IBM meeting about a U.S. Air Force request for proposals concerning development of a so-called Materiel Information Flow Device (MIFD). The objective of MIFD was largely to automate the inventory accounting and control job for airbases, a job that required transactions to be processed as they arrived. This requirement essentially ruled out serial files consisting of decks of cards or reels of magnetic tape. As a result, Endicott and Poughkeepsie had nothing to propose except magnetic drums—drums too expensive and too low in storage capacity to support a truly convincing proposal.[16]

Stevens came back with news that large-capacity storage devices must be of general interest because the MIFD request had gone to thirty firms. He also brought statistics suggesting that storage capacity should be viewed in grander terms. Where the San Francisco branch office thought a useful random-access device should store the equivalent of perhaps five thousand punched cards, analysts in Future Demands and salesmen familiar with air force applications favored several times that much capacity.

Although Johnson had nearly sixty employees by the end of 1952, few of them had enjoyed an opportunity to meet professionals in IBM's older laboratories. Several engineers in those laboratories had known of the work of Jacob Rabinow, a government-employed inventor, for at least eighteen months.[17] Yet it was around December before Critchlow learned that Rabinow had written of magnetic-disk storage in the August issue of an engineering journal. The second paragraph of the article summarized Rabinow's project:

A magnetic information-storage device now being developed at the National Bureau of Standards (NBS) combines advantages of large storage capacity and rapid access time. The new "memory" stores data in the form of magnetic pulses on both sides of thin metal disks, which are mounted in a doughnut-shaped ring with the planes of the disks vertical. Each disk has a deep notch, and the notches are normally aligned so that a bank of magnetic recording-reading heads can be quickly rotated into position at any desired disk. Test results demonstrate that stored data can be reached in times of the order of 0.5 second. This memory was devised at NBS by request of the Ballistic Research Laboratory of Aberdeen Proving Ground, Md. Two models are nearing completion.[18]

Disks were justified, Rabinow argued, because three-dimensional storage of information uses space efficiently. His disk device, he wrote, was analogous to a book with round pages that could be read without opening the book. Assuming that the entire book was notched part-way to its center and that the page format presented lines of text as arcs (circles made incomplete by the notch), a page could be made visible by rotating it past the notch. After considering a long cylindrical array of magnetic disks, he had decided on a bent shaft that gave the array the form of a doughnut. The notches, aligned to the doughnut hole, made room for heads mounted on a centrally pivoted arm to whirl directly to a selected disk. Once the bank was positioned at a selected disk, the relative motion needed for a read-write operation came as a quick, incomplete rotation of the disk.

The NBS doughnut came to Critchlow's attention at a time when every conceivable low-cost storage technology was still open for consideration. But Johnson, hoping to accelerate progress, soon narrowed the investigation to magnetic surfaces. There followed a review of surface geometries: short tapes and wires, plates, drums, disks, tape loops, and sundry hybrid configurations. In January 1953, during this exercise, a newly hired engineer jotted down the outlines of a storage device in which an array of disks spaced along a straight shaft would spin continually.[19] In Rabinow's device, the pivoting head bank was whirled within one channel of notches, a circumstance that made it impractical to consider having more than one bank. With a rotating array of disks, on the other hand, several access mechanisms could be stationed at angles to the array, thereby permitting head-positioning operations to be performed in parallel. Access to a rotating array, of course, had the disadvantage of requiring two distinct motions, one for moving an access station to a selected disk and another for extending a suitable read-write arm into the array to a desired area of disk surface.

During January, Johnson chose the magnetic disk as the most promising medium for direct-access storage.[20] Critchlow, pushing ahead with a written proposal in early February, formulated challenging goals for a system with fifty disks, a capacity of 4 million characters (the equivalent, that is, of 50,000 IBM cards), and an access time of less than 1 second.[21]

One of the major problems expected with a disk concerned head-to-disk relationships. The rigidity of a drum made it mechanically feasible to maintain a small gap between surface and read-write head. A tape was sufficiently pliable and light to make head-to-surface contact workable. But Rabinow had written of permitting heads to rub disks and then carefully added, "No data are as yet available as to the wear of the heads or of the disks." Johnson and Stevens, starting from the assumption that disks were more drumlike than tapelike, suspected that the data, when available, would rule out rubbing. Rabinow had mentioned some expedients being investigated in case rubbing turned out to be impractical, among them an attempt "to develop methods of keeping fixed, non-contacting, disk-to-head spacing by air-bearing techniques." If the answer truly lay in the direction of air bearings, a good deal of pioneering could be involved. In the face of this, the project continued to go over alternatives, hoping a less difficult one might turn up. For example, when McDowell in February first visited the laboratory, glass disks were being considered as a way of avoiding some of the wobble in thin metal disks.[22]

Stevens and Critchlow flew to New York in February to attend another meeting concerning the MIFD. They learned that Johnson was to be responsible for IBM's proposal, a task that came at an awkward time. Disk storage was a promising vision, but Johnson had little empirical evidence to show that it could be made to work. On the other hand, if he expended resources pursuing a less daring technology such as drums, much of the momentum toward disks would be lost. Time was short; the proposal had to be completed in the first week of March so that corporate departments could review it before a 1 April deadline. Johnson favored disks but compromised on the issue of engineering feasibility by agreeing to propose ten magnetic drums and to say in an appendix that discovery might at some point make other forms of storage more attractive than drums.[23] Participating with Stevens in the detailed preparation of the proposal were Haanstra and others, including William A. Goddard, who had been a research engineer in an aircraft company before joining IBM San Jose in December 1952.

During February and March, Johnson assigned a few more engineers to the disk project in an effort to accelerate preliminary studies of air bearings and magnetic recording. Although air bearings have experimental roots that go back to the nineteenth century, Johnson had no lubrication specialists in his laboratory, and textbooks did not provide answers to his novel requirements. One initial question concerned the likely merits of "hydrostatic" versus "hydrodynamic" air lubrication. The film of air that separates two approaching surfaces is maintained by forced air in the former case and by self-acting physical phenomena in the latter.

In February, the long-influential Future Demands department at IBM headquarters was replaced by an organization of wider scope, Product Planning and Market Analysis. The new organization was headed by J. W. Birkenstock. With Tom Watson's support, Birkenstock gave a high priority to weeding out all activities that seemed divergent from IBM's main data processing business. High on his list of questionable activities was San Jose's data reduction work, which he viewed as narrowly specialized.

8.3 Disk-Array Feasibility and Early Development

On 9 and 10 April, Johnson attended an IBM sales convention in Los Angeles. He was stimulated by the change in scene to a product-oriented world and the chance to talk to corporate people. For one thing, headquarters had turned cool to the data reduction project, and he discussed with Birkenstock a recent corporate decision to abandon the field. Mulling this over and thinking that he should waste no time in reallocating resources, Johnson decided that the planning phase of his storage project was ending and that it was time for design engineering. To push the magnetic disk effectively, he saw that a reorganization was needed: feasibility studies had to be accelerated, specialized groups had to be formed, and personnel strengths had to be reoptimized. Promising project managers, he decided, were Haanstra, who had been a leader in the data reduction program, and Goddard. Stevens would continue as his technical assistant.[24]

Upon returning to San Jose, Johnson announced that the laboratory was committed to engineering development of a storage device with rotating disks and movable heads. To justify further the utility of such a device, he asked Haanstra to lead a two-week task force for considering the applicability of a low-cost system based on disk storage, Critchlow being among the five in the task force. Two days later, Goddard was placed in charge of four engineers and given responsibility to develop a disk device. A small group formed to design electronic circuits for experimental heads was soon assigned to Haanstra.[25] The physics department was asked to develop a read-write head of thickness 0.1 inch, which seemed the maximum thickness consistent with an acceptably small distance between disks.

Goddard's team soon gave Johnson some encouragement regarding the structural feasibility of disks. In experiments during late April, a shaft-mounted array of 120 aluminum disks was rotated at various speeds up to a thousand revolutions per minute. All went well, although the air between the disks was "accelerated radially, and sufficiently, to cause a low frequency oscillation of the disks, a sort of 'breathing.' "[26] Arrays were adjudged structurally safe, but to dampen the oscillations, disks were strengthened.

In early May, firmly convinced that forced air offered the only practical way of providing for a small and relatively uniform spacing between a disk surface and a read-write head, Goddard gave his engineers a crude drawing of an "air head" that might be expected to glide on an air film and be capable of incorporating and supporting a read-write element. Before the month was over, preliminary designs and tests had shown that pressurized air escaping through orifices in a spring-loaded head formed a cushion that separated the head from a disk and that whenever the head was gently disturbed, a restoring force tended to return it to the stable spacing. These constructive demonstrations apparently cleared away some doubts, for Johnson wrote McDowell that the drums specified in the MIFD proposal should be respecified as a disk device because his engineers had come to regard the engineering problems associated with disk storage as no more formidable than those associated with the use of ten drums.[27] Shortly thereafter, when IBM learned that its MIFD proposal had been rejected, the matter of respecification was dropped.

For recording experiments, Haanstra's electronics and magnetics team first used an aluminum disk 16 inches in diameter and 0.038 inch thick. The disk was sprayed with a paint base containing particles of iron oxide and then smoothed with a fine grade of emery paper. A joint effort between the Goddard and Haanstra teams produced an aluminum air head fitted at the center with a modified read-write element of the kind used for the drum unit of the IBM 701 computer. The head support consisted of two rodlike arms that straddled a disk

Figure 8.2
Test bench and equipment used during summer 1953 magnetic-disk recording
and reading experiments. Among the factors varied and observed were disk diameter, disk thickness, revolutions per minute, runout, surface smoothness, surface flatness, recording density, and applied air pressure. Air escaping through
orifices in the face of the head formed a film that yielded a stable 0.002–0.003
inch (2000–3000 microinch) head-to-surface spacing over a wide range of air
pressures. Indicative of the state of the art was a test that read a recorded track
repeatedly for 4 hours before dropping a pulse: the disk rotated at 632 rpm, and
the track contained approximately 50 pulses per inch.

Figure 8.3
IBM San Jose's first air-bearing head incorporating a magnetic element. The
combination first worked successfully on 2 June 1953.

and provided a head for each of its surfaces (figures 8.2 and 8.3) Many
experiments were performed after Haanstra recorded and then correctly read back a digitally encoded message early in June. Although
the disk swayed nearly a tenth of an inch, the air head followed it
without any detectable evidence of contact between head and surface.
Typical head-to-surface separation was estimated to be about 0.002
inch. This estimate was based on measurements made in experiments
with a stationary surface because the experimenters still had no way
of accurately measuring the distance between a head and a spinning
surface.[28]

The air head experiments of May and early June were very encouraging, but a host of engineering problems remained. The head
flew less stably with an encapsulated read-write element than without,
highlighting the lack of understanding of the interrelated factors affecting stability. To rectify this lack, many experiments were conducted
with various heads (some of which are shown in figure 8.4). Spray
coating, which yielded an uneven coat that interfered with head stability when a disk was speeded up, had to be replaced by spin

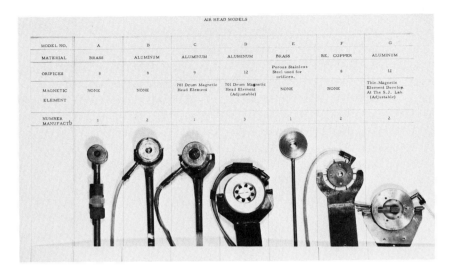

MODEL NO.	A	B	C	D	E	F	G
MATERIAL	BRASS	ALUMINUM	ALUMINUM	ALUMINUM	BRASS	BE. COPPER	ALUMINUM
ORIFICES	8	8	9	12	Porous Stainless Steel used for orifices.	8	12
MAGNETIC ELEMENT	NONE	NONE	701 Drum Magnetic Head Element	701 Drum Magnetic Head Element (Adjustable)	NONE	NONE	Thin-Magnetic Element Develop. At The S.J. Lab. (Adjustable)
NUMBER MANUFACT'D	1	2	1	3	1	2	2

AIR HEAD MODELS

Figure 8.4
Face view of seven experimental heads tested in 1953. The heads and accompanying display were photographed on 5 November 1953.

coating. Other problems concerned coating paints, head mountings, and methods for disposing a head toward a surface with a suitable force.

While the work on heads and surfaces continued, July saw the beginning of an intensive study of methods for (1) moving an arm-supporting carriage to the edge of a specified disk and (2) extending the disk-straddling heads of the forked arm inward to a specified track on the disk. Teams of engineers competed in an effort to assess the relative merits of servomechanisms and electronic feedback techniques versus classical electromechanical methods. The feedback principle, combined with electric motors, magnetic powder clutches, cables, and mechanical detents that aligned and firmly held the carriage when it reached a destination, was soon selected for method 2. By late October, after a number of redesigns, the system could locate a track. Before long, a way was conceived of jointly handling tasks (1) and (2) by controlling the servo-controlled cable drive in two modes of operation. In essence, a cable that ran over pulleys governed both carriage (disk-to-disk) and arm (track-to-track) motions, but whenever the mechanical detents barred one motion, the cable's force came into play for the other motion. The simplification obviated the need for a good deal of mechanism.[29]

In November, Johnson promoted Stevens to senior engineer, taking the opportunity to place him in charge of the whole disk-based project, which included about a dozen engineers.

The first successful writing and reading operations involving disk-to-disk motion were achieved in February 1954, as was the first transfer of a message from card reader to disk and then from the disk back to punched card. By this time, the project was hewing to tight deadlines, and the step came during a feverish effort required to complete the first version of an operable disk mechanism. After an assessment that started in March, Stevens instructed his engineers to scrap the existing unit and to design a Model II. In one of many improvements suggested by experience, the shaft of the disk array was realigned from the horizontal to a vertical position. Authorization was received to construct five prototypes for engineering purposes, and by January 1955, one of them was fully operable.[30]

In May 1955, the Model II was publicly demonstrated as an experimental engineering development with product potentialities.[31] By the end of June, test exercises on one of the prototypes had passed the millionth movement of the access arm. Still required, of course, was a great deal of refinement, testing, and manufacturing engineering.[32]

The resulting disk-storage mechanism was first described in detail at the Western Joint Computer Conference in February 1956. It had a stack of fifty coated aluminum disks. Each disk was 0.1 inch thick and 24 inches in diameter. Disks were separated by 0.3 inch spacers, making the height of the disk stack approximately 20 inches. In use, the stack rotated at 1200 revolutions per minute and, as stated, "The spacing of the heads from the disk is maintained by an air bearing obtained from minute air jets in an annular manifold surrounding the magnetic elements. The 0.001-inch spacing is held despite the axial runout in the disk so that there is never physical contact between the heads and the magnetic coating."[33] The approximate 0.001 inch head-to-disk spacing was maintainable despite appreciable warping in the disks. Although a disk had to be very smooth, and out-of-flatness had to be avoided in localized regions of the surface, a disk could have "as much as 0.030-inch runout" in its surface as a whole. Since "runout" refers to maximal departure from an ideally true disk, this is to say that a disk could sway 0.060 inch from one side to the other. Hence, a disk was permitted to sway about sixty times the average head-to-surface spacing.

Each disk surface contained 100 concentric recording tracks in the outermost 5-inch band used for storage. An NRZI recording method similar to that employed in IBM's tape devices was abetted by a special self-clocking system.[34] Bits were recorded on the innermost track at 100 per inch and on the outermost track at about 55 per inch, densities that permitted 500 encoded alphanumeric characters per track. Hence, the 10,000 tracks (100 surfaces times 100 tracks each) were capable of storing 5 million characters. In describing their device, the San Jose engineers vindicated Johnson's faith in the geometry of disks by mentioning that "an equivalent storage capacity on a magnetic drum would require a drum 13 inches in diameter and 42 feet long. Such a drum would have about seven times the volume of the disk array."

The disk unit discussed at the computer conference, later announced as IBM 350 Disk Storage, was destined to be the first movable-head disk unit in production.[35]

8.4 Record Addressing and RAMAC

At first, the idea of replacing a tub file by a disk-storage unit may seem to involve a simple substitution that raises no difficult system problems. For reasons to be discussed, this was not the case, and the data processing industry had to develop entirely new methods to support the substitution.

Electronics, a trade magazine for electrical engineers, carried in 1950 a thought-provoking article by a member of the research arm of a mail-order firm. One theme stressed was that a "selective-sequence" calculator capable of solving complicated equations was not necessarily an economical machine for mundane business applications. The author's main concern was with inventory-related applications, where his experience told him that invoices "must be prepared as goods are shipped. They cannot be held until a convenient batch of work has accumulated. What this means from a machine-design point of view is that the clerical machines must be able to take work in random order."[36] Noting that magnetic tapes could not provide for random access and drums appeared to be too expensive, the author argued the need for large, low-cost, random-access storage devices wherein any record of an inventory file could be consulted promptly.

The author did not explain how records, once stored, were to be sought when needed. Instead, he resorted to an analogy that viewed the part number in an incoming order, as well as the address of the storage location containing the corresponding record, as akin to telephone numbers. (The analogy was imperfect in that part numbers are typically less compact, and therefore less amenable to automatic switching, than telephone numbers.) In his words, "The problem is similar to that of a telephone exchange. Telephone calls are received, by the central exchange, in random order. Selectors must be used to connect with the parties called. Were it not for their relatively low speed, telephone selectors could be used, as is, to solve many selective memory problems that will be encountered in designing machines for business use. The computing companies must find a faster and less expensive solution." Here the author left the reader at an industry frontier: even if a large random-access storage device were available, nobody knew an efficient automatic way of finding a business record stored within it. Seen in this light, the searches conducted by tub-file clerks take on added interest.

A clerk's search task was similar to the chore of looking up a telephone number (not to the problem of connecting two telephone numbers). In consulting a telephone book, a searcher judiciously views entries, narrowing the search with information so gained. Although the searcher's method defies explicit definition, it is akin to the following formal procedure. Open the book near the center and compare the given name with an observed name. If, as is unlikely, the two names are identical, the search is over (the desired telephone number being then at hand). If the given name is of lower rank than the observed name, repeat the centering-and-comparing task using the first half of the book; if it is of higher rank, repeat using the second half of the book. Continue with a quarter of the book, and so on. Thus, at each comparison, the search either ends, or the segment eligible for further search is approximately halved. In principle, each step of the search is like the first step, the practical difference being in the proportion of book remaining for scrutiny. Finally, if no match has yet occurred, the remaining segment will narrow down to one entry (and a match is assured at the next step if the name is in the book). The method so outlined is the "binary search," a procedure with roots in mathematical methods and intellectual games.

The binary search lends itself to a systematic procedure, that is, one that goes through identical steps whenever repeated under identical circumstances. In searching N ordered entries, the procedure requires nearly $\log_2 N$ comparisons on the average. Rounding slightly, easily remembered benchmarks for $\log_2 N$ are ten (for N equal a thousand) and twenty (for N equal a million). Hence, given the large files of interest to disk designers, a binary search would require well over ten "seeks" (head movements) to find a desired record. Given that each seek might take a second, this meant that the expensive machine could hardly compete with a clerk. As a result of this and of the prospective difficulties in maintaining an ordered file, nobody considered the binary search a suitable method for searching a large random-access storage device.

Critchlow knew the task of finding the location of a desired record as the "addressing problem." In February 1953, when he postulated the hardware parameters of a disk device in some detail, for lack of a better answer to the problem he specified semiclerical addressing, that is, a clerk in conjunction with an experimental device for storing identifiers and storage addresses and performing lookups.[37] (Because the device was never completed, its cost-effectiveness—relative to that of clerks and card files, say—remained undetermined.)

Fortuitously, at about this time, a better solution to the addressing problem was documented by Hans Peter Luhn of the Poughkeepsie laboratory.[38] An established inventor before T. J. Watson hired him in 1941, Luhn had made himself an expert in relay circuits and had then emerged as a busy internal consultant on topics such as checking methods, coding principles, and scanning techniques, meanwhile obtaining patents in many contexts. He worked in New York City until the late 1940s, then relocated to Poughkeepsie. In 1951, Ralph Palmer, Poughkeepsie laboratory manager, appointed Luhn his coordinator with IBM's Washington office on matters concerning the needs of the armed forces for data processing in logistics.[39] As a result, Luhn was fully acquainted with the late-1952 MIFD request from the air force; very likely, the request stimulated him to work on addressing.

Let part numbers ("numbers," incidentally, that often contain alphabetic characters) and other record identifiers be termed "keys," a familiar term in business data processing. Keys are often much lengthier than logically necessary because human beings prefer in naming and discussing objects to rely heavily upon mnemonic and descriptive aids— for example, a driver license number may include indicative information, such as the driver's year of birth. In general, the larger an organization and the more difficult the circumstances under which it must be prepared to operate, the greater the incentives for lengthy keys. In the 1950s, for instance, U.S. Air Force part numbers consisted of over twenty characters.[40]

In developing keys, Luhn noted, people often assign upwardly increasing integers to subfields, with the result that small digits tend to occur more often than large digits. Practices of this nature, he observed, invest keys with a "structure" that works against uniformity in the distribution of digits or characters. Although the natural reaction for casual observers was to ask how these smatterings of regularity could be turned to use in solving the addressing problem, Luhn came to view structure as a bane. His fundamental insight was to see merit in deliberately abusing keys, thereby attempting to destroy every vestige of structure. The lack of structure he wanted has its mathematical counterpart in the uniformly distributed random variable, a concept illustrated at its simplest by random decimal digits. A random digit, in principle, represents the outcome of a ten-way choice influenced by nothing but chance. Random digits, and their generalization, random numbers, follow laws of probability that support conclusions about average behavior.

After trials with small numbers of keys, Luhn became confident that for any given file a simple "shrinking and randomizing" procedure could be found that would transform the keys of the file into numbers that fell into some desired interval of storage addresses and effectively possessed the property of randomness. The procedure could "be carried out along several lines," as Luhn put it, by starting with selected subfields and fashioning a number of desired length by choosing alternate digits, transposing digits, adding digits ignoring the carries, or other jumbling operations. Alphabetic characters could be treated as numbers by making substitutions or by considering the numeric portion of an alphabetic code. A given procedure would serve permanently as a basis for loading and searching the file.

The details of Luhn's suggested search method make for rather tedious reading, but the main ideas of the method can be presented by analogy. Imagine a birthday dinner for thirty guests. The sole stipulation for the invited guests is that they be born in September. When places are set, chairs are numbered from 1 to 30 with the aid of white cards. Before the dinner, guests line up behind the chairs numbered with their birthdays. Because birthdays are essentially random, the pattern of line lengths is known in a statistical sense—that is, as an average over a great many cases. Although chance leads to variations in any given case, the broad pattern expects about three-eighths of the possible lines to be vacant, about the same proportion to consist of only one guest, a little more than a sixth to consist of two guests, and the proportions for longer lines to continue declining— a line of five or more guests being expected less than once per 300 lines.

The guests just behind the chairs are termed "designees" and told to sit down. Then, one by one, the still-standing guests, termed "overflows," are led by the butler to vacant chairs. There being as many chairs as guests, there is a chair for every overflow, but they are scattered here and there around the table. The master of ceremonies has told the butler to be prepared to play covert pranks upon all guests born on a given day, a day that he will quietly specify while the guests are eating. To assist in promptly associating guests with days, the butler has attached a second card, a blank red card, to the back of each chair. Before seating the overflow in a line of length two (that is, a line consisting of one designee and one overflow), the butler writes the number of a still-empty chair on the designee's red card, then seats the overflow at that chair. Thus, if designee and overflow were born on 15 September, say, the butler can later find them by going to chair 15 (which seats the designee) and then as specified by its red card to a second chair (which seats the overflow). The red card on the overflow's chair is blank, indicating the end of the line. This red card technique lends itself to longer lines as follows: on the red card of the first overflow is written the chair number of the second overflow, on the red card of the second overflow is written the chair number of a third overflow, and so on as many times as necessary. The red card of the last overflow, being blank, signifies the end of the chain.

One obvious advantage of chaining is that all guests with a specified birthday can be found by looking at the cards on at most a few chairs. Another strength of the method becomes clear if one imagines a September with N days. The line-length pattern already discussed for $N = 30$ remains about the same, remarkably, for increasing values of N. For example, if somehow N could equal 3000 and the butler could wing himself directly from chair to chair at a table for 3000, the task of finding all the people with a given birthday would be no more difficult, on the average, than for the case $N = 30$. About five-eighths of the guests would still be designees, and the chain-length proportions would be virtually the same.

To grasp the outlines of Luhn's search method from the analogy, substitute for the chairs a random-access storage device, for the guests a file of business records, for numbered white cards the addresses of storage locations, and for red cards a "chaining field" in each storage location. Luhn intended his key transformation to yield numbers with the randomness of birthdays. His broad objective was to reduce the task of searching a file to the task of searching one chain.

Once the records of a file have been properly deployed in storage, Luhn pointed out, any record called for by a transaction key can be located by transforming the key to obtain the address of a designee record and examining the chain of records that starts with the designee. The sought-for record, of course, is the one whose key matches the transaction key. A match is obtained immediately in chains of length one. In longer chains, half of the overflows, on the average, have to be consulted in the course of reaching the desired record (assuming every record has equal likelihood of being sought). Luhn did not provide a detailed analysis of the efficacy of his method, being content to say (conservatively) that the method reached a desired record "on the first try in one out of two cases." Had he carried his analysis further, he might have shown that his assumptions implied an average of 1.5 comparisons per search, which in the case of large files constituted roughly a tenth of the comparisons required by the binary search.[41]

He also pointed out that where some records were known to be needed more often than others, comparisons could be saved by placing the most-active records first in their chains. Moreover, he mentioned that where an addressable storage location could contain ten or a dozen records, as might be the case for drum bands or disk tracks, the randomizing-and-chaining scheme could be used in a different mode. Assuming this modification, the odds of finding a desired record in the first-consulted band or track went up to "9 in 10" (but the desired record still had to be located within the band or track).

The report that Luhn finished in March 1953 did not receive widespread attention in the Poughkeepsie laboratory. The idea that chain lengths are independent of N is far from intuitive, and there were legitimate doubts whether a satisfactory key transformation could be found for every file. Furthermore, Luhn aimed his proprietary report at the patent department. Busy inventor and consultant that he was, he did not return to randomization and chaining to explicate and promote the subject by analysis, experiment, or mathematical derivation, although he unsuccessfully recommended to Palmer that someone should further develop the method. One prompt follow-up occurred in Endicott, where shrinking and randomization was tested on selected key sets, among them the encoded representations of all entries in a 25,000 word dictionary. These empirical studies soon lent support to Luhn's predictions about chain lengths.[42] The results were not immediately influential in Endicott because designers there were still not facing the search problem inherent in large storage devices. For decades, batch sorting had sufficed.

But in the San Jose laboratory, Luhn's method met an urgent need that had been highlighted by the MIFD discussions. By April 1953, when Haanstra was asked to lead a short-term study of possible applications and configurations for a low-cost disk-based machine, "addressing" was recognized as a truly fundamental problem. At the first opportunity after his initial disk-recording experiments, he returned to the problem. The following is from the summary page of a July report he wrote with colleagues:

The problem of automatic addressing for a random access storage unit is outlined and certain fundamental characteristics of this problem are given. Various methods for solving the problem and evaluations of these methods are presented. A solution is presented which offers complete automatic addressing at a cost of about 20 percent of the random access memory storage capacity and an access time twice that of the basic random access memory. This appears to be the minimum cost now known for automatic addressing.[43]

Using the term "external address" for key, the authors posed the question, "Is there some manner in which a random-access storage unit can automatically determine the correct internal address for any given external address?" By asking the right question and coming to a relevant answer, this study constituted a big forward step in the evolution of a disk-based system.

Although the summary mentions "various methods for solving the problem," this is misleading in that of the five basic methods discussed, four were either straw men set up to be instructively toppled or specialized methods with limited applicability.[44] The first toppled was do the job clerically (forget automatic addressing). The second was search by scanning consecutive storage locations, in which case, on the average, "half of memory would be scanned for each inquiry." (But because magnetic tape could be scanned at less expense than disks, this option vitiated the whole rationale for disks.) The third and fourth methods required unusual sets of keys. After the weak candidates were eliminated, Haanstra's one promising alternative was the Luhn method.

While Haanstra fully accepted Luhn's ideas concerning shrinking and randomization, he rejected the basic form of record chaining as too complicated for a low-cost system. (Much later, product planners would alter this conclusion.) Instead, choosing to supplement a data file by a smaller file of index (key and address) terms, he proposed a method of index searching that employed key randomizing but used extra storage as a way of simplifying the handling of overflowing index terms. Haanstra became convinced that the desired simplicity could be obtained by visiting two tracks per search—one in the index file and one in the data file—at the cost of 20 percent unused storage. The second visit would simply obtain the desired record using an address obtained during the first visit. Assuming that key transformations were carefully selected, the analysis left little doubt that addressing could be done systematically at reasonable cost. Haanstra also concluded that the functional machine capabilities needed for

Figure 8.5
Artist's conception of a disk-based substitute for the tub file. (By J. Welsh)

programmed addressing—which is what "automatic addressing" had come to mean—were essentially those needed for accounting applications.

Although Haanstra recommended further study of addressing methods, his July report sufficed, and other matters deserved higher priorities. At the time, the disk-based system was envisioned as fairly rudimentary (figure 8.5 conveys the view). But for Haanstra, the next big question was whether a disk-based system could be viewed as something more than an automatic tub file; obviously, even inventory applications posed occasional needs for summary reports that required a file to be scanned systematically in a mode akin to batch processing. This question led to a study that postulated a low-cost stored-program system and programmed it for some "batch" jobs (traditional processes requiring scanning), as well as for some "in-line" jobs (involving tub-file transactions). One example of the former went as follows: during in-line processing a journal record of each transaction is placed sequentially in unoccupied storage; then at the close of day, activity is summarized while scanning the journal file. Processing of this nature appeared feasible if adjacent tracks could be accessed about tenfold faster than randomly addressed records. The conclusion reached by Haanstra and others in a December 1953 report on their postulated "Magnetic Disk Processing Machine" was that the disk-based system could and should be general purpose in nature.[45]

The December report pointed to the consequences of machine failures as a still-unresolved concern. This concern arose because disk-contained records were to be updated in place, whereas systems based on punched cards or magnetic tape preserved old information in the course of newly punching decks or writing tapes during each updating pass. The study assumed "a printed register containing sufficient information to allow reconstruction or auditing of machine operations" but could not verify whether this would suffice in practice. Later, card decks proved useful for such purposes.

During 1953, the potential advantages of large random-access storage began dawning on more and more product planners. In early 1954, when L. H. LaMotte's sales staff in New York became keenly interested in disk storage, McDowell counseled that the San Jose laboratory required more time for engineering development.[46] Later, in October, an influential member of the staff, F. J. Wesley, made a strong plea for attacking accounting problems "under the philosophy of handling each business transaction as it occurs."[47] The response was swift. Johnson was directed to complete the design of a disk-based system and build copies for field trials. Stevens then chaired a team effort that produced a December report on a low-cost Direct Reference Accounting Machine (DRAM). This report contained details down to the level of instruction set.[48] As a member of the team would later recall, "Most of us in those days were plugboard men. There were a few stored program people, but not many. We decided what we wanted was the best of both worlds. . . . We decided one could transfer data best with stored programs—that was always a nuisance with all those wires to string—but one could make decisions a lot easier on plugboards."[49] The result was a compromise between control-panel and stored-program principles. The system was endowed with a small magnetic drum for memory, a card reader, a card punch, and an inquiry station with an electric typewriter, units based largely on extant IBM equipment. The other main units were a 40-character-per-second serial printer that had been developed in Poughkeepsie by H. S. Beattie and, of course, disk storage. One hundred characters constituted the unit of information in transfers between the drum and the disk device; later, a 100-character, magnetic-core buffer was included to facilitate such transfers.

At about the time of the DRAM report, Remington Rand announced a drum-based Univac File Computer that was said to be suitable for inventory control and other applications and to combine the advantages of plugboards and stored programs.[50] Since San Jose was far from ready for a DRAM announcement, this meant that IBM was lagging in the marketplace. Moreover, because Remington Rand was an experienced drum manufacturer, it was clear that drum potentialities would be thoroughly exploited.

DRAM was renamed RAMAC in February 1955, abbreviating "Random Access Memory Accounting Machine" at the suggestion of J. A. Haddad, the director of advanced machine development on McDowell's staff.[51] During 1955, as plans for manufacturing RAMAC matured, there were various organizational changes, with Stevens's activity becoming the product-engineering arm of a new San Jose manufacturing organization. Fourteen prototype RAMAC systems, known as IBM 305As, were built for field trials and internal testing. These systems provided much preannouncement information concerning system reliability and file-updating operations. The first delivery to a customer site occurred in June 1956.[52] By this time, news from the marketplace was intensifying the pressures on IBM San Jose. The first production Univac File Computer was delivered in August 1956; this product offered as many as ten drum units, each storing 180,000 characters, for a system capacity of 1.8 million characters. Average access time to a drum sector was an impressively short 17 milliseconds, but average transaction-processing time was over ten times longer.[53]

The production RAMAC was announced in September 1956 as the IBM 305 RAMAC, and a simultaneous announcement of an IBM 650 RAM system made disk storage an option for the 650. But after "RAM" was deemed objectionable on copyright grounds, the disk-expanded 650 became the IBM 650 RAMAC and "RAMAC" came to mean Random Access Method of Accounting and Control, alluding to the fact that all related accounting ledgers could be updated every time a transaction card was read.[54] The system organization of the 305 was reported in a paper presented at the Eastern Joint Computer Conference in December 1956.[55]

The IBM 305's disk unit (separately called IBM 350 disk storage) was configured with 50,000 sectors identified by the numbers 00000 to 49999. Each sector held 100 alphanumeric characters, yielding a system capacity of 5 million characters. The execution of a "seek" instruction positioned a read-write head to the track that contained the desired sector and selected the sector for a subsequent read or write operation.[56] Seek time could vary from a low minimum (when the arm was already at the desired track) to a maximum of about 800 milliseconds, the experience-based average being about 600 milliseconds.

Product manuals for the IBM 305 and the IBM 650 discussed randomization and chaining as a useful search method. First the method was called "indirect addressing," but soon it came to be the "chaining method," a term that persisted for Luhn's method.[57] By this time, the idea of key transformation was being generalized to include saving the remainder from a division or selecting central digits from the product obtained in multiplying two subfields.

One of the disadvantages of the chaining method is that worst-case chain length is limited theoretically only by the number of records in a file. In practice, fortunately, a user did not have to worry about rare events because he could try the method in advance with punched-card machines; given a candidate key transformation and a deck of cards containing the keys of a file, the addresses yielded by the transformation could be punched and processed to determine the actual pattern of chain lengths. Moreover, if the deck contained a little additional information, it could serve later as a useful adjunct during batch processing runs. The deck having been sorted into some desired order, an application program could read record addresses from the cards in the very order that records were needed. Thus, randomization and chaining, together with card sorters, could be tailored to a wide class of applications.

Although usage of the chaining method required forethought, the method and its variations answered the need for automatic addressing. Not until years later, when large main memories, faster processing units, and more elaborate programming systems made other search methods feasible, would the class of general search methods be widened significantly.

Upon devising the chaining method in early 1953, Luhn had followed his customary practice of seeking patent protection for IBM. However, viewed as an invention, Luhn's contribution was marred by an apparent inconsistency that impeded patent recognition. After describing his method as one for searching "automatically," Luhn noted that shrinking and randomizing could be carried out "along several lines," correctly suggesting that a different key transformation might be required for every file and that designing a transformation might be a job for someone acquainted with the characteristics of a file's keys. This subjective factor, in conjunction with probabilistic chain-length considerations, hampered the Poughkeepsie patent department, and the matter dragged on for some time. In mid-1955, at an IBM conference concerning addressing, Luhn was the first speaker, and his early con-

Figure 8.6
An IBM 305 RAMAC system at work on a customer's premises. The system, as announced on 4 September 1956, consisted of a 305 processing unit, 323 card punch, 340 power supply, 350 disk storage, 370 printer, and 380 console. Capacity of the fifty-disk array was 5 million characters. Disks rotated at 1200 rpm, tracks (20 to the inch) were recorded at up to 100 bits per inch, and typical head-to-disk spacing was 800 microinches.

tribution was recalled.[58] Yet the idea of randomizing had already taken wing—perhaps by hearsay, perhaps by independent formulation—and reached people who knew little or nothing of its history. In August 1956, the IBM Poughkeepsie patent review board informed Luhn that its counterpart in San Jose had ruled against patent application for at least two reasons: first, randomization and chaining were nowhere embodied in RAMAC's hardware design, and second, addressing by programs was not germane because IBM had deemed programs unpatentable.[59]

Late in 1956, an industry consultant published an article mentioning randomization and chaining as a search technique.[60] This and other events effectively deprived Luhn of recognition for work that had helped Haanstra over a serious obstacle during the evolution of RAMAC.[61]

The 305 RAMAC (figure 8.6) was one of the last vacuum tube systems designed in IBM. Transistors were considered and rejected because San Jose management already had its hands full tightening up the design and establishing product test and manufacturing capabilities. The first production unit came off the line in June 1957.[62] The basic system rented for $3200 per month, an attractively low price for the time.[63] In 1958, the system was enhanced to permit an optional additional 350 disk storage unit, thereby doubling storage capacity; an additional access arm for each 350 unit; and cable connectors to an IBM 407 accounting machine, a provision particularly useful for big printing jobs.[64] Over a thousand 305s were built before production ended in 1961.[65] Among the customers was the U.S. Air Force, which employed RAMAC for inventory control at numerous airbases.[66]

8.5 Slider Development in San Jose

During 1954, engineers at two IBM locations experimented with "gliding shoes" meant to be used in separating a read-write head from a magnetic-drum surface by hydrodynamic air lubrication, which relies on self-acting forces for creation of an air film. Experimentation was initiated at the Watson Laboratory in New York City; later in the year, work began in Vestal, New York, at the IBM Airborne Computer Laboratory, an outgrowth of nearby IBM Endicott.[67] That year, also, one of Johnson's engineers began experimenting with hydrodynamic lubrication as a means of floating a disk read-write head.[68] Some of the associated phenomena had been treated by textbooks and other technical literature in the field of mechanical engineering under the term "plane-slider bearing."

A slider essentially is any smooth plate that relies on hydrodynamic lubrication to separate it from a larger surface during relative motion between plate and surface.[69] To be useful in conjunction with a disk surface, a slider would have to incorporate a read-write head. Because the air compressors required for hydrostatic lubrication tended to be bulky, a disk unit that obviated the need for compressed air would remove one of the practical limitations on the number of heads. With more heads—one per disk surface, say—electronic switching could replace the awkward disk-to-disk mechanical motion, thereby substantially reducing average seek time. Moreover, if one track and its positional counterparts on all other disk surfaces—a set of tracks called a "cylinder"—could be read one after the other simply by switching through a set of heads, then a disk device could read cylinders of information at data rates comparable to those obtainable with drums.

Early in 1955, by which time Stevens's project had attained product-development status, Johnson established among his exploratory projects one known for a time as "Advanced RAM." This project set out to expand storage capacity "on the order of twenty times" and make "1/10 second access time the standard."[70] Central to the objectives was a comb of "gliding heads" (as slider heads were then termed) that would move as a unit and provide one head per disk surface. The plan for the disk array included up to three combs. Among the items for investigation were smaller recording devices, better read-write amplifiers, and stronger actuator mechanisms.

Later in 1955, Johnson moved his exploratory projects to a building on West Julian Street, San Jose. The early work on Advanced RAM led to a capacity goal of 50 million characters, ten times the capacity of a RAMAC disk unit. The first experimental actuator for the Advanced RAM moved a comb of heads in and out under cable control; a dozen or so pulleys could be moved to adjust effective cable length, the factor that determined comb position. This work turned up many problems, and project engineers began voicing the need for a better understanding of "disc surfaces, air bearing heads, access mechanisms, magnetic heads and magnetic recording techniques."[71] Among the items being explored was a method of recording whereby the orientation of the magnetic field runs perpendicular to, rather than parallel to, the surface of the medium. Although the method held promise for inexpensive, high-resolution recording elements, it required a ferromagnetic substrate and therefore could not rely on the coated aluminum disk being readied for RAMAC.[72] A specially treated steel disk was under consideration.

In January 1956, the IBM Research organization was formed in Poughkeepsie. One of the responsibilities of its acting director, Ralph Palmer, was to coordinate with Johnson's group. The move tended to strengthen relationships between Poughkeepsie and San Jose. Haanstra, even while helping Stevens on RAMAC engineering, had been laboring to cement the future of disks by promoting new applications. As a result of negotiations among Johnson, Haanstra, and S. W. Dunwell of Poughkeepsie, a special version of Advanced RAM was envisioned and nominated for high-speed auxiliary storage in a Stretch supercomputer proposal (see chapter 11). Given two access combs, the idea ran, one could be moving from cylinder to cylinder while the other was reading or writing, thereby providing for continuous transmission. Dunwell's proposal called for simultaneous reading (or writing) of disk surfaces and for handling all bits of a Stretch word in parallel, thereby yielding a transmission rate of one word every 4 microseconds. That rate was impressive, even though in negotiating with Dunwell, Haanstra at one point had suggested an even faster rate.[73]

In 1956, Goddard became project leader for Advanced RAM. He was joined by John M. Harker, a mechanical engineer with a master's degree from the University of California. After being hired by Johnson in May 1952, Harker had worked on various projects, among them the Model II disk unit. Harker became preoccupied with the inexplicable "head crashes" occasionally experienced by the self-acting sliders. Whenever the slider rubbed the coated disk surface, damage could result to both the disk coating and the slider. These failures were reminders that the project was pioneering at the limits of lubrication theory and being handicapped by practical difficulties in measuring air-film thickness and other parameters. (As someone noted, if a slider the size of a nickel could be scaled upward to the size of a football field, the corresponding air film would be less than an inch thick.) In an attempt to formulate and quantify better some of the relationships that governed slider behavior, Harker made the slider a focal point of research.

Harker was being encouraged, and perhaps goaded, by results obtained in other laboratories. In late October 1956, when the Poughkeepsie laboratory convened an IBM conference on air bearings, an engineer from Vestal reported "satisfactory" operation with slider-mounted drum heads.[74] Engaged in slider-related investigations at the time were engineers in San Jose and four laboratories in the state of New York: Endicott, Poughkeepsie, Kingston, and Vestal. All but those from San Jose were dealing with drum surfaces that could be built with far less wobble than disks, thereby easing some of the difficulties in managing a slider. But the RAMAC announcement had truly raised the expectations of product planners, who by this time were actively considering the potentialities of random-access devices for various business files, and it was disks, not drums, that were being eyed most closely in corporate headquarters.

An optimistic mood prevailed in IBM San Jose at the close of 1956. Tom Watson had just announced a sweeping reorganization that created, among other divisions, the Data Processing Division (DPD). Headed by Executive Vice-President L. H. LaMotte, DPD embraced all punched-card and computer development, manufacturing, and marketing activities. Palmer, newly appointed director of product development for DPD, recognized the RAMAC-development activity as a full-fledged IBM product-development laboratory and Stevens as its head (for some time, Stevens had been reporting through the growing manufacturing organization in San Jose).

In January 1957, as a result of DPD's growing interest in having a range of large-capacity storage devices, Poughkeepsie Research management assigned three engineers the job of devising a mechanism that could store a billion characters and access a sector, on the average, in a tenth of a second. After choosing tape strips as a suitable medium, the team dubbed their mechanism SCRAM (Strip Circular Random Access Memory).[75]

By April, as luck would have it, Johnson felt constrained to cut back on advanced development and lend some of his engineers to Stevens, who was undermanned for the difficult RAMAC release-to-manufacturing exercise. But despite the manpower shortage, Harker was still able, during the first half of 1957, to attack the vexing slider failures with a small team that combined mathematical, computational, and experimental talents. The technical literature on air lubrication was combed and digested, methods of measurement were improved with suggestions from other IBM laboratories, and solutions to relevant equations of slider behavior were programmed for an IBM 650. Then the summer was devoted to an intensive investigation of slider behavior. By iteratively comparing experimental results with computationally predicted results, Harker's team ascertained the basic causes of head crashes. Where existing mathematical models had usually assumed air an incompressible fluid for the practical purpose of reducing computational effort, the additional fidelity gained by treating air as a compressible fluid assisted in explaining some of the important nuances of slider behavior. Moreover, where Harker had once assumed that inability to flatten a slider surface perfectly was a limitation, the summer study affirmed that slight convexity of the surface was critical to bearing stability. The study produced handbook data with which a slider designer could make good decisions concerning the surface convexity and film thickness compatible with a desired slider load.[76]

The results of the summer study being truly encouraging, Harker with part of his team was transferred from Johnson to Stevens to expedite development of the slider-based Stretch File and a derivative suitable for wider usage. Others of Harker's team completed the slider study as members of Johnson's research activity. The study was documented the following year as a series of internal reports. Subsequently published, these reports long served as basic works in the field of slider technology.[77]

About the time of Harker's move, Haanstra left Johnson's research organization to become one of the development managers under Stevens. Disk-storage development had reached a juncture that required carefully considered decisions between new and old technologies; for example, when Stevens acquired the slider project, he still had a project for producing a 25-million-character file with RAMAC's pressurized-air technology. LaMotte, moreover, having become convinced that many files—some of those in insurance companies, for example—could be maintained most efficaciously with random-access storage, had made it known that "time was running out."[78] As a result, Palmer authorized Haanstra to chair a task force for reviewing relevant developments and formulating DPD's probable needs for direct-access storage.

In November 1957, Haanstra's task force recommended a vigorous three-pronged approach to large-capacity storage development. Stevens was asked to develop a billion-character device based on tape strips, a 50-million-character disk file, and a million-character, fast-access device. The average goals for access-time were 0.5 second for the tape-strip bin, 0.1 second for the disk array, and 0.01 second for the fast-access device. Postulated delivery dates for the three storage devices were 1961, 1960, and 1960, respectively.[79] Following the study, Stevens combined his large-capacity disk-storage work into one Advanced Disk File (ADF) project, a project committed to using slider technology.

The task force had examined several exploratory developments, including a magnetic wire device at Endicott, a tape-loop device at Poughkeepsie, the aforementioned SCRAM, and Telecomputing's tape-strip device (to which IBM held joint license). For various technical reasons, none of these seemed to fit smoothly into Haanstra's plan, and the new arrangement had the effect of strengthening San Jose as IBM's main center of expertise in large-capacity random-access storage. Palmer, impressed with the work of the task force, soon persuaded Haanstra to come East as his assistant manager. Thus Stevens, having accepted a very heavy engineering burden, shouldered the load without the help of Haanstra.

ADF project manpower was increased to hasten testing of a comb of slider-borne heads in conjunction with a hydraulic actuator. Two kinds of hydraulic devices were being considered: a "fluid adder" that delivered exact quantities of fluid to a single cylinder whose piston displacement was proportional to fluid volume, and a "piston adder" in which serially connected pistons contributed strokes proportional to powers of two in a binary number. The latter kind was chosen for the test. In February 1958, under Harker's direction, the first tests of the actuator were conducted with a test bed consisting of forty-two steel disks mounted on a horizontal shaft. Heads were tested on five coated disks using perpendicular recording.[80] The trials were sufficiently encouraging to justify a year-end target date for an engineering model of the ADF.[81]

Concurrently outlined was a tape-strip device with a rectangular bin, interchangeable containers of strips, and strip compositions and coatings compatible with San Jose disk-manufacturing techniques. Some of the resources of the SCRAM project were transferred to San Jose. The projected device was termed Very Large Capacity Memory and assigned an announcement target of early 1961.[82] A project aimed at a million-character device was also established.

The research laboratory under Johnson was not directly affected by Haanstra's plan. Work continued on photochemical and optical principles that held out hope of providing for economical treatment of huge masses of information. Also continuing were magnetic-recording studies led by Albert S. Hoagland. In the late 1940s at the University of California, Hoagland had worked with fellow graduate students Haanstra and Stevens on the design and construction of a navy-sponsored drum computer. After further pursuing the subject of magnetic recording while acquiring a Ph.D. in electrical engineering, Hoagland had become an instructor and a magnetic-recording consultant to Stevens. He joined Johnson's organization in mid-1956 and subsequently headed research in disk recording.

To test new ideas, Hoagland established at least two research projects in 1957, one concerning a small-scale magnetic-strip file and the other a single-disk file. The former employed a replaceable cartridge with enough strips to provide for 10 million characters of storage. The replaceable disk of the latter also provided capacity for 10 million characters, making its capacity superior to RAMAC technology by a factor of a hundred (the 350 disk unit stored a tenth of a million characters per disk). Hoagland's laboratory devices served for trying out various substrates, surfaces, recording techniques, head designs, and the like during 1958 and 1959.[83] With the disk, Hoagland also tested a track-following servo technique that appeared in a product years later.[84]

In early 1958, Palmer decided that San Jose's product-development charter should encompass, in addition to storage devices, data processing systems with rentals no higher than those of the 305 RAMAC. Faced with this new mission, Stevens removed Harker from the ADF project and assigned him to a small team that was trying to define a "Small RAMAC" of about half the 305's cost and capability. After talking to product planners, the team pondered whether a few million characters of capacity could be provided inexpensively by a few disks the size of phonograph records and whether small magnetic tapes or some degree of disk replaceability should serve the needs for additional capacity.[85] A preliminary report in June recommended work in four areas: applications and systems, processing unit, printer, and file. Stevens gave Harker responsibility for development of a low-cost file. This development work moved in the direction of using ADF slider and recording technology in conjunction with a simplified actuator and comb mechanism. By February 1959, Small RAMAC was being dropped, but Harker was setting objectives for a disk unit that would accommodate a removable disk pack of capacity 2 million characters.[86] Given a disk of 13-inch diameter, an array of a dozen disks would provide twenty surfaces for data, a pair for control information, and an unused outer pair.

Meanwhile, the ADF project had been experiencing many difficulties and falling behind schedule so that a fully assembled prototype module did not become available until August 1959.[87] When the module proved less reliable than expected, the project found itself at the vortex of an IBM-wide crisis. Dunwell's Stretch project, laboring toward completion of a supercomputer for the Los Alamos Scientific Laboratory, was expecting its variant of the ADF in March 1960. The Project SABRE system (see chapter 12) for American Airlines was relying on the ADF. Much of IBM's future product line was predicated on the ADF, which was expected to improve computer-system operation by providing faster access to library programs, as well as by holding large data files.

The bad news about ADF came at a time when IBMers were still adjusting to a host of organizational changes made in May 1959. Although the Data Processing Division had retained its marketing and service responsibilities, its development and manufacturing activities had been split between two new divisions, the Data Systems Division (DSD) for large computer systems and the General Products Division (GPD) for smaller systems. Also created were the Federal Systems Division—which replaced the federal sales office and the former Military Products Division—and the Advanced Systems Development Division (ASDD), which assembled system-related projects from various laboratories.

As a result of the changes, Johnson's research organization of approximately two hundred people was divided into an ASDD laboratory, which Johnson headed, and a scaled-down research laboratory, which was later assigned a new head. Hoagland and his group remained in the research organization. Palmer became corporate director of engineering, a staff position in headquarters. Haanstra became GPD assistant general manager; his office was at divisional headquarters in Westchester County, New York, and his jurisdiction included the San Jose product development laboratory directed by Stevens. When Ste-

vens accepted an opportunity to join Palmer's staff in corporate headquarters in November, Haanstra named V. R. Witt, an engineering
manager who had gained recognition in the magnetic-tape area (see
chapter 6), as Stevens's replacement.

8.6 IBM's First Slider Product.

In January 1960, Haanstra asked for a technical audit of the ADF
project. The audit committee, which included Hoagland, observed that
"the successful development of the ADF is dependent upon the proper
application of three new technologies, namely: a gliding head-disk
combination, high-speed high-accuracy hydraulics, and high density
vertical magnetic recording."[88] It concluded that the three technologies
had not been tested sufficiently under nonlaboratory conditions. The
committee presented a list of engineering tasks that deserved attention
before the ADF could reasonably be expected to pass its scheduled
tests. Since the deadline for the Stretch disk unit was imminent, the
committee recommended that ADF commitments be renegotiated and
the program strengthened.

The audit committee's findings and recommendations stimulated
many changes. Harker, the Low Cost File manager, was replaced in
that capacity and made available to the ADF project as manager of
air bearing development. Hoagland was borrowed from Research and
placed on a special assignment as ADF recording manager. Alan F.
Shugart (who had joined IBM in 1951 as a field engineer and subsequently gained experience in several RAMAC development, assembly, and product-engineering assignments) was named ADF engineering
manager. One victim of manpower reallocation was the million-character file project, which was dropped. Out of need for rapid access,
this project had involved experimentation with the voice coil actuator
(a component destined to become important years later).[89] Witt was
persuaded to give up the broad-gauge position of laboratory manager
and became technical manager of storage products.

It was not long before the new regime dropped perpendicular recording and the associated steel disk. Then, to expedite the parallel
version of ADF for the Stretch project, it cut back on recording density—
effectively halving capacity to 2 million words, data rate to one word
every 8 microseconds—and reverted to familiar RAMAC air-fed head
techniques. Although the decision encumbered the Stretch system with
air compressors, Witt was able to ship a parallel disk file to Dunwell
in the fall.[90]

Meanwhile, work continued on the main version of the ADF. Pressure for an ADF product announcement was heightened by the fact that Bryant Computer Products was readying a slider-technology disk unit for a military application (after the unit was delivered in November 1960, Bryant began designing a unit more suitable for commercial installations).[91] Engineering progress improved the slider operation, which was made more reliable by experiments that provided tolerance limits for disk "out-of-flatness" and particle contamination.[92] Various other ADF problems were isolated and remedied. For example, the hydraulic actuator, which had come to employ both a fluid adder for coarse positioning and a piston adder for fine positioning, tended to fail because of sticky valves after a few hundred hours of operation; careful studies disclosed that corrosion was being caused by minute amounts of hydrochloric acid, which in turn were traced to chemical changes in a cleaning agent used for rinsing parts and hydraulic-oil containers.[93]

The ADF, with its slider technology, was announced in June 1961 as IBM 1301 Disk Storage (figure 8.7). The 1301 could be ordered either with one twenty-five-disk module or with two modules, one mounted above the other on the rotating vertical spindle. Each module was served by a comblike access mechanism that moved twenty-four arms in concert. Each arm had two slider-supported recording heads, one to serve the surface above the arm and one the surface below. Once the comb had been positioned, the active head was selected by electronic switching. A module provided storage capacity for 28 million seven-bit characters. Since a 1301 unit could contain two modules and up to five units were attachable to a computer, maximal system capacity was 280 million characters.[94]

Where the RAMAC technology of 1956 had been limited to twenty tracks per inch and one hundred bits per inch of track, the 1301 technology of 1961 provided for fifty tracks per inch and the recording of up to 520 bits per inch of track—gains attributable in part to a reduction in average head-to-surface distance from 800 to 250 microinches. The net result was that storage capacity per square inch of surface had risen over thirteen-fold. Also, the 1301 designers had added to the functional versatility of disk units by permitting the user to specify sector lengths within each cylinder and by providing input-output instructions for cylinders of data, as well as for tracks and sectors. As a result, the 1301 vied with drums at reading or writing large blocks of data and programs.

A few days before the 1301 announcement, an engineering model of the 1301 was shipped to IBM Poughkeepsie for use in tests of the

Figure 8.7
IBM 1301 Disk Storage unit containing two storage modules, announced 2 June 1961. Module capacity in the 7000 series computer context was 28 million characters and in the 1410 computer context 25 million characters. As many as ten modules (five units) could be attached to a computer system, providing maximal capacity of 280 million characters for 7000 series systems (250 million for the 1410). Disks rotated at 1800 rpm, tracks (50 to the inch) were recorded at up to 520 bits per inch, and typical head-to-disk spacing was 250 microinches.

SABRE reservation system.[95] Plans for that system called both for 1301 disk units and for drums (later, in full operation, the SABRE system attached six drums and sixteen 1301s).[96] Two drum units had been delivered to Poughkeepsie about three months earlier. These units were based on a technology developed at the Kingston laboratory of the Federal Systems Division for possible use in upgrading SAGE installations; each drum rotated on a vertical shaft and was endowed with a slider-supported head for each track. Although the drum stored only about 1.1 million characters, versus 56 million for the 1301, it could access a track in about a twentieth of the time required by the 1301. After studies had shown that the drum could enhance the efficiency of memory usage in large systems, the Kingston unit was announced in December 1962 as IBM 7320 Drum Storage for the 7090 and 7094 computers.[97]

September 1963 saw the announcement of IBM 1302 Disk Storage.[98] The 1302 provided four times the storage capacity of the 1301: two recording parameters, the number of tracks per inch and the number of bits per track, had been doubled to quadruple areal storage capacity. A fourfold improvement in two years, following on a large initial improvement, made the promise of slider technology seem bright indeed.

8.7 Collateral Storage Development

Ten years after Johnson had staked his career on the possibility that a recently assembled group of a dozen or so engineers could develop a disk-storage product, IBM San Jose employed nearly three thousand people and comprised manufacturing facilities, a product-development laboratory, a research laboratory, and the advanced systems development laboratory that he headed. He was still at work on technologies for storage.

"Walnut," an information-retrieval system for the U.S. Central Intelligence Agency, was developed in a project initiated by Johnson in 1957. Walnut was publicly demonstrated in July 1961 and delivered in late 1962. It was the first mechanized system that could feasibly store and search millions of pages of documents.[99] It was analogous to a library with a hundred very long book shelves, each capable of holding about three thousand books. To pursue the analogy, a tiny photographic image on a filmstrip corresponded to a page, a desk-sized bin of filmstrips to a shelf, and a disk array to the library's index-card file. The disk file used in Walnut was the IBM 1405, announced in October 1960. (By improving the RAMAC technology, the 1405 engineers had doubled two parameters, tracks per inch and bits per inch of track, yielding a fourfold increase in capacity.)

The library analogy is necessarily less direct in the matter of usage. Walnut, the automated library, did not offer the luxury of visually browsing through book shelves or index cards. Rather, documents were described by "key words," a technique that H. P. Luhn had experimented with extensively, and the user called for documents by entering topical key words.[100] After consulting the disk-file index, an IBM 1401 computer responded with punched cards on which were printed summaries of possibly relevant documents. The user selected the cards of interest and, after returning them to the system, received "aperture cards" with heat-developed images of the relevant pages. The aperture card was an IBM card with a window of light-sensitive material capable of receiving four images. Each image could be visually scanned with a special reader or used as a negative for page reproduction.

Walnut did not contend for product development; Johnson was considering another system, called Walnut II, that seemed to open up more possibilities for product spin-off, particularly in the field of engineering drawings. In April 1961, Stevens returned to San Jose to head up this work, which was superseded in a year by a project called Cypress. The main Cypress system, designed to store all information in digital form, was sometimes called the Trillion-bit File. This system was very exploratory and expensive; it necessitated mastery over several technologically advanced engineering fields, among them electron-beam recording. (The project continued for several more years and five systems were delivered—three to AEC laboratories and two to NSA.)[101]

The most capacious direct-access development of broad product interest was the magnetic-strip device. In mid-1960, coincident with adoption of a rotary configuration wherein the tape bin moved around a stationary strip-picking mechanism, the project name was changed from Very Large Capacity Memory to MARS (standing for Modular Access Random Storage). In October 1962, a MARS unit was turned over to the Product Test organization. The test results were discouraging, and in a few weeks the unit was withdrawn from testing. Shugart, who had led the ADF project during a period of difficulty, was named project leader for MARS. Required development delayed product announcement for another year and a half.[102] With its planned direct-access properties and interchangeable cartridge of strips, MARS had figured importantly as a tape successor in IBM's system plans for large computers. Disappointment in the delay was aggravated by concern over the reported success of competitive technologies. The field of large-capacity storage was much in the news after 1960, and industry products based on magnetic cards, strips, drums, and disks were frequently forthcoming.[103]

8.8 The Removable Disk Pack

Benefiting as it did from the existence of the ADF project, the Low Cost File (LCF) project that Harker started in 1958 was able to focus narrowly on the engineering implications of working with a removable, interchangeable product. The prospect of a surface written by one head being read years later by another head forced a reconsideration of all troublesome facets of disk technology, among them various sources of contamination and vibration.

In latter 1960, when removable packs of up to ten 13-inch diameter disks were being considered, Haanstra took the position that a suitably configured pack should have ten usable surfaces.[104] In negotiations over a pack of six disks, the San Jose engineer responsible for recording technology balked at further raising the bits per inch of track goal. Agreement was finally reached on six disks and an enlarged diameter of 14 inches. Since the two outer surfaces of a pack cannot easily be protected from damage, the resultant disk pack provided ten recording surfaces for a comb with ten heads.

To achieve their goal of a recording density of a thousand bits per inch (about twice that of the 1301) on the inside track, the LCF engineers halved the 1301's head-to-surface distance by experimenting with slider modifications, the final solution being to drill small holes in the forward part of the slider. Since the reduction in distance was making loose particles an even greater hazard to disk and slider surfaces, the engineers carefully analyzed the potential for damage as a function of particle size. Then they went to great lengths to minimize the number of harmful particles introduced by manufacturing and assembly processes. Also, they found a way to make the rotating disk pack act as a pump that ventilated itself with filtered air and thereby excluded unfiltered air. Among other advances were a tougher, thinner disk coating and more-rigorous quality control procedures.[105]

In October 1962, the LCF was announced as the IBM 1311 Disk Storage Drive. Its interchangeable pack (figure 8.8) was jointly announced as the IBM Disk Pack; later this pack was given the number IBM 1316. The first hosts for the 1311 were IBM's smaller computer systems: the 1401, 1440, 1620, and 1710. The pack, with a standard

Figure 8.8
IBM 1316 Disk Pack, announced 11 October 1962 in conjunction with IBM 1311 Disk Storage Drive. The pack contained an array of six disks and with its protective covering weighed less than 10 pounds. The ten recording surfaces provided, in normal usage, a storage capacity of 2 million characters. The 1311 rotated the disks at 1500 rpm, tracks (50 to the inch) were recorded at up to 1025 bits per inch, and the typical head-to-surface spacing was 125 microinches.

capacity of 2 million characters, was addressable in sectors of a hundred characters each. For systems that could handle thirty sectors en masse, an extra-cost feature permitted each track to be treated as a block, thereby eliminating the spaces between sectors and raising capacity by 50 percent. The hydraulic actuator in the 1311 used a two-speed drive and was much lighter and simpler than the 1301 actuator. Its cost-conscious designers saved on actuator control logic by having the comb return to an initial position after every seek, a scheme that yielded an average seek time of 250 milliseconds. An optional feature that provided for track-to-track movement without initialization brought average seek time down to 150 milliseconds.[106]

The IBM 1311 met a need for versatile storage and became a very influential product. Whereas the technologies of tapes and disks had always favored expensive drives and control units, the 1311 offered some of the advantages of both tapes and disks at a relatively low rental. A disk pack, the equivalent in storage capacity of roughly 25,000 punched cards or a fifth of a tape reel, served well as auxiliary storage in many system environments and, in particular, provided an excellent functional balance between a low-cost computer and a medium-to-low-volume accounting application. As a result of this balance,

many of the smaller punched-card installations became a growth opportunity for low-cost computers.

The removable disk pack not only opened a new era for disk storage,
it augured the end of the punched-card machine era.

9

Programming

The subroutine library. Two IBM assembly programs. The Speedcoding language and interpreter. The FORTRAN language and compiler. Programming as a marketing aid. SHARE, a user organization. IBM's organization for programming. Early experience with operating systems. A proliferation of machine types and programs. A conference on programming.

By the time IBM's RAMAC made its debut in the fall of 1956, it was clear that the introduction of electronics into computing machinery had been merely the first step in a continuing revolution of major importance to the business world. Rapid developments in the key areas of internal and external storage had brought the technology from counter wheels and punched cards to magnetic cores, tapes, and disks in only ten years. And those advances, however remarkable, would soon be eclipsed by the introduction of transistors to replace vacuum tubes, promising the opening of a vast market for smaller machines in which a vendor might sell thousands, as against mere tens, of a single model. The early apprehensions that users might not commit their business records to magnetic files and that there were not enough scientific problems to keep more than a few of the largest machines working were dispelled and forgotten.

As the excitement of the early 1950s mounted, IBM planners and engineers were concerned about a possible limiting factor: the capability of users to put the new machines to work and to keep them busy. Neither computers nor calculators before them could be sold like kitchen appliances, with their schedules of operation built in. Each customer's procedures were unique, and it would fall to him with computers as it had with punched-card machines to adapt the equipment to the computing tasks of his business or enterprise.

This process of adaptation was known as application development. In EAM practice it began with identification of the overall data processing task, subdivision into constituent tasks, collection of information pertinent to each such task (such as record sizes and volumes), division of the task into "machine runs," and finally control panel wiring for each run, all in the context of the specific equipment to be used.

With the advent of computers of enhanced storage capacity and flexibility relative to their punched-card forebears, there would, of course, be large changes in the amount of work that could be performed in an individual machine run, as well as in the speed at which complete applications would run. But the fundamental change in the application-development process would be in the final step, where programming would replace control panel wiring.

The notion of a program, a sequence of discrete processing steps to control an automatic computing engine, goes back to Babbage. IBM's association with the concept began with the ASCC and continued with the SSEC and 604. An ASCC program, while not stored in the memory, was nonetheless expressed and manipulated by the programmer in a numerically coded form: a punched-tape sequence of numerically coded program "steps." To the programmer, therefore, the ASCC is a closer ancestor of the computer than is the ENIAC, whose program took the form of the interconnection of machine components by plugwires.

Since IBM donated the ASCC to Harvard University and had no use of it after that time, the company derived practically no programming experience from the machine. The SSEC had greater influence in that respect on IBM because IBM kept the machine, operated it as a service bureau for solving problems, and thereby established a group of about a dozen experienced programmers in the period 1948–1952. It soon became apparent that it could take one or two of them as long as three months to program a problem and get it running. But the hybrid nature of the SSEC, most notably its lack of a large and fast addressable memory, isolated it from the groups modeling the Test Assembly, the TPM, and the Magnetic Drum Calculator in the Poughkeepsie and Endicott laboratories. The economics of SSEC programming and operation did not influence their planning.

The 604 was introduced early in the SSEC era. While not a stored-program machine, it offered a control panel on which could be wired a "program" of up to forty steps (later expanded to sixty). Users of it were thereby introduced to processing card-recorded data by means of a planned, purposeful sequence of rudimentary operations. The CPC appeared about a year later and added to the 604 mechanism another level of sequence control (the input card deck) and up to fifty-six more storage registers.

But crucial programming differences distinguished the computers being planned and built, as the 1950s began, from the ASCC, 604, and CPC. Neither the ASCC, as it was originally built, nor the 604 included the facility of program "branching." A branch instruction causes normal instruction sequencing to be altered by transferring control to some instruction other than the one that would normally be next executed; the program then continues from the transferred-to instruction. In its most useful form, the branch instruction is executed conditionally; that is, control is transferred only if a specific condition obtains (for example, if a number just calculated is negative); otherwise the normal sequence continues. In this way the sequence of instructions performed in successive executions of a program can be made to vary, based on the input data or on results achieved in the course of a calculation using the data. An elementary application of the branch instruction in a billing program would invoke alternative courses of action based on the sign of the balance in a customer account following processing of a batch of transactions against it. Other uses, in both scientific and business applications, abound. Moreover, a choice may be made among several alternatives, instead of just two, and the alternatives may themselves lead to alternatives. A computer program thereby exhibits a logical structure considerably more complex than the single-path programs of the ASCC and the 604. The complexity was not new, but it was now to be embodied in programs rather than in the multiple EAM machine runs and manual procedures performed by operators working with card decks segregated and combined by sorting and collating operations.

Other differences also served to complicate the task of computer programming. The programmer's needs to write programs consisting of hundreds of interrelated instructions, to keep track of data and program steps distributed throughout a large memory, and to write programs that metamorphosed during execution sharply increased the complexity of programming computers relative to the earlier calculators.

9.1 The Subroutine Library

By late 1950, engineering models of the 650 and the TPM were being constructed, and the Defense Calculator project was being formulated. The objective was to build machines that could be programmed to solve a broad range of problems and would be efficient in solving them. The programs would be written by customer staffs, as a part of installation and operation, supported by manuals of operation, customer education classes, and trained IBM representatives. Thus while IBM would build the machines, others would put them to use.

Other early builders of computers were to be responsible for programming and operating their completed machines and had looked closely at the cost implications of program complexity. A solution that emerged well before any machine was completed was that a program could be developed at less cost if a way could be found for it to exploit sections of code previously written and checked.

Such sections were identified by J. P. Eckert, Jr., and J. W. Mauchly in a progress report on the EDVAC written in September 1945, when they were finishing construction of the ENIAC at the Moore School of Electrical Engineering at the University of Pennsylvania. Under the heading "The Economics of Computing Machines" they considered means for reducing the cost of programming. They observed that in a typical application,

the same sequence of arithmetic processes must be carried out over and over again, but each time on a new set of numbers. To repeat such arithmetic orders each time they are to be used would be wasteful of memory capacity as well as wasteful of coding time, and is obviously unnecessary. . . . The directions for carrying out this work need be inserted in the memory only once, and the basic order code must provide for finding these instructions each time that they are needed, and for returning to *different* parts of the problem orders after each use.[1]

Eckert and Mauchly described code sharing, then, initially in this narrow context: a single section of code (stored only once) could be shared among multiple executions in a single program. When the program arrived at a point where the process represented by such a section was to be executed, a branch instruction would transfer control to the first instruction of the section. When execution was finished, control would be transferred back to the point from which the transfer was made; that point would be different for different executions. They saw that the code of such a multiply executed section could itself transfer control to another such section; for example, a section for solving a quadratic equation might utilize a section for calculating a square root. They concluded that "compounding of orders at different levels . . . constitutes the most important strategy for easily organizing and writing down the instructions for a large computation." Eckert and Mauchly used the phrase "computational routine" to designate a major computing procedure that might be formulated, in part, from such "subsidiary routines." Later in their report the latter phrase appears contracted as "subroutines."

By this time, A. M. Turing was planning a computer for the National Physical Laboratory in England. Turing's interest in computing went back to pioneering theoretical work he had done in the mid-1930s.

In 1945 he had read John von Neumann's "First Draft of a Report on the EDVAC," which articulated and elaborated early plans developed by the Moore School group. His plan for a machine to be named ACE (Automatic Computing Engine) included a careful examination of how programming might be accomplished. He saw that the programmer's job could be simplified by keeping the instructions of frequently used subroutines punched in cards in "a sort of library," so that they could be shared among different programs. This would be useful, he felt, because the typical program would consist "almost entirely of the initiation of subsidiary operations and transfers of material."

Turing realized that the detailed coding of a subroutine would differ in different programs because of the impracticality of specifying that the subroutine occupy the same storage locations in every program into which it was incorporated. To account for this he proposed a "permanent form" in which each subroutine would be maintained in the library, with each individual instruction identified by a subroutine name and a sequence number. The subroutine card decks selected for use in a particular program would be reproduced and "renumbered" for loading (each instruction would be assigned to a storage location punched in the reproduced card) in a systematic way. References by one subroutine to its own instructions or to those of another subroutine would have to be fixed before loading to account for the renumbering, said Turing, without detailing the process except to note that it was "a straightforward sorting and collating process."[2] Years later, many of the users of the first computers would assemble their programs on EAM equipment, before their machines were installed, in precisely the manner Turing anticipated.

In mid-1946, the idea of a memory-stored program began to reach more people through the agencies of lectures at the Moore School of Electrical Engineering at the University of Pennsylvania and the report by A. W. Burks, H. H. Goldstine, and J. von Neumann concerning a proposed computer for the Institute for Advanced Study. Although the IAS paper addressed order code and hardware organization principally, the authors foresaw great utility in a "library of . . . general sequences" with "facilities provided for the convenient insertion of any of these into the coded statement of a problem."[3]

The next year, Goldstine and von Neumann began an intensive study of the programming process for their machine. In the third and final volume of "Planning and Coding of Problems for an Electronic Computing Instrument," completed in August 1948, they considered how a subroutine library might be utilized. Subroutines were by then in regular use on IBM's SSEC and the ASCC at Harvard, the major enabling units on the SSEC being paper-tape readers; a subroutine was a loop of tape. The ASCC had, in addition to the original single sequence tape, ten twenty-two-step pluggable control panels, each driven by a rotary stepping switch; control could be transferred conditionally or unconditionally among the eleven units. For the IAS machine, in which subroutines would instead be stored along with data and other program components in a serially numbered memory, the dependence of a subroutine's code on its location presented the additional problem Turing had noted. In the body of their paper, Goldstine and von Neumann specified and coded in detail a "preparatory routine" whereby the IAS machine would load and adjust a set of subroutines being combined into a single program. Their assumed form of a library subroutine was a set of instructions followed by data areas, programmed to occupy a contiguous set of storage words. The programmer, after choosing the set of subroutines to be used, planned the storage layout of the combined program, noting the displacements in storage thereby implied for each subroutine. The preparatory routine, consisting of about 100 program steps, first loaded each subroutine into its relocated position and then adjusted the address parts of intrasubroutine references to account for the displacements. Necessary values such as subroutine lengths and displacements were provided to the routine by a typewriter connected to the machine. The adjustment process did not establish intersubroutine references; Goldstine and von Neumann had not developed a subroutine library format in which such interrelationships could be expressed, as Turing had. Their program's novelty was in its purpose: to facilitate the preparation of other programs for the machine on which it would run.[4]

During the summer of 1948, when the final paper on programming the planned IAS machine was completed, programming effort at IBM was focused on the application of the SSEC to a variety of scientific problems. By September, results had been obtained for two substantial problems, supplementing the results of the lunar position problem. The first was a problem in the field of atomic physics. The second, performed for the U.S. Naval Ordnance Laboratory, concerned the reflection and refraction of a shock wave at the interface between two gases.[5] The evaluation of mathematical functions on the SSEC was usually accomplished by the machine's table-lookup feature, using the high-speed paper-tape readers. Decks of cards containing tables of frequently used functions, from which table tapes were made for individual problems, were the principal resource shared by the programmers. There was no analogous library of subroutines.

The first subroutine library was realized and used at Cambridge University in England, where EDSAC began running in May 1949. The computers under construction at NPL and IAS, for which such libraries were planned, were not operable until later. M. V. Wilkes, director of Cambridge's University Mathematical Laboratory, had been at the Moore School during lectures given there in the summer of 1946 and had begun to design a computer upon his return to England.[6] When the computer became operable, he was soon galvanized into starting a library of carefully tested subroutines. Later he recalled, "Somehow, at the Moore School and afterwards, one had always assumed that there would be no particular difficulty in getting programs right. I can remember the exact instant of time at which it dawned on me that a great part of my future life would be spent in finding mistakes in my own programs."[7]

In June 1949, when the first conference in England on computers was held at Cambridge, Wilkes's plan for a subroutine library was outlined by a member of his staff, David J. Wheeler. Among other advantages in the library, Wheeler noted, "Library subroutines are known to be correct, thus greatly reducing the overall chance of error in a complete routine, and making it much easier to locate errors." He also observed that a library "enables routines to be more readily understood . . . as conventions are standardized and the units of a routine are much larger, being subroutines instead of individual orders."[8]

Wheeler planned that subroutines would be "adjusted" by the same program that loaded them, in contrast to the Goldstine-von Neumann scheme of loading followed by adjustment. His adjusting routine processed subroutines in a library form wherein each instruction on the input paper tape carried with it an additional line of information for the adjusting program. Such a line might mean, for instance, "to the address part of this instruction, add the memory location of the first instruction in this subroutine."[9]

Later in 1949, Wheeler established a standard two-instruction form by which control might pass from a main-line routine, by a branch instruction, to a subroutine.[10] Each usage of a subroutine would have to be associated, of course, with an instruction somehow establishing a correct return from the subroutine. As Turing had observed earlier, "We need only make a note of where we left off the major operation. . . . When the subsidiary is over we look up the note and continue." Also, for a typical subroutine, the branch would have to be accompanied by the subroutine parameters, that is, information ascertaining the data to be operated upon.[11]

Wheeler decided that a subroutine should, whenever executed, first construct its own return branch instruction from information (Turing's "note") provided by the main routine. Each EDSAC instruction contained an operation code and an address, and the address part sufficed for a "note." He chose EDSAC's single accumulator to hold the note and cleverly had a main-line load instruction, whose address comprised the note, load itself into the accumulator. Hence, if the load instruction occupied location 100, it contained 100 in its address field. The following instruction, which branched to the subroutine, was followed by parameters, if any. If there were no parameters, the subroutine established a return address by adding 2 to the accumulator and then moved the accumulator-contained address into the return instruction. If the subroutine required parameters—for example, the starting locations of required data—the subroutine took this into account in developing the return instruction. Wheeler felt that placing subroutine parameters in the main routine at the branch point promoted "economy of thought," since the programmer would be required to consider them at the very time he was writing the orders invoking, or "calling," the subroutine.[12]

It is evident that the "calling sequence" for a subroutine affects its coding. For a library of subroutines to be most useful, the calling sequence for each subroutine should follow the same pattern. Moreover, calling conventions are costly to change because every subroutine in the library has to be modified, as do application programs that rely on the library. In 1949, Wilkes was already envisioning that when a number of subroutines were in use, "There would be almost as much capital sunk in the library of sub-routines as the machine itself and builders of new machines in the future might wish to make use of the same order code as an existing machine in order that the subroutines could be taken over without modification."[13]

By the end of 1950, Wilkes's library contained over eighty subroutines in some eighteen categories, including Division (EDSAC had no divide operation), Power Series, Logarithms, Trigonometric Functions, and Print and Layout. In 1951, a book describing the EDSAC and its subroutine library was published; the authors were Wilkes, Wheeler, and a colleague, Stanley Gill. As a first textbook on programming, it had the merit of being based on actual operating experience.[14]

During 1950, while completing the design of the TPM, Nat Rochester surmised that a means for incorporating library subroutines would be needed for programming it. Since the Test Assembly would soon be available, he decided to write a TA program to load and relocate library subroutines punched in one-instruction-per-card format.

The program he tested late in September was similar to Wheeler's in that it utilized a library form for each subroutine in which each instruction of a subroutine identified, by code, a number to be added to its address part upon loading. The codes were the digits 0 to 9, where 0 meant "add nothing," 1 meant "add the address at which the first instruction of this subroutine is to be located," and the meaning of the remaining eight were assigned by the programmer to govern adjustment of address parts representing intersubroutine references. Code assignments were punched on "setup cards" preceding each library subroutine deck. As in EDSAC usage, the beginning memory location of each subroutine was determined by the programmer, and the resulting storage layout determined the content of the setup cards. Rochester decided not to combine relocating with loading. Instead his program punched out a "load deck" that could be used to load the composite program prior to executing it. This procedure allowed for somewhat larger programs, since the relocating program need not occupy memory during the loading process.[15]

At about this time, in the early autumn of 1950, Wheeler's two-instruction subroutine calling sequence was shown to William F. McClelland of IBM by von Neumann, to whom Wilkes had described it during a summer visit to the IAS machine site at Princeton. McClelland had been an SSEC programmer in his first year with IBM in 1948 when he was assigned to help von Neumann attempt to solve the high-speed fluid-flow problem (see chapter 2). Their continuing relationship nourished McClelland's interest in machines of the IAS type. He joined Cuthbert C. Hurd's Applied Science department in 1950 and later supervised that department's participation in Defense Calculator planning.[16]

The Wheeler calling sequence was used in the earliest Defense Calculator documentation, specifically in a programming example in the February 1951 manual written by Rochester and his staff (figure 9.1).[17]

9.2 Two IBM Assembly Programs

Von Neumann had observed, on the first page of his 1945 "First Draft of a Report on the EDVAC," "The instructions which govern . . . operation must be given to the device in absolutely exhaustive detail." Rochester and McClelland were by 1951 well aware of the drudgery of programming suggested by von Neumann's observation. Rochester had written and tested programs on the Test Assembly. McClelland had programmed the SSEC for two years and even devised a way in subprogram for writing on Tape   2-12-51

SERIAL NUMBER	OPERATION	TENTATIVE ADDRESS	COMMENT	SERIAL NUMBER	INSTRUCTION
	Main Program Detail				
1.1	TAPE	—			
1.2	R ADD	1.2			
1.3	X	2.1			
1.4	Address	of	first word to be written		
1.5	Number	of	words to be written		
1.6	Next step				
	Subprogram for writing on Tape				
2.1	ADD	K.2			
2.2	STORE A	3.1			
2.3	Add	K.1			
2.4	STORE A	3.3			
2.5	STORE A	3.4			
2.6	ADD	K.1			
2.7	STORE A	3.11			
3.1	R ADD	(1.4)			
3.2	STORE A	3.6	Insert address of 1st word		
3.3	SUB	(1.5)			
3.4	SUB	(1.5)	} Calc. end word		
3.5	STORE A	K.3			
3.6	WRITE	— c(1.4)			
3.7	R SUB	K.2			
3.8	ADD MEM	3.6	} Step address to next word		
3.9	R ADD	K.3			
3.10	SUB	3.6	} Test for end of record		
3.11	X +	(1.6)			
3.12	X	3.6	End of record		
K.1	1				
K.2	2				
K.3	WRITE	—			

Figure 9.1

Programming example: main program and subroutine for Defense Calculator. Copied from a handwritten page of "Type 60X Electronic Computer Operator's Reference Manual," 12 February 1951. To enhance comprehensibility, arbitrary designations are used in the "serial number" and "tentative address" columns instead of memory addresses; "operation" is indicated by an abbreviation instead of a numeric operation code. The example shows how a subroutine could be used to write on tape a list (any length) of numbers located in any set of contiguous storage locations, using the Wheeler subroutine calling sequence. In the main program, instruction 1.2 loads itself into the accumulator, and instruction 1.3 transfers control to the subroutine beginning at 2.1. Two parameters needed by the subroutine are stored, as Wheeler had suggested, immediately after the two-instruction linkage. The subroutine, using the constants "2" and "1," calculates the addresses of these parameters and plants them in the three instructions that need them, then calculates the return address and plants that. The main body of the subroutine begins at 3.1 with initialization of the WRITE instruction and calculation of the word with which that instruction will be compared, after each execution, to determine whether all words have been written. Instructions 3.6 through 3.12 constitute the tape-writing program "loop." (At the time this subroutine was prepared, WRITE provided, for tape output, functions later incorporated in the COPY instruction.)

which parts of each SSEC program could be produced automatically. In the mode of SSEC operation favored by its programmers, the instructions, fetched and executed in pairs, duplicated operations at each line, varying machine elements or operand designations. In multiplication, for instance, multiplicand and multiplier were reversed in the second instruction. Since the purpose of duplication was to detect hardware failures promptly, after every few instruction executions the program compared the arithmetic results of the two instruction sequences and, if they were unequal, the machine was stopped, and the sequence tapes were manually restarted at a preceding checkpoint. Thus dependable results could be obtained despite intermittent faults, and evidence of "solid" failures could be established before much time was invested in incorrect results. The cost was to run the machine at about half its potential speed.[18]

It was customary to write one set of instructions and then prepare the analogous second set. Since the translation from first to second could be done systematically, McClelland devised an EAM procedure — the key element being a 604 run — to read the first set from cards and punch the second. The last step of the process recorded both sets on SSEC paper tapes.[19]

McClelland wanted to extend mechanization to the clerical aspects of Defense Calculator programming, preferably using the machine itself to perform the work involved. He found a kindred spirit in Rochester, who had recently finished just such a program, the Test Assembly subroutine relocator. They agreed that an "assembly program" should assemble into an executable whole a program prepared in parts (to include previously written subroutines) that could be formulated independently.[20] Another of their objectives was to eliminate the time-consuming, error-prone "renumbering" task that bedeviled programmers. Writing a program consisted, in its simplest form, of writing a column of successive instructions adjacent to a column of "location numbers" designating a memory location for each instruction. For the Defense Calculator, a line began with a four-digit location number, followed by an instruction sign, a two-digit operation code, and a four-digit address designating the operand of the instruction. (As related in chapter 5, decimal-to-binary conversion routines were embodied in loading programs, enabling programmers to write and punch programs in decimal notation.) Whenever an instruction served as an operand or branch-to point, its location number appeared as the address part of another instruction. Often, after writing a dozen or more instructions, a programmer would decide to insert one or more instruction lines, provoking a renumbering of all lines below that point. Any address parts designating the renumbered instructions then had to be changed as well. A common blunder was to fail to revise an affected address part, the risk of such blunders mounting as a program grew in length.

McClelland observed that such program revisions were simply special cases of subroutine relocation. An insertion of two instructions, for example, entailed relocating by two half-words all instructions below the insertion point. The assembly program he designed and wrote for the Defense Calculator was capable both of combining library subroutines with a main program and of performing the fix-ups entailed by program changes. Programs to be assembled were punched one-instruction (or data item)-per-card, using a special "relative address" form for location numbers and address parts. A "relative address" consisted of a three-character index (two digits and a letter) designating the block of code of which the instruction was a part, followed by a four-digit number indicating the sequential position of the instruction within its block. Decks of punched cards comprising code blocks were first read by the Defense Calculator and written on magnetic tape. A control card prepared by the programmer then initiated an assembly "run" selected from among several types; each type read the tape and wrote a new one embodying insertions, deletions, or corrections suggested by trial executions of the program.

For example, the "relocate" run simply applied a specified increment or decrement to the numeric portion of each relative address in a specified code block, or (for insertion/deletion) to some subset of those addresses each of which exceeded a specified "cut address" at which the insertion or deletion was to be made. A "binary punching" run prepared a compressed program load deck. The load address for each instruction or data item was taken to be the numeric part of its relative location number; the programmer was expected to invoke the necessary relocation runs so that all such addresses would be unique. But that function was automatically performed by a "consecutive address assignment routine," which checked successive location numbers. When one was encountered in which the numeric part was not equal to its predecessor plus one, a relocation run was automatically performed to make it so, using the appropriate cut address and increment.[21]

The highly structured addressing convention implicit in "SO2," the name given to the system, seems unnecessarily stringent by hindsight, but McClelland's SSEC experience had convinced him of the value of programmed checking. With his scheme the data on the input and output tapes for any SO2 run were arithmetically related. For instance, for a relocation run, the arithmetic sum obtained by simply adding up all instruction and data elements on the new tape was equal to the old-tape sum plus the product of the designated increment and the number of instructions to which it was applied. After any run, the new-tape sum was checked by reading the tape backward. If the check failed, the run was automatically repeated. It was vexing for a programmer to find a routine thought to be error-free failing after being introduced into a new program. While a latent program flaw was the probable cause, there was also the possibility of human or machine error during program assembly. SO2 reduced new-program checking costs by substantially reducing that possibility.[22]

From the outset, Rochester was dissatisfied with McClelland's assembly plan. Early in 1950, while investigating methods of sorting on a hypothetical TPM-like machine, he had tried using relative addresses. On coding sheets he wrote blocks of instructions bearing successive location numbers such as $B, B + n, B + 2n, \ldots, B + 18n$ and $U, \ldots,$ $U + 37n$ (n represented the as-yet-undetermined number of memory characters per instruction.)[23] This procedure drew him immediately into the tedious chore of additions and corrections. He found relief from it in the flowchart programming practices proposed by Goldstine and von Neumann for the IAS machine in 1947.[24] They had recognized that, following preparation of a "flow diagram," coding would be accomplished in two stages: a "preliminary enumeration" followed by a "final enumeration." In the first, location numbers of instruction and data words were represented with the aid of labels that designated boxes (units of code) on the flowchart: "the numbers we assign at this stage are not those that will be . . . the actual position in the . . . memory." The final enumeration followed, "assigning all storage positions and all orders their final numbers."

On the flow diagram, each "operation box" (block of instructions with a well-defined processing function) was labeled with a Roman numeral. In the initial enumeration, an instruction within an operation box was labeled by the Roman numeral followed by a comma followed by an Arabic numeral indicating sequential position. Blocks of data were labeled with capital letters. As in the case of a librarian's Dewey decimal system, labels could be extended to accommodate insertions: "decimal fractions may be used for further subdivisions or in order to interpolate omissions, etc." Goldstine and von Neumann gave examples to illustrate their method. In the first, which evaluated a function of six numbers, eight data areas were labeled A.1, A.2, . . . , A.8. The code enumeration consisted of fourteen program steps labeled I,1 through I,14. In the second example, which derived another program by elaborating the first example, one change required that six new instructions precede I,1; they were simply labeled I,0.1, I,0.2, . . . , I,0.6.

Rochester switched to this system early in 1950, when detailed TPM planning began. A page of a TPM program written by W. Buchholz, his planning colleague, is shown in figure 9.2; the IAS numbering scheme for instructions is evident, except that the unwieldy Roman numerals are not used.[25] Rochester's subroutine-relocating program for the Test Assembly, written in September, is shown in figure 9.3.[26] Note that a decimal point has replaced the comma in instruction labels and that letters are used for data areas. Labels with two decimal points were being used, although none appear in the programs of figures 9.2 and 9.3. "Operation" is written as an abbreviated descriptive word. The "comment" area of the coding form, a feature important to enhanced comprehensibility, also had been anticipated by Goldstine and von Neumann, who called it the "explanatory column."[27]

Until they had a machine to test their programs on, Rochester and Buchholz did not bother to translate from "preliminary enumeration" to "final enumeration." When the Test Assembly began operating in the autumn of 1950, translation became necessary; they did it by a clerical process in which actual operation codes and memory addresses were substituted for the preliminary ones, as Goldstine and von Neumann had done to make their examples complete (see figure 9.3).

With the advent of the Defense Calculator project in early 1951, Rochester joined McClelland in studying the feasibility of automatic assembly but clung to the style of programming he had found most useful. Referring to his decimal and alphabetic-decimal labels as "symbolic addresses," he asserted, "It is possible for a machine to convert a program which is written in symbolic addresses into a program with actual address [sic]. This process will require a program which is fairly lengthy, but which would be fully manageable for either the Tape Processing Machine or the new proposed computer."[28]

His outline for the conversion process contemplated several machine passes over a programmer's "symbolic program." First, transfer instructions from cards to tape, forming one record per instruction; next, sort the tape records into ascending order of labels, an order presumed to be the intended sequence for the assembled program (although there was provision for rearrangement of major blocks); next, append location numbers, sequentially assigned, to the records, thereby establishing for each label an equivalent actual memory address. After a second file consisting only of instructions was created, the symbolic address parts were replaced by actual addresses; this required sorting on address parts and then collating with the main file, copying equiv-

PROGRAM FOR MERGING TWO FILES   2/13/50
                                                       W. Buchholz
4
(5½ Instructions)

SERIAL NUMBER	OPERATION	TENTATIVE ADDRESS	COMMENT	SERIAL NUMBER	INSTRUCTION
1,1	FT	0001			
1,2	R-ADD	00XX	$+C_1'+$		
1,3	ADJOIN	00YY	$+C_1''C_1'+$		
1,4	ADJOIN	00ZZ	$+C_1'''C_1''C_1'+ = C_1$		
1,5	TO MEM	0800			
1,6	FT	0202			
1,7	R-ADD	02XX	$+C_2'+$		
1,8	ADJOIN	02YY	$+C_2''C_2'+$		
1,9	ADJOIN	02ZZ	$+C_2'''C_2''C_2'+ = C_2$		
1,10	TO MEM	0900			
1,11	COMPARE	0800			
1,12	X	2,1	$C_1 > C_2$		
1,13	X	1,14	$C_1 = C_2$		
1,14	INTERCH.	0004	$C_1 < C_2$		
1,15	PTT	0403			
1,16	FT	0001			
1,17	XET1	3,1			
1,18	XET3	8,1			
1,19	R-ADD	00XX			
1,20	ADJOIN	00YY			
1,21	ADJOIN	00ZZ			
1,22	X̶ TO MEM	1̶,1̶1̶ 0800			
1,23	R-ADD	0900			
1,24	X	1,11			
2,1	INTERCH.	0206			
2,2	PTT	0603			
2,3	FT	0202			
2,4	XET2	4,1			
2,5	XET3	7,1			
2,6	X	1,7			
3,1	INTERCH.	0206			
3,2	PTT	0603			
3,3	FT	0202			
3,4	XET2	5,1			
3,5	XET3	10,1			
3,6	X	3,1			
4,1	INTERCH.	0004			
4,2	PTT	0403			
4,3	FT	0001			
4,4	XET1	5,1			
4,5	XET3	9,1			
4,6	X	4,1			

Figure 9.2
Page from an early 1950 program. Copied from IBM Technical Report "A Program for Merging Two Files," by W. Buchholz, dated 13 February 1950.

ASSEMBLY PROGRAM   N. Rochester   11-7-50

SERIAL NUMBER	OPERATION	TENTATIVE ADDRESS	COMMENT	SERIAL NUMBER	INSTRUCTION
			READING		
1.1	F1→Mem	A.1		001	60037
1.2	Add	A.1	A&C XYY) Separate	002	01037
1.3	Store	3 A.1	} A from C	003	74037
1.4	Sub.	3 A.1	Just A YY)	004	13037
1.5	Add	A.3	J = D + A	005	01039
1.6	RR	1.13		006	86013
1.7	Add	A.1	X C	007	01037
1.8	Add	A.2	F + C + 01000	008	01038
1.9	RR	1.10		009	86010
1.10	- From 1.9	--	Get E	010	--
1.11	G 12→Mem	A.1		011	80037
1.12	Add	A.1	G = B + E	012	01037
1.13	- From 1.6	--	Store G	013	--
1.14	PPX	1.1		014	50001
			PUNCHING		
2.1	Add	F.1	) Set Initial	015	01051
2.2	Sub	A.4	} Value of H	016	11040
2.3	RR	A.5	)	017	86041
2.4	Add	A.6	) Set Initial	018	01042
2.5	RR	2.18	} Value of K	019	86032
2.6	Add	1.13	86000 + D + A = 86000 + J) Set Up	020	01013
2.7	Sub	A.7	01000 + D + A } Stopping	021	11043
2.8	RR	A.8	) Point	022	86044
2.9	Add	2.18	) Increase K	023	01032
2.10	Add	A.4	} by 1	024	01040
2.11	Store	2.18		025	76032
2.12	Sub	A.8	) Test K for	026	11044
2.13	End -	--	} Stop	027	28000
2.14	RR	000		028	86000
2.15	Add	A.5	) Increase H by 1	029	01041
2.16	Add	A.4		030	01040
2.17	RR	A.5	)	031	86041
2.18	- From 2.11	--	Get Instruction) Prepare to	032	--
2.19	RR	A.1	} Punch	033	86037
2.20	Mem→G12	A.1	) Instruction	034	88037
2.21	Add	4 A.5		035	04041
2.22	PPX	2.9		036	50023

ASSEMBLY PROGRAM (CONSTANTS)   N. Rochester   11-7-50

SERIAL NUMBER	OPERATION	TENTATIVE ADDRESS	COMMENT	SERIAL NUMBER	INSTRUCTION
A.1	Manipulation			037	--
A.2	F + 01000			038	01050
A.3	D + 86000			039	86060
A.4	00001			040	00001
A.5	H			041	--
A.6	D - 1 + 01000			042	01059
A.7	85000			043	85000
A.8	01000 + Final Address Used (Stopping Point)			044	--
F.0	00000			050	
F.1			)	051	
F.2				052	
F.3			) Relative	053	
F.4			} Address	054	
F.5			) Constants	055	
F.6				056	
F.7				057	
F.8				058	
F.9				059	

Figure 9.3
Program for the Test Assembly. It read a main program and a number of library-form subroutines from cards and punched a load deck for a composite program. Constants and work areas follow the instructions. The Serial Number and Instruction columns on the right, needed for loading the program into the Test Assembly, were written after the program had been designed and detailed using the notation on the left. Copied (with minor corrections) from pages 7 and 8 of IBM Technical Report "Assembly of Programs on the Test Assembly (Revised)," by N. Rochester, dated 24 October 1950.

alent actual addresses. Final sort-collate operations created records with actual instructions and constants in correct sequence ready for compressing into a tape that could be used to load the assembled program.

By the end of April, Rochester had flowcharted and written a 750-instruction Defense Calculator program to perform assembly. A label contained one, two, or three numbers, in the range 1–99, separated by one or two decimal points. Instead of the unwieldy, multiple-run sort-collate process, all instructions and data complete with symbolic labels and assigned actual addresses were held in memory, and the actual equivalents of symbolic address parts were obtained simply by searching a "symbol table" for the appropriate "symbolic: actual" entry. Although the task had been reduced to table setup and lookup operations, the improvement brought the disadvantage that the amount of needed memory grew with length of program being assembled, the Defense Calculator memory accommodating a program of no more than 300 or 400 instructions. So Rochester added a provision that permitted larger programs to be processed in segments, the intermediate results for successive segments being stored on tape. A subsidiary table provided for symbolic address parts that had to be finally specified by reference to segments out on tape.[29]

A second improvement dropped the notion of a relationship between labels and the sequence in which instructions and data would reside in memory at execution time. Instead, the programmer established storage sequence simply by ordering the program cards prior to assembly. Although labels still followed a decimal format, this change enhanced the programmer's freedom to choose labels that matched his concept of program structure. Most assembly programs written later provided this freedom. Another contribution was made in 1951 when Wilkes proposed that only those instructions referred to by other instructions need be labeled.[30] This led to less clutter in written programs, to smaller symbol tables, and to faster assembly processing.[31]

When an assembly program was used, there were conspicuous differences between the source document that a programmer wrote in assembly language and the counterpart machine-language program that a 701 could execute. The programmer could use relative or symbolic addresses and alphabetic abbreviations for operations, while the executable program consisted of binary numbers and codes. In testing a program, as a result, the programmer could be faced with the problem of matching two dissimilar representations. The problem was mitigated by having assembly programs produce a printed list wherein the two representations were exhibited side by side.

Rochester's and McClelland's assembly programs were described to 701 customers during the winter of 1951–52, but the two had to wait for consistent operation of the 701 engineering model before they could try out their programs. This occurred in the spring of 1952; Rochester's program, by then recoded, was working by the end of June.[32] McClelland's SO2 was running before August. By then, McClelland's conventions were being called "regional programming" by Applied Science programmers, after the practice of allocating storage into functional blocks called regions. Standardized letter designations were used for regions: A for "universal" constants, B for program constants, C for input, D for output, and so forth. The letters appeared in the programmer's relative addresses; for example, 01B0005 might designate the fifth program constant in a block designated 01B.[33]

In August 1952, some thirty 701 customer representatives and the same number of IBM engineers and programmers participated in a one-week meeting at Poughkeepsie.[34] The 701 engineering model was by then in operation, and the customers tried out some of their first programs, written earlier in the year. During the week, IBMers described their two assembly programs and perhaps three dozen shorter programs, collectively known as "utilities," for input, output, loading, decimal-binary conversion, copying tapes, and similar functions. The programs had been contributed by Applied Science and by Rochester's planning group, two groups that had been actively trying to educate themselves in how a 701 should be used.

Nobody at the meeting expected that the IBM programs would be used unchanged at 701 installations. Their purpose was to serve as models that might be used in developing basic operational tools, making more time available for the development of application programs.[35] As for the customers, each installation had already formulated ideas on how to accomplish programming. The exchange of ideas occasioned by the Poughkeepsie meeting was stimulating, but each attendee could see ways to improve methods proposed by others. The freedom to design afresh was exhilarating enough to make improvements always seem worth some programming effort.

Subsequently, most 701 customers used programs written on their own premises or adapted from those obtained elsewhere.[36] For example, at the Los Alamos Scientific Laboratory, the first customer to receive a 701, regional programming was used, but the assembly program SO2 was modified to suit the installation's operational modes and standards.[37] Programmers at Douglas Aircraft Company in Santa Monica wrote an assembly program embodying features from both of the IBM assembly programs (for example, standardized regions and symbolic addresses) and tested the system before their 701 was shipped in May 1953.[38]

9.3 *The Speedcoding Language and Interpreter*

The time-consuming nature of 701 programming, by contrast with the evident speed of the machine, was a prominent subject of discussion at the August 1952 Poughkeepsie meeting. The usefulness of the machine was questionable where results were required soon after problem formulation, or where the expected value of results might justify the cost of executing a program but not the additional cost of writing and debugging the program.[39] ("Bugs" are errors in programs; "debugging" is the process of testing a program and correcting its errors.) Assembly programs were a step in the right direction but did not go far enough to help in time-critical circumstances. One of the principal contributors to von Neumann's "exhaustive detail" was the need to know the decimal point (or binary point) position in every operand, so that during arithmetic operations points could be properly aligned by shifting. That part of programming directed to alignment was known as "scaling."[40]

One of the attendees was John W. Sheldon, who as supervisor of IBM's Technical Computing Bureau had directed the preparation of dozens of CPC applications and had consulted often with Rex Seeber and his SSEC programmers.[41] During the meeting, Sheldon demonstrated the most comprehensive application program theretofore written for the 701, one that obtained solutions to a partial differential equation in the field of atomic physics.[42]

Sheldon had been impressed by a special mode of CPC operation devised in mid-1950 at the Los Alamos Scientific Laboratory. In the normal mode, the unique arithmetical manipulations for a particular problem solution, including attendant scaling operations, were governed by a program plugged on the control panel of the 604 calculating unit. The Los Alamos method, by contrast, employed a general-purpose 604 control panel wired to perform the basic arithmetic operations of addition, subtraction, multiplication, division, and square root on numbers in a floating-point format. Each number was represented by ten digits, of which eight represented value and two represented position of decimal point. Thus if the programmer prepared data in floating-point format, the CPC would perform card-prescribed operations, which, although selected from a limited repertoire, correctly adjusted decimal points. Programmers using the general-purpose panel were relieved of the burden of scaling and, in the bargain, of the task of control panel plugging. Operations on the 604 were typically fast enough to permit program execution at the full speed of 150 cards per minute.[43]

This development had revolutionized CPC usage. At the Technical Computing Bureau, where the economics of machine use were given substance by Sheldon's monthly statement showing income and expense, a similar control panel was soon developed; it served in most scientific jobs done on the CPC thereafter.[44]

Sheldon had felt that something similar should be done for the SSEC. Two or three programmers sometimes worked for several weeks to prepare and test an SSEC program. The situation was tolerable only because each problem was tested, corrected, and run to completion before the next one was applied. There was always a waiting list of users, and so each program was written during the weeks that its sponsor waited for access to the machine. Sheldon and others developed a proposal: a special set of general-purpose fixed-point panels would be developed for the CPC; program decks written to run using those panels would be amenable by design to translation by an SSEC "translation sequence" into an equivalent SSEC program. A program would be written and then checked on the CPC. When time on the SSEC opened up, the checked program would be translated for the most part automatically. Some hand adaptation would be required, but Sheldon thought he could reduce program preparation time on the SSEC to a week. This plan, devised in the fall of 1951, was completed too near the time of the mid-1952 dismantling of the SSEC to be carried out.[45]

In Poughkeepsie in August 1952, Sheldon found that customers for the 701 shared his concern about programming efficiency. The most promising avenue seemed to be an "interpretive" system of programming. An early exposition of this idea had been set forth by Wilkes and his colleagues in their 1951 book. The problem of scaling had been a motivation. They had defined pseudo-floating-point operation codes, abiding by the single-address instruction format of EDSAC. They had adopted the convention that each sequence of floating-point instructions in a program would be preceded by a branch to an "interpretive subroutine," which analyzed each instruction in turn, performing the indicated floating-point operations by carrying out appropriate fixed-point arithmetic and shifting operations on the value and decimal point position parts of the floating-point factors. A pair of EDSAC memory locations was reserved as a "floating-point accumulator" to receive results.[46] Members of the EDSAC staff later observed that an interpretive subroutine "enables the programmer to use a new order code of his own choice."[47]

By early 1952, Whirlwind programmers at MIT also were experimenting with a number of single-address floating-point interpretive systems similar to EDSAC's. In May, an MIT speaker suggested that the surface had not yet been scratched: "Future interpretive systems may be of a different logical type—perhaps three-address with programmed B-boxes and logic similar to the University of Manchester machine."[48] The word "three-address" denoted an instruction format wherein three storage locations, two for operands and one for result, were associated with each operation code. Using an interpretive routine to make a one-address fixed-point machine appear to be a three-address floating-point machine was an appealing idea to a CPC customer striving to program the 701, as was apparent at the Poughkeepsie meeting. At the Los Alamos Scientific Laboratory, where interpretive methods were characterized as "shorthand" in contrast to the "longhand" methods of assembly language coding, a system called SHACO (Short Hand Coding) was already being developed.[49] Portions of another system, dubbed FLOP (for Floating Octal Point), were run during the week by two representatives of Lockheed Aircraft Corporation.[50]

Sheldon had reason to be interested in these user initiatives: his Technical Computing Bureau had been charged with operating a 701 in a service bureau and customer program testing role, continuing service bureau use of the CPC and 604, and staffing a series of EDPM classes for customers. Even given the opportunity to add experienced SSEC programmers, he needed better programming tools as urgently as any 701 customer.[51]

He had enlisted John W. Backus, of the SSEC programming staff, for the unfinished CPC-to-SSEC program translator.[52] Backus had been hired into Seeber's programming group in 1950 after earning a master's degree in mathematics at Columbia University. From the beginning he had shown an interest in improvement of inefficient programming and operating practices. He and a colleague, Edgar F. Codd, an Oxford University graduate who joined IBM in 1949, had worked out a method of error checking for the SSEC that improved on the scheme whereby the results of twin instruction streams were compared every few instructions. Backus and Codd compared far less frequently, repeated the computation from the last compare point if the comparison failed, and switched to an error routine if the comparison failed a second time. The error routine essentially reran the faulty portion of the computation with comparisons as frequently as possible, thereby identifying the program step at which the fault was occurring, an elaborate operator procedure in the usual mode of operation.[53]

Now Sheldon asked Backus to supervise the development of a floating-point interpretive system for the use with the 701 to be located at the Technical Computing Bureau, a job that had to start with definition of a convenient "new order code." Although they had their own ideas on the subject, before settling the matter they chose to seek the counsel of interested 701 users, among them Willard G. Bouricius,[54] who was directing the development of SHACO at Los Alamos,[54] and Walter A. Ramshaw, who was working on an interpretive system at United Aircraft Corporation in Hartford, Conn. With Ramshaw, who was close enough to New York to visit frequently, they maintained a continuing association. In February 1953, Ramshaw wrote a first brief description of the "IBM Shorthand Coding System" and illustrated its use by programming some simple problems.[55]

During a period of intensive programming and testing that began in January 1953, Backus and five principal colleagues built a system that acquired the descriptive name "Speedcoding." It became evident that its use would not be limited to Sheldon's activity.[56] By September, five 701 installations were using or planning to use Speedcoding.[57] A few months later Backus reported extensive use at several installations; by then, users were extending the system's functions and sending copies of their changes to other installations.[58]

Based on CPC usage, the Speedcoding statement format provided fields for a floating-point operation code (denoted by OP_1), the addresses of two floating-point operands (denoted by A and B), and the address of a floating-point result (denoted by C). But a problem not encountered in the CPC immediately arose. Address modification, a crucial function that confers great flexibility on stored-program computers, is by nature a fixed-point operation. Backus chose to meet the difficulty by expanding the statement format to include a field for the address of a fixed-point operand (denoted by D) and a fixed-point operation (denoted by OP_2). During interpretation of a statement, the OP_1 operation was executed first and the OP_2 operation second.

OP_1 operations went beyond add, subtract, multiply, and divide to include square root, sine, arctangent, exponential, and logarithm functions. The OP_1 list also included input-output and move-within-memory operations. OP_2 operations supplied conditional and unconditional branching. Other OP_2 operations performed address arithmetic, in a fixed-point accumulator established by the system, on addresses extracted from the Speedcoding statement designated by the D-address;

"store" instructions caused the accumulator contents to be planted in an address field of the designated statement.

A Speedcoding program was written as a sequence of Speedcoding statements, each with two three-digit operation codes and four four-digit addresses and each assigned to a location in the address range 300–1013. The Speedcoding loader loaded the program, with decimal-to-binary conversion of the operation code and address fields, into the assigned locations, each of which mapped into two 701 thirty-six-bit words. Control was then transferred to the Speedcoding interpretive program, which executed each statement in turn by formulating and then executing the appropriate 701 instructions; subroutines necessary to the execution process were read into memory from one of the 701 drums when needed.

An important subset of the OP_2 operations performed setting, manipulating, and testing of three address-format numbers called "R-quantities" in the Speedcoding manual. They were associated with the A, B, and C addresses, respectively, of statements. Further, a one-digit "R-code" in each statement (eight possible values) determined whether none, one, two, or all of the R-quantities would be added to their respective associated addresses just prior to execution of the statement. None of the addresses was changed in storage by that process, but its effect was different by virtue of the address modification; hence the term "effective address" was used in the manual to distinguish such a transitory address from the one stored in the statement in memory.[59]

The R-quantities facilitated programming of iterative routines dealing with strings or arrays of operands. The capability may be built into the native order code of a computer instead of being added by a system of programming. The idea had, in fact, been originated by engineers at the University of Manchester in England, led by F. C. Williams, soon after the first, limited model of their machine began to operate in mid-1948. Cathode-ray tubes were used for number and instruction storage. An additional tube, designated "A," was used as the accumulator; another, "C," stored two control registers, the instruction counter and the instruction register. When they conceived of a special storage register whose contents would selectively modify instruction addresses during execution, they wired up a third tube for the purpose and called it the "B-tube" because, as Williams put it, "the letters A and C had already been used up."[60] The casually chosen name, with variants such as B-line, B-box, and B-register, was not replaced by a more descriptive one for about four years.

A Williams colleague, Tom Kilburn, described the B-tube idea at the Cambridge University conference in June 1949, and Williams told IBM engineers about it on a visit to the Poughkeepsie and Watson laboratories in August. At that time the only instruction affecting the B-tube contents was one that transferred a number from main storage to the B-tube.[61] The key to exploiting the idea for both shortening programs and speeding up applications was to specify more such devices and more instructions to manipulate their contents. This was done at Manchester, IBM, and elsewhere. By early 1953, when ideas for an improved 701 were beginning to surface, B-tubes exploited in that way were being called "index registers" in IBM. One proposed associated instruction would test the index register contents; if not 0, the contents would be decremented by 1, and control would transfer to the address specified in the instruction; if 0, control would pass to the next instruction in sequence. Thus the index register would contribute both to address modification and to the associated program loop control.[62]

Speedcoding's users, for the privilege of writing programs in a "shorthand" code featuring floating-point operations and index registers, had to endure some hardships. Each instruction was written as a string of some twenty-three decimal digits; there was no assembly program to translate mnemonic operation codes or allocate storage.[63] Against the saving in programmer time and the prompter results obtained through Speedcoding, the user had to reckon a problem execution time that was typically fifteen times longer than an equivalent program written in assembly language.[64] Since interpretation was part of execution, the penalty was paid at every run of a program. This meant that Speedcoding was more appropriate for transitory computations than for those performed regularly. Nevertheless, the popularity of Speedcoding was a clinching factor in the decision to include built-in floating-point operations and high-speed index registers in the improved 701 announced in May 1954 as the IBM 704.[65]

9.4 The FORTRAN Language and Compiler

In mid-1953 Sheldon left IBM to devote full time to his graduate studies at Columbia University.[66] C. C. Hurd asked Daniel R. Mason, head of the mathematical planning group at Poughkeepsie, to replace Sheldon as manager of the Scientific Computing Service, a name that replaced "Technical Computing Bureau."[67] The SCS continued the service bureau function, the original basis for the CPC-and-604-equipped bureau, but with greatly enhanced capacity afforded by the

701. With a portion of the staff engaged in development projects like Speedcoding and in conducting training sessions for customers, employees, and Applied Science trainees, more programmers were needed, and Mason's department became a hiring and training center with a continuous schedule of classes; training activities increased after announcement of the 650 in July. The third activity involved assistance to 701 customers who, prior to delivery of their own machines, came to test their initial programs.[68]

The service bureau business was lively because the 701 at the Scientific Computing Service in New York was the most powerful computer available with attendant programming services. The one-of-a-kind machines in the government and the universities were largely restricted in use to the purposes of their builders. UNIVACs had so far been delivered only to government agencies; the first commercial firm to install a UNIVAC was General Electric Company at Louisville in April 1954,[69] whereas eight 701s were delivered to private companies in 1953. With one shift devoted to service bureau work, a second to customer program testing, and a third to machine maintenance, the 701 was busy around the clock. Because setup time was low, perhaps a dozen user groups would be on the premises for a portion of each day, in sharp contrast to the SSEC practice of serving only one user for a period of days or weeks.

Given the great variety of programs being tested and run and the careful records of income and expense necessarily being kept, Backus was afforded an excellent glimpse of computer-usage economics. His perception was broadened at a conference of 701 users hosted by Douglas Aircraft in August 1953. Five of the customers who attended had received their 701s; the others were well along in planning. The sizes of programming and operating staffs were surprising. With thirty people, Mason was low on the scale; two users reported forty-five-person staffs. At $15,000 per month, 701 rental was roughly equivalent to the pay of thirty employees, and so computer cost was doubled or more when staff cost was added. Backus heard, moreover, that about 40 percent of useful machine time was used for preparing and debugging new programs.[70] All told, nearly three-quarters of the expense of operation involved programming and debugging.

Backus first expected Speedcoding and similar systems, as they came into use, to moderate this figure. But it soon became clear that the situation would instead deteriorate. First, the maturing plans for the 704 indicated substantial performance gains at surprisingly little additional hardware cost, implying that programming costs would become an even higher proportion of total costs. Second, Speedcoding had little to offer the 704 programmer; its main advantages were built into that machine in the form of floating-point operation codes and index registers.[71]

Backus decided that a practical system for programming the 704 would have to be a "compiler," a program that would process a program written in some user-oriented language and produce a machine-executable program. The concept of a compiler had been advanced in May 1952 by Grace M. Hopper of Remington Rand Inc. while investigating the use of UNIVAC for scientific problems. She shared the prevalent view that the key to efficient application development was a library of subroutines and a multiaddress order code containing codes for the subroutine operations. But an interpretive system was only one way to exploit such a facility. A second way would be to process the programmer's code and construct a program to execute it, but to defer execution until later. Subroutines invoked by the code would be copied into the growing program (properly adjusted for relocation) rather than executed on the spot.[72] Hopper's first compiler was written in the winter of 1951–1952 and was running when she presented a paper on the subject at a meeting of the Association for Computing Machinery in May 1952. She cited the advantage of faster program execution as compared with an interpretive system, while conceding that some logically unnecessary data-shuffling operations seemed unavoidable in compiled programs.[73]

A-0, as Hopper's compiler subsequently was named, was augmented, and some UNIVAC customers began using the A-2 version in late 1953. Statements written in the A-2 language were similar in format to the OP_1 segment of a Speedcoding statement: a floating-point operation code and three addresses. A-2 lacked the control and indexing features afforded by Speedcoding's OP_2; instead a facility for interjecting machine language code between stretches of "pseudo-operations" was provided.[74]

Backus outlined to Mason and Hurd, late in 1953, his reasoning that a compiler would be needed for the 704. As a result, he was allowed to start a compiler project at the Scientific Computing Service.[75] In January 1954, he was joined by Irving Ziller, supervisor of the EAM section of the SCS, the descendant of the original Technical Computing Bureau. Ziller, who had joined the bureau in 1952 after graduating from Brooklyn College, had transferred many of the CPC service bureau applications to the more cost-effective 701, taking advantage of the similarity between Speedcoding and CPC programming.[76] The third project member was Harlan L. Herrick, a mathematician with five years of SSEC and 701 programming experience; while a graduate student at Yale University in 1948, he heard about the SSEC, wrote to Wallace Eckert, and was hired for the programming staff.

At a May 1954 conference entitled "Automatic Programming for Digital Computers," Hopper pointed out in the opening paper that whereas the word "automatic" had often modified "computer" (as in the expansion of the acronym UNIVAC), that usage had become redundant and the currently useful phrase was "automatic programming," which identified the class of aids to programming represented by assembly, compiling, interpretive, and other systems.[77] Backus and Herrick described Speedcoding, explained its lack of suitability for the IBM 704, and indicated the new direction of their thinking by listing "the advantages of being able to state the calculations, decisions, operations on ordered arrays of data . . . necessary for a problem solution in a concise, fairly natural mathematical language." More specifically, "the programmer would like to write 'X' instead of some specific address, and if he wants to add X and Y he would like to write 'X + Y.' " They implied that the next step beyond Speedcoding would not only replace interpretation by compilation but would provide a programmer's language based on algebraic expressions rather than on fixed-format, operation-code-oriented statements. Significantly, a programmer would represent a variable to be processed, such as "X," by its algebraic denotation, not by a name associated with the storage location at which the numeric value of the variable would be stored.

Backus and Herrick posed a "vital question" for automatic programming efforts: "can a machine translate a sufficiently rich mathematical language into a sufficiently economical machine program at a sufficiently low cost to make the whole affair feasible?"[78] The question of feasibility was far from settled by a speaker from MIT, who described an algebraic compiler already being used on Whirlwind, a machine with 1024 sixteen-bit words of memory. Limitations on the structure of compiled programs were lengthening running times almost ten to one compared with assembly-language-coded programs; the speaker estimated that any satisfactory improvement would require considerably more work.[79] Backus visited MIT and was given a demonstration of the MIT compiler in June. He returned impressed by the pioneering aspect of the MIT work but realizing that his own goal, a much more efficient compiler for a more versatile language, represented a long step beyond Whirlwind's program.

The basic features of a proposed language were established by Backus and his colleagues during 1954. The critical question, for which the traditional formulations of algebra provided little guidance, was that of the control statements: how to provide for conditional transfer of control, for iterative program loops, and for signaling the systematic processing of arrays of data, the procedures for which the OP_2 codes of Speedcoding had been developed. One element of the solution was to permit variable names to carry subscripts (the subscripts themselves being variables or simple expressions involving variables); subscripts were written in parentheses following a variable name. Another was a "DO formula" for specifying that a subsequent sequence of statements be repeated in the computation, a given variable being augmented during successive iterations until it reached a prescribed value. The variable (the "index" of the DO formula) could be used in subscripts in the sequence of statements, and since DO statements (as they were later called) could be "nested" (a given sequence of statements to be repeated could itself include a DO statement), data arrays of more than one dimension could be processed. Figure 9.4 shows how compactly a matrix multiplication could be expressed by this formulation.

In November, Backus's group published "Preliminary Report, Specifications for the IBM Mathematical FORmula TRANslating System, FORTRAN." This first description of the FORTRAN language served during calls that Backus, Ziller, and Herrick made during the winter, on half a dozen customers who had ordered 704s, for the purpose of obtaining reactions. For the most part, the results were discouraging. Most 701 users, already busy developing their programming skills and keenly aware of the limitations of much less ambitious assembly and interpretive systems, were dubious about the FORTRAN project's prospects of success. The key component of Backus's "vital question," efficient use of computer resources by the compiled programs, evoked particular skepticism. One encouraging response was from United Aircraft. Walter Ramshaw agreed that Roy Nutt, an accomplished UA programmer, would assist Backus in compiler development. By 1955, the long job of writing the compiler was underway.[80]

9.5 Programming as a Marketing Aid

The plan for FORTRAN had evolved over a period of years beginning with the programming of the SSEC for scientific work and was significantly stimulated and advanced by contact between Applied Science representatives and the imaginative users of the IBM CPC and 701. The 701 assembly programs, utility routines, and Speedcoding had established that IBM programming initiatives were useful to customers in installing their machines. In early 1954, orders for the 702 were coming in. T. V. Learson, the new director of EDPM, established in late April in Poughkeepsie a new department managed by W. H. '

|
|
|

$$DO \quad 8 \quad I = 1, 5$$
$$DO \quad 8 \quad J = 1, 5$$
$$C(I, J) = 0.$$
$$DO \quad 8 \quad K = 1, 5$$

8    $$C(I, J) = C(I, J) + A(I, K) * B(K, J)$$

|
|
|

Figure 9.4
Part of a FORTRAN program to compute the product of two matrices. The 704 program that results from compilation of the above segment of a FORTRAN program computes the twenty-five elements of a 5 × 5 matrix C (five rows and five columns) by multiplying two 5 × 5 matrices A and B stored in fifty 704 memory words in floating-point format. Each of the twenty-five result elements is the sum of five products obtained by taking the elements of the corresponding row of A and column of B in pairs (in FORTRAN the asterisk (*) indicates multiplication).

Each DO statement causes the sequence of subsequent statements up to and including statement 8 to be executed repetitively, first with the indicated subscript set to 1, then 2, 3, 4, and finally 5. The initial effect of the first two DO statements is to set subscripts I and J to 1. The next statement initializes the value of C_{11} at zero. Then five executions of statement 8 provoked by the third "DO" cause C_{11} to be replaced by its former contents plus, in turn, $A_{11} \times B_{11}$, $A_{12} \times B_{21}$, $A_{13} \times B_{31}$, $A_{14} \times B_{41}$, and $A_{15} \times B_{51}$.

The third DO having been "satisfied" by this process, control reverts to the second DO. Subscript J is advanced to 2, and result element C_{12} is initialized to zero and calculated by execution of the third DO and by the attendant five executions of statement 8.

The process continues until C_{55} has been computed. At that point each of the three DO statements in the "nest" terminating at statement 8 will be found to be satisfied, and execution will proceed to the part of the compiled program corresponding to the next FORTRAN statement.

Johnson. Titled Programming Research, one of its functions was to develop 702 programs for customer use.[81]

The considerable programming done in establishing the TPM as a product had been application programming, as, for example, in the studies that were part of the "tape survey" of 1952. There had been no work of general applicability, such as the 701 assembly programs, because the opportunities for such programs seemed very limited for the alphanumeric 702. Binary-decimal conversion subroutines were unnecessary, and indeed the entire notion of subroutine libraries seemed inapplicable because no common functional elements were perceived in the applications of diverse industry groups.

Programs that demonstrated particular applications seemed important, however, because prospective 702 customers, unlike 701 users, would be making the leap from EAM equipment to EDPM without the mediating influence of the CPC. Moreover, there were as yet no success stories; UNIVAC, always a spur to 702 development, was still six months away from regular operation at its first publicized accounting installation at the General Electric Company's Major Appliance Division in Louisville.[82] In the light of this, a second function of Programming Research had to be development of demonstration programs and assistance to the sales organization.

The first major programs written by the department were a symbolic assembly program and a sort program. The assembly program provided labels of the general form devised earlier by Rochester. The location field had to be completed for each statement, but to reduce symbol-table length and thus increase the size of the program that could be assembled, a column on the programming form was reserved for flagging "each instruction whose location is used as an address by another instruction." Only flagged instructions produced table entries; if the programmer failed to include a needed flag, the assembly program noted it. A "patch" card supplementing the load deck or tape could be used to avoid reassembly.

Sorting, a fundamental task in most accounting applications, had been studied during TPM planning. A basic logic for sorting with magnetic tapes had been established. During a first "internal sort" pass of a file, a group of a few records was read, examined, and written in sorted sequence on an output tape. The next group was treated similarly, except that a second output tape was used if the first record of the new sequence did not follow, in sorting sequence, the last record of the previous one. By this process, the internal sort pass wrote an equal number of "strings" (sequences of sorted records) on each of two output tapes. "Merge" passes followed, each merging strings from two tapes in pairs, writing longer strings alternately on two tapes, until a string consisting of the entire sorted file was written on an output tape. Although the basic logic of sorting is actually simple, among the several parameters involved are number of characters per record, number of characters per sorting (or "control") field, and location of control field or fields within record. To write a sort program that could be easily adapted to some portion of the wide variety of files maintained by 702 users was a considerable challenge. This first IBM sort program was written for sorting unblocked (records written one at a time, and therefore separated by "gaps" on the tape) eighty-character records with the control field as the first nine characters; records were written twenty to a block on the merge tapes. These numeric parameters, however, and others were provided as constants in the symbolic sort program and used at the beginning to initialize instructions in the sort program proper. Thus users who understood the program could readily adapt it to a variety of sort applications.

The assembly and sort programs were tested on the 702 engineering model during the summer 1954 Poughkeepsie plant vacation period. The programs used tape heavily, and numerous tape reading and writing errors interfered with the testing schedule by requiring the programmers to spend considerable time with engineers. Nevertheless, both programs, and three demonstration programs as well, were substantially tested during the two-week period. A 702 programming manual printed in November presented the two general-use programs at a level of detail that included not only flowcharts but the symbolic instructions as well. The sort program, which contained over 1000 instructions, was presented "for study and actual application if desired."[83]

During 1954, the members of Programming Research, some twelve to eighteen people, were frequently called upon to assist IBM salesmen. Although a special sales department had been established at headquarters to assist in 702 sales, it did not serve as a center of technical knowledge.[84] For the 702, as a result, Programming Research temporarily played a role somewhat similar to the role Applied Science played for the 701. In the fall, with the programs completed, this role became the dominant one, and the department was disbanded, most of its members going either to the product planning function or to the Education department at Poughkeepsie. The product planning group retained a general responsibility for developing advanced programming techniques. After improving the usability of the 702 assembly program, this group defined and wrote an early version of an improved assembly program called "Autocoder."

The IBM 705 was announced as a successor to the 702 in October 1954. The Education group's first task was preparation of a table giving 705 sorting times, based on the 702 sort program, for a plethora of combinations of sizes of files, records, and control fields. Because customer plans were already indicating that 702s and 705s might be used a third or more of the time in sorting tape records, prospective 705 customers wanted fairly precise tools for estimation. The computations that generated the table were done by a program written for the 702. The 705 sort programs themselves were deferred until this work was completed.

702 customers began testing sessions late in 1954 on the 702 engineering model at the Poughkeepsie laboratory annex and continued at the plant on the first production machine after it was completed in February 1955. The Education programmers, while assisting in sessions, also wrote a 705 assembly program, designed and documented an EAM assembly procedure (one had been done earlier for the 702) that permitted customers to arrive at the 705 test site with programs already assembled on their own equipment, and prepared a 702 program that simulated a 705.[85] The third of these, a "simulator," was in principle a specialized interpreter; it was done in anticipation that early customers for the 705 would be ready to test programs before a 705 test site could be prepared. (Though 705 deliveries were not scheduled to start until 1956, by late May 1955 nearly a hundred 705s had been ordered.)[86] The simulation program processed 705-language programs on the 702, producing the results that a 705 would.

The simulator was first used in June 1955 at the Poughkeepsie 702 test site. Its use continued that summer at headquarters when a second production 702 was installed there. Even after this 702 was replaced by the first production 705, which became available for customer testing in January 1956, the customer-testing load continued to justify simulated testing on the Poughkeepsie 702 into the spring of 1956.

Meanwhile, in March 1955, the Programming Research department was reestablished in a one-story building in Red Oaks Mill, a crossroads community a few miles east of the Poughkeepsie plant. The programmers debugged on the plant 702, competing for time with six other activities that included customer program testing, IBM methods departments (the bona fide "users" of the machine), sales demonstrations, and general sales use that included training of marketing representatives and instructors.[87]

While Autocoder and sort development continued at Red Oaks Mill, the focus of programming activity shifted to New York in summer 1955. With a 701, a 702, and a 650 in operation in the ground-floor data processing center, that location became the showplace for 702 customer testing and demonstrations. Mason, who managed the center, had one main unit for the 702 and another for the 701 (the latter being the former Scientific Computing Service). His staff included over sixty programmers, those for the 701 being busy with the service bureau and those for the 702 being largely concerned with program testing and demonstrations. Service bureau work had been planned for the 702 but was not done because of the heavy load of the other functions. The main bond linking the two groups was that functionally similar utility programs were sometimes needed for both machines.[88]

Later in the summer group distinctions deepened into an organizational one, and the marketing orientation of the 702 group intensified. Installations of the 702, which had begun in March 1955, were not proceeding as smoothly as desired. The problems ranged from 702 reliability to lack of needed capability at the branch offices responsible for installation. Publications and training programs to distribute needed information and skills had not been adequate. The 702 unit at headquarters was made the nucleus of a new Customer Assistance department under Walter Johnson and charged with the task of supporting branch offices by providing direct service to installed and to-be-installed accounts. Members of a "flying squad" began visiting customer sites to advise on all aspects of planning and operating and to provide liaison with IBM testing, programming, and engineering functions. Training was stepped up, particularly for candidate representatives to user sites. Others of the experienced programmers were assigned to Poughkeepsie to assist with Autocoder development; work on utility programs was stepped up; and for documentation and distribution of IBM's programming results, a separate function was established.[89]

By early 1956, the nine programmers on the 705 side of the New York Data Processing Center were but one unit, named "Applied Programming," of a marketing support organization that included units for customer testing, field contact, training, competitive equipment review, methods study, and recruiting. They were fully occupied maintaining existing assembly, demonstration, and utility programs and updating them to accommodate more 705 storage and enhanced input-output facilities.[90]

9.6 SHARE, a User Organization

At the Eastern Joint Computer Conference in Washington, D.C., in late 1953, Bouricius described eight months of operating experience with the 701 at Los Alamos. Most application programs had been written using Regional Coding (an assembly program adapted from IBM's SO2) or one of two floating-point interpretive systems, SHACO and DUAL. A set of utility programs was also available. In response to a question about these programs after the presentation, Bouricius said, "A complete description, and the code itself, for any of our programs, will be sent to anyone who writes for it."[91]

Although this statement illustrates the willingness of most 701 programming managers to share programs of general applicability, the sharing that actually took place was very limited. The notion that "we can do it better for our particular needs," naturally prevalent in installations experimenting with a novel machine, was one reason. Another reason was simply inoperability; a subroutine written using one set of coding and linkage standards could require a tedious rewrite before fitting into another system. Finally, the level of documentation that sufficed locally seldom served for effective exchange.

By the summer of 1955, however, when a number of customers were preparing to receive 704s early in the next year, the stage was set for program sharing to become an integral part of planning. For one thing, a cadre of 701 programmers had met sufficiently often to develop respect for one another's abilities. Relevant meetings included a 1949 meeting at Endicott of early CPC customers, the CPC-oriented IBM scientific computation seminars in 1949–1951, the Poughkeepsie preinstallation meeting of 701 users in August 1952, the meeting at Douglas Aircraft in Santa Monica in August 1953, and a 701-oriented computation seminar in Endicott in May 1954 at the time of 704 announcement. In southern California, moreover, in late 1952, a series of informal dinner meetings had been organized (and the first one hosted) by R. Blair Smith, an IBM salesman, because "it was clear that the 701 customers needed to share information and know-how." This group adopted the name Digital Computer Association (DCA).[92]

Further evidence that sharing might be beneficial was provided by a cooperative programming project started in November 1954, by which time a number of users who had decided to replace their 701s by 704s were beginning to estimate the task of program revisions. Each had a substantial library investment in 701 programs designed solely to assist in preparing application programs. Such a library— consisting of at least an assembly program, one or more interpretive systems, and subroutines for frequently used procedures—was needed to hold down application costs, but obviously the expense of rewriting it for the 704 would be substantial. Beyond this, there was some dissatisfaction with the current assemblers and interpreters. The former did not sufficiently alleviate the awkwardness of machine language, while the latter imposed a heavy performance penalty.

North American Aviation proposed that a compiler be jointly developed. Representatives of four user installations approved the idea during a meeting at Douglas Aircraft Company, El Segundo, California, in November 1954. The compiler would be written for the 701, proved feasible, and then revamped for the 704. A suitable language was formulated, and by year-end 1955 some fifteen programmers from six 701 installations in the area completed a compiler. The joint effort went by the name Project for the Advancement of Coding Techniques, the compiler by the acronym PACT.[93]

In early August 1955, when the success of PACT was assured, members of three of the cooperating corporations (Lockheed Aircraft, North American Aviation, and RAND) considered broadening their objectives and embracing more participants. An IBM symposium in Los Angeles for 704 customers in the West during the week of 8 August afforded an opportunity for further discussions of the idea. Scheduled 704 deliveries, to begin near the end of the year, added a sense of urgency. A 9 August letter from Fletcher Jones of RAND, sent to organizations that had ordered 704s, brought representatves from seventeen installations to a meeting at RAND during the week of 22 August. A new organization, which took the name of SHARE, was formed with the following objectives: the standardization of machine language and certain machine practices, the elimination of redundant effort expended in connection with the use of the computer, the promotion of interinstallation communication, and the development of a meaningful stream of information between the user and the manufacturer. Within nine months, forty-seven installations were members of SHARE, and three hundred machine-checked 704 programs had been placed in an IBM-maintained library that could be drawn on by members.[94]

Through the deliberations of its technical committees, the new organization provided a focus for the creativity of the users of IBM 704 and successor machines. SHARE resolutions, as a consensus of user opinion, became a powerful force in shaping IBM's programming undertakings.

9.7 IBM's Organization for Programming

Early in 1955 Hurd became director of EDPM, replacing Learson, who had moved on to vice-president in charge of sales. The new director of Applied Science was Charles R. DeCarlo, who, like his predecessor, held a Ph.D. in mathematics. DeCarlo had joined IBM as an Applied Science representative in 1951 and had become assistant director of the function in 1954. His responsibility as director included the Scientific Computing Service, which was reorganized at the same time, in anticipation of the installation of a 702, into the Electronic Data Processing Service. The dual scientific-commercial nature of that department lasted only a few months, however; later in 1955 the commercial side became part of the Customer Assistance department. The scientific side, which remained in Applied Science, was sometime thereafter renamed the Scientific Computing Center.

The 701 service bureau had been generally successful, both as a business undertaking and as a training and customer program testing site. But a flaw in this otherwise favorable picture was noted early in 1955 by the technical supervisor, Frank S. Beckman.

Beckman, while assistant professor of mathematics at the Pratt Institute of Engineering, had joined IBM in June 1951 as an SSEC programmer trainee. He had developed his programming skill rapidly and had been involved in planning for the Technical Computing Bureau's 701. He was one of three supervisors reporting to Sheldon (the others were Backus and Ziller) when the 701 was unveiled in April 1953.[95]

After Backus and Ziller left the Scientific Computing Service staff in late 1953 to develop FORTRAN, Beckman became the supervisor responsible for all of the technical aspects of operation of the 701. The normal procedure was to prepare time-to-complete and cost estimates for every computing job submitted by a prospective customer. As experience accumulated, Beckman was distressed to find that estimates too often proved optimistic. Yet the information he gleaned from other users of large-scale machines suggested that by comparison with others, his estimates were conservative. He expressed his concern in March 1955 to Mason. Groping for an explanation to the generally poor record for estimates, he noted a lack of correlation between the length of problem formulations and the length of programs required to solve them, wide variations in programmer productivity, and difficulties in predicting machine running times. In addition to the attendant disservice to customers, Beckman was concerned about programmer overtime, which was causing "great . . . personal sacrifice" for the staff. The estimating problem that Beckman noted in connection with the 701 would prove to be an increasingly intransigent problem for the computer industry.[96]

In 1955, William P. Heising headed 701 operations at the New York Data Processing Center. As a graduate student in physics at Columbia

University in the late 1940s, Heising had taken an interest in numerical analysis and availed himself of the computational facilities at the Watson Laboratory. In mid-1950 he joined IBM and began working for Sheldon at the Technical Computing Bureau. Later he managed a similar IBM bureau in Washington, D.C., and was the IBM member of a three-man team that programmed the 701 for weather-prediction equations in a competition that involved the ERA 1103. In February 1955, he attended an early 650 course at Endicott and began planning for a 650 soon to join the 701 at the data processing center.[97]

Heising noted that plans for the 650 did not include an assembly program. Elmer Kubie and a colleague in Endicott had written some load routines and a small mathematical library, including some floating-point subroutines incorporated into a simple interpretive system.[98] But for the work at the center, Heising wanted an assembly program. Kubie had developed an algorithm for choosing instruction and data locations that a 650 programmer could apply in trying to reduce execution-time slowdown due to drum storage latency. Heising thought the optimization algorithm could be automated and somehow applied during assembly by the 650 itself.[99]

Heising found the programmers at the center indifferent about the impending 650 arrival; they were looking forward to the 704 scheduled to replace the 701 later in the year. When Applied Science conducted a 650-oriented computation seminar in August, Heising attended with a recent hired member of his staff, Stanley Poley, who described a 650 program he had written before joining IBM. Heising was impressed by the quality of work described in the twenty-four papers by 650 users. Several papers described assemblers; one, by a speaker from John Hancock Mutual Life Insurance Company, which—eight months earlier—had been the first customer to receive a 650, mentioned provisions for automatic optimization.[100]

Heising asked Poley to join with a colleague, Grace E. Mitchell, in writing a 650 assembler that would combine mnemonic operation codes and "free" mnemonic labels, the latter being a relatively new idea that permitted the assembly language programmer to identify conveniently an instruction or operand by a short term chosen to suggest the function of the instruction or data. Examples in an accounting context might be SUBR or TAX. Heising had learned of free labels through an enhancement of Rochester's original symbolic assembler done by 704 planners at Poughkeepsie. The idea was feasible because the 650 at the center was to be equipped with a newly announced "alphabetic device." Also to be adopted from the Poughkeepsie assembler was a novel form of symbol table wherein table entries could be stored and rapidly retrieved during assembly at locations determined with a "hashing" algorithm (the "open method" of search described in note 61 of chapter 8). Finally, the assembler would assign "optimum" drum locations to assembled instructions and data.[101]

Poley and Mitchell completed their assembler in three months and named it SOAP (Symbolic Optimal Assembly Program). In November 1955, their first mimeographed programmer's guide gave instructions for use and included a wiring diagram for a control panel to be used in printing input and output card decks on the IBM 407 tabulator. Figure 9.5 shows an example of a SOAP output listing for an illustrative problem.[102]

Heising had wanted the program only to enhance programming productivity at the center. SOAP came to be used, however, by almost all 650 installations, after a slow start due to the requirement for the alphabetic device, a reluctance to step away from the machine-language coding procedures familiar from the 650 manual and IBM courses, and the low-key manner of promotion of programs at that time.[103] In September 1956, DeCarlo wrote a letter to Sales and Applied Science representatives stating that SOAP could double programming effectiveness. He attached a detailed description of the alternative coding procedures (one titled "The Programmer as Clerk") for comparison.[104]

While SOAP was being written, Beckman had a number of utility programs under development for the 650 and 704 at the Scientific Computing Center. The 704 work was supervised by John L. Greenstadt, a Brooklyn College graduate who had known Sheldon at Yale University graduate school and whom Sheldon had hired a few months before the 701 was installed. Greenstadt had been impressed by the quality of utility programs brought to the center by 701 customers for use during their preinstallation tests. Therefore, while planning 704 utilities, he made it a point to visit some 701 customers. His trip, in early 1955, followed soon the one made by Backus to gather views on his compiler project.[105]

In August 1955, several months before arrival of the 704, the 701 at the Scientific Computing Center was moved to The Glenn L. Martin Co., a defense contractor. The consequent lull in service bureau work permitted programmers to step up preparations for the 704. Greenstadt and two colleagues requested and got the assignment to write an assembler. By the time of the first SHARE meeting in August, they had completed a first version. A novel assembly language feature was dual address fields. The two fields were used individually for the two conventional address forms: symbolic (alphanumeric) and actual (whereby the programmer specified a 704 word by its actual numeric

5   PROGRAM FOR EXAMPLE I

1		1951	1960	RESERVE READ				
3		P0027	0028	RESERVE PCH				
4		LOOP	U0000	FIRST INSTR				

LOC	OP	D	I	REMARKS	LOC	OP	D	I
LOOP	RAU	XI		CALCULATE	0000	60	0003	0007
	MPY	A1		NEW XI	0007	19	0010	0015
	SRT	0005			0015	30	0005	0077
	ALO	A2			0077	15	0030	0035
	STL	XI		STORE XI	0035	20	0003	0006
	RAU	YI		CALCULATE	0006	60	0009	0013
	MPY	A3		NEW YI	0013	19	0016	0021
	SRT	0005			0021	30	0005	0033
	ALO	A4			0033	15	0036	0041
	STL	YI		STORE YI	0041	20	0009	0012
	RAU	8001		CALCULATE	0012	60	8001	0019
	MPY	XI		XIYI	0019	19	0003	0057
	SRT	0005			0057	30	0005	0069
	AUP	S1		ADD XIYI TO	0069	10	0022	0127
	ALO	S2		PARTIAL SUM	0127	15	0080	0085
	STU	S1		STORE NEW	0085	21	0022	0025
	STL	S2		PARTIAL SUM	0025	20	0080	0083
	RAL	M		REDUCE M	0083	65	0086	0091
	SLO	ONE		BY 1	0091	16	0044	0049
	NZA		OUT	TEST FOR	0049	45	0002	0053
	STL	M	LOOP	END OF LOOP	0002	20	0086	0000
OUT	LDD	S1		PUNCH	0053	69	0022	0075
	STD	P0001		SUM	0075	24	0027	0130
	LDD	S2			0130	69	0080	0133
	STD	P0002			0133	24	0028	0031
	PCH	P0001			0031	71	0027	0177
	HLT	1111	8000	STOP	0177	01	1111	8000
XI	00	0000	0000	INITIALIZE	0003	00	0000	0000
YI	00	0000	0000	XI YI	0009	00	0000	0000
S1	00	0000	0000	AND S	0022	00	0000	0000
S2	00	0000	0000		0080	00	0000	0000
ONE	00	0000	0001	CONSTANT	0044	00	0000	0001

Figure 9.5
Printed result, from an output card deck, obtained on the 407 Accounting Machine, of the assembly of a program on the IBM 650 by the SOAP assembly program. The right-hand four columns show the locations and contents of the assembled instruction and data words. The remaining information was written by the programmer on a coding form and punched on cards as input to the program. Illustrated are: (1) a "comments card" (first line), used only to annotate the printed result, (2) mnemonic operation codes, (3) symbolic (alphanumeric) and actual (numeric) addresses, (4) "remarks" field, a documentation aid, and (5) action of the optimizing feature: the locations of successive instructions are not in numeric sequence. Copied from *650 Programming Bulletin 1, Symbolic Optimal Assembly Program (S.O.A.P.)*, IBM Form No. 22-6285-1, 1956.

address). By making an entry in both fields, the programmer could refer to a location symbolically without assigning a label to it. For example, entries of LIST and 5 in the two columns would result in an assembled address referring to the fifth 704 word in sequence after that assigned to the label LIST. This capability, borrowed from the more rudimentary relative assembly systems, permitted use of a relative address whenever that form was more meaningful to the programmer; also, it saved symbol table space.[106]

At the August SHARE meeting, members were disposed to agree on a single assembly program for the 704 so as to facilitate interinstallation communication and program exchange. They heard Greenstadt's plans and equally detailed plans from three other member installations also writing assemblers: Los Alamos, General Electric at Evendale, Ohio, and United Aircraft at Hartford, Conn. They voted that the IBM assembly program, augmented by favored features of the other proposals, would be the SHARE assembler.

But in mid-September, at the second SHARE meeting, the question was reopened. Roy Nutt of United Aircraft divulged that his symbolic assembly program already included many of the features Greenstadt would have to add and that therefore it could be ready sooner. Nutt's plan extended Greenstadt's two-column address feature by allowing an address to be an arithmetic expression involving symbols and integers. The reconsidered decision of the members was to adopt Nutt's program instead of Greenstadt's, an action that symbolized the independence of the new user organization from its single supplier.

Nutt tested his program on the 704 engineering model at the Poughkeepsie laboratory prior to the December delivery of the United Aircraft machine. Its availability was announced at the February SHARE meeting.[107] At the Scientific Computing Center, which was a member installation of SHARE as well as the focal point of IBM development of 704 library programs, Heising soon decided to use Nutt's assembler, although he did not relish appearing to repudiate the enterprise of his colleagues.

By early 1956, IBM had begun to recognize a common purpose among its various programming groups. The Scientific Computing Center, as a service bureau, traced back to the Technical Computing Bureau and before that to long-established EAM service bureau activity. The programming section of the Customer Assistance department was one of a number of marketing support activities; it maintained and augmented existing general-use programs and developed new utility programs. A group at an Endicott test center had been operating for some time in a similar role in support of the 650. The Poughkeepsie

Programming Research group was developing 705 Autocoder and sort programs. The FORTRAN activity had become a long-term project meant to advance programming technology.

In the ten years since Turing had postulated a library of subroutines, automatic coding, the use of computer programs to increase the cost-effectiveness of application programming, had become an established technology. Initial programs were in use, and more advanced ones were being developed by manufacturers and users. IBM saw such programs as "necessary" to the operation of an EDPM installation and saw development of them as the common programming activity accounting for the resources of the various groups. IBM was distributing such programs through a variety of informal publications and from program libraries at headquarters.[108]

In January, John McPherson surveyed the situation and concluded that programming research activity in IBM was far below that rendered appropriate by the level of programming activity. The preponderance of IBM programming was devoted to making established-technology programs available to customers. There was too little work on "improving the effectiveness of machines, programs and instruction in programming." One significant problem not being addressed was "the rigidity to change of a large program"; he argued that too much development activity was being devoted to improving and adapting completed large programs such as assemblers and sorts. Also, he found that programming groups suffered from inadequate exchanges of information. He recommended that research be strengthened under a single manager, communication between IBM programming groups and customers be improved, and seminars for programmers be established.[109] The immediate result of these recommendations was that the ongoing work on FORTRAN and Autocoder was made McPherson's responsibility, and he was given staff responsibility "to see that from a technical viewpoint" the other development groups were serving customers adequately. The staff responsibility, as usual, carried no authority to redirect development plans, but it gave him a formal right to monitor and criticize the plans.[110]

705 Autocoder was largely written during 1956. The system permitted the programmer to identify any frequently used short sequence of instructions, place it in a library with an abbreviated name, and later while writing programs include it simply by writing the name followed by the labels of the relevant data. Such statements, expected to produce multiple instructions, were called "macro instructions." A number of them, deemed broadly applicable, were provided with the system.

Autocoder also introduced "literal" operands: constants entering into a calculation were written directly (literally) into the address fields of the instructions manipulating them. They eliminated the need for the programmer to lay out and name constant areas and messages before writing the program steps that processed them. Autocoder was released in March 1957.[111]

The programming and testing of the FORTRAN compiler was done between early 1955 and late 1956. The initial plan postulated a compiler of three sections, each a 704 program to process predecessor output. The first would process the user's FORTRAN "source" program. The third would be an assembler to process symbolic instructions and produce a relocatable machine-language "object" program. By late 1955, the planned number of sections had doubled, due to the project's preoccupation with the objective that the computer should produce efficient programs, that is, programs that would compare well in execution speed with programs written by skilled programmers in machine or assembly language.[112]

The most critical of the many problems posed by the objective was that of establishing the addresses corresponding to subscripted variables in the source program. Since arrays of data were stored in contiguous memory locations, such addresses could be calculated at each encounter by evaluating a function of the subscript expressions. For two-dimensional arrays, the function would involve a multiplication using one of the array dimensions. But the evaluation would be unnecessary in cases where the subscript variables had not changed since the previous encounter and would be unnecessarily elaborate in cases in which a single subscript variable had changed in a systematic way under control of a DO statement. Beyond this, the 704 had only three index registers for doing address arithmetic. They would have to be shared among the various subscript combinations appearing in a source program in a way that minimized instructions for saving and loading index register values.[113]

A determined attack on these and other programming problems of unprecedented complexity expanded the initially planned compiler section 2 into four sections. By late 1956 there were over a dozen persons working on the compiler. Program debugging was done on the Scientific Computing Center 704, mostly at night, when sufficiently long periods of time were available. To conserve time and energy, rooms were rented at a nearby hotel. Backus later recalled, "We'd sleep there a little bit during the day and then stay up all night."[114] A programmer's manual, much admired at the time and after for its conciseness and clarity, was published in October.[115] While in Los

Angeles to present a paper on the system at a computer conference in February 1957,[116] the program authors borrowed time on North American Aviation's 704 to continue the debugging process.[117] A few programs prepared at that installation were the basis for a favorable first impression of object program efficiency reported at the conference by programmers from North American.[118]

Shipment of the completed FORTRAN system began in April 1957.[119] Its acceptance grew steadily; a year later a SHARE survey of twenty-six 704 installations revealed that over half were using it for a majority of their problems. The trend soon accelerated when an improved version (see next section) was released.[120] Productivity studies at the General Motors Research Laboratories installation showed that compared to assembly language FORTRAN reduced programming and coding effort by a factor of between five and ten. Taking into account machine and programmer costs for programming, compiling, and debugging, development cost was reduced by a factor of 2.5.[121]

Late in 1956, a second user group, GUIDE, was formed by customers of the 702 and 705. Its purposes, and its method of operating through technical committees, paralleled those of SHARE. IBM programmers attended meetings of both organizations in the substantial numbers necessary to furnish information on programming developments at the level of detail requested, which was particularly stringent at SHARE. Communication was two way, the reactions of members being very useful to IBM in determining future specifications.

In January 1957, as the result of settlement a year earlier of a lawsuit initiated by the U.S. Department of Justice, IBM collected its service bureau operations into a separate subsidiary. The Scientific Computing Center, its managers, and a number of its experienced programmers became part of the new Service Bureau Corporation.[122] The SHARE library and the distribution function remained in the IBM Corporation. Taken together with other events, particularly the imminent release of 705 Autocoder and 704 FORTRAN and the maturing of user relationships, a consolidation of IBM's programming activities in support of its EDPM products seemed indicated.

DeCarlo picked Jack T. Ahlin, an Applied Science representative, to head a new department called Applied Programming. Ahlin became responsible for planning and developing programs of wide applicability, including automatic coding systems, for distribution to and use by customers. Managers were named for 704/709, 702/705, and 650 programming. Later in 1957, a unit of McPherson's Programming Research department was transferred in, strengthening Ahlin's advanced development capability; still later, a 305 manager was named.

Unfortunately, Ahlin's department, which occupied one floor of an office building a few blocks from corporate headquarters at 590 Madison Avenue, had no machine room or machines. Debugging time had to be negotiated with the data processing center at headquarters, the Service Bureau Corporation, or the plants and laboratories.

The discipline of programming had gained an integrated organization, and thereby more recognition within the company, but it was still seen as a "marketing service" of the Data Processing Division's sales activities. Organizationally, it was still far removed from the product-development laboratories.[123]

9.8 Early Experience with Operating Systems

For months after the release of 704 FORTRAN in April 1957, Backus's group maintained the system, distributing corrections in the form of small card decks that users incorporated by a system editing program.[124] The group also added improvements that permitted an application program to incorporate previously compiled or assembled subroutines. This brought the facility of a subroutine library, the earliest type of programming aid (see section 9.1), to FORTRAN users in a practical way. One important result was to reduce compilation time; tested subroutines no longer needed to weigh down the recompilations of a program being debugged. A compiler for the revised language, FORTRAN II, was released in the spring of 1958.[125] Beckman, 704/709 manager in Applied Programming, was asked to take over the maintenance of both FORTRAN compilers. He had to form a group for this purpose from programmers unacquainted with compilers. Heising, erstwhile manager of the Scientific Computing Center and now an assistant to Ahlin, was assigned to help Beckman with training and in planning the transfer of responsibility.[126]

Beckman and the remainder of his group were heavily occupied with another commitment. By the time the IBM 709 (successor to the 704) was announced in January 1957, SHARE members wanted a programming system that would truly capitalize on their years of 701-704 experience. Some innovative work had already been done to reduce the "between-jobs" periods during which one programmer was removing card decks and tapes and the next-scheduled programmer was mounting his. The proportion of time devoted to setdown and setup could be high in installations where numerous jobs were being debugged and run. The first corrective step had been to hire and train operators to accomplish the changeovers expeditiously. The next improvement partially automated the operator's job by turning job control over to a supervisory control program that occupied a small area of 704 memory throughout the day. Incoming job programs and attendant data were "stacked" on magnetic tape as a preliminary step, typically by card-to-tape operations on peripheral units. Every job program concluded by branching to the control program, which then completed the log, directed the operator regarding setdown and setup, and initiated the next job in the stack. Certain installation standards relative to utilization of peripheral devices aided this procedure. Since the control program allocated tape units, it could exploit unoccupied units by directing the operator to mount tapes ahead of actual need. An early program of this type, called simply "the Input-Output System," was completed by General Motors Research Laboratories in collaboration with North American Aviation by the time GMR's 704 was installed in May 1956.[127]

At its December 1956 meeting, SHARE established a 709 System Committee to design and write, after the manner of PACT, an improved system for using the 709. A chairman was elected, Donald L. Shell, from the General Electric installation at Evendale, Ohio. Ideas suggested by over forty attendees at an organizational meeting showed that users were preoccupied with operational features; hence what was most needed was an "operating system." Programming languages were not an issue; the assembly language processed by the system assembler would be an extension of the 704 SHARE assembly language with a macro instruction facility.[128]

In early 1957, Shell filled out his committee. Four members were from IBM, the remaining eight from organizations that had been 701 customers. At the eighth SHARE meeting in April, Shell reported that the committee had met for three days in February and ten in March, was working individually between meetings, and in May would be "in essentially continuous session until the job is done." He expected complete specifications by June.[129] The energy SHARE devoted to the specification task reflected the users' need to have the SHARE 709 system available when machine deliveries began in mid-1958. Otherwise they would have to use contrived procedures and write programs that would later have to be modified to fit the system or qualify for the SHARE library.

One example suggests the challenging specifications of the SHARE 709 system. Assembler designers had typically assumed that debugging corrections would require reassembly of the entire source program, even if only a few instructions were to be changed. But the eightfold increase in the size of 704 memory (to roughly 32,000 words) had permitted much longer programs, making the system time required for reassemblies intolerably long. Programmers therefore began making corrections by inserting machine-language "patches" into their binary load decks (the decks yielded by assembly). The clerical task of reflecting patches back into the source program was conducive to blunders, so that the source program's symbolic representation, vital to further changes and maintenance, could easily be ruined.

In the new SHARE 709 system, the assembler was specified to produce a load deck that retained source-program symbolic information, rearranged and tightly encoded so that the deck would be of manageable size. The system loader, while loading the assembled program, was to process program corrections expressed in the symbolic terms of the original program, producing a revised deck and listing. The required assembler and multifunction loader promised to be complex.[130]

While the specifications of the SHARE Operating System (SOS) for the 709 were being firmed up, IBM agreed to build SOS and deliver it in early 1958. The reason was the "shortness of the time schedule and the sheer magnitude of the job. . . . It was felt that the manufacturer was the only party capable of committing sufficient personnel to complete the entire project in time."[131] However, no one in IBM had much experience in developing systems as complicated as SOS. Beyond that, the specifications were controlled by SHARE, reducing freedom to deal with unanticipated difficulties best resolved by relaxing requirements.

Beckman had about a dozen programmers working on SOS, including the IBMers who served on Shell's committee. They worked in New York City and debugged in Poughkeepsie, a two hour drive up the Hudson River. The task overwhelmed the group; despite intensive work schedules, which for some programmers lasted well over a year, SOS was far from available when 709 deliveries began in mid-1958.[132] In a report to SHARE in February 1959, IBM stated that "as a final shakedown of the system, we are now processing the 46,000 instructions of SOS through the system itself."[133] In August, the chairman of the SHARE SOS committee reported that "SOS was distributed on August 7. Although there are still many bugs in the system it operates correctly in all important respects, and many packages of additional corrections are in the late stages of completion or distribution."[134]

The delivered supervisory control program did not operate in the specified "multiphase" mode; it was a limited version agreed to early in 1959 when SHARE had volunteered to code the specified control program if IBM would maintain it as well as the limited version.

Although in August the multiphase control program was expected in October, it was not distributed until early in 1960.[135]

The scheduling difficulty with SOS matched a similar miscalculation for the FORTRAN compiler, which Backus had originally expected would take about six months to write.[136] Because no customers had been depending on FORTRAN, that circumstance received little notice. In September 1959, Beckman linked scheduling lapses with "large programming problems of this kind," but Applied Programming would subsequently experience difficulty in setting accurate completion dates for programs of all sizes.[137]

Some of the 709 customers waiting for SOS were helped by FORTRAN, maintenance of which was Beckman's second major responsibility. With Heising's help, a half-dozen people assigned to FORTRAN learned the structure of the new 704 FORTRAN II compiler. To support the 709, they undertook the limited task of copying that structure, making only changes mandated by new machine features, which mostly involved input and output. They were able to release a 709 FORTRAN II compiler in mid-1958.

Some experienced users solved their initial 709 needs by developing a limited operating system around the FORTRAN II compiler. Mindful of their success, Heising wanted a similar system for distribution to less-experienced customers. Knowing that Beckman's group was not staffed to undertake such a system, Heising asked SHARE for help. Members were not at first inclined to help, at least with SOS unfinished. But after the Rocketdyne division of North American Aviation volunteered its system as a base, the SHARE FORTRAN committee designated members to help Heising specify a combination of functions likely to satisfy most users.

Ray A. Larner, one of Beckman's programmers, went to the Rocketdyne installation in Canoga Park, California, where he spent a few weeks studying the system. Upon returning to New York, he took the lead in adapting Rocketdyne's system, benefiting from a wide range of expert-user opinion. Distributed in the fall of 1959 as the 709 FORTRAN Monitor, the result became very popular, riding the crest of the mounting acceptance of FORTRAN. A FORTRAN Assembly Program (FAP), an assembler that yielded output compatible with FORTRAN-compiled programs, was later added by UCLA's Western Data Processing Center. Built in several stages and based on a wealth of practical experience, the FORTRAN Monitor System (FMS) continued to be heavily used in the later 7090 era.[138]

9.9 A Proliferation of Machine Types and Programs

The macro instruction facility of 705 Autocoder became the basis for further development of programs for successor machines. The 705 Model III, announced in September 1957, provoked design of a new Autocoder-based programming system, the 705 Processor. By the provision of a greatly expanded library of "decision making" and "report writing" macro instructions, the programming of two familiar tasks was simplified: the selection of tape records from an input file for processing and the specification of formats for output files and printed reports.

The major advance of the 705 Processor over previous systems was embodied in a collection of routines for performing input-output operations. The instructions for reading and writing tape files were the most difficult parts to write of any application program, for they involved considerations relating to the equipment being used rather than to the data processing purpose of the program. For one thing, records on tape were written and read in blocks of typically two to ten, to reduce the number of time-consuming tape start-stop operations per record. Thus successive records were delivered to and dispatched from different storage areas. For another, speed considerations similarly demanded that tape records be "buffered" by, for example, reading successive blocks of high-activity files alternately into two storage areas, so that the reading time of one block could be "overlapped" by processing of the predecessor block. The input-output channel announced with the 705 Model III (see chapter 5) enabled such simultaneity but complicated programming planning and writing.

Another tape-oriented programming task was the detection (by interrogation via conditional branch instructions) of reading and writing errors and attempted correction (by rereading or rewriting) followed by suitable procedures when correction failed. Label writing and processing was still another: files of tape records had come to be preceded and followed by single "label" records identifying the tape reel and indicating the file(s) written on it, the date following which the file could be safely destroyed, and other similar data. These records were processed by routines that ensured that the input file intended by the programmer had in fact been mounted by the operator and protected files intended for retention from being overwritten by new data.[139]

In 1956 some users found error-correction procedures in particular to be susceptible to standardization through the medium of installation subroutines. One type of subroutine became known as a "transfer any" routine, after the 705 instruction that branched conditionally upon the setting of any one of several machine check indicators; programmers could meet their obligations to incorporate standard error procedures into their programs by using "transfer any" following input-output operations to invoke a standard routine. The routine identified the particular indicator(s) that had been set and took the appropriate actions.[140]

Other piecemeal and scattered solutions to input-output programming followed, often taking the form of Autocoder macro instructions in 1957.[141] In 1958 Richard L. Cline, who as a new employee in 1953 had worked on a 701 commercial application for the Naval Aviation Supply Office and was now head of the 705 section of Applied Programming, proposed to fit the planned 705 Processor with subroutines to accomplish all input-output-related tasks, available to the application programmer through simplified macro instructions. For the user, these routines would involve acceptance of certain "standards" previously installation-defined, for example, the format and content of tape labels. The standards and other specifications were established in collaboration with GUIDE, and the "Data Synchronizer Input-Output Package" was available with the other components of the 705 Processor in October 1959 when 705 Model III deliveries were beginning.[142]

Similar systems were soon thereafter developed for other IBM computers; they were generally called "IOCS," for Input-Output Control System. They enabled application programmers to define the files relevant to an application in simple terms, translated by IOCS into a set of file tables relating file names to input-output units and file properties. In the initial part of the body of his program, the programmer typically wrote an "OPEN" macro instruction for each file to be used, resulting in the case of tape input files in the generation of instructions to read and process tape labels and to read blocks of data records into buffer areas. Subsequent "GET" instructions generated instructions making successive records available for processing, for instance, by providing the correct buffer area address. Necessary tape unit read instructions, such as those to refill a just-emptied buffer area, were placed by IOCS in the assembled program so that they were executed when needed. IOCS enabled programmers to write input-output-related code in an idealized manner independent of the physical properties of input-output devices.[143]

In mid-1956, McPherson asked his most experienced programmers whether a "business language" might facilitate commercial accounting applications in roughly the degree that FORTRAN had facilitated scientific applications.[144] Early in 1957, he launched a project in Programming Research to develop such a language, to be called

COMTRAN. The task was removed to Applied Programming in mid-1957 and divulged to the user organizations later in the year.[145]

At a GUIDE meeting in November 1958, Roy Goldfinger, a leader in COMTRAN development, described the proposed language. IBM's motivations, he said, went beyond the programmer convenience and efficiency purposes that had provoked FORTRAN:

COMTRAN . . . represents a blueprint of what we think programming should be in the future. We are motivated by two interests. The first is to produce a large-scale programming system which is going to apply over a fairly wide range of machines. We are looking forward to the day when conversion problems are eliminated through having a single programming language that applies to many different machines. FORTRAN is an excellent example of a language for scientific users which permits a program to be written once, and then with little or no modification may be extended to machines other than the one for which the program was written originally. We would like to accomplish the same thing for the commercial data processing user.

Our second motivation is also on behalf of the data processing user. We want to arrive at a language which is best for defining commercial programs to the computer . . . which talks directly about the problem, a language which has to depend for its interpretation as little as possible on a knowledge on the part of the programmer of the precise logic that is built into the hardware.

His example of a conditional statement illustrates the character of the language:

IF AGE IS MORE THAN 21 AND (SINGLE OR MARRIED AND NO DE-PENDENTS) THEN SET DRAFT STATUS EQUAL TO 1.)[146]

Subsequently, the language was renamed Commercial Translator.

Grace Hopper of Remington Rand had long advocated an English-like programming language, it should be noted. A compiler for an early version of her language, later called FLOW-MATIC, was being tested on one of Metropolitan Life Insurance Company's UNIVACs in late 1956.[147] The possibility of a language at once convenient and applicable to a variety of machines had become a matter of keen concern to large organizations, such as the military branches, that managed scores of diverse computers. At the suggestion of a broadly constituted group that met to discuss the objectives in April 1959, the U.S. Department of Defense in May sponsored a meeting that resulted in an industry-wide project, manned by committees of volunteers, to develop a business programming language. The principal result was specifications a year later for a common business-oriented language (COBOL). Six persons, two of them IBM programmers, worked almost continuously during the fall of 1959 to develop a document synthesizing and reconciling decisions made by a larger committee during the summer. The definitions of FLOW-MATIC and Commercial Translator were of significant technical influence in the work. The specifications of COBOL, dated April 1960, were printed and distributed in June.[148]

In August 1959, IBM had announced that in 1961 it would provide Commercial Translator compilers for the IBM types 705 III, 7070, and 709/7090.[149] Later in the year, while the COBOL document was being written, IBM found itself at odds with its customers on how to arrive at a shared long-term goal: a single business programming language, supported by one compiler for each IBM machine. In November, GUIDE members passed a resolution asking that IBM develop compilers only for COBOL.[150] IBM was not willing to link its support for higher-level language programming of business applications to an as-yet-unspecified target, one that indeed might prove to be a moving target as revised versions of COBOL were developed. At a SHARE meeting in February 1960, Alvin L. Harmon, successor to Ahlin as Applied Programming head, stated that the Commercial Translator language would be modified to include new developments "from . . . efforts . . . of the COBOL Committee" and that customers could use the modified language for programming in anticipation of compilers for the 705, 7070 and 709/90.[151] The revised specifications were published in June, the same month that the COBOL specifications appeared.[152]

In April 1960, IBM announced that the Commercial Translator compilers would be available in the second quarter of 1961 and that COBOL compilers would follow later.[153] At the May GUIDE meeting, a number of users pressed vigorously for COBOL compiler availability dates. Harmon declined to set dates, mindful of both evident and probable lurking ambiguities in the COBOL specifications, which he knew the industry committee would have to resolve.[154] In September, nevertheless, he committed to deliver COBOL compilers in the third quarter of 1961.[155] However, the COBOL specifications were substantially revised: at the June 1961 GUIDE meeting, following a report on initial user experience with the 705 and 7070 Commercial Translator compilers, a member of the industry COBOL project's Executive Committee confirmed that new specifications, called COBOL-61, would be published a month later. He said, "The changes are sufficient in scope that a program written in COBOL-60 will not compile properly using a compiler specifically written for COBOL-61 specifications."

Harmon then stated that IBM's compilers, written for COBOL-61, would not be available until the fourth quarter of the year.[156]

The COBOL compilers for the machines used by GUIDE members — 1410, 705 (and its successor 7080), and 7070 — were finished and delivered during the first four months of 1962, a period that followed by less than a year the delivery of the Commercial Translator compilers. The work occupied a significant proportion of the Applied Programming work force, located in new quarters on two floors (including an onsite machine room) in the Time-Life Building in New York City. Since IBM began late in 1962 to phase out its support of Commercial Translator in favor of COBOL, the dual effort of the period 1960–1962 was deemed by some to have been ill advised. Nonetheless, it was the only course consistent with IBM's objectives: to meet its mid-1959 commitment to provide Commercial Translator compilers, to provide business language compilers at the earliest possible time, and to give each customer the choice between beginning higher-level language programming with Commercial Translator (switching later to COBOL) and waiting for COBOL.[157]

Later in 1962 two COBOL compilers for the IBM 1401 were delivered, one of them operable on a model with only 4000 characters of storage. These products culminated efforts to extend program types proved on large-scale machines to considerably smaller machines. Deliveries of two such machines, the 1401 and 1620, had begun in the fall of 1960 (see chapter 12). Assembly support for the 1401 was initially a fixed-form Symbolic Programming System (SPS) in two versions, one operable, using punched-card input-output only, at the lowest core capacity offered, 1200 characters. An Autocoder system was later provided, supporting 4000-character systems with four tape units. Macro instructions and literal addresses, features of 705 Autocoder, were included.[158]

An assembler with floating-point macro instructions was written for the 1620, a 20,000-digit machine for scientific applications, but the principal support was a FORTRAN compiler. It was, however, delayed until several weeks after machine shipments began. Substantial efforts at early installations by IBM Systems Engineers (successors to the earlier Applied Science Representatives and Field Technical Representatives) helped with the problems; a few of them joined the Applied Programming department temporarily to help complete and document FORTRAN. An interesting 1620 program was GOTRAN, which interpretively executed a subset of the FORTRAN language. Initially lacking a floating-point hardware feature, the 1620 sparked a renaissance of the interpreter.[159]

A FORTRAN compiler for the 1401 became popular for two reasons. First, the 1401 served many 7090 installations as an off-line peripheral device for preparing stacked input and for printing output tapes; now, with the compiler, it could serve as a test stand for small FORTRAN programs. Second, the compiler was of novel, innovative design. By conventional compilers, the source program was read, processed, and written on tape a number of times under control of the several compiler phases before a loadable machine-language program resulted. The 1401 FORTRAN compiler read the source program just once, held it in memory throughout, and then read from tape programs for sixty-four processing steps in turn; each contributed something to compilation and then was replaced by its successor. At close, the compiled ready-for-execution program in storage could be optionally punched into a load deck. The input-output overhead associated with conventional compilers was eliminated, and in fact 1401 FORTRAN could be executed on a machine without tape units. Compilation speed was startlingly high.[160]

SOS was not further developed by IBM after its release in 1960. Its basic concepts and all of its ingenious operational features were inextricably associated with efficient operation of an installation at which programs were written in assembly language. Installation managers were by 1960 preoccupied with the more fundamental application-development efficiency offered by higher-level programming languages. New operating systems, signaled by the FORTRAN Monitor System's popularity, would have to include scientific and business language compilers among their program-preparation components. A substantial SOS legacy was integrated input-output: IOCS-type routines embodied in operating systems to serve the input-output needs of compilers and application programs alike.

Later operating system support for 709 and 7090 customers was provided at two levels identified by names of the basic control program components: IBSYS and IBJOB. The former was released in November 1961 simultaneously with a Commercial Translator compiler; by mid-1962, programs modified to run under its control included FORTRAN II, FAP, and a generalized sorting program. Released in February 1963, IBJOB provided more sharing of facilities among its subsidiary processors and became the monitor for subsequent programs, which initially included a new assembler, a COBOL compiler, and a compiler for FORTRAN IV (a level of FORTRAN language significantly advanced beyond FORTRAN II). The two monitors were not independent; IBJOB was designed to be invoked by IBSYS, a scheme that enabled older programs, as well as newer, to serve under unified control.[161]

9.10 A Conference on Programming

Fundamental to the concept of the general-purpose digital computer was its adaptability to a wide variety of computing tasks. The instrument of that flexibility was the program, whereby the capabilities of the machine were marshaled and orchestrated to accomplish a specific purpose: the processing of a specific set of data to produce a new and more useful set. A data processing system useful to any enterprise necessarily included both machines and programs. During the 1950s IBM came to realize through its own undertakings and those of its customers that, for any general-purpose machine, programs could be written that were themselves general purpose in nature. The most useful were of two major types: those designed for processing-oriented tasks, such as sort and utility programs, and "system programs" designed to make programming and operation more efficient, such as assemblers, compilers, and supervisory monitors.

General-purpose programs, being amenable to exchange among users and to cooperative development, provided a basis for the formation of SHARE and GUIDE. But such programs were also plausible as components of data processing systems offered by vendors, for the same reason that the machines themselves were: the savings achieved through their use were substantial. The availability and quality of such programs had come to be one of the factors by which users differentiated among competing machines. This was very apparent to IBM's programmers, since they had been involved in most of the technical contacts with users throughout the 1950s. By contrast, the programmers knew little about IBM's product-development procedures until the latter portion of the period, when the increasing complexity and variety of machine components and the need for product information earlier in the development cycle forced them into frequent contact with their engineering counterparts. As a result, they began to perceive that program development lacked many of the disciplines and supporting services that aided development engineering. The uncertain availability and distant locations of machines on which to check their programs was one example. The exclusion or token inclusion of programs in IBM's product division plans was another. Job codes and position descriptions were still provisional. Programmers felt, in short, that IBM's approach to programming was inconsistent with the significance of programs.

In early 1961 these perceptions were of concern to David Sayre, the first incumbent of a new position on the corporate staff: director of programming. Sayre had participated in the development of the

704 FORTRAN compiler and had written the October 1956 FORTRAN manual. His manager, who a few months earlier had acted to meet related needs in the sales division,[162] had suggested that Sayre organize a conference of IBM programmers with the purpose of synthesizing their views on what should be done. Sayre enlisted a FORTRAN colleague, Ziller, to help. They organized and issued invitations to a conference that would divide into workshops, for which chairmen were selected, to develop objectives and recommendations for achieving them.

Learson, meantime, had received from a customer an unsparing criticism of the quality and timeliness of IBM programs. Learning of Sayre's plan, he made a forceful case that something should change as a result, insisting that workshop chairmen be named from the ranks of product and marketing division executives. He further directed that presidents of the relevant IBM divisions appear at the conference for the last day or two, receive recommendations, and make firm action plans before leaving.[163] The mid-June conference, held at the Bald Peak Colony Club in Melvin Village, New Hampshire,[164] began with a speech by chairman of the board Tom Watson, Jr., that acknowledged the increasing importance of programming and noted the expensiveness of scheduling failures. Expressing confidence that the assembled group could prescribe means to fix the problems, he urged it to do so.

The temperature rose to over 90° in New Hampshire early in the week and stayed there; windows and doors were opened wide and informal attire was in order. The workshops met their schedules to set down by Tuesday evening objectives, recommendations, and supporting data. At plenary sessions on Wednesday, the chairmen presented their results. On Thursday and Friday the presidents of the sales division and the two product divisions studied the results and drafted an "Action Program," a tersely worded document setting out some thirty-five actions. The actions included a corporate-wide career ladder and recognition and reward system for programmers, recognition of programs in divisional plans, expansion of the product-testing departments' responsibility to include programs, and increasing by over 50 percent the corps of sales division programming specialists. Also included was the following action: "The product divisions will establish unfettered 'programming technology' organizations to pursue advance programming concepts, applied research, automatic program production techniques, etc. by August 1, 1961."[165] The Bald Peak conference, IBM's first major programming conference,[166] led to significant changes in development and marketing. New computer systems concepts continued to evolve rapidly, however, all of them depending for their realization on new levels of achievement by programmers of system programs.

One avenue for improving system cost-effectiveness, for instance, was minimization of "idle" time, fractions of a second when instruction execution was suspended to await completion of the operation of an attached mechanical device, or longer periods when operators dealt with events demanding their attention. Tape units, however buffered, slowed applications in which record processing time could not fill the time required to read and write records. A program that needed a subroutine or record stored in disk storage lost the time in which thousands of instructions could be executed while an access mechanism moved to the required disk track.

Since different parts of a computer system could operate concurrently, as long as there was no program-imposed reason for operating them sequentially, a solution was to have computers work on a batch of several independent programs in main storage at once. When operation of one program was necessarily suspended, another could be invoked and utilize the otherwise idle time of the processing unit and other devices.[167] When execution of a program was completed, another might be selected for loading from a program "staging" area in disk storage. New machine facilities, first implemented by IBM in its Stretch computer (see chapter 10), were needed to make this "multiprogramming" mode of operation feasible, but most of the burden fell on the supervisory control program. It would have to schedule the execution of programs staged in disk storage rather than accept them in a fixed sequence determined by the operator, and then allocate the system resources (main storage, I/O devices, channels, and disk access mechanisms) among scheduled programs on a dynamic basis with the objective of keeping all of them busy.[168]

At the time of the Bald Peak conference, a multiprogramming control program for Stretch had been planned and was being written by Edgar F. Codd and others. Many complex functions not needed in "uniprogramming" systems had to be identified, and strategies for achieving them defined. Among these were optimizing techniques such as "queue selection," the set of rules used to select among a line-up of "requests" for a machine facility (occasioned by the collection of programs in main storage at some instant) at the time that facility signaled its availability.[169]

Codd and his colleagues completed their program in 1961 and used it on a Stretch machine in conjunction with an application program pool of fifteen programs from which sets were selected to form execution batches. The program was fitted with a routine that printed execution statistics useful to evaluation, such as the percentage of total batch execution time each machine component was busy. It was designed so that it could be easily crippled to the extent that it would run as a uniprogramming control program for comparison.

The results were encouraging. Component utilization was increased by an amount that more than compensated for the overhead of the new control program functions. The speed of the system, in terms of time to complete execution of program sets, was increased from 30 percent to 100 percent by the multiprogramming control program. The program required some 10,000 words of Stretch storage (exclusive of those used for gathering execution statistics), however, suggesting that multiprogramming, in the generalized form embodied in the Stretch program, could be exploited only by the largest systems.[170]

The work of Codd's group had demonstrated the appropriateness of the Bald Peak conference conclusion that advanced technology work was essential to the development of system programs. Before programming could attain the same footing as engineering, improved methods of formulating objectives, writing specifications, forecasting usage, predicting schedules, and estimating resource requirements still were needed, as were better criteria for evaluating program performance and reliability. But the importance of programs as elements of cost-effective systems had at long last been established.

10

Transistors

The first transistors at IBM. Entering the solid-state era. Point-contact to junction transistors. Drift transistors. Current-switch circuits. Development and manufacturing. Standard Modular System.

In December 1947, less than two years after Ralph Palmer began building IBM's capability in vacuum tube electronics in the Poughkeepsie laboratory, John Bardeen and Walter H. Brattain successfully operated the first transistor, a device destined to replace vacuum tubes in electronic circuits. The invention of the transistor was the culmination of years of research with William Shockley and others at the AT&T Bell Telephone Laboratories—research for which Bardeen, Brattain, and Shockley were awarded the Nobel Prize in 1956. Brattain recorded the event in his notebook as follows: "Using the germanium surface . . . and the gold contacts the . . . circuit was set up. This circuit was actually spoken over and by switching the [transistor] device in and out a distinct gain in speech level could be heard and seen on the scope with no noticeable change in quality."[1]

Germanium was selected for this experiment because of its semiconductor properties. With almost all of the electrons bound to atoms, as they are in semiconductors, the number of *conduction electrons*—those free to move through the solid—can be altered significantly by adding small amounts of *impurity* elements. Impurities that supply extra electrons are called *donors*, whereas those that reduce the number of free electrons are known as *acceptors*. Each acceptor atom creates a site in the semiconductor to which electrons can be bound. If enough acceptor atoms are added, there will not be enough electrons to attach to them, thus creating vacancies or *holes* in the distribution of bound electrons. In this case, electrical conduction occurs not by conduction electrons moving freely through the solid but rather by bound electrons jumping from one electron vacancy site to another. The consequent "movement" of vacancy sites (i.e., holes) is described as *hole conduction*, where holes—much like bubbles in water—represent the absence of electrons in a sea of electrons.

Semiconductor material, doped with impurities so as to exhibit hole conduction, is called *p-type* because the holes are positively charged relative to the sea of electrons, whereas material exhibiting electron (negative charge) conduction is called *n-type*. Holes or electrons injected into the device through external leads can temporarily alter the conduction characteristics, thus permitting a transistor to perform the same functions in a solid that an electron tube performs in its evacuated chamber: conduction, modulation, switching, and amplification of electrical signals.[2]

The transistor invention was reported by the *New York Times* on 1 July 1948—among news items on summer changes in radio programming—in a brief story beginning, "A device, called a transistor, which has several applications in radio where a vacuum tube ordinarily is employed, was demonstrated for the first time yesterday at Bell Telephone Laboratories . . . where it was invented."[3] Most newspapers ignored the event entirely. But its significance was not lost on scientists in other laboratories who had been following or participating in developments in solid-state research; they eagerly devoured every technical detail contained in the one and one-half page article by Bardeen and Brattain, which appeared in the July 1948 issue of *Physical Review*.[4] The importance of the invention was also not lost on Halsey Dickinson, who had succeeded James Bryce as head of IBM's Patent Development department located in the corporate headquarters building at 590 Madison Avenue, New York City. Although Dickinson's group had no expertise in solid-state physics, it was continually on the lookout for new ideas.

10.1 The First Transistors at IBM

Less than two weeks after the Bell announcement, a member of Dickinson's group sent a copy of an article on the transistor to John McPherson with the comment, "It would appear that this device should have considerable application in our business."[5] That fall, M. Loren Wood, another member of Dickinson's group, came across an article that discussed the operation of a bistable circuit made with transistors. Wood recalls that although the article did not explain the operation of the transistor circuit, he "finally conjured up a concept as to how it might work." He described his ideas to Dickinson, and the two of them went to Bell Laboratories to see if they could obtain some transistors. Returning with half a dozen devices, Wood attempted to create the bistable circuit he had envisioned, but without success. He determined the reason his circuit failed was that the transistors received from the Bell Laboratories had a current amplification less than unity — the output current was less than the input current.[6]

This was Wood's first experience with solid-state devices or theory, and his experience with vacuum tube circuits was limited. After receiving the bachelor's degree in power engineering from MIT in 1940 and a one-year stint designing washing machines for the Maytag Company, he had spent the wartime years with the Curtis Wright Corporation and the Cornell Aeronautical Laboratory, developing instrumentation for wind tunnels. During this time, he met Dickinson in connection with special equipment built by IBM for the Cornell Aeronautical Laboratory wind tunnel in Buffalo, New York. In March 1946, he accepted Dickinson's invitation to join IBM, where he spent much of his first two years working on systems to convert the readings of scales and other analog devices to punched-card output.[7]

Although Wood had no background in solid-state devices, he concluded he could not devise successful transistor circuits unless he made his own transistors. Lacking any facilities for processing materials, he purchased germanium crystal diodes, broke off the covers, carefully leaving the two leads of each attached, and with the help of a microscope attempted to attach the necessary third lead. The resulting transistors were similar in structure and function to those first made at the Bell Telephone Laboratories.

Known as *point-contact* transistors, such devices consist of two thin wires in point contact with the surface of a piece of germanium and a third wire attached to the base. One of the point-contact leads is called the *emitter* because it is used to emit *minority* charge carriers into the base region of the transistor, that is, electrons into p-type or holes into n-type material. The other point contact is called the *collector* because it collects minority-charge carriers from the base.[8] Point-contact devices failed to achieve significant use in computers because they depend on a difficult-to-control metallurgical formation where the collector is attached to the germanium. Junction devices, the theory of which was published by Shockley in 1949, ultimately provided the stable characteristics needed for large, transistorized computers.[9] But point-contact devices were discovered first and were the basis of all early efforts to develop and use transistor circuits.

Wood says he "fumbled around a lot and learned a lot" making his own point-contact transistors but did not make much real progress until he hired a young assistant with the Ph.D. in physics from MIT.[10] Working together, they found that probes made of silver and gold wires did not give current gains greater than one but that a certain copper-alloy wire did. Merely touching the copper-alloy wire to the germanium crystal was not sufficient, but if a large current was passed through the collector wire in contact with the crystal, the wire bonded itself to the germanium and created a transistor with good current amplification. This bonding process was called *burn in* or *forming*, a metallurgical process, poorly understood at the time, that gave point-contact transistors their unique characteristics. Wood and his assistant correctly speculated that the copper-alloy wire contained elements that entered the germanium and helped create the desired structure.[11] Most of what they learned about the mysteries of transistor forming was presumably already known to those who had invented the transistor at Bell Laboratories; but such information was not yet generally available, and in such a new field there was always the chance of unexpected discoveries leading to new inventions.

By the spring of 1950, Dickinson's group had made substantial progress in the fabrication and use of transistors. The fabrication process began with 1N48 germanium crystal diodes purchased from the General Electric Company. These were chosen because they had "a satisfactorily high impedance in the reverse voltage or back direction" and because they exhibited "a livelier surface." The group soon developed techniques for optimizing the placement of both the emitter and collector leads instead of using the lead attached by the diode manufacturer as one of the transistor point-contact leads. A transistor triode test unit was constructed that automatically plotted the collector current versus its voltage for six different values of emitter voltage (and emitter current for later versions) on the screen of a cathode-ray oscillograph.[12] Using this test unit, a technician in Wood's group—who also served as elevator operator and chauffeur for T. J. Watson, Sr.—could electrically form transistors in steps, testing the device after each step and adjusting the position of the whisker (metal wire) contact to achieve the desired transistor properties.[13] Later it was found that the transient currents of the curve tracing system were so large that they were sufficient to form the contacts automatically as the technician moved the electrodes over the surface of the germanium.

This was not a delicate operation by today's standards. The piece of germanium was placed in a cavity in a steel slug. A fiber cylinder, through which two metal conductors passed, was fitted tightly into the top of the cavity. Two metallic whiskers, to be placed in contact with the germanium, were attached to the input conductors of the fiber cylinder, and the output leads were connected to the curve plotter. Using two pairs of pliers built for holding small gas pipes, the technician held the steel cylinder containing the germanium in one hand and the fiber cylinder with the emitter and collector whiskers in the other hand. "Then," according to one observer, "he'd just sit there and wiggle these things until the curve tracer, which plotted out on the CRT, produced something that looked like a transistor."[14]

Wood described this part of the transistor assembly process as the only part that could not be automated for manufacturing because the current gain depended on the amount of jiggling done by the technician. Experience indicated that a transistor with current gain less than one could be assembled in less than 2 minutes, a current gain between one and two required about 5 minutes, and a current gain greater than two could take half an hour or more.[15] Using transistors fabricated in this somewhat primitive manner, Wood and Dickinson devised a variety of flip-flop circuits, which they and others at IBM called triggers for many years; but because of the nonuniformity and relatively low current gain of their devices, all of these circuits used vacuum tubes in combination with transistors.[16]

In a May 1950 memorandum, "Transistors in IBM," Dickinson reported that more than one hundred transistors had been constructed for use in various devices. He added that fabrication of devices of uniform characteristics was "hampered by the fact that the surface receiving the whiskers is inherently nonuniform in electric properties." A variety of circuits had been designed using voltage amplification, and others had been designed using current amplification. Phototransistors and devices with three whiskers plus the base contact (tetrodes) had also been explored. Noting that complete substitution of transistors for vacuum tubes "is dependent upon whether or not research and development work produces devices or circuits having improved characteristics," Dickinson urged that more work be done on transistors.[17]

Dickinson attempted to justify an increased effort by calculating the financial savings if future Type 604 calculators were built with circuits combining vacuum tubes and transistors. Since transistors were too new to have meaningful prices, he assumed they would cost the same as solid-state diodes, about $2 each. This was four times the cost of 12SN7 vacuum tubes, but by assuming a ten times lower failure rate for transistors than the 0.46 percent per month of the tubes, he arrived at an estimated annual savings of $4800 to $48,600 in projected 604 production alone. Using his rule-of-thumb that five times the first year's saving could be spent on research and development, he arrived at a project level of up to fifteen engineers at $16,000 each. The annual cost of $16,000 per engineer was equally divided between salary and overhead.[18]

Dickinson's cost analysis and rule of thumb hardly seem adequate in the light of the dramatic technological changes then occurring in IBM's business. John McPherson provided a broader perspective by calling for "further expansion of our development in engineering in 1950" because "electronic units will accelerate the obsolescence of many business machines." He also expressed the growing view of corporate management that the 1949 development expenditure of $4 million (2.3 percent of income) was inadequate. Of the 466 persons in development, 42 percent were working on new electronic products, 40 percent on nonelectronic EAM products, and the remainder on a variety of projects including electric typewriters. McPherson specifically noted that only eleven people — all in Dickinson's or Samuel's groups — were doing what he considered to be "long-range research in electronics." Urging greater emphasis on long-range research in such areas as new vacuum tube structures, magnetic delay line memories, and semiconductors, he asserted, "We must go beyond the obvious fields and investigate electrochemical phenomena, ferro-electric phenomena, and other unusual physical effects to see their possible application to our business."[19]

These ideas were discussed at an important engineering and development meeting in April 1950, following which Wallace McDowell became director of engineering and Ralph Palmer was appointed laboratory manager of Poughkeepsie. Palmer then assigned Arthur Samuel the job of building IBM's expertise in transistors and other solid-state technologies. It was an appropriate choice. Although Samuel had no direct experience with solid-state devices or theory, he did have close ties to the University of Illinois and Bell Laboratories, which possessed two of the strongest programs in solid-state research in the country. In the summer of 1950, Loren Wood and his technician—no longer an elevator operator and chauffeur—were transferred from company headquarters to Samuel's group in Poughkeepsie. There they set up shop on the second floor of the former pickle factory and went to work on semiconductors.[20]

Meanwhile, Dickinson and the Patent Development department at 590 Madison Avenue continued to work on transistors and other inventions. During 1951 and 1952 the department reported work on transistor-tube circuits, photographic data recording, magnetic recording, sequential line printing, and methods for measuring whole or fractional rotations of a shaft. In July 1953 the Patent Development department was transferred from IBM corporate headquarters to the Watson Laboratory at 612 West 115 Street. Here it continued to operate in the traditional mode of the IBM inventor and his group, but the move from corporate headquarters eliminated the last vestiges of an era in which nearly autonomous inventors had taken their instructions directly from Watson, Sr. The small Patent Development department of Bryce and Dickinson had compiled quite a record: from 1932 through 1954, a total of 243 patents were issued to members of the department and 56 were still pending.[21]

10.2 Entering the Solid-State Era

In June 1951 Samuel's group received strong reinforcement in the person of Lloyd P. Hunter, a physicist who arrived at IBM with thirteen years of experience in solid-state research. His credentials included a Ph.D. from the Carnegie Institute of Technology, several years at Westinghouse, and a few years at the Oak Ridge Laboratory during World War II. While this was just the background needed in Samuel's group, Hunter's recruitment apparently resulted from a chance meeting with Cuthbert Hurd at a technical society meeting in New York City in February 1951. Hurd, who had known Hunter at Oak Ridge, brought him to corporate headquarters, where Hunter met with McDowell, McPherson, and Samuel. Not long after, Hunter joined Samuel's group and was given one overriding assignment: "to develop solid-state components to replace vacuum tubes in the electronics of machines, whether it involved semiconductors, magnetics, ferroelectrics, or anything else."[22] Loren Wood, who had initiated IBM's transistor work, was given an engineering staff assignment reporting to Palmer.

Following these changes, Samuel described his semiconductor effort as "finally in high gear." He now had three physicists with Ph.D.s, four engineers with bachelor's or master's degrees, and two technicians. Four more people had accepted offers, and at Palmer's urging, Samuel had proposed an expanded program utilizing ten more people.[23]

An important member of Hunter's team was Robert A. Henle, who had arrived in April 1951 with a master's degree in electrical engineering from the University of Minnesota. For his master's thesis, Henle had attempted to use point-contact transistors obtained from Bell Laboratories to build a trigger (flip-flop) circuit. These transistors had a current gain of less than one, as did so many of the other early experimental transistors supplied by Bell Laboratories. This made them "kind of useless in a trigger circuit," Henle recalls; so he began making his own transistors by forming point contacts on germanium crystals supplied by Sylvania.[24]

The critical characteristic of a point-contact transistor was its gain, defined by the parameter alpha (α), which is simply the ratio of the change in output collector current (ΔI_C) to the change in input emitter current (ΔI_E) (that is, $\alpha = \Delta I_C / \Delta I_E$). A good point-contact transistor had an alpha greater than one. Transistors with alpha greater than one also possessed another important characteristic. They exhibited two stable conducting states, which could be used to represent the binary 1s and 0s used in digital logic and memory. Indeed, it was this bistability of "good" transistors that made it possible to design flip-flops with only one transistor, whereas two vacuum tube triodes were required to perform the same function. Point-contact transistors with alpha less than one were regarded as "kind of useless" by Henle and others, even though flip-flops with two transistors could have been designed, because the high cost and inherent instability of point-contact devices made this unattractive.

Continuing his graduate-school research at IBM, Henle began designing a variety of transistor circuits, including adders, shift registers, and a binary-coded decimal counter. Unlike the circuits designed by Dickinson and Wood, Henle's circuits used no vacuum tubes. Henle described his transistor adder circuit, for example, as "consisting entirely of transistors, diodes, and pulse transformers," capable of operating "at repetition rates as high as 40,000 pulses per second" using "pulses of from 12 microseconds to 3 microseconds duration."[25] He described the basic, bistable transistor circuit in the shift register as similar in operation to a circuit described two years earlier in the *Review of Scientific Instruments.*[26]

Toward the end of 1951, circuit designers were placing demands on transistors that could not be met by the fabrication methods originally devised in Dickinson's group. Transistors were needed "with a current gain greater than 1.5 and a back resistance of the collector, at zero emitter current, not less than 10,000 ohms." To meet these requirements, a new process was devised that began—as had the original process—with purchased germanium diodes. The outside casings of these were first cracked; then the germanium crystals, mounting studs, and attached wire leads were carefully removed. Thereafter, several fabrication improvements were implemented. These included cutting the 5 mil phosphor bronze wire to create a "sharp chisel edge" for the emitter and collector contacts; preparing the germanium surface by sand blasting with a number 500 mesh carborundum; then oxidizing the surface by an anodizing process. Finally, the collector was formed by a "defined series of steps" in which the contact wire was "wiggled over the surface of the germanium" while being subjected to current pulses.[27]

It was not until early 1952 that IBM began to grow its own germanium crystals for device and circuit studies. The vacuum furnace used for the purpose was similar to one used by Hunter when he was at Westinghouse. A two-stage mechanical forepump was used in conjunction with an oil diffusion pump to achieve a pumping speed of about 300 liters per second at 10^{-4} mmHg (Torr). The vacuum was maintained in a large quartz tube into which a cylindrical resistance heating coil was mounted. Inside the heating coil was the crucible containing germanium. The germanium ingot was melted in the vacuum to maintain its purity and then cooled very slowly to freeze into large single crystals.[28] By the end of 1952, all of the essential elements of a transistor-processing capability had been established at IBM, and people had been recruited who were capable of understanding the work of others and then making their own innovations.

While all this work on transistors was underway, Samuel and Hunter were recruiting people to work on ferrite-core devices and materials. The magnetic-core device effort had begun at IBM late in 1950, and ferrite-core fabrication was underway by early 1953 (see chapter 7). Just as the MIT Lincoln Laboratory provided leadership in the development and use of ferrite cores, so Bell Laboratories provided leadership in the development and use of transistors. The result was a rapid buildup in both technologies throughout the industry.

In September 1951 Samuel reported to McPherson, McDowell, and others that a series of meetings on transistors at Bell Laboratories had attracted over 300 people. Furthermore, at an IRE conference on electron devices, there had been 21 speakers who dealt with transistors: 11 from Bell Laboratories, 4 from GE, 3 from Sylvania, 2 from RCA, and one from Yale. Samuel then noted, "At least 15 additional persons took an active part in the discussion." He estimated that at least 400 people were working full time on transistors, including about 168 at Bell Laboratories. His most provocative observation was that "The Bell Telephone Laboratories has an all-transistor computer in operation and is nearly ready to make a public announcement of this fact."[29] The "computer" was actually a simple multiplying unit, which would constitute only a small part of a modern computer, but even this was considered a significant accomplishment.

Samuel's report of Bell's all-transistor multiplier was soon confirmed in a memorandum from McPherson to Watson, Jr. Citing conversations with various people during a professional society committee meeting, he wrote: "A representative from MIT at our meeting stated that he had seen this [all-transistor multiplier] first about three months ago and reported it back to the head of MIT Project Charles with the result that today all the good electronic engineers at the Institute are working on electronic computers without tubes, and they have effectively abandoned their work on ordinary electronic tube type computers. It was the feeling of the group I was with that this is the most important development in the computer field, and that within a year all effort will be channeled in this new direction."[30]

In May 1951, four months before writing this memorandum to Watson, McPherson had expressed his conviction that transistors would become important to IBM, saying to McDowell, "We should assume that better transistors will be available and immediately set up a group on transistor circuitry to explore and experiment with, on a broad scale, various transistor circuits for all our principal electronic tube calculator functions. Because of the difference in characteristics, it may be necessary to design and build a complete set of new circuits to produce the result, say, of the present 604 or of one of the more advanced electronic computer designs. I feel this should be done as soon as we clearly see the possibility of completing such an engineering model effectively."[31]

In 1951, however, IBM's development resources in electronics were already overcommitted. The decision to build the Defense Calculator (IBM 701) had been made at the beginning of the year, and there was increasing pressure on resources for its design and construction. Not until mid-1952 was an opportunity found to experiment with the use of transistors in a practical application. It was then that Henle was assigned to develop transistor circuits for a small accounting machine being designed by H. S. Beattie. The proposed machine was to use a rotating magnetic drum to store data, and transistor circuits were to be used both in the write and sense circuits for the drum and for the arithmetic operations. Henle designed the transistor circuits and participated in assembling them with the machine. Except for a few vacuum tube cathode followers, all electronic circuits in the machine were built with germanium point-contact transistors made in Hunter's group. The rate of failure of the transistors was so high, however, that Henle was soon spending most of his time locating and replacing faulty devices.[32]

The solution, ultimately, was to shift from point-contact to junction transistors. But this was not obvious early in 1953 when the effort to use point-contact transistors in the small accounting machine was mercifully terminated. Both types of transistors had unique advantages and disadvantages, and both types required fundamental improvements to be satisfactory.

10.3 Point-Contact to Junction Transistors

The junction transistor resulted from studies initiated at Bell Laboratories by William Shockley, in whose laboratory the point-contact transistor had been invented. The first junction transistors were made by growing a cylindrically shaped single crystal of germanium with p-type impurities in a thin cross-sectional region, on each side of which the crystal was doped with n-type impurities. Several transistors could be made by cutting the crystal parallel to its length. Using the central p-type material as the base and the n-type regions on either side as the emitter and collector, a so-called npn device was created with two pn junctions.[33]

A power gain in the collector output could be obtained for a given emitter input, but current gain could not be achieved by junction transistors that were wired in circuits in the manner of point-contact devices. Current gain could be achieved, however, using a so-called grounded-emitter wiring configuration. Junction transistors wired in this manner exhibited large changes in output collector current (ΔI_C) for small changes in the input base current (ΔI_B). In this configuration, the critical gain parameter was called beta (β), where $\beta = \Delta I_C / \Delta I_B$. The gain was much larger than 10 for typical junction transistors because $\beta = \alpha/(1 - \alpha)$ and the value of α was typically between 0.95 and 0.99. The grounded-emitter configuration thus became the standard way to use junction transistors. (Point-contact transistors could also be wired in this way, but the difficulty in controlling α resulted in very large variations in β, making circuit characteristics exceptionally hard to control.)

An alternative way to make pn junctions was proposed by research workers at General Electric toward the end of 1950.[34] They placed a small metallic dot on the surface of a thin germanium wafer and melted the metallic dot in a vacuum furnace. This caused the metal to alloy with a thin layer of the germanium. If a p-type germanium wafer was used, an n-type alloy region could be formed with a metal such as lead-antimony. By 1952 substantial progress had been made in developing this simple process for making npn and pnp devices by alloying metallic dots on opposite sides of very thin germanium wafers.[35] This process provided an economical means for producing many devices simultaneously on the same wafer, and a number of new companies were started to make these devices. Like all junction transistors of that time, the alloy devices were much slower than point-contact transistors, but they were more reproducible, more reliable, and cheaper to make.

Some limited evaluations of alloy-junction transistors were carried out in Poughkeepsie toward the end of 1952, but the results generated very little interest. It was widely believed that all junction transistors were too slow to be useful in computer logic; furthermore, they failed to exhibit the two stable conduction states possessed by good point-contact transistors.[36] Significant work on junction devices, therefore, did not take place until after work on the IBM 701 was completed, permitting additional resources—and new approaches—to be applied to the problem.

In December 1952, Jerrier Haddad, engineering manager of the 701 project, asked Joseph C. Logue to become involved with the group that was designing transistor circuits. He had known Logue from the early 1940s when they were both engineering students at Cornell. Haddad had joined IBM immediately after graduation in 1945, whereas Logue had remained at Cornell after getting his bachelor's degree in electrical engineering in 1944 to teach electrical engineering laboratory and electronics courses and to earn a master's degree. In 1949 Logue left Cornell to join the Brookhaven National Laboratory, working on radio-frequency controls for the Cosmotron proton accelerator. A chance meeting with Haddad and Palmer at the American Physical Society Meeting in New York City in early 1951 led to his joining IBM that May to work for Haddad on the Defense Calculator (IBM 701). One of his accomplishments was to achieve a substantial improvement in the "read-around ratio" of the Williams-tube storage unit. This is the number of times storage spots can be accessed before information in an adjacent spot is destroyed. After carrying out experiments that showed a strong correlation between instabilities in the power-supply voltage and variations in the read-around ratio, Logue designed more stable power supplies that resulted in significant improvements in the Williams-tube storage capability.[37]

Finding that the "transistor circuit design group" to which he was now assigned consisted of individuals working on different projects without any overall supervision, Logue decided to fill the void. His experience on the 701 caused him to become disillusioned quickly with the lack of predictability and reliability of point-contact devices, no two of which ever seemed to perform the same way. Upon learning about the slower but more predictable junction transistors, Logue began urging more work with them.[38]

In January 1953, shortly before the effort to develop transistor circuits for the small accounting machine was terminated, Henle began designing replacement circuits using junction transistors. It is not clear whether Logue influenced this work or was merely an early observer;

but by April, Logue's transistor circuit design group had become a formal entity, Henle was a key member of the group, and Logue had established the goal of designing a complete set of circuits using junction transistors.[39]

Each flip-flop circuit required two junction transistors, compared to only one point-contact transistor. The junction devices were also slow, operating at maximum frequencies of less than 100 kilocycles per second, but their large current gain (β) in the grounded-emitter configuration contributed to their predictable and reliable operation and made them highly favored by the circuit designers.[40]

In the summer of 1953, Palmer asked Logue to organize and conduct a course to train IBM engineers in the use of transistors and magnetic cores. In all, twenty-eight engineers attended this course, which Logue organized into three weeks of classes followed by six weeks of laboratory work. The class was divided into six groups for the laboratory portion, and each group was asked to design a practical machine using transistor circuits. After the course was completed, three of the machines were actually built.[41]

One of these machines was a transistorized version of the Type 604 calculator in which junction transistor circuits were used instead of vacuum tubes. On 7 October 1954, this "experimental all-transistor calculator" was demonstrated at a press preview of the opening of the company's new Research Laboratory in Poughkeepsie. (During the same week, IBM also announced the 705 computer with core memory and the availability of ferrite-core main memories for the 701 and 704 computers; see chapter 7.) The "experimental all-transistor" calculator was described as "comparable in capacity to IBM's 604 electronic calculator of which over 2000 are in use." Although it used 2200 transistors versus the 1250 vacuum tubes in the 604, it occupied less than half the volume. All switching and storage circuits, the power supply, and the output circuits were built with transistors—without any vacuum tubes—marking the first time all the functions of a large electronic calculating machine had been implemented with junction transistors. As reported by the *New York Times*, "This is believed to be the first fully-operative transistorized computer complete with automatic input and output."[42]

The circuits contained pnp and npn germanium junction transistors, purchased from outside vendors, with current gains (β) of 40 to 90 and minimum operating frequencies of up to 1 megacycle. This was about ten times faster than the first junction devices studied in IBM, less than two years earlier, but it was only the beginning of a long-term trend toward faster junction transistors.[43]

To accomplish the arithmetic and control functions of the 604, a variety of switching and control circuits were employed, including inverters, emitter followers, flip-flops, logical circuits, and output drivers. Special care in the circuit designs was required to be sure the temperature-sensitive junction devices would operate at the elevated temperatures in the machine.[44] The use of both pnp and npn junction transistors was found to provide the designer with an advantage not realized with vacuum tubes. Inverter circuits, for example, designed with npn devices were capable of producing rapid negative voltage changes, analogous in that respect to vacuum tubes; but inverters designed with pnp devices provided rapid positive voltage changes, a capability not directly available in vacuum tubes. The design of high-performance logic circuits was facilitated by using pnp inverters when a positive output was needed and npn inverters for a negative output. The use of pnp and npn devices for the logical AND and OR circuits, respectively, is indicative of the type of circuit designs developed for the transistorized 604 (figure 10.1).

The logic functions in the experimental transistorized 604 were performed both with transistor-driven diode logic and with all-transistor logic. Diode logic was well known to IBM circuit designers, who had used it in the company's first electronic stored-program computer products: the 701, 702, 650, 704, and 705 computers. Vacuum tube circuits had been used in these products to drive the diode logic, whereas transistor drivers were used in the experimental 604. Full transistor logic was used in the experimental 604 wherever greater speed was required. Pluggable circuit units were used to facilitate assembly and repair. Each unit consisted of a 3-by-5$\frac{1}{2}$-inch "printed-circuit card" on which transistors and other electrical components had been soldered to interconnecting conductor lines prefabricated (printed) on the surface of the card. A total of 595 cards, representing forty different circuit types, were used. Total power consumption of the calculator was only 310 watts—95 percent less than the vacuum tube machine—a result not only of the smaller sizes and lower current and voltage levels typical of transistors but also of the fact that considerable power was required merely to heat the cathode of vacuum tubes to the high temperatures needed to eject electrons. Future miniaturization of transistors was possible in part because of their inherently lower power characteristic.[45]

With the experimental transistorized 604 running successfully, Palmer immediately began pressing for the use of transistors in the product line. In 1955 an attempt to use transistor-support circuits for IBM's first megabit ferrite-core memory, the Type 738, failed because tran-

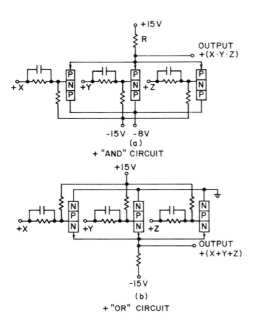

Figure 10.1
Junction transistor logic circuits. The AND operation of circuit *a* is performed by means of pnp emitter followers paralleled with a common load resistor, the output being at ground if X and Y and Z are each at ground. The output of the npn-implemented OR operation of *b* is at ground if either X or Y or Z is at ground. (From G. D. Bruce and J. C. Logue, "An Experimental Transistorized Calculator," *Electrical Engineering*, Vol. 74, pp. 1044–1048. ©1955 AIEE [now IEEE].)

sistor circuits were not able to supply enough current for the drivers; but the effort did result in the use of transistor sense amplifiers. Thus the Type 738 memory, first shipped in April 1957, became IBM's first product to make use of transistor circuits (see chapter 7).

The first IBM product to use transistor circuits without any vacuum tubes—also believed to be the world's first all-transistor calculator to be manufactured for the commercial market—was the IBM 608 calculator, first shipped in December 1957. (The 608 calculator is properly called a calculator, not a computer, in today's terminology because its small ferrite-core memory was not used for stored-program operation.) All the circuits and circuit-packaging techniques were based on those used in the experimental transistorized 604. Its small ferrite-core memory was driven and its output sensed by transistor circuits. The 608 contained more than 2100 transistors on 600 5 inch, printed wiring cards and was capable of performing addition in 0.22 millisecond, multiplication of two nine digit numbers in 11 milliseconds, and division of eighteen digits by nine digits in 13.5 milliseconds.[46] It was intended to be the smallest in a series of machines known as the MAC system, but because of changing product plans, it was the only member of the MAC series ever shipped (see chapter 12).

Long before the Type 608 was completed, Thomas Watson, Jr., had become concerned that other development projects were not converting to transistors fast enough. He believed sufficient tests had been made to ensure the reliability of solid-state devices and that the costs of transistor circuits would be less than vacuum tube circuits once sufficiently high production was achieved. If each project was left to make its own decision, vacuum tube circuits would be perpetuated in the product line, and transistor costs would come down only very slowly—a rate of progress unacceptable to Watson. Accordingly, he asked W. W. McDowell to establish a date after which no future products based on vacuum tube circuits could be introduced.

In October 1957, two months before the first 608 was shipped, McDowell issued a corporate policy statement asserting, "It shall be the policy of IBM to use solid-state circuitry in all machine developments. Furthermore, no new commercial machines or devices shall be announced which make primary use of tube circuitry. . . . Any variations of this policy must be approved in writing through this office."[47]

The subsequent success of transistors—and more particularly IBM's successful early entry into solid-state computers—gave Watson considerble pride. Years later, he enjoyed citing his "visceral decision" forbidding further development of vacuum tube machines to illustrate that authoritarian management is sometimes required to move an organization rapidly. The last two IBM computers of the vacuum tube era, the 705 Model III and the 610 "personal computer," had been announced the previous month (see chapter 12). The new corporate policy probably had little effect on development work in Poughkeepsie where Palmer had been pushing transistor devices for many years, but it did have a significant effect on development projects in other IBM laboratories.[48]

A manufacturing line was established in IBM to make the alloy junction devices used in the Type 608; whereas by contrast, all of the transistors used in the transistorized 604 had been purchased from outside vendors—with one exception. This was an experimental transistor, designated the IBM X-4, which had been developed for use as a relay driver—a function it performed in the transistorized 604. A cross between a point-contact and a junction transistor, the X-4 had an alloy junction emitter and an electrically "formed" point-contact phosphor-bronze wire collector. It was used in the grounded-emitter configuration but made use of the fact that it had an alpha greater than one.

The X-4 was called a "thyratron transistor" because its operation was analogous to that of a grounded-cathode thyratron (gas-filled) tube, in which a relatively small reverse-bias voltage to the grid prevents charge flow between the cathode and plate. Removal of the bias voltage initiates ionization of the gas, resulting in a large current that is no longer controllable by the grid; to stop the current, the plate voltage is reduced. In the X-4 transistor, a relatively small reverse-bias voltage applied to the base kept the current between the emitter and collector low. When the bias voltage to the base was removed, a large flow of charge occurred between the emitter and collector and through the external load. This large current was caused by the positive feedback within the transistor, resulting from the electrically formed point-contact collector. To turn off the current, the base voltage was returned to its initial value and the collector voltage momentarily reduced to a very low value. An important advantage of this structure over earlier point-contact transistors was the good heat-removal capability provided by the large surface area of the alloyed emitter, which was soldered to the copper header. This good heat sink, combined with the relatively low internal impedance in the high-conduction state, permitted the device to handle much higher currents than earlier devices. It was capable of switching current loads of approximately 0.1 ampere at pulse rates of 1 megacycle per second.[49] (See figure 10.2.)

The inventor of the X-4 was Richard F. Rutz, who had joined IBM in August 1951 after spending several years working on radar in the Los Alamos Scientific Laboratory in New Mexico. Compared to Los Alamos, Rutz recalls, "IBM was the pits," with very little equipment for experimental work. Assigned to the same group as Henle, Rutz spent the first month learning about transistors until Samuel told him to "stop studying and do something because we are not running a university." Rutz was then assigned to build a read amplifier for the magnetic-tape recording head for the Defense Calculator. He completed the multistage, point-contact transistor amplifier by April 1952, but the point-contact transistors were not reliable enough for use in a product. Rutz then began working on combined point-contact and alloy junction transistors that resulted in the X-4 transistor.[50]

Of greater interest to Rutz and his research colleagues was his work on point-contact transistors with more than the conventional three terminals. Early in 1953, Rutz showed that the current amplification

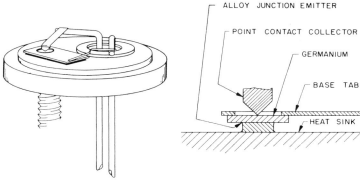

Figure 10.2

X-4 Thyratron transistor. The body of the Rutz thyratron transistor (see schematic) is a thin wafer of n-type germanium of about 6 ohm centimeter resistivity. A circular p region about 40 mils (0.04 inch) in diameter is formed on the bottom of the wafer by alloying with indium. This region is attached to the copper heat sink by indium solder. The base tab is a 5 mil nickel strip with a 60 mil hole, which is soldered to the upper face of the germanium wafer so that the hole in the base tab is concentric with the p region. The collector is a pointed phosphor-bronze wire or strip, which is electrically "formed" in the same manner in which point-contact transistor collectors are formed. An experimental X-4 transistor is shown standing on its three electrical leads. The large cylindrical copper heat sink, which dominates the photograph, is connected to the chassis by the screw and nut of the closest lead. (Schematic from A. W. Berger and R. F. Rutz, 26 May 1955: "A New Transistor with Thyratron Like Characteristics," IBM Technical Publication.)

of a point-contact transistor could be increased to values in excess of 20 by the addition of a third point-contact whisker placed far from the collector and biased so as to act as a second emitter.[51] Even more exciting was a transistor with two collectors that was able to function as a full adder for binary numbers in computer circuits. The emitter of the full adder was an alloy junction, but the two collectors were "formed" point contacts. Three input signals—one each for the binary 1 or 0 of the two numbers to be added and the carry—were fed in parallel into the emitter. A single input to the emitter caused the first collector to conduct. A double input caused the first collector to become saturated because of the voltage drop across its load resistance. This caused the second collector, which was connected to a two-times-smaller load resistance, to conduct. Once it started conducting, it ended up carrying the entire signal because of a "carrier-robbing" phenomenon. Finally, a triple input signal to the emitter saturated the second collector, forcing both collectors to carry the output current. The device thus had four stable output states.[52] Interest in the "Rutz Commutator Transistor" was heightened by the discovery that the two-collector transistor not only operated as a full adder but could be used to achieve directly the binary logical functions of "and," "or," "exclusive or," "if-and-only-if," "neither-nor," "not both," and "not." The versatility of the two-collector device meant that it could replace five to six standard transistors in logic circuits.[53]

The possibility of implementing complex logic functions with a single device, plus the much higher speeds of point-contact devices, had convinced Lloyd Hunter and his group that the future of transistors lay with point-contact devices and that it only remained to make them as reproducible and reliable as the slower junction devices. On the other hand, Logue, Henle, and other engineers were eagerly using the slower, more reliable junction devices. They contended ways would be found to speed up junction transistors—and they were right. But before that prediction was realized, many inventions and process improvements were needed.[54] In retrospect, failure to shift the research effort to junction devices sooner was "a serious mistake," a physicist in Hunter's group acknowledges. "I think we did not have the vision in that group to realize that there were other ways of making junction transistors."[55]

10.4 Drift Transistors

By September 1954, Logue's circuit design group had completed work on the emitter-follower logic circuits used in the IBM 608 and had turned its attention to "the development of high-speed building blocks" for computer logic. They began by reviewing the work of others and by a "theoretical and experimental study to determine how transistor parameters affect the speed of response of circuits." They considered a variety of devices, including point-contact transistors, junction transistors, a modified junction transistor proposed at Bell, field-effect transistors, and surface-barrier transistors.[56]

Of particular interest were the surface-barrier devices, first publicly described by members of the Philco Corporation Research Division in December 1953. The surface-barrier structure consisted of a very thin n-type germanium wafer with a metal emitter on one side and a metal collector on the other. Seemingly similar to the alloy device, it was actually quite different in structural detail and electrical operation. The germanium wafer was electrochemically etched to a thickness of only 0.0002 inch. Conduction electrons trapped in unfilled covalent bonding states on the germanium surface created the "surface-barrier" region, which together with the thinness of the germanium accounted for the very fast 50 megacycle performance.[57]

The announcement of the new devices created a lot of interest, and by January 1955 Philco had obtained a subcontract with the MIT Project Lincoln to develop surface-barrier transistors for digital computers.[58] Jay Forrester, who played such a key role in developing ferrite-core memories for SAGE, and others in the industry were enthusiastic about surface-barrier devices, but Lloyd Hunter was not convinced. He noted that surface-barrier devices were slower than point-contact devices and were made by an electrochemical etching process that would be difficult to automate.[59]

Early in 1955, Hunter read about yet another type of transistor structure in a series of theoretical papers by H. Krömer, which were published the previous year in a German journal.[60] The first of these papers proposed that holes would "drift" more rapidly across the n-type base region of a pnp transistor if the impurity concentration in the base was made to decrease exponentially from the emitter to the collector. The gradient in impurity concentration created an internal electric field that would drive the hole conductors across the n-type base region. With such an impurity gradient, fast transistors could be constructed even with relatively wide base regions. The second and third papers by Krömer were particularly helpful since they anticipated many of the problems and limitations of these devices.[61]

As soon as he read these papers, Hunter recalls, he was convinced they pointed the best way to make high-performance junction transistors; he asked Rutz to initiate the effort. At that time, Rutz was still working with alloyed emitters and point-contact collectors, but he had also been studying ways to make so-called hook collectors and other structures about the collector by diffusing gold and other impurities in from the surface. He and Hunter noted that it should be possible by this type of diffusion process to create the exponential impurity gradient proposed by Krömer. Rutz immediately undertook experiments to do so, and by May he had measured the properties of the first devices made in this manner.[62]

Initiation of work on "drift transistors" came at a critical time for IBM. Early in 1955, C. C. Hurd had stimulated an engineering activity to develop a proposal for a high-performance "two-megapulse" computer requested by the University of California Radiation Laboratory at Livermore, California. It was essential that some type of high-speed transistor circuit be part of this proposal because Edward Teller, associate director of the laboratory, had specified that the machine use transistors—not vacuum tubes.[63]

In March 1955, following an interdepartmental planning meeting on high-speed transistor structures, Hunter observed that there was general agreement that direct coupled, low-voltage operation of high-speed transistor circuits was the correct approach. He noted that a variety of junction and point-contact devices had been considered but added, "There was no general agreement on the type of compromise which would be best in a high-frequency transistor." He therefore asked Gardiner L. Tucker (a young physicist who had transferred to Poughkeepsie from the Watson Laboratory in New York City) and another member of his group to join with Logue and Henle of the circuit development group in studying this problem and making a recommendation.[64] One of the conculsions that Hunter particularly regretted was that work on the drift transistor had not progressed far enough for it to be recommended for use in the proposed machine.[65] Thus, it was decided that Philco surface-barrier transistors would be specified in the IBM proposal for the 2-megapulse Livermore Automatic Research Computer (LARC).

At this point, Palmer stepped in and dramatically altered the thrust of the proposal. Believing IBM's drift transistors would be superior to Philco's surface-barrier transistors if sufficient resources were available to develop them, he strongly opposed entering into a contract that would result in government funds being spent to develop Philco rather than IBM devices.[66] In April 1955 IBM made a proposal for LARC but—reflecting Palmer's philosophy—indicated it would prefer to work on a much higher performance machine with a longer development schedule. It was a bold decision by Palmer, demonstrating remarkable confidence in his semiconductor group; but the immediate result was that Remington Rand was awarded the contract for LARC (see chapter 11).

Meanwhile, Hunter, Tucker, and Rutz collaborated in an effort to build the proposed drift transistor. By May they had obtained promising results using diffusion of impurities into the germanium wafer from a heated vapor, and by August they had developed a recipe for making the drift transistor using vapor diffusion.[67] Beginning with a p-type germanium die, typically 0.08 by 0.08 by 0.009 inches in size, the die was annealed for 25.5 hours at 800°C in the presence of arsenic vapor. During the annealing process, arsenic atoms from the vapor diffused into the germanium. This created a strongly n-type material near the surface whose n-type impurity density fell off nearly exponentially. At a depth of about 0.03 inch, the transition to the original p-type impurity dominance was reached. This created an npn germanium die with n-type material on the surface and p-type in the center. The next step was to grind off all the n-type material on one side, leaving a simple pn junction with an exponential increase in n-type impurities going from the junction to the surface. A p-type emitter was then alloyed into the surface of the n-type region. This created the desired drift transistor structure and was the basis for a patent application filed by Hunter, Rutz, and Tucker in November 1955.[68] (See figure 10.3.)

As Hunter recalls, he did not expect to get a patent from the application. He believed their application would come into interference with patent applications by Krömer, thus helping to learn who had patent rights to the drift transistor. There was considerable uncertainty on the point because Krömer had left Germany and joined RCA during 1954. To their surprise, it turned out that Krömer apparently had not applied for any patents; his proposal was strictly theoretical.[69] The only patent interference was with an application of Shockley and coworkers at the Bell Laboratories. Although the Bell application was filed eight months before IBM's, the interference was settled in IBM's favor in 1960 for reasons having as much to do with the manner in which the patent attorneys had written and prosecuted the applications as with differences in technical content. In particular the patent application emphasized the unique electrical specifications of a "switching transistor," thus distinguishing it from the Bell invention as well as from prior art, all of which was directed to different devices.[70]

Following the loss of the contract for LARC to Remington Rand in 1955, IBM continued to seek government funding for some of its advanced-technology efforts. Early in January 1956, the company ob-

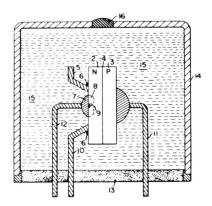

Figure 10.3
Drift transistor. U.S. Patent 2,810,870, granted to L. P. Hunter, R. F. Rutz, and G. L. Tucker on October 22, 1957, describes the left figure as follows: "a PNP junction switching transistor is shown, constructed and encapsulated in such a manner as to provide performance especially suited to information handling operations. The transistor . . . comprises a **N** type body region **2** and a **P** type collector region **3** joined at a junction barrier **4**. On one surface of the base region **2** a circular base tab **5** makes an ohmic connection **6** to the base region **2**. In the center of the opening of the base tab **5** an alloy junction emitter **7** joins the base **2** forming a **P** region **8** and a junction barrier **9** in the base region **2**. Connections **12**, **10** and **11** are attached to emitter, base and collector regions respectively and pass through a suitable insulator and sealer **13** such as glass. An airtight package cover **14** such as a metal can is sealed as by soldering to the sealing mount **13**." An experimental drift transistor is shown (right) supported by three leads to a subminiature, glass tube header, which is about 1/4 inch long. The germanium die is soldered to the back side of the rectangular nickel base tab, which is itself supported by the electrical lead at the center, rear. The emitter lead contacts the germanium through the small hole in the nickel base tab, and the collector lead contacts the germanium die directly from the back side. The product versions used in Stretch and the 7000 series had a smaller and simpler structure.

tained a contract with the Bureau of Ships to develop advanced memory technology (see chapter 7) and Palmer also formalized an effort to define a high-performance, 10-megapulse computer, which was proposed in March 1956 to the AEC at Los Alamos. The project was named Stretch, underscoring Palmer's goal of "stretching the technologies." A critical element in the proposal was IBM's new drift transistor, with which a delay of 0.02 microsecond per stage of logic was ultimately achieved.[71]

10.5 *Current-Switch Circuits*

In July 1955 Hannon S. Yourke, whose master's thesis at MIT involved nonsaturating point-contact transistor devices for flip-flop circuits, joined IBM and Logue's group. Yourke was at first put to work studying the characteristics of alloy-junction transistors and later surface-barrier transistors purchased from Philco. The surface-barrier devices were readily destroyed by voltages larger than about 5 volts. Yourke recalls a technician destroying a box of expensive Philco transistors by putting the transistors one by one on a tester that applied a voltage higher than 5 volts. The technician, who reported they were all "defective," was dismissed, showing there were limits to IBM's "full employment" policy.[72]

Noting that "the Philco devices were fantastic in performance except for very large saturation storage delays," Yourke began studying ways to use them in an unsaturated mode. A transistor is said to be *saturated* when the minority-charge carriers are emitted faster than they can be collected. When a transistor is operated in a saturated condition in digital circuits, excess minority carriers become lodged in the base region and must be removed before the transistor can be returned to its cutoff condition. The time required to remove the minority carriers can be even longer than the turn-on time and is a serious impediment to high performance.

Working on unsaturated device operation was a natural follow-on to Yourke's thesis at MIT and also consistent with interests of the IBM circuit design group. Logue himself had filed for a patent in 1953 on a "diode clamp" that prevented saturation of transistors by shunting current away from the collector through a diode. The resulting patent was first issued in 1959 and then reissued with broader claims in 1963 following an interference with a Philco patent. Logue's patent applied to many transistor circuits used in computers beginning in the late 1950s and is the forerunner of what is now known as the Schottky clamp circuit used in very large scale integration (VLSI) logic and memory chips. However, the diode itself had recovery time problems, causing Logue and others to continue seeking better ways to keep transistors out of saturation.[73] At the time Yourke joined the group, Henle was experimenting with various nonsaturating npn-pnp logic structures, but he had been unable to control the collector current adequately without using excessive power in the circuit.[74]

During early 1956, Yourke began exploring diode clamping versus feedback clamping as a means of limiting current, and there were many entries in his notebook on the stability of transistors operating out of saturation. In June he made notebook entries describing work on a two-transistor feedback clamp inverter and a pnp-npn direct-coupled inverter flip-flop. Then in July, he began work that was to lead to one of the more significant inventions in semiconductor switching circuits. His beginning entry for the month showed how to switch a well-controlled current between the emitter circuit of a transistor and a diode sink. At that stage, Yourke was simply looking for a nonsaturating, high-speed switching mode of operation. Later that month, he made an entry with the heading, "A scheme for current-mode logic relatively independent of diode voltage drops." This was the start of his use of a true current-clamping arrangement in the emitter of the transistor, but he still had not discovered how to use the concept in a logic circuit. At the time, he was thinking in terms of a type of Kirchoff logic, in which a well-defined current could be switched on and off, steered into a node, and then added.[75] But Henle, who remained technically involved in spite of his responsibilities as a second-level manager, prodded him on, telling him, "There has to be a better way."[76]

Responding to Henle's prod and to his own determination to find a better way, Yourke conceived the basic idea of switching a constant current between a diode and one or more transistors, thus permitting the use of a constant-current source with a well-defined power level. He quickly followed this with another significant idea: the replacement of the diode in the emitter circuit with a transistor. This provided a complemented output, both positive and negative output. An entry dated 30 August 1956, the day he says he "dreamt up how to use them in logic," began with the statement, "A method of doing logic with current clamps in the emitter of all transistors is developed." (See figure 10.4.) This was followed by specific circuit designs such as a pnp, N-way complemented OR circuit.[77] The patent application, filed by Yourke two and one half months later asserts the invention provides "a maximum of switching speed" using the "grounded base type of operation":

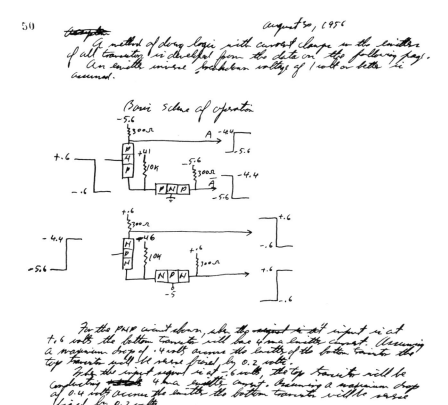

Figure 10.4
Current-switch circuit invention. This entry in H. S. Yourke's engineering notebook, accompanied by specific circuit designs on succeeding pages, was marked, "Read and Understood By J. L. Walsh at Poughkeepsie, N.Y. on this 30th day of August 1956."

This is accomplished by providing a transistor switching circuit having a common point to which is attached a constant current source. Multiple current paths are provided between the common point and the reference potential, each of which has an asymmetric impedance and at least one of which is a transistor. With this configuration a difference of potential may be applied between points in the paths to control the path through which constant current flows.[78]

Only five days after Yourke filed his patent application, the contract for Stretch was signed, committing IBM to design and build a computer about five times more powerful than LARC—the contract for which had been awarded to Remington Rand the previous year. Current-switch (originally called current-switching) circuits using drift transistors were targeted for use in Stretch and were also used in the IBM 7000 series of computers. The design philosophy of these circuits ran counter to the industry trend toward reduced transistor count, but it provided a cost-effective solution for high-performance circuits. Now more generally called emitter coupled logic (ECL), current-switch circuits soon became the dominant type of high-speed switching circuits used throughout the computer industry.[79]

The current-switch circuits developed for the IBM 7000 series have another important distinction: they were the first circuits designed for IBM computers using statistical design criteria. In contrast to the worst-case design methods used in SAGE, which assured in theory that no circuit would fail during the life of the machine, the statistical approach merely assured that the probability of failure was adequately low. Because statistical design methods reduced the cost of circuits without a significant sacrifice in machine reliability, they soon became standard engineering practice. Mathematical techniques for statistical designs were simple in principle but required thousands of individual calculations, which would have been impractical without the aid of electronic computers. Therefore, statistical design proposals made in the 1940s were largely ignored, but by the mid-1950s there was an increasing trend to use existing computers to help design new computers. Describing the statistical design methods developed at IBM beginning early in 1957, an engineer in the project summed up the contribution as follows:

Thus we are not announcing a new basic technique, although some of the details and refinements which are the results of several years' experience with Monte Carlo analysis and design programs may be new. What we are announcing is a way of life. Statistical design is here to stay and our engineers now take it for granted as an everyday tool. . . . We believe this is so because the computer is taken for granted in our development laboratories, and this, in combination with methods like Monte Carlo, facilitated the coordination of specialized effort which was necessary for practical statistical design.[80]

10.6 Development and Manufacturing

An important element of the company's success with electromechanical equipment and then vacuum tube devices had been its ability to design products that could be manufactured in large quantities at a low cost. As in the case of ferrite cores, the development of a manufacturing process and tools for making transistors was originally assigned to the component development group in research. However, the decision in 1956 to make research an entity separate from development (discussed in chapter 13) created a need for a new transistor-development group to be responsible for developing devices and processes suitable for large-scale production.

Bernard N. Slade was hired in June 1956 to establish this group. He had spent the previous eight years working on transistor technology at RCA, having coincidentally joined that company on the very day the transistor was first announced. With a bachelor's degree in electrical engineering from the University of Wisconsin in 1948 and a master's degree from Stevens Institute in 1954, his experience was well suited to the new assignment.[81]

Slade's initial task was to develop a pilot line and process for making alloy transistors for use in the proposed IBM 608 calculator. The transistors themselves were similar to alloy devices available from outside vendors, and much of the preliminary design and process work had already been done by people in Research. An n-type germanium chip with indium alloyed to either side was the basic pnp device, and a p-type germanium chip with lead-antimony alloyed to either side was the basic npn device. The processing and assembly of these transistors was done by hand, as it was in other organizations.

At Palmer's urging, Slade also initiated a project to automate transistor production using the mechanical expertise available in IBM.[82] Palmer believed that automatic production equipment not only would reduce the cost of transistors but would also turn out a more uniform product. This was important because digital circuits built with transistors reportedly had higher error rates at that time than those built with vacuum tubes.[83]

The lead mechanical engineer for this automation effort was Elliott L. Fritz, who had joined IBM in 1948 with a bachelor's degree in mechanical engineering. He had spent his first few years as a customer engineer, servicing electrical accounting equipment, before he was given an assignment in the Poughkeepsie development laboratory. There he worked at first on a stick printer for RAMAC and then on the banking program, especially the reader-sorter that read, handled, and sorted checks. In October 1957, as the reader-sorter project neared completion, Fritz accepted an assignment, reporting to Slade, to develop what became the world's first automated assembly line for alloy transistors.

In December, while Fritz was still formulating plans for a thirty-person effort during 1958, William E. Harding joined IBM and was assigned to the automated transistor assembly project. With a master's degree in physics from Brooklyn Polytechnic in 1950 and seven years of experience designing transistors at the Radio Receptor Corporation, Harding's job was to define a transistor-fabrication process that could be mechanized.[84] An important early decision attributed to him was to limit the equipment to making only one transistor type, an npn lead-alloy transistor expected to be used in large quantities. Previously the plan had been to design the equipment to produce as well a pnp indium-alloy transistor and the npn and pnp drift transistors for Stretch. This would have complicated the automated assembly process, which was already complicated enough. A particular challenge was the handling of parts so tiny that their total dimensions were smaller than the tolerances then required for conventional parts.

The project evolved rapidly during 1958, the first full year of the effort. Numerous experiments were run to check out processes and materials to ensure that they resulted in good transistors and were compatible with the proposed mechanization. Equipment design for the handling of parts began in April, and by July turntables, conveyor ovens, and other equipment for the automatic production line had been purchased. Final systems design began in September. Constant liaison was maintained with manufacturing to be sure the automated line would be compatible with all manufacturing procedures including those being developed for inserting components into printed circuit cards. In December, Fritz was transferred to the manufacturing organization and given responsibility for completing the line.[85]

The system was completed and demonstrated to management in July 1959. Transistors were fabricated from preformed components: two small metal-alloy dots (spheres) for the emitter and collector, a single-crystal germanium disk, a washer-shaped metallic base contact, two contact wires for the emitter and collector, and the mounting base (header). Each transistor was assembled in its own machined carbon jig, called a boat, which was used to confine and position the components during the alloying process. This made it possible to reject individual faulty transistors at each stage of the process. Assembly functions were performed on internally driven and controlled turntables. The total process, which began by loading the collector dot into an empty boat on the first turntable, was described by the lead manufacturing engineer as follows:

At the first index of the [turntable] . . . a photoelectric detector checks for the presence of the boat. The check at this point permits the automatic inhibiting of the dot loading operation if the boat is not present. At the next station the collector dot is inserted into the cavity of the boat. Before leaving the turntable, the boat is again photoelectrically checked to insure proper positioning of the dot. If the dot is absent or improperly positioned, the boat is rejected at the output station of the unit. Accepted boats are placed on a conveyor for transport to turntable 2.

A build-in float or overload between all units in the machine permits a predetermined number of boats to arrive at the input of each unit. An over-supply will automatically restrict the output of the preceding unit.

At turntable 2 the boats are loaded with the germanium disks and checked. The disks are fed into and oriented in a rotary Syntron feeder which will remove chips or broken disks. Accepted disks are then fed into a linear feeder track for delivery to a pickup station. During their trip down the track, the disks pass below two control points called bridges, which prevent out-of-tolerance, dirty, or double disks from reaching the assembly point. At the end of track, accepted disks are picked up by a vacuum probe, carried over, and dropped into the orifice of a cone, which guides them to their proper position in the boat. Another photoelectric check determines the presence and proper position of the disk in the boat. Accepted boats are transported along the conveyor; rejects are removed from the assembly process.[86]

And so the process continued, with automatic assembly and checking to turntable 3 for the emitter; through a five-zone alloying oven to turntables 4 and 5 where the base tab, emitter wire plug, and emitter were loaded; through a three-zone bonding oven to turntable 6 where the collector wire was inserted; then back through the bonding oven, to the starwheel assembly (three adjacent turntables) where the carbon jig (boat) was disassembled automatically and the extracted transistor was automatically welded to a three-lead stem. This was the last step performed by the automatic production line. Completed transistors were then chemically etched, cleaned, enclosed with an hermetically sealed cap, and individually tested. The entire sequence took only 3 hours, and the system could be operated, at variable throughput rates, to a maximum of 3600 units per hour (figure 10.5).

This automatic system contrasted sharply with the manual assembly lines then in use, which depended on the dexterity of experienced operators, often working with microscopes. Only three people were now required to monitor the status of the entire system and to direct corrective action as required. Once the system was installed and debugged, the quality of the product improved rapidly. Within three months, its yield surpassed that of the manual assembly line. In one ninety-day period, operating continuously except for adjustment and maintenance, it yielded an average of 2600 good transistors per hour at final test. The success of this system was not confined to economics. It showed that what was originally perceived as artful technology could be understood and controlled.[87]

Among the interested observers of IBM's automated transistor production line were representatives of Texas Instruments. They were on hand as a result of a policy decision made by McDowell, Birkenstock, and others that IBM would purchase transistors from outside vendors in order to save its own capital funds for expanded production of data processing systems. Texas Instruments (TI) had been selected as a primary supplier in December 1957, and to ensure that IBM obtained the best possible devices for its needs, an agreement had been concluded that provided for "exchange of patent licenses, purchasing arrangements, interchange of technical information, and joint development" of transistors and diodes.[88]

At the time, TI had its own program to mechanize transistor production. But soon after the TI representatives saw the IBM system in operation, the TI program was terminated. In October 1959, the IBM automated transistor production line was disassembled for shipment to TI. Placed in production at TI in 1960, it was replicated several times and was kept running for many years, supplying transistors to IBM and to other TI customers as well.[89]

About a year before this project was completed, Slade was asked to become one of a three-man engineering management team to develop manufacturable transistors for Stretch. The other two members were from Research. Out of this effort came the post-alloy-diffused method for making the graded-base logic devices used in Stretch and the IBM 7000 series of computers.[90] Post-alloy-diffused pnp devices were fabricated on p-type germanium with a narrow n-type layer on one side created by gaseous diffusion of antimony or arsenic. A small lead-alloy dot containing minute quantities of an acceptor (gallium) and donor (antimony) impurities was then placed on the n-type layer.

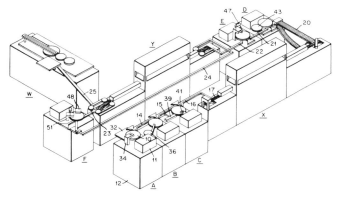

Figure 10.5

Transistor assembly machine. The photograph (top) shows the automated transistor production line completed by IBM and turned over to Texas Instruments in 1959. The drawing (bottom) shows how the line is composed of independent assembly units A, B, C, D, E, and F (each with its own turntable), two ovens X and Y, and a welder W. (Schematic from E. L. Fritz, W. A. Kauffman, and T. J. Leach, April 1960: IBM Technical Disclosure Bulletin.)

These impurities were selected because the antimony diffused into the germanium crystal about 750 times faster at elevated temperatures than did the gallium. The lead-alloy dot on the germanium chip was heated to about 750°C, causing a lead-gallium-antimony-germanium alloy metallic emitter to form. By holding the unit at that temperature, the antimony could be caused to diffuse into the germanium, thus creating a thin n-type exponentially graded-base region near the p-type emitter. As reported by Slade, "This technique provides a closely controlled method of obtaining a thin base region, since the diffusion is controlled only by time and temperature." A metallic base ring was then soldered around the emitter, and a collector contact was made to the opposite side of the chip.

Taking advantage of these diffused-base fabrication methods, IBM engineers also devised a medium-power, graded-base npn transistor needed for driving the 2.18 microsecond cycle ferrite-core memory used in Stretch and the 7000 series of computers. The device was described as being "very similar to conventional npn diffused devices for low power levels and high frequencies except that the junctions are considerably larger in area to permit high current and higher power characteristics."[91]

In 1959 William Harding, Walter Mutter (who had shifted his interests from Williams tubes to transistors), and others in Slade's group released to manufacturing a double-diffused npn "mesa" transistor that was to be the last of IBM's germanium transistors. Like other mesa transistors, its characteristic shape was created by etching away the semiconductor material surrounding the base and emitter contacts, leaving the transistor junctions in a small, raised, mesa-shaped region supported by the more massive part of the semiconductor wafer. Unlike the pnp germanium mesa transistors with alloyed emitter and diffused base-junctions then being manufactured throughout the industry, the IBM npn device had both the emitter and collector junctions created by high-temperature diffusions from one side of the wafer—a precursor of processes later used to make planar silicon transistors.

The p-type base diffusion, which created the base-to-collector junction, was performed uniformly over the surface of the n-type wafer. This was followed by a shallower n-type diffusion through a silicon-oxide mask, which created the emitter-to-base junction and completed the npn structure. The thickness of the base region was defined by the difference in depth of the two diffusions, both of which could be controlled accurately by time, temperature, and other parameters of the diffusion process. (See figure 10.6.) Even in this early application, the control of donor and acceptor distributions by diffusion was almost

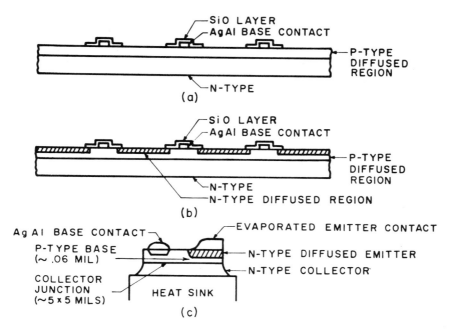

Figure 10.6
Double-diffused npn transistor process. First, as shown in *a*, a graded region of
p-type is formed by diffusion of an indium vapor onto an n-type germanium
wafer. A matrix of Ag-Al base strips is next evaporated onto the p-type region
through a mask. A suitable mask with apertures lined up over the base strips is
now placed onto the wafer and silicon monoxide evaporated through the mask.
The mask is now removed, and an n-type vapor diffusion is carried out; see *b*.
Since the silicon monoxide acts as a mask against the diffusion of donor impurities, the diffusion has occurred only in selected regions, leaving several npn diffused-base transistors, which need contacts made to the emitter and collector.
Evaporation techniques are used to make contact to these two regions. After the
individual transistor assemblies are separated, as in *c*, the collector is attached to
a heat sink, and a mesa is now etched to reveal the collector and reduce the
collector to its final desired area. This technique permits extremely small emitters
and collectors to be formed through masks with apertures of desired dimensions
and geometry; furthermore, the transistors can be made in large batches on one
wafer by simultaneous diffusion through one mask. (From B. N. Slade, 1962: in
Handbook of Semiconductor Electronics, 2d edition, ed. L. P. Hunter, New York: Mc-
Graw-Hill, p. 10–7. Reproduced with permission.)

an order of magnitude better than the control achieved by alloying techniques. Unlike silicon devices subsequently developed for System/ 360, however, this device was still a double-sided structure with electrical contacts on one side for the base and emitter, and on the other side for the collector.[92]

An automated transistor assembly line was developed for the mesa device and placed in production at IBM in 1962. But its use was quite limited because of the shift to single-sided (planar) silicon transistor technology for System/360. Furthermore, mechanical assembly of transistors, so useful for alloy devices, was less important for the mesa device, whose production called for many process steps to be performed over the entire surface of the wafer before it was diced into chips.[93]

10.7 Standard Modular System

Ralph Palmer, who had introduced the single-tube pluggable unit with the 604 calculator, was dismayed when the number of standard circuit types grew from fewer than ten to more than forty.[94] He was even more dismayed when the number of types of eight-tube pluggable units required to service the 700 series of computers grew to more than two thousand.[95] He was determined not to let this happen in the new transistor technology. In March 1957, he and H. S. Beattie asked Logue, who had served for a year as engineering manager for Project Stretch, to establish a group in the Poughkeepsie laboratory with division-wide responsibility for developing standard circuits and packaging for Stretch and what later became the 7000 series.

Palmer suggested that a movie be made, to be shown at the laboratories, that would extol the virtues of standardization. After giving this some thought, Logue had a movie made that included a view of a shelf of eight-tube pluggable units. When the camera dolly backed off, the viewer saw that it was not a shelf these pluggable units were on but was in fact the gym floor in the Poughkeepsie IBM Country Club, literally covered with a sea of over two thousand pluggable unit types needed to service the 700 series machines. It was a staggering scene. Beattie ordered the film put under lock and key after Palmer observed, "If anybody saw that movie, I would get fired." The movie was obviously more effective than desired. It ended Logue's short career as a movie director but not his effort to achieve standardization in semiconductor circuits and packaging.[96]

At the same time, Palmer was seeking ways to automate the production of transistors and the interconnection of transistors with other circuit components. Automation of transistor production was assigned to Slade in the fall of that year, but neither the problem nor the solution for automated component assembly was easily defined because so many different component packaging structures had been proposed. Palmer himself had helped to create this variety by challenging a number of groups to devise component packing schemes that could be mass produced with automated equipment.

This challenge was of particular interest to Edward J. Garvey, who had established a small manufacturing research group in the Endicott laboratory. Garvey had joined IBM in 1938 in the product engineering department in Endicott and had held a variety of engineering and manufacturing positions there and in Poughkeepsie, including a year or so as laboratory manager in Endicott, prior to joining manufacturing in mid-1953.[97] He is credited with making important contributions to the manufacturability of the 604 and was coinventor of the eight-tube circuit package used in the 701.[98] By 1957 Garvey's manufacturing research group had several projects underway to automate the mounting and interconnecting of components on flat circuit cards similar to those used in the transistorized 604 and the Type 608 calculator. Garvey believed IBM could use printed circuit technology effectively if a manufacturing system with considerable flexibility were devised. The television industry was making extensive use of printed circuits at that time, but it used a large number of identical cards, whereas IBM needed smaller quantities of many different types.

By the end of 1957, the Endicott manufacturing research group had developed a machine for automatically inserting 1 and 2 watt resistors into predrilled holes on a printed circuit card. Known as PROSERT, for Programmed Component Inserter, this machine inserted resistors into preselected locations under the control of an electronic controller, receiving instructions from a Type 026 card reader. PROSERT had a servo-table with a 10 inch by 10 inch travel, over which the insertion equipment was constructed. Resistors stored in twenty hoppers (one for each resistance value) were fed into a central hopper. The resistor leads were then bent by a forming tool into the shape of a staple and the resistor inserted into the card, which had been positioned by the servo-table. The insertion rate was about one component per second. Punched-card control eliminated human error in selecting the correct resistor and card location.

Although cards with printed wiring on both sides were used by others to permit one wire to cross over another, Garvey's group believed cards with printed wiring only on one side would better meet IBM's requirements for automated production. They therefore developed a machine for cutting and bending conductor wires into staple shapes for insertion in a manner similar to that used for resistors. The inserted jumper wire in effect caused one printed wire to cross over another without touching it. Thus the printed wiring was on one side of the card, and all components (including jumper wires) were mounted on the other, with their leads protruding through holes to the side with the printed wiring. The ends of these leads, which had been mechanically crimped after insertion, were then soldered to the printed wiring to complete the electrical circuit. This could be accomplished automatically by a wave-soldering technique in which the printed circuit side of the card was placed down over a bath of molten solder and allowed to touch the crest of a wave created on the solder surface.[99]

In April 1958 Palmer announced his intention to have a meeting in the Glendale laboratory at Endicott to select a circuit packaging system for all future products. With so much effort invested in automating the use of planar circuit cards, the Endicott group was deeply concerned about the possible outcome of this meeting. Some of the packaging schemes then under consideration were sufficiently different in structure that—should they be selected—the PROSERT equipment would have little if any use.

Of particular concern was an advanced circuit packaging approach being developed by Logue's group in Poughkeepsie. Called the "bird cage" because of its appearance, this package consisted of discrete electronic components—transistors, resistors, capacitances, and inductors—interconnected by wires in a three-dimensional configuration. An automatic "wire-wrap" technique was used to make electrical contact between the interconnecting wires or with the component leads. Based on developments at Bell Laboratories, the wire-wrap method consisted of placing two electrical pins in contact and then tightly wrapping a wire around them to ensure good electrical contact. If the pins were rectangular instead of round, their edges made good electrical contact with the wrapped wire, even without soldering.[100] This proposal was of concern to the Endicott group because it appeared to provide more density and design flexibility than large planar cards. More important, it had been devised by IBM's leading circuit design group, which had company-wide responsibility for developing standard circuits and packaging.

Garvey immediately got together with people in his manufacturing research group to discuss ways to respond to this threat. It was agreed that a complete packaging scheme, compatible with automated fabrication methods, should be devised in time to be presented at Palmer's meeting the following week. The basic elements of the scheme were quickly established, and one of the engineers undertook to create a detailed proposal. Only a few days, including the weekend, were available to define a packaging system that was soon to become IBM's highly successful Standard Modular System (SMS).[101]

In this system, circuit cards about 2.5 inches by 4.5 inches in size were selected to provide the space believed to be needed for standard circuit parts. Eight of these cards could be handled at a time on the PROSERT servo-table. Contact tabs to the printed lines were spaced at 1/8 inch increments on one of the 2.5-inch sides of each card. Critical to this approach was the creation of a socket into which the cards could be inserted so as to make reliable electrical and mechanical contact. The contacts within the sockets were made of phosphor bronze springs under tension so that when a card was inserted, each contact was overstressed, causing it to exert nearly the same force on the card. The tabs at the ends of the printed copper lines on the epoxy-paper card were gold plated to ensure good electrical contact. Two rows of pins on 1/4 inch centers, sticking out the back side of the glass-filled-epoxy socket, provided a means for interconnecting the leads from one card to another. Although no work on automatic wire wrap had been done in Endicott, wire wrap was selected for interconnecting the pins of the sockets, and the sockets were stacked so as to form a regular array of pins on the back panel.[102]

All of this was defined in time for the meeting with Palmer, and models of the entire system were made, including circuit cards with components inserted and a wooden mock-up of a socket. During the presentation, emphasis was placed on the existence of an operational PROSERT system for 1 and 2 watt resistors and jumper wires. Additional insertion units would have to be built to handle half-watt resistors and transistors, and an automatic soldering unit was needed. Functional sockets and back-panel wire-wrap equipment would also have to be designed and built. (See figure 10.7.)

Palmer was impressed with what he saw and made the decision on the spot to implement the Endicott-developed SMS proposal, reportedly saying, "Just tell me what you need, and you'll have it."[103] Palmer says he was able to make this decision quickly for three reasons: the proposal appeared to be "reasonable from an automatic manufacturing point of view," he was "really impressed by the competence of the group," and he "knew Garvey wouldn't take on a thing unless he planned to see it through."[104]

Of Palmer's decision on SMS, Garvey says, "Generally you find that you need one good idea, not an assortment of mediocre ones or even an assortment of good ones. . . . Ralph Palmer was magnificent in his ability . . . to make some very tough basic decisions in this business,

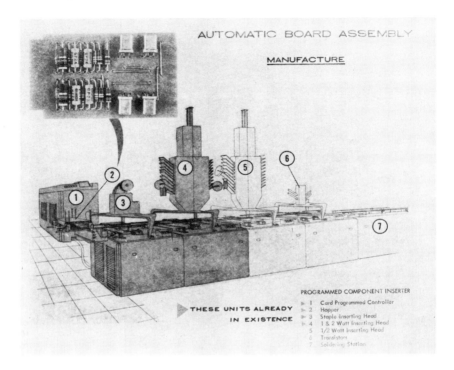

Figure 10.7
SMS manufacturing proposal. This figure was used by the Endicott manufacturing research group to explain their SMS proposal in April 1958. At the upper left is an SMS card with components inserted: transistors to the right and resistors and capacitors to the left.

and a lot of them were associated with SMS. . . . He was willing to make the decisions and take the consequences." Following the meeting in Endicott, Palmer asked Garvey to give presentations to the engineers in Poughkeepsie "to accomplish two things: to demonstrate that the decision was made and to make it clear what the decision was, so the engineering people and management would act accordingly."[105]

SMS packaging was first shipped on the 7090 computer in December 1959. Following this, the PROSERT equipment was replicated, modified, and ultimately replaced as production of SMS was increased to meet ever-expanding requirements. SMS was used on all IBM computers after the 7090, until Solid Logic Technology (SLT) was introduced in 1964 as the new logic technology for System/360. Even then, SMS continued to be used—in larger quantities than ever—for the lower-performance circuits of peripheral equipment attached to System/360 central processing units. Thus, SMS served not only as the primary circuit packaging technology for IBM's first generation of transistorized computers, but it remained a reliable, cost-effective part of the company's circuit technology even into the early days of integrated circuits. (See figures 10.8 and 10.9.)

The wire-wrap method, originally studied by Logue's group for the "bird-cage" package, found its first IBM use in the back-panel wiring of SMS. A paper-tape-controlled wire-wrapping machine, designed by engineers of the Gardner-Denver Company in close cooperation with IBM, was used for wiring back panels for well over a decade. The use of digital information to drive the Gardner-Denver machines represents one of the early transfers of digital design data from development to manufacturing. The logic design engineers determined the physical layout of the logic and specified which SMS cards were to be used and which pins were to be connected on the back panel, but a computer program calculated the actual back-panel wiring pattern, using constraints imposed by the circuit design as well as by the Gardner-Denver machine.

Finding ways to provide computer assistance in all aspects of research, development, and manufacturing had been a goal of the Poughkeepsie engineers for some time. The pressing need to reduce paperwork associated with the design and test of large systems had become evident during the design of the 701 and 702 computers. To help control this problem, information about the characteristics and form of standard circuit elements was stored in the computer, and methods were developed to enable the computer to print out logic block diagrams. Engineering changes were facilitated by the records kept in the computer, and the introduction of new errors was reduced. It was the beginning of design automation in IBM; the term itself came into common use at this time.[106]

Equally as important as the development of standard circuits and packaging was the enforcement of their use. SMS, it should be noted, soon encompassed not only circuits, cards, and boards but also power supplies, memories, frames, and covers. Engineers had many reasons not to use the new system. First of all, SMS restrained them in their desire to invent new and better circuits. Second, the size of the card and number of interconnection pins limited circuit density and performance for large machines and could be a constraint on low-cost designs for smaller machines. Finally, as with any other new technology, SMS had high initial costs that had to be borne by early users. It was precisely this high initial cost, however, that convinced Palmer to select only one packaging system so that the cost could be spread over many programs.

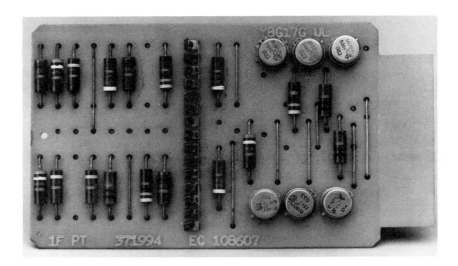

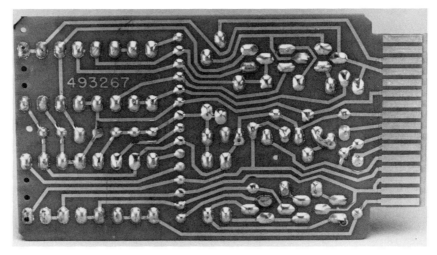

Figure 10.8
SMS card. The 2.5 inch by 4.5 inch SMS card is shown (top) with six transistors and assorted resistors and jumper wires inserted. The back side of a card (bottom) reveals the printed lines soldered to crimped component leads and the sixteen gold-plated tabs to the right.

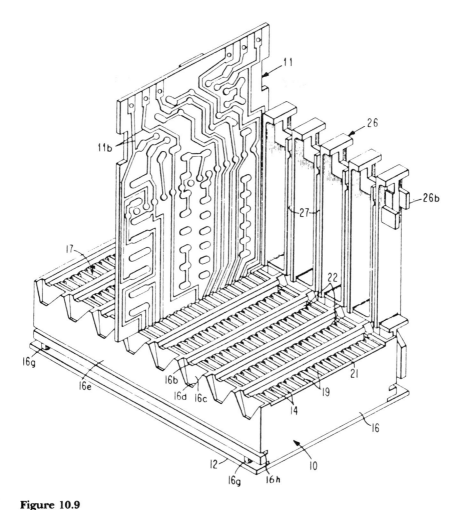

Figure 10.9
SMS card in socket. An SMS pluggable card (11) is shown inserted in one of the grooves (22) of an eight-socket receptacle (10). Sixteen phosphor bronze springs (14) electrically isolated from each other by separators (19) make electrical contact with the gold-plated tabs on the end of the card. The guide and separator element (26) has longitudinal guideways (27) corresponding to the grooves (22) of the receptacles (10). The card was made of epoxy paper and the receptacle of glass-filled epoxy. (From U.S. Patent 3,008,113, filed 30 July 1958: A. H. Johnson, "Electrical Interconnecting and Mounting Device for Printed-Circuit Boards.")

To achieve compliance with SMS, Palmer, as manager of product development for the Data Processing Division, took over management of the program. He arranged to have Logue, with overall circuit responsibility, report directly to him; and he gave special enforcement responsibility to N. P. Edwards, whom he brought to White Plains as director of standards for the division.[107] It was not an easy task because inventive (and frequently strong-willed) engineers were continually demanding consideration of their "special" requirements. An early enhancement of SMS resulted from insistance by Erich Bloch that the required performance of Stretch could not be achieved without a so-called two-wide card, designed to occupy the space normally allocated to two cards. In certain cases these two-times larger cards could hold four times as many circuits as a single card and greatly enhance performance by permitting direct interconnection among these circuits on the same card. While highly desirable for large computers, the two-wide card resulted in many more parts that had to be fabricated, tested, and retained in inventory. Edwards's job was to fight all such extensions to SMS until they were proved to be essential to the products in question and not too great a burden to the total collection of systems using SMS.

Speaking from his experience in this role, Edwards describes Palmer as "the Henry Ford of computers whose goal was to mass-produce computers on an assembly line."[108] It was a goal Palmer achieved for IBM both in vacuum tube machines and in the newer generation of solid-state computers. In doing so the problem of ever-expanding part numbers was never fully solved, but it was controlled.

While production automation and component standardization was important, it would be wrong to minimize the importance of IBM's growing strength in advanced technology. Despite heavy product pressures during the 1950s, basic research had been supported. Experimental and theoretical studies had been carried out on the electrical properties of semiconductor materials. Epitaxial growth and other new processes had been investigated, and novel devices, such as high-speed tunnel diodes, had been explored. The shift from germanium to silicon transistors in IBM's commercial products was not made until the 1960s, but Logue had obtained government contract support for work on silicon devices much earlier. In 1956, for example, Henle and others had designed servo-amplifiers and other circuits for a high-precision bombing and navigation system, using some of the first silicon transistors produced by Texas Instruments.[109] The use of silicon was initially motivated by its ability to operate at higher temperatures than ger-

SEMICONDUCTOR PATENTS AWARDED PER YEAR

	'52	'53	'54	'55	'56	'57	'58	'59	'60	'61	'62'	'63
AT&T	34	47	36	27	48	34	51	72	67	67	55	54
IBM	1	1	0	1	4	6	15	22	25	37	96	53
GE	5	7	6	11	25	13	35	34	26	36	42	35
RCA	14	19	16	10	44	45	57	46	34	33	33	27
TI	0	0	0	0	0	2	9	8	22	13	20	24
Westinghouse	2	6	2	4	9	7	21	25	30	21	23	18

Figure 10.10
Semiconductor patents. AT&T, IBM, GE, RCA, TI, and Westinghouse—listed
here in order of the number of semiconductor patents awarded in 1963—each
had more patents on semiconductor technology issued in each of the years from
1960 through 1963 than any other U.S. company. The next three companies in
1963 were Honeywell, Sylvania, and Philco-Ford. Note that ninety-six patents
were awarded to IBM inventors in 1962.

manium, but the existence of oxides of silicon to serve as process
masks and passivation layers became even more important as planar
transistor structures were developed. By 1960, IBM had two major,
advanced development thrusts in transistor technology: Project IMPACT
(Integrated Machine Program in Advanced Computer Technology),
which addressed problems of ultra-high-speed circuits and packaging;
and Project COMPACT (Cost-Oriented Machine Program in Advanced
Computer Technology), which addressed problems of cost-performance
circuits and was the forerunner of SLT circuits and packaging introduced
in the IBM System/360 in 1964.[110]

The growing expertise in semiconductor technology in IBM not
only made SMS possible, but it also placed the company in a strong
position to participate in and benefit from technology developments
of the 1960s. Patents are not the sole measure of technological achievement, but they are useful indicators. Prior to 1955, fewer than a
handful of patents in semiconductor technology had been awarded
to IBM engineers and scientists. But by the early 1960s, patents on
semiconductor technology were being awarded to IBM employees at
an average rate of more than fifty per year—a rate matched only by
AT&T, where the transistor had been invented.[111] (See figure 10.10.)

11

Project Stretch

"We must take a giant step." Project Stretch formulation. System planning. Logical design and engineering. The Type 7090, first Stretch-technology product. The 7030 program. Stretch delivery and assessment. Epilogue.

The year 1954 saw "the firm establishment of the large electronic computer in industry."[1] Or so an IBMer cheerfully reported. At year's end, eighteen IBM 701 Electronic Data Processing Machines were in use by customers (see chapter 5), as were about two dozen large Remington Rand computers.[2] Having endured the delays and shakedown difficulties that attended these first large computers, users were fired by thoughts of better programming methods, more efficient operating modes, and improved hardware.

Still, the business prospect for large computers was plagued by uncertainty. While ideas clamored for development resources, nobody had convincing data from which to predict returns on investment. In IBM, for example, the Poughkeepsie-based strategy for employing the vacuum tube had produced a 604 electronic calculator and a 701 electronic computer. Over 2000 604s had been produced.[3] Clearly, until large computers could be produced in greater volume, the burden of development and production start-up expenses implied high rentals. And as long as large-computer costs remained inflated, volume production would be inhibited by price competition from 604-like calculators.

Financial considerations were not the only source of uncertainty nagging at IBM management. Industry opinion was questioning whether the accounting-oriented IBM 702 system, announced in September 1953 for delivery in 1955, would better the performance of Remington Rand's UNIVAC, extant since 1951 and still gathering sales momentum. Many in IBM's sales force, ill at ease with 702 concepts and unfortified with tested answers to numerous questions, would have preferred to face the future with improved 604-like machines. It was partly in response to the mounting confusion that T. J. Watson, Jr., IBM president, in April 1954 named sales manager T. V. Learson to the new post called director of EDPM (electronic data processing machines). Learson's charge was to "coordinate all the company's engineering, manufacturing, sales and service activities in the electronic business machines field."[4]

Learson formed a council of EDPM-associated managers in the Poughkeepsie laboratory, including R. L. Palmer, laboratory manager, and N. Rochester, engineer in charge of EDPM development. He also established departments for EDPM product planning and EDPM programming research. Exploiting his coordination mission to the fullest (as discussed in chapter 5), he undertook to accelerate actions that would encourage the sales force. In May, the IBM 704 was announced as successor to the 701; in October, the IBM 705 was announced as successor to the 702. Learson's enthusiasm helped rid computers of the aura of laboratory instruments, making it easier for the sales force to view them as viable products.

By 1954, vacuum tubes had lost their savor for Palmer, who had supervised 604 development and managed the Poughkeepsie laboratory during 701 development. His attention, which necessarily ranged ahead of marketing and manufacturing activities, had gravitated toward solid-state switching devices. The demise of the vacuum tube had often been predicted. For example, in early 1953, before the first 701 shipment, *Fortune* magazine had opened an article by saying,

For nearly five years the electronics industry has been living with a pea-sized time bomb called a transistor, a device that can replace vacuum tubes for many jobs. This is the explosive year when the transistor goes into volume production. . . . the transistor will, to a large degree, free electronics from the vacuum tube's onerous limitations—relatively short life, high power consumption, bulkiness, and fragility.[5]

Further down, the article duly noted that transistors were still very expensive and that 1953's "volume production" had been allocated to military needs. At the time, of course (see chapter 10), close observers knew that technical difficulties still obscured the outlook for cost and speed. But Palmer felt sure that transistors were coming and that his laboratory was lagging in know-how. Although L. P. Hunter, one of Palmer's project managers, headed a small group that was attempting to identify serviceable transistors for computer circuits, no small group was likely to match the work underway in Bell Telephone Laboratories, Radio Corporation of America, General Electric, and Philco.

Despite Learson's attack on immediate problems, many hurdles remained to be cleared. In addition to the need for developing new computer components, a host of ideas merited investigation. Among these were ideas for speeding up computer operations by overlapping instruction executions to a greater degree, reducing programming costs by providing standardized aids, reducing installation costs by designing computer systems with more flexibility and modularity, and further automating computer design and production tasks. To sift out the real opportunities required answering an unprecedented number of technical questions. And the 701 exercise had shown that answers could be elusive and costly.

Computers had arrived and with them Palmer's realization that research and development expenditures commensurate with the opportunities were beyond IBM's modest resources. Additional funding had to be found. This realization was to govern IBM's technical strategy for several years.

11.1 "We Must Take a Giant Step"

S. W. Dunwell, an engineer who had long been a member of the Future Demands staff in headquarters, joined Palmer in summer 1954 for the purpose of working on "advanced concepts." Despite their divergent career paths, the two had much in common: both had joined IBM in the 1930s, gotten involved with electronics while in the armed forces, and been influential in shaping IBM's postwar response to electronics. Palmer could fairly be considered the foremost electrical engineer in the company, Dunwell the foremost product planner. Dunwell had played prominent roles in formulating specifications for the 604, the CPC, the 650, the TPM, and the 702 (see chapters 2–5).

As early as 1952, Palmer had informed the manager of Future Demands that Dunwell was needed in Poughkeepsie.[6] But Dunwell had insisted on a special assignment in IBM's Washington, D.C., office in order to obtain training he felt he needed. So during part of 1953 and about half of 1954, he had aided the manager of the Washington office and surveyed data processing requirements in federal agencies, among them the Federal Bureau of Investigation, Social Security Administration, Treasury, and Weather Bureau. Also, he had brushed up on the requirements being postulated by staff members of the National Security Agency (NSA). While in the army during World War II, he had headed a large data processing machine installation at one of NSA's predecessor organizations.[7]

Having been stimulated by his discussions in Washington, Dunwell came to Poughkeepsie brimming with aspirations. Also, like many other IBMers, he was smarting over IBM's public image as second best in large computers because of the mounting reputation of UNIVAC. His suggestions for a more effective 702 had been rejected in 1951 on the grounds that they would raise costs and rentals and further delay announcement and delivery. Now, before first delivery of the 702, improvements were considered urgent.

Dunwell's assignment to Poughkeepsie, coming shortly after announcement of the IBM 704 as a successor to the 701, coincided with a review of prospects for the large-computer line. One machine on Learson's mind was the Watson Scientific Computing Laboratory's soon-to-be-completed NORC (Naval Ordnance Research Calculator), which promised to be the fastest computer anywhere. Other prospects consisted of the in-development SAGE computer and a still-nebulous successor to the 704. Because all designers were endowing their computers with highly distinctive characteristics, performance comparisons tended to slip away into qualifications and footnotes. J. W. Backus of Applied Science helped to clarify one contrast in June 1954 by obtaining general agreement that the decimal NORC possessed 1.7 times the internal performance of the binary 704 on floating-point computations where the 704's precision — the equivalent of about eight decimal digits — sufficed.[8] Where more precision was needed, its precision of thirteen decimal digits gave NORC a higher margin of superiority.

NORC, with roughly twice the hardware of a 704, was creating interest on the part of various research laboratories. As a result, B. E. Phelps was asked to lead a technical committee in assessing NORC's engineering and design features. While trying to find an optimal balance between design and construction costs, the NORC engineers had carried circuit standardization to a degree that required some of the circuitry to contain more components than logically necessary. Faulting the degree of redundancy, Phelps recommended that NORC hardware not be used in commercial systems, even though he found points to commend in the standardization, wiring-chart, and testing techniques developed by the project. To best exploit these techniques, he urged "a strong transfusion" of experienced NORC personnel into product-oriented groups.[9]

Learson's late July conclusion was that the job of making a product of NORC would absorb engineering resources that could better be spent in designing "a new machine which might be a combination of 702-704-NORC-High." ("High," at the time, was still a designation for the SAGE computer.) Faced with mounting demands for development funds, Learson was willing to listen to proposals for unifying the whole large-computer aggregation.[10]

Rochester's chief computer planners were G. M. Amdahl, who was in charge of engineering work on computers for scientific computing and had led in the 701 redesign that yielded the 704, and W. Buchholz, who earlier had contributed to the system designs of the TPM, 701, and 702, and was now finishing up on a 702-improvement study. While the results of the study were being groomed for an October announcement of the 705 (as the 702's successor), Dunwell and Buchholz began pooling ideas about a system that might supplant the 704 and 705. Dubbing their conjectural system "Datatron," they began issuing a series of numbered technical memoranda under that name. Datatron Memo No. 1, appearing in late August, discussed microcoding, a still-new design idea that seemed to open up the possibility of modifying a computer's instruction vocabulary without altering circuits or soldered wires.[11] They were intrigued by the thought of tailoring one computer to the tastes of disparate classes of customers by reloading a control memory or replacing a plugboard. Other memoranda—variously authored by the two and a few associates—followed, addressing specific topics in lean, technical-paper style.

Dunwell soon felt a need to explain the motives and objectives of the Datatron work. Since the manifesto style of his explanatory memorandum was out of character with the existing series, he chose to back-number the document to zero rather than to label it No. 20. The following excerpt is from the first page of Datatron Memo No. 0, authored by Dunwell and Buchholz and dated 25 October 1954:

The Datatron Program is intended to assure IBM a pre-eminent position in the field of electronic data processing. To do this we must take a giant step and make substantial advances on all fronts. . . . The Datatron is to be equally usable for commercial and technical applications. . . . It is hoped that the scope of the Datatron will extend considerably beyond that of present EDPM machines, and that this will open up entirely new areas of applications. Success in this will permit production facilities to be concentrated on one rather than three machines and will result in a similar concentration in the areas of sales, training and customer engineering.[12]

The authors went on to mention some of the advances they had in mind: solid-state electronics, faster pulse rates, microprogrammed instructions, design automation, automation of manufacture, automatic checking, failure diagnosis, random-access auxiliary storage units, faster input-output units, and improved programming methods. Their reference to "three machines" was to the Type 704, Type 705, and a magnetic-tape sorter that never reached the standard market. From their vantage point as advanced planners, they naturally thought of the announced but undelivered 704 and 705 as "present" machines.

Although Dunwell's brusque style in the memorandum was nicely calculated to attract notice, it was his breadth of vision that held interest. At a time when Learson's council was unsure how to formulate a cohesive development program, Dunwell brought a message about unifying computers. For example, to the oft-debated question whether an arithmetic unit should be designed for decimal or binary arithmetic, his answer was that a system with sufficient flexibility and modularity could provide either or both.

EDPM planners knew that some customers were already demonstrating accounting applications on their binary 701s. This raised the question whether a 704-like system could better the alphanumeric 705's performance on the 705's own ground of accounting applications. If the answer was yes, then one of the stumbling blocks in the way of product unification—customer taste—might disappear; after all, given a little time, tastes have a way of adjusting to product economics. To help settle matters, the director of applied science, C. C. Hurd, arranged for a study of the question and gained the "rational first evaluation" he desired during the second day of a November work session with consultant John von Neumann, Dunwell, and others.[13] Material assembled for the session included various programming exercises comparing the 704 and 705 computers. The binary 704 was duly charged for the processing time required by input-output radix conversions. Offsetting this, it was expected to do some computing during tape operations. The study did not purport to be a product-planning exercise because, as Hurd explicitly noted in his summary, user attitudes, personnel training requirements, and ease of programming were not considered. The only question addressed was how two differing machines with roughly equal amounts of hardware compared in job performance. The study tentatively concluded that a 704 with the input-output units of a 705 should be able to handle a wide range of accounting applications at least as fast as the 705. In jobs with substantial computing, the 704 was clearly the faster system.

About three weeks later, on 2 December 1954, IBM held the first public showing of the NORC. At the invitation of T. J. Watson, Sr., IBM chairman, von Neumann delivered the main address. After complimenting the NORC designers, von Neumann explicitly ignored the ordnance computations that "ordinarily come into one's mind" and mentioned some geophysical problems of increasing importance, notably meteorology, tidal motions, and the hydrodynamics of the liquid core of the earth. Also, as areas ripe for the fastest computers, he nominated "statistical experiments of complicated situations" and "logistic programming"—nontechnical language he chose for referring to Monte Carlo simulation and linear programming, two new mathematical applications. Conceding that profit-and-loss considerations must govern in most circumstances, he then concluded on an emotional note:

It is very important, however, that there should be one case in a hundred where it is done differently. . . . That is, to do sometimes what the United States Navy did in this case, and what IBM did in this case: to write specifications simply calling for the most advanced machine which is possible in the present state of the art. I hope that this will be done again soon and that it will never be forgotten.[14]

In making this point, von Neumann undoubtedly was speaking for the physicists in the audience. Computational limitations had long forced them to approximate complicated interactions among physical laws with highly simplified mathematical models. But they had been finding that relatively modest refinements in the fidelity of a model could greatly magnify the implied computational task. This being the case, computer power had to be recognized as a critical resource in the race for scientific discovery.

Perhaps von Neumann was also speaking directly to the two Watsons, for he knew that at least two of their customers were projecting needs for computers faster than the NORC or 704. These two were laboratories managed by the University of California for the U.S. Atomic Energy Commission (AEC): Los Alamos Scientific Laboratory (LASL) in New Mexico and the University of California Radiation Laboratory (UCRL) at Livermore, California. Two IBM 701s were installed at LASL and one at UCRL. And as an active consultant to Hurd and others, von Neumann knew that nobody in IBM was prepared to write specifications for another "most advanced" machine.

The engineering sector of IBM's business had grown to over 3000 people, in large part because of SAGE and other defense programs. This growth had brought many administrative problems, and W. W. McDowell, engineering director and newly elected vice-president, had been energetically attempting to strengthen his management organization. Among others he had recently brought into his headquarters were Palmer and J. A. Haddad, former managers, respectively, of the Poughkeepsie and Endicott laboratories. Palmer became responsible for all engineering, Haddad for advanced computer development. While these moves were being completed, Learson became vice-president for sales, replacing L.H. LaMotte, and LaMotte and A. L. Williams were named executive vice-presidents. LaMotte's main responsibilities became sales, service, engineering, product planning, sales promotion, and advertising, while Williams took charge of the finance, manufacturing, purchasing, defense contracts, personnel, and legal staffs. By the end of the year, when Hurd succeeded Learson as director of EDPM, the executives expected to cover the large computer area were Haddad, Hurd, and Palmer.[15]

Meanwhile, once his "giant step" memorandum had attracted interest, Dunwell had begun holding occasional meetings concerning the Datatron. Among the fourteen invitees to his late-1954 meeting in Poughkeepsie were Amdahl, Backus, Buchholz, W. J. Eckert, Hurd, and J. C. McPherson.[16] When McPherson wrote the newly appointed Poughkeepsie laboratory manager, H. S. Beattie, for a description of the Datatron, he received a summary ascribed to the "Datatron Committee."[17] The summary postulated a modular solid-state system in which decimal digits were to be represented by a four-bit code and alphabetic characters by an eight-bit code. Features were to include variable field and record lengths (as in the 702), concurrent input-output and computing operations, and automatic checking. Assumed were magnetic-core memory units with cycle times of 6 to 8 microseconds. Assumed also was a 1-megacycle pulse rate. (Among the vacuum tube computers designed with 1-megacycle oscillator circuits were the NORC and the 700 series machines.) In arithmetic speed, Datatron I was projected to be about half, Datatron II roughly equal to, and Datatron III twice the speed of an IBM 704. Hence Datatron III contended not as a superspeed computer but as the top of a modest product family. The summary was boldest on three points: the intention to make the system all purpose; the intention to store inactive programs and business files in a large random-access storage device, "either a disc or airfile device, depending upon the direction taken by the Company"; and the expectation that machine instructions would be executed under the control of microprograms stored in a fast memory or wired in plugboards.

In late December, by which time UCRL was known to be very interested in obtaining a superspeed computer, Dunwell's emphasis veered toward higher speeds. As a result, Datatron figured in McDowell's meeting of 14 January 1955 concerning the "next large technical computer to be produced following the Type 704."[18] McDowell outlined six alternatives: (1) produce NORC, (2) improve NORC, (3) improve the 704, (4) modify the Project High computer, (5) adapt the Datatron to technical work, or (6) develop faster components "for a machine of one hundred times the speed of the 704." Amdahl discussed the outlook for redesigning the 704 and NORC; assuming magnetic-core memory with a cycle of 8 microseconds and a faster multiplication scheme for the 704, he explained, redesigns of both the 704 and NORC would be limited by memory rate to about twice the speed of the current NORC. The Project High machine was discussed only briefly, the consensus being that it lacked product suitability. Buchholz wrote the memorandum of record for the meeting and included a summary of the remarks he had made on the Datatron:

To go beyond the factor of 2 over present NORC speeds obtainable by improving either the NORC or the 704, it is necessary to overcome the limitations set by the 8-microsecond core memory. The 70X (Datatron) does this by providing a small fast memory (equivalent to multiple registers) with 1 or 2 megacycle transistor arithmetic circuits, essentially a computer within a computer. A microprogram system provides the high-speed control necessary to keep the fast computer going efficiently and to reduce the references to the main memory. The 70X may provide a factor of 10 in performance. As long as we are limited by present core memory technology, this seems to be the best performance available.[19]

The new elements proposed for the Datatron consisted of a fast arithmetic unit and of a set of transistorized registers, that is, "small fast" memory for reducing the number of accesses to main memory. Attendees agreed that larger main memories were needed in some technical computations as a way of reducing input-output operations. The meeting did not address McDowell's seemingly rhetorical point concerning components for a machine of one hundred times the speed of the 704. In closing the meeting, McDowell stated that Engineering should develop a solid-state Datatron as rapidly as possible and seek a development contract for a very large core memory.

Hurd's promotion made him fully responsible for pulling together the sales aspects of advanced-machine plans and taking recommendations to senior management. This he did energetically. In a meeting with LaMotte, Learson, McDowell, McPherson, and others on 20 January, he was empowered to "seek Government money to assist us in producing the model for a combined computer and data processing machine."[20] Next day, he made an appointment to visit Edward Teller of UCRL on 26 January.

LaMotte, Learson, McDowell, Birkenstock, and Haddad met with Hurd on 24 January to rehearse questions and answers for Hurd's forthcoming meeting with Teller. It was agreed that Hurd should seek a NORC-type contract (cost plus $1), target delivery for no earlier than

July 1957, specify memory capacity of at most 100,000 words, speak of a solid-state decimal machine with a 2 megacycle pulse rate, and mention 10 to 20 microseconds as the time for floating-point multi-plication. Inasmuch as a majority of computer designers had employed a 1-megacycle clock, the phrase "2 megacycle" hinted at transistor circuits that would at least double the speed of vacuum tube circuits. But overall performance was expected to more than double: lavish use of hardware, combined with a larger instruction set and overlapped input-output operations, would make it possible to outstrip NORC several-fold.[21]

In his meeting at UCRL, Hurd was disappointed to learn that the parent AEC organization wanted a fixed-price contract. Teller was thinking in terms of a $2.5 million contract, and his general require-ments were reasonably compatible with Hurd's projections. Teller was indeed serious; his schedule was to publish system specifications in March, receive bids in April, and make decisions regarding machine and manufacturer in May.[22]

After his return to New York, Hurd urged Amdahl and others to pursue the design of a high-speed computer on a crash basis. The Datatron series of memoranda was soon closed out while a "Nova" series was being launched.[23] But a nova brightens only to fade, someone sourly noted, and the new series faded in a month—perhaps because events were moving too swiftly to permit the preparation and editing of technical memoranda.

Meanwhile, at headquarters, McDowell's management team was slipping into a mood of cautious reassessment. Palmer knew of Hunter's excitement after reading an article on the nature of a "drift" transistor. Hunter was no admirer of the surface barrier transistor, the leading candidate for 2 megacycle circuits, because he felt that its characteristics inherently worked against uniformity in production. The "drift" idea tantalized him with a promise of superior circuit speeds as well as high manufacturing yields, but his laboratory work on it was still inconclusive (see chapter 10). All of this posed a problem for McDowell, who was being urged to clarify goals.[24]

In February, Beattie in Poughkeepsie assigned a dozen key men to a UCRL computer proposal team.[25] Surface barrier transistors were assumed. UCRL's detailed written specifications arrived in mid-March.[26] By late March, the proposal team was keenly aware of an unchar-acteristic lack of enthusiasm on the part of Haddad and Palmer. At headquarters, on 4 April, in a presentation for Haddad, Hurd, and Palmer, the team urged a bid on the Livermore Automatic Research Computer (LARC) and delivered a written recommendation to that effect signed by eight engineers including Amdahl, Buchholz, and Dunwell.[27] The theme of the several-page document was set forth in two early paragraphs:

We are proposing a machine employing the latest and most advanced engineering techniques. The program will force development of transistors, magnetic cores, new components, and system logic to the highest level of the art. The IBM LARC proposal includes automation of construction and design as an integral part of the program.

The proposed technical computer has been specifically designed with the purpose of obtaining a good commercial machine as a modular by-product of the same program.

The proposed computer, referred to in the bulk of the document as the "707," was not outlined in detail. Rather, the power of the 707 was suggested by a comparison attributed to experienced programmers, the gist of the comparison being that "the combined computing and tape speed of the 707 is estimated to be ten to twenty times the speed of the NORC." At the time, the draft proposal for UCRL envisioned a fast memory unit (of capacity 800 words and cycle time 2 microseconds) and two main memory units (each of capacity 20,000 words and cycle time 10 microseconds). Memory accesses could be partially overlapped. Floating-point addition and multiplication were to require 6 and 10 microseconds, respectively. In floating-point format, the sixty-bit word was to represent a twelve-digit decimal fraction accompanied by an exponent and sign.

Haddad and Palmer listened and reserved judgment. The conjectural 707 might suffice, but their main concern had passed from tactical to strategic questions. While proposal plans went forward, headquarters staffs debated the consequences of winning the LARC contract. As recently as January, McDowell had agreed that Hurd might negotiate toward July 1957 delivery; now, in April, he argued that 1957 delivery was made risky by manpower shortages. An exasperated Learson advised LaMotte to proceed "despite the squeeze it puts on us in Engineering" and solve the resource problem by subcontracting.[28] Hurd continued to argue that IBM needed LARC as a product. On 18 April, after all concerned staffs had firmed up their positions, Haddad sought to document Engineering's position, which had come to be that IBM should defer action in the large machine area "until we are ready to talk about machines having 10,000,000 pulses per second or more." It was known, he wrote, that the Bell Telephone Laboratories were working on transistors and circuits in that pulse region.[29] The tug of war within headquarters continued to the last possible moment, at length delaying the team scheduled to fly to Livermore for an oral presentation. The final compromise was to go on with the exercise but to qualify the proposal with a renegotiation clause.

IBM's written proposal of 20 April 1955 to UCRL's purchasing agent comprised a letter and supplementary documents.[30] The letter, signed by Hurd and McDowell, contained this plea:

The University's attention is particularly invited to the fact that, as a result of our study of this program and in the course of preparing the attached proposal, we have become convinced that far greater strides in the computer art than are specifically proposed herein will be possible within the next few years. Accordingly, it is our recommendation that between the time this proposal is accepted by the University and prior to January 1, 1956 the specifications be renegotiated in order that the University will be provided with a well-balanced machine operating in the eight to ten megacycle range similar in character to that proposed herein. Such a machine, which will be delivered in lieu of that specified herein, will be installed on the same time schedule as that for the machine proposed herein but at a cost of $3,500,000. The University's favorable consideration of this alternative is strongly urged since the resulting computer will far surpass that outlined in this proposal.

Consistent with the idea of renegotiating toward a faster computer in lieu of the 2 megacycle machine actually discussed, the proposal mentioned a development period of forty-two months, a period unresponsive to the requirements. UCRL's purchasing agent wrote Hurd on 10 May of a decision to recommend an award to Remington Rand, noting that "predominant in our considerations was the factor of delivery."[31] Remington Rand had proposed delivery in twenty-nine months from date of contract.

Straws of information collected during the proposal exercise reinforced LaMotte's fund of compliments for Remington Rand products, a fund he occasionally drew upon to taunt IBM engineers to additional effort. Hurd, who kept LaMotte informed through summary memoranda, admitted having been shaken when told that UCRL's IBM 701 and its Remington Rand UNIVAC were equally available for customer use, each about 80 percent of the time.[32] Hurd had assumed that the 701, designed later than UNIVAC, would naturally excel in availability.

Palmer's reservations had been instrumental in convincing McDowell that a straightforward LARC contract could shackle IBM to a second-best technology during a period of critical opportunity, thereby jeopardizing the future of the company.[33] The renegotiation idea having failed, the only reasonable strategy left seemed to be to attempt to leapfrog LARC technology. As the funds this strategy was likely to require for circuit and memory development were unavailable within IBM, Palmer soon found himself playing the role of a technical salesman. In May and June, he and Hurd discussed with NSA scientists a plan whereby IBM would undertake two development tasks, one to consist of formulating the functional characteristics of a high-speed computer appropriate to NSA's growing work load, the other to consist of advanced development of the switching and storage components required for such a machine.[34] NSA's experts rejected the plan, judging that the goals for component speeds were too high to be convincing on the basis of existing knowledge.

The rejection was a grim disappointment, as it had been hoped that the plan would lead to an order for a supercomputer. Presumably McDowell and Palmer read of the June 1955 merger that brought Remington Rand Inc. and other firms into a new Sperry Rand Corporation. The merger brought together several strong engineering traditions and created a firm that exceeded IBM in annual revenue. With its LARC contract, the new firm was ahead in the supercomputer race.

Hurd and Palmer visited NSA's research and development director again in late July to see whether any attitudes might be undergoing change. Perhaps because his staff maintained working relationships with Bell Telephone Laboratories and Philco, recognized leaders in transistors, the director still saw no merit in supporting circuit work by IBM. He was cool, also, to the idea of supporting memory research, although Palmer's offer to conduct a seminar for NSA concerning memory was accepted and scheduled for 12 August.[35]

The date agreed to for the memory seminar posed an awkward scheduling problem for Palmer. He made the commitment on Thursday, 28 July, which fell in the first week of a two-week vacation for IBM plants and laboratories. As a result, everybody needed to help prepare the seminar was away. The next day, he reluctantly interrupted the vacations of nine engineers, asking them to return the following week for the sake of merging and discussing ideas about magnetic-core memory. Fortunately for his reputation in Poughkeepsie, the effort produced technical rationales that NSA officials deemed worthy of support.[36] A development task, named "Silo," was assigned to IBM; the task's goals called for cycle times of 2 microseconds in main memory and 0.5 microsecond in fast memory. (See chapter 7.) Another task, named "Plantation" and projected as a study of extraordinary computer capabilities likely to speed the processing of NSA applications, also received informal approval in August (formal approval came the following January).[37]

The $1.1 million that NSA budgeted for Silo and Plantation did not begin to satisfy Hurd and Palmer, who believed that IBM's one good chance of gaining leadership in the large computer race was to contract for a solid-state supercomputer. Since the practical effect of the NSA contracts was to postpone any such opportunity at NSA until the Plantation study ended in 1957, they decided to try selling a super-computer elsewhere, using a preliminary 10-megacycle computer pro-posal prepared under Dunwell's leadership. This proposal was founded on predicated goals for circuits and memories, not on demonstrated versions of such components. Although the goals had been rationally based on IBM's best expertise, unforeseen difficulties might delay their attainment. All development plans involve some degree of uncertainty, but this preliminary proposal clearly went beyond the usual degree. The SSEC, NORC, and 701 designers had followed safer courses, and it may be recalled that von Neumann in December 1954 had called for the most advanced machine possible "in the present state of the art." Nevertheless, in August 1955, under the spell of what they per-ceived as a fleeting opportunity to rectify IBM weaknesses in solid-state technology, Palmer and McDowell agreed to push the capabilities of the Poughkeepsie laboratory to the very limit.

The planned departure from conservative technical policies was no secret, as indicated in August by the term "Stretch" that came to designate the still informal endeavor involving the 10-megacycle ma-chine.[38] Never dignified as an acronym, the term clung as a cryptic reminder of the endeavor's determination to stretch technology.

11.2 Project Stretch Formulation

On the strength of their limited success at NSA, Palmer and Hurd obtained internal approval of a plan for discussing the supercomputer with potential customers. Hurd in a memorandum to LaMotte, Wil-liams, and Palmer summarized agreements reached by the four on 23 August 1955:

1. That I should prepare immediately to obtain a contract for the construction of the machine using ten megacycle transistor circuits with a high speed one-half microsecond memory and a large two microsecond memory. With the above will be appropriate input-output, including high speed card reader, high speed punch, high speed printer, very high speed tapes.

2. The contracted price is to be $3,500,000.

3. . . . we may need to supplement the above amount by $1,500,000.

4. . . . certain risks are involved in going to several agencies simultaneously. We will certainly need to be prepared to accept letters of intent from an agency who wants the machine but does not reply as quickly as some other agency.

5. . . . we would present design objectives with the understanding that the complete specifications would be arrived at following a joint study between the contractors and ourselves specifying the exact set of orders which would need to be agreed upon.

6. . . . we could quote 36 months delivery.

7. . . . the AEC, Navy, Air Force, and RAND constitute good prospects.

8. . . . the market survey indicated 37 machines during the first five years of production at a monthly rental of in the neighborhood of $100,000.[39]

By "set of orders," in point 5, Hurd alluded to "instruction set" in the parlance of the day. RAND, the nonprofit research organization cited under point 7, was being funded by the armed forces.

The participants in this meeting returned a week later to a larger meeting attended by McDowell, Dunwell, and others. It was agreed that Hurd should first contact representatives of the Los Alamos Scientific Laboratory (LASL). Hurd, in his summary report of the meeting, mentioned that he had reviewed for McDowell's benefit what had been done in the way of obtaining research contracts and added that "emphasis was put on the fact that we should not appear to be desperate."[40] He tacitly feared that LASL would order a LARC.

In mid-September, J. P. Eckert of Sperry Rand Corporation outlined his plans for LARC at a national meeting of the Association for Computing Machinery.[41] Floating-point addition and multiplication were to require 4 and 8 microseconds, respectively. The 20,000 word memory planned for UCRL consisted of eight units; the unit cycle time was 4 microseconds, but units could be referenced one after another at intervals of 0.5 microsecond. Magnetic drums would provide for high-speed auxiliary storage. As a result of the technological improvements and additional instructions, Eckert expected LARC to be 200 to 1000 times faster than UNIVAC over a wide range of applications. Eckert was free to discuss his plans because the contract with UCRL had just been signed. He mentioned that Sperry Rand was already planning to build more LARC-like systems.

Meanwhile, Hurd managed to schedule a September meeting at Los Alamos. After hearing IBM's preliminary proposal, LASL management expressed interest.[42] As a result, Rochester's EDPM design department was asked to give increased aid to Dunwell in the form of design studies. The first of a series of technical "Stretch Memos" was dated 1 November 1955. By year end, nineteen of these memos had been authored by Dunwell and others, with Amdahl playing a prominent role in outlining system characteristics. Amdahl, the practiced designer whose soon-to-be delivered 704 was meeting with praise, was envisioning the world's fastest computer to be. Dunwell, the veteran product planner, was thinking not only of such a computer but of the many technical advances and products that would ensue if a suitably large development program could be "sold" to IBM management. As a spokesman for the endeavor, Dunwell began to find the phrase "100 to 200 times the 704" useful as a way of crystallizing the power of the projected Stretch computer. Indeed, assumptions and studies provided him a case for a large improvement. In an IBM 704, a floating-point multiplication took 204 microseconds and a typical floating addition about half that time. Much of the time required for these 704 operations was owing to inexpensive, serial methods of shifting operands and propagating carries; he expected to speed up these processes at the expense of more logical circuitry. If, as projected, floating-point multiplication could be done in less than 2 microseconds and if most supporting activities could be overlapped (that is, the arithmetic unit could be kept fairly busy), then indeed the hypothetical Stretch could run over a hundred times faster than the 704.

Throughout 1955, the mounting expectations engendered by the supercomputer studies had stimulated excellent teamwork within the Poughkeepsie laboratory. But the rapidly shifting organizational patterns required by the studies naturally had encouraged a good deal of jockeying for position. Foremost contenders for Stretch project leadership were Amdahl and Dunwell, two accomplished individuals with sufficiently different backgrounds and interests to hold disparate views concerning design methods and product emphases. Palmer and Haddad favored Dunwell, the long-term IBMer, for a top managerial role. In late December, after learning that Dunwell was soon to be named head of a formal Stretch Project, Amdahl resigned from IBM.[43] (Amdahl was rehired by IBM in 1960.)

In January 1956, Poughkeepsie laboratory activities were realigned into separate research and product development organizations (see chapter 13). Palmer, named acting director of research, acquired responsibility for the activities most concerned with future technologies and for coordinating with research-like work underway in the Endicott and San Jose laboratories. Project Stretch was given a budget and established as a research department headed by Dunwell.

During January, also, LASL formally sought bids for an advanced computer. IBM's proposal, completed in February, requested a year of joint IBM-LASL deliberation concerning user-oriented features of the computer. Proposed floating-point times for the primary arithmetic unit were 0.6 microsecond for addition, 1.2 microseconds for multiplication, and 1.8 microseconds for division. Assumed was a sixty-bit word consisting of a forty-eight-bit fraction, ten-bit exponent, one-bit exponent overflow tag, and one-bit sign. Cycle times were listed as 2.0 microseconds for the 8192-word magnetic-core unit (four of which would comprise main memory) and 0.5 microsecond for the 512-word core unit (two of these were to comprise fast memory). Overlapped memory accesses were proposed as a way of yielding higher effective memory rates than suggested by the cycle time. For intermediate storage, a multiple-disk device with one read-write head per surface was proposed; additional storage was to be provided by magnetic tape.

Nothing was said of "throughput" in the specification section of IBM's proposal to the AEC, but the three-page cover letter included the statement: "The general design criteria for this computer include: suitability and ease of use for atomic energy computing problems, a speed at least 100 times greater than that of existing machines, unattended operation for long periods of time, very great reliability, and ability to expand capacity in modules."[44] The letter also noted that "IBM proposes to perform the work contemplated hereby at a fixed price of $4,300,000." The price came as a shock to LASL managers, who had hardly dared to ask the AEC for $3.5 million, the amount that Hurd had previously discussed with them. The price rise represented a concession that Hurd and McDowell had made to obtain approval from Williams, whose staff had argued that prior discussions should not be construed as including the final proposal's expensive quota of test equipment. Hurd had argued to no avail against risking rejection of a contract that would obtain LASL consulting help and direly needed funding for Stretch.[45]

Dunwell and others made an oral presentation to LASL in March.[46] In April, Hurd received informal reports that LASL's technical committee had decided in favor of IBM's proposal.[47] During the AEC procedural interim that preceded formal approval, the joint IBM-LASL mathematical planning group met to begin considering suitable system characteristics. Contract approval came in November 1956.[48]

The delay in contract approval was advantageous to Dunwell; it meant that the date of delivery, set at forty-two months from date of contract, had slipped to May 1960, giving him extra time for project staffing. Technical personnel were in short supply, as suggested by this item in an IBM Poughkeepsie newsletter: "We have sent 200 recruiters directly to some 37 campuses."[49] Fortunately, high-speed computers had acquired an aura of glamor that aided Dunwell in attracting talent. During summer 1956, his technical planning staff was augmented by Gerrit A. Blaauw, who had joined IBM in 1955, and Frederick P. Brooks, Jr., a recruit. Each had earned a Ph.D. at the Harvard Computation Laboratory for work on the design and application of computers. Also joining the staff, directly from Ph.D. studies at Duke University, was mathematician John Cocke, who had a strong interest in computers. These men were to serve Dunwell's rather fluid organization in various planning and design roles.

Meanwhile, about March 1956, J. C. Logue had become Stretch engineering manager. Previously, as manager of transistor circuit development, he had started complaining that the term "10 megapulse circuit" was insufficiently meaningful for the circuit engineers, who were being forced to mediate between the language of physicists on one hand and that of system planners on the other. Boolean algebra had become familiar, making it convenient for circuit engineers to think of a circuit in terms of numbers of input and output lines, intrinsic logical task (AND, for example), and circuit delay. For the typical switching network, where circuits would have to feed others stage by stage, Logue viewed delay per stage as the critical circuit parameter. He viewed the related question of the number of stages that might be managed before the process had to be resynchronized with a clock signal as a secondary matter governed by numerous engineering choices. The contention over the drift-transistor circuit goal ended when Dunwell agreed with Logue on an average per stage switching delay of 20 nanoseconds under representative operating conditions.[50] (Before 10^{-9} second was termed "nanosecond" by standards organizations, engineers actually used "millimicrosecond," meaning a thousandth of a millionth of a second.) If attained, the 20 nanosecond delay would be shorter by a factor of two or three than the comparable delay for a surface-barrier transistor—a gain that would represent a splendid accomplishment. The decision regarding an appropriate clock frequency was implicitly postponed by adoption of the new goal.

When Stretch managers confidentially described their project in June to an IBM research and engineering audience, Dunwell mentioned in his overview that "the problem testing which we have done to date leads us to believe that the STRETCH machine will be approximately 200 times as fast as the Type 704, and about 170 times as fast as the

NORC."[51] Dunwell also described the current formulation of an input-output system:

> The input-output section of the STRETCH system including the input-output units, the input-output exchange, the input-output computer and the memories has been given the name LINK, to signify that it provides the link between the outside world and the high-speed section of the machine. This portion of the machine is a complete computer with all of the capabilities of our present Type 704 and Type 705 machines. It is capable of operating upon technical problems at approximately ten times the speed of the Type 704 machine, and upon commercial problems at speeds of up to possibly 20 times that of the 705. The LINK system is being designed as an eventual replacement for both the Type 704 and Type 705 EDPM systems. In addition, it would appear to have all of the central computer requirements necessary for the guidance and interception of aircraft and missiles. We think it quite possible that the systems produced by Military Products will use the LINK input-output computer and exchange sections coupled to input-output units of their own design.

Such were his high expectations for a unified product line. He also noted that work was underway on design automation, error checking and correcting, and improved maintainability.

At the same conference, Logue mentioned the circuit goal of 20 nanosecond switching, noting that if attained the goal would permit a computer to operate at many times the speed of a vacuum tube machine. He attributed much of the prospective gain in speed to the reduction in stray capacitance afforded by two inherent advantages of the transistor over the vacuum tube: its smaller dimensions and its capability for operating at lower voltages and with smaller signal swings. Nevertheless, in high speed operation of "upward of 50,000 transistors" packaged within a single machine, he foresaw a formidable problem in the tendency for the rapidly changing electrical signals to radiate energy, thereby attenuating the signals and perhaps inducing harmful signals in nearby lines. One remedial answer being considered was use of coaxial cables in back-panel wiring.

In July, Stretch technical staff manager Buchholz wrote a report listing the advantages of a word length of sixty-four bits. Assuming an m-bit binary field for addressing a sixty-four-bit memory-contained word, he noted, $m + 1$ bits could address a half-word, $m + 2$ bits a quarter-word, $m + 3$ bits an eight-bit segment, and so on until $m + 6$ bits could address a single bit. Using this systematic addressing principle, one class of instructions could address words, and other classes could address shorter operands by increasing the length of an address field.

By this time, the term "byte" had been coined as a way of avoiding typographical confusion between bit and "bite," a term that project personnel had been using to designate small, character-oriented word segments. The sixty-four-bit format was adopted in September; like the previous format of sixty bits, it was accompanied by redundant bits for use by error-detection and -correction circuits.[52]

Emanuel R. Piore, former research vice-president for Avco Manufacturing Corporation and before that chief scientist of the Office of Naval Research, was announced as IBM's director of research in September 1956. In November, as part of a sweeping IBM reorganization, Palmer became manager of product development for the new Data Processing Division. EDPM coordination as a special mission was dropped, and Hurd became director of automation research. Haddad became manager of a newly formed Special Engineering Projects Division.

Meanwhile, IBM and Sperry Rand had been invited to discuss their plans for high-speed computers at the December 1956 Eastern Joint Computer Conference. The UCRL and LASL contracts were no secret, and their technological implications, combined with the drama of a supercomputer contest, lent them audience appeal. Dunwell's planned submission, which concerned Stretch design objectives, was a revision of his June talk to IBM personnel. McPherson wrote Piore in October that Dunwell's paper contained "some very extravagant statements which are hard to justify on the basis of the more specific information included" and advised further internal review of the document.[53]

In the paper that Dunwell presented at the conference, the performance expectation for Stretch on typical technical applications was toned down to "at least 100 times that of the fastest general purpose computer now in use." Dunwell outlined the broad organization of his intended computer system as follows:

The three sections of the computer are an input-output section to maintain communication with the individual input-output units, a serial computer section for editing the flow of input-output data, and a high-speed parallel arithmetic section to operate upon the organized data of the problem. The division of the computer into separable major sections . . . allows . . . the choice of a serial arithmetic mechanism for the complex editing of data, and of a parallel arithmetic system for high-speed operation upon previously organized data.[54]

The serial computer section was described as a versatile computer that could operate in both decimal and binary arithmetic modes and would include instructions for fixed-point and floating-point operation as well as for handling data with fields of variable length.

Dunwell's short description of the parallel-arithmetic section mentioned two floating-point speeds—0.6 microsecond for addition and 1.2 microseconds for multiplication—noting that "approximately 0.2 microsecond should be added to these times for each data word transferred over the bus system between the arithmetic unit and the memory." To these numerical goals, all from the LASL contract, Dunwell added another in the form of a percentage range: "Since the other sections of the system relieve it of all secondary responsibilities, the high-speed computer section will be able to perform useful work on the arithmetic portion of the problem at between 75 percent and 90 percent of its theoretical maximum rate. This compares very favorably with present computers, which spend a large part of their time on secondary operations." The parameters being "stretched" came, with this statement, to include average arithmetic-unit utilization as well as circuit and memory speeds. Dunwell skirted the topic of circuits, referring his listeners to a companion paper in which R. A. Henle discussed IBM's 20 nanosecond goal and the promising results to date with drift transistors.[55]

Dunwell noted that his project was still in the research phase and a number of important design decisions still had to be made. He added that while he was confident continued research would provide satisfactory solutions, forthcoming decisions might have some influence on ultimate speeds. The term "research phase" is often interpreted by skeptical listeners to mean "the outcome is unknown." But this was not what Dunwell meant. His view had been expressed by a clause in the LASL contract that permitted unit capacities and speeds to vary from given specifications by plus or minus 25 percent.

In making his presentation, Dunwell followed J. P. Eckert, who was already a widely known computer engineer. Eckert, whose LARC contract was about halfway to scheduled delivery, reported that his system would be "over 100 times faster than today's scientific computer and internally 1,000 times faster than today's business data-processing system." (These unexplained round numbers, like the one given by Dunwell, are indicative of the feverish atmosphere that prevailed.) The broad outline of LARC had changed little since his description of it fifteen months earlier. The system was being designed as two computers, one for processing input-output data and one for performing main computations. Time was divided into 0.5 microsecond periods by a 2 megacycle clock. In discussing his surface-barrier transistor circuits, Eckert noted that up to eight stages of logic could be fitted into a time period. Including some looseness of fit for safety's sake, this implied an average delay per stage of under 60 nanoseconds.[56]

11.3 System Planning

In January 1957, Project Stretch was reassigned from the research organization to product development, Dunwell's publicly stated need for "continued research" notwithstanding. As Dunwell was learning, compromises have to be made in guiding a large project through the unpredictable circumstances of a changing company environment. The seemingly premature reassignment was urged by a plan for Research to move southward, into Westchester County, to a location some 50 miles away from the Poughkeepsie product development laboratory, Project Stretch's intended home.[57] Dunwell needed a base in Poughkeepsie if the difficulties inherent in two unnecessary moves were to be avoided.

At the time of the reassignment, Project Stretch's broad scope included activities responsible for system planning, parallel computer planning, serial computer planning, exchange planning, design automation, maintenance planning, engineering development, memory development, transistor circuit development, and magnetic-core circuit development. Magnetic-core circuits were thought to hold promise as an economical substitute for transistors in relatively slow applications such as input-output units.[58]

At about this time also, the tests on a novel current-switching mode of operation confirmed that drift-transistor circuits could usefully function at the agreed-upon goal of 20 nanoseconds per level of logic (see chapter 10). This noteworthy achievement gave IBM the basis for a very effective circuit technology.[59]

As a result of work under the Plantation task, the major features of a system suitable for NSA emerged in February.[60] Bearing the NSA-coined name "Harvest," the projected system required high-speed magnetic-tape units (see chapter 6), a central processing unit (CPU) with unusually flexible provisions for handling varied data formats, and a novel unit capable of executing a number of "streaming" commands in conjunction with the CPU. Although the notion was reminiscent of a punched-card collator with its input and output decks of cards, the intended streaming mode of operation was far more versatile than anything previously imagined. Typically, it was postulated, a command would convoke two operand strings by making repetitive memory fetches, perform tasks repetitively upon operand pairs, and return a string of statistics to memory. The command set was assumed

to include matching, substituting by table lookup, tallying the occurrences of specified logical relationships, and other operations of interest
in cryptanalysis. NSA representatives were sufficiently involved and
pleased to strengthen the prospect of a subsequent machine contract.

At this point, Dunwell was not sure how best to mobilize his resources
toward satisfaction of the LASL contract, the anticipated NSA contract,
and a "stripped-down version of Harvest for commercial use."[61] The
degree of uncertainty did not appeal to the engineering manager,
Logue, who argued that basic hardware considerations deserved a
louder voice in the planning deliberations. Logue left Project Stretch
in March to work on standardized circuits (see chapter 10).

The first Harvest manual, which summarized NSA requirements
and discussed the Plantation study's proposed response, became available in May.[62] A few days later, Dunwell commissioned a "3-In-1
Committee" "to study the various proposals for several advanced
solid-state computers to see if a compromise solution could be achieved,
such that IBM could develop three machine systems with a single
integrated engineering program."[63] The committee decided to restrict
its deliberations to the CPUs of the three proposed systems, since
memories, bus systems, and input-output equipment were deemed of
secondary importance in reaching a compromise. Because the Harvest
manual provided more detail than the Stretch plans, the committee
agreed upon Harvest as the starting point for its study of compromise
configurations.

Since Dunwell wanted a response by June, the committee rapidly
narrowed its focus to three hardware units, a CPU called "Basic," a
high-speed floating-point unit called "Sigma," and a Harvest streaming
unit. These names, in turn, were abbreviated B, S, and H. Three
configurations—B and a register bank, B + S and a larger register
bank, and B + H and a still larger register bank—were postulated,
respectively, as the systems needed to provide a successor to the 700
series computers, a senior technical computer (that would also satisfy
the LASL contract), and a specialized system for NSA.

A sixty-four-bit word and binary addressing were assumed for all
systems. Sigma was assumed to consist of an ultraspeed unit for binary
floating-point arithmetic augmented by a "lookahead" unit that could
hold several ready-to-execute instructions and marshal associated operands. Basic was described as an unusually versatile computer with
an instruction set that not only duplicated most Sigma instructions
but included supplementary instruction sets for logic operations and
for decimal and binary arithmetic on variable-length fields. In all
configurations, Basic contained the instruction counter, instruction reg-

ister, index registers, and index adder. In the simplest configuration, Basic was expected to execute binary floating-point instructions, but in the B + S configuration, it was expected to pass such instructions to S for execution. To support Harvest in the course of streaming tasks, the variable-field-length instructions in Basic were required to contain flexible provisions for addressing, reformatting, and code-to-code transformation.

The committee reported two main advantages in having Basic common to all configurations: customers could grow from B into B + S and commonality could reduce engineering, education, maintenance, and manufacturing efforts. It did its best to assess trade-offs involving duplication and unit interconnections. It asked the Stretch engineering groups for first approximations of the number of transistors needed. "Based upon preliminary layouts," the estimate for B was 65,000 transistors. "Based upon extrapolation rather than estimation," B + S and B + H were judged to take about 130,000 and 175,000 transistors, respectively. The hardware duplication caused by including Basic in all configurations was estimated to be well under 10 percent at worst, which was reassuring because a modest amount of duplication seemed a reasonable price to pay for the advantages of commonality.

The committee unanimously concluded that Stretch goals could be met by a three-in-one system, "with the possible exception of price," which was not quantified. It did not comment on the estimate of 65,000 transistors for Basic, a number much higher than the combined numbers of vacuum tubes and diodes contemplated for the IBM 709, which had been announced in January 1957 as a successor to the IBM 704.

Some of the committee's sessions had been stormy. The committee of six consisted of three of Dunwell's engineering planners and three product planners not under Dunwell's command. The latter trio, who argued for a more straightforward approach to the design of the LASL computer and were concerned about the risks inherent in the three-in-one novelties, considered writing a minority report but chose not to prolong a debate that seemed to have considered all available facts. The three-in-one proposal proved attractive to Dunwell, who used it as a guide in reorganizing project assignments.[64]

At the time, all computers popular for accounting applications used decimal arithmetic, and, in the supercomputer class, both IBM's NORC and Sperry Rand's planned LARC were decimal. On the other hand, the fastest computers being marketed on a routine basis, the IBM 704 and Sperry 1103A, had been influenced by von Neumann's early convictions and therefore were binary. At about the time of the three-in-one report, Buchholz wrote a technical memorandum concluding that Stretch would be "binary throughout except for a second decimal adder in the serial computer." His main arguments for the superiority of binary to decimal were threefold: the binary radix involves less round-off error in arithmetic operations, more efficient storage utilization, and less equipment complexity; instruction-contained binary addresses require fewer bits and can be decoded with less circuitry; and binary addressing is particularly convenient for operations involving operand segments and table-lookup conversions. Because of the third advantage, he thought that binary addressing deserved wide use in programming logical expressions, interpreting codes, packing and unpacking data fields that contained leading zeros, and editing of input and output data.[65]

During the summer, Dunwell's circuits group, as well as his design automation group, were split off as independent departments, an action that substantially increased Project Stretch's burden of coordination. Also, as a way of reducing the cost of memory-attendant electronics, Dunwell's memory group recommended doubling the sizes of the fast memory unit (from 512 to 1024 words) and the main memory unit (from 8192 to 16,384 words).[66] In the latter half of 1957, the functional specifications of the LASL computer were agreed upon by Dunwell's system planners, the product planning group, and the IBM-LASL joint mathematical planning group. The focal point of much work had been the instruction set, which had become increasingly elaborate. The "stretch" principle that infected planners made it easier to accept than reject ideas, perhaps especially so because they were in no position to assess accurately the direct and indirect costs of each embellishment. After empirical studies had indicated that instruction fetch was likely to be a system bottleneck, the full-word instruction format was supplemented with a half-word format for floating-point instructions. In November, a preliminary manual that described the instruction set and related facets of the LASL system marked the conclusion of work by the IBM-LASL joint group.[67]

By this time, detailed engineering descriptions were expanding the role of Sigma, which contained the parallel arithmetic unit and the lookahead unit. Functionally, Basic was conceived of as two parts, an instruction unit and a serial arithmetic unit capable of executing byte-by-byte arithmetic and logical instructions. The instruction unit fetched all instructions from memory, indexed instruction-contained addresses to yield effective addresses, and passed the indexed instructions to the lookahead unit in Sigma. Each level of lookahead typically was assigned an in-process instruction. Lookahead not only directed the fetching of operands, coordinated arithmetic tasks, and controlled all store instructions, but it conducted tests to avoid problems of the form where an instruction fetches an operand from memory location m before a previously encountered instruction has completed storing a result in m. Once the complicated logical task of preventing overlapping executions from subverting the instruction-by-instruction intention of a program was allocated to lookahead, the unit became an important control center.[68]

Dunwell's organization consisted of about 180 people in November 1957.[69] This being a large activity, great returns were expected from it. These hopes were dampened late in the year when the air force's Strategic Air Command, while seeking transistorized high-performance computers for a worldwide control system, rejected Basic as too costly. Though Dunwell immediately launched work on the design of a simpler version of Basic called the 7000A, IBM finally won the contract in 1958 with the aid of a design being prepared by its Military Products Division for the (never realized) objective of replacing vacuum-tube SAGE computers. Involved was a binary computer with a 48-bit word, parallel arithmetic, a generous complement of input-output units, a peripheral control unit for handling input-output operations independently of the central processing unit, and four units of core storage— each of capacity 16,384 words and cycle 2.3 microsecond. (In 1961, three of these machines were delivered to the air force under the name AN/FSQ-31(V). The engineering prototype, which was embellished with real-time provisions for managing dozens of telephone and teletype messages, went to the System Development Corporation as the AN/FSQ-32.)[70]

During 1957, it had become increasingly clear that the performance of the LASL computer would be difficult to predict. The usual estimation techniques were simply inapplicable. Typically, the 704 CPU time required of a computation could be estimated by isolating a "kernel," that is, the main program loops known to account for much of the CPU activity; programming the kernel; estimating the number and kinds of instructions to be executed; and then deriving CPU running time from instruction-execution times. This method worked well because 704 instructions were executed one at a time, and the CPU time required for any given operation was independent of the operations that preceded it. These conditions did not hold for Stretch because the design called for a high degree of concurrency among units whose task initiations had to be governed by task completions in related units.

Harwood G. Kolsky, a former LASL mathematician who joined IBM in mid-1957 to work with Poughkeepsie product planners, teamed with J. Cocke, a Stretch system planner who was formulating analytical methods for assessing the relative effects of individual unit speeds upon Stretch program execution. One objective was to throw empirical light upon how many lookahead levels optimized system performance. The idea of studying the internal behavior of computers by simulation exercises was still new at the time, and the two had to pioneer for IBM. They prepared a summary of the delay-producing interactions that governed functional units in responding to requests for service. Given assumed service-completion times for each of the units, their summary made it possible to analyze the activities of the various units during simulated execution of a Stretch kernel by counting the intervals during which each unit was busy, idle (not requested), or waiting (unable to respond to a request because of some logically necessary interlock).

For step-by-step simulation of unit activity, they decided, a step should represent 0.1 microsecond. Given about twenty units to track, clerical simulation was ruled out by the implied volume of tallying, and so their simulation method was programmed for an IBM 704 in November 1957. During execution of their simulator program on a Stretch kernel, one user option was to print raw results as a table in which the typical column corresponded to a given unit and each row to a step. Each printed line displayed the state of all units at the beginning of the step, and simulation of a short Stretch kernel could easily yield a listing 50 feet in length. Very soon, the standard procedure became to print summary statistics instead of raw results.

At the end of 1957, the principal units being considered for the planned LASL system were:[71]

index storage section
fast memory (two units)
main memory (four units)
fast memory bus
main memory bus
input-output exchange
high speed exchange
instruction unit
Basic arithmetic unit
Sigma arithmetic unit
lookahead levels (number to be decided)

The main utility of the Cocke-Kolsky simulator lay in the fact that inputs that could be varied from one run to another. Among the inputs were test kernel, numbers of units (within certain constraints), and unit service times. In the five kernels chosen as representative of the classes of problems most likely to be encountered by Stretch, the percentage of floating-point instructions varied substantially, from 47 to 90 percent.[72] The simulator, liberally designed to accommodate up to eight main memories, four fast memories, and eight lookahead levels, played a significant role in providing information concerning suitable configurations. Because the elapsed times indicated by the simulation studies were dependent upon still-tentative unit speeds, the times taken by one configuration relative to another were given far more credence than were specific timings. That is, the programmed simulator was regarded as an indicator of configuration optimality, not as an accurate indicator of ultimate Stretch performance. A simulator for the latter purpose would have had both to represent even more interactions and to undergo much revamping during later engineering phases of the project.

In April 1958, Dunwell abandoned the three-in-one plan.[73] The truth had to be faced: Basic was too ponderous to be useful to the regular product line. Sigma was redefined to include Basic's functional capabilities, among them serial arithmetic, making it essentially a Stretch CPU. Since cost considerations were urging that equipment be shared wherever feasible, the consolidation was accompanied by considerable engineering redesign of Sigma.

IBM's proposal for Harvest was accepted by NSA in May 1958.[74] Harvest engineering was headed by James H. Pomerene, who before coming to IBM in 1956 had been chief engineer for von Neumann's computer project at the Institute for Advanced Study, Princeton, New Jersey. After the demise of the three-in-one plan, Pomerene's team, which was preoccupied with the streaming unit, redefined Harvest as a Stretch plus the streaming unit.[75]

As a product-design exercise, the three-in-one interim had failed to make Basic a viable product. Viewed sympathetically as an opportunity for intensely motivated systems research, the exercise was more successful; for almost a year it helped make Project Stretch an exciting center for computer-organization studies. True to the venturesome origins of his project, Dunwell had provided a goal-directed climate in which new ideas could be explored and documented. Several of the technical analyses written by Blaauw, Brooks, Buchholz, and others were touched up and published as technical papers.[76] Among the subjects treated were program-controlled interrupts, new uses of control words, ways of harmonizing diverse data formats, and look-ahead principles.

11.4 *Logical Design and Engineering*

Erich Bloch became Sigma engineering manager in early 1958. He had been engaged in research on magnetic-core logic devices, but when that technology was dropped as a serious contender to transistor logic, he was persuaded by Dunwell to help on Stretch. When he arrived, Project Stretch was deep in engineering studies based upon alternative assumptions regarding components, arithmetic-unit algorithms, and system organization. Still needed were firm specifications and conventions for the current-switching drift transistor circuits in the forthcoming Palmer-sponsored family of circuit components. These components consisted of printed circuitry, transistors, and other circuit components packaged on plastic rectangles called "SMS cards." (SMS stood for Standard Modular System, a term seldom used in full.) Palmer had given SMS development a very high priority, and his staff was intent on forcing IBM engineering groups everywhere into using the cards. Bloch found Stretch engineering highly dependent on forthcoming details about the characteristics of the new components; for example, a decision among three competing designs for the parallel arithmetic unit was still hanging on such details.[77]

The information needed became available around April 1958, the very time at which the functional capabilities previously allocated to Basic were being assigned to Sigma. In May, Dunwell's central planners issued a comprehensive manual of operation, thereby providing the engineering group with the last set of specifications needed before starting a detailed logical design of Stretch.[78]

As is well known, the speed of light, approximately 1 foot per nanosecond, limits the speed at which electrical wave fronts can be conducted in circuits (the actual speed being somewhat lower than the limit). In designing with a circuit capable of switching in 20 nanoseconds, the lengths of the wires and cables that interconnect circuits can materially affect operation times; hence circuit-to-circuit distances and wiring methods become critical factors in determining overall speeds. It soon became evident that for some purposes the new SMS card afforded insufficient packaging density. Bloch faced this unhappy prospect by setting up his own circuits organization, which in 1958 developed a so-called "double" card holding four times the transistors of the standard SMS "single" card. His engineers also developed a special circuit discipline, called "third-level logic," that economized on transistors and space in the arrays of circuitry required for the double-word registers of the arithmetic unit.[79] But despite these and other valiant efforts, the prospect of meeting the goals for arithmetic speeds dimmed with every new engineering insight.

In October 1958, Bloch's engineers tested a simplified version of their planned arithmetic unit. This "data-flow model," so called, was carefully debugged and operated in all intended modes of operation. Some difficulties were experienced with faulty transistors, which was not surprising because the transistors used were from early production batches. But the engineers were sobered by the arithmetic speeds they observed. Even after making allowances for the speed-enhancing effects of the double cards still being ironed out with Palmer's SMS standards team, the tests cast doubt on IBM's ability to meet the conditions of the AEC contract. The disappointing results were duly discussed with LASL.[80] Barring the unexpected, it seemed that the contract would have to be modified, perhaps compensating for lowered arithmetic speeds by providing larger storage capacities and higher input-output rates.

During 1958 and into 1959, the engineering groups diligently tuned the system design for a reasonable balance between complexity and cost. Along with other studies, the Cocke-Kolsky simulator was exercised more than a thousand times. Some of the major simulation studies concerned lookahead levels and memory configurations. These studies indicated that Stretch performance would be about as well served by storing instructions in two main memory units (each of capacity 16,384 words) as in two fast memory units (each of capacity 1024 words).[81] The studies also justified a choice of four lookahead levels and six main memory units.

Assembly of the Stretch engineering model began in January 1959. Because the assembly of Harvest also began in 1959, the hard-pressed Poughkeepsie laboratory began to borrow manpower from manufacturing. The Project Stretch headcount in 1959 averaged around 300 as compared with 200 in 1958.[82]

Development uncertainties and seemingly endless design and assembly difficulties, combined with the asynchronous character of the Stretch system, continued to obscure Stretch's ultimate processing power. To avoid wasting time on arguments over still-tentative estimates, Dunwell avoided statements about the subject. The result was confusion. In July 1959, IBM's corporate publication, *Business Machines*, reported that Stretch would be "about 100 times faster than the most advanced computer working today."[83] Ironically, the report appeared while the LASL contract was being modified to permit a slower arithmetic unit and to forgo the 0.5-microsecond memory boxes, embarrassments being compensated for by increasing the capacities of the main memory and the parallel-disk device and by specifying faster tape units. Shortly thereafter, an item buried in an industry publication quoted Bengt G. Carlson, group leader in LASL's theoretical division, as saying of Stretch, "On the average, it will show a 60-fold improvement over IBM 704 speeds, and it will be 100 times as fast in some areas of operation."[84] The article reported that the speeds expected of floating-point operations were, in microseconds: 1 for add or subtract, 2 for multiplication, 7 for division, and 0.65 for loading or storing one word. Possessed of information from Bloch's engineers, Carlson was in a sound position to estimate the average power of Stretch versus the IBM 704 on his applications.

Bloch went to the Eastern Joint Computer Conference in December 1959 with a long, fact-filled report on the engineering characteristics of the Stretch computer.[85] He described Stretch components and organization. He attempted to convey some of the complexity of the system by noting that its operation codes and their modifiers gave Stretch a vocabulary of 735 instructions, several times the number in most computers. He reported that the Stretch CPU contained 169,000 transistors. After mentioning floating-point operation times that agreed with those previously reported by Carlson, Bloch added, "Simulation of Stretch programs on the 704 proved a performance of 100x704 in mesh-type calculations. Higher performance figures are achieved where double or triple precision calculations are required." Because Stretch performance was expected to be highly application dependent, he was in no position to make general statements.

11.5 The Type 7090, First Stretch-Technology Product

During the second quarter of 1958, the manufacturing engineering department in IBM Poughkeepsie renovated portions of a plant building, adjusted the atmospheric conditions in the new area, tested some new equipment, and announced that it was beginning to manufacture drift transistors for use throughout IBM.[86] The transistors that met specifications would go into various kinds of SMS cards and then into computers. What Palmer had dreamed of years earlier was coming true.

Palmer, it seemed, had been impatiently awaiting the new components. While considering the possibility of doubling the power of the IBM 709 (the 704 successor) by redesigning the machine for circuits based on alloy-junction transistors, he had asked an engineering team whether twelve months would suffice for the job. After arguing that no period under eighteen months was feasible, the engineers had returned in March 1958 with an estimate of the cost, adding that a version built of Stretch components would cost only 10 percent more and yield a machine with the power of six 709s. Palmer, who as mentioned earlier was heading product development, asked the team to lay out a design for the faster machine, soon termed 709TX.[87] He did not bother to inform the Data Processing Division's product planners, who were advocating a Stretch-related 7000A machine with a forty-eight-bit word and later were distressed to find Palmer endorsing a transistorized machine with the conventional thirty-six-bit word.

Things were brought to a head when Sylvania Electric Products Inc. became interested in transistorized computers. Sylvania was the data processing subcontractor to RCA Corporation, prime contractor to the U.S. Air Force for BMEWS (Ballistic Missile Early Warning System). While Sylvania was considering suitable computers, the military mandated the use of solid-state computers. Sylvania was forced to shop for transistorized computers on a very taut schedule—it needed first deliveries in about eighteen months. The new requirement became known at a time when IBM's computer plans were in disarray. Stretch and Harvest were demanding more and more manpower, and it was questionable whether Stretch memory development could support an eighteen-month schedule. But Sylvania's needs seemed to Palmer a fine business opportunity and he brushed all reservations aside. Every possible short-cut to 709TX implementation was seized upon: not only memory unit and circuits but back panels, frames, and power supplies were borrowed from Stretch designs. In late June, the 709TX was proposed to Sylvania.[88] In competitive bidding, the 709TX had one distinctive advantage: Sylvania could write programs for the 709 and soon obtain a 709 on which to debug them. The 709TX, which would execute 709 programs, therefore could protect Sylvania's investment in programs with minimal disruption to schedules.

By October, when Sylvania tendered an order for 709TXs, Learson had decided to announce the system as the 7090 Data Processing System, a product with five times the CPU performance of a 709 at a price increase of a third.[89] The memory was announced with a 2.4 microsecond cycle, making it five times faster than the 12 microsecond 709 memory.

Shortly after IBM Poughkeepsie had begun manufacturing drift transistors, plant management realized that its facility could never meet the growing demand. Although hurried arrangements were made for Texas Instruments to manufacture additional transistors, the components were in short supply for an uncomfortably long interim. By July, the Stretch project was contending with the 709TX project over priorities.[90] When Bloch's engineers needed more transistors for their arithmetic data flow model, Dunwell flew to Texas and persuaded TI management to remove "a thousand or so" transistors from test racks. He carried the transistors to Poughkeepsie, boasted of his success to Palmer, and was thoroughly outraged by Palmer's decision to allocate them to the 709TX project.[91] Dunwell's subsequent allegation that the 709TX manager had overstated requirements forced a laboratory investigation, but no impropriety was discovered.[92] Before long, the 7090 program was aiding Dunwell by sharing the responsibility for Stretch-component debugging.

Until mid-1959, the 7090 designers made do with test equipment that simulated some of the behavior of a Stretch memory unit. Since the cycle of the forthcoming memory was predicted to fall in the range 2.0 to 2.4 microseconds, they provided for some give and take in timing. They assumed a 5 megacycle clock, which yielded a clock period of 200 nanoseconds, and based their design on twelve periods per memory cycle. Working with six to eight stages of logic per period, they assured themselves a sufficiently loose fit to permit some reduction in period length. When the memory group finally assured them a cycle of 2.2 microseconds, they decided to speed up their machine. Since the 5 megacycle clock suited a memory cycle of 2.4 microseconds and it was easy to see that a 6 megacycle clock implied a memory cycle of 2 microseconds, someone hastily assumed that a 5.5 megacycle clock would match the desired 2.2 microsecond memory cycle. Quartz crystals, duly ordered, had arrived before it was noted that twelve of the new periods would actually sum to 2.181818 . . . microseconds. Probably no designers in IBM's experience had ever been more schedule-conscious. So rather than spend time reordering crystals, they badgered the memory group into agreeing to the slight additional speed-up.[93] Henceforth the memory cycle would be expressed as 2.18 or 2.2 microseconds, depending on the speaker's choice in rounding.

While accommodating the 2.18 microsecond memory, the 7090 designers incorporated other improvements that reduced the time required for multiplications, divisions, and some of the other instructions. Where the 7090 had been announced as five times faster than the 709, these changes made it over six times faster.[94] Stretch technology reached the marketplace on 30 November 1959, when the first two 7090s were delivered to Sylvania at Needham, Massachusetts.[95] The 7090 went on to become an exceptionally successful IBM product.

Later, many IBM designers were to employ Stretch components. The IBM 7080, announced in January 1960 as a higher-performance successor to the IBM 705 III, was constructed of the same components as the 7090. The IBM 7094, announced in January 1962 as having 1.4 to 2.4 times the internal speed of the 7090, was based heavily on the Stretch double-card circuits and a memory-cycle reduction to 2.0 microseconds. The 7090 designers had been able, by a fortunate coincidence, to pack two 7090 words (each of thirty-six bits) into the Stretch memory word (seventy-two bits). The 7094 designers further exploited this coincidence to reduce substantially the number of instruction fetches. Further technological improvements and various degrees of overlapping gave the 7094 II, announced in May 1963, about twice the speed of the 7094.[96] Beyond these direct applications of Stretch technology, many others filtered into the product line.

11.6 *The 7030 Program*

In May 1959, an IBM reorganization carved two new divisions, called General Products Division (GPD) and Data Systems Division (DSD), from DPD. The missions of the two were to develop and manufacture data processing systems—GPD the smaller systems, DSD the larger. The Stretch and Harvest systems being well into their assembly phases, Dunwell was promoted to DSD systems development manager, reporting to assistant general manager C. R. DeCarlo. Buchholz remained with Dunwell. Blaauw was already at work designing a new product system for DSD. Brooks and Cocke had joined the Research organization.

After the reorganization, DSD's plan for an IBM 7030—a top-of-the-line product version of Stretch—soon ran into obstacles raised by schedule slippages and concerns over mounting costs. As a result, DeCarlo arranged for a technical audit, that is, a review by IBM experts not connected with the project. In December, the audit foresaw a three-month delay in Stretch and urged that various risks be countered by delaying 7030 announcement until Stretch had been tested and delivered to LASL. The audit committee noted that Project Stretch had contributed much to the development of memory, disk, tape, and system technologies, as well as frames, cards, circuits, and power supplies for the SMS program. It defended the Stretch-related cost overruns, saying "it is doubtful that a complete financial control procedure would have reduced significantly the cost of these same accomplishments."[97] As one result of the audit, the assembly effort was strengthened by a loan of twenty engineers from the Federal Systems Division.

Since the Stretch project was in trouble, Dunwell stepped down to devote full time to it, and a new DSD systems development manager was appointed. More bad news came in January 1960 when a substantial delay in the Stretch disk file was predicted by a technical audit in San Jose.[98]

While the sales organization worried about the negative impact of a delay in 7030 announcement, inquiries about Stretch were coming in from various computing centers, among them Lawrence Radiation Laboratory (formerly known as UCRL), the U.S. Weather Bureau, and Dahlgren Naval Proving Ground. Finally, in April 1960, IBM's intentions were clarified when shareholders at the annual meeting were told by Tom Watson of a new class of computers. As described in a press release:

The $10-million-and-up class computers are the world's fastest and most powerful. They are similar to the STRETCH computer which IBM is now completing for the Atomic Energy Commission at Los Alamos, New Mexico. IBM will now contract with business firms and government agencies to build STRETCH type computers. They can complete 100 billion computations in a day. The new machines are seventy-five times faster than the large-scale IBM 704 computer, yet occupy no more floor space than a single 704. STRETCH class computers will perform more computations per dollar than any other system in the world.[99]

At the time of this announcement, the Federal System Division, having passed its peak work load in building SAGE computers, was preparing to construct 7030 computers at its plant in Kingston, New York.

During 1960, the 7090 computer was proving to have about seven to eight times the power of the 704 in scientific computations. DSD product-planning studies placed 7030 average performance at about eight times that of the 7090, but some analysts were nevertheless concerned about the ambiguities underlying the estimate. They worried lest they be misled by estimates too heavily predicated upon the times required for arithmetic operations.

In December 1960, after IBM's indecision over contract terms had occasioned considerable delay, an AEC purchasing agent ordered a 7030 on behalf of Lawrence Radiation Laboratory (LRL).[100] The contract called for a 7030 functionally equivalent to the LASL Stretch system at a price of $13.5 million with delivery in October 1961. Subject to an imprecision of 10 percent, the average times for floating-point operations were given as follows (in microseconds): load or store (0.83), add or subtract (1.38), multiply (2.48), and divide (9.00). Disk storage capacity was 2 million words with a read-write speed of one word every 8 microseconds, thereby halving the capacity and data rate expected a year earlier.

In early February 1961, by which time Stretch was operable, DeCarlo wrote a sobering memorandum to the DSD general manager. The subject was Stretch. Unhappily, after two weeks of trials with IBM and LASL programs, it appeared that the system was slow by a factor of two; it was operating at "approximately four times 7090 performance." The reasons for this were still not clear: "With respect to raw operation speeds—mentioned in the Livermore contract—it appears that the machine executes according to specifications. The one possible exception to this is the *Store* instruction. However, when the machine executes all of its instructions in complicated programs, the actual efficiency of the system falls below what these raw speeds might indicate."[101] Not only were Store operations lagging, but it was soon discovered that most program branches were taking longer than expected. Too often, the effect of such delays was to idle the arithmetic unit. Although no contract had mentioned branch times, the omission had little bearing on IBM's predicament. In discussions of the fate of the 7030 computers, it was not the letter of the LRL contract that prevailed—it was the spirit expressed by an anguished IBM salesman, "I feel that I have sold something that does not do the job reputed to it."[102]

On the basis of additional Stretch runs in February and March, LRL observers rated 7030 performance for their work load at about five times 7090 performance—versus an expected eight times. DSD management agreed in principle and, after some hurried analyses, reduced the price of the 7030 from $13.5 to $7.78 million. The system was then reoffered to eight potential customers with whom negotiations were underway. Beyond that number, the system was withdrawn, since each 7030 was calculated to lose money. Tom Watson, keynote speaker at the May 1961 Western Joint Computer Conference, broke the news of the 7030 price reduction at a WJCC press conference.[103] The LASL Stretch could not well be celebrated in the fashion of the ASCC, SSEC, and NORC ceremonies; in an ironic contrast, this press conference served as its main completion fete. Watson pointed out that Stretch was late in delivery, failed to meet its specifications, and cost IBM far more than expected, confessions that muted his point that it was the world's fastest and most capable computer. IBM had been humbled, and Watson's embarrassment touched the whole IBM technical and sales community.

11.7 Stretch Delivery and Assessment

Stretch left Poughkeepsie in vans on Sunday evening, 16 April 1961, bound for Los Alamos. A month later, after acceptance tests had been successfully completed, custody of the system passed to LASL.[104]

Kolsky, by this time a manager in the San Jose research laboratory, went to a July 1961 meeting at LASL. His trip report included the cheering note that "the people at LASL who are actually using STRETCH . . . are almost uniformly happy about the machine. They feel that it is very reliable (having run as much as 17 hours without stopping and without a single error), easy to use, and quite fast."[105] LASL operated its Stretch system for ten years.

The LASL Stretch system included a bank of six core storage units that communicated with a central processing unit, an input-output exchange, and a special exchange called the disk synchronizer. A word consisted of sixty-four information bits plus eight check bits, and each storage unit held 16,384 words—the six units as a bank providing a memory of 98,304 words. Since the storage units could operate on an overlapped basis, as many as six memory accesses could be in various stages of completion at any given time. Memory addresses 1 through 31 were reserved for special registers (addresses 1–15) and index registers (addresses 16–31). These registers were variously constructed of fast cores or transistors, and two of the special registers served as a double-word accumulator.

The design of the CPU's instruction and lookahead units provided for a high degree of concurrency. Up to eleven successive instructions could be in CPU registers at various stages of execution: undergoing address modification, awaiting operands from memory, waiting for or being processed by arithmetic units, or waiting for a result to be stored in memory.

A disk file of 2^{21} (2,097,152) words was connected to the disk synchronizer (additional files could be accommodated, and LASL later obtained a second). The disk array transmitted at a rate of 125,000 words per second, which meant that in less than a second the entire content of memory could be copied or reloaded. Attached to the input-output exchange, through control units, were twelve IBM 729 IV magnetic tape units, a 1000-card-per-minute card reader, a 600-line-per-minute printer (the chain printer described in the next chapter), a 250-card-per-minute card punch, and an operator's console.

Among the advanced features of Stretch were sophisticated provisions for multiprogramming, a mode of operation in which two or more application programs share the capabilities of a CPU. Such a mode permits an application with sporadic demands for service to interrupt another program of lower priority; it also facilitates fuller utilization of system resources, as when an application with heavy usage of the arithmetic unit is run in conjunction with an application mostly concerned with input-output units. To manage multiprogramming activities safely, the hardware design provided for memory protection and for program-controlled interruption, while the software plans assumed a control program for monitoring all input-output instructions and managing (interrupting or starting) all application programs. Two special registers set by the control program determined the sector of memory available to an application program; any attempt to outreach the limits resulted in an interruption that activated the control program.

No computer design can guarantee error-free operation, the most likely error usually being that of garbling one bit during transmission of a word. While the Stretch designers could hold this probability to a very low level, the margin of safety was tempered by the large number of words their machine would move per day. To meet this problem, they designed checking hardware that with the aid of the check bits in every word could detect and immediately correct a one-bit error. The less likely event of an error involving two bits of a word was detected, at which point an indicator in a special register was set and the active program was interrupted momentarily to permit the system control program to turn off the indicator and repeat the faulty transmission, which usually corrected matters. The designers applied the principle of internal indicators and interruption to a number of other exceptional events as well, among them errors detected by special circuits for checking arithmetic processes.

The Stretch instruction set included rich subsets for floating-point arithmetic operations, binary indexing operations, and VFL (variable field length) operations. Greatly expanding the effective number of VFL instructions were modifiers that controlled the radix (binary or decimal), sign usage, disposition of result (to accumulator or memory), and other choices. A field was addressed at the left-most bit, the length was specified, and the field could cross word boundaries. There were provisions for logical operations and radix-conversion operations as well as for arithmetic operations.[106]

In view of the disappointments attending Stretch, various levels of IBM management naturally sought after-the-fact analyses. Carlson's informal judgment that "the most impressive thing about Stretch is that it works" was apparently intended as an accolade to Bloch and his engineers for carrying through an obviously difficult job.[107] Carlson, it seemed, was resigned to the problems of pioneering. He had suffered a delay as the first 701 customer, and he had done so again with Stretch.

Palmer reviewed the technical facets of the Stretch project in a six-page memorandum. In referring to the 1954–1955 period, he summarized technical motivations that most IBMers had either forgotten or never known: "IBM was behind competition both in device and circuit development. In view of the state of knowledge on transistors and core memories, the STRETCH program was a high risk program intended to force IBM by firm commitment into a lead position."[108] Written in May 1961, his memorandum had a dispirited tone that conveyed disappointment. It concluded, "My own opinion is that the STRETCH program did provide IBM satisfactory product material."

Other experts were consulted as well. Ralph E. Meagher of the University of Illinois, a highly regarded IBM consultant, conducted the analysis that proved to be influential with key executives. He commended the many technical achievements of Project Stretch and observed that the project had needed and benefited from Dunwell's strong leadership. He thought that the Stretch computer had been endowed with too many instructions and embellishments, thereby adding to the difficulty and cost of design and construction. But his most incisive conclusion was that a fundamental mistake had occurred early in the project when attainable circuit speed must have been misjudged from sparse experimental evidence. Although he could not reconstruct how this had happened, he recalled that his colleagues at the University of Illinois computer laboratory had been unable to substantiate the original Stretch goals "by about a factor of 2." Meagher was not asked to address the soundness of IBM's commitment to Project Stretch, a matter concerning which he revealed some puzzlement. Thus it lends perspective to his conclusion to recall that McDowell and Palmer had gambled with the project before their physicists, circuit engineers, logical designers, and system planners had been given the usual amount of time to take careful stock of their work and develop adequate means of communication among disciplines. The "10 megapulse" terminology that took root in 1955 and persisted into 1956 illustrates the kinds of problems that resulted. The pulse rate finally adopted as optimal was a third of that, partly as a result of advances in circuits and circuit usages that increased the reasonable number of stages of logic per clock period, and partly because the delay per stage proved to be longer than originally implied.[109] For the

confusion, a toll was eventually paid in the form of serious misun-
derstandings and bitter disappointments.

Tom Watson asked Learson for a report on the lessons learned
from Stretch. The reply was organized around important management
points, tangible gains, and recommendations for avoiding similar situations. The management points were:

1. To undertake a product development project that represents 100 times
    improvement over the existing State of the Art, with guaranteed spec-
    ifications and delivery dates, is fundamentally unsound.
2. To endeavor to estimate correctly at the outset the cost of such a project
    is not possible. . . .
3. That compromises in the original concept and design were made during
    the next five years is par for the course, that the effect of these com-
    promises on throughput was not known until the machine was operable,
    was an error that could have been avoided. Simulation methods would
    have determined this to a large degree, but were dropped because
    expenses for the project were so out of balance with projected cost.
4. To establish a marketing program for additional models, particularly
    since throughput could not be guaranteed, was an error.
5. To plan to go into production on additional models with full knowledge
    that the technologies involved in the model equipment had been ob-
    soleted represented poor management coordination.[110]

No summary of business principles and mistakes could more succinctly
pinpoint the main sources of difficulty in the Stretch and 7030 programs.
Point 5, however, probably mischaracterized Stretch technology as
"obsolete"—the crux of the matter being that IBM laboratories had
continued some work on faster circuits while the Stretch schedule was
slipping a year.

The tacit scapegoat in Learson's report to Watson was the management process that had endorsed the 7030 product program. Concerning a modus operandi for the future, the report commended the
wisdom of more carefully separating product development from advanced development, of basing advanced-development projects strictly
on incurred costs and best-effort commitments, and of always evaluating new products in the cold light of empirical performance data.

Both Meagher's analysis and Learson's report were prepared within
the context of a computer industry that in five years had advanced
remarkably in sophistication. Neither document was able to recreate
the almost pathological atmosphere of optimism—and its corollary,
fear of being left behind—that had characterized the 1954–1956 era
and produced the Stretch program. Dunwell had been trapped, un-

fortunately, in an endeavor that by its very nature lacked a carefully planned "fall-back" alternative in case of a circuit-speed or memory-speed disappointment. (Years later, he would recall that "the transistor circuits did not run as fast as we hoped they would. They were slow by a factor of two.")[111] The attractive course of action had been to attempt to compensate by obtaining an extra measure of improvement from parallelism. This turned out to be impossible in the given time frame and the attempt finally had to be subordinated in a desperate effort to complete the system.

Dunwell knew that Project Stretch had yielded superior technologies and system concepts and believed that this would become obvious in retrospect. But the Stretch disappointment and adverse publicity had undercut his effectiveness as a product-development manager. In latter 1961, he began a second career at the Thomas J. Watson Research Center. Since his transfer from Research at year-end 1956, in Pough-keepsie, the organization had grown, moved to northern Westchester County, and greatly changed in circumstances. The main Research Center, where he was to work, occupied a curved laboratory building designed by Eero Saarinen. The quiet tenor of the place contrasted with all his many years of experience. He put big computers out of mind and began a study aimed at developing methods for the new field of computer-aided instruction.

Harvest was accepted by NSA in February 1962. This massive system, said to be almost twice the size of Stretch, was extolled ten years later at an NSA honorary event for Harvest designers; it was operated for fourteen years. Nine Stretch machines were built: the original for LASL, seven under the 7030 program, and one as part of Harvest. LASL, after operating its Stretch for a decade, held a seminar on the "Historical Importance of the Stretch Computer." Among the assembled Stretch contributors were Buchholz and Dunwell, invited speakers.[112]

11.8 Epilogue

In early 1963, IBM inaugurated a fellowship program intended to reward the creativity of engineers, programmers, and scientists with exceptionally distinguished records of achievement. Appointees were to be given full freedom in choosing and carrying out research projects within their fields. The program was advanced as IBM's highest form of recognition for technical employees. Among the first round of IBM Fellows was Ralph Palmer, who was cited for conceiving the 604 calculator, directing development of the 701 and 702 systems, and assisting in the development of the 7000 series systems.[113]

On 8 April 1964, one day after IBM had announced a sweeping new product line called System/360, Dunwell wrote to Tom Watson.[114] The text of his letter follows:

The new System/360 is in many respects the image of STRETCH. It is important to me that you know this, for I hope that in time you will look upon the STRETCH contribution to our technical heritage as an excellent bargain.

Attached is a partial list of System/360 system features whose first appearance in an IBM machine was in STRETCH.

Also attached is a book edited by Dr. W. Buchholz setting forth the design considerations for STRETCH. This book contains sections by several of the principal contributors to System/360. Most of the new system features of System/360 are discussed between its covers.

Among the concepts listed were multiprogramming, memory protection, generalized interrupt, memory interleaving, lookahead, eight-bit character, and standard interface for input-output equipment. The book that Dunwell attached had previously explained them and provided a permanent record of the detailed characteristics of the Stretch computer.[115]

Watson replied a few days later, making two points: "There has never been any question in my mind but that the money we spent on STRETCH has been a good investment from the standpoint of technological fall-out of the project. I do believe, however, that our customers and the top management of this corporation were led to believe that the performance objective was being achieved when, in fact, we were falling short of it."[116]

At IBM's Annual Awards Dinner in March 1966, at the close of the awards ceremonies, Dunwell was one of two men named an IBM Fellow. Tom Watson, the invited speaker, set aside his prepared notes and explained that he was limiting his remarks to Dunwell because some events "over the last few years" had not been fair to him and because "Red Dunwell in his STRETCH machine, as well as in many other machines, has been a major contributor to the success of this business." Recalling the 7030 price reduction at the press conference in 1961, Watson went on to say,

What I didn't stress and what I should have stressed was the fact that this was the lead machine at the time in the whole world. . . . from this machine derived most of the commercial features that enabled us to prolong the

700 line into the 7000 line. . . . I fear . . . the great contribution of STRETCH to our whole future in IBM got obscured and muddy. And I think tonight at long last the situation is clarified. I think that the Corporation, perhaps belatedly, has shown Red and his family what we really think of him, how much we prize his contributions, and I just thought I would take the opportunity of publicly trying to correct the record in saying that as an old-time salesman I repriced a product so that it would sell and in doing so perhaps besmirched some of the great contributions of that product.[117]

Watson, speaking in early 1966, carefully limited his remarks to the benefits derived from Stretch by way of the 7000 series. At the time, the unqualified success of his new product line—a family of compatible computers that accommodated both the binary scientific and decimal accounting traditions—was still beclouded by a host of software difficulties. Had he been speaking one or two years later, by which time full success was assured, he might have dwelled upon the role that Stretch had played as an experimental testing ground for daring ideas and upon Project Stretch as the regimen that had cleared the way for the "giant step" of System/360.

Dunwell had helped develop a bold plan, suffered the indignity of having much of it fall apart piece by piece, and yet by steely determination saved enough to leave deep imprints upon all subsequent IBM computers.

12

Broadening the Base

Electronics and accounting machines. The Type 1401 data processing system. Other 1400 series computers; the Report Program Generator. High-speed printers; the chain and train. Document reading machines. Small scientific computers; process control. Teleprocessing and the SABRE system.

In the early 1950s, even the smallest stored-program computer was more expensive than a typical installation of punched-card machines. The $3250 minimal monthly rental of IBM's 650 — the least expensive computer the company had installed by 1956 — would support an impressive array of punched-card machines. That figure would cover, for example: two accounting machines (Types 402 and 407); two re-producers, usable also as summary punches for the accounting machines; two sorters; a collator; an electromechanical multiplying punch; half a dozen keypunches and verifiers; and several hundred dollars for miscellaneous equipment and supplies.

Thus the computer was as irrelevant to many punched-card users as to the small businesses whose accounting procedures were un-mechanized. It also left unchanged the practices of many firms whose accounting involved special types of documents and industries with information processing requirements (such as process control) that were not yet widely viewed as applications for digital computers. Nevertheless, before the computer could realize its potential, these small businesses, special industries, and unfamiliar environments would have to be considered in its planning. This chapter is concerned with technical developments that began with the earliest efforts in IBM to widen the range of enterprises and applications its computers could serve effectively.

12.1 Electronics and Accounting Machines

IBM had continued after World War II to develop and introduce "unit record" machines, as punched-card equipment was called in the computer era. Outwardly, "modernized" gray covers distinguished the new products from the somber black prewar machines. New electromechanical components such as the wire-contact relay were substituted for less efficient ones. But the functions of the machines were largely unchanged. New machines of traditional types announced in the ten years from 1946 through 1955 included the Types 602 and 602A electromechanical multipliers (introducing division), Types 402 and 407 accounting machines, sorters, collators, reproducers, interpreters, keypunches, and a long list of others. As late as 1959, the Type 84 sorter was introduced, operating at 2000 cards per minute—twice the speed of the Type 83 announced only four years earlier.[1]

The 603 and 604 electronic calculators appeared also during that period. And the 607, announced in 1953, had more than triple the flip-flop storage of the 604. But the electronic calculators were essentially only elaborations on their predecessors, the electromechanical multipliers. They did not alter in any dramatic way the procedure of carrying decks of cards from machine to machine for the successive processing steps of an accounting application.

IBM's product forecasters expected no reduction in the field inventory of unit-record machine installations for many years, and they were right.[2] The company's annual income from traditional punched-card machines exceeded that from electronic data processing equipment through the 1950s and was still growing until the early 1960s.[3] This trend long encouraged advocates of unit-record equipment, who could always point out applications in which the convenience and simplicity of punched-card methods outweighed the higher speeds and greater economy of storage afforded by tape.[4]

The accounting machine, or tabulator, was the mainstay of the unit-record product line, being essential for the preparation of printed reports and documents. But its arithmetic capability, limited to accumulation in wheel-type counters, invited electronic enhancement. The resulting faster, more versatile machine could be expected to eliminate the need for costly stand-alone calculators such as the 604 and to withstand the competitive onslaught that many IBM product planners felt was bound to occur. Several planning and exploratory engineering projects in the Poughkeepsie laboratory sought as early as 1953 to apply electronics to accounting machines.[5]

Initially, there was no great urgency about these projects. It appeared that the combination of a 604 or 607 calculator and the efficient new 407 accounting machine would meet the needs of U.S. customers. In Europe the situation was different. Accounting practices there—in banks, for example—required more calculations per account each week than those in the United States. Furthermore, import restrictions and high tooling costs deprived the European marketplace of the 407 accounting machine.[6]

IBM had done business overseas for decades, and that business had expanded rapidly after World War II. By 1949, when the IBM World Trade Corporation was formed as a wholly owned subsidiary to centralize the top management of its overseas activities, IBM products were installed in seventy-nine countries.[7] Some of the European companies of World Trade had their own manufacturing plants. Laboratories or engineering departments in those countries developed special versions of IBM machines, or standard-machine attachments for which there were requirements in Europe. The most experienced engineering staffs were those of the French and West German laboratories, then located in Paris and Sindelfingen, respectively.

Arthur K. Watson, the Yale-educated younger brother of Tom Watson, Jr., became general manager of the IBM World Trade Corporation in 1952. The debut in that same year of a competitive calculator from the French Bull Company caused concern in the marketing departments of the European IBM subsidiaries. IBM's French laboratory had developed an accounting machine that vied in performance with the 407 despite its bar-type printer technology. But the Bull Gamma 3, as the new competitive entry was named, consisted of a 604-like electronic calculator attachable not only to a reader-punch but to an accounting machine. Delay-line memory gave various models of the Bull machine greater storage capacities, at lower rentals, than the corresponding models of IBM's 604 and 607 calculators. Its calculating speed, and the fraction of the card cycle available for calculation, exceeded those of the IBM calculators. The Bull machine's reader-punch was faster by 20 percent and the cable-attached combination of calculator and accounting machine was unavailable in IBM's product line.

Top executives of World Trade companies made their discomfort known in communications and personal visits to corporate headquarters. The result was that a committee consisting of engineering and planning people in the domestic laboratories met frequently during 1954 to consider the feasibility of building a "modular" line of electronic calculators and accounting machines. The goal was to employ functional elements (such as arithmetic units and registers) of common design in a large variety of machines capable of covering a wide range of applications.[8] It was a general assumption that transistors offered the best hope of meeting this need. This assumption was not based on any successful experience, as early as 1954, with procurement or manufacture of consistently good transistors at low cost. It derived, rather, from engineering considerations that pointed to the likelihood

of continuing improvement in quality and reduction in cost of transistors. For tubes and their associated components, by contrast, there
seemed little hope of substantial cost reduction.

Committee deliberations continued for many months, during which
the membership of the committee changed frequently.[9] There was no
real consensus during 1954 on the kind of machine that would best
meet the need—whether its features should be primarily those of an
accounting machine or those of a calculator. Some favored stored-
program control; others advocated plugboards as the most efficient
form of control for small-to-medium machines.

The last report, issued in February 1955, did not address the matter
of control. It simply proposed establishing a "modular accounting
calculator" (MAC) development program to replace a group of at least
five projects then in the planning stage. Economic feasibility of a MAC
line had been shown, it stated, for the range from a "calculating
accounting machine" at the low end to just below the announced 700
series computers at the top. Technical feasibility, the report added,
extended further downward to the 604. MAC was proposed as the
only means of guiding "through a series of system expansions . . . a
large group of accounting machine customers who will someday employ
EDPM systems." "Modularity" was left almost completely undefined,
but considerable power was attributed to the concept: "One production
line would surely be more efficient than twelve."[10]

There was a good deal of support for a MAC program, although
it left unanswered many questions besides that of stored-versus-plugged
program. One unanswered question was whether "modularity" truly
could reach downward to the 604-607 area—that is, whether the solid-
state successor to the company's popular electronic calculators could
be part of the MAC program. Particularly interested in this question
was Maxwell O. Paley, an engineer who had joined IBM at Poughkeepsie early in 1949 and had helped to solve problems on the 604
during its early production phase. He had later been the engineer in
charge of the 607 calculator development and thereafter the experimental "transistorized" 604. (See chapter 10.) The latter machine
having been successfully demonstrated, Ralph Palmer argued for limited announcement of a similar machine that would include core storage
as well. By taking advantage of the relative simplicity of the electronic
organization of the 604 and its rather low circuit speed requirements,
he could thus prove the feasibility of transistors in an established
product architecture.

In the spring of 1955, Palmer established the MAC program with
Paley as manager.[11] Palmer had moved to headquarters in New York

City early in the previous fall, as director of engineering. H. S. Beattie had succeeded him as manager of the Poughkeepsie laboratory. Palmer, Beattie, and Paley agreed that the 608, as the transistor-core version was designated, should be a member of the MAC family. They also agreed that the new transistor 608 should retain the parallel-digit, serial-bit-count design of the 604 and 607.[12] That, in fact, was the plan for the MAC family in general as visualized at the time. By adopting it for the 608, Paley could better rationalize including the 608 in the MAC program.[13] At Palmer's continued urging, the 608 was given a limited announcement in April 1955. Palmer had garnered considerable support for the idea of getting early experience with the design, manufacture, and maintenance of a transistor product.[14] The 608, with twice or more the speed, storage capacity, and number of program steps obtainable in the 607 and with a more than 50 percent faster reader-punch (155 cpm), was announced at a monthly rental of $3000—approximately twice that of the 607.[15] Although few orders were expected at such a high rental, even the few would provide the experience so urgently desired.

From its beginning, the MAC program enfolded proposed machines of such widely varying (and vague) descriptions that it was hard to define the common denominator. A list compiled by Paley in May 1955 included five machines:

1. 604-608
2. Intermediate calculator
3. Accounting machine
4. Random-access machine
5. Scientific calculator[16]

Of these, only the first two machines had already received more than superficial planning. The 604 was a long-established product. The 608 had been announced but without a specific delivery schedule. There seemed to be an understanding that the "low-end" MAC machines would supplant both machines, without clarification as to whether the 608 first shipped would be identical to the MAC 608 or even resemble it physically. There was, in fact, prolonged discussion as late as November 1955 of whether the 608 in the MAC program should use serial-digit or parallel-digit circuits.

The intermediate calculator was defined as "a larger version of the Type 608 to cover the area below the 705." It was to have a wide variety of highly overlapped input-output equipment including magnetic-tape units and up to 10,000 words of alphanumeric storage.

According to a contemporaneous report it would be controlled by either a plugboard or a stored program, or by a combination of the two, "because of the extreme flexibility of the various control panel features." This member of the family was a close relative in concept to the "Wooden Wheel" (see chapter 5).[17]

The accounting machine—the third item on the MAC family list—was referred to as the 750, and by mid-year 1955 a special committee had addressed the question of whether the machine could be enhanced sufficiently to perform as a successor to both the 704 and 705 computers. The conclusion was that it could, by the substitution of 2 megapulse transistors and circuits. In this case, the 100 kilopulse 604-type serial-by-bit, parallel-by-digit organization would be replaced by 2 megapulse circuits operating in serial-by-digit (character) mode.[18] By autumn the enhanced member of the proposed MAC family was known by both the designations 751 and SAMAC.

It began to seem that there was no planned machine whose intended place in the IBM product line could not be filled instead by the MAC program—properly redefined. But in the process of attempting to be "all things to all people," the MAC team was seriously delayed in establishing final specifications for most of its proposed machines. Many months passed, and it was still unclear how the machines formed a family. Even the term "modular" seemed to have been adopted more for its agreeable implications than for any examples of common use of functional units or circuit components beyond that which had occurred among, say, the 700 series machines.

Time was running out for the MAC program. By 1956, the 704 and 705 engineering groups were well along with plans for successor machines—the 709 and the 705 Model III, respectively—which were announced the following year. Moreover, in each case it would require only rather straightforward design steps to develop later transistor versions. The 750 accounting machine thus missed the opportunity to serve as the replacement for the established large-scale 700 series. The MAC program, as such, did not continue beyond 1957. Of the machines considered part of the MAC series, only the 608 calculator was produced. Only two dozen or so of those were delivered, starting in 1957. The machine served its intended purpose, however, as a first step in the production of digital equipment using transistors. It is believed to be the first all-transistor calculator made commercially available by any manufacturer.

The 750 continued for a time as a development project. In the latter half of 1957 it found itself in a lively competition for the "intermediate" data processing area with a contender from the Endicott laboratory known as the 660. That machine had originated in 1955 as a proposed successor to the 650, featuring mainly improved instructions and a more efficient register organization. Enhancements proposed for the 660 during the two ensuing years included a larger-capacity drum memory, an optional magnetic-core supplemental memory, and finally solid-state circuits.[19] It was an uneven contest—the relatively new 750 design based from the start on transistors and cores against the aging and increasingly cluttered 660 organization, not easily freed from the peculiar requirements of a rotating drum memory. Intensive studies by the Applied Programming department showed the 750 to be easier to program than the 660.[20]

The results of the programming evaluation were revealed early in 1958, and the 750 was selected for development by agreement among all departments concerned. Soon thereafter, Ralph Palmer assigned the task to Endicott—partly, perhaps, because of the increasing commitment of the Poughkeepsie laboratory to the Stretch project and partly because of the enthusiasm Endicott had shown for the intermediate computer assignment.[21] The machine that eventually emerged from that laboratory bore as litle resemblance to the planned 750— or to any of the existing 700 series—as to the old 650. Known briefly as the 785 during development, it was announced in September 1958 as the IBM 7070 Data Processing System. It was the first IBM computer of the solid-state generation to be announced, but its first shipment lagged by six months the November 1959 delivery of the 7090. Timed poorly with respect to 700 series improvements and offering little inducement to users of those machines to change their programming styles, the 7070 was not notably successful. The 7070 family, consisting of the original machine and two improved models, failed to leave a lasting imprint on the product line.[22]

12.2 The Type 1401 Data Processing System

By early 1955, when the MAC program was launched, the domestic argument over small-to-medium electronic calculators had become largely self-sustaining and independent of the European crisis that had triggered it. This did not escape the notice of the French and German engineers, who proceeded to take the initiative in solving the competitive problem posed by the highly effective Bull Gamma 3 electronic calculator. The German IBM design group at Sindelfingen played host to a group of ten or so engineers and planners from France, Germany, and the United States during June and July 1955. The purpose of the seven-week conference was to propose several accounting machine designs. The idea was that all candidate designs would later be refined and the best one chosen.[23]

From each of the three countries came a design proposal. The most distinctive came from representatives of the French laboratory in Paris, who endowed their machine with variable field length, a characteristic of the 702 and 705 with which they were familiar. They felt, however, that the 702-705 method, with end characters to delimit fields and with special instructions for adjusting field lengths, was wasteful of memory space. They believed the familiar plugboard could be used to advantage and at lower cost. With serial handling of data, plugwires would be required only to indicate field boundaries and not for the parallel transmission of all characters of a field as in the traditional card machine control panels. The German and American proposals, which did not differ greatly from each other, were based on fixed field lengths.[24]

The report produced by the conference in Sindelfingen explained that the objective of that effort was to gain economy of manufacture by satisfying both European and domestic U.S. market areas with a single machine. The domestic and World Trade corporations would both manufacture the machines, each to meet its own requirements.[25] Although a particular machine design was yet to be selected from among the three proposals, the anticipated product of the Sindelfingen conference was known thereafter as the Worldwide Accounting Machine (WWAM).[26]

To take advantage of the transistor experience of circuit design groups in the U.S. laboratories and to consider additional machine design alternatives, the members of the Sindelfingen conference reconvened in Poughkeepsie in September 1955. By year end, they had examined the engineering prototype of the transistor 608 and thus acquired a first-hand appreciation of transistor circuit design and packaging requirements. In December, the group produced a joint recommendation to select the French proposal—including transistor technology, ferrite-core memory, and the variable-word-length characteristic.[27]

The French engineers stayed in the United States for about one year, working in Poughkeepsie and Endicott. They adopted a variation of the circuits designed for the 608, along with that machine's electronic packaging design (circuit cards, panels, and so forth), and counted heavily on the assumption that a large share of program costs would be borne by the 608 and other machines of the MAC program.[28] When they returned to Paris, some time after mid-1956, it was with the understanding that design of the electronic calculator portion of the machine would be the responsibility of the French laboratory. The German engineers, meanwhile, had agreed to develop the card reader and printer. The latter was to employ the same stick printing mechanism—based on a development by H. S. Beattie in Poughkeepsie—that was being used in the RAMAC system. The Germans chose a configuration involving a large number of the type-bearing metal sticks, each of which printed only a few columns in succession. They hoped thus to achieve a much higher line speed than that of the single-stick RAMAC printer, while keeping the cost of the machine as low as possible. (See section 12.4.) A model was eventually operated at 300 lines per minute.[29]

As matters stood in June 1956, the WWAM was to have a serial-by-character arithmetic unit, being in that respect unlike the 604, the 607, or the 608 from which its circuits derived. It was an add-to-memory machine, having no accumulator and therefore requiring that each arithmetic instruction specify two memory operand locations (one of which was also the result location). As a plugged-program (control panel) machine, it relied on its serial electronic design to keep the size, complexity, and cost of the control panel small by comparison with the panels of traditional punched-card accounting machines. Magnetic-core working storage (used entirely for data, since no stored program was involved) could be as large as 1900 seven-bit characters.[30]

Viability of the WWAM project depended on the realization of a number of key engineering objectives. In addition to the obvious matter of meeting the estimated costs of the new printer and card reader-punch, there was the requirement to show that the control panel and associated electronic driving circuits would also meet their cost estimates. Furthermore, there was the assumption that the MAC program, which provided a basis for the assumed costs of circuits and electronic packaging, would remain healthy through the production stage.

The WWAM project had hardly become established in the European laboratories when it encountered serious problems with estimated product cost, including the cost of electronic circuits and packaging.[31] After basing its circuit cost estimates on the assurance that the MAC program was solid, the WWAM group faced spiraling increases in those estimated costs as the MAC program began to slip.[32] Furthermore, the WWAM project suffered from a lack of confidence at corporate headquarters in the ability of the relatively small and inexperienced European laboratories to manage a major product development program, one on which a large amount of revenue might depend over the years. As early as April 1956, sales vice-president T. V. Learson had told his superior L. H. LaMotte that, from the viewpoint of the sales department, WWAM was the "number one" item in importance, outweighing the 750 "by a country mile." But he cautioned against putting the program in "unknown hands" (overseas) and expressed skepticism that the machine could range downward to meet its low-end cost and price objectives, when the 400 series accounting machines had never been able to do so: "The stick [printer], I assume, will be given as the new and different reason. I don't believe it."[33]

McDowell and Palmer worried, too, that the accounting machine end of the business was not being given enough attention by the domestic engineering organization. By February 1957 they had appointed Ralph G. Mork in the Endicott lab as manager of the WWAM program, with responsibility also for any other accounting machine activity "in the same general area."[34] Mork had joined IBM in 1949, had worked on CRT printing and other electronic projects, and had been a charter member of the bombing navigation system project when the Vestal laboratory was set up to fulfill that government contract around the start of 1951. (See chapter 5.) Having been responsible for the radar display part of that project, he had gone on to take charge of display console engineering for SAGE.

Shortly after acquiring responsibility for the accounting machine area, Mork turned his attention to the WWAM product-cost problem. He learned that the plugboard—along with all the electronics to drive the signals and to ensure against damage arising from an operator's plugging errors—accounted for several thousand dollars of estimated product cost. Rather than upsetting the French laboratory by asking them to redirect their efforts in midstream, Mork asked Francis O. Underwood of the Endicott engineering planning group to study the problem and recommend a more economical approach to the organization of the machine.[35]

Underwood had participated in WWAM planning meetings in Poughkeepsie during 1955—in fact, had helped design a control panel for the machine. As he recalled later, his study of the design revealed that 45 percent of the cost of the WWAM was attributable to the control panel. Underwood was charged with retaining the logical organization that had originated in the French laboratory, including such features as variable field length and the method of arranging (editing) data in memory for printing. He set out to accomplish all the WWAM functions through stored-program control, which he believed was achievable at much lower cost than the plugboard control originally proposed.[36]

Thus, for at least the fourth time, a variable-field-length stored-program computer was designed—the TPM, the somewhat different

702-705, and the 305 RAMAC having been three earlier examples.[37] Underwood dismissed the 702-705 method of field delimitation as too expensive. What was wanted, he later recalled, was a machine capable of replacing three 407s at the roughly equivalent rental of $2500 per month, including card reader, punch, printer, and processor.[38]

In the method he chose for marking the boundaries of fields, Underwood retained a good deal of the logic of the plugboard. He proposed simply to add an eighth core plane, called the "word-mark plane," to the seven-plane array originally required for storage of seven-bit characters (702 style) in the machine's main memory. The eighth core for each storage location would be set to 1 or 0, depending on whether that was the location of the left-most character of a field. This approach in a sense kept the word mark separate from the data, just as the "storage-split" wiring of the WWAM plugboard had been outside the data stream. The method was described in Underwood's first report on the project in August 1957.[39]

A month later, responsibility for the accounting machine area shifted again. Mork had been assigned to give direction to the World Trade engineering laboratories, which until that time had been under no common technical management.[40] His former responsibility had been handed to Charles E. Branscomb, a mechanical engineer who had joined IBM in 1950 with a master's degree from North Carolina State College. Assigned initially to the "Transcriber," an electromechanical 400-line-per-minute accounting machine that might have reached the market but for the impact of electronics, Branscomb had participated in the design of several new card machines including a high-speed collator and sorter.[41] Components such as the card feeds used in these products were part of a standardization effort in card handling and provided mechanisms widely used in subsequent computer systems as well as in unit-record machines.[42]

A few weeks after Branscomb became responsible for accounting machines, a market research report made it clear that, since the lowest estimated monthly rental for the European laboratories' WWAM was some $900 more than that of roughly equivalent capability in the form of two 407s plus one 604, the market for the machine would be nonexistent.[43] McDowell made it equally clear to LaMotte that, if the product was important and urgent to the Data Processing Division, it should be transferred to the domestic engineering organization. Palmer agreed and added that the project should be located in Endicott.[44] Still, no action toward that end seems to have been taken for several months. Underwood, meanwhile, had submitted a second report on the proposal for the stored-program version of the machine, in which he introduced the idea of variable-length instructions as well as variable-length data words. It was important to minimize the memory requirement because core memory could be expected to account for around $10 of monthly rental for each one hundred characters. Underwood's proposal was still preliminary in nature, but the memory-conserving principle of variable instruction size had been established.[45]

Palmer and others in engineering continued to express concern over various aspects of the WWAM project in Europe—not only the rising estimates of product cost but such matters as the German laboratories' departure from the new standard designs, developed at Endicott, for card feeding and reading units.[46] But a top management decision would be required to move so important a project from World Trade to a domestic laboratory; and LaMotte, for one, was being told that substantial delays might be the price to be paid for an unnecessary move.[47] Then, late in 1957, Tom Watson, Jr., expressed dissatisfaction with the program.[48] Branscomb later recalled that in March 1958 the Endicott proposal for a stored-program WWAM was given formal approval as the company's approach to meeting the need for an electronic accounting machine.[49] The French and German engineers, and the product planners who shared their convictions, had kept the Worldwide Accounting Machine idea alive during a crucial period; beyond that, they had contributed a logical machine organization that survived a translation, essentially, from plugged- to stored-program form.

The electronic accounting machine project, in its stored-program reincarnation, had an auspicious beginning in Endicott.[50] Since the reorganization following the Williamsburg Conference in late November 1956, the manager of that laboratory had been James J. Troy, an engineer originally from Endicott, who had served for the preceding two years as director of product development on the corporate staff. Troy had vigorously opposed occasional suggestions from headquarters that all computer work should be in Poughkeepsie and that the Endicott laboratory should concern itself with input-output products. His belief that Endicott could never realize its full potential without a reasonable share of the electronics and processor development was almost an obsession, and over the years it guided his reaction to various plans to specialize the missions of the laboratories by system function.[51]

When the Endicott laboratory was given responsibility to develop the electronic accounting machine, Troy's position on such matters was not especially difficult to maintain. The 650 Magnetic Drum Calculator, after its long and precarious journey to the announcement stage, had very quickly become an outstanding success. By the beginning of 1958, there were over 800 of the machines installed and hundreds more on order. Because of the modest rental of the 650, it was within financial reach of many universities and colleges; and it is safe to say that, for several years, far more computer scientists had their first experience on that machine than on any other electronic computer.

The newly assigned project, which for a time carried the acronym SPACE (for Stored Program Accounting and Calculating Equipment) and which was to culminate in the announcement of the 1401 data processing system, depended for its success on much more than a clever logical design for storing in memory the equivalent of plugboard control. There was need for electronic circuits and circuit packaging that could be economically applied to a computer requiring only a few thousand decision elements and also a memory technology that would be economical for a total capacity of as few as 1400 characters. There also had to be fast, inexpensive card reading and punching devices for input-output and a reliable and economical printer to run at more than 450 lines per minute (lpm), more than three times the speed of the 407 accounting machine.

Considering all these essential ingredients, the timing of the SPACE system could hardly have been better. The SMS (standard modular system) electronic packaging technology was hurried along by the requirements of the Stretch program. It was further refined for the 7070 project, by then settled in Endicott and calling for economical circuits of intermediate speed. A "data flow" model of the 7070 had been built using current-switch circuits, but subsequent analysis showed that greater economy was to be gained by the use of a family of circuits known as "complementary transistor diode logic" (CTDL). Consisting of conventional diode-logic circuits using alloy-junction transistors between logic stages, this circuit family achieved its economy in part by alternating the use of pnp and npn transistors. The technique made use of the fact that every pnp circuit provided output signals of the polarity desired for input to npn circuits, and vice versa, thus frequently avoiding the use of additional transistors for signal inversion.[52] CTDL circuits were used to great advantage in the SPACE machine.

The development of core memory, too, was timed conveniently for the new machine. Magnetic-core tape buffers of 800 characters had been in use as early as 1955 in the 702 system, and core main memories of much larger capacities had been part of all 704 and 705 systems, first shipped early in 1956. (See chapter 7.)

The standardized approach to design of card feeds and other card-handling devices had just yielded such machines as a high-speed collator with two independently clutched card feeds operating at 650 cards per minute (cpm), much faster than any predecessor. A reader-punch was designed for the SPACE system, employing the same feed for reading and replacing the second reading unit with a punching station; it read and punched cards at 800 and 250 cpm, respectively.[53] By contrast, the fastest electric accounting machine (the 407) read 150 cpm, and the fastest punches available with unit-record systems operated at 100 cpm.

Perhaps the most fortunate aspect of the timing of the SPACE project was the completion, in time for announcement with that system, of the "chain" printer, a machine that was to introduce radical innovation into the design of high-speed printers for computer systems. At the time Branscomb became manager of the SPACE project, this fast, relatively economical, and versatile printer was far enough along in development to provide an admirable answer to the printing requirements of the system.

In July 1958, Branscomb was made "area manager" for accounting machine development. In a novel approach to engineering management that had begun early in 1957, "area managers," while reporting personally to the managers of the laboratories, were responsible directly to Ralph Palmer for the technical and business management of their programs. The laboratory managers, for whom this was not the happiest of arrangements, became keepers of resources (people, space, technology centers, and so forth), while important decisions about the course of a particular product program might be made with little or no involvement on their part. Most IBM product-development activity fell under the area managers by the time Branscomb joined their ranks.

For the next fifteen months or so, Branscomb directed his efforts to completing the SPACE project on schedule and without any significant rise in estimated product cost. The plan was to get the equipment into the product-testing laboratory by early July 1959 and to have the system ready for announcement by September. There was no shortage of distractions. Competitive machines or proposals for machines arose from outside as well as inside IBM, affording innumerable opportunities to engage in a contest over performance, memory capacity, or attractive special features. The chief competitive entry from within IBM was an expanded version of the 305 RAMAC from the San Jose laboratory—a proposed machine known at various stages as the 306 and the 310—which, in the opinion of Endicott engineering planners, could easily be dispensed with, assuming certain modest enhancements in the design of the SPACE system.[54]

Branscomb resisted the pressure to incorporate features that might have driven the cost of the SPACE system beyond an acceptable range. There was, however, one proposed enhancement that even Branscomb had to entertain: the inclusion of magnetic-tape units in the system at the time of its announcement. The plan to that point had been for announcement initially of strictly a punched-card system, with magnetic tape to be added at some unspecified later date. In January 1959, Bob O. Evans had moved to Endicott and had taken over the management of the 7070 computer development. This had become rather a large and ambitious project whose most ardent supporters expected it to bring forth a common successor to at least the 650 and the 705, thereby reducing the number of computer "families" that would be perpetuated. Evans had been installed as manager in order to extricate the 7070 from difficulties encountered in getting the system into production on schedule. Quite soon after assuming command, he found that the 7070 needed a companion system capable of reading its magnetic tapes, editing their data, and printing reports in any desired format. This would free the 7070 of the requirement to deal directly with slow input-output devices such as printers or punches. The group in Poughkeepsie responsible for the 7090 expressed a similar need. But to fulfill the role of a report-editing system, Branscomb's machine would have to be capable of tape operation.[55]

This and other arguments in favor of attaching tape were persuasive, and the decision was made in March 1959 to do so with the initial announcement of the 1401. As Branscomb recalled, that decision cost a month or so in the product-testing and announcement schedule,[56] but for several reasons it was never regretted. For one thing, it made possible a larger market forecast for the 1401 system, including now not only steadfast punched-card users but also those interested in acquiring small tape processing systems. Second, the existence of tape in the system would greatly ease the upward movement of 1401 users to larger computers as their data processing needs expanded. Finally, the availability of a tape-connected 1401 eliminated entirely the need for a control unit that had been planned for the chain printer.

The IBM 1401 Data Processing System—comprising a variety of card and tape models with a range of core memory sizes and configured for stand-alone use as well as peripheral service for larger computers— was announced in October 1959 (figure 12.1). It quickly became one of the most important and successful products IBM had ever announced, with many thousands of systems delivered starting in 1960.[57] A small configuration, without tapes and with the minimum memory capacity of 1400 characters, was available for just under $2500 per month, a

Figure 12.1
IBM 1401 data processing system, including, from left, card-reader punch, processing unit, chain printer, and tape units. The tape units shown, type 7330, were actually introduced almost a year after the 1401 system. They were smaller, less expensive, and somewhat slower than the 729s, which were available at the time of 1401 system announcement.

much lower rental for much higher performance than three 407 accounting machines plus a 604 calculator. It is no exaggeration to say that the 1401 opened the world of electronic data processing for the first time to a broad range of small and medium-sized users of IBM's punched-card systems. It was not the first IBM computer to use transistors instead of tubes—the 7070 and the 7090 computers, as well as the 608 calculator, were announced and delivered ahead of it—but it was undoubtedly the product that gave IBM its first realistic glimpse of the size and importance of the computer market that was unfolding.[58]

12.3 Other 1400 Series Computers; the Report Program Generator

The 1401 was the first of a family of data processing systems known as the 1400 series. The second machine in this line evolved in a curious way from the Advanced RAMAC System—a project in the San Jose Laboratory known also as the 310—which had risen earlier to challenge the SPACE system for the lead position in the series. Having lost in that contest, the 310 was transplanted to Endicott around November 1958 by the edict of Ralph Palmer, who hoped to guide its development in the direction of the technology and organization of the 1401.[59] It was to be a larger, more powerful machine than the 1401 and—while retaining its disk-storage orientation—it was to cover the range from just above the 305 RAMAC to well beyond the 650 drum computer. One of the most prominent features of the 310, technologically and in terms of improved performance, was the Advanced Disk File (ADF), a basic component of the planned system as it stood in January 1959.

The 310 would seem to have been in an enviable position as the development engineers, engineering planners, and product planners prepared to apply the final touches to its organization and design. It was not constrained as rigidly by the requirement for minimal product cost as the 1401 had been. It was provided with the competitively superior ADF, with its several modules of 25 million characters each, accessed by comb-type parallel head arrays. The 310 project group had been free to use the higher-speed circuits and other results of the latest technology to ensure superior performance while keeping their machine within the "intermediate" size and cost range. Moreover, it appeared to be a powerful answer to several competitive machines of concern at the time: the NCR 304, the Datatron 220 of ElectroData (a division of Burroughs), and the RCA 501.[60] But things did not proceed entirely as Palmer had intended. By mid-1959 the 310 had lost a good bit of its similarity to the 305, but it still fell far short of compatibility with the 1401 in terms of instruction and data format.[61]

At this point, Bob Evans came into the picture. Having helped to rescue the 7070 from its immediate problems and restore its schedule to something like the one on which manufacturing and marketing commitments had been based, Evans became available for an important post created as a result of the IBM reorganization that took place in May 1959. (See chapter 8.) The new General Products Division (GPD) had acquired planning, engineering, manufacturing, and testing responsibilities for the punched-card product line and for small-to-intermediate systems, as well as for most of the company's computer input-output products. Included among GPD systems were the 305 RAMAC, the 650, and the soon-to-be announced 1401. "Intermediate" computers, the largest systems within the division's purview, were to be the responsibility of a manager of Processing Systems in the Endicott Laboratory. This was the post Evans was offered and accepted. He reported to Donald T. Spaulding, manager of Systems Development, located at GPD headquarters in White Plains N.Y. Among Evans's responsibilities were the 1401, nearly ready for announcement, and the 310, still in development.

A serious controversy that arose concerning compatibility between these two computers threatened the unity of Evans's organization. Neither he nor Spaulding looked favorably upon the 310 as a machine with unique instructions and data formats. They understood that some aspect of the new computer's performance—speed, capacity, or versatility—would undoubtedly be compromised if it were constrained to machine-language compatibility with a smaller machine. They were much more impressed, however, by benefits that would accrue from program compatibility between the new machine and the 1401, which was close to announcement. The engineers who had been developing the new machine fervently disagreed. As Evans later recalled, they were emotionally committed to presenting something new and to providing the highest possible performance within the allowable cost and available technology. "Unfortunately," he added, " . . . that does not represent a systems viewpoint. It fails to take into account programming, customer transition, field service, training, spare parts, logistics, etc." It was hard to discipline computer engineers in an era when there were so many new machine organizations to explore. "Processors were the rage," he recalled. "Processors were getting the resources, and everybody that came into development had a new way to design a processor."[62] Often, as in the case of the 310, the new way entailed a new instruction set and thus the abandonment of program compatibility.

Evans's insistence on machine compatibility was influenced by an understanding of why Palmer had moved the 310 to Endicott in the first place and by a desire to do what he could to return the program to the course Palmer had intended. His later comments, concerning Palmer's influence on engineering and technology in IBM, shed light on that motive:

He is largely responsible for a lot of the basic thinking in the engineering fraternity in IBM and has led us to the position of product eminence that IBM now enjoys. Ralph was successful at standardizing technology and in forcing the engineering groups to reach out for new technologies. But I think that the systems people let Ralph down when they got to the point of making the systems themselves compatible. . . . The engineering fraternity . . . seems to have a penchant for looking at a problem, discarding other people's solutions, and inevitably coming back with a different way of doing anything. And so it went with the 310. The 310 in Endicott became neither like the 305 nor the 1401, but instead a third type of architecture.[63]

In September 1959, just a few weeks before announcement of the 1401, Spaulding and Evans took a group of engineers, programmers, and planners from both the 1401 and the 310 projects to Rocky Point, a resort in upstate New York. There they "nailed the door shut" and conducted a thorough analysis of the issues, with no aspect of compatibility or its effects upon performance or programming left unexamined. Some of the proponents of a unique machine were firmly set in their convictions. "There were people that threatened to quit the company if we made the decision [for a compatible machine],"

Evans remembered. But when the evidence was in, he and Spaulding made the decision that the 310 (soon renamed the 1410) would be "upward compatible" with the 1401—meaning that, with few exceptions, programs written for the 1401 should run on the 1410.[64] The consequences of that decision extended well beyond the 1400 series and its whole generation of computers. The 1410 experience deepened the convictions of Evans, Spaulding, and E. S. Hughes (engineering manager for the systems area under Evans) about system compatibility, a concept that would find its most significant application in IBM's System/360, introduced about five years later.

In the process of becoming more like the 1401, the system became decreasingly disk storage oriented; by the time it was ready for announcement, it was just a computer with a generous complement of disk storage. As a matter of fact, the 1410 was announced twice: first in September 1960 with no mention whatever of disk storage and in the following month with disk storage units quite different from the Advanced Disk File.

The apparent explanation for this strange sequence of events is that by 1960 the sales organization was clamoring for a larger machine, compatible with the 1401, that would offer a path of expansion for 1401 users. Evans and Spaulding had been right, perhaps more so than they realized, in their insistence on compatibility. And although the ADF had run into serious technical difficulties and fallen many months behind schedule, the 1410 was quite capable of operating as a tape system. Thus, when needed to assure prospective 1401 customers a convenient avenue for growth of their applications, the 1410 was ready for unveiling. (Hughes recalls that it was a significant factor in the outstanding market acceptance of the 1401.)[65]

Meanwhile, with the severity of engineering problems confronting the ADF better understood, a decision had been made to substitute in the 1410 system two modified versions of the RAMAC disk file. Named the 1405 and operating at twice the track and bit densities of the original RAMAC, the storage units were available in twenty-five-disk and fifty-disk models, having 10 million and 20 million characters, respectively. The 1410 was capable of controlling up to five of the larger model 1405s, with a total of 100 million characters. (At the same time, the 1405 disk storage was made available for attachment of one unit—either model—to the 1401 system.)[66]

The next 1400 series computer to be introduced was known during much of its development as the 11LC. Like the 1410, it originated in the San Jose laboratory and was transferred to Endicott prior to its announcement. This system was designed to be substantially lower in cost—hence the "LC" in its name—and in overall speed of operation than even the 1401. The project was started by Lawrence A. Wilson, who had been Branscomb's superior in Endicott until 1958, when Wilson moved to San Jose and Branscomb assumed responsibility as area manager for the SPACE system.

Wilson was a self-trained statistician turned self-trained engineer, who had originally joined IBM as a junior salesman in 1939. During World War II, he became chief of data processing for the U.S. Census Bureau, where he noted the large number of special-purpose machines in use, many of them designed and constructed by that agency. While there he laid out a plan for a multifunction machine, a statistical tabulator that included sorting capability. Returning to IBM after the war as a special sales representative, he found an opportunity to interest Tom Watson, Jr., in the idea and was transferred in 1947 to the Endicott laboratory. There he worked in "an equal partnership" with C. D. Lake and B. M. Durfee to develop the IBM 101 Electronic Statistical Machine, a product announced in mid-1949, which combined sorting and accumulating capabilities.[67]

During the mid-1950s Wilson acquired increasing responsibility for the company's punched-card machine development, of which a rapidly growing share was directed toward computer system card input-output equipment. By 1958 he was unquestionably the principal successor to the card-machine inventors of the preceding era. During his years in Endicott, he had become convinced of the need to produce much less expensive card readers, punches, and other card-handling machines. He believed that the steady encroachment of magnetic storage media would restrict the role of cards to recording, verifying, and editing—in general, to the system data-entry function—for which increased market acceptance would depend on lower product cost. Truly low-cost design, he reasoned, would require the combination of serial (column by column instead of row by row) reading and punching of cards, along with the application of more advanced mechanical design and technology to maintain reasonable performance in spite of the serial mode.[68] After moving to San Jose in 1958, Wilson pursued these ideas as part of the 11LC system design. It was in connection with the 11LC that J. M. Harker and his associates in the San Jose laboratory developed the first removable-pack disk-storage unit.

Wilson was fully prepared to complete the development of his 11LC, now enhanced with an economical "bar" printer (to be described further on) as well as the serial card devices and the removable disk storage. But a familiar problem arose: compatibility with the 1401. The specific issues were much the same as with the 1410, which had started in San Jose as the 310.[69] The inevitable showdown with Evans occurred; once more Evans prevailed, and for the second time a new member of the 1400 series (by then known as the 14LC) was transferred from San Jose to Endicott for completion of its development. The system was announced in October 1962 as the IBM 1440 Data Processing System, with a core memory of 4000 to 16,000 characters — the capacity to which the 1401's memory had been increased in mid-1960.

Although it served to introduce the removable-pack disk file concept and, along with the 1410, to broaden the application range of the 1400 line of systems, the 1440 was a disappointment. For one thing, its serial card reader-punch and bar printer were not of sufficiently low cost, in comparison with the 1401's input-output devices, to compensate for their reduced speed of operation. Furthermore, the 1440 was introduced initially without even the capability of attaching magnetic tape; and perhaps IBM's plan for a transition to disk storage was too sudden and too absolute, or perhaps disks simply had not reached a level of capacity and performance adequate to support such a transition.

The company offered a tape unit attachment for it just one year after the original system announcement, but the 1440 remained a mere shadow of the 1401 in terms of product acceptance. However, with its new transistors and circuits faster than those of the 1401, it provided a design upon which the 1460, a later and much higher-performance machine in the series, would be based.

No account of the introduction of the 1400 series should fail to include a description of an unusual development in the programming field that proved important to the success not only of that group of machines but also of subsequent generations of computers. The 1401, although designed primarily by and for EAM-experienced people, still presented programming requirements. In the months between its announcement and the earliest deliveries, there was concern in both the marketing and product divisions that programming difficulties might be an obstacle to acceptance or successful installation of the 1401.

As a result, in 1959 two members of the applied programming department of the General Products Division were assigned the task of providing a software method of easing the transition from the wiring of control panels to the preparation of programs for the 1401.[70] Wiring a "plugboard" to prepare a printed report was a familiar task among users of EAM equipment such as the 407 accounting machine; however, writing a program to cause the machine to print a similar report using the 1401 instruction set could be far more burdensome, especially for a first-time user of computers.[71] Report preparation being a frequent requirement, the programmers were asked to design a system that would assist customers in preparing report-writing programs.

They responded by creating a "language" whereby the user could specify the features desired in any report and a "generator" (a translating program) that could convert those specifications to a 1401 program capable of producing the report. The name RPG (for Report Program Generator) was applied to both the language and the generator program, separately or in combination, in the rather indefinite style of reference that had become accepted for languages and compilers. Happily, the programmers kept constantly in mind the need to satisfy inexperienced users and to avoid "the considerable temptation to orient the language instead to people who were already programmers."[72]

RPG was made available early in 1961, within about three months after shipment of the first 1401 system to a customer. Applicable in its initial form to card 1401 systems only, it was soon adapted to the tape system and to the RAMAC version of the 1401 announced in 1960. (In each case, it required that the computer memory have a capacity of 4000 or more characters.) Accounts vary as to the amount of users' programming effort RPG saved, but it was not unusual to read of programs that had taken days to write in 1401 assembly language being completed in hours using RPG. Made available also for later computers of the 1400 series, adapted to subsequent generations of computers, and widely used throughout the industry, RPG played an important part in the successful introduction of computers into small businesses.[73] Furthermore, the concept of a report program generator, more generally defined, was to acquire even greater importance in later decades, when further technological improvements brought the computer to a much larger community of users.

12.4 High-Speed Printers; the Chain and Train

The ability to prepare printed reports and documents of high visual quality was taken for granted by users of punched-card systems. Required only to match the modest speeds of electromechanical accounting machines, new printing devices were carefully designed to maintain or improve upon the print quality of their predecessors. The timely introduction of an entirely new class of printing devices was an important factor in the success of the 1401 computer system. It is appropriate to consider events leading to the chain and train printers in the context of IBM's effort to gain wider acceptance for computers among users of traditional unit-record machines.

The only "high-speed" printer available for the early 700-series computers was the wheel-type printing mechanism from the 407 accounting machine, which operated at 150 lpm. This form of wheel printer was originated by H. S. Beattie in the late 1930s, while he was assigned to IBM's East Orange, N.J., laboratory. Alphanumeric accounting machines then used in punched-card systems had vertical bars containing the complete font of characters—one bar for each column to be printed—and these bars moved up and down to select the desired character for each line of printing. The need to carry all the alphabetic as well as the numeric characters made the bars long, heavy, and relatively difficult to position at high speeds. The highest speed of alphanumeric printing achieved in such IBM machines prior to the 407 was 100 lpm. Beattie, who joined IBM in 1933, had begun thinking of a wheel printer while he was still quite new with the company.[74] Reasoning that by using type wheels instead of bars he could minimize the inertia of the type carrier, he devised an ingenious method for printing whereby the speed of the type (parallel to the surface of the paper) was reduced to zero at the instant of impact.

Using 120 wheels, it was possible to print any of 48 characters (numerals, alphabetics, or 12 special symbols) in 120 columns across the paper. The 48 characters were arranged in 12 sectors on the periphery of each wheel, each sector corresponding to a row (or combination of rows) on the IBM punched card. Nine of the sectors corresponded to the rows 1 to 9, and each carried its decimal digit along with three nonnumeric characters represented by a "zone" punch (0, 11, or 12) in combination with the numeric punch in the card. Two more sectors corresponded to the numeric pairs 8-3 and 8-4 along with the various zone combinations, providing for most of the special symbols such as percentage and dollar signs. A last sector was reserved for characters represented in the punched card by zones only, including the 0 as well as three more special symbols.[75]

Each wheel was caused to start rotating at high speed at just the right time to bring the leading edge of the desired sector to the print line shortly before impact. The speed of the wheel was then reduced and the wheel pivoted toward the paper at a time calculated to select the desired one of four characters in the sector for printing. The pivoting action provided just enough angular velocity to offset the low speed of rotation of the wheel, and the effect achieved was that of impelling a nonrotating wheel against ribbon and paper. Although the speed of 150 lpm does not seem spectacular today, the 407 was hailed as a great improvement over machines then in existence. And because its print mechanism was used in the output printers for IBM's first generation of general-purpose computers, it set a standard for print quality that profoundly influenced the company's selection of higher-speed mechanisms for later printers.

The 407 accounting machine had been completed in Poughkeepsie under Beattie's management in the years following his move from East Orange in 1944, and it was announced in 1949. During the extended period of testing to which that machine was subjected, Beattie had time to work on other printing methods as well. One involved a mushroom-shaped type element whose surface (a portion of a sphere) held fifty-two raised characters and was positioned angularly to select the desired character for printing. Although this device, demonstrated in 1946, was purely experimental, the basic idea was carried forth some years later in the widely used IBM Selectric typewriter with its interchangeable spherical type elements.[76]

Two years later, Beattie demonstrated a "stick" printer, so called because of the shape of its four-sided type element, each side of which carried one-fourth of the characters of the font. Its low moment of inertia permitted the stick to be positioned more rapidly than the "mushroom," and it was shown that 2000 characters per minute could be printed with each stick. Various configurations of this printer were proposed, with the sticks either horizontal or vertical and with multiple sticks printing several columns, or several lines, concurrently. An improved version, using an eight-sided stick but limited to about 30 lpm by the single-stick configuration, was introduced with the 305 RAMAC. Multiple sticks were employed in the WWAM engineering model to achieve 300 lpm. The stick printing mechanism never saw commercial use, however, in that configuration or in any other high-speed printer for computer systems.

A wire printer, in which each character was formed by the combination of dots printed by selected wires from a 5 by 7 array—in much the same manner as the printers that became common in terminals and smaller computers more than two decades later—was developed by Reynold B. Johnson and others in Endicott and introduced with the Type 26 keypunch in 1949. This keypunch contained only a single matrix of wires, since it had only to print across the top of the card the characters being punched sequentially. However, it did have to respond to high instantaneous character speeds under special conditions, such as the operator's "rippling" from key to key. The printer Johnson designed for this keypunch incorporated at the rear extremity of the pack of wires a code plate, which was moved laterally to select a pattern of raised dots corresponding to the character to be printed. When the plate was then moved forward to advance the selected wires in their longitudinal direction, the projecting ends of those wires formed the pattern necessary to print the character. Actual printing was accomplished by a rapid forward thrust of the head, or front end, of the entire pack of wires.

At least as early as 1950, with increasing recognition of the need for a printer capable of 1000 lines or more per minute as a computer-output device, W. W. McDowell was urged by both Beattie and Johnson to consider the advantages of their respective inventions. Each had built models to demonstrate feasibility, and Johnson had incorporated in his wire printer some design improvements over the Type 26 key-punch version. One of these was a long, thin code rod used in place of the code plate. Rotated and moved along its axis to present any desired surface pattern to the lower ends of the print wires, it took less space per column than the earlier version and was thus better adapted to a line-at-a-time printer. The grounds for the eventual decision between the stick and wire printers are not fully documented or well remembered, but headquarters executives were impressed with the apparent flexibility of the wire printer with respect to both character format and applicability to a variety of products. (Its wide use in recent years attests to that flexibility.) Mechanical considerations presented in various technical reports and discussions of which records survive seem to have provided little basis at the time for choosing one high-speed printing method over the other; neither was judged to be more or less sound overall from an engineering viewpoint than the other.[77] In any case, by the end of 1952 it was understood by the Endicott laboratory manager that wire printing was the technology to be used in high-speed printers developed by IBM "in the near future."[78]

A wire printer development effort, based on Johnson's designs, had been underway in Endicott for a year or so, with the initial goal of providing a printer for a planned 400 lpm accounting machine. After the formal selection of wire printing, emphasis was placed on developing a 1000 lpm computer-output printer. Responsibility for the project was assigned to Frank J. Furman, whose association with the company dated back to 1920 when he joined the accounting machine firm of J. Royden Peirce in New York City as a draftsman. Two years later, that company was acquired by CTR (see chapter 1), and Furman was transferred to Endicott in 1933 when IBM opened its new laboratory there.

The choice of wire printing was confirmed in a sense in 1954 when Control Instruments, a subsidiary of Burroughs Corporation, announced a wire printer producing 100-character lines of printing at 1000 lpm.

Although IBM's 407 had set a standard of print quality, the company was embarrassed that the Control Instruments machine was faster by more than six times. Furthermore, at about the same time, competitive wheel-type printers designed specifically for computer systems began to appear on the market. These printers (to be described later on) were all several times faster than IBM's 407-derived computer-output printers.

The competitive need was thus formally established, and the wire printer project at Endicott received increasing management attention. The Control Instruments printer was installed at Prudential Insurance Company of America. It was reported to be very complex mechanically and to have been withdrawn from the market in 1957, but by then the Endicott project was heavily committed.[79] IBM's wire printer was to fare no better, and its failure was all the more conspicuous because it had been the object of a full-fledged product program.

In June 1955, IBM announced two wire printers with the type numbers 719 and 730, both capable of printing 1000 lpm—the former to print 60 columns and the latter 120 columns across the paper. In each of these machines, the basic print mechanism was capable of printing 2000 characters per minute. The 719 used thirty heads, each indexing horizontally once to print a second column; the 730 used sixty heads in a similar way. The column span was thus twice the number of print heads, each head being the forward termination of a flexible assembly of thirty-five print wires in a tube. At the lower end of the tube, the wires needed for a particular character were advanced by means of a suitably positioned code rod designed in this case so that holes drilled in the rod came into alignment with wires not to be moved forward (figure 12.2).

It had been intended all along that the high-speed printer should be capable of operation either connected to a computer, as an ordinary output unit of the system, or connected to a tape unit. The latter mode was becoming increasingly of interest in balancing the components of a system to maximize "throughput"—that is, to get as much work done as possible. Magnetic tape was still the only output medium that could keep pace with computers, and the growing tendency, as noted in the case of the 7070, was to permit the computer to deal directly with tape only and let the printer perform "off-line." The wire printers were provided with a control unit that was capable of operation in either mode and included all the necessary controls for a tape unit when operated in a tape-to-printer subsystem. This control unit, designated Type 760, contained a 1000-character core

Figure 12.2
Laboratory "plate" model of the wire printer in a February 1955 photograph showing setup mechanism, code rod, and print wires. The thirty-five wires for one print head were contained in the curved guide tubes visible near the center of the photograph. To their right is the vertical code rod (shown magnified, with housing tube removed, in inset). Each code rod was positioned under the control of a set of six electromagnets, grouped vertically at the right and identifiable by their white-covered windings. The model, which could print an eight-character line, contained four setup mechanisms, two of them visible here. A full-sized printer required thirty setup mechanisms to print either 60 character lines at 1000 lpm or 120 character lines at 500 lpm.

buffer memory and had the additional feature of being usable as a tape buffer for the 705 computer without regard to a printer.

The requirement of multiple print heads—one for every two columns—made these "line" printers far more complicated than the single-head (serial) wire-matrix printers commonly used with the small computers of a later generation. The print head, its actuator, its tube of print wires, and its entire setup mechanism had to be designed to fit into a space only two print columns wide. The difficulty of adjustment and maintenance and the probability of component failures were exacerbated by the complexity of the machines. Neither of the two 1000 lpm models was ever delivered in the form of its original design. Less than two months after their announcement, problems of maintenance, cost, and high noise level prompted the company to introduce a stopgap model, operating at 500 lpm, in which 30 heads printed 4 columns each to produce a width of 120 columns at the reduced speed. After five of these slower machines had been installed, production was stopped for several months while design improvements were incorporated. Although about 200 were eventually installed (including only about fifteen operating at 1000 lpm), they were beset by a seemingly endless list of mechanical problems.[80]

The wire printer never filled its intended niche in the marketplace, but the impressive engineering effort that was mounted to solve its problems yielded valuable knowledge about high-speed, high-impact mechanisms and about the requirements of high-speed paper handling. As in the case of other apparently expensive failures, the education it provided added to the success of later products. For example, the engineers had found it necessary to replace the original electric-motor-driven paper carriage of the wire printer with a hydraulically operated one in order to achieve the necessary precision in paper control. (The requirement to move paper rapidly and still bring it to a complete stop before printing each line was fundamental to high-speed printers and would have been encountered in any mechanical printing device operating at comparable speed.)

The new carriage was used soon afterward in the outstandingly successful chain printer to be described. The experience with hydraulics thus acquired in engineering and manufacturing at Endicott was applied only a few years later in manufacturing the actuators needed for disk files in San Jose. Furthermore, problems of high acoustical noise level and of "fretting" corrosion, both encountered in mechanisms involving high speeds and impacts, were greatly reduced in later machines because of the wire printer experience.

By early 1957 it had become clear to the engineers and planners in Endicott that the wire printer would never qualify as the common high-speed output device for IBM's computers. The cost was too high, the list of mechanical problems too long, and both were increasing. Therefore an engineering planning committee was formed in February of that year to study high-speed printing requirements.[81] In May, the committee delivered a report recommending that a magnetic matrix printer be developed and that this "ferromagnetographic" technology be designated as the one to serve high-speed printing needs.[82] It was apparently a premature recommendation—one born of desperation over the problems with the wire printer—since IBM had never built a full-scale working model based on magnetic printing technology.

Magnetic printers, on which exploratory work had been done in IBM and elsewhere, employed the principle of magnetizing the surface of a metal drum in a pattern corresponding to the shape of the character to be printed and then permitting a "toner" made of magnetic particles and ink to be attracted to the magnetized regions. The characters were subsequently transferred to paper by means of pressure and the image "fixed" by means of heat. The process was entirely analogous to the xerographic process widely used in office copiers except that the image on the drum was magnetic instead of electrostatic and the toner was attracted to the drum by magnetic rather than electric force. The magnetic image on the drum was usually, but not always, formed of spots by means of electromagnetized wires corresponding to those of the mechanical wire printer. A wide range of wire configurations was possible. In some, for example, a single row of wires across the drum created characters one row of dots at a time. In other magnetic printers, the image was formed by magnetizing an engraved metal type slug on a rotating wheel as it passed the surface of the drum.

Magnetic-printer exploratory projects were carried on for five years or more following the committee recommendation, but no product ever resulted. For one thing, although the dots forming the character image on the drum fused into one another in the fixing process, thus producing a high visual quality in the final printed character, there was difficulty in obtaining good adhesion to the paper; the characters literally fell off when the paper was shaken.[83] For another, the method did not offer enough advantage in speed to offset certain limitations (such as inability to provide simultaneous carbon copies) or to justify the development of an entire new technology. Furthermore, the printer would have required a supply of magnetic toner, for which no source existed—and that was an important consideration.

Other "nonmechanical" approaches to high-speed printing were also explored by IBM in the 1950s and early 1960s. Notable among these was the CRT-film printer, in which a form of cathode-ray tube was used to generate a display of characters, and each screenful of information was photographed on microfilm. The resulting microfilm could then be viewed directly or used to prepare hard copy through a xerographic microfilm printer which had become available from the Haloid Corporation (later the Xerox Corporation). Such a printer was under development in Endicott when Jonas E. Dayger became area manager for printer development early in 1957.

Dayger had joined IBM in 1929, at age twenty-four, as a draftsman at the Varick Street laboratory in New York City. He held a degree in electrical engineering from Rensselaer Polytechnic Institute. From 1933 to 1944 he worked in various departments at headquarters in New York City—sales, commercial research, and sales engineering— acquiring what he later described as the most valuable experience of his career.[84] He went next to Endicott as assistant to an executive there and in 1946 became manager of a "special engineering" department, in which capacity he assumed responsibility for engineering management of the Card-Programmed Calculator three years later.

When it became clear that the high-speed wire printer had an unpromising future, Dayger attempted to get the microfilm printer announced as a product to meet at least part of the need for high-speed printing. That printer employed a Compositron tube, made by RCA, with an electron "beam" of large diameter. A stencil disk placed over the photocathode from which the beam originated produced cross-sectional electron densities in the beam corresponding to the character shapes of windows in the stencil. A character was selected by deflection of the entire beam so that only the portion representing the desired character passed through an aperture within the tube and was thence accelerated to the phosphor screen where it formed a light image of the character. This arrangement had the advantage that the stencil disk carrying the font of characters was external to the Compositron tube and could easily be changed, providing for alternate fonts. A contemporary project, at the Stromberg-Carlson Corporation, made use of their proprietary Charactron tube, which had a corresponding character stencil inside it.[85]

IBM's microfilm printer project did not yield a product for the line. As a machine with vacuum tube logic in the year of a corporate decision to announce thenceforth only transistor machines, it was badly timed.[86] Upper management was distracted by an offer by Stromberg-Carlson to provide its printer under a special contract—

one that, after acceptance by IBM, was not fulfilled on schedule by Stromberg-Carlson. After reevaluating the market, IBM dropped its microfilm printer, although a single machine using transistor circuits was delivered to the Social Security Administration offices in Baltimore. It operated there quite satisfactorily for many years, but as replacement components such as the Compositron tube became difficult to obtain, the machine was displaced by printers from Stromberg-Carlson.

The high-speed printer planning committee had hardly documented its recommendation of ferromagnetography when Ralph Palmer requested the formation of another committee, this time to recommend a method of printing for the intermediate-speed range. In less than two weeks, the new committee had finished its study and was urging that printing in the range of 200 to 600 lpm be provided by the development of a chain printer.[87] This recommendation stemmed from exploratory work by Fred M. Demer in the Endicott laboratory, based on a principle that dated back to experiments in the early 1930s using a horizontal bar carrying type and reciprocating horizontally at high speed. Each character on the bar was presented at some instant to each column of the paper, and it required only the proper timing of a print mechanism to cause impact between type and paper. Those earliest experiments had also included a variation on the bar mechanism, in which the type slugs were affixed to an endless horizontal belt or chain, permitting constant speed to replace the reciprocating motion.[88]

The mechanical "analyzer" necessary to select characters and control the timing of hammer impact was enormously complex and seems to have been the stumbling block to the early realization of a practical printer. Beattie recalled that the original bar printer had been in contention with his own wheel printer before the latter was finally chosen for the 407 accounting machine. Both mechanisms were, he said, taken to headquarters in New York City and put on a continuous and grueling test under the supervision of J. W. Birkenstock. The wheel printer came through 24 hours of this pounding with only a few columns out of working order, while the bar printer had only a few columns still printing. That test was apparently the basis for a final decision in favor of the wheel printer for the 407.[89]

By 1954, however, when Demer began his own exploratory work with chain printing, electronic circuits had advanced to the stage where they appeared capable of performing the selection and control of hammer firing reliably and fairly economically. He proposed to use the principle of the electrostatic clutch for actuating the hammer, in a "back printing" scheme. In back printing, character formation resulted from striking the rear surface of the paper—with a small hammer provided in each column position for the purpose—rather than by impelling the type forward against ribbon and paper as in "front printing" methods. Because the electrostatic clutch (mentioned earlier in connection with magnetic-tape transport) was an unproved component, the committee's recommendation to Palmer included a six-month study of that device as a safeguard against its premature application.

Significant in the report of the committee on intermediate-speed printing is its recognition of certain basic advantages in the horizontally moving chain as a carrier of printing type slugs. Competitive printers that had appeared in the mid-1950s for use with computers were based on a drum or stack of type wheels, much like those of the 407 accounting machine, the drum with its axis horizontal and rotating at constant speed. Companies that introduced such printers included ANelex, Shepard Laboratories, Potter Instrument, and Sperry Rand. Capable of speeds up to 600 lpm, they represented an embarrassment to IBM, which could offer only a choice between its 150 lpm 407-derived printer and its still-unsuccessful wire printer. Drum printers were used in computer systems of Honeywell, Burroughs, General Electric, Bendix, Philco, Datamatic, and Ramo-Wooldridge, as well as those of Sperry Rand. Like IBM's proposed chain device, they were all back-printing, "on-the-fly" printers (printers in which the type-carrying elements were in constant motion).

On-the-fly drum printers presented several problems. One of the most serious was the difficulty of maintaining horizontal alignment of printed characters produced from type moving at high speed in a direction perpendicular to the print line. It was necessary to move the type wheels or drum at high speed in order to present the full set of characters to the paper within the time available—for example, considerably less then one-tenth of a second for 600 lpm printing (allowing also for line-spacing the paper). But the smallest variations in hammer-flight time caused the hammer to strike at an instant when the character was not in precisely the desired position. The eye is particularly sensitive to vertical misalignment of characters on a horizontal line (waviness), and the timing problem increased noticeably as attempts were made to obtain operation at speeds over 500 lpm or so. Other disadvantages of drum printers related directly to the need to provide a full font of characters for each column to be printed. At a spacing of ten characters per inch along the line, "shadow printing" resulted from the proximity of adjacent-column characters to the one being printed. Moreover, since the tooling for type was quite expensive, the cost of the machine was greatly increased by the need for 120 sets of type to print a page of 120 columns.

The chain was clearly worth pursuing, since it was much less affected by any of these problems. The type slugs (fastened to a steel band, forming the "chain") moved horizontally; imprecision of hammer flight resulted in variations of character spacing along the line, a defect to which the human eye seems relatively tolerant. Shadow printing could, for all practical purposes, be eliminated by the adequate horizontal spacing of individual characters of the type. (Since each character would at some instant be presented to any given column of the page, there was no need for a type character on the chain for each column.) The cost of type was thus radically reduced; in theory, a single set of characters would serve for all columns. For reasons of timing and to keep the speed of the chain within desired limits, the full font was repeated for a total of five appearances on the chain.

Chain printing offered certain advantages beyond those suggested by the problems inherent in drum-type printers. The one most immediately apparent was the ability to incorporate a larger character set, at reduced printing speed, with fewer than five copies of the font on the chain; or to print faster by including more than five copies of a smaller (for example, purely numeric) font thereon. Even the uniqueness of the chain among competitive products was an attractive aspect of the device. There was also interest fairly early in the project in taking advantage of the lower cost, lower weight, and greater simplicity of the chain to design operator-interchangeable print chain "cartridges."

By July 1957, Dayger had made the decision to gamble on the chain.[90] As a new, high-speed, fairly complex mechanical device, the printer posed many serious problems on its way to announcement in 1959. One was breakage of the type-bearing chain, under the stress of frequent hammer blows, at its high speed of 90 inches per second. Another problem was simply print quality. Although better than the drum, the chain was still an on-the-fly printer, and with rapidly moving type it proved difficult to approach the standard established by the 407 for quality of printing. These problems were solved through the persistent efforts of the engineering team, and at least one alternative to the chain—a train, with type slugs pushed along a track—which had been conceived to solve the chain breakage problem, was used instead in a subsequent, faster printer.

By the end of 1957, it had been decided to energize the hammers by electromagnets rather than by electrostatic clutches, since the latter had not proved reliable. The hydraulically operated paper carriage, developed for the wire printer, was substituted for an electrical stepping

Figure 12.3
Print chain used in the IBM 1403 printer

motor on which some effort had been expended. During 1958, a rather
major change in the program took place when the chain printer was
adopted as a unit of the emerging 1401 system. Shortly after Branscomb
had agreed to add magnetic tape to the 1401, he raised the question
of whether the chain printer needed a control unit, which (as in the
case of the wire printer) had been planned for tape-to-printer operation.
As it turned out, the 1401 was so well suited to (and in such large
part designed for) the editing of data and the control of printing that
it was itself the most economical and generally desirable "control unit"
that could be devised for the printer. Thus, it was in the 1401 processor
that IBM introduced its first "intelligent" (programmable) control unit.

The chain printer was announced in October 1959 as a unit of the
IBM 1401 data processing system and was given the type designation
1403—available in Models 1 and 2 with 100 and 132 columns, respectively. (The card reader-punch of the system was designated the
1402.) The printer had a maximum speed of 600 lpm and printed at
10 characters per inch horizontally from a font of 48 characters. The
machine could be set by the operator to print either 6 or 8 lines per
inch, and it was able to skip groups of 8 or more lines at more than
twice normal line-spacing speed. The 240 characters, representing 5
sets of the font around the chain, required 120 type elements each
carrying the raised type for two characters. (See figure 12.3.)

Regions of the core memory of the 1401 processor were designated
for use as input-output buffer memory, with two regions of 80 characters each reserved for the card reader-punch and one of 132 char-

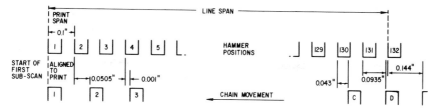

Figure 12.4

Diagrammatic representation of the spacing of characters on the chain relative to print hammer (or print column) spacing in the 1403 printer. Because the type elements on the chain were more widely spaced than the print hammers, on each "subscan" of the buffer memory, every third hammer in succession was presented with a properly aligned type slug. In three such subscans (a full scan) the entire buffer memory was examined once. A font of forty-eight characters required forty-eight full scans for each line printed.

acters for the printer. (These regions were usable as ordinary main memory when input-output instructions were not being executed.) As each character of type came into alignment with a column, the buffer memory location corresponding to that column had to be interrogated. If the character stored there agreed with the character on the chain (as indicated by a "print compare counter" in the 1401 processing unit), the hammer was actuated by current in its electromagnet from the transistor drive circuit for that column. Thus, the entire buffer memory had to be scanned once for every passage of the time interval required for a single character alignment in each column; the total number of such scans was 48, the number of characters in the font. (See figure 12.4.)

Because of the high speed of the chain (90 inches per second), good print quality required that the hammer flight time be held to within a few percent of a constant value.[91] The requirement was met, and the chain printer became an unqualified success. Uniquely an IBM product for many years, it set a standard for print quality in its speed class and added immeasurably to the popularity of the 1401 system. Early in 1961, the 1403 was enhanced by the announcement of two new features: an operator-interchangeable chain "cartridge," to permit convenient selection of alternate fonts; and the capability of higher-speed printing—up to 1285 lpm—in purely numeric mode.

We digress briefly to mention the bar printer, whose development partly overlapped that of the chain. L. A. Wilson had transferred his bar printer project to Endicott in the last weeks of 1960, as part of the 1440 project. In this printer, the type slugs were affixed to finger-like springs projecting vertically from a horizontal bar along its length.

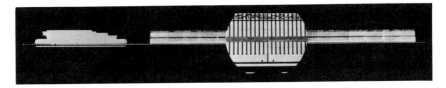

Figure 12.5
Type bar from the 1443 printer. Portions of two of its type-carrying segments are shown enlarged. The metal "flag" at left was used in combination with photosensing circuits to control hammer timing and bar motion.

(See figure 12.5.) This was a front printer operated at 150 lpm, a speed low enough to permit the hammers to deflect the desired type fingers and withdraw without interference from adjacent fingers. In Wilson's original design, in fact, the bar moved in horizontal increments, stopping each time the type was aligned with the hammers opposite the print-column positions. The main advantages of the bar printer over the 407 wheel printer, in which a separate type wheel was used for each column of printing, were its much smaller size and lower cost and the convenient interchangeability of bars for font selection. Print quality was higher still than that obtainable from the chain printer, both because of the absence of shadow printing in a front printer and because the effects of horizontal motion had been eliminated.

In Endicott Frank Furman was placed in charge of the printer, and he made improvements prior to its announcement in 1962 as the 1443 printer in the 1440 system. Furman found that the incrementing motion of the bar could be replaced by a smooth, reciprocating motion without noticeable degradation of print quality. In fact, the simpler motion permitted operating the machine at 240 lpm with the full normal font of fifty-two characters and faster with numeric or other special fonts. The machine was offered in two models, with full-font speeds of 150 and 240 lpm, both using the smooth, reciprocating motion. The quality of printing obtainable from the horizontal-bar mechanism was good enough to permit its use in the printing of bank checks to be read by magnetic-ink character recognition equipment.[92] (See next section.)

Meanwhile, there were many improvements on the original chain printer. Chief among these was the train printer, designated 1403 Model 3, which made use of the principle considered earlier as a remedy for chain breakage. The chain was eliminated, and the type elements were guided around a track—their rear surfaces toothed to engage driving gears and thus push each other around the track. Announced in 1963, this printer was capable of printing alphanumeric data at 1100 lpm; later enhancements provided for the printing at still higher speeds of characters in a "preferred" set. The 1403-3 was still a "back printer," but the chain-train family was to continue for many more years, ultimately producing a front-printing machine that operated at 2000 lpm.[93] After a few years, the train printer design was adopted by numerous other manufacturers and became by far the most widely used high-speed printer in the data processing industry.

12.5 Document Reading Machines

The initial preparation of data for machine processing was a costly step, even in punched-card accounting systems. In a typical accounting application, at least a portion of the information about each transaction had to be keypunched manually before that transaction could be processed. Applications in which the original record was at least partly in the form of controlled printing were seen as opportunities for minimizing the keypunching requirement by providing a means of optical character recognition (OCR).

In oil-company credit-card transactions, for example, the embossed card provided a controlled font for the imprinted account number. Keypunching of that information could be largely eliminated if OCR machines were available in the accounting center. The handwritten dollar amount of the transaction would, at first, still have to be keypunched, but envisioned transaction recorders would eventually imprint that information also. A variety of retail credit transactions could be processed with similar equipment.

In other applications, such as customer billing, a "turnaround" or "reentry" document was often involved. This might be a typed or printed statement bearing the customer's account number and the amount due, in which case OCR machines would again replace key punches. In some cases the customer was sent an IBM card containing, in machine-readable punched form, all the information required for processing the transaction upon its reentry into the accounting system. Keypunching was not a major requirement in such systems. But since the information had to appear in printed form also for the customer to read, the cost of card (and punching) over regular printed documents could be eliminated if an OCR machine were available. The volume of such documents in public-utility billing, for example, often justified consideration of special equipment. Beyond the matter of cost, there were considerations of the better visual quality and greater information capacity of printed paper documents compared to punched cards.

In computer systems, capable of handling thousands of characters per second, the manual entry of data became even more wasteful of time and money. IBM and other manufacturers of computers and business machines recognized in the early 1950s that OCR machines would have to be provided if businesses of the type just mentioned were to be fully served by computers.

Fundamentally, OCR involved scanning a document with a controlled beam of light—with photocells positioned to receive the reflected light—and analyzing the resulting voltage variations to identify each character scanned. An OCR machine would contain the mechanisms for feeding and stacking the documents, the scanning and sensing devices, and the logic circuits necessary for character identification. Farrington Electronics, a division of Farrington Manufacturing Company, pioneered in the development of machine-readable fonts, imprinters, and OCR machines, with special emphasis initially on the credit-card application.[94] Work on character recognition in IBM's Endicott laboratory was reported at least as early as 1936. Such innovators as Reynold B. Johnson and H. P. Luhn turned their attention to the problem in the 1940s. Most projects in those years depended on the simultaneous printing of human-readable characters and machine-readable codes, usually on opposite surfaces of the same document, but they attacked the same general problem as machine-reading ordinary printing, for most character recognition schemes actually used have depended on some constraint or control over printing. Johnson also studied properties of handwritten numerals and later obtained a patent on a method of recognition based on the intersections of a character with "rays" (radial lines) emanating from an upper and a lower point within it.[95]

From 1950 to 1954, several members of N. Rochester's group at Poughkeepsie investigated machine recognition methods, and performed experiments with a cathode-ray-tube "flying-spot" optical scanner attached to the 701 computer. (The computer was programmed to perform the logical analysis for which special circuits would have been provided in a complete OCR machine.) They investigated shape recognition in particular, as distinguished from the more obvious method of matching an unknown character against an ideal pattern of black and white areas. One of the techniques they pursued, called "lakes and bays," involved identification of white areas completely enclosed by black (lakes) and areas partially enclosed (bays), and their relative positions in a character. An experimental lakes-and-bays machine was completed in 1954.[96]

At Endicott, during the same period, at least two groups investigated character recognition. In 1954 the responsibility for OCR development was assigned to Endicott, and the flying-spot scanner and the lakes-and-bays machine were moved there. Although the recognition method employed by the latter would not appear in an IBM product, the machine and the experiments it made possible were helpful in understanding the problems to be solved. Evon C. Greanias had by then emerged as the laboratory's technical leader in the recognition field. Greanias had joined IBM at Endicott in 1952, after five years as a research physicist with the Standard Oil Company of Indiana.[97] Greanias approached the subject initially with what he called the "proportional parts method." Using this technique, a character was dissected into thin, vertical strips by a number of scans and each strip assigned a three-digit code in which the individual digits represented such characteristics as the distribution of black and white regions, the local slope of the uppermost black region, and the maximum height of the character.[98]

There followed a period, covering much of 1955 and 1956, when the Endicott laboratory's hopes for an announceable OCR product were tied to a program known as VIDOR (Visual Document Reader). From time to time competitive announcements, particularly by Farrington and Burroughs, caused a flurry of excitement among IBM's product-planning and marketing executives, but efforts by the engineers to define a product were hampered by lack of agreement on what constituted acceptable performance. Particularly controversial was the question of what percentage of documents the machine could be permitted to reject—that is, classify as containing one or more characters that could not be identified reliably.

The nature of human-readable information and the processes by which it was printed introduced into the design of OCR machines trade-offs that were quite different from those in punched-card reader design. The quality of printing or the physical condition of a document might dictate that, in order to hold instances of incorrect identification down to a very low percentage of characters read, the machine must be permitted to reject several percent of the documents scanned. A machine might, in fact, perform quite acceptably from an economic viewpoint even if it read only 80 percent of the documents and required the remaining 20 percent to be routed through manual operations, for example, copied by a keypunch operator. But such percentages were alien to planners and marketing representatives accustomed to the reliability of card reading, and the VIDOR program languished.

Events in a related area may have helped to generate a more favorable climate in IBM for OCR products. In July 1956, the American Bankers Association (ABA) selected magnetic-ink character recognition (MICR) and a particular font as its proposed "common machine language" on which to base the mechanization of check handling in banks. Up to that time, the only product IBM provided for the automatic sorting of bank checks (by account number, for example) was the punched-card sorter, and it was useful only with special-account checks printed on punched cards. For several years, the ABA had been studying various methods of reading information preprinted on checks in order to mechanize accounting operations. IBM had been aware of the ABA's leaning toward magnetic ink (for its supposed superior freedom from spurious signals caused by smudges and similar problems) but apparently misjudged that organization's determination to proceed directly to MICR as opposed, for example, to the use of a machine-readable code placed near each conventionally printed character.

For several years, there had been a project in IBM's Poughkeepsie laboratory under J. A. Weidenhammer to study the mechanical feeding, transporting, and stacking of paper checks. Lacking the thickness or the uniform length and width of punched cards, paper checks could not be handled by the time-honored method of "feed knives" and narrow "throats" used to select and feed cards one at a time and in proper sequence. Weidenhammer and his colleagues devised instead a system of friction wheels and belts that acted on the surface of the paper to feed the desired check and restrain those following.

Another group, working on magnetic inks and printing, had collaborated with Weidenhammer on a method involving a machine-readable bar code: groups of vertical bars, representing digits and other symbols in a binary-coded decimal format, printed simultaneously with, and under, the human-readable characters on the check.[99] A relatively simple recognition scheme involving a magnetic sensing head, amplifiers, and decoding circuits sufficed to give reliable reading of the preprinted bar code. The ABA concluded, however, that the cost of printing any such combination of coding and characters would be prohibitive and furthermore that the appearance of the bar-coded check was aesthetically unsatisfactory. The ABA's midyear decision on a font for MICR required an immediate turnabout in IBM's bank project. Late in 1956, Greanias in Endicott was commissioned to recommend the most reliable character recognition scheme that could be economically employed.[100]

The font selected by the ABA, along with an associated character recognition technique, had been developed by Stanford Research Institute (SRI) under contract to Bank of America. Highly stylized for the purpose, the characters lent themselves to recognition by analysis of the unique voltage variations each character induced in the winding of a single magnetic read head. As the check moved in its longitudinal (or "horizontal") direction, one character after another passed the head's single gap, a slit extending the full height of the character. The head thus sensed variations in the magnetic field of the ink. Carefully chosen horizontal placements and widths of the lines forming each character gave it the desired unique signal. Because of the single sensing gap, the method did not yield information about the vertical placements of parts of a character.

IBM's competitors, among them NCR, Burroughs, Sperry Rand, and General Electric (which had contracted to manufacture for Bank of America the SRI-developed machine known as "ERMA"), all adopted the SRI recognition scheme. But the IBM engineers, led by Greanias, were reluctant to do so. The OCR technique then showing the most promise involved, first, subjecting each character to many single-line vertical scans as the character moved horizontally, and then analyzing the data resulting from all scans in a single shifting register.[101] Greanias was convinced that the vertical information obtained about the character by this method was sufficiently important to be worth the cost to obtain it, even in the MICR machine. To do so would apparently require a multitrack (or "multigap") head—a composite of many thin heads, each with its separate winding—so that each head would yield information for a separate band across the character. Greanias proposed such a composite head, in which ten adjacent tracks would cover the height of any character. In order to allow for the ABA-prescribed range of positions of the print line relative to the lower edge of the check, it was necessary to make the width of the composite head three times the height of a character. The composite head was therefore constructed of thirty track heads, with sets of three tracks (for example, the first, eleventh, and twenty-first) wired in series to provide a logical OR function. Once the position of a character was determined, anywhere within the range of thirty heads, it could be shifted into a standard registration within the electronic shift register.

The engineers on the IBM bank project in Poughkeepsie were highly receptive to this proposal. They had considered the possibility that their machine might find application beyond the reading of checks—perhaps even to reading normal printing such as that produced using a magnetic-ink ribbon on an IBM 407 accounting machine. In that case, the multigap head would certainly be required, the single-gap head being limited in its usefulness to a highly stylized font such as the one the ABA had chosen. Furthermore, although the multigap head and the associated amplifiers and switching circuits of Greanias's scheme would undoubtedly cost more, the engineers agreed that it should result in significantly more reliable recognition of the ABA font than the single-gap method.

The recognition logic developed for use with the multigap head was based on representation of the character in a matrix of cells, seven wide by ten high. Storage for the matrix of 1s and 0s, representing ink or no ink, was actually in the form of a shifting register, permitting the character to be analyzed in any desired position relative to horizontal or vertical axes. Each character in the allowed set of numerals and special marks (fourteen characters in all) was defined by a logical statement or specification of "black" and "white" cells that must exist in combination in the matrix in order to be recognized as that character. This technique of character recognition was well adapted to simulation by computer and to rapid evaluation of the effects of any proposed changes in ideal character shape.

The ABA's decision in mid-1956 to adopt the SRI font and recognition technique did not amount to a final selection of precise character shapes or dimensions; these were matters to be worked out by a committee of representatives of the manufacturers, including IBM. In December 1958, agreement on a font called Type E-13B was reached after a cooperative effort involving not only the ABA and the bank equipment manufacturers but also ink manufacturers and suppliers of bank checks, who would have to ensure that specified standards of quality and uniformity were maintained in the printing.[102] (See figure 12.6.)

The IBM bank machines, announced in January 1959, included the 1210 sorter reader; magnetic-ink inscribers by means of which the amount could be keyprinted on the face of a check; and control units to permit operation of the sorter reader with a computer, a magnetic-tape unit, or an accounting machine. The sorter could feed, read, sort, and stack checks (of regular paper or punched-card stock and of intermixed sizes) at rates of up to 900 per minute, the feeding rate varying inversely with check length. As a stand-alone sorter, the machine was used to sort on one column at a time, like a card sorter. Connected to a computer, it could be controlled to distribute checks to any of its thirteen stacker pockets (including a reject pocket) based on the reading of an entire field. Much faster and generally improved machines were introduced, starting in 1961, which eventually supplanted the original sorter reader. The reliability of character rec-

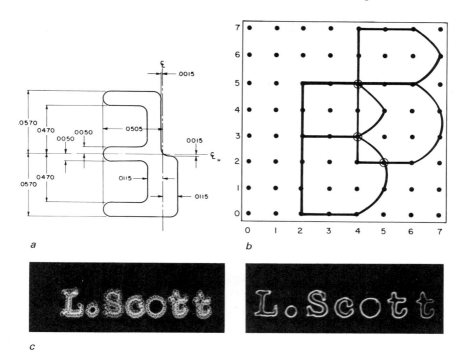

a

b

c

Figure 12.6

Illustrations representing character recognition methods. At *a*, the numeral "3" is shown with standard dimensions for magnetic ink character recognition in the language known as E-13B. As the character moves to the right, its unique magnetic pattern may be sensed by either a single-gap or a multigap magnetic reading head, IBM having chosen the latter for its bank check reader-sorters. (From *The Common Machine Language for Mechanized Check Handling*, The American Bankers Association, 1959.) At *b*, coincidences of a pattern representing the character "B" in its initial position (lower left) with the same pattern displaced to another of sixty-four possible positions in a storage matrix, provide one term of a value used to identify the character in the autocorrelation method of optical character recognition. The oscilloscope traces at *c* represent unfiltered (left) and filtered (right) deflection voltages generated in tracing characters by the curve follower method.

ognition achieved with the multigap head appears to have justified the selection of this relatively elaborate device.[103]

At Endicott, techniques that contributed to the bank program were further developed for use in OCR machines designed to feed and read one or two lines of printed information from paper documents of a wide range of sizes, the maximum dimensions being considerably larger than those of a standard IBM card. Two such machines, the 1418 numeric reader and the 1428 alphanumeric reader, were announced in September 1960 and August 1961, respectively. In use, they were cable connected to either the 1401 or the 1410 data processing systems. In each of these character readers, a mechanical image dissector (related to the Nipkow disc of early television) caused the character to be scanned in a series of vertical bands, each band consisting of a "tall, thin raster" of short horizontal sweeps. In a data consolidation step in the recognition process, information from several sweeps was combined into a single black or white cell of a shift-register-stored matrix much like that of the MICR machine. Again, the contents of the shift register were tested, in various positions, against the digital logic statements for characters of the set. The 1418 was able to read numerals of a standard font printed in either of two sizes by the popular 407 accounting machine. The 1428, having a larger set of logical statements from which to select a match for the character being analyzed, was constrained to reading a special font that, while somewhat stylized for the purpose, was less so than the E-13B bank font.[104]

Certain OCR applications required reading printed information from an IBM card and punching it into the same card; gasoline credit-card accounting was an example. Machines for this purpose had already been supplied commercially by at least one manufacturer, Farrington Electronics, when in October 1963 IBM announced its 1282 optical reader card punch. This machine represented the realization of plans laid in the early 1950s by engineers at Endicott. Simpler in its scanning mechanism than the character readers announced before it and described as requiring only a "fairly trivial logic" for identification of the stylized credit-card characters, it filled an important need in the marketplace. Within two years, one hundred of the machines were installed or on order.[105]

By the early 1960s, with several MICR and OCR products on the market, the company was in a position to take a larger view of character recognition. There was interest, in Research as well as in the product divisions, in understanding the limits of character recognition and underlying technologies. The Social Security Administration (SSA) had for some time been studying the possibility of machine reading information on some portion of its large and growing volume of employer quarterly earnings statements. At IBM's 1962 research and engineering conference, it was reported that while some employers, with SSA encouragement, were submitting reports in computer-processable form (on reels of magnetic tape), there remained about 57 million lines of employee information that required manual conversion by keyboard each quarter. The forms received by the SSA, carrying one line of information per employee, were prepared on every form of typewriter, tabulator, bookkeeping machine, or other printer in use, as well as by hand.[106]

The SSA wanted machines that could perform the conversion on a significant fraction of the printed or typewritten statements. In October 1961, it requested proposals for page readers from manufacturers of OCR equipment. Goaded by E. R. Piore, vice-president of research and engineering, by T. V. Learson, group executive over the data processing divisions, and by executives in the Federal Systems Division, which had responsibility for the government as a customer, IBM's Research and divisional engineering managers deliberated for months over the OCR techniques to propose. The chief contenders, early in 1962, were a "curve follower" method of Greanias (by then in the Advanced Systems Development Division laboratory at Ossining, New York) and an "autocorrelation" method that had originated in the Research laboratory. It had been decided that, should IBM be the successful bidder, the General Products Division would design and build the actual equipment.

Greanias's curve follower consisted of a CRT flying-spot scanner in which the position of the spot was controlled by superimposing a small-diameter circular scan on a coarse vertical scan. After encountering a character as a result of the vertical scan, the spot of light was controlled by the circular scan, which caused continuous exploration of the character's periphery. (See figure 12.6.) Successive explorations yielded information about the character's size and shape through analysis of average beam-deflecting voltages after circular-scan components were filtered out. An interesting feature of the curve follower was that since its scanner was controlled by encounter of the flying spot with the character, it was neither dependent on character registration (exact positioning) nor constrained to reading characters of rigidly fixed shapes (machine-printed characters). For this reason, in fact, it was considered and extensively tested during 1962 for the recognition of handprinted numeric information.[107]

Unlike the curve follower, the autocorrelation method proposed by investigators in Research required a systematic scan of the character and the development of an image made up of 1s and 0s, corresponding to black and white regions, in a storage matrix of suitably small cells. The image was analyzed by counting the coincidences (black superimposed on black) that occurred between the image in its original position and that obtained by shifting the original image to every other position in the storage matrix. (See figure 12.6.) The sum of such counts for all possible positions of the image was supposedly a unique number for each character and was therefore used for identification. It is fairly evident that the number so obtained was independent of the original horizontal or vertical position of the image in the storage matrix and therefore that the autocorrelation method essentially eliminated registration problems. It was, however, very sensitive to variations in character size and shape.[108]

While showing great promise as a theoretical approach, the Research proposal was less convincing to the engineering managers in the General Products Division than that of Greanias. Therefore, IBM's initial response to SSA in February 1962 was based on the curve follower. No decision by that agency resulted from the initial proposal; instead, a more detailed one was requested in May 1963. By then, the engineers had developed a preference for statistical decision techniques, which (although vastly more sophisticated) bore a closer relationship to those already in use in the commercial OCR machines than to the curve follower. Research Division people continued to work closely with the General Products Division engineers on the project (by then located in GPD's Rochester, Minnesota, laboratory.) The selection of significant features to be used in character identification, and methods of measurement of those features, and the development of "reference" values corresponding to characters in the allowed set, were a joint project of the two divisions. The machine actually delivered to SSA late in 1965 was capable of reading well over 200 typed and printed fonts. Its performance exceeded the expectations of all concerned, and it remained in service for at least twelve years.[109] Meanwhile, the curve follower found application in commercial OCR products, announced in 1964 and later, that were capable of reading a variety of printed fonts.

The MICR and OCR products described here, taken all together, accounted for a very small fraction of IBM's annual revenue, small even in comparison with that from the single most popular type of keypunch. But they filled their intended purpose. They helped to make possible the effective use of computers in businesses and applications whose special requirements could not have been met by the better-established product types.

12.6 Small Scientific Computers; Process Control

The high cost of early computers, along with the burdensome nature of programming in machine language, discouraged their use during the 1950s by scientists and engineers concerned with solving small problems. For digital computations involving too few repetitive steps to justify the use of a computer, electromechanical desk calculators were usually relied upon.

The need for computers to solve small scientific problems commanded little attention at IBM during the decade, perhaps in part because of the company's lack of experience in that application area. The use of punched-card machines in the solution of such small problems was rare. IBM's first effort to provide a small scientific computer was not primarily in response to demands from the marketplace. It resulted, rather, from the fact that IBM had a growing population of scientists and engineers of its own who were accustomed to solving their problems on desk calculators.

This was especially true in the environment of Wallace Eckert's Watson Laboratory in New York City. (See chapter 13.) It was there that the Personal Automatic Calculator (PAC) project was undertaken by John J. Lentz. He was one of three engineers hired by Eckert from the MIT Radiation Laboratory in 1945.[110] Familiarizing himself with all activities of the laboratory, Lentz observed that programming the SSEC was more laborious than specifying a sequence of operations on a keyboard. He became interested in designing a small automatic calculator or computer that an operator could use without writing a program in the usual sense of the word.

Lentz began by experimenting with circuits designed for economical storage and accumulation of digital information in decimal form. Most of his early investigation involved the storage of electrical charges on capacitors to represent information—initially only the presence or absence of a bit—the charge being restored periodically. Then, after conversations with Halsey Dickinson in which Lentz learned how digits were stored, transferred, and added to one another in wheel-type electromechanical counters, he saw a useful analogy between the rotary position of a counter wheel and the electrical charge of a capacitor. He devised a counting circuit in which a capacitor was discharged in uniform steps, by two sets of pulses. The number of pulses in each set was controlled by the timing of an input pulse representing one

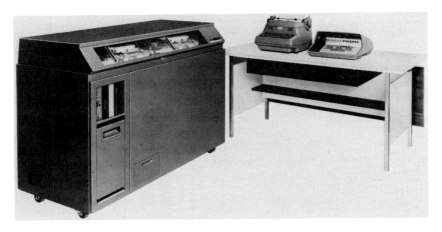

Figure 12.7
IBM 610 Auto-Point Computer announced in 1957. It was known during its development phase as the Personal Automatic Calculator.

of two digits to be added. Thus the final state of charge of the capacitor depended upon the combined values of the two inputs. "Rolling" the counter subsequently with a fixed train of pulses—in a manner not unlike that used to transfer data from Phelps's BCD counter (described in chapter 2)—produced an output pulse timed to represent the sum of the input digits. (Any such pulse that occurred during the adding portion of the digit cycle was stored and treated as a decimal carry.)

Finding this method of decimal digit representation more economical than binary-coded decimal registers, Lentz designed a complete calculator. All digits to be remembered were stored on a small magnetic drum, each digit space on the drum consisting of twelve pulse spaces. The first space was for a "tag" pulse, which might be present or not, and which served control purposes including that of the "cursor" in later terminals and small computer displays.[111] Of the next ten pulse spaces, only one contained a recorded pulse, its position representing the decimal value of the digit. The final space held a pulse only when a decimal point was associated with the digit.[112]

The engineering model of the PAC, described by Lentz in December 1954, was similar in its operation to the product finally announced in 1957 as the IBM 610 Auto-Point Computer.[113] (The delay in introducing the machine resulted from the company's preoccupation with the 700 series computers, the 650, and the RAMAC.) The 610 consisted of three separate physical units (figure 12.7). The largest component was a floor-standing cabinet, which housed a magnetic drum, the arithmetic control circuitry, a plugboard, and separate paper-tape readers and punches for program and data. Cable connected to this cabinet were two desk-top units. The first, an operator's keyboard for control and data entry, incorporated a small cathode-ray tube on which the contents of any desired register could be displayed. The second desk-top unit was an electric typewriter for all printed output. The magnetic drum was used only for numeric registers, of which eighty were general arithmetic registers, each holding thirty-one digits plus sign and decimal point, and four more were special registers (of the same size) involved in multiplication, division, and square-root operations. The machine was capable of operation in either fixed-point or controlled-point mode, the latter being essentially that of the familiar hand-held electronic calculators of later decades.

On the simplest level, the 610 could be used much as a desk calculator, with manual entry of each instruction and all data. At an intermediate level, it could be "programmed" to repeat the instructions keyed in by the operator for a sample set of data simply by capturing the keystrokes on a punched program tape; the operator then had only to key in new sets of data each time the machine stopped. At its most sophisticated level, the 610 could operate indefinitely under control of such a program, calling for new data from a second paper-tape reader and delivering results to the associated data punch and/ or the typewriter. The power of the machine at any of these levels was enhanced considerably by the inclusion of a pluggable control panel in the main cabinet. When the control panel was invoked by an appropriate command from either the keyboard or the program tape, its stepping switch caused the execution of up to 200 program steps in sequence. Often used as a source of prewired subroutines, the control panel could call for any operation available on the keyboard or from tape.

IBM's first "personal computer" was available at a rental of $1150 per month, or purchase price of $55,000. Physically large by the standards of a later generation and one of IBM's last two vacuum tube computers (the large-scale 705 Model III was announced on the same day in September 1957), the 610 was capable of an impressive range of operations. But because of its delayed introduction, the 610 Auto-Point Computer was technologically obsolescent when it became available. Too costly for its performance, it had little impact either in the marketplace or on IBM's product line. Only about 180 were produced, and no successor was planned.

The IBM 650 drum computer, as noted in chapter 5, was very well accepted in both business and scientific applications. But with its monthly rental of at least $3250, it was regarded as an "intermediate" computer. Thus IBM had failed to meet the need for a small scientific computer in a competitive way, and several other companies seized the opportunity. Their machines were typified by the G-15 of Bendix Aviation Corporation and the LGP-30 of Librascope, Inc. Both were in the field as early as 1955; both used the combination of vacuum tube logic circuitry and magnetic-drum storage. The LGP-30, in particular, was a very simple binary machine with only sixteen instructions in its repertoire. It contained only about 100 tubes (fewer than half the number in IBM's 610), had a large, relatively slow drum memory holding 4096 thirty-bit words, and was offered at a purchase price even lower than that of the 610.[114]

By spring 1958, as a result of increasing pressure from the sales organization, the manager of IBM's Poughkeepsie laboratory had asked Wayne Winger to study the small scientific computer requirement and propose a response. Following his early work on magnetic-tape circuits, Winger had served in engineering and planning assignments on the 702 and 705 computer projects, ultimately becoming engineering manager for the latter. At the time of the request just mentioned, he was a member of a small planning group assigned to the laboratory manager.[115] Although price and performance objectives for the small scientific computer seem not to have been stated clearly at the outset, as planning progressed it was understood that an acceptable rental would be in the $1600 to $2000 per month range—about half the rental of the 650 drum computer—and that the arithmetic speed should be at least half that of the 650.

The assumption, Winger recalls, was that he would propose a small drum calculator as a challenger to the machines of that nature already in the marketplace. Drum storage was widely believed to provide the best basis for the design of a low-cost computer. But Winger had made considerable use of magnetic cores in early magnetic-tape buffer storage units and in the memory of the 705, and he included a sizable magnetic-core memory among features for consideration. IBM had no special advantage in magnetic-drum technology or any reason to expect that it could price below its competitors, technology for technology and function for function. But magnetic-core memory was another matter entirely. The company was rapidly accumulating expertise in that technology, and a small scientific computer with core memory would have an enormous edge over its competitors—access times being measured in microseconds for cores and in milliseconds for drums. A decision was made rather early in the planning to use cores in CADET, as the small machine was named during development.[116]

Because core memory was still new and (compared with drums) expensive, Winger and his small engineering group realized it would be important to hold the cost of other parts of CADET to a minimum.[117] They decided to take advantage of the speed and capacity of the core memory to keep the number of arithmetic circuits and registers as small as possible. They planned to store tables of results of addition or multiplication for single-digit operands and require the processor to consult such tables repeatedly in order to build up the complete result of an arithmetic operation. There had been proposals from time to time to use information in stored high-speed memory to replace logical decision circuits. In 1949, N. Rochester had described a machine based on "memorized" rather than logically formed results in, for example, arithmetic operations.[118] Although there is no indication that Winger or anyone else on his project had read Rochester's technical report, the computer they proceeded to define resembled in some respects the machine he had proposed.

Announced in October 1959, about two weeks after the 1401, the CADET computer was officially designated the IBM 1620 System.[119] It was a serial, decimal machine, with fixed twelve-digit instructions, and variable-length data words. Since it had neither an arithmetic unit in the conventional sense nor general data registers, the desired results for addition or multiplication were obtained, digit by digit, from stored tables. Pairs of digits, formed by taking one digit from each operand, were used as table addresses for successive digits of the result, proceeding from lowest order to highest. Subtraction was like addition, except that the complement of either of the operands or the result was produced, when necessary, by circuitry. There was no DIVIDE instruction; the equivalent result had to be achieved either through programming or through multiplication using previously developed reciprocals. Both operands involved in an arithmetic operation were taken from the main-memory locations specified in the first and second address parts of the instruction, and the result placed in the first of these or (as in MULTIPLY) in a predetermined, standard memory location.

Each digit was represented by six bits, of which four were used for the binary-coded decimal (BCD) representation of the numeric value. The fifth was an odd-even parity check bit; and the sixth was a flag bit used to indicate the sign of a number or the end of a word, depending on whether it appeared in the lowest-order or highest-order digit in the field. Alphanumeric characters could be handled, but each was represented by a pair of digits inside the computer.

Input-output equipment was limited to a paper-tape reader and punch and a typewriter whose keyboard served as a manual data-entry device.

By reducing the circuits and other hardware to little more than the bare essentials for storing and retrieving 20,000 digits in core memory, the CADET group had achieved its objective of a computer with approximately half the power of the 650 drum computer at no more than half the cost. Moreover, at a monthly rental of $1600 and purchase price of $74,500, the 1620 provided about four times the computing speed of the LGP-30 at less than twice its cost.[120] With a straightforward and convenient instruction set and a large memory for its time, the 1620 was a successful machine. Supported from the outset with FOR-TRAN as well as a symbolic assembly program and numerous application programs, it was repeatedly upgraded thereafter: its memory was expanded to 60,000 positions; punched-card input-output equipment was added; improvements were made in its operation repertoire, including a DIVIDE instruction; and additional programming systems were provided. Well over a thousand systems had been delivered by the end of 1963.[121] IBM had responded late to the demand for a small scientific computer, but the 1620 was well designed to help the company establish a position in that area of applications.

The 1620 was also the digital computer chosen for IBM's entry into industrial process control. In the IBM corporate reorganization announced at the Williamsburg Conference of November 1956 (see chapter 5), it was officially recognized that electronic data processing machines had become part of the company's product line. The co-ordinating role of director of EDPM, which for nearly two years had been played by C. C. Hurd, was no longer considered as necessary. As a result Hurd, long interested in such extensions of scientific computation as computer simulation and control, was named director of IBM automation research. It had been recognized for some years that industrial processes such as petroleum refining, steel and paper making, and the production of chemicals could benefit from the application of computers. Industrial control systems that had been developed over the years, long before the advent of digital computers, employed devices that were actually analog computers. A process plant would typically use a variety of such analog devices, each tailored to a particular process parameter and supplied with inputs from appropriate sensing devices for temperature, pressure, and so forth. The signals fed to an actuator—which in turn controlled a process variable—might depend on a combination of input conditions, such as the difference between a temperature reading and a preset value, the rate of change of that difference (error derivative), and the accumulation of that difference over time (error integral). It was clear in principle that a digital computer with its flexible stored-program control could take over the functions of a number of such analog computers in much the same way that digital computers had replaced large numbers of single-purpose machines in punched-card installations. The analog controller functions were all describable in mathematical terms and were therefore capable of being executed through the numerical methods developed for digital computers. There was, however, an important difference between existing digital computers and process control equipment. Computers, accounting machines, sorters, and the like all operated in the same sheltered business-office environment. To compete with established industrial controllers, the computer would have to perform in places without temperature or humidity control, in corrosive and grime-filled atmospheres, and with personnel more accustomed to turning valves and throwing heavy switches than dealing with the keys and buttons of a data processing system.

Moreover, to replace a number of analog controllers a digital computer would have to be fast and exceptionally reliable: fast because it would have to match the combined speed of the controllers while keeping pace with a process in "real time" (on a schedule determined by the requirements of the process); and reliable because computer failure might cause serious financial loss or even danger to personnel or equipment. Furthermore, a digital computer used for process control would generally require additional equipment, and therefore system cost, in the form of analog-to-digital conversion at its input and digital-to-analog conversion at its output. This was because process sensors usually produced analog signals, and actuators were usually driven by them.

Beyond all those considerations, there was the problem that any attempt to replace small, distributed, and carefully tailored individual devices with a single large machine was likely to leave unsatisfied a number of small or highly specialized applications. Hurd recognized this problem and approached it with caution and respect. He recruited a small group of engineers and planners and began to study the process control requirements of specific plants in petroleum refining, chemicals, steel, and a number of other industries. The 1401 and 1620 computers were considered the best candidates for use in the first control systems, and around the end of 1959 the 1620 was chosen on the basis of performance, cost, and relative straightforwardness of instruction set.[122]

Early in the automation research program, the engineers who had been assembled by Hurd were made part of the Special Engineering

Figure 12.8
1710 Control system, with 1620 central processor

Products Division, of which J. A. Haddad was general manager and which had a laboratory in Poughkeepsie. A small group of highly technical planners reporting to Hurd was responsible for the requirements of the application and the environment at each site studied. Arrangements were made with three customers, after study of their requirements, to install preliminary models of IBM control systems. These systems, comprising the 1620 computer and analog-to-digital conversion equipment, were enclosed in special covers and originally planned to have a considerable tolerance to hostile environments. As early cost estimates revealed the extraordinarily high cost of a completely "hardened" system (one laboratory model of which was built), it was decided to proceed with simpler enclosures for the equipment and to require air-conditioned and temperature-controlled rooms in the test locations.[123]

In the IBM reorganization of mid-1959, both the 1620 computer and the control systems project were assigned to the General Products Division and designated for transfer to San Jose, California, one of the GPD locations. The three field-test control systems, with their special enclosures, were referred to as 1720s.[124] The first of these was completed in October 1960, before the move to San Jose. By the time comparable systems were made generally available, it had been decided for reasons of product cost to use the standard 1620 computer, an additional frame being provided for the analog-to-digital conversion equipment.[125] The IBM 1710 Control System, as initially offered in March 1961 (figure 12.8), was useful only in "open-loop" control systems—that is, where results computed from sensor readings were printed on the output typewriter of the 1620 and used to direct operators in the manual adjustment of process parameters. By August, "closed-loop" 1710 control systems were available, providing electrical output signals of the analog type suitable for the direct operation of actuators to control the process.[126]

The announcement of the 1710 control system in 1961 represented a significant milestone in the development of IBM's electronic digital computers. It meant that commercially priced machines had reached a level of reliability where they could be trusted not only with the traditional kind of data processing, which could usually be done as well at one time of day as another, but even with the supervision and control of ongoing processes for which interruption or loss of control could have serious consequences. Hundreds of 1710 systems were installed, and these were followed by several generations of faster, more flexible, and still more reliable and economical control systems.[127]

12.7 Teleprocessing and the SABRE System

A wide range of important applications for computers became practical only after techniques were developed for the reliable transmission of digital information between widely separated locations. The history of IBM's involvement in data communications can be traced to events in 1940. In that year IBM began to receive inquiries from customers in various lines of business, all expressing a similar need. They wanted to be able to take information from remote sources, such as branch sales offices or plants, and process it quickly and reliably at a central location. These customers already had punched-card equipment, but they depended on keypunch operators to read and manually punch into cards the lists of data received by printing telegraph from remote locations. Not only was this procedure costly and time-consuming, but it also provided opportunities for potentially serious errors in such transactions as orders for products to be manufactured and securities to be bought or sold. In each case the customer expressed interest in obtaining from IBM a special machine that would read the information punched on paper tape by telegraph devices and automatically punch it into cards without the need for human intervention.

These commercial inquiries stirred little enthusiasm at IBM's headquarters; they were followed, however, late in 1940, by one that the company found more difficult to resist. The U.S. Army Air Corps was anxious to improve its method of preparing balances on hundreds of thousands of stock items, which at that time involved the laborious, error-prone, manual keypunching procedure. IBM expressed interest and was invited to send representatives to a meeting in February 1941 at Wright Field in Dayton, Ohio. The meeting had been called by the army air corps and was attended also by representatives of American

Telephone and Telegraph and its subsidiary, the Teletype Corporation. IBM was represented by L. H. LaMotte, head of its Washington Federal Office (which was responsible for all the company's dealings with the government), and Charles R. Doty from the Commercial Research department at headquarters in New York City. "Specifications were discussed," according to Doty, "and IBM was requested to proceed with the development of a trial machine."[128]

Charles Doty was a self-made inventor-engineer who had experimented with electronics since his early years before World War I. Hired by IBM in 1925 at the company's main office at 50 Broad Street in New York City, he worked at first as a secretary but managed to be transferred to the engineering laboratory at 225 Varick Street. Although assigned there as a purchasing agent, as he recalled much later, he contrived "to do some engineering work on my own."[129]

In his Commercial Research assignment, it was Doty's responsibility to write the specifications for the tape-to-card converter for engineers in the Endicott laboratory, where a first model was to be built for the air corps. This model was delivered and placed in operation on a test basis in mid-May 1941, just three months after IBM had been given the go-ahead. It consisted of an IBM keypunch to which had been added relays to convert from the code of the paper tape to the code of the punched cards, plus an attached paper-tape reading device. Within another three months or so, the air corps received the first ten production copies of this machine, known as the IBM 40 Tape-Controlled Card Punch. In the same year, the air corps requested and received its first model of a machine to perform the inverse function: to read IBM punched cards and prepare perforated tape for use in telegraphic transmission. This machine, derived from an IBM punched-card verifier and fitted with the necessary relays and paper-tape unit, was called the IBM 57 Card-Controlled Tape Punch.

IBM took its first step toward data communications with these two products, which became widely used and were followed by improved machine types within a few years. One might wonder why this first step was based on telegraph networks rather than the faster circuits of the telephone system and why IBM's first data-communications-related product dealt with paper-tape devices as intermediaries instead of being attached directly to communication lines. The answer to both questions lies in the urgency of the government's original request and the existence at that time of widespread telegraph facilities with paper-tape readers and perforators matched to them.

In 1949, Doty was assigned to the Special Engineering department of the Poughkeepsie laboratory. He assisted initially with matters relating to production of the card-tape machines, which were to be manufactured there; but soon he began work on a machine that would eliminate the paper-tape link from card-data communications, improving both speed and accuracy. The code used in transmission between paper-tape devices contained no provision for the automatic detection of errors in transmission. Doty proposed to introduce a card-to-card transmitter and receiver that would employ an error-detecting code and be capable of using not only telegraph circuits but also higher-speed telephone and radio communication facilities.

An eight-bit code was chosen in which every character or control combination would include exactly four "1" bits. This four-of-eight code provided for seventy different combinations, of which only fifty were used for printable characters and four more for control signals such as "end of card" and "end of transmission." It was a well-checked code because all single-bit errors and most errors involving multiple bits would result in combinations that failed the count-of-four test at the receiving end of the line.

When connected to telegraph circuits, Doty's machine transmitted data from three to five cards per minute, applying and sensing direct-current pulses by means of relays. Telephone lines permitted higher-speed transmission. It was possible, within the 4000-cycle-per-second range of frequencies handled by so-called voice-grade circuits, to assign four separate audio frequencies, each to serve as the carrier for a separate data channel in which the signals consisted of on-off modulation of the carrier. The four frequencies chosen were separated by 500 cycles per second: 800, 1300, 1800, and 2300 cycles per second. Prevented by electrical filtering from interfering with each other, four pairs of transceivers could be accommodated on a voice-grade channel simultaneously. Each pair of machines, one transmitting and one receiving, operated at eleven cards per minute, a speed corresponding to sixteen characters per second. The signals were synchronized by the "start-stop" method, which was in common use for telegraphic transmission. With this method the transmission of a single character or control signal occupied ten time intervals: the start interval, the eight code-bit intervals, and the stop interval.

The IBM 66 Data Transceiver, as the card-to-card machine was named, incorporated all circuits necessary for applying the appropriate signals to the line—presence or absence of a direct current in a telegraph line and presence or absence of the audio-frequency carrier in a telephone line. Later, devices containing circuits with this capability became known as "modems" (for *mod*ulating-*dem*odulating), and telephone companies maintained tight control over attachment of such devices to their lines. That issue was avoided in the case of the Data Transceiver, mainly because its use was restricted initially to leased and private telephone lines. The system was tested in February 1952, when information read from punched cards in one transceiver in Poughkeepsie was transmitted to New York City and back and punched into cards in a second transceiver. A more impressive demonstration was given to IBM executives on 7 and 8 July 1953, when the machines were similarly used to transmit data from the board room in New York City to Roanoke, Virginia, and back over a path including open wire, carrier, submerged cable, and microwave telephone links.[130]

The IBM Data Transceiver was announced in 1954 when IBM's first computers were already in the field, thus adding communications capability to the new electronic data processing systems. The machine was limited to batch transmission of data and therefore represented only another step toward modern-day data communications. It was followed by higher-speed batch-transmission devices, the first of which was the 7701 Magnetic Tape Transmission Terminal, a machine whose objective was to make full use of the 1200-bit-per-second data rate of voice-grade channels. Announced in March 1960, it included an incremental magnetic-tape drive (one that started and stopped for each character) at a tape-recording density of 200 bits per inch and an electronic innovation for line control called the Synchronous Transmitter Receiver. STR permitted much faster transmission, retaining the four-of-eight code but eliminating the start-stop signaling method and holding transmitter and receiver in synchronization for an entire message rather than for one character at a time.

A significant project in the development of commercial computer applications involving data communications was known as SABRE. This project originated after discussions between American Airlines and IBM executives in 1953. The airline company approached IBM for assistance in studying the application of computers to its passenger reservation system.

Since at least 1946, IBM sales executives had been aware of an electrically controlled reservation system installed in the American Airlines office in Boston by the Teleregister Corporation. Built around a central, manually plugged control panel, and lacking the element of digital data communication, it nevertheless represented an important move toward coordinating the reservation process.[131] This system, named the Reservisor, was limited to indicating the availability of space—"open" or "closed"—on a given flight.

A more advanced system in operation by mid-1952 employed a magnetic drum to store the seat inventory. Known as the Magnetronic

Reservisor, the new Teleregister system was installed in the American Airlines office at LaGuardia Airport in New York. It provided a significant advancement in capability over its predecessor: it permitted agents not only to determine seat availability on a flight, but to sell or cancel seats directly and leave the resulting seat inventory stored on the drum. W. W. McDowell had been urging action by IBM in the airline reservations area since 1950 when he moved to headquarters. In 1952, referring to the specially developed Teleregister system, he told LaMotte and Roberts "I think we are going to have to take developments on somewhat the same basis if we are ever to be successful in some of the tough applications, such as Banks, Department Stores, Railroads, etc."[132]

Then a chance meeting that took place late in the spring of 1953 — appropriately enough on an airplane — helped to elevate the airline reservations problem to the status of a project. R. Blair Smith, a senior salesman for IBM in Santa Monica, California, found himself on a transcontinental flight with C. R. Smith, president of American Airlines.[133] Their conversation turned to the airline's most pressing data processing problem. For all its efforts to provide the most advanced reservation system possible, the airline was prevented by storage limitations from doing more, automatically, than keeping track of seats sold and seats available, by flight. Lists of passenger names, and essentially all other information that applied to the individuals reserving the seats, were maintained by hand. The complications arising from human error and the inability to keep details up to date with changes in people's travel plans represented a problem that grew by leaps and bounds as airline travel became ever more popular. Clearly, a much more comprehensive, integrated data system was needed.

The airplane conversation left Blair Smith in no doubt about the pioneering attitude of American Airlines and its determination to solve the reservation problem by means of the most up-to-date automatic equipment obtainable. There were already three IBM 701 computers installed in his sales territory, and he was on his way to Poughkeepsie to attend the first sales class on the soon-to-be-announced 702. He was convinced that a computer like the 702 could handle a much larger portion of the reservation process than methods or equipment then in use. The conversation intensified C. R. Smith's eagerness to see an answer to his company's large and growing need and initiated a new flurry of contacts between the engineering and planning staffs of the two companies.[134]

At IBM, the problem was assigned to a small study group led by Hans Peter Luhn and Perry O. Crawford. The latter (mentioned in chapter 7) had joined IBM in the headquarters Product Planning department in 1952 and had been especially interested in information organization, storage, and retrieval. (For Luhn's earlier contributions in that area, see chapter 8.) By March 1954, McDowell and Birkenstock had been informed that "the study group concurs with American that development of an efficient, highly mechanized system should proceed in steps to obtain guidance from operating experience." In June they had a draft proposal for an "integrated data system" for the airline.[135] By mid-year a good deal of discussion had taken place at high levels of the Engineering and Product Planning staffs, but it was not unanimously agreed that IBM should undertake such a seemingly large, resource-consuming project for what was believed to be a specialized and somewhat limited area of the market.[136] Nevertheless, the dedicated small study group maintained its zeal and, in July, recommended that IBM undertake a three-or-four-man joint study with American for a year or so to work up a proposed set of specifications for equipment.[137]

In early correspondence concerning the airline's requirements and possible solutions, little if any mention was made about the specific form of storage that might solve the problem. It seemed to be understood that the introduction of vastly more data would require much more advanced storage than any under development. Drums were inadequate, but development of the 305 RAMAC system had been underway at San Jose for more than a year. It was expected that the airline requirement would not only assist the infant random-access storage program by providing the specific parameters of a real and urgent application but also benefit in return from the results of that program.

IBM continued working closely with American Airlines, and the study continued for the better part of four years—1954 through 1958. It became the responsibility of an advanced product-planning function at corporate headquarters and an advanced engineering planning group in Poughkeepsie in 1955 when those two groups were formed. Then at the beginning of 1957, the project was established formally as SABER (Semi-Automatic Business Environment Research) in the newly created Research organization in Poughkeepsie. There, it was managed by William J. Deerhake, who transferred to Poughkeepsie from Watson Laboratory. Deerhake had worked at the MIT Radiation Laboratory during World War II. He joined IBM at Watson Laboratory in 1948 and shortly began working on electrostatic storage of the Williams type. As the NORC project developed (see chapter 5), Deerhake assumed responsibility for the memory. With that machine delivered, he was free to take on SABRE, as it became known, but that project remained in Research for only about eighteen months.

It was moved (with most of its personnel) to the Special Engineering Projects Division (SEPD) under J. A. Haddad in November 1958.[138] SABRE was one of several system efforts that were incorporated in the Advanced Systems Development Division (ASDD) when that unit was formed in 1959 with Haddad as general manager. The project remained ASDD's responsibility through completion of the system and its installation at American Airlines.

In the course of SABRE's planning and design, a succession of computers spanning two technological generations had been considered for its control. The earliest plan had been based on a decentralized system — a number of computers in centers scattered across the country. Because a duplex arrangement of computers emerged as the best solution for dependable operation, and because that increased the cost of a center, and finally because SEPD had acquired responsibility for the real-time channels of the BMEWS 7090s (see chapter 11), the SABRE system became a single-centered one using duplexed 7090 computers.[139] One of the computers was normally used to perform the data processing essential to the reservation application and the other, acting as a standby available to substitute in that role at any time, was normally occupied with lower-priority, routine batch jobs.

Similarly, as SABRE took form a whole succession of automatic file storage devices was considered, including punched or printed cards, photographic storage, the RAMAC disk storage, and finally the one that was chosen: the IBM 1301 (the Advanced Disk File) with its 50 million character capacity per storage unit, for which the SABRE project had represented the first and most pressing need.

It has often been said that without the SAGE project, there would have been no SABRE — for a long time at least. SABRE did indeed bear a resemblance to SAGE — a scaled-down SAGE, to be sure, since the whole central computing complex of SABRE could be compared in form to only a single direction center of the air-defense system. Even so, in its early years the American Airlines reservation system was recognized as the largest commercial real-time data processing system in operation.[140] Where SAGE had surrounded each twin computer with a vast communication network of radar data sources, the pair of 7090s in SABRE was surrounded by a network involving agent terminals at more than 1000 reservation desks and ticket counters. (See figure 12.9.) While lacking the SAGE center's huge array of special CRT consoles, SABRE had its two processors connected in common to sixteen 1301 disk storage units with a combined capacity of about

Figure 12.9
SABRE system reservation desk of American Airlines. Agent terminals consisted of the IBM input-output Selectric typewriter, a director console at the operator's right for push-button entry of such information as the date of the flight and the number of seats required, and an air information device (AID) above the Selectric. The operator inserted into the AID a special card displaying information about all flights between two cities. Special punching in the card, automatically sensed by the AID, identified that card to the computer. The operator selected a specific flight by depressing row and column buttons adjacent to the card.

800 million characters—the largest on-line and directly accessed storage subsystem that had ever been assembled—and to six high-speed magnetic drums of SAGE design.

Introduced specially for SABRE were agent terminals based on a special input-output version of the IBM Selectric typewriter with its spherical, interchangeable type element. The "I/O Selectric" had just been developed by the Electric Typewriter Division laboratory under H. S. Beattie in Lexington, Kentucky. This new device possessed important advantages over the traditional electric typewriter when operated as a printing terminal. It was inherently less complex and lower in cost, partly because its print element was positioned under control of seven electromagnets rather than requiring one for each key. The print element moved across the paper, eliminating the inconvenient and space-demanding movable carriage of other typewriters then available. It was also faster, by perhaps 50 percent, providing output messages at approximately fifteen characters per second. All in all, the I/O Selectric contributed significantly to the competitiveness of SABRE, and it would become an increasingly familiar component of reservation systems as well as of other, more generalized data communication systems over the years.

The equipment for the SABRE central processing installation at Briarcliff Manor, about thirty miles north of New York City, was delivered in January 1962 and checked out during the year. In addition to providing the machines, IBM developed the control program. This was a programming innovation of major importance. It controlled all major aspects of operation of the 7090s and the transfer of American Airlines' operating programs as required between main memory and large drum memory units, and of passenger and flight information between main-memory and the huge disk storage, all in a real-time, communication-based application. "Real-time" in this case is characterized by a specification that had been set by American Airlines at the outset and maintained throughout the project: there would be a less than 3 second delay between the keying in of data by an agent and the response received at the agent's terminal.

It was for the SABRE system that IBM first used the term "teleprocessing," at the suggestion of J. A. Haddad. For airline and agents, SABRE provided a much-needed expansion of reservation service—from a mere count of seats sold and seats available on each flight to a constantly updated and instantly accessible file of information about the passenger, including telephone contacts, special meal requirements, and hotel and automobile reservations. Beyond that, the power and flexibility of the machines and the control program permitted American

Airlines to extend the system to flight planning, maintenance reporting, crew scheduling, fuel management, and essentially all other real-time aspects of its total operation.[141] The SABRE system became fully operational in 1964, when the last of the major cities was brought "on line."[142] Reservation systems using a variety of computers were subsequently placed in service by many other airlines. But the influence of the SABRE project extended far beyond the airlines and other companies offering comparable reservation services. SABRE helped to prove the effectiveness and economic value of the computer in a wide range of industries where distributed operations needed better central control.

Thus, in order to extend the computer's range of usefulness, IBM had mounted technical efforts as varied as the factors seeming to limit that range. At the very low end of the cost scale, a solution was found in the 1401, designed to be so economical that it could replace even modest-sized installations of traditional punched-card machines. At the other end of the scale, a large central computer was linked to a vast network of terminals to provide a nationwide service that would have been impractical without a variety of technical accomplishments, including reliable data communication techniques, large-capacity disk storage, and a control program for real-time, on-line operations. These achievements, along with many others—higher-speed and better-quality printing, machines to handle and read printed documents, systems that could operate reliably in hostile environments—met essential needs of the computer age.

13

Research

The Watson Laboratory. Research in Poughkeepsie. Separating research from development. Basic research in Zurich. Restructuring the San Jose laboratory. Preparing for the new research center. Exciting projects. Growing problems.

Prior to World War II, IBM's electromechanical product technologies had evolved at a relatively slow pace. The company's success derived primarily from its responsiveness to customer needs and its ability to design and manufacture reliable, serviceable products. Supported by engineers and draftsmen, inventors provided IBM with new products, and T. J. Watson, Sr., aware of the importance of this process, involved himself personally in hiring creative people and establishing product development projects.

Watson was keenly interested in science and technology generally. In 1947, for example, he began supporting the work of a physician, John H. Gibbon, Jr., who was developing a mechanical heart and lung to take over the functions of the human counterparts during operations. In 1954 Gibbon wrote to Watson praising the "inventiveness and ingeniousness" of IBM engineers in Endicott who had "enormously improved and simplified" the device. He added, "It is a beautiful piece of work and will do the job of the former machine, I am sure, with far greater safety and simplicity. We are, of course, greatly indebted to you for making these changes and improvements."[1] Turned over to another company for production, the machine became known as the Gibbon-Mayo Pump-Oxygenator and was in use in eight hospitals by 1959.[2]

Watson also had a near-reverence for education that caused him to support a variety of activities at Columbia and Harvard universities. It will be recalled that in consultation with his "chief scientist," James Bryce, he had donated punched-card equipment to establish the Columbia University Statistical Bureau that began operation in 1929, supplied modified IBM machines to Wallace Eckert for astronomical calculations in 1934, and established the Astronomical Computing

Bureau at Columbia University in 1937. He had also become a trustee of Columbia in 1933. In 1939, he had signed an agreement with Harvard to construct an automatically operated assemblage of calculating machines, proposed by Howard Aiken. The resulting IBM Automatic Sequence Controlled Calculator (ASCC), later known as the Harvard Mark I, was dedicated in August 1944. (See chapter 1.)

Watson's primary motives in supporting these research activities appear to have been a sense of duty to society, pride in IBM, and recognition that fundamental advances in automatic computation might result in new uses for the company's products. He knew that IBM's product line traditionally had been enhanced and broadened in response to new applications suggested by customers, and scientific computation using punched-card equipment was one such application.

In the fall of 1944, Watson invited Wallace Eckert, who had served as director of the Nautical Almanac at the U.S. Naval Observatory since 1940, to join IBM and form the Department of Pure Science. It was Watson's desire that this department would become the premier organization in the country for developing and using automatic calculation methods in science. Although the term "pure science" may seem inappropriate for describing some of the proposed activities of this department, it did help distinguish them from IBM's advanced engineering that Watson liked to refer to as "science." Eckert himself provided the following clarification: "By pure science we mean scientific research where the problem is dictated by the interest in the problem and not by external considerations. In other words, he [Watson, Sr.] wished to set up a research group which would function in a manner similar to those in academic institutions." The laboratory facilities established for this department were officially known as the Watson Scientific Computing Laboratory at Columbia University.[3]

The timing of Watson's decision to establish the new department—perhaps the decision itself—appears to have been influenced by Howard Aiken's snub of IBM at the ASCC dedication earlier in the year and by Aiken's plans to build even bigger automatic calculating machines without IBM's help. Watson did not want to lose preeminence in the construction and use of the most advanced automatic calculators in the world. Accordingly, one of Eckert's first assignments was to establish specifications for a supercalculator that would eclipse the ASCC and any calculator Aiken might build in the future (see chapter 2). From a broader perspective, however, establishing the new department under Eckert was a continuation of Watson's long-established policy of contributing to the advancement of education and science while promoting new uses for IBM equipment.

In accepting the offer to join IBM, Eckert became the first scientist with a doctorate to be hired by the company. The research and instructional resources of Eckert's laboratory were to be made available to scientists, universities, and research organizations throughout the world. According to the official news release, "the laboratory is designed not only to increase the already notable contribution of high efficiency calculating machines to the war effort, but by a broad interest in the computational problems of all branches of the physical and social sciences to strengthen the scientific and educational foundations of our national security and the welfare and peace of the world."[4]

It was soon evident, however, that even this broad mission of the laboratory was too narrow to satisfy IBM's technological requirements in the postwar era. Thus, Ralph Palmer, who had just returned from the navy, was asked to move from Endicott to Poughkeepsie early in 1946 to establish an engineering group to work on vacuum tube electronics.

Less than a year later, Wallace Eckert joined John McPherson in writing to Watson, Sr., warning of serious competitive threats presented by developments in digital electronics. Noting that the National Bureau of Standards had embarked on a program to develop electronic digital calculating devices, the letter asserted, "This program parallels several other developments now being financed by the Army and Navy at the University of Pennsylvania, the Institute for Advanced Study, Harvard University, MIT, and other places. Several commercial concerns in addition to IBM have been developing electronic computing machines, including RCA, National Cash Register, and Eastman Kodak." Concerning the significance of these efforts, Eckert and McPherson made the following observations:

Whereas before the war IBM was the only organization able and willing to carry on large scale development of calculators, such development is now taking place on a large scale.

The trend from mechanical devices to electronic ones carries the development into fields where other organizations such as RCA have a wide background of experience and an extensive basic patent structure.

In view of these facts we can expect important developments on a large scale in electronic calculation both from government financed research and from industry. These developments which are directed at ultra high speed calculators will eventually affect business machines as well.

McPherson and Eckert pointed out that these outside activities presented IBM with a serious dilemma. If the company maintained its traditional policy of secrecy and attempted to develop all required electronic capability internally, it might fail to keep pace with companies that used government money to finance their development efforts. Because of the "wide scope of outside development," they asserted, "it is doubtful if IBM could or should try to match them in extent." On the other hand, if the company involved itself in government-funded research and development, it would necessarily forfeit some of its patent rights.[5]

While others debated these policy issues, Tom Watson, Jr., who had returned from the service late in 1945, pressed for increased involvement in electronics, and Ralph Palmer developed the needed expertise in Poughkeepsie. By 1950, the Type 604 electronic calculator had been introduced successfully to the market, an aggressive recruiting program for electronics engineers was underway, Wallace McDowell had become director of engineering, and Palmer had been designated manager of the Poughkeepsie laboratory with prime responsibility for developing IBM's capabilities in electronics.[6]

A year earlier, Arthur Samuel, with more than twenty years of experience in vacuum tube research and development, had been hired to establish an advanced development effort in vacuum tube devices and to provide technical support for the proposed vacuum tube production by IBM. By mid-1950—less than one year after Samuel arrived—the potential importance of transistors and other solid-state devices was recognized, and the Poughkeepsie laboratory under Palmer was given responsibility for establishing a capability in this area as well.

So it came about that IBM had scarcely established the Watson Scientific Computing Laboratory to develop automatic computation methods when vacuum tube electronics became the primary technological requirement of the company; and barely had work in electronics been started in Poughkeepsie when solid-state devices were identified as an equally urgent need. These rapid shifts in emphasis reflect not only the rapid technological changes then taking place in the industry but also the difficulties IBM faced as it attempted to meet the challenge.

In addition to uncertainty concerning the direction of technological advances, there was also uncertainty as to how research and development should be managed. It was not clear whether research and development should be carried out in the same group or separate groups or whether they should have the same or separate management. If separate, how should one define what was research, development, and advanced development, and how should interaction among the groups be achieved?

Most of IBM's technical management had had little time to worry about such matters during the first decade following World War II. They were much too busy doing what was necessary to get IBM started in electronic data processing and in the new field of electronic stored-program computers to worry about how research and development should be organized and managed. But by the mid-1950s, the issue became more important, largely because of the success the company had already achieved but also because two very different management philosophies had emerged within IBM. One was the pragmatic, results-oriented, R&D philosophy practiced in Poughkeepsie; the other was the university-oriented, separate research practiced in the Watson Laboratory. These two management philosophies were brought into sharp focus and became an increasing source of conflict as the company worked to strengthen its research and development activities during the late 1950s and early 1960s.

13.1 The Watson Laboratory

Wallace Eckert's decision to accept the offer to head IBM's first laboratory devoted to pure science was influenced by many years of association with Watson, Sr. Eckert was convinced of Watson's genuine interest in promoting science. He knew Watson believed a corporation should participate in the cultural life of the community and that because IBM reaped the benefits of science, it should contribute to science. Watson had, in fact, emphasized to Eckert that only by maintaining the ideal expressed in its name could the Department of Pure Science render its best service to the company. The department was intended to assist the engineering and development work within the company but not to become another development group. It was to assist in selling scientific installations but not become a sales group; to assist in public relations in connection with scientific subjects but not become a public relations office; and to provide education in scientific calculation for members of IBM, customers, and scientists but not become an educational institute. In early discussions with Eckert, Watson had urged him to maintain his own standing as an astronomer. Noting that a scientist should contribute to activities that were not pure science, Watson had asserted that the contribution would be effective only so long as he remained primarily a scientist.[7]

Consistent with these views, Eckert proposed that the department's facilities be located on the Columbia University campus where research could be carried on in an academic setting with easy contact with other scientists. Temporarily located in Pupin Hall on the Columbia campus, the laboratory moved in November 1945 into new quarters in a townhouse at 612 West 116 Street where facilities could be provided for two to three dozen professionals. The building was 25 feet by 90 feet, with five stories above ground and a basement and cellar below ground. About half of each of the lower three floors held punched-card and other computing equipment. There was also a library, reception lounge, and a small machine shop.[8] Officially designated the Watson Scientific Computing Laboratory at Columbia University, the facility was more commonly referred to simply as the Watson Laboratory, and by 1963 this shorter name was officially adopted in recognition of the broader scope of the research activities. (See figure 13.1.)

One of the first persons hired by Eckert was Robert Seeber, who had worked for Aiken programming the IBM Automatic Sequence Controlled Calculator (Harvard Mark I). At IBM, Seeber became the chief architect of the Selective Sequence Electronic Calculator (SSEC), which was designed at Watson's request to outperform the ASCC and any other machine Aiken might build. Another early employee was Llewellyn H. Thomas, a world-renowned applied mathematician and theoretical physicist who is best known for the Thomas-Fermi approximation for describing degenerate electron gases and for the Thomas precession of electron spins. He is also credited with first suggesting strong focusing in particle accelerators (using shims on magnet pole pieces), and he had even received a medal from the army for his analysis of mortar lap joints.[9] Thomas had left Ohio State University to join the new Watson Laboratory in order to work on the adaptation of mathematical problems to automatic calculating machines. His bibliography lists nearly fifty publications after he joined IBM, with titles such as "Stability of Solutions of Partial Differential Equations," "Use of Large Scale Computing in Physics," and "Relativistic Particle Dynamics."[10] He also involved himself in practical engineering problems and collaborated with an engineer in the laboratory in early experiments using magnetic rings for information storage (see chapter 7).

The decision to hire Thomas had been made following the recommendation of I. I. Rabi, a Nobel Prize–winning member of the Columbia University physics department who had served as associate director of the MIT Radiation Laboratory during the war. Recognizing the need to hire specialists in electronics, Eckert had also sought Rabi's advice in hiring Byron Havens and John J. Lentz, both of whom had

Figure 13.1
IBM Watson Laboratory buildings. A five-story townhouse (top) at 612 West 116 Street in New York City housed the Watson Laboratory from 1945 until 1953 when a larger building on 612 West 115 Street (bottom) was purchased by IBM and donated to Columbia University to serve as the Watson Laboratory. This facility was closed in 1970 when its research activities were transferred to the IBM Thomas J. Watson Research Center in Yorktown Heights, New York.

worked at the Radiation Laboratory on radar and advanced electronic circuitry.[11] It will be recalled that Havens initiated development of the Naval Ordnance Research Calculator (NORC), the most powerful computer in existence for many years, and designed an electronic delay circuit, which was also used in the IBM 701 computer (see chapter 5). Among other activities of Lentz was his experimentation, starting around 1948, with circuits for use in a "personal computer." In 1957, still uncertain of the market for small computers, IBM introduced the IBM 610 Autopoint Computer that Lentz had developed in the intervening years (see chapter 12). There were, of course, many other outstanding individuals at the Watson Laboratory, but the activities of these few provide some sense of the breadth and depth of the work.

Besides serving as director of the laboratory, Eckert was also appointed professor of celestial mechanics at Columbia in 1946, and joint appointments with Columbia University soon became a common practice. Teaching was not to be used by laboratory members to supplement salaries, all of which were paid by IBM; but involvement in the academic life of a major university was intellectually stimulating and one of the many attractions of the Watson Laboratory. Academic freedom was emphasized.[12] "The relations of IBM with the Columbia University are unprecedented and ideal," Eckert wrote in 1947. "There are no formal agreements or regulations; the entire arrangement is based on Mr. Watson's statement that the Laboratory is for Pure Science. We collaborate on matters of mutual interest. The University makes no inquiries concerning our relations with our customers, members of IBM, visitors from elsewhere, or our development work. Our staff is free to use all the facilities of the University, and we try to reciprocate where we can be of use."[13]

The primary missions of the laboratory during its first ten years were to develop scientific computation techniques, contribute to the design of new computers, and educate people inside and outside IBM in the use of automated computation methods. Its missions were carried out in a variety of ways. Many people were trained on the SSEC and NORC projects. The SSEC programming group included John Backus, who subsequently worked on 701 programming before transferring to the Applied Science Department where he led the development of the still-popular FORTRAN language.[14] The Watson Laboratory's "Three-Week Course on Computing" was started in 1947 to teach others how to use punched-card equipment for sophisticated calculations. Ultimately attended by more than 1500 persons from over twenty countries, this highly successful course influenced IBM's decision to create computer instruction centers throughout the country in 1957.[15]

Although the Watson Laboratory had no mission as such in solid-state technology, Eckert in 1949 had taken advantage of an opportunity to hire Léon Brillouin, whose interest in being in the New York City area had earlier influenced his decision to leave Harvard to become director of engineering education in Poughkeepsie.[16] One of the world's leading scientists in solid-state physics, Brillouin is probably best known for his theory of "Brillouin Zones," a central feature of the quantum mechanical theory of the solid state. Part of his assignment was to establish educational programs, and many IBM engineers received their introduction to solid-state theory in a series of lectures given by Brillouin in Poughkeepsie early in 1950. This was only a few months before Loren Wood was transferred from corporate headquarters to Poughkeepsie to establish a transistor research effort under Samuel.[17] Brillouin, whose personal contributions and interests extended to engineering of radio antennas, electric wave transmission in cables, and electron beams in traveling wave tubes and magnetrons, also served as a consultant to engineers in Poughkeepsie on practical development problems.[18]

Meantime, the relatively dormant issue of how research and development should be managed began to surface. During 1951, several management committees were formed according to Watson, Jr., in order to "enable us to make decisions in the light of all the best available facts and opinions. We used to be able to do this by individual personal contact, and I don't want to lose one bit of that," he asserted, "but IBM is growing and a great deal is happening, so these get-togethers should give us perspective and a unity of interests."[19] Eckert, McDowell, McPherson, and Samuel were assigned to one of these management committees, the function of which was to review IBM's progress in pure research.[20]

At the first meeting of the Management Committee on Pure Research, held in July 1951 and attended by Watson, Jr., a primary topic was Eckert's proposal for an expanded program. During 1950, the Watson Laboratory had employed 40 people, occupied 13,000 square feet, and spent $275,000. Eckert proposed a three-fold increase to 130 people with appropriate increases in space and expenditures. The expanded program was to deal with all aspects of "information handling: the nature of information, means of representing it, and its movements and manipulations." Three-quarters of the effort was to be divided nearly equally among mathematics, physics, and electronic engineering, with smaller efforts in chemistry and metallurgy.[21]

There seems to have been little disagreement about the desirability of increasing basic research in the company, but there was substantial discussion of what distinguished research from development, how it should be managed and related to development and manufacturing, where it should be located, and how to obtain outstanding people. One problem was that of definition: two projects could be doing essentially the same work, yet one was called research and the other development. No clear definition resulted during these meetings, although Eckert proposed that a project done to specification was engineering, whereas one done without specification was research. A more pragmatic view expressed during the discussions was that projects performed in research laboratories were called research whereas projects undertaken in engineering or development laboratories were not.[22]

In the fall of 1951, Watson, Jr., requested McPherson to contact leading research administrators at Princeton University, RCA, and Bell Laboratories to seek their guidance. Of particular interest to Watson was the possibility of gaining the benefits of pure research by funding the work of others. By the end of November, McPherson reported that all those contacted had agreed with the following four points:

1. Support of fundamental research programs of interest to IBM is welcomed . . . *provided* we place no restrictions on freedom of research communication or publication and do not ask for patent rights.
2. No direct benefit to IBM can be assured from such a program.
3. The recommended way to benefit from this support of university research is to have these programs set up and guided by an IBM fundamental research group familiar with our needs and working in fields of interest to the Company.
4. The IBM research group will not be effective if it is an administrative or staff function only and not an organized working group.[23]

These outside views clearly indicated that the benefits of pure research could not be obtained merely by funding the work of others. The company would have to participate in all areas relevant to its needs. The way this participation should be structured was a problem turned over to a subcommittee consisting of Eckert, McDowell, McPherson, Palmer, and Samuel. The most substantive differences of opinion arose over the appropriate geographical location for research and its organizational relationship to development. Samuel, speaking from his experiences at the Bell Laboratories and the IBM Poughkeepsie laboratory, recommended close organizational and geographical proximity for development and research. Eckert, on the other hand, emphasized the importance of close ties with a major university. He minimized the problems of achieving good internal communication and the possible loss of propriety information through university contacts. Much more important in his mind were the availability of a good library, association with university people, opportunities for advanced education, and the attraction this relationship would have for new employees.[24]

Eckert's views prevailed, and by 1952 he had obtained approval from IBM and Columbia University to expand the mission and facilities of the Watson Laboratory. To accommodate the planned expansion, a second, larger building—a former women's residence club at 612 West 115 Street—was bought by IBM, renovated, equipped with physics laboratories, and donated to the university. (See figure 13.1.) It was fully ready for occupancy in September 1953, with some laboratories in service as early as July. Meanwhile with the help of Rabi and others of the Columbia Physics Department, Eckert had set about to recruit Ph.D.s who could be turned loose, with little direction, to examine various areas of the newly evolving discipline of solid-state physics.[25]

That July, Eckert was pleased to advise Watson, Jr., that he had already hired eight outstanding scientists with doctor's degrees: seven physicists and one chemist. Among those cited was Richard L. Garwin, who had arrived before the end of 1952. "A student of Enrico Fermi and later an assistant professor at Chicago University. He is extremely well informed in all fields of physics," Eckert reported, "and is full of ideas and enthusiasm on matters of both scientific and practical interest. He has been a consultant for the AEC at Los Alamos for several years. He is now 25 years old." Another was Erwin L. Hahn, previously an instructor at Stanford, who Eckert said, "has all the earmarks of the potential Nobel Prize winner. His overwhelming interest is in pure fundamental physics; yet his first experiment resulted in the discovery of 'Spin-Echoes' whereby one can now store information on the nucleus of the atom." A third was Gardiner L. Tucker, who received the Ph.D. under Rabi at Columbia and to whom reference has already been made (see chapter 10) as a co-inventor of IBM's first process for making the all-important graded-base, drift transistors for Stretch.[26] Showing an interest in research management from the beginning, Tucker later served as manager of semiconductor research in Poughkeepsie from 1954 to 1957, manager of the San Jose laboratory from 1959 to 1961, and director of the Research Division from 1963 to 1967.

The opportunity to extend their education in New York City while working at the Watson Laboratory was an attraction for many. Arthur G. Anderson, for example, who had worked in the applied mechanics laboratory in Poughkeepsie since 1951, transferred to the Watson laboratory in 1953 to pursue graduate studies in New York. After building an electromagnetic delay-line device for Thomas, he was given an assignment on the spin-echo memory project.[27] By the end of the year, he and two associates wrote an internal report that evolved into a very extensive paper in the *Journal of Applied Physics* titled, "Spin Echo Serial Storage Memory," coauthored by Anderson, Garwin, Hahn, Tucker, and others. Following Hahn's earlier work, the authors had utilized the method of pulsed nuclear magnetic resonance to store radio-frequency energy serially in the form of pulses in a sample of nuclear spins and to recall the stored information at an arbitrary later time, within the relaxation time of the sample. Experiments revealed that approximately 1000 pulses could be stored and recalled in a proton sample several cubic centimeters in volume within a memory time of 10 to 50 milliseconds. The best storage media were found to be liquids such as glycerine and solutions of paramagnetic ions in water. The authors acknowledged that "a severe limitation against greater series storage capacity is imposed by the fact that a large [magnetic] field inhomogeneity over the sample volume to produce short echoes accentuates a loss of spin phase coherence due to the self-diffusion of molecules in the liquids."[28]

When Anderson joined the spin-echo project in 1953, the mercury-delay line memory on UNIVAC was the most reliable memory in use. Cathode-ray tubes were faster but less reliable. In this context the serial storage of information by pulsed nuclear magnetic resonance seemed promising, but by the end of 1953 a 17,408 bit ferrite-core memory had been operated successfully for several months in the Whirlwind I computer at MIT (see chapter 7). The speed and reliability soon achieved with ferrite-core memories caused loss of interest in the spin-echo memory and many other alternative storage technologies. Indeed the *Journal of Applied Physics* article, published toward the end of 1955, signaled the end of the Watson Laboratory work on spin-echo memory and coincided with Hahn's decision to accept an appointment as professor of physics at the University of California, Berkeley.[29]

Meanwhile, Anderson turned his attention to the design of very high-frequency vacuum tube circuits. In 1957, he joined three other members of the Watson Laboratory in reporting on the design of an arithmetic unit that performed binary addition, multiplication, and dynamic storage at a pulse repetition rate of 50 megahertz, using the highest-speed logic pulse techniques to that time.[30] In 1958 Anderson received his Ph.D. in physics from New York University and transferred to the IBM Research Laboratory at San Jose, in his native state of California. Three years later he was appointed manager of the San Jose laboratory.

The extent to which basic research was encouraged at the Watson Laboratory is evidenced by experiments on muon decay conducted in January 1957 by Garwin, in conjunction with Leon M. Lederman of the Columbia Physics Department. These experiments confirmed the suggestion of C. N. Yang of the Institute for Advanced Study at Princeton and T. D. Lee of Columbia University that the long-held space-time principles of invariance under charge conjugation and space reflection (parity) are violated by the "weak" interactions responsible for decay of nuclei, mesons, and "strange" particles.[31] On 4 January 1957, Garwin and Lederman first discussed the possibility of detecting whether muons formed during meson decay in the normal beam of the Columbia cyclotron were polarized. If they were, it would indicate that parity had not been conserved in this process. Quickly working out experimental details, they enlisted the apparatus and help of a graduate student of Lederman. During a nighttime vigil beside the equipment, Garwin made the critical observation and immediately telephoned Lederman, announcing, "Leon, we're in. . . . It's just come through. Parity is good and dead."[32]

Their paper describing these results was received by *The Physical Review* on 15 January 1957, the same day a paper by Chien-Shiung Wu of Columbia University and four colleagues from the National Bureau of Standards in Washington, D.C., was also received. Wu's paper described the experimental results of a half-year's effort using the decay of ^{60}Co to demonstrate the lack of parity conservation. In fact, it was knowledge of Wu's results, achieved late in December, that had triggered Garwin and Lederman to devise their own experiment beginning in January. These experimental results contributed to the selection of Lee and Yang for the Nobel Prize in physics later that year.

In 1960 Garwin extended the techniques and experience gained from the Columbia experiments to another series of experiments conducted at the Geneva, Switzerland, headquarters of the European Organization for Nuclear Research (CERN). In these experiments, the anomalous magnetic moment of the mu meson was precisely measured; the result showed that the mu meson might be regarded simply as a heavy electron.[33]

Another Watson Laboratory member, Byron Havens, having completed NORC, also ventured into basic physics. Shortly after his former Cal Tech classmate, Charles H. Townes, developed the first ammonia maser in 1954, Havens turned his attention to masers. Havens had concluded, correctly but prematurely, that someday computers would be interconnected all over the country. He reasoned that a well-engineered maser might serve as a highly stable clock to synchronize this communication.[34]

Havens collaborated with Townes in performing a sophisticated alternative to the classical Michelson-Morley experiment of 1887. The equipment consisted of two ammonia masers aligned antiparallel to each other and able to rotate about an axis perpendicular to the earth's surface. The basis of the measurement was the difference in Doppler effect in the two masers for radiation emanating from the beams of ammonia molecules moving parallel to the cavities but in opposite directions. If Einstein's Special Theory of Relativity was correct, no difference in Doppler effect in the two masers would be observed even when the masers were pointed parallel to the direction of the earth's rotation. Indeed no difference was observed. The resulting measurement was about fifty times more precise than previous measurements using the method of Michelson and Morley. The primary interest, however, lay in the fact that the theory was now confirmed by a different physical phenomenon.[35]

In providing so much freedom for scientists to choose their own projects, Eckert was acting in accordance with the well-documented observation that major advances often are achieved through unexpected developments in apparently unrelated areas of research, a philosophy that also helped attract some of the most outstanding scientists in the country. His management of the Watson Laboratory was modeled after that used in many successful universities. It was, however, a very different philosophy from that held by Palmer in the Poughkeepsie laboratory.

13.2 Research in Poughkeepsie

Ralph Palmer, who had initiated work on vacuum tube circuits in IBM's Endicott laboratory before the war, returned from the navy late in 1945. A results-oriented engineer, Palmer was not interested in research for the sake of research, but he was willing to take big risks to achieve major product improvements.[36] When the Poughkeepsie laboratory was given the mission to develop solid-state devices as well as vacuum tube electronics, Palmer turned to Arthur Samuel to establish the needed capability. Although Samuel's background was in vacuum tubes, he understood good research, and his experience at the Bell Laboratories and the University of Illinois provided him with connections to two of the country's leading institutions in solid-state technology. The arrival of Lloyd Hunter in Samuel's area in June 1951 reinforced the solid-state effort with the necessary technical leadership.

The two largest solid-state projects under Samuel and Hunter were ferrite cores and transistors, selected as the most promising alternative approaches for high-speed memory and logic for digital computers. M. K. Haynes initiated work on ferrite cores that led to IBM's first commercial ferrite-core memory, and the company's efforts to make its own cores were also initiated under Samuel. However, the cooperative project with MIT to build ferrite-core memories for SAGE quickly eclipsed the small research effort, which nevertheless supplied trained personnel and consultation for the larger effort on SAGE and explored a variety of logic and memory concepts. The transistor research effort headed by Hunter was sometimes criticized for staying too long with point-contact devices; other times, it was applauded for initiating work on drift transistors. But it was always recognized as a significant factor in IBM's transistor development effort. (Research's activities in ferrite cores and transistors are extensively treated in chapters 7 and 10, respectively, together with the associated development projects.)

Early transistors were sensitive to heat, moisture, vibration, and stray electric fields. In short they were not reliable. Magnetic-core logic was expected to provide greater reliability and was the primary thrust of Haynes's research at the University of Illinois and at IBM. But even while magnetic-core logic was being considered as an alternative to transistors, alternatives to magnetic-core memories were also under study.

The ferroelectric device effort initiated by Donald R. Young was probably the most significant of these activities. Young, who had joined IBM in August 1949 after getting his Ph.D. in physics from MIT, soon joined Walter Mutter who was experimenting with barrier-grid concepts for improving cathode-ray tubes used in Williams-tube memories. Becoming disenchanted because it took nearly six months to get a newly designed tube built, Young began looking for new areas in which to work.[37] In April 1951 he published a paper on the enhancement of hysteresis in barium titanate, with the objective of using this ferroelectric material for the storage of digital information.[38] The hysteresis loop obtained by plotting the electric polarization versus applied voltage for barium titanate had a nearly rectangular shape similar to the hysteresis loop (magnetization versus drive current) exhibited by magnetic cores used for information storage. This suggested that a stable direction of electric polarization in a ferroelectric device could be used to store information just as stable magnetic polarization was used in ferrite cores.

In October 1951 Young suggested using ferroelectric barium titanate capacitors to create a coincident-voltage selection memory array similar to the type Haynes had proposed for ferrite cores. Specifically, Young proposed an array organization in which any one capacitor could be selected for writing a 1 or 0, but all of the capacitors in a row were read simultaneously by driving the appropriate word line.[39] The details of this proposal were unique to Young, but the general concepts were similar to those being discussed by workers in several other laboratories.[40] "At the present time ferroelectric materials are not as well developed as ferromagnetic materials," Young asserted, "however, it is felt that the simplicity of a condenser [capacitor] as compared with a magnetic core with associated winding may warrant some work in the direction of improving the materials."[41] The best ferroelectric materials available at that time for information storage, according to Dudley A. Buck of MIT, were barium titanate ceramics with unidentified additives made by the Glenco Gulton Corporation in New Jersey. Switching times of the order of 1 microsecond were reported, but the energy consumed per unit volume during switching was about one hundred times that of the ferromagnetic materials under study, suggesting very high-powered circuits would be required to drive the device at acceptable speeds.[42]

Then at the AIEE Winter Meeting in January 1952, workers at the Bell Laboratories described the superior electrical properties of single crystal barium titanate crystals, which they had recently learned to grow. Reporting on these results, Young wrote, "It now appears that practical ferroelectric materials have been developed that are comparable to the better magnetic materials. This opens up the possibility of a large number of storage and switching applications."[43] Bell researchers initially refused to divulge their crystal-growing method, causing the IBM group to develop its own. The resulting crystals, grown in a flux, looked like butterflies with each wing a single crystal, perhaps 1 centimeter on a side and 0.1 millimeter thick.[44] As proposed by the group at Bell, a two-dimensional selection array could be created by depositing a set of parallel metal conductors on one side of the crystal and an orthogonal set on the other side. At each location where these lines crossed, a small square-shaped capacitor was defined within which the ferroelectric material could be switched from one stable polarization state to the other.

Early in 1954, a young theoretician named Rolf W. Landauer was asked to help the ferroelectric group understand the basic polarization reversal mechanism. He had received the Ph.D. in physics at Harvard in 1950 and had spent two years with the National Advisory Committee for Aeronautics at the Lewis Laboratory in Cleveland before joining IBM in 1952 to work with Lloyd Hunter.[45] In his first year at IBM, he had started a calculation of the energy levels in a one-dimensional model of a disordered crystal using numerical techniques programmed on the IBM 701 computer. The distribution of electronic energy levels in perfectly periodic crystals or periodic crystals with well-defined defects had been widely investigated previously, but as Landauer observed, "The effect of a complete departure from periodicity, such as occurs in disordered alloys and also in liquids, has not received much attention." The results of his calculation were published in the *Journal of Chemical Physics* in 1954 and are believed to be the first time an electronic stored-program computer was used to model a solid-state system.[46] Landauer was also interested in more practical problems, having worked with experimentalists such as Richard Rutz, who credits him with explaining how the Rutz Commutator Transistor and other novel semiconductor device structures worked.[47]

Landauer's assignment to the ferroelectric project helped provide a stimulating intellectual environment for the more application-oriented individuals, and Landauer speaks with evident nostalgia of the close-knit group effort managed by Young, saying, "It was a very good group effort and it would be wrong to separate out the contribution of any one person."[48] Of particular interest to the group was the study of the polarization reversal mechanism in barium titanate crystals. Using a phenomenological theory of ferroelectricity developed at Bristol University and extended by workers at Bell Laboratories, the IBM group came to understand the idiosyncrasies of these materials and contributed to the growing scientific and applications-oriented literature.[49]

Work on ferroelectric memories continued long after the decision was made in 1954 to use magnetic-core memories on IBM's commercial computers. An important advantage anticipated for ferroelectric devices was batch fabrication as contrasted to the individual fabrication, testing, and hand-wiring of ferrite cores. By vapor depositing ten 0.5 millimeter wide conductors on each side of a 1 centimeter wide single crystal of barium titanate, an array of 100 bits was created. Larger crystals would permit thousands of bits of memory to be made at once. By 1956, Young had divided his group into an applied and a basic research section and was coordinating his work with that of a small activity at the Watson Laboratory where the properties of alternative ferroelectric materials such as potassium niobate and triglycerin sulphate were under study.[50]

Three problems of ferroelectric materials were never overcome, however: the large energy loss per unit volume during switching made it difficult to achieve high-speed operation, the switching threshold was frequency and time dependent, and the ferroelectric properties changed slightly each time the polarization was reversed so that an acceptable lifetime was never achieved.[51]

In 1959, the ferroelectric memory effort was terminated and replaced by a joint project with the phosphor materials group under Hunter. Work on phosphor materials that store energy when radiated with ultraviolet light and emit energy when radiated by infrared had been initiated in 1953 by Hunter, who believed these materials could be used for digital information storage. After a year or so, he decided the device possibilities were not promising but continued to support the research, believing it was an interesting field that might lead to new discoveries and inventions.[52] The purpose of the new joint project was to develop low-cost logic and memory devices using layered structures of electroluminescent (EL) and photoconducting (PC) materials. Integrated circuits were to be achieved by screening the EL and PC materials onto glass substrates and then interconnecting them by conductors, vapor deposited through a mask. The so-called ELPC devices were almost a thousand times slower than transistors, making low-cost fabrication essential to achieving cost-effective circuits. This effort was also not successful, partly because of rapid progress in transistors and ferrite-core memories but more specifically because EL materials with stable electrical characteristics were never achieved.[53]

Even while ferroelectric devices were being studied as possible replacements for magnetic cores in memories, the excellent reliability of magnetic cores led to their consideration as replacements for some of the transistors in logic circuits. This was a continuation of Haynes's work on magnetic logic begun at the University of Illinois and initiated by him in IBM in 1950. In January 1955, Palmer learned that Engineering Research Associates (part of Remington Rand since 1952) had contracted to build special-purpose computers for the National Security Agency using a combination of diodes and magnetic cores for logic.[54] Palmer responded by increasing Haynes's research on magnetic logic, and in 1956 he asked Erich Bloch to develop magnetic logic for computers.[55]

By November 1957, some of the technological uncertainty was resolved when Bloch's effort to develop magnetic logic for input-output units on Stretch revealed that nearly as many semiconductor devices were required to drive and detect magnetic devices as were required to do the same logic without any magnetic elements at all. Even more important was the growing confidence in the high-speed drift transistors developed in Lloyd Hunter's group and the invention of current-switch transistor circuits by Hannon Yourke. These junction devices were expected to be much more reliable than point-contact devices, making the superior reliability of magnetic devices less important. Accordingly, Bloch's effort to develop magnetic logic was terminated. It was the last serious consideration of magnetic logic for products in IBM, although exploratory studies continued for several years in Research.[56] (Sperry Rand did not terminate its effort until several years later, after it had delivered a number of machines with magnetic logic. These machines were reported to be very reliable.[57])

With regard to the important shift from point-contact to junction transistors, Byron Phelps, who served as manager of component development beginning in 1953, recalls Samuel and Hunter agreeing early on that IBM should not waste time on junction transistors because they would always be too slow. This was a view Phelps recalls also being expressed by the people he knew at Bell Laboratories. Joseph Logue, on the other hand, was enamored of junction devices because their electrical characteristics were dependable. He believed they would always be more reliable than point-contact devices and that, in time, people would learn how to make them operate just as fast. "I really don't think I thought he was right," Phelps confesses, "but I was willing to give him a chance to find out because that's the way Palmer taught me."[58]

Phelps's statement reveals much about the way Palmer operated and what made the Poughkeepsie laboratory successful. People with good records of achievement and strong convictions were given an opportunity to test their ideas even when those ideas ran counter to the judgment of their managers. Palmer believed in having exploratory studies of all possible alternative technologies, and he wanted people who could investigate and understand the fundamental phenomena.

Hunter adds that Palmer gave very few specific directives, even though he had strong views about the general direction projects should take. He held weekly staff meetings at which the activities of the various groups were discussed and criticized by the participants, but those in charge of projects were given a lot of freedom to make their own decisions. Hunter says he was expected to recruit and hire good people and to undertake appropriate projects, but Palmer saw to it that he never had to worry about administrative or budgetary matters. Any time his account got low, more money was added.[59]

For many, the Poughkeepsie environment was ideal. Product development, advanced development, and research projects flourished side by side. Palmer had little interest in one-of-a-kind machines such as the SSEC or NORC. His objective was clear: to develop technologies for products that could be mass produced at a good profit. Projects such as the Tape Processing Machine and Stretch were pursued as a means to develop new product technologies; they were not an end unto themselves.

Under Palmer, the research and development activities in Poughkeepsie grew from fewer than 200 people in 1950 to 1440 by 1954. During this period the total IBM research and development activity grew from just over 600 to about 3000 employees: approximately 1440 in Poughkeepsie, 1400 in Endicott, 110 in the Watson Laboratory, 80 in San Jose, and 25 at corporate headquarters.[60]

Because rapid expansion had resulted in numerous small facilities in Endicott and Poughkeepsie, a construction program, favoring Poughkeepsie, was initiated to alleviate the problem. In October 1954, the 701 Building, situated on the Kenyon Estate in Poughkeepsie and given the same number as IBM's first electronic stored-program computer product, was dedicated as the IBM Research Laboratory. It was especially designed for research and development activities, with a variety of electrical voltages, gases, and distilled water piped through the building to support activities in electronics and materials research. (See figure 13.2.) Two new buildings, the 702 and 703 development buildings, were soon under construction behind the 701 Building. When completed in 1956, they added 100,000 square feet of laboratory and office space to the 179,000 square feet of the 701 Building. These three buildings were intended to provide space for 1300 employees.[61]

A bust of Edison was placed in the 701 Building to symbolize the type of results-oriented research Palmer liked.[62] "I think we were a little bit touchy about using the word research," Palmer confesses, because research for the sake of research would be "just wasting our money."[63] As the move into the 701 Building took place, Arthur Samuel confidently advised new employees that Poughkeepsie would be the final location of IBM Research.[64] But this was not to be.

A review of IBM's development organization in 1954, supported by a report prepared by outside consultants, recommended that a number of changes be made. The primary recommendation dealt with coordination and management of development activities in Endicott and Poughkeepsie—both of which engaged in research, development, release engineering, production engineering, and special product en-

Figure 13.2
IBM Research Laboratory. The 701 Building in Poughkeepsie, New York, was
dedicated in 1954 as the IBM Research Laboratory. It was Palmer's pride and joy
and served as headquarters for research and advanced development activities until 1957.

gineering functions. The report urged that a technical staff be established to assist the director of engineering in his tasks.[65]

This recommendation was carried out. W. W. McDowell was promoted from director of engineering to vice-president in charge of
research and engineering in July 1954, and two months later, R. L.
Palmer became director of engineering with an office at corporate
headquarters in New York City. Reporting to Palmer were J. A. Haddad,
director of advanced machine development, and J. J. Troy, director
of product design. At the same time, H. S. Beattie replaced Palmer
as manager of the Poughkeepsie laboratory and F. E. Hamilton replaced
J. A. Haddad as manager of the Endicott laboratory.[66]

A secondary recommendation of the consultants dealt with concerns
that the company's research activities were too closely tied to immediate
product objectives. Suggesting that more basic research was needed,
the report observed that research in Endicott and Poughkeepsie was
"primarily applied research" and that "very few of the research projects

are in fields foreign to the Company's current lines of business."[67] These observations were consistent with those expressed earlier by the Management Committee on Pure Research, which had led to the expansion of the Watson Laboratory in 1953.

13.3 Separating Research from Development

Following his promotion in July 1954 to vice-president in charge of research and engineering, McDowell sought help in determining how best to organize research and development. He established a task force of laboratory representatives, including B. L. Havens from the Watson Laboratory, N. P. Edwards, M. E. Femmer, J. C. Logue, and G. L. Tucker from Poughkeepsie, and E. S. Hughes from Endicott. B. O. Evans, then on a staff assignment to McDowell, served as secretary. During the spring of 1955, the task force met for several weeks at the Fox Hill estate in Connecticut, pondering how best to organize and manage research.[68] In reviewing the methods of other companies, the group was impressed by Westinghouse's distinguished research organization, for example, but concluded that it had not contributed sufficiently to the company's product line. Westinghouse had apparently tried to correct this situation by placing research in the engineering organization, only to cause many of its scientists to leave. This experience helped to highlight the complexity of managing industrial research.

The Fox Hill study concluded that research activities should be organized so as to permit independence in determining areas of research, provide for awareness of corporate problems, and ensure that contributions were made to IBM products. The report included four recommendations: that research activities be separated organizationally from development; that a distinguished scientific executive not currently employed by IBM be hired to head the research activities; that Research report directly to corporate management; and that Research be held accountable for the relevancy of its projects to IBM.[69]

McDowell accepted the report, and in January 1956, the Poughkeepsie Engineering Newsletter announced his first step in implementing the recommendations: "IBM has established a new independent research organization to develop the business machines of the future. The new group will remain within the company's research and engineering department, but will operate independently of its parent. It will be headed by Mr. R. L. Palmer, formerly IBM Director of Engineering." The announcement also disclosed that a portion of the company's engineering operations at Poughkeepsie would be reorganized into a product development laboratory to be directed by H. S. Beattie, formerly manager of the Poughkeepsie Engineering Laboratory.

The "new independent research organization" was intended to provide greater concentration on "the basic and applied research which must precede the development and production of new products," and it was to aid in recruiting and training top technical talent to meet IBM's growing requirements. As reported in the newsletter, "The problem of recruiting top-caliber engineers in sufficient quantity to meet the company's ever-increasing needs is probably the most important single problem facing us today." Over 1300 engineers were to be hired in 1956 alone.[70] In addition, a program had been developed in cooperation with Syracuse University to provide IBM engineers with graduate-level courses in electrical and mechanical engineering and physics leading to a master's degree.[71]

These announcements failed to note that Palmer's assignment as head of the independent research activity was only temporary. Despite his success in bringing the company into the solid-state electronics era, Palmer's model for research was not the one selected for the new organization. Instead the new research organization was to be patterned more on the model of the Watson Laboratory, which had given IBM prestige and recognition in science—but little in the way of products.

Consistent with the recommendation of the Fox Hill study, corporate management was looking for a distinguished scientist to manage the new research function. Palmer's job was to pave the way for a new director of research by extracting a research organization from the combined engineering and research activities in Poughkeepsie. Whatever Palmer may have thought of this assignment at the time, he later asserted that separating research from development was not an entirely pleasant assignment because it "shattered what we had thought was a pretty well grounded organization."[72]

Palmer initiated the reorganization process at meetings with about fifteen key technical managers in Poughkeepsie in April 1956. He told the group that three main things would have to be considered: getting new projects started in research, managing research projects, and transferring projects out of research and into manufacturing. He was particularly concerned with the third problem. In the past, development projects initiated in the Poughkeepsie research laboratory went straight into manufacturing, often accompanied by engineers who had worked on the project. The new, separately managed research organization was not expected to take product technologies directly into manufacturing—this was to be the job of development. The change created immediate as well as long-term problems.[73]

The immediate problem related to projects then being transferred, or readied for transfer, from research to manufacturing. For example, magnetic ink and a reading head had been developed for check-handling equipment, and there was a small pilot line making magnetic tape for tape storage units. Also ready for transfer was an improved technique for making printed wiring cards of the type used in the IBM 608. Drift transistors for Stretch had been developed to a stage where pilot-line production was being considered. Finally, there was a most critical situation in ferrite-core technology.

In the middle of 1955, an impasse had occurred in negotiations with the General Ceramics Corporation for the use of its MgMn ferrite-core material. IBM's search for alternative compositions had resulted in a decision to work with the Philips corporation to improve its CuMn ferrite-core material and process. Rapid progress was being made on the pilot line under J. W. Gibson, and transfer of the process to manufacturing was being discussed. But there was a serious problem posed by the separation of research and development. Gibson was believed to be the only person in his small group with sufficient experience to work both with research people and with the engineers in manufacturing. Thus, it was impossible to divide the group into two parts, one in development and one in research. To solve this problem, Palmer proposed that John B. Little, under whom Gibson worked, be given a rather special assignment.

Little had joined IBM from Bell Laboratories in 1950, at Samuel's urging, to assume responsibility for the manufacture of vacuum tubes. Little's experience at Bell had been primarily with vacuum tubes, but he also had worked on magnetic recording and semiconductors. In particular, he had collaborated with G. K. Teal in the first growth of germanium single crystals for junction transistors.[74] His understanding when he left Bell was that he would not work on transistors at IBM for over a year, an agreement to which he rigorously adhered. Thus, when IBM decided not to make its own standard vacuum tubes, Little did not move immediately into transistor work. Instead, he undertook to develop mechanical assembly techniques for manufacturing Williams tubes. By mid-1953, when he hired John Gibson to establish the ferrite-core production line, Little had about twenty-five people working for him on a variety of component development projects.[75]

The new assignment defined by Palmer for Little in mid-1956 was to continue the task of transferring projects from research to manufacturing, while quietly creating a technology transfer group within

Research that might later be moved to development. Because of the uncertainties of the future and because most of the people were expected to prefer to remain in Research, Little was told not to discuss this plan with the people in his group. It was a difficult assignment, and Little recalls that he "went through hell" attempting to handle it.[76] His department, known as Components Research, occupied much of the north wing of the 701 Building in Poughkeepsie and included a number of people who played major roles in future developments. Among them were Gibson, who became the first manager of IBM's Components Division in 1961, and V. R. Witt, who managed the development of magnetic-disk technology in San Jose from 1960 to 1970 when he became an IBM Fellow.[77]

Occupying much of the south wing of the 701 Building was L. P. Hunter's Physical Research department, which—more than any other group—formed the nucleus of the new research organization. M. K. Haynes, who had started ferrite-core device work in IBM, led a magnetics-device group, and A. H. Eschenfelder, who had made the first ferrite cores in IBM, headed the work on magnetic materials. G. L. Tucker, who had worked with Hunter and Rutz in the early stages of the drift-transistor development, was now in charge of semiconductor materials research, and D. R. Young was responsible for ferroelectric research. Other major areas of research under Hunter included information-processing theory, phosphorous materials, microwave resonance in solids, and cryogenics.[78]

S. W. Dunwell, manager of Project Stretch, continued to report to Palmer, as did N. Rochester, manager of research projects on magnetic-core logic, applied logic, speech recognition, learning machines, programming research, circuit theory, and mathematical analysis. Also reporting to Palmer were A. L. Samuel, serving as a consultant on research; N. P. Edwards, responsible for liaison with the product divisions; and M. E. Femmer, the recently named associate director of Research with responsibility for various functions such as patent engineering, contracts, services, finances, and personnel.[79]

During the early meetings in which Research was established, Palmer specifically highlighted automation research as critical to IBM. Citing techniques being developed to facilitate the design and construction of Stretch, Palmer asserted, "We need another research activity that stretches even beyond Stretch, in other words a permanent part of our research program." Rochester reinforced these views, saying, "Computing machines are tools that can enable us to do a tremendous amount of work that people used to do with their brains. . . . People really shouldn't have to do this [menial work], it generally dulls them. . . .

All through our activities there are places where we can put machinery to work, relieving people of what they are doing . . . and then we'll really start to move, I mean multiply the amount we can achieve by a very large factor: not 10 percent, but a factor of 10 or something like that."[80]

The views expressed by Palmer and Rochester on automated design and assembly were remarkably farsighted. Palmer's proposal that automation research should be "a program of very broad spectrum, all the way from very fundamental research to manufacturing," clearly revealed his preference for overlapping the functions of research and development. As it turned out, design automation studies remained with Project Stretch, which was moved from Research to development early in 1957. The result was the elimination of all work on design automation in Research, an area not reentered by Research until 1962, when a design automation group was started as part of the newly established project on large-scale integration (LSI) of semiconductor devices.[81]

While Palmer was busy creating a separate research organization in Poughkeepsie, others searched for a distinguished scientist to lead it. At a meeting in January 1956, Eckert, Hunter, Hurd, McDowell, McPherson, and Samuel agreed that they "must obtain a recognized scientist and one who has had at least some administrative experience." Their preference was for a young man, perhaps forty to forty-five years old, but they agreed that "if such a person seems to be unavailable, then there should be no objections to getting someone fifty to fifty-five years of age who has ten good years ahead of him."[82]

In September 1956, some 350 executives and research engineers from corporate headquarters, Poughkeepsie, Endicott, and Kingston were invited to a special luncheon at the IBM Country Club in Poughkeepsie. The occasion provided the forum for Watson, Jr., and McDowell to introduce Emanuel Ruben Piore who had joined the company to become the director of research. Simultaneously, Palmer was made director of research and development liaison reporting to McDowell. Soon thereafter, as part of the company-wide reorganization announced at the Williamsburg Conference of November 1956, Palmer was appointed manager of product development for the newly formed Data Processing Division.[83] Femmer, the first engineer to be hired into IBM by Palmer in Poughkeepsie, continued as associate director of Research under Piore.

The forty-eight-year-old "Mannie" Piore, born in Wilno, Russia, had come to the United States at age nine. He had earned his Ph.D. in physics at the University of Wisconsin in 1935 and had held a variety of positions prior to the outbreak of World War II. During the war, he had served as a lieutenant commander on the staff of the deputy chief of naval operations for air. From 1946 to 1955, he had been associated with the Office of Naval Research, serving as the ONR's chief scientist during the last four years. He was hired by IBM after one year as vice-president in charge of research for the Avco Manufacturing Company.[84] The decision to hire Piore had been made by Watson based on the strong recommendation of James R. Killian, president of MIT and a member of the IBM board of directors.[85] Piore was particularly respected for his contributions to the postwar policies and practices of the Office of Naval Research that provided continuity of funding for military research projects established during the war at colleges and universities.[86] By facilitating an orderly transition of academic research from military to civilian projects, the ONR funding made a significant contribution to the postwar technological strength of the nation's universities and colleges and ultimately to the economy.

The new Research organization under Piore was to consist of the Poughkeepsie Research Laboratory as reorganized by Palmer, the Watson Laboratory in New York City, the San Jose Research Laboratory, and a research laboratory established one year earlier in Zurich, Switzerland.[87] Piore lost no time in shifting the emphasis of that organization to basic research. To help formulate judgments, the new director of research assigned three knowledgeable young technical people to report directly to him. Soon labeled "the three wise men" by their contemporaries, M. C. Andrews, J. W. Gibson, and G. L. Tucker were asked to review ongoing programs and to determine which projects were not appropriate to Research and which new fields should be entered. Piore's goal was to create an industrial research organization second to none; he often cited as models the well-established research organizations of the General Electric and American Telephone and Telegraph companies.[88]

During the first week of June 1957, a Research planning conference was scheduled to help define the research program. Senior Research members presented proposals for studies in areas including theoretical physics, chemistry, ferroelectrics, phosphors, magnetics, surface physics, semiconductors, cryogenics, mechanics, hydraulics, computing systems, programming, psychology, and economics.[89]

It was the first of a series of annual Research planning conferences to which senior Research members and selected technical leaders from the development organizations were invited. These conferences not only helped to identify the company's requirements in technology, but they also brought into sharp focus differences of opinion as to what constituted basic research, applied research, and development. For example, what experienced IBM development engineers considered "basic research" was regarded by Piore as "product development," and what Piore called "research" was often so far removed from the work of the development engineers that they saw no reason for it at all.[90]

13.4 Basic Research in Zurich

Piore's convictions about basic research were emphasized during a visit he and Watson, Jr., made to the Zurich laboratory in February 1957. The laboratory, consisting of approximately thirty people housed in a rented facility in Adliswil just outside Zurich, had been established a year earlier through the efforts of A. L. Samuel.[91] Working directly for McDowell, Samuel had toured European technical universities and research facilities for several years, reporting back on developments of interest to the company and attempting to communicate IBM's growing technical interests to the European community. Toward the end of this assignment, he began looking for a site and a director for an IBM research facility to provide the company with first-hand knowledge of technical developments in Europe. Late in 1955, he hired Ambrose P. Speiser to establish the laboratory in Switzerland. The University of Zurich and the Eidgenössische Technische Hochschule (ETH)—Swiss Federal Institute of Technology—from which Speiser had been hired, were expected to make Zurich an attractive place for technical people from all over Europe.[92]

During his visit to the Zurich laboratory, Piore asserted that it should concentrate on basic research because it was too far away from IBM development activities to affect them; furthermore, a basic research effort would facilitate the laboratory's interaction with activities in the European scientific community. According to Speiser, "Piore's influence was decisive." Moreover, Watson reinforced Piore's comments, saying that technical people who wanted to build machines should go to the IBM manufacturing engineering laboratories in France or Germany.[93] It was not a welcome message for many who had engineering backgrounds and a greater interest in designing and building new computers than in doing basic research, even in closely related topics.

Speiser himself had a keen interest in computers. After graduating in 1948 as an electrical engineer from the Swiss Federal Institute of Technology (ETH), he had spent eight months at Harvard with Howard Aiken and two months at Princeton with John von Neumann during 1949 learning all he could about computer technology. He had then returned to the ETH to obtain his Ph.D. and to help establish and manage a project to construct Switzerland's first electronic computer. Known as ERMETH (the Elektronische Rechen Maschine of the ETH), this machine used a magnetic-drum memory and vacuum tube logic. "The ERMETH combined features of Mark III and IAS," according to Speiser, who says, "It was also strongly influenced by Konrad Zuse's designs and by the fact that our group had several years of practical experience with the operation of Zuse's Z4."[94]

As a Swiss national with responsibility for the new laboratory, Speiser found the emphasis on basic research most welcome. He was sensitive to the hostile reaction of many Swiss toward foreign-based companies. To help counteract this, he had already determined that the laboratory would not become a conduit for engineers and scientists seeking employment in the United States. The emphasis on basic research helped to serve this purpose. It was also useful in establishing cooperative research projects with universities and in ensuring that the work in the Zurich laboratory could be presented at European technical meetings.[95]

One of the first persons hired by Speiser was Walter E. Proebster, whom he had met in 1953 at an early European conference on computers. Proebster was then a graduate student at the Technical University in Munich, where he was developing high-speed electronic vacuum tube circuits for the university's computer, PERM (Parallel Elektronische Rechen Maschine). Proebster accepted Speiser's offer in February 1956, immediately after receiving his doctor's degree. During the Research planning conference of 1957, he gave thought to Piore's mandate on basic research and to his own more practical interests. He had been working with ferrite cores and transistor devices but took the opportunity while in the United States to become familiar with thin magnetic films, which had been proposed as high-speed memory elements. On seeing some of the thin magnetic film work underway in IBM's Military Products Division, he concluded that the technology provided an excellent vehicle for basic physics and engineering studies and that it might become a significant device for advanced computers. Returning to Zurich, he and Speiser agreed that basic studies of magnetic films would be a major focus for the laboratory.[96]

Fortunately, an engineer in Zurich had already begun work on a high-speed sampling oscilloscope of the type described in 1957 by a researcher at the Brookhaven National Laboratory. The Zurich oscilloscope was originally intended to measure the properties of fluorescent materials to be used for information storage on a rotating mechanical drum, but in the light of the new laboratory mission, it was used instead to provide detailed studies of high-speed switching in magnetic films.[97] The first experimental observations of rotational switching, with times under 1 nanosecond, were made in magnetic films driven perpendicular to the easy axis of magnetization.[98] Films driven parallel to the easy axis were shown to switch more slowly due to "partial rotation" effects, which were discovered and analyzed by the physicists at the laboratory.[99] The sampling oscilloscope's resolution capability of 0.4 nanosecond made it the fastest one in the world and led to a decision to build ten additional units for other IBM laboratories.[100]

Taking advantage of the abundant supply of highly skilled technical people in Europe, the IBM Zurich laboratory soon had acquired one of the world's most expert groups in thin magnetic film technology. When an urgent need to develop high-speed memories using thin magnetic films was identified in 1960, the laboratory was ready.[101]

Low-cost circuit technology was another focus of the Zurich laboratory. One of the more interesting approaches, initiated in April 1956 before Piore's arrival, was hydraulic logic. By 1960, a wide variety of devices had been designed and tested in the laboratory, including three-stage and ten-stage adders and shift registers. Each stage of the adder, for example, was 19 × 22 × 4 millimeters; the moving pistons that served to open and close internal valves were about 1.3 millimeters in diameter. Speeds of a few milliseconds per logical operation were achieved with liquid pressures of a few atmospheres. These hydraulic elements were "faster and smaller than [mechanical] relays, and also cheaper," according to the researchers, who suggested they were particularly "attractive for applications requiring mechanical output."[102]

Making use of boundary layer effects that caused a stream of liquid to adhere to one of two surfaces, the Zurich engineers also created hydraulic logic devices that had no moving parts and could be carved or molded inexpensively in plastic sheets—thus creating "integrated circuits." These devices failed to provide as much logical capability as devices with moving pistons, however; and the fact that the input and output circuits had common paths was a serious drawback. Nevertheless, the lack of moving parts, precision bores, and closely fitting pistons was reported to be a distinct advantage.[103] In the light of the later era of low-cost, integrated semiconductor circuits, this approach to logic seems almost inconceivable, but in the late 1950s it appeared to be a promising alternative, with unique advantages of compatibility with mechanical input-output devices and the ability to operate over a broad range of temperatures and in environments hostile to semiconductor devices.

13.5 *Restructuring the San Jose Laboratory*

Initially, Piore's call for more basic research had far less effect on the San Jose laboratory than on the laboratory in Zurich. Reynold Johnson, an innovative technical leader who had initiated the RAMAC project, had strong ideas about the management of research and development. In 1955 he had already established a separate engineering effort for RAMAC so that he could spend most of his time on advanced development. Two projects of great interest to him were the advanced disk file—intended to be a dramatic improvement on RAMAC—and an entirely new image storage system intended to store written documents and photographs (see chapter 8). When corporate-wide research was separated from development, Johnson's advanced development group formally became part of Piore's domain. But with three thousand miles separating San Jose from corporate headquarters and with announcement of the successful RAMAC disk file product the same month Piore joined IBM, Johnson was in a strong position to set his own direction.

In mid-1958, when A. G. Anderson transferred to San Jose from the IBM Watson Laboratory, two hundred people were in Johnson's organization. About 80 percent of them were doing applied research and engineering, and the rest were engaged in basic studies involving physics, chemistry, mechanics, and electrical engineering. Anderson himself initiated basic studies of magnetic resonance, which, like most of the other small physics efforts, was unrelated to exploratory development projects. Other basic studies were, however, primarily in support of exploratory projects on magnetic recording or the new initiatives in image storage.[104] The organization and operation of the San Jose laboratory resembled those in Poughkeepsie, under Palmer, before Piore arrived.

However, a dramatic restructuring of the San Jose laboratory and a further shift by Research out of applied work and into more basic work was implemented when the Advanced Systems Development Division (ASDD) was formed in May 1959. Replacing the Special Engineering Products Division (SEPD), the new division was established to explore new opportunities in the electronic data processing industry such as information retrieval, industrial process control, and airline reservations systems. Jerrier Haddad, previously manager of SEPD and now general manager of ASDD, said the division's mission was to "probe and develop products" for "future markets for all of the divisions."[105]

To help establish the new division, projects with the most likely near-term payoff were transferred into it from Research. One of these was Project SABRE, actually transferred to SEPD five months earlier. In May 1959 Piore wrote, "We are making profound rearrangements as we transfer projects to the Advanced Systems Development Division."[106] Just prior to the formation of ASDD, out of a total of 640 IBM Research professional and technical employees, 41 percent were described as in science and 59 percent in systems design and exploratory development. Piore's plan called for nearly inverting this ratio, with 57 percent in science by the end of 1960.[107] Among the projects transferred out of Research to ASDD in San Jose were a small business systems project intended to expand the use of machines through terminals, a communications project, and the image storage project known as Walnut.

A month after ASDD was created, Gardiner Tucker arrived in San Jose to manage a small Research group that had been separated from Johnson's laboratory and oriented toward basic research. All that then remained in San Jose Research were eighteen people, including Tucker and two managers reporting to him: Arthur Anderson, now in charge of physical science, and Albert Hoagland, in charge of engineering science.[108]

A vigorous hiring effort during the next year and a half resulted in a threefold increase in the size of the effort. Hoagland's group carried out technology studies intended to improve future disk products: signal processing, servomechanisms, and air bearings for sliding the magnetic head over the disk surface (see chapter 8). Under Anderson, the chemistry effort provided support primarily for the image storage effort in ASDD. It gradually became evident, however, that it would be difficult to make very large automated image storage files inexpensive enough to be successful products. Meanwhile, there was growing recognition that copier technology was important not only in itself but also for use in high-speed printers attached to computers. There were also a number of small development projects throughout the company that were independently attempting to develop various types of machines to handle aperture cards and other types of image storage media.[109]

In mid-1961, the San Jose laboratory was given a corporate mission to develop photomaterials and to coordinate the related development activities throughout the company. Out of this mission ultimately came the organic photoconductor and other technologies used in IBM's first copiers, introduced in 1970. At the time, however, photomaterials represented only a challenge—one soon inherited by Anderson, who

Figure 13.3
Temporary IBM Research headquarters. The main building on the former Robert S. Lamb estate near Ossining, New York, became the temporary Research headquarters in 1957 in anticipation of the planned move to Yorktown Heights.

took over as manager of the San Jose Research Laboratory when Tucker accepted the position of director of development engineering, IBM World Trade.[110]

13.6 Preparing for the New Research Center

Consistent with Piore's plans for expansion and emphasis on basic research, a decision was made to change the location of the main research facility from Poughkeepsie to Westchester County, where it would be farther from development laboratories but closer to universities and also easier to reach from major metropolitan centers. Implementation of this decision began in 1957, when some 125 scientists and administrative staff members were moved into the former Robert S. Lamb estate near Ossining, New York.[111] The grand three-story building, with a fine view of the Hudson River, served for some time as Research headquarters and housed research groups requiring offices but no laboratory facilities.[112] (See figure 13.3.) M. E. Femmer set up his office here. In addition to overall administrative responsibility for Research, he was assigned management of several groups headquartered at the Lamb estate or expected to be located soon in Westchester County.

Not long afterward, the Spring Street laboratory was established in Ossining to house about 100 scientists and engineers; and by August 1958, the Mohansic laboratory in Yorktown was completed, providing 75,000 square feet of laboratory and office space for about 400 persons.[113] These three facilities were, however, only staging grounds for the final location of IBM's main research facility, which was to be built near Yorktown Heights in Westchester County.

An aggressive recruiting program was also initiated. Engineers and scientists with Ph.D.s in solid-state physics, electrical engineering, mathematics, and chemistry were in particular demand. Newly hired scientists had considerable freedom to define their own assignments, often selecting projects that were continuations of their thesis research. This made it easier to attract good people and reduced the problem of providing appropriate assignments. At least as much emphasis was placed on the scientific significance of their work as on its product significance. Indeed many new Ph.D.s reflected the then-prevalent academic view that no scientist worth his salt would work on applied problems.

Finding people skilled in what later became known as computer science was not easy; university departments of computer science did not yet exist.[114] Piore, like Palmer before him, therefore encouraged experienced engineers and scientists to pursue novel ideas in systems design and information research. One of the more inventive individuals reporting to Femmer was H. P. Luhn, who headed the Information Retrieval Department.[115] By 1957, he had already been issued more than fifty patents for inventions filed since joining IBM in 1941.[116] Most of his inventions related to electromechanical devices for punched-card equipment, but Luhn had a growing interest in the storage and handling of information. In 1953 he devised the randomizing generation of file addresses used with RAMAC. This method, which was the basis for most file addressing schemes for many years, was never patented because it lent itself to program implementation and IBM did not attempt to patent programs (see chapter 8). Luhn had already begun attending meetings of librarians and documentalists to gain a better understanding of the possibilities of applying machines to literary data processing. In January 1953, his first nonpatent publication appeared in *American Documentation*, describing a new method for recording and searching for information; and by 1956, Luhn's interests had turned almost entirely from electromechanical devices to information storage and retrieval.[117]

In February 1958, an auto-abstracting system for the 704 computer was announced. As described by Luhn, "Statistical information derived from word frequency and distribution is used by the machine to compute a relative measure of significance, first for individual words and then for sentences. Sentences scoring highest in significance are extracted and printed out to become the auto-abstract."[118] A more pictorial description was provided that May by the *New York Herald Tribune*:

H. P. Luhn inserted a roll of magnetic tape into the big International Business Machines Computer. On it in the form of electrical signals were 2,326 words of an article from the Scientific American on hormones of the nervous system. He pushed a button and the tape began to spin. . . . Three minutes later, the machine's automatic typewriter started clicking . . . four statements represented the gist of the article. The machine had made an abstract.[119]

In May 1958 Luhn described his ideas for a system to provide Selective Dissemination of Information (SDI), whereby people listed their areas of interest and were then sent reports or publications in these areas. By the end of 1960, it was reported that 450 of the company's managers and professional people were using SDI for abstracts of scientific and management information. At the International Conference on Scientific Information held in Washington, D.C., in November 1958, Luhn helped arrange IBM's display. This included two products to which he had contributed: the 9900 Index Analyzer and the Universal Card Scanner. His new Keyword in Context (KWIC) indexing technique was also introduced and demonstrated in the form of an index to the titles of the papers presented at the conference. In 1960 the American Chemical Society adopted KWIC indexing to produce *Chemical Titles*, which was projected to have about 3000 titles in each of the twenty-four issues planned the following year. But in 1961, three years before his death, Luhn was still dissatisfied with the acceptance of these systems, complaining, "Information retrieval is not well enough known to those who could use it most."[120]

One of the largest and most successful activities under Femmer was Project SABRE. A working agreement had been established with American Airlines permitting IBM personnel to study its operations in detail in order to devise what was to be IBM's pioneering computerized airline reservation system. Interest in developing an airline reservation system dated back as early as 1950, but the project was not formally initiated until early 1957 as one of the projects of the new Research organization. Under the direction of W. J. Deerhake, this project grew to a twenty-man effort in less than a year.[121] By the end of 1958, the project was transferred to the Special Engineering Projects Division, and it became part of the Advanced Development Division when that unit was formed in 1959. Equipment for the central processing installation of this pioneering airline reservation system was shipped in January 1962 and successfully checked out during the year.

By 1964 all major cities served by American Airlines had been placed on line. (See chapter 12.)

Three other technical departments also reported to Femmer: the Machine Organization department, primarily involved in designing special-purpose systems such as Harvest for the National Security Agency; the Systems Research department, established to study the feasibility of advanced systems software and hardware components; and the Information Research department, with projects on character recognition, speech recognition, engineering psychology, switching and mathematics, information theory, and theory of automata. Headed by Nathaniel Rochester, Information Research was the largest and most diverse department.[122]

All of the projects in Rochester's department represented relatively new research initiatives, with the exception of character recognition, which had a long tradition dating back to the 1930s in Endicott. Therefore, the character-recognition work in Rochester's group during the 1950s was done in cooperation, or competition, with the Endicott laboratory. An early contribution was the "lakes-and-bays" approach suggested by Walter Mutter in Poughkeepsie and successfully tested in Endicott in several prototype systems. The method finally found expression in a much simplified version in the Type 1282 optical reader card punch, announced in 1963. Beginning late in 1961, Research and the General Products Division cooperated in responding to a request of the Social Security Administration for an optical character recognition system to read information supplied in every form, from typewritten to handwritten characters.[123] An autocorrelation technique, originated in Research, was a strong contender for several years; and although this technique was not finally selected, the system delivered in 1965 was the result of a continuing cooperation between the two divisions. (See chapter 12.)

Among the various new technical initiatives in Rochester's area, perhaps the one with the most immediate results was the application of sophisticated mathematical techniques to the design and layout of logic circuits. An early technique was the extraction algorithm, developed in 1957, which made it possible to compute the minimum-cost implementation of a specified logical function.[124] In contrast, work in engineering psychology was slow to provide practical concepts and approaches, but it was significant in that it may have been the first time professional psychologists were hired to help improve IBM products.[125] During a four-year period beginning in 1958, Rochester's group published a number of papers in a field soon known as artificial intelligence. Of particular interest was work on a geometry-theorem-proving machine, which was simulated on an IBM 704 using a program written in standard FORTRAN notation to which a large set of list-processing functions had been appended.[126] In developing geometrical proofs, the machine, according to the researchers, "uses no advanced decision algorithms, but relies rather on rudimentary mathematics and 'ingenuity' in the manner, for example, of a clever high-school student."[127]

Work on artificial intelligence was not limited to groups reporting to Femmer. Arthur Samuel, who served as manager of the Pough-keepsie Research laboratory during much of this period, also found time to pursue ideas in artificial intelligence. In 1956 he had pro-grammed a 704 computer to play checkers, using a method in which the computer would look ahead several moves and then choose a course of action based on the anticipated results. The program per-mitted the machine to learn from experience which choices were desirable. "In terms of games," Samuel asserted, "this means writing programs where it is possible for the machine to 'learn' to play a very much better game than that played by the man who writes the pro-gram."[128] In 1959 Samuel's studies received national attention. A *New York Times* science writer said of his work, "A machine is winning at checkers from Dr. Arthur L. Samuel, the IBM scientist who taught it the game. He is delighted."[129]

Between 1956 and 1960, the relatively modest growth in the number of IBM research professionals from 420 to 506 fails to indicate the dramatic changes that had taken place. During that four-year period, more than 500 professionals were brought into Research. Of these, 100 were transferred in from development divisions. The remaining 400 were new employees, a number that corresponds almost exactly to the number of research professionals who were either transferred out to development organizations or who had left the company.[130] At the same time, a dramatic change in the educational level of the Research professionals occurred. In 1956 only 58 Research members had Ph.D.s, many of them in the Watson and Zurich laboratories. But by the end of 1960, 243 persons—nearly half of all Research profes-sionals—had Ph.D.s; among them were many individuals with well-established reputations.[131]

In January 1958, Gilbert W. King joined IBM as consultant to the director of Research. Later he headed the Experimental Systems de-partment, which developed a Russian-language translation machine. King had received his Ph.D. in chemistry from MIT in 1935 and had served as an operations analyst with the Office of Scientific Research and Development during World War II.[132] In January 1961, he succeeded Piore as director of research, following Piore's promotion to IBM vice-president for research and engineering.

Also hired in 1958 was Herman Goldstine, who joined IBM Research from the Institute for Advanced Study at Princeton, where he had collaborated with John von Neumann in the design and development of the IAS computer. At IBM, Goldstine formed the company's first department of mathematics, which soon became one of the country's leading centers of applied mathematics. He hired Richard Courant, of the Courant Institute of New York University, as a consultant to help identify important topics and promising candidates for employment in classical mathematics. The major thrust of the new department, however, was in nonclassical mathematics—that is, new areas of mathematics oriented toward the special needs and capabilities of electronic computers. To provide close interaction between mathematicians and people operating and using computers, the computing center was included in the department. One of the many outstanding people recruited by Goldstine was Ralph E. Gomory.[133]

According to the official announcment, Gomory was hired in 1959 to do "fundamental research of a mathematical nature in the area of large business firms"—in other words, operations research, a field that had been little known before World War II.[134] He had received his Ph.D. in mathematics from Princeton in 1954. Following three years' active duty in the U.S. Naval Reserve, he had returned to Princeton as Higgins Lecturer in Mathematics and had also served as a mathematics consultant to the U.S. Navy, the RAND Corporation, and IBM. At Princeton he developed the first systematic and finite algorithm for obtaining integer solutions to linear programming problems.[135] This work, and Gomory's subsequent contributions made at IBM, established the still-flourishing subject of integer linear programming. Gomory also made major contributions to other topics in operations research—from minimizing the paper wasted when cutting large paper rolls into stock sizes to handling the flow of messages in networks of many terminals.[136] In 1964 he became an IBM Fellow. Then, after a series of management positions beginning with director of the mathematical sciences department, he became IBM Director of Research in August 1970, a position he had held, by mid-1984, longer than all of his predecessors combined.

In 1960, Leo Esaki joined IBM Research after spending four years at the Sony Laboratories while working toward his Ph.D. in physics at the University of Tokyo.[137] In 1957–1958 he had observed electron tunneling in heavily doped pn junctions of germanium. The significance of the discovery was immediately recognized, and a new type of semiconductor junction soon became known as an Esaki (or tunnel) diode. In 1973 Esaki won the Nobel Prize in physics for his discovery, sharing the honor with Ivar Giaever (for his observation in 1960 of tunneling in the superconductor gap) and with Brian Josephson (for his prediction in 1962 of tunneling supercurrents in superconductors).[138] For many years, researchers attempted to use the tunneling phenomenon as the basis for high-speed devices, but this interest faded because of inherent limitations of tunneling devices (in particular the lack of an independent control terminal) and because of continuing progress in integrated silicon circuits with which the tunnel diode was not compatible.

Tunnel diodes did find limited use in communication and instrumentation equipment. More important, tunneling phenomena continued to provide new insights to electronic transport in solids. Investigations by Esaki into the properties of semimetals such as bismuth and bismuth-antimony led to the use of tunneling through an insulator to a semimetal to study the band structure of the semimetal. Subsequently applied to a variety of semiconductors, this technique became known as "tunneling spectroscopy."[139]

So it was that IBM Research already had a diverse set of projects, bright new engineers and scientists, and established technical leaders when the long-awaited move to the new research laboratory in Yorktown Heights took place. Set on a 240 acre site and designed by the world-renowned architect, Eero Saarinen, the new Thomas J. Watson Research Center had the shape of a 73 degree arc, 146 feet wide, with a 1091 foot front wall and a 900 foot rear wall. Saarinen's design allowed for future extensions of the building on either end. (These were completed in 1979 and 1984, respectively, with a resulting increase in the arc from 73 to 118 degrees, the front wall length from 1091 to 1769 feet, and floor space from 459,000 to 757,000 square feet.)[140] The long, curved, glass front wall overlooked the rolling wooded hills of Westchester, just south of the town of Yorktown Heights, approximately 25 miles from the northern borders of New York City. Ground had been broken in October 1958. Construction began the following spring of the original central section of the research center, designed to house up to 1500 research staff members and support personnel.[141] Much of it was ready for occupancy by the summer of 1960. (See figure 13.4.)

At 6 A.M. on Friday, 12 August 1960, the first of a series of moving vans left Building 701 in Poughkeepsie for Yorktown Heights. By seven the next morning, the Magnetics department and its 80 tons of equipment had been moved. Five hours later, according to official reports, some of that equipment was already in operation in the new research

Figure 13.4
The IBM Thomas J. Watson Research Center. An aerial photograph (bottom) reveals the arc-of-a-circle shape of the structure, designed by Eero Saarinen and dedicated on 25 April 1961. Situated in Westchester County about 40 miles north of the center of New York City, its mailing address and common name is Yorktown Heights. The photograph of the front entrance (top) reveals the floor-to-ceiling glass front wall and one of the two Argonauts (right), designed by the artist, Seymour Lipton, to "symbolize man's eternal quest for the ideal through research and knowledge."

center. But many months passed before all of the sophisticated laboratory equipment was again in operation.

The Thomas J. Watson Research Center formally received its name at a dedication in the spring of 1961 during a week-long series of events in which thousands participated: members of the press, stockholders, employees with their families, and even neighbors living near the site. The dedication ceremony itself took place in April, immediately before the annual stockholders' meeting, which was held at the new facility. Nelson Rockefeller, the governor of New York State, was a featured speaker, as was Thomas J. Watson, Jr., who named the new building after his late father—the man who had shaped and guided the destinies of IBM for more than four decades.[142]

13.7 Exciting Projects

As the 1960s began, one of the most important achievements of IBM Research was the creation of the second and third lasers on record. An important contributor to this effort was Peter P. Sorokin, who had been hired in the fall of 1957, immediately after receiving the Ph.D. in applied physics from Harvard. His thesis research was in nuclear magnetic resonance. Motivated in part by the suggestion that paramagnetic resonance in diamond might be used for a spin-echo type of information-storage system, Sorokin spent his first few days at IBM studying microwave resonance in diamond.[143] Then seeking additional ideas for research, he became involved in discussions with Rolf Landauer and H. Juretschke (a frequent visitor to the IBM Poughkeepsie laboratory from the Brooklyn Polytechnic Institute) that led to new ideas concerning the theory of ferroelectric materials.[144] These ideas, which related the dielectric properties near the Curie Temperature to optical lattice vibration modes, provided a basis for theoretical work by Landauer and L. H. Thomas (of the IBM Watson Laboratory) on the structure of electromagnetic shock waves formed by propagation in ferroelectrics.[145]

Sorokin had been with IBM only a year when A. L. Schawlow of the Bell Telephone Laboratories and C. H. Townes of Columbia University published their 1958 paper suggesting that stimulated emission devices operating in the infrared and visible portion of the electromagnetic spectrum could be realized.[146] Such devices, now known as lasers, were first referred to as optical masers.[147] At the urging of his manager, Sorokin turned his attention to this challenge.[148]

Two fundamental decisions, based on theoretical considerations, were made by Sorokin. First, because maximum reflectivities achievable with metallic or multiple dielectric surfaces were unknown, he decided to investigate the possibility of using optical cavities based on total internal reflection. To do this, a solid-state cavity structure in the form of a rectangular block with accurately cut and highly polished edges was planned. The idea was that the coherently generated light could circulate in a low-loss manner in the cavity, with the light rays internally reflecting at an angle of about 45°. This imposed the requirement that the material have a dielectric constant greater than 1.41 (the square root of 2). The coherence of the light would be best if the value was not much greater than that. Sorokin determined that fluorite, with a dielectric constant of 1.43, was ideally suited for the optical host material.

Sorokin's second decision was to seek a material with a four-level electron energy system, so that optical stimulation could be achieved at low power. Specifically, he planned to stimulate the material with white light, driving the electrons from the first level (ground state) to a broad-band fourth level. Electrons dropping from the fourth level to the third level would create a greater population of the third than the second level (population inversion) with a resulting optical emission as the electrons fell from the third to the second level. A search of the literature revealed two promising four-level ionic systems in CaF_2: trivalent uranium and divalent samarium. Two outside vendors were immediately given orders to grow the special crystals.

Before either of these crystals arrived, however, T. H. Maiman of Hughes Aircraft electrified the scientific world with the June 1960 announcement that he had achieved stimulated emission in the visible region with a ruby crystal fabricated in the form of a plane-parallel resonator—the same geometry originally proposed by Schawlow and Townes. Maiman had demonstrated the world's first laser.

The ruby laser had a simple two-level electron system, requiring very high stimulation power, which Maiman cleverly supplied with a helical-shaped pulsed xenon flashlamp, commonly used for flash photography.[149] The IBM group quickly changed to this geometry and high-powered method of excitation. Within a few months, they had successfully demonstrated stimulated emission in $CaF_2:U^{3+}$ and $CaF_2:Sm^{2+}$—the second and third solid-state lasers. When cooled to cryogenic temperatures, both systems operated as true four-level lasers. Threshold pumping energies were reduced by two to three orders of magnitude from levels required by ruby lasers.[150] This important feature touched off intensive research efforts in several laboratories to find a suitable rare-earth ion for four-level laser operation at room temperature. More than a year later, such an ion (the neodynium ion

Nd^{3+}) was found.[151] Because it operates in a four-level manner at room temperature, Nd^{3+} became the most widely used ion in solid-state optically pumped lasers produced for a variety of industrial and scientific uses.

In the midst of the excitement over lasers, even greater publicity was accorded to the machine translation of Nikita Khrushchev's speech of May 1960 to the Supreme Soviet. Translated by the IBM Mark I language translator and submitted to the Congressional Committee on Science and Technology less than ten days after it was delivered, the speech dealt with the U-2 flight over the Soviet Union.[152]

The concept of machine translation of natural languages was not new, having been proposed at least as early as 1947.[153] IBM had become involved in 1952 when it was asked to participate in a conference on mechanical translation at MIT. From the beginning, it was understood that, in addition to a dictionary, the computer would have to possess some knowledge of the structure of each language. By the end of the year, IBM had agreed to participate with the Georgetown University Institute of Languages and Linguistics in an experiment to translate Russian into English.[154] In January 1954, a successful test of the concept was run on the 701 computer at IBM World Headquarters on Fifty-seventh Street and Madison Avenue in New York. With 250 Russian words and their English equivalents stored in the rotating magnetic drum and with six rules of operational syntax, the 701 computer quickly printed out correct English sentences when simple Russian sentences were inserted.[155] Following this, the company entered into a contract to develop specialized language-translation systems for the government.

The Mark I Translator had been developed under air force sponsorship in the experimental systems department headed by Gilbert King.[156] An improved Mark II Translator was completed only two months after Khrushchev's speech was translated by the Mark I. The heart of the new system was a 10-inch diameter read-only optical storage disk containing 55,000 Russian words and their English translations. Capable of translating Russian at the rate of thirty words a second, it represented a significant improvement over the Mark I, which had recently received so much publicity.

It was in this atmosphere of exciting research that E. R. Piore was elevated to the position of vice-president for research and engineering in July 1960 and G. W. King to his replacement as director of research in January 1961, only a few months before the new research laboratory at Yorktown Heights was dedicated.[157]

13.8 Growing Problems

During his first few years at IBM, Piore had defined a threefold mission for Research: (1) ensure the company's technological future by providing basic understanding of the anticipated relevant sciences and engineering, identifying future trends in these, and helping to maintain a good patent position; (2) support current IBM technologies by excelling in branches of science and engineering on which current products are based; and (3) provide guidance on matters involving science and technology, contribute to the formation and staffing of new projects in the development division, and ensure an eminent position for IBM in the scientific and industrial community by "publishing a large volume of productive scientific work of highest quality in areas germane to its business."[158]

As the organization moved into its new facility, Piore could point with pride to the progress made toward fulfilling this mission, to the quality of the people in Research, and to the recognition their work had received in the scientific community. Much had been accomplished, but the benefits derived by separating research from development and by the thrust into basic research were not achieved without cost to near-in product developments. These costs were always evident, but their importance seemed to increase when some of the more highly publicized Research projects ran into technical difficulties.

In describing the performance of the Mark II language translator, Gilbert King had modestly asserted, "We still have a long way to go, but we have gotten over the first hump."[159] It is doubtful, however, that he realized how far away was the second hump. The distance from the almost-useful translations produced by the Mark I and Mark II to truly satisfactory ones was in fact so great that even a quarter of a century later, an expert in the field could only report that "current developments in machine-translation research provide some basis for optimism."[160] Meanwhile, IBM Research, under the prodding of Piore, pushed ever further into the fundamental underpinnings of all areas of computer science and closely related fields, attempting to build bridges between theory and practical applications—bridges that are still under construction more than a quarter of a century later.

An even more basic orientation for Research's activities in solid-state technologies was encouraged by formation of the Components Division in August 1961. Organized on the recommendation of Piore, Palmer, and others, its mission was to develop and manufacture, or purchase, all components required for IBM's products.[161] Its staff came primarily from the components department in the Systems Development Division, but a significant number came from Research, including the first general manager of the new division, John Gibson.[162]

Formation of the Components Division and the Advanced Systems Development Division was consistent with the view that Research was to provide basic scientific understanding of product technologies and to identify completely new alternatives. The creation of these new divisions, plus the move of Research to Yorktown Heights, separated Research geographically and intellectually even more than anticipated from product requirements. New problems were created.

Without the test of product contribution, success in research was difficult to measure. What was the value of improved understanding, and how should it be measured? A count of the number of publications and presentations at technical conferences was a frequently used—but inadequate—measure. Concern was expressed that few Research members had been elected to Fellow status or had received other recognition from the major technical societies. That such recognition tended to come late in life and that most Research members were young was not a completely satisfying explanation.[163] Many managers and executives from the development organizations openly expressed concern that the separation of research from development had gone too far, that work in Research was so esoteric that it no longer had value to IBM.

In attempting to explain how Research measured its progress and selected new areas, Piore wrote in 1959:

Recommendations that come from the Corporate Staff, such as Advance Product Planning, or from an operating division go directly to the "Tucker Staff" for analysis; and recommendations for action, whether negative or positive, are made by me. . . . There are times when programs are started by "command decision." Examples are cryogenics and microwaves. There was not sufficient information around to determine whether there was pay dirt for our business. There were a number of schools of thought, pro and con, within IBM. There was no way to get the answers without experimentation. Even the critical experiments could not be ascertained without rolling up one's sleeves and going to work. It was my decision to get into both fields with large groups so that answers could be forthcoming in two to three years, rather than in five to ten years.[164]

By 1960, the two major projects Piore had started by "command decisions"—cryogenics and microwaves—were in trouble. The microwave project was an attempt to create computer logic and memory using the interaction between oscillatory waves rather than base-band voltages and currents. This work, led by Byron Havens, was based on John von Neumann's patent (filed in 1954 and assigned to IBM), which proposed constructing a computer using nonlinear resonant devices. A collection of such devices, constructed with the same resonant frequency and driven at that frequency, has two stable oscillation states with a phase difference of 180°. These two states can be used to represent the 1s and 0s of binary logic. A simple majority logic scheme was proposed, and elements of the logic were to be interconnected with wave guides or coaxial cables. The nonlinear element von Neumann favored was the solid-state crystal diode, which he said was "up to 1000 times faster than the conventional vacuum tubes."[165] A similar proposal, using a nonlinear magnetic element (the parametron), was made apparently independently by E. Goto in Japan in 1955. In the late 1950s, a number of industrial laboratories had activities in this field, but by 1960 evidence was accumulating that nonlinear resonant devices could never be made as compact and efficient as transistor circuits.[166]

The cryogenics project, also started by "command decision" according to Piore, had become one of the largest projects in Research by 1960. The objective was to make a computer using devices called cryotrons. These devices, invented by Dudley Buck of MIT, made use of characteristics of certain metals that exhibit superconductivity, fundamental to which is zero electrical resistivity at very low temperatures. Buck described his cryotron invention in June 1955 at the summer general meeting of the American Institute of Electrical Engineers. His manuscript, submitted five months later, contains the following description:

The cryotron, in its simplest form, consists of a straight piece of wire about one inch long with a single-layer control winding wound over it. Current in the control winding creates a magnetic field which causes the central wire to change from its superconducting state to its normal state. The device has current gain, that is, a small current can control a larger current; it has power gain so that cryotrons can be interconnected in logical networks as active elements. The device is also small, light, easily fabricated, and dissipates very little power.[167]

Less than two weeks after Buck's talk at the summer general meeting, a number of members of the IBM Watson Laboratory began analyzing the cryotron.[168] Richard Garwin was particularly interested. He proposed that cryotrons could be made to operate at high speeds if constructed of thin superconducting films instead of the bulk wires originally proposed by Buck. In particular, Garwin showed theoretically that gain could be obtained in the device nearly in proportion to the difference in width between the control line and the signal line.[169] By October 1956, Garwin had outlined a program to make a superconducting computer. The objectives of the program were to achieve a large-scale computer in four or five years; use Stretch-type logical organization; achieve 100 megacycle operation; and provide a 10^6 to 10^8 word memory accessible at a 100 million cycle per second rate.[170]

The Arthur D. Little company in Boston was hired to design and build the refrigeration unit for maintaining the devices at liquid helium temperatures. The Military Products Division in Kingston, New York, started a project to make a cryogenic computer as an enhancement to the SAGE air-defense system. Central to that effort was the Crowe Cell—named after its IBM inventor—which represented a substantial improvement over Buck's original proposal.[171] Finally, a group was established in the Poughkeepsie laboratory to study the switching times of thin film and bulk devices. During 1956, the cryogenics computer effort at IBM was large and growing. Garwin was becoming increasingly frustrated by management burdens and eager to return to personal research. Young, by now convinced there was little future for ferroelectric devices, was pleased to replace Garwin in January 1957 as manager of the cryogenic project in Research.[172]

The early euphoria gradually faded, however, as numerous technical problems were encountered. A cryogenic computer could not be developed rapidly enough for a SAGE enhancement, causing that government contract to be terminated at the end of 1958. Cryogenics projects in the Kingston Military Products Division and in Research continued, however, with a mixture of funding from IBM and Project Lightning, a National Security Agency–sponsored program to achieve a very high-speed computer system.[173]

Approximately thirty-five employees were still on the cryogenics project when the final report for Project Lightning was submitted in July 1961. Optimistic in tone, the report stated that detailed analyses suggest that "cryotron densities of several thousand per square inch can be operated at a kilomegacycle rate." Concerning the processing of actual devices, the report acknowledged that "additional control of evaporation conditions must be achieved to obtain the maximum operating speed capabilities of in-line cryotrons." But even this statement proved to be optimistic. The last remnant of the IBM cryogenic effort was finally terminated in 1965, after it had been transferred first to the Systems Development Division and then to the Components Division. The cryotron devices had been found to be slower than originally projected; more serious, the thin film fabrication techniques were not capable of providing the very tight control of device parameters required by cryotrons.[174]

By the end of 1961, Piore had been given a relatively free hand for five years to establish Research. Under his leadership, it had grown in size and changed in character. It had made contributions, but many of these had come from individuals hired or projects established before Piore arrived. It was still too early to evaluate most of the people hired and the projects started after he had arrived. Some projects— cryogenics, microwave logic, language translation—would glitter and fade away. Others—organic photoconductors and lasers—would make contributions of lasting value. But the long-term value of the scientific efforts and exploratory projects were largely unknown when Piore was promoted to vice-president for research and engineering and when Gilbert King succeeded him as director of Research in January 1961.

Piore had created the separate research organization desired by McDowell, Eckert, Watson, Jr., and others. Its contributions to science were beginning to be recognized, but its thrusts into advanced technologies were in difficulty. Adherents to Palmer's results-oriented, combined-research-and-development philosophy were becoming more vocal, whereas those who supported the university-style, separate research espoused by Eckert and Piore were on the defensive. The new director of Research, and those who followed him, would have to learn how to manage Research with sufficient independence to provide technical leadership yet with close enough coupling to product divisions to ensure relevance to the company's needs and to facilitate technology transfer. Together with engineering and corporate management, they would also have to gain experience in the difficult task of evaluating and measuring the contributions of Research.[175]

14

The Architectural Challenge

Adjusting to new technology. The changing environment. Coping with growth. Product diversity. Architectural considerations. Commitment to change.

Until 1946, when IBM announced its Type 603 electronic multiplier, an electromechanical technology had sufficed for the company's products. Much of this technology was rooted in the distant past; IBM's inventors, draftsmen, modelmakers, and machinists—and even the specialists who helped them in chemical and electrical design—had been dealing with slowly accumulating bodies of knowledge. But the vacuum tube, which until World War II had been considered essentially a communications device, had been pressed into service for military applications, and the data processing industry had suddenly become susceptible to a higher rate of technological change. The prospects for change were considerably heightened by the 1945 conception of the stored program.

Although by 1946 IBM was already designing the SSEC in Endicott and establishing a small electronics activity in Poughkeepsie, the company was far from ready for abrupt technological change. T. J. Watson, Sr., and his staff had never been forced to come to grips with close relationships between science and technology. As a result, they had tended to emphasize the broad social benefits of science rather than specific applications to product technologies. Moreover, the traditional IBM views concerning patent policy and product secrecy needed overhauling in America's postwar society, where the government was becoming increasingly disposed to support computer development in university, national, and private laboratories.

Watson had built a company with an exceptional record for customer service and employee loyalty. It is noteworthy that Ralph Palmer and a number of other engineers returned to IBM after having tasted the excitement of wartime electronics. Moreover, Watson had an excellent manufacturing organization, and his product-development laboratories were successful at improving punched-card machinery. Most important, he had created a company with a rare unity of purpose; he and his managers were completely preoccupied with data processing.

By capitalizing on old strengths while gradually developing new ones, IBM made a satisfactory adjustment to electronics and the stored program in the period 1946–1955. Well before the end of the period, most of its engineering activities had been redirected toward computer systems. Computer production increased between 1956 and 1961, even though the growing revenues from EAM products exceeded those from computer systems throughout that period. Some of the trials IBM went through after 1946 have been recounted in previous chapters. In the course of those trials, the company was extensively refashioned, but care was taken to preserve its reputation for service to customers and its dedication to data processing.

Before discussing how success led the company into a new predicament, it is helpful to recapitulate the adaptive responses through which IBM accomplished its transformation.

14.1 Adjusting to New Technology

IBM took its first significant commercial step into the era of electronics with the pluggable vacuum tube circuit and announcement of the 604 electronic calculator. The step, taken in 1948, was a modest one, but it met a widespread customer need and provided experience in designing, manufacturing, and servicing vacuum tube machines. The 604 preserved product continuity and bolstered an already successful line. Ralph Palmer, who led the engineering development of the 604, derived from the experience a basic formula for advanced development: develop and test general-purpose components, commit to their initial usage in a realistic setting (preferably a product), and then go on to develop and pioneer even better components. As a result of ongoing advanced development, the formula permitted most development activities to rely on field-tested components—or, in the terminology that soon emerged, field-tested "technology"—much as had been the case in the electromechanical period.

The critical matters for advanced development, those upon which its effectiveness largely rested, concerned the choice of components to be seriously pursued, the excellence of the components finally obtained, and the availability of challenging commitments. Much depended on these matters, and preceding chapters have treated some of the drama attending them. Among the most successful components were the vacuum-column tape unit, current-switch circuits, SMS circuit packaging, mass-produced ferrite-core memories, RAMAC disk file, slider disk file, chain printer, and removable disk pack.

IBM's determination to learn by bold commitment led to the Defense Calculator, NORC, SAGE, FORTRAN, Stretch, Harvest, and SABRE—to mention only major projects. Each of these involved risks of one kind or another, a good deal of technical and managerial effort, and the support of high-placed management. The diverse technological benefits that resulted defy a summary, but all of the projects added to the number of trained IBM engineers and programmers. The challenges presented by such undertakings aided greatly in recruiting technical people who would otherwise have been deterred by the pervasive view that IBM, as a respected but conservative supplier of punched-card machines, had little appetite for advanced technology.

In the electromechanical era, design engineers had gained professional recognition through their patents, and business-machine companies had relied heavily on patent protection. These circumstances, coupled with the senior T. J. Watson's penchant for dealing directly with his engineers, fostered an atmosphere of secrecy within the Endicott laboratory. This IBM tradition of secrecy and patent protection was initially antagonistic to any acceptance of government funding for advanced development, but by 1949 the tradition was being eroded by the influx of electronics engineers and other technical personnel. In the dynamic field of electronics, scientific information was shared at professional meetings, and the pace of technological change reduced the scope of proprietary information. The concurrent rise of solid-state physics, with its heavy demands for research and development funds, ended the tradition. By 1954, IBM was avidly seeking government development contracts, as were its competitors, in an attempt to defray the rising cost of advanced development.

Even after IBM's attitude toward outside funding had changed, nevertheless, most of the company's successful advances in computer components and automated manufacturing were internally funded. Skills previously used in developing electromechanical punched-card equipment were applied, with remarkable success, to speed up the tasks of handling, testing, and wiring the thousands of ferrite cores used in memory arrays. Later, IBM built the first fully automatic production line for transistors and developed many techniques for efficiently manufacturing the Standard Modular System (SMS) cards and circuits that until 1964 remained the company's primary solid-state computer components.

14.2 The Changing Environment

While IBM was taking its first lessons in rapid technological change and tentatively forging policies for dealing with it, the business environment also was changing. Two factors were especially important. First, the U.S. postwar perception of a Soviet threat was followed by heavy emphases on research and development in ballistics, nuclear physics, aerodynamics, and related technical fields. This, in turn, led to mounting interest in faster computation and in stored-program computers on the part of universities and national laboratories, to the convening of influential technical conferences, and to the formation of professional groups concerned with computers.

Second, a large-scale computer known as the UNIVAC, designed by the Eckert-Mauchly Computer Corporation and partially funded by a government contract for three units, was accepted by the U.S. Bureau of the Census in 1951. The machine was accepted from Remington Rand, which had absorbed EMCC the previous year. Census personnel, who were relying on UNIVAC for help with the 1950 census, operated the system in the factory for nearly two years to postpone the substantial down-time of a move. UNIVAC, a computer with a thousand words of delay-line memory, had been heralded for years, and its availability signaled the beginning of an era of commercially available computers. After falling behind in the punched-card machine market, Remington Rand had acquired in UNIVAC an automatic system that was capable of displacing a whole installation of punched-card machines as well as most of the operators required for carrying card decks from machine to machine.

Since census taking stands as a prominent symbol of nontechnical data processing, the bureau's acceptance of a UNIVAC soon began changing the public view of the electronic computer as a laboratory curiosity. The thought of performing applications in a better way began to catch the interest of methods supervisors in large corporations everywhere. They could foresee possibilities for improved data processing services, even though the cost reduction attainable in replacing punched-card machines with large-scale computer systems was often debatable. Within IBM, the result was a tug of war between computer and card-machine advocates concerning the true needs of the marketplace.

As the tide slowly turned toward the use of computers, the period 1952–1955 became one of great tension for IBM engineers, executives, and salesmen. The company's initial computer, the 701, first delivered about two years after Census accepted the first UNIVAC, was designed for mathematical applications. IBM's direct response to the UNIVAC, the accounting-oriented IBM 702, was first delivered almost four years after the Census Bureau had accepted a UNIVAC. Despite the gratifying early sales of the relatively small IBM 650 computer, first delivered in 1954, the future of the data processing industry came to be perceived, within IBM and elsewhere, as heavily dependent upon large computers and magnetic-tape units.

Remington Rand management presumably viewed its acquisitions of EMCC—and in 1952 of Engineering Research Associates (ERA), a company whose computer soon vied directly with the IBM 701—as the best way of recovering from a product-line weakness caused by its several-year lapse in fielding a suitable counterpart to the IBM 604 electronic calculator. In fact, IBM's degree of success with card machines led the U.S. Department of Justice in 1952 to sue the company for monopolizing the punched-card accounting machine industry, an action that ended with a 1956 consent decree under which IBM agreed to sell (as well as rent) its machines and to license certain data processing patents at reasonable royalties and certain card-machinery patents without charge. At this time, IBM adopted the policy of making all patents pertaining to the manufacture, sale, and use of data processing equipment available at reasonable fees. Under this policy, the company's patent portfolio merely assured freedom of action, while product superiority was to be achieved by using all available knowledge rather than excluding competitors from patents.[1]

By an ironic twist, the 1952 to early 1956 duration of the antitrust action corresponded closely with a period during which the highly visible presence of UNIVACs prompted some industry observers to speculate about the possible eclipse of IBM by Remington Rand.

But in acquiring pioneering computer products, Remington Rand executives had also acquired formidable marketing problems. At the time, experience upon which to estimate ultimate customer receptiveness was nonexistent. After the first UNIVAC was accepted in 1951, UNIVAC deliveries curved as follows: 1952 (three), 1953 (three), 1954 (seven), 1955 (seven), 1956 (fifteen), 1957 (six), and 1958 (one). Although these numbers were augmented by less-publicized deliveries of ERA-developed scientific computers, they well indicate the early hesitancy in the marketplace. Perhaps Remington Rand management was beguiled by the extraordinary public acclaim accorded to UNIVAC (eventually called UNIVAC I), but much of the initial acclaim was based more on awe and curiosity than on readiness to buy. UNIVAC II, a successor machine with ferrite-core memory, was announced later than might have been expected; its completion was delayed, moreover, by a diversion of skilled personnel to the superspeed LARC project.[2]

During the initial years of the UNIVAC challenge, IBM's Card-Programmed Electronic Calculator (based on the 604) served much of the nation's need for computational equipment. The presence of the CPC was helpful in showing IBM's comprehension of the pervasive role that data processing was to play. Then, in 1953, deliveries of a production run of nineteen 701s began. In late 1954, also, the completion of the superspeed NORC provided additional evidence of IBM's technical capabilities. IBM's commitment to the future of computers was further demonstrated in mundane but telling ways. For example, IBM computer products were designed as units that could pass through standard doorways, thereby ensuring that the computer systems could be installed conveniently. Moreover, before the company delivered the first 702 system, it had programmed its Poughkeepsie area payroll and a number of other applications; by early 1955, prospective customers could watch an IBM payroll being run on a 702. Meanwhile, in 1954, IBM had announced the performance-enhanced, core-memory 704 and 705 systems as successors to the 701 and 702. IBM's coordinated response to computers was convincing, and by late 1955 Tom Watson, Jr., could breathe a sigh of relief: his large-scale computers were leading Remington Rand's in installations and the company he managed had apparently weathered a critical challenge.[3]

14.3 Coping with Growth

In the first half of the 1950s, IBM experienced rapid growth as a result of defense programs and brisk EAM sales and, by 1956, continuing growth seemed assured by a mounting list of orders for computers. As a result, the corporate offices were overloaded with responsibilities and the burdens were increasing. After careful study, a thorough reorganization was undertaken in late 1956. Some new divisions were created, and many divisional responsibilities were realigned. Responsibilities were also clarified, permitting more of them to be decentralized. Aside from a class of important decisions specifically reserved to corporate headquarters, divisions became free to conduct their affairs under guidelines provided by the written policies and procedures of a watchful corporate staff.

The resultant organization gave the Data Processing Division (DPD) responsibility for developing, manufacturing, and marketing EAM and computer product lines. Because revenue growth was the measure of DPD's success, actions naturally focused on the short run, with heavy emphases being placed on system improvement and embellishment and on programming aids that might increase the appeal of revenue-producing products. These tactics proved successful in terms of sales, but they also contributed to the untidiness of a product line that already contained several computers of divergent design.

As a result of DPD's growth, another companywide realignment of responsibilities and resources occurred in May 1959. This reorganization, which among other things carved the General Products Division (GPD) and the Data Systems Division (DSD) out of DPD, was an additional step in the direction set in 1956. As Tom Watson said, "The management concept is decentralization, wherein more of the responsibility for key decision-making and for profit is set at operating levels below corporate headquarters."[4] And according to D. T. Spaulding, GPD's manager of systems and product development, the new organization made the product divisions into profit centers and gave each "accountability from conception to death of . . . a segment of the product line."[5] One purpose of the new organization clearly was to facilitate management of a sprawling product line.

The boundary between GPD and DSD products was loosely understood in terms of rental, with systems renting at $10,000 or more per month assigned to DSD and those below that figure to GPD.[6] As explained by the company's news magazine: "The General Products Division is responsible for all product planning, development and manufacture of equipment presently represented by the punched card, RAMAC and 650 class. The Data Systems Division does the same for equipment in the 700-series class and up."[7]

The new alignment motivated the product divisions to plan and design computers of long useful lives, rather than to opt for the quickest means of exploiting every opportunity sighted by the marketing organization (the surviving Data Processing Division). But it did not preclude interdivisional quarreling over the middle ground—often the most lucrative region of the market—and it did little to reduce proliferation of dissimilar families.

14.4 Product Diversity

IBM's first three marketable computers—the 701, 650, and 702—exhibited little kinship in their instruction sets and data formats. The engineers who championed these computers were influenced by differing backgrounds and were forced by the high costs of hardware to warp their designs toward specific customer needs and device characteristics. The 701 designers stressed arithmetic speed, the 702 designers character-handling convenience, and the 650 designers low manufacturing cost. Once the pattern of diversity was set, other distinctive systems followed, the 305 RAMAC being an early example.

At an early stage, Stretch planners argued for a unified product family, emphasizing potential savings in hardware development and manufacture. These were sound reasons, but potential savings in program development later proved to be far more compelling. The Stretch planners also foresaw the value of being able to expand a customer's installation without serious disruption, but this argument did little to advance their case because other planners found little difficulty in developing feasible growth paths for 704 users (to the 709 and 7090) and 705 users (to the 705II, 705III, and 7080).

By September 1960, just two years after announcing its first transistor computer, IBM had eight solid-state computers in its sales catalog. In order of announcement date, these were: 7070, 7090, 1401, 1620, 7080, 7030 (Stretch), 7074, and 1410. The last two provided a measure of compatibility in that programs written for the 1401 could be run on the more powerful 1410 and programs written for the 7070 could be run on the faster 7074. But among the first six, none could execute a program written for another.

Moreover, the development plans of the laboratories were fostering future diversity. Of particular concern was the preoccupation of GPD and DSD with new midsized computers. While GPD's 1410—planned long before the divisional split and announced a year after—could be configured below the $10,000 per month rental line, typical 1410 configurations were priced well up within the DSD range. In fact, prior to its September 1960 announcement, the 1410 had been challenged by a DSD design called the 70AB.

Meanwhile, DSD Poughkeepsie was developing an "8000 series," a computer family intended not only to supplant all DSD computers but, circumstances permitting, to supplant the GPD product line. F. P. Brooks and B. A. Blaauw, veterans of Project Stretch, were involved in this effort. Furthest developed in this series was a midsized machine called the 8106, a reincarnation of the 70AB. The family, intended for both scientific and business applications, ranged in projected performance and cost from GPD's low-cost 1620 well into DSD's 7030 (Stretch) region.[8]

Considerably conditioned by pleas from the sales force for immediate responses to the need for a more dollar-worthy product line, the plan for the 8000 series was somewhat shortsighted. To permit announcement of the 8106 in mid-1961, DSD had ruled out significant improvements in circuit technology; thus, the planned series would be making its debut as another line of SMS products, even though the company had by then begun developing a form of integrated circuits and packaging.[9] Furthermore, a full solution to compatibility was lacking. Some machines were to be word-organized and others to operate on characters, and economy was to be served by varying the instruction sets.[10]

During 1960, there appeared yet another challenger for a portion of the GPD product line. The Hursley, England, laboratory in the IBM World Trade Corporation touted a small binary computer intended to strengthen the company's bid for certain technical applications where the relatively slow 1620 could not vie on a performance basis. Known as SCAMP, the Hursley computer included among its novel features a form of control using read-only memory.[11]

In February 1960, John McPherson dusted off a year-old memorandum that he had previously circulated within corporate headquarters. It recommended a unified product line. Sending a new version of it to C. R. De Carlo, DSD assistant general manager, he noted: "The amount of common knowledge which has to exist to use stored-program data processing machines is so great that I feel we need the advantage of a single system which makes a single community of all our customers. If all our customers today were able to interchange program information, the progress in programming would be even more rapid than it is, and our contributions to programming could be much more significant and more widely useful."[12]

McPherson was well aware that customer data processing managers with two or more kinds of IBM computers were encountering formidable obstacles to optimal resource allocation. Among the biggest obstacles were the proliferations of incompatible program libraries and of differing personnel-training requirements. Programmers and computer operators suffered a temporary but substantial loss of productivity in reassignments that moved them from one computer family to another. The more an organization came to depend upon computers, the more obvious such inefficiencies became. IBM, as a heavy user of computers, faced them itself.

The most critical problem for IBM nevertheless lay in the huge task of developing and upgrading system programs and general-purpose routines of the kinds increasingly desired by computer users. By supporting half a dozen computer families, IBM was reducing its capacity for advanced work on programming technology. And improvements in programming technology had been clearly recognized as necessary counterparts to technological improvements in hardware components.

Improvements in both technologies were important to continued growth of the computer industry.

Once again, McPherson's plea added more to an understanding of the problem than to formulation of a remedy. However, the disharmony among divisional plans was soon to catch the attention of a strategically placed member of management with a strong inclination toward action. T. V. Learson, the group executive who had been heading DSD and GPD since May 1959, had operated for a year and a half without a staff organization, following his natural preference for direct and personal management. Then, in October 1960, growing weary of visiting laboratories scattered across the country and attempting to rationalize the potpourri of projects they housed, he called upon Spaulding to head a small group staff that would assist in reviewing divisional plans.

Spaulding believed the 8000 series plan, while bold and novel, was not likely to succeed because it represented the planning of a single division, lacked an improved circuit technology, and did not represent a sufficiently firm commitment to compatibility.[13] He recommended that Learson appoint Bob Evans, a GPD systems manager, to manage DSD systems and product development. It was a natural suggestion in the light of the effectiveness with which Spaulding and Evans had worked together earlier to save the 1410 from incompatibility with the 1401. For the first time apparently, compatibility had been gained deliberately and at the expense of a tough fight among competing design groups. Evans's disposition toward the new challenge was influenced by the 1410 experience, which he later described as one of the "milestones in compatibility that shaped my thinking for the years to come." He accepted Learson's charge to "examine the proposed 8000 series and if it was right, to build it as fast as we could; and if it was not right, to build what *was* right as fast as we could."[14]

After about two months, Evans concluded that the 8000 series might "commit IBM to a major program of mediocrity." He felt that a satisfactory reduction in the cost-performance ratio demanded new technology. He recommended, in place of the 8000 series, a multi-divisional program with "a charter to develop a total cohesive product line with a target of 1965 availability." He also recommended enhancements to the current set of products, among them a 7090-like medium-priced scientific computer, a faster version of the 7090, and a faster version of the 1410.[15]

Brooks fought for his 8000 series, but after several presentations to corporate management, Evans emerged the victor. Then Evans surprised Brooks by asking him to lead in planning a next-generation-technology line of computers.[16]

In May 1961, toward the end of the debate over the 8000 series, Evans requested studies of whether the product line would sustain sufficient improvement to provide an acceptable prospect for sales growth while a new product line was being developed. Because upgradability of the 1410 was already planned, the truly urgent question was whether the 7090 could be enhanced by a factor of two or more. Later, Evans would recall that a small study group, led by Gene Amdahl (who after resigning from IBM in late 1955 had returned in 1960) and John Cocke, "came in with literally a hundred things you could do to speed up the 7090."[17]

Armed with answers, Evans convened a number of "the bruised people" from the 8000 team in Saratoga Springs, New York. Together they addressed the question of how to fill the void caused by the demise of the 8106, previously planned for announcement three months later, in August 1961. The mere existence of a formally approved strategy for dealing with next-generation products was immediately beneficial. The 8000 series, promised for early introduction, had been stifling improvements to contemporary DSD products by making it pointless to expend resources on them. But with the next generation deferred to 1965 delivery, the division was again free—indeed, compelled—to enhance existing products and programming systems.

At the Saratoga Springs meeting, a "temporizing plan," as Evans called it, took shape. The former 8106 development leader agreed to manage an upward 7090 successor announced in January 1962 as the IBM 7094 Data Processing System. Also defined were medium-priced 7090 derivatives announced in December 1961 as the 7040 and 7044. A 1410 extension was later announced in October 1962 as the 7010. Soon after the 7094 announcement, the IBSYS operating system for the 7090 and 7094 was respecified to provide a higher degree of integration embracing FORTRAN, COBOL, a new assembler, and the application programs produced by them. Before the end of 1963, the 7090 family also included a 7094 Model 2.

The temporizing plan encompassed improvements in GPD products as well. In 1962, a faster version of the 1620 was announced, as was the low-cost 1440 with disk storage. In 1963, the 1460 bettered the 1401 with a faster memory and a train printer that nearly doubled the speed of the chain printer. Also in 1963, the 1620 system was provided with disk storage and substantially enhanced by provision of a disk-oriented operating system.

14.5 Architectural Considerations

With the time provided by the temporizing tactics, Brooks, Evans, and Spaulding set about analyzing the problems in creating a unified line that would benefit from recent advances in transistor circuit technology. Obviously, several disparate needs had to be reconciled in the design of the new line.[18]

First, the prevalent distinction between computers for science and computers for accounting needed to be erased because, as the variety of applications and operating modes widened, more and more computer installations needed capabilities for both floating-point arithmetic and character-handling convenience. Brooks and Blaauw were experts on the possibilities for marrying the two viewpoints, having studied the problems and the prospects extensively while working on Project Stretch and the 8000 series.

Second, core-memory technology was continuing to enhance the prospects for larger memories—much to the satisfaction of customers, whose requirements for larger memories were steadily increasing. This meant that the computer programs of the future would have to address much larger memories. The need for longer addresses, which was already stretching instruction formats in large computers, obviously posed serious problems for anyone proposing to reconcile the addressing structure of more powerful computers with that of small computers.

Third, the six-bit character sets in use were becoming an intolerable limitation that barred the use of both uppercase and lowercase alphabets and of suitable variety in special symbols. As a result of his Stretch experience, Brooks favored standardizing upon an eight-bit byte that could be used for one alphanumeric character, two decimal digits, or a segment of a binary number.

Fourth, the increasing variety of attachment methods for input-output units had become a hindrance to the design of optimal hardware and software. The possibility of standardized input-output interfaces had received considerable attention in the design of Stretch.

These needs, and others related to promising new modes of computer operation and maintenance, made it clear that the hypothetical product line would have to constitute a radical departure in design. Moreover, the effort as a whole would shake the entire corporation as never before. Attitudes toward computer design would have to be changed, as would the provincial attitudes of divisional management. So vast an undertaking would require the concerted effort of everyone in IBM.

In November 1961, as a way of indicating the seriousness of the task and of mobilizing technical know-how and support, a companywide task force called SPREAD was convened at Spaulding's suggestion. The task force members, thirteen in all, worked for about sixty days and produced a final report on 28 December 1961. The technical substance of the report is beyond the scope of this book, as are the misgivings and struggles that it provoked. But in essence, the report recommended that IBM create a compatible family of computer models spanning an unprecedented range of performance. The models might differ in design and construction, as well as in price and performance, but all should present the same outward aspect to a user. In other words, they should share a common computer architecture.[19] (The family of computers that resulted was announced in April 1964 as IBM System/360.)

14.6 Commitment to Change

When Tom Watson, Jr., became president of IBM in 1952, EAM products and electric typewriters were the company's major sources of revenue. Revenue from computer products was nil. In 1962 the company's U.S.-based annual revenue from computer products reached $1 billion and for the first time surpassed the corresponding revenue from EAM products.[20]

In the course of a decade, the data processing industry had relied heavily upon vacuum tubes and then gone about replacing the tubes with solid-state devices. Storage had come to include various kinds of new devices, among them ferrite-core memory units and direct-access magnetic disk files. Software technology had produced compilers, operating systems, and various other programs intended to facilitate the programmer's task or contribute to more efficient computer operations. IBM's organization had changed dramatically and instituted a large, clearly delineated research activity with several laboratories equipped for exploring future technologies.

During the decade also, the growth prospects for electronic computers had attracted many entrants to the data processing industry. By 1962, Remington Rand and IBM were competing with many firms, among them General Electric, RCA, Philco, Burroughs, National Cash Register, Honeywell, and Control Data Corporation.

In 1962, while IBM's technical community was preparing for its huge task of product-line renewal, Watson took time to give a series of seven lectures at the Graduate School of Business of Columbia University. Published as *A Business and Its Beliefs: The Ideas That Helped*

Build IBM, the series highlights the importance of human values, communication, and service. But in his own relaxed way, Watson also paid his respects to the importance of technology in the fifth lecture, "What Growth and Change Have Taught Us." Referring specifically to IBM's travail in introducing stored-program electronic computers, he observed, "Unless management remains alert, it can be stricken with complacency—one of the most insidious dangers we face in business. In most cases it's hard to tell that you've even caught the disease until it's almost too late."[21]

After suffering from the malady of complacency for a time following World War II, IBM management had confronted the existence of stored-program electronic computers and undertaken the technological buildup essential to a rapid transformation of the IBM product line. Then, in the course of satisfying a wide variety of specific customer requirements, the firm had become a computer company, meanwhile finding itself at the forefront of an unusually dynamic industry. Not only was technology advancing rapidly, but customer requirements were dictating greater unity in computer architecture. An early phase of the computer era was closing, and the manner in which IBM would respond to the SPREAD Report was destined to have a profound influence on the company's future.

Appendix A
Sequence Control in the SSEC

The line of sequence as it was read from storage and held in the relays of the sequence control unit in the SSEC is represented below. The first row indicates the name of each field. Six of the fields had subfields s, b, and r, as shown in the second row. The number of digits in each subfield (or field, in the other six cases) is indicated in the third row.

P	Q	R	SH1	OP1	S1		T	U	V	SH2	OP2	S2
s b r	s b r	s b r					s b r	s b r	s b r			
$\frac{1}{2}$1 3	1 1 3	1 1 3	1	2	2		$\frac{1}{2}$1 3	1 1 3	1 1 3	1	2	2

Each half-line, sometimes referred to as an instruction, occupied nineteen and one-half decimal digits on tape. Since these were in binary-coded form, each digit required four columns, and the instruction in each half-line of sequence required seventy-eight columns (hole positions) across the card-width tape. The remaining two positions were used for sprocket holes—one at each edge of the tape.

The fields P, Q, R, T, U, and V specified twenty-digit operand or result storage locations. Fields P and V specified only storage-out and storage-in transfers, respectively, whereas fields Q, R, T, and U specified transfers to or from storage depending on the values of their subfields. The s subfields also indicated operational signs and the tens order of shifting of a result field. The b subfield indicated which of the storage-in or storage-out bus-and-register pairs was to be used for each field. The r subfield specified the storage source of destination for a twenty-digit operand or result. These locations might be paper-tape readers or punches, relay storage units, or dial or pluggable storage units; if the r subfield was zero, only the indicated electronic register was involved, becoming the source or destination rather than merely a buffer.

The SH1 and SH2 fields indicated the units order of shifting to be performed on results in their respective half-lines of sequence. The OP1 and OP2 fields specified the arithmetic operations for their half-lines, including whether rounding of a result was required. It should be understood that the line of sequence could be used quite flexibly in the SSEC, either to perform two separate operations such as $a + b = c$ and $d + e = f$, or to perform a single operation such as $a + b + c + d + e = f$.

The S1 and S2 fields indicated the sources of the next left and right half-lines of sequence respectively. Being only two-digit fields, however, they could not specify every relay, tape, or other storage unit in the SSEC, in a given program because the number of such devices was well over two hundred. Instead an S1 or S2 value of 00 to 99 was translated to one of one hundred plug hubs through a network of relay points. The assignment of these hubs to storage units was established by plugboard wiring. Little flexibility of sequence control was forfeited in this way, since nearly half of all storage units could be identified as sources for "next" lines of sequence.

The fields of the entire line of sequence standing in the sequence control were "scanned" at electronic speed, from left to right, and the specified data transfers to or from the arithmetic unit occurred one twenty-digit unit at a time. But data paths to and from the much slower electromechanical storage units had to remain set up during execution of the entire line of sequence. The overlapped transfer of so many twenty-digit numbers or instructions required an elaborate system of buses. Comprising eight storage-out and eight storage-in buses, each having eighty conductors (seventy-eight for data and two for control), the busing system thus contained well over twelve hundred wires, and these extended over the full length and breadth of the machine.

Each in-out pair of eighty-wire buses was permanently connected to one of the eight electronic storage registers. These were ordinarily used to buffer data being transferred to or from the slower storage units, and instruction fields P, Q, R, etc., contained subfields designating the direction of data flow (to or from storage), the bus-and-register pair to be used, and the storage unit involved. By omitting the storage-unit designation, any of six electronic registers could be used as data source or destination; the remaining two, as the machine was actually used, were dedicated to transfer of the two instructions that made up the next line of sequence.

A better understanding of sequence control is gained by considering how the result of a computation might determine the course of a program. Assume that a main sequence on tape was to be followed until the need arose to determine a square root. The iterative square root procedure would then require a subsequence to be executed repeatedly until a key value in the computation changed sign. The sign of the key value in this case would indicate whether the two most recent approximations to the square root differed by more or less than a predetermined amount. When the sign of the key value changed, the main sequence would resume.

Thus the S1 and S2 fields in each line of the main sequence would have specified the same two sources (their respective tape readers) repeatedly for next left and right half-lines of sequence until a square root was needed. The S1 and S2 fields at that point would specify sources for the subsequence, which might be stored in five or so pairs of the twenty-digit relay storage units. As each line of subsequence was read into the sequence control from a pair of storage units, the values found in its S1 and S2 fields would be larger by one, thus specifying the pair of storage units holding the next line of subsequence.

The last pair of relay storage units might be empty except for S1 and S2 fields, each of which contained a preset value minus or plus a fixed number (e.g., 5), depending on whether the key value, initially negative, had become positive. The positive increment in S1 and S2 would cause the next line of sequence to be read from the main sequence tapes. It would not have been necessary, incidentally, to store all five lines of the subsequence in relay storage as assumed in this example. It is more likely, in fact, that all but the final line would be stored on a pair of subsequence tapes—endless loops from which the first four lines could be read as often as required. In that case sequence selection by the results of computation would require only two (one pair) of the 150 relay storage units.[1]

The machine was asynchronous in that the time taken to execute an instruction depended on the speeds of the functional units involved. A system of "forward" and "back" signals, carried over separate wires in each data bus, indicated whether sending and receiving storage units were ready for the transmission of data. Otherwise identical instructions would take less time to execute when, for example, only relay and electronic storage locations were addressed, than when paper tape was addressed. Furthermore, since the execution of a next instruction could proceed any time the required buses and storage units were free, parts of several instructions might be in the process of execution at a given instant. Toward this end, the relays of the sequence control were provided in duplicate sets, so that while one set controlled operation, a second set could receive the next line of sequence.[2]

Appendix B
TPM Organization and Operation

The outline of the Tape Processing Machine prepared in March 1950 by N. Rochester and W. Buchholz described in all important respects the machine that was subsequently designed and constructed. The features and details of operation given here accord with those in the TPM as actually constructed.[1]

As a result of character-by-character discipline, the system required virtually no flip-flop registers for operands or results; execution logic, on the other hand, required more sequencing circuits than would be needed in a fixed-word machine. For the sake of economy, a compelling consideration, plans called for each character to be transmitted internally as a sequence of seven bits; the machine was as serial in nature as if it had contained a mercury-delay-line memory. As seen from a user's viewpoint, the basic unit of time was a "character cycle," the period required for fetching, processing, and replacing a CRT-stored character, including an allowance for regeneration. During the planned character cycle of 128 microseconds, either or both memory and accumulator storage could yield and store (or restore) one character.

An instruction was allocated six memory characters: one for the operation code, four for an address, and one for a field mark. The sign of an operand was indicated by its right-most field mark. An addition required six character cycles for reading the instruction and its field mark, one for the sign of the memory-stored operand, one for each digit of the longer operand, and one for the final field mark. Thus, to add operands with two-digit fields required ten cycles, or 1.28 milliseconds; and to add operands with twelve-digit fields required twenty cycles—twice that time.

The period of each programmed operation was divided into "instruction time" and "execution time." During the former, an instruction was read from memory and execution circuits were activated. CRT deflection circuits were controlled by a "program counter" during instruction time and by a "memory address counter" during execution time (except during the regeneration part of each cycle, when a "regeneration counter" assumed control and proceeded from the last bit-cell that had been refreshed). (See figure B.1.) The instructions comprising a program could be located anywhere in memory, as could operands. Memory locations increased to the right, in the order that information is normally read by human beings. (See figure B.2.) A memory field was addressed by referring to the location of the field mark just to the right of its least significant digit or right-most alphanumeric character.

The arithmetic element of the TPM included a decimal adder, true-complement controls for both adder inputs, a comparator, and the accumulator. The adder operated serially upon the low-order four bits of its two incoming characters. During most character cycles of an operation such as ADD or SUBTRACT, one character came from memory and one from the accumulator. The 100-character capacity of the accumulator, in serving the variable-field-length feature of the TPM, could hold a result of up to ninety-eight digits, two positions being reserved for left and right field marks.

Unlike the wheel accumulators of electric accounting machines and their early electronic counterparts in the SSEC and 604, the accumulator was endowed with no arithmetic capability; it might better have been named "general register" or "arithmetic storage." Arithmetic was accomplished by formation of sums in switching circuits capable of nothing much more complicated than binary addition. The basis for addition of bits being simple, sums can be formed, bit by bit, with a few AND, OR, and NOT (or inverting) circuits. Consider the first (lowest-order) bits arriving at an adder from two binary numbers. The sum bit is 1 if either but not both of the input bits is 1. The sum bit is 0 if both inputs are the same. Only if both are 1 is a carry generated as an additional input to the next binary column. The adder circuit is made somewhat more complex, of course, because a possible carry-in from the next-lower column must be included in forming a sum; in a decimal machine using four-bit groups to represent digits, a correction is required every four bits (for sums in the range 10 to 19) to obtain a decimal result; and subtraction is obtained as a slight generalization of algebraic addition. In the TPM, subtraction of a positive value, like addition of a negative value, was accomplished by adding

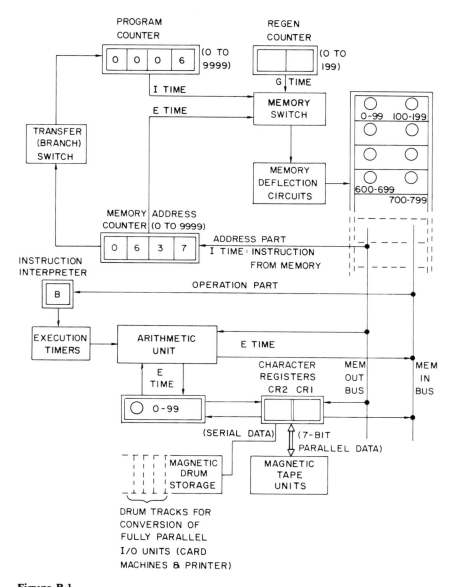

Figure B.1
Logical organization of the TPM. The instruction B0637 (RESET ADD 0637) has been read from word location 0006 during instruction time (I time). During the following execution time (E time), a word will be read from memory location 0637 and placed in the accumulator. Character registers CR1 and CR2 held the current characters from memory and accumulator and, during input-output operations, held alternate characters from tape, to buffer the main frame circuits against timing variations in tape data rate.

CONTENTS	+ B 0 6 3 7 + A 0 6 4 3 + • • • + 7 3 2 + 1 0 1 4 9 − • • •
MEMORY LOCATION	0000 0001 0002 0003 0004 0005 0006 0007 0008 0009 0010 0011 0012 • • • 0633 0634 0635 0636 0637 0638 0639 0640 0641 0642 0643 • • •

Figure B.2
TPM memory address assignment. When the TPM was turned on and the START button was depressed, control circuits caused an instruction to be read from the word location 0006 (addressed by the character location of its right field mark). Actually, the program counter was set to 0000 and caused to step one position just before each of six characters was called from memory. In this manner it read, from locations 0001 through 0006, the operation code, the four-digit address part of the instruction, and the right field mark. As the operation part (or "operation code," as this single character was often called) was read, bit by bit, from memory, its first six bits were stored in a register of flip-flops in a part of the machine called the instruction interpreter. Its seventh bit, the parity bit, was used only in determining that the character passed the parity test: that the total number of "1s" it contained was odd. This test was performed on all characters read from memory or from input-output devices. In this example, the operation code of the first instruction to be used is B, which is the code for RESET ADD. (See table B.1.)

The four decimal digits of the address part of the instruction (0637) were read from memory next. They were used to set up the memory address register, which would provide an initial setting for the memory deflection circuits during execution time. Finally the last character of the instruction, which was really its right field mark, was read. It was used in this case only to confirm that the machine was reading its program from the correct memory locations. There were, however, both "+" and "−" field marks, and a "−" field mark would be placed at the right of an instruction if the machine was intended to stop before executing the instruction. This would mean going into repeated regeneration mode until the START button was depressed again.

After the instruction had been read, the state of the machine was switched from "instruction time" to "execution time." The number 732+ (or plus 732) was next read from right to left, starting with the +FM at location 0637, under the control of the execution timer appropriate to the instruction that had just been read and interpreted—in this case RESET ADD. There were many execution timers in the TPM, each consisting of from one to sixteen flip-flops. Some served for groups of closely related instructions and some for single instructions. After executing the RESET ADD instruction, the state of the machine switched again from E to I, and the second instruction was read, beginning with its operation code A (for ADD). During the next E time, the five-digit number 10149− would be added to the three-digit number that had just been placed in the accumulator.

the ten's complement of the value to the accumulator. The ten's complement of an n-digit decimal integer is the result obtained by subtracting the entire number from 10^n. In the accumulator, negative results remained in ten's complement form until converted to true form during the course of an accumulator-to-memory operation. The sign of the accumulator contents, frequently needed for controlling the course of the program, was kept available in a special "accumulator sign" flip-flop. The sign of a number in memory, on the other hand, was indicated by the right-hand field mark.

Decimal digits were represented in the "excess-three" code, so called because the binary value of the low-order four bits is higher by three than the digit represented. (See table B.1.) The digit 5, for example, was encoded as 0 00 1000 (where spaces have been inserted only to aid in explanation). The left-most bit, the parity bit, was set to 0 or 1 as required to make the count of 1s odd; the next two bits, called "zone bits," were always 00 for decimal digits; the low-order four bits, the digit part of the character, corresponded to the binary columns 8, 4, 2, 1, respectively, and in this case their combined weight is 8, three in excess of the 5 represented. The excess-three code, apparently originated by G. R. Stibitz[2] and used in the first of the Bell Telephone Laboratories relay calculators in 1938, had also been selected by Eckert and Mauchly for their UNIVAC.

Use of the excess-three code facilitated taking the ten's complement of a number "on the fly" (without a special pass through the adder) by deriving the nine's complement and adding one. The nine's complement of a number is formed by subtracting each digit from nine and substituting the difference for the original digit. To obtain the nine's complement in excess-three code, it sufficed to invert digit-part bits, changing 1s to 0s, and vice versa. Consider the digit 5, encoded as 1000 in its digit part. Inverting the bits produces 0111 with binary value 7 as the proper excess-three representation of 4—the desired nine's complement of 5. The ten's complement was generated in the TPM by turning on a "carry" flip-flop before processing the nine's-complement number through the adder; this carry-in to the least significant position provided the additional 1 required.

Since the sum of two digits, each increased by three, is six greater than the sum of the digits themselves, a correction was required to restore the sum to excess-three form. This did not imply an extra operation; it was combined with the adjustment required in any case to correct from base 16 to base 10. (See chapter 2 for for a discussion of how this correction was effected in the counting type of accumulator.) In the TPM, both the excess-three and the decimal correction were

Table B.1
Character code chart for the TPM.

C BA 8421	C BA 8421	C BA 8421	C BA 8421
I II 0000	0 I0 0000 ∓ (RECORD MARK)	0 0I 0000 ⧺ (TAPE MARK)	I 00 0000 b (BLANK)
0 II 0001	I I0 0001	I 0I 0001	0 00 0001
0 II 0010 — (HYPHEN)	I I0 0010	I 0I 0010	0 00 0010
I II 0011 & AMPERSAND	0 I0 0011 — (FIELD MARK)	0 0I 0011 + (FIELD MARK)	I 00 0011 0 NO OP
0 II 0100 A ADD	I I0 0100 J SHOR	I 0I 0100 / (SLANT)	0 00 0100 1 STORE
I II 0101 B R ADD	0 I0 0101 K COMP	0 0I 0101 S SUB	I 00 0101 2 ST AFM
I II 0110 C R ADD-R	0 I0 0110 L LENG	0 0I 0110 T SEL	I 00 0110 3 ST BFM
0 II 0111 D DIV	I I0 0111 M MPY	I 0I 0111 U DRUM	0 00 0111 4
0 II 1000 E TREEF	I I0 1000 N BLANK	I 0I 1000 V SET FM	0 00 1000 5 ST NFM
I II 1001 F REW	0 I0 1001 O	0 0I 1001 W WRITE	I 00 1001 6 ST + FM
I II 1010 G ADD MEM	0 I0 1010 P SECT	0 0I 1010 X TR	I 00 1010 7 ST – FM
0 II 1011 H CTRL	I I0 1011 Q ROUND	I 0I 1011 Y TR +	0 00 1011 8 WR ER
I II 1100 I	0 I0 1100 R READ	0 0I 1100 Z R SUB	I 00 1100 9 ASTK
0 II 1101 (DECIMAL POINT)	I I0 1101 $	I 0I 1101 '	0 00 1101 #
0 II 1110 ⊐	I I0 1110 ✶	I 0I 1110 %	0 00 1110 @
I II 1111 (INVERSE BLANK)	0 I0 1111	0 0I 1111	I 00 1111 ∞ (INFINITY)

Note: The four columns of the chart correspond to the four combinations of the zone bits, usually labeled A and B. The "digit part" of each character was represented in its 8, 4, 2, and 1 bits; and in the excess-three code used, each decimal digit was given a binary code value greater by three than the decimal value it represented. The C bit, or parity bit, was chosen to keep the total count of 1s odd. Shown below each character is an abbreviation of the instruction type, if any, for which the character is used as the operation code.

accomplished within each character cycle by sending the uncorrected decimal digit of the result from the "sum register" through the adder in a second pass, during which it was combined with either binary 0011 (decimal 0) or 1101 (decimal 10), depending on whether a carry had occurred in the first pass.

The comparator consisted of circuits that performed the equivalent of subtraction upon the "zone" bits of two characters being compared, taking into account the ranking desired for certain special characters. Together with the adder circuits, which processed digit parts, the comparator was capable of indicating whether a memory field outranked the accumulator field in a "collating sequence" like the one commonly observed in punched-card systems.

The TPM was endowed with capabilities for interpreting and executing a variety of instructions, many of them made novel by the variable-field-length requirement. (See table B.2 for a summary list of instructions.) Some understanding of the system can be conveyed in comments on a few representative instructions. In ADD, the number whose right field mark was at the memory location specified by the address part of the instruction was added to the number in the accumulator; the sum, allocated the number of digit positions in the longer of the two operands, appeared in the accumulator between field marks and could be as long as ninety-eight digits. Nonnumeric operands were permissible, but the adder considered only the digit parts and yielded a numeric result. ADD TO MEMORY was like ADD except that the sum replaced the memory operand instead of the accumulator operand and was of memory-operand length.

In MULTIPLY, a number in memory was multiplied by the number in the accumulator to yield a product in the accumulator of length equal to the sum of the lengths of the multiplier and multiplicand. The product could contain up to forty-seven digits, a restriction arising from the use of the accumulator to store not only the multiplier and the product but also the multiplicand and three field marks. Multiplication was achieved by repeated addition with successively doubled multiplicand; the original multiplicand was moved to the accumulator for safe keeping so that, at the end of the process, it could be used to replace the by-then-octupled multiplicand in memory. In DIVIDE, the number in the accumulator was divided by a number in memory to yield a quotient in the accumulator. The length of the quotient equaled dividend length minus divisor length. An execution timer used repeated subtraction to achieve the result.

In SET FIELD MARK AND SKIP, the left field mark in the accumulator was so positioned that the resulting length of the accumulator

Table B.2
Instruction set of the TPM

ADD: Algebraic sum of (memory) and (accumulator) replaces (accumulator).

SUBTRACT: Same as ADD, with (memory) sign changed.

RESET ADD: (Memory) replaces (accumulator).

RESET SUBTRACT: (Memory) with sign changed replaces (accumulator).

RESET ADD RESET: Same as RESET ADD, with (memory) then set to zero.

MULTIPLY: Algebraic product of (memory) and (accumulator) replaces (accumulator).

DIVIDE: Quotient of dividend (accumulator) by divisor (memory) replaces (accumulator).

ADD TO MEMORY: Algebraic sum of (memory) and (accumulator) replaces (memory).

SET FIELD MARK AND SKIP: Set (accumulator) length. Skip if only zeros deleted.

LENGTHEN RIGHT: Lengthen (accumulator) by moving right field mark.

SHORTEN RIGHT: Shorten (accumulator) by moving right field mark.

ROUND OFF: Same as SHORTEN RIGHT, after half-adjusting (accumulator).

TRANSFER: Branch to instruction at specified location.

TRANSFER ON PLUS: Branch only if (accumulator) positive (incl. zero).

TRANSFER EXCEPT AT END OF FILE: Branch unless end of I/O file is sensed.

COMPARE AND SKIP: Skip one instruction if (memory) = (accumulator); two if (memory)<(accumulator).

STORE: (Accumulator) replaces (memory). Fields must be same length.

STORE AND ALTER FIELD MARKS: Same as store, with fields of different lengths.

STORE BETWEEN FIELD MARKS: Store as much of right portion of (accumulator) as fits.

STORE WITH NO FIELD MARKS: Store, omitting (accumulator) field marks.

STORE PLUS FIELD MARK: Set (memory) sign by storing positive right field mark.

STORE MINUS FIELD MARK: Set (memory) sign by storing negative right field mark.

SELECT INPUT-OUTPUT UNIT: Designate device for next I/O instruction.

READ: Read one record from selected input device to memory.

WRITE: Transmit one record from memory to selected output device.

WRITE AND ERASE MEMORY: Write, leaving memory blank except for field and record marks.

REWIND: After recording tape mark (if appropriate), rewind selected tape.

DRUM SELECT: Select the one of 200 (25-character) drum sections for starting READ or WRITE.

SECTION-OF-DRUM SELECT: Same as DRUM SELECT, but read/write *ends* at first field mark or section boundry.

CONTROL: Effects various controls on selected printer, card reader or punch.

NO OPERATION: Instruction is bypassed.

STOP: (Negative right field mark on any instruction stops machine before execution.)

BLANK: Blank non-significant left (accumulator) zeros. Insert decimal point as specified.

ASTERISK: Same as BLANK, but asterisks replace blanks.

Note: Contents of accumulator or of specified memory location are indicated by "(accumulator)" or "(memory)." Instruction descriptions are neither rigorous enough nor complete enough for programming and are shown merely to indicate the nature of the machine's capabilities.

field (excluding field marks) equaled the number in the address part of the instruction. If no characters but zeros were deleted in the process, the next instruction was skipped; if nonzero characters were deleted, the next instruction was executed, providing an opportunity to branch to a subprogram for handling this case.

In COMPARE and SKIP, a field (or the absolute value, in the case of a number) in memory was compared to that in the accumulator. If the memory field was higher, the next instruction was executed in sequence. If the fields were equal, the program counter skipped over the next instruction. If memory was lower, the next two instructions were skipped. Alphabetic characters ranked lower than numerics, and the "blank" and a group of special symbols (such as "*") ranked lowest of all.

There were several instructions for moving accumulator content to memory under various conditions. In STORE BETWEEN FIELD MARKS, useful when the accumulator field was longer than the memory field, the right field mark from the accumulator replaced the field mark at the specified memory location, along with as much of the right-hand part of the accumulator word as would fit in the memory field without changing the left field mark in memory. Two instructions were usually required to initiate an input or output operation. In READ, a record was read into memory from the input device specified in the last-executed SELECT I/O UNIT instruction. The record was entered in memory from left to right, proceeding upward through memory addresses, starting at the field mark location specified by the address part of READ. Thus, for input-output operations information was handled highest order first, whereas in arithmetic operations it was handled lowest order first. In WRITE, a record was sent from memory to a previously selected output device.

The data rate of the fastest input-output devices—tape and drum— was approximately 7000 characters per second, the corresponding interval for each tape or drum character being therefore 140 microseconds. The TPM interspersed additional regeneration cycles among its full 128 microsecond character cycles as required to achieve synchronization with the I/O data stream.

Appendix C
Havens Delay Unit Circuit Operation

The Havens delay unit is described in B. L. Havens's patent "Pulse Delay Circuit," U.S. Patent No. Reissue 23,699, and in a paper by H. D. Ross, Jr. The circuit diagram and waveforms of figure C.1 are adapted from the latter source: H.D. Ross, Jr., "The Arithmetic Element of the IBM Type 701 Computer," *Proceedings of the Institute of Radio Engineers*, Vol. 41, pp. 1287–1294. © 1953 IRE (now IEEE).

Assuming first that the input is at -30 volts (low level) for several cycles, the left-hand tube (amplifier) is cut off. Successive CLAMP pulses hold the top plate of the 22 mmf capacitor at a level of -30 volts. It is not driven to a lower level because of the connection to the -30 volt supply by crystal diodes A and B. Between CLAMP pulses a small amount of the 30 volts of charge is lost due to current flow onto the top plate from these sources: (1) the CLAMP line, through the 1.5K resistor and the back resistance of diode C, and (2) the capacitor bottom plate, through the capacitor dielectric. But the charge lost during that time is not sufficient to change the voltage across the capacitor appreciably, and is restored by each clamping pulse. Thus the output remains at the low level.

When the input does rise to the upper level, the AND-type coincidence circuit at the grid of the amplifier tube causes the tube to conduct fully during the SYNC pulse. The tube current partially discharges the 47 mmf coupling capacitor so that when the tube is cut off by the fall of the SYNC pulse, the positive pulse on its plate is coupled to the 22 mmf capacitor. The "peaking" circuit consisting of the induction coil and resistor in the amplifier plate circuit ensures that the coupled pulse endures until the CLAMP line begins to rise, whereupon current is still available to discharge the 22 mmf capacitor, bringing its top plate up to about the upper level of the CLAMP line.

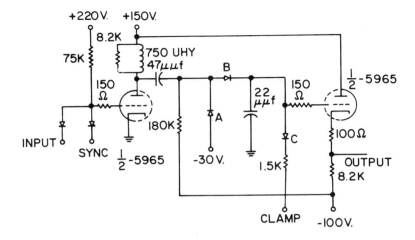

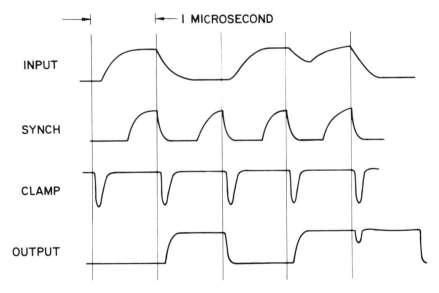

Figure C.1
Havens delay unit circuit and waveforms. The voltage levels for all waveforms
are about $+10$ volts (upper level) and -30 volts (lower level) except for CLAMP,
for which the lower level is -40 volts.

The capacitor voltage provides the circuit output by the right-hand tube, a cathode follower that supplies the output waveform to other circuits.

We see that the output rises at the end of the CLAMP pulse that begins a particular 1 microsecond period if the SYNC pulse that concluded the preceding 1 microsecond period has been gated by the input line to the amplifier tube grid.

The next CLAMP pulse will charge the 22 mmf capacitor back to -30 volts, causing the ouput to fall to the lower level, unless the just-preceding SYNC pulse has been applied to the amplifier grid. In that case the clamping action is opposed by current from the amplifier peaking circuit; the output falls momentarily but is restored when the CLAMP rises to its upper level.

Thus during the period from the end of a particular CLAMP pulse to the beginning of the next, the output is at the upper level if and only if the SYNC pulse in the preceding 1 microsecond interval has been gated to the grid of the amplifer tube; otherwise the output is at the lower level.

The output waveform is a replica of the input with these qualifications: it is delayed by 1 microsecond, and the leading and trailing edges of the pulses are steeper and more precisely timed with respect to the time base defined by the SYNC and CLAMP pulse trains.

Appendix D
701 System Design Summary

Tables D.1 and D.2 are reproduced from a paper by W. Buchholz, "The System Design of the IBM Type 701 Computer," *Proceedings of the Institute of Radio Engineers*, Vol. 41, pp. 1262–1275. © 1953 IRE (now IEEE). Until mid-1952, the machine was called the Defense Calculator. The operation times shown in column 3 of Table D.2 invite discussion of the memory regeneration process. Taking the memory cycle of 12 microseconds as the basic unit of time, the 701 designers treated memory cycles as of four kinds: I, E, E/R, and R. During an I cycle, an instruction was obtained from memory. During an E cycle, an operand was obtained from, or stored in, memory. Some operations involved E/R cycles that invoked execution circuitry only—not memory—and could therefore permit regeneration to proceed. During R (regeneration only) cycles, instruction sequencing deferred to regeneration, the process with the higher priority. All operational patterns were suggested by the maximum times for four prototypical operations:

TRANSFER	I, E/R, R, R	48 microseconds
ADD	I, E, E/R, R, R	60 microseconds
STORE	I, E, R, R, R	60 microseconds
MULTIPLY	I, E, 36 E/R	456 microseconds

Multiplication was lengthy because one E/R cycle was set aside for each of the possible thirty-five times that the multiplicand might be added under control of the bits being shifted out of the multiplier; division functioned analogously with thirty-five possible subtractions. As indicated by the first three timing patterns, the 701 designers meant to ensure at least three regeneration cycles per executed instruction. But since a multiplication or division operation moved regeneration ahead of schedule, they provided for suppression of R cycles during twelve subsequent operations—unless another multiplication or division intervened, in which event the count of twelve was restarted. The minimum (parenthesized) times of table D.2 prevailed during these periods when R cycles were being omitted.

Rochester had decided early in 1951 that there would be no restrictions imposed on Defense Calculator programmers to help defeat the effects of "spill." Two words were regenerated on every 12 microsecond regeneration cycle. Thus six were regenerated for each instruction execution, and each of the 2048 words in storage would be regenerated every 342 executions (counting multiply and divide as 12 each). In the final tests of the memory units, they were made to operate with a read-around ratio of 400 to 1.

Table D.1
Summary of 701 system characteristics

General:
  Parallel operation.
  Binary notation internally.
  Control by stored program.
Word Size:
  Either 36 bits or 18 bits, including sign; approximately equivalent to 10 or 5 decimal digits and sign.
  Accumulator has two extra bits for overflow.
Instructions:
  Single-address system.
  33 distinct operations.
  Instructions are 18-bit words.
Computing Speed:
  Multiplication or Division: 0.456 millisecond.
  Addition or Subtraction: 0.060 millisecond.
Electrostatic Storage:
  Capacity—2048 words of 36 bits each.
  Each full-word location may store a pair of 18-bit words.
  72 tubes, 1024 bits per tube.
Magnetic Drums:
  Four drums, each with a capacity of 2048 words of 36 bits each, in basic system.
  Average access time to first word of block—40 milliseconds.
  Reading or writing rate—800 words per second.
Magnetic Tapes:
  Four magnetic tape units in basic system.
  Material: Oxide-coated plastic tape, 1/2 inch wide.
  Recording in 7 parallel channels, 6 for information and 1 for redundancy checking.
  Tape may be written forward, read forward, or read backward under program control.
  Density within a unit record: 200 words per foot.
  Distance between unit records—1 inch.
  Maximum tape length on reel—1400 ft.
  Access time to start of unit record—approx. 10 milliseconds.
  Reading or writing rate within unit record—1250 words per second.
Page Printer:
  Rate—150 lines per minute.
  Prints numeric, alphabetic, and special characters.
  Prints at full speed in decimal form using simultaneous conversion program.
  Prints 72 characters in any of 120 character positions on one line, more at reduced speed.
  Automatic line spacing or skipping, under control of stored program.
Card Reader and Card Punch:
  Reads or punches any 72 of the 80 card columns.
  Reading rate—150 cards per minute.
  Punching rate—100 cards per minute.
  Reads or punches cards in standard IBM decimal code at full speed using simultaneous conversion program.
  Reads or punches cards in binary form at full speed with 24 words of 36 bits each to a card.

Table D.2

LIST OF 701 INSTRUCTIONS WITH BRIEF EXPLANATIONS

Code	Short Name	Time[6]	Full Name and Explanation[7]	Code	Short Name	Time	Full Name and Explanation
00	*Stop*	—	*Stop and Transfer* Stop, and prepare to transfer to *x* (see *Tr*) when the computer is started again.	18	*Div*	456	*Divide* Divide contents of the accumulator and *MQ* register, taken as a unit, by the contents of *x*. Contents of *x* must exceed in magnitude the accumulator contents. The resultant quotient appears in the *MQ* register, and the remainder is left in the accumulator.
01	*Tr*	48 (24)	*Transfer* Take the next instruction from half-word address *x*.				
02	*Tr Ov*	48 (24)	*Transfer on Overflow* Transfer to *x* only if the overflow indicator is on; then reset the overflow indicator.	19	*Round*	48 (24)	*Round* Increase the magnitude of the accumulator contents by one in position 35, if there is a one in position 1 of the *MQ* register. The *MQ* register is not changed.
03	*Tr +*	48 (24)	*Transfer on Plus* Transfer to *x* only if the accumulator sign is plus; the other accumulator positions are ignored.	20	*L Left*	48 (24)[8]	*Long Left Shift* Shift both the accumulator and *MQ* register contents as a unit to the left by *x* places (*x* not greater than 255). The accumulator sign is set to that of the *MQ* register.
04	*Tr 0*	48 (24)	*Transfer on Zero* Transfer to *x* only if the accumulator contains zero; the accumulator sign is ignored.	21	*L Right*	48 (24)[8]	*Long Right Shift* Shift both accumulator and *MQ* register contents as a unit to right by *x* places. *MQ* register sign is set to that of the accumulator.
05	*Sub*	60 (36)	*Subtract* Subtract the contents of *x* from the accumulator.	22	*A Left*	48 (24)[8]	*Accumulator Left Shift* Shift accumulator contents to left by *x* places. Sign is not changed.
06	*R Sub*	60 (36)	*Reset and Subtract* Reset the accumulator to zero before subtracting.	23	*A Right*	48 (24)[8]	*Accumulator Right Shift* Shift the accumulator contents to the right by *x* places. The sign is not changed.
07	*Sub Ab*	60 (36)	*Subtract Absolute Value* Subtract the absolute value of the contents of *x* from the accumulator.	24	*Read*	48 (24)[9]	*Prepare to Read* Prepare to read one unit record from the input component specified by *x*. Start mechanical movement forward if necessary.
08	*No Op*	48 (24)	*No Operation* Do nothing.	25	*Read B*	48 (24)[9]	*Prepare to Read Backward* (For tape only.) Same as *Read* except tape is moved backward.
09	*Add*	60 (36)	*Add* Add the contents of *x* to the accumulator.	26	*Write*	48 (24)	*Prepare to Write* Prepare to write one unit record on the output component specified by *x*. Start mechanical movement forward, if necessary.
10	*R Add*	60 (36)	*Reset and Add* Reset the accumulator to zero before adding.	27	*Write EF*	48 (24)[9]	*Write End of File* (For tape only.) Write an end-of-file gap on the tape unit specified by *x*.
11	*Add Ab*	60 (36)	*Add Absolute Value* Add the absolute value of the contents of *x* to the accumulator.	28	*Rewind*	48 (24)	*Rewind Tape* (For tape only.) Rewind tape unit specified by *x* to starting point.
12	*Store*	60 (24)	*Store* Store the accumulator contents (except the two overflow positions) at *x*, replacing the previous contents; the accumulator is left unchanged.	29	*Set Dr*	48 (24)	*Set Drum Address* (For drum only.) Set up *x* as the drum address of the first of a sequence of words to be read or written on the drum specified by the last preceding *Read* or *Write* instruction.
+13	*Store A*	60 (24)	*Store Address* Store the contents of bit positions 6 through 17 of the accumulator in place of the rightmost 12 bits at half-word address *x*. Note: Instruction must have a + sign part.	30	*Sense*	48 (24)	*Sense and Skip, or Control* If *x* specifies an input, sense input line for a signal; if a signal is present, skip the next instruction. If *x* specifies an output, send out a control signal; do not skip.
−13	*Extr*	60 (24)	*Extract* Wherever an accumulator bit position contains a zero (or +), store a zero (or +) in the corresponding position at memory address *x*; leave all other bits in memory unchanged. Note: Instruction must have − sign part.	31	*Copy*	60 (24)[9]	*Copy and Skip* 1. If reading, store one word arriving from the input at memory address *x*. At the end of a unit record, skip *two* instructions. At the end of a file (i.e. after the last record is read), skip *one* instruction. Otherwise do not skip. 2. If writing, send one word from memory, address *x* to the output; do not skip.
14	*Store MQ*	60 (24)	*Store Number from MQ Register* Store the contents of the *MQ* register at *x*.				
15	*Load MQ*	60 (24)	*Load MQ Register* Load the contents of *x* into the *MQ* register.				
16	*Mpy*	456	*Multiply* Multiply the contents of *x* by the contents of the *MQ* register. The most significant 35 bits of product are left in accumulator and the others in *MQ* register, in place of their previous contents.				
17	*Mpy R*	456	*Multiply and Round* The same as *Mpy* followed by *Round*, giving a rounded 35-bit product.				

[6] The normal time is given first. The time in parentheses applies only if this is one of 12 instructions immediately following *Mpy, Mpy R,* or *Div.*
[7] *x* denotes the address part of an instruction.

[8] These are minimum times. Time to shift $= 12(1+K)$ microseconds where K is smallest integer $\geq x/8$, provided this exceeds the minimum of 48 (24) microseconds.
[9] These times may increase if input-output synchronization requires a delay.

References and Notes

Chapter 1

1. T. G. and M. R. Belden, 1962: *The Lengthening Shadow: The Life of Thomas J. Watson* (Boston: Little, Brown).

2. G. D. Austrian, 1982: *Herman Hollerith: Forgotten Giant of Information Processing* (New York: Columbia University Press). Chapter 1 relies on this biography for background on Hollerith. The School of Mines became Columbia University's engineering school.

3. L. E. Truesdell, 1965: *The Development of Punch Card Tabulation in the Bureau of the Census, 1890–1940* (U.S. Department of Commerce). A basic source for census events, machines, and applications.

4. A. Hyman, 1982: *Charles Babbage, Pioneer of the Computer* (Princeton: Princeton University Press).

5. T. C. Martin, 11 November 1891: "Counting a Nation by Electricity," *Electrical Engineer*, pp. 521–530. In this article, decimal positions are said to be connected, but the carry mechanism is not explained.

6. Austrian, 1982, pp. 124–141. Also see *American Machinist*, 31 July 1902: "The Electric Tabulating Machine Applied to Cost Accounting," pp. 1073–1075.

7. E. W. Bryn, 19 April 1902: "The Mechanical Work of the Twelfth Census," *Scientific American*, p. 275.

8. Austrian, 1982: p. 242.

9. Apparently the size of the dollar bill varied slightly from mint to mint. See A. Pick, 1973: *Paper Money, Catalogue of the Americas* (Munich: Ernst Battenberg Verlag).

10. W. E. Freeman, June 1915: "Accounting Session," *Convention Record of the National Electric Light Association*, p. 30.

11. G. F. Daly, January 1955: "Historical Record of Card and Machine Development," IBM staff report. In this authoritative record of CTR and IBM products, dates for first use and public announcement can differ. Chapter 1 relies on the former.

12. G. F. Daly, 1953: "Development of IBM Unit Record Equipment, Inventors and Laboratories," IBM staff report. Also see *IBM Think*, April 1949 and *IBM Endicott News*, 23 December 1958 and 15 November 1961.

13. A. E. Gray, undated: "IBM Development Manual, Book I, Numerical Tabulators," IBM staff report.

14. B. M. Durfee, December 1969: interview by L. M. Saphire.

15. Daly, 1953.

16. Durfee, 1969. Also see *IBM Business Machines*, 12 January 1933.

17. Daly, 1953. Ford had remained a CTR consultant.

18. IBM Principles of Operation Manual, 1942: "Alphabetical Accounting Machine, Type 405." Also see Gray, undated.

19. E. J. Rabenda, August 1969: interview by L. M. Saphire.

20. IBM Principles of Operation Manual, 1947: "Electric Multiplier Type 601" (IBM Form 52-3408-1).

21. IBM Customer Engineering Manual, 1948: "Electric Multiplier, Type 601" (IBM Form 22-3672-1).

22. W. J. Eckert, 1947: "Calculating machines," *Encyclopedia Britannica*, mentions a similar method of multiplication invented by Léon Bollée in 1887.

23. A small group under Frederick L. Fuller (1861–1943) moved to New Jersey.

24. *Endicott IBM News*, September 1968, in a reprint.

25. W. W. McDowell, November 1970: interview by L. M. Saphire.

26. *IBM Business Machines*, 7 November 1946. See also J. C. McPherson, September 1941: "On Mechanical Tabulation of Polynomials," *Annals of Mathematical Statistics 12*, pp. 317–327.

27. *IBM Business Machines*, December 1961.

28. IBM Principles of Operation Manual, 1942: "The Alphabetical Accounting Machine Type 405."

29. The Tabulating Machine Division in 1937 was renamed Electric Bookkeeping and Accounting Machine Division, which in early 1939 was merged with the Proof Machine Division to form the EAM Division.

30. IBM brochure, 1950: "Accounting Machine Functions."

31. Machine Inventory, a file maintained by J. C. McPherson.

32. Let $u_9, u_8, \ldots, u_2, u_1$ denote a series of nine numbers. From this series, two stages of progressive totals leads to a last sum, denoted, say, by S, where $S = 9u_9 + 8u_8 + \ldots + 2u_2 + u_1$. Let T denote a sum of products, xy; that is, $T = x_1y_1 + x_2y_2 + \ldots + x_ny_n$. To see that T may be derived by adding and sorting operations, consider the case where x consists of one decimal digit. Assuming a punched card for each x,y pair, the cards are sorted by x value—that is, into subdecks for values 9, 8, $\ldots$, 1. (Those with a zero multiplier are temporarily set aside.) Multiplicands (ys) are then summed within each subdeck, to obtain nine sums labeled $u_9, u_8, \ldots, u_1$. This series, after two stages of progressive totaling, yields S, which under the assumed conditions is, of course, identical to T. In the general case, where multipliers have more than one decimal place, the procedure has to be iterated once per multiplier digit, each iteration yielding a value of S; then the final step in obtaining T is to sum the S's, shifting each as appropriate to its decimal position— that is, power of ten—in the multipliers. The method's efficiency goes up for larger n and down for longer multipliers. The term "progressive digiting" was probably coined as an extension of "progressive total," which originated as the term for a sum that was not cleared when printed.

33. H. R. J. Grosch, August 1946: "Harmonic Analysis by the Use of Progressive Digiting," *Proceedings of the IBM Research Forum*, pp. 81–84.

34. L. J. Comrie, April 1928: "On the Construction of Tables by Interpolation," *Royal Astronomical Society Monthly Notices 88*, pp. 506–523; L. J. Comrie, May 1932: "The Application of the Hollerith Tabulating Machine to Brown's Tables of the Moon," *Royal Astronomical Society Monthly Notices 92*, pp. 694–707. For another instance of early usage, see G. W. Snedicor, April 1928: "Uses of Punched Card Equipment in Mathematics," *American Mathematical Monthly 35*, pp. 161–169.

35. W. J. Eckert, May 1963: "Early Computers," *IBM Research News*, pp. 7–8; W. J. Eckert, 1947: "The IBM Department of Pure Science and the Watson Scientific Computing Laboratory," *IBM Educational Research Forum Proceedings*.

36. D. R. Piatt, 19 December 1949: to W. J. Eckert, "Statistical Calculator."

37. Eckert, 1947.

38. S. W. Dunwell, August 1967: interview by L. M. Saphire. Long after his employment, Dunwell took some graduate-level courses.

39. W. J. Eckert, 1940: *Punched Card Methods in Scientific Computation* (New York: Columbia University Press), p. 77.

40. Eckert, 1963. On the general usage of punched-card machines in universities, see G. W. Baehne, ed., 1935: *Practical Applications of the Punched Card Method in Colleges and Universities* (New York: Columbia University Press).

41. L. J. Comrie, October 1946: *Mathematical Tables and Other Aids to Computation*, a quarterly published by the National Research Council, pp. 149–159.

42. V. Bush, 1931: "The Differential Analyzer, A New Machine for Solving Differential Equations," *Journal of the Franklin Institute 212*, pp. 447–488.

43. H. H. Goldstine, 1972: *The Computer from Pascal to von Neumann* (Princeton: Princeton University Press).

44. I. B. Cohen, foreword to G. C. Chase, July 1980: "History of Mechanical Computing Machinery," *Annals of the History of Computing 2*, pp. 198–200.

45. H. Aiken, 3 November 1937: to J. W. Bryce.

46. H. Aiken, August 1964: "Proposed Automatic Calculating Machine," *IEEE Spectrum*, pp. 62–69.

47. H. E. Pim, 17 December 1937: to J. W. Bryce; and J. W. Bryce, 20 December 1937: to H. E. Pim.

48. H. E. Pim, 7 January 1938: to J. W. Bryce.

49. F. E. Hamilton, 3 March 1938: to A. H. Dickinson. Also F. E. Hamilton, 21 August 1944: "History of the Harvard Machine," IBM staff report.

50. J. W. Bryce, 18 January 1939: "Memorandum re Computing Mechanisms for Harvard University." The memorandum, Bryce explains, resulted from conferences with Aiken and Dean H. M. Westergaard of Harvard. Also see J. G. Phillips, 3 April 1939: to J. W. Bryce.

51. J. B. Hayward, 1 March 1939: to J. W. Bryce; J. W. Bryce, 12 May 1939: to C. D. Lake.

52. *IBM Business Machines*, 28 September 1950.

53. Goldstine, 1972.

54. IBM brochure, 1945: "IBM Automatic Sequence Controlled Calculator."

55. Staff of the Harvard Computation Laboratory, 1946: *A Manual of Operation for the Automatic Sequence Controlled Calculator* (Cambridge: Harvard University Press). See p. 245.

56. A. G. Oettinger and T. C. Bartee, August 1964: "A Note on the Twentieth Anniversary of the Mark I Computer—August 7, 1964," *IEEE Spectrum*, pp. 62–63.

57. T. J. Watson, 20 December 1943: to J. B. Conant, noting that Norman Bel Geddes & Associates had been retained by IBM to assist in designing the covering.

58. J. O. Harrison, Jr., 1948: "The Preparation of Problems for the Mark I Calculator," *Annals of the Computation Laboratory of Harvard University 16*, p. 210.

59. L. J. Comrie, 26 October 1946: "Babbage's Dream Comes True," *Nature 158*, pp. 567–568. A review of Harvard's manual of operation for the ASCC.

60. Harvard University press release 1944-80, 7 August 1944: "World's Greatest Mathematical Calculator." Release 1944-81 the next day, covering the ceremonies, was generous to the IBM engineers. (Both releases courtesy of Harvard University files.)

61. IBM brochure, 1945: "IBM Automatic Sequence Controlled Calculator."

62. U.S. Patent 2,616,626, filed 8 February 1945: C. D. Lake, H. H. Aiken, F. E. Hamilton, and B. M. Durfee, "Calculator."

63. *Wall Street Journal*, 14 January 1948: P. H. Buck, "Letter to the Editor."

64. Computer industry usage of the term "architecture" dates back at least to 1959. In L. R. Johnson, 10 December 1959: "A Description of Stretch," IBM Research Report, "system architecture" is used to suggest a level of computer structure that subordinates details of logical and circuit design. Later, "computer architecture" was defined as the "art of determining the needs of the user of a structure and then designing to meet those needs as effectively as possible within economic and technological constraints" by F. P. Brooks, Jr., 1962: "Architectural Philosophy," in *Planning a Computer System*, ed. W. Buchholz (New York: McGraw-Hill).

65. Staff of the Harvard Computation Laboratory, 1946, p. 105.

66. Goldstine, 1972: pp. 136–138.

67. H. H. Aiken and G. M. Hopper, November 1946: "The Automatic Sequence Controlled Calculator—III," *Electrical Engineering*, pp. 522–528.

68. Aiken's original estimate of ASCC speed, as reported 7 August 1944 by the *New York Herald Tribune*, was fifteen to fifty times the desk calculator.

69. Goldstine, 1972: p. 138. In some rough comparisons, Goldstine finds relay calculators about equal to the differential analyzer at computing shell trajectories.

70. W. J. Eckert, July 1948: "The IBM Pluggable Sequence Relay Calculator," *Mathematical Tables and Other Aids to Computation*, pp. 149–161. After joining IBM in 1945, Eckert obtained two of these "Aberdeen" calculators for his computation center.

71. J. C. McPherson, 11 January 1945: "Memorandum re Improved ASC Calculator."

Chapter 2

1. R. L. Palmer, July 1967: interview by L. M. Saphire.

2. F. E. Hamilton, 21 August 1944: untitled report describing development of "the Harvard machine," sent with cover note by J. J. Robbins to C. D. Lake 28 January 1949.

3. T. J. Watson, 1 June 1922: to G. W. Spahr; G. F. Daly, 3 December 1981: conversation with C. J. Bashe. Daly, a senior engineer and inventor of the punched-card era, spoke with great admiration of Bryce and his contributions. He said Bryce

was "nothing short of a genius" and referred to him as "the patron saint of IBM engineering." With 400 patents to his credit by 1936, Bryce was honored as one of the ten "greatest living inventors" by the U.S. Patent Office at its centennial celebration that year. IBM *Think*, April 1949: "The Light He Leaves Behind."

4. Gunne Lowkrantz, who headed the electrical laboratory when R. L. Palmer was hired, had worked with Bryce on the Difference Tabulator.

5. R. L. Palmer, July 1967.

6. A. H. Dickinson, July 1967: interview by L. M. Saphire.

7. C. E. Wynn-Williams, 1932: "A Thyratron Scale of Two Automatic Counter," *Proceedings of the Royal Society (London)*, A Vol. 136, pp. 312–324.

8. U.S. Patent 2,580,740, filed 20 January 1940: A. H. Dickinson, "Accounting Apparatus." Said to be the earliest electronic computing patent application. B. E. Phelps, 1980: "Early Electronic Computer Developments at IBM," *Annals of the History of Computing*. pp. 253–267.

9. E. C. Stevenson, and I. A. Getting, 1937: "A Vacuum Tube Circuit for Scaling Down Counting Rates," *Review of Scientific Instruments*, pp. 414–416; W. B. Lewis, 1937: "A Scale-of-Two High-Speed Counter Using Hard Vacuum Tubes," *Proceedings of the Cambridge Philosophical Society*, pp. 549–558.

10. B. E. Phelps, October 1967: interview by L. M. Saphire; H. J. Reich, August 1939: "Trigger Circuits," *Electronics*, pp. 14–17; H. Lifschutz and J. L. Lawson, 1938: "A Triode Vacuum-Tube Scale-of-Two Circuit," *Review of Scientific Instruments*, pp. 83–89; W. H. Eccles, and F. W. Jordan, 1919: "A Trigger Relay Utilizing Three-Electrode Thermionic Vacuum Tubes," *The Radio Review*, pp. 143–146.

11. A. W. Burks, 1947: "Electronic Computing Circuits of the ENIAC," *Proceedings of the Institute of Radio Engineers*, pp. 756–757. Although great care was later taken in the computer industry to distinguish between the terms "calculator" and "computer," their usage was evolving rapidly in the late 1940s. A few years earlier, "computer" referred to a person who performed computations, with or without the assistance of machines. By the early 1950s, the term was usually understood to describe a stored-program, electronic digital computer; but IBM applied the term "calculator," internally or publicly, to several machines that were in every sense general-purpose, stored-program, electronic digital computers. While it may be no more appropriate to call the ENIAC (which had a manually plugged program) a computer than to call those machines calculators, the term "computer" is used here because it was part of the full name given to the machine: Electronic Numerical Integrator and Computer.

12. Phelps, 1980. Phelps recalls that he had tried both ten-stage ring circuits and a five-stage ring preceded by a flip-flop, which also produced a carry on the count of ten. B. E. Phelps, 26 September 1984: conversation with C. J. Bashe.

13. U.S. Patent 2,584,811, filed 27 December 1944: B. E. Phelps, "Electronic Counting Circuit." The experiences related here do not necessarily reflect the knowledge of codes or number systems among computing people or electronic engineers generally but only the awareness of Phelps and his colleagues at the time. B. E. Phelps, 22 April 1981: conversation with C. J. Bashe.

14. Phelps later wrote, "In 1946, I, at least, had never heard the terms *logical and* or *logical or*." B. E. Phelps, 1982: "Computer Circuit Design in the 1940's," *Annals of the History of Computing*, pp. 368–370. Phelps's examination of the circuit diagram

of the experimental multiplier in 1981 confirms that the "twin-triode switch" was not used in that machine, except as a blocking tube in the counter. B. E. Phelps, 29 April 1981: conversation with C. J. Bashe.

15. R. L. Palmer, September 1969: interview by L. M. Saphire.

16. Phelps, 1980.

17. Ibid.

18. Dickinson, July 1967.

19. S. S. Snyder, 1980: "Computer Advances Pioneered by Cryptological Organizations," *Annals of the History of Computing*, pp. 60–70. For a description of British government work on specialized digital electronic devices during World War II, see I. J. Good, 1979: "Early Work on Computers at Bletchley," *Annals of the History of Computing*, pp. 38–48.

20. H. H. Goldstine, 1972: *The Computer from Pascal to von Neumann* (Princeton: Princeton University Press).

21. W. J. Eckert, 1948: "The IBM Pluggable Sequence Relay Calculator," *Mathematical Tables and Other Aids to Computation III*, pp. 149–161; C. B. Smith, with foreword by G. F. Daly, October 1964: "IBM Pluggable Sequence Calculators."

22. Comment on inadequacy of IBM's work in electronics is from Anon. (initials BEW:HC), "Minutes of Engineering Meeting Held in Mr. Watson's Office, October 6, 1943."

23. Dickinson, July 1967.

24. J. C. McPherson, 28 November 1944, 9 April 1945: to F. W. Nichol; W. W. McDowell, 10 March 1945: to J. C. McPherson.

25. The engineer from Dickinson's group who worked with Phelps on the 603 multiplier was Carl A. Bergfors. See C. A. Bergfors, December 1967: interview by L. M. Saphire. Division was not included in the 603 because the length of result produced by that operation—which had been incorporated in the engineering model—was deemed inadequate by the Future Demands department. B. E. Phelps, 13 May 1981: to C. J. Bashe; Phelps, October 1967.

26. J. C. McPherson, 9 May 1946: to C. A. Kirk.

27. Phelps, 1980; Phelps, October 1967. For Tom Watson, Jr.'s, support of the 603 program, see also Palmer, July 1967.

28. J. C. McPherson, October 1980: conversation with C. J. Bashe and J. H. Palmer.

29. W. J. Eckert, July 1967: interview by L. M. Saphire.

30. W. W. McDowell, 10 March 1945: to J. C. McPherson.

31. F. E. Hamilton, August 1945–March 1948: "IBM Calculator for Scientific Computing," monthly progress reports; F. E. Hamilton, 12 March 1945: to J. C. McPherson; J. C. McPherson, 29 March 1945: to F. E. Hamilton.

32. R. R. Seeber, Jr., August 1967: interview by L. M. Saphire. Supplementary biographical information about Seeber is found in the *Harvard Yearbook of 1932* and in the 10th, 15th, 25th, and 35th anniversary reports. In the 25th anniversary report (1957), he states: "I took a major active part in all phases of conception, invention, design, construction, and testing (and naming!) of the I.B.M. selective sequence electronic calculator. . . . As co-inventor of this computer, I have several patents issued, one of which contains claims fundamental to the entire computer field."

33. Ibid.

34. B. E. Phelps, April 1981: conversation with C. J. Bashe and J. H. Palmer.

35. F. E. Hamilton, August 1945–March 1948. Also attending the meeting in Pough-keepsie on 27 and 28 September were H. S. Beattie, M. Cunningham, G. F. Daly, B. M. Durfee, E. W. Gardinor, H. P. Luhn, and R. E. Page.

36. W. J. Eckert, 6 December 1945: to J. C. McPherson.

37. W. J. Eckert, 29 March 1946: to J. C. McPherson; F. E. Hamilton, 14 March 1946: to J. C. McPherson. Attached are proposed specifications for IBM calculator.

38. E. S. Hughes, Jr., November 1968: interview by L. M. Saphire; J. J. Troy, 7 May 1970: interview by L. M. Saphire. Russell A. Rowley, already a member of the Endicott group, designed many of the relay circuits and data transmission paths of the SSEC. George E. Mitchell played a large part in developing the electronic arithmetic unit. Many others who contributed are mentioned in IBM brochure, 1948: "IBM Selective Sequence Electronic Calculator"; C. J. Bashe, 1982: "The SSEC in Historical Perspective," *Annals of the History of Computing*, pp: 296–312.

39. Hughes, November 1968.

40. J. C. McPherson, F. E. Hamilton, and R. R. Seeber, 1982: "A Large-Scale General-Purpose Electronic Digital Calculator," *Annals of the History of Computing*, pp. 313–326. This article was written in 1948, although not published until 1982. See also W. J. Eckert, 1948: "Electrons and Computation," *The Scientific Monthly*, pp. 315–323; IBM brochure, 1948: "IBM Selective Sequence Electronic Calculator." As noted earlier IBM continued to use the term "calculator," even in the early 1950s, in naming some of its fully electronic, fully stored-program computers.

41. There was great flexibility in the way the "fields" of an instruction were allocated to specifying sources and destinations for the transfer of data. The description given is intended mainly as an example and couched in terms with which the modern reader may be familiar.

42. H. K. Clark, 22 November 1948: to J. J. Robbins, "Possible Sequence Modifications on SSEC."

43. Many details of the system's organization and operation must be excluded from this account. They are described in detail elsewhere. McPherson, Hamilton, and Seeber, 1982; Eckert, 1948; IBM brochure, 1948; A. K. Bhattacharya, 22 January 1982: "The IBM Selective Sequence Electronic Calculator," IBM Research Report; U.S. Patent 2,636,672, filed 19 January 1949: F. E. Hamilton, R. R. Seeber, Jr., R. A. Rowley, and E. S. Hughes, Jr. This patent described the machine and its operation in great detail and with numerous examples of instruction layout.

44. Hughes, November 1968: interview by L. M. Saphire.

45. Seeber, August 1967. Seeber recalled that Hamilton, during one of his trips to New York in the winter of 1945–1946, was invited into Watson's office and informed that Watson was depending on him personally to get the machine built promptly.

46. W. F. McClelland, May 1982: conversation with J. H. Palmer and C. J. Bashe.

47. A small but representative subset of the list of attendees: Dr. L. Brillouin, Harvard University. Dr. Irving Langmuir, associate director, General Electric Research. Dr. A. T. Waterman, chief scientist, Office of Naval Research. Prof. S. S. Wilks, professor of mathematical statistics, Princeton University. Dr. S. Chandrasekhar, Yerkes Observatory, University of Chicago. Prof. John von Neumann and Dr. Oswald Veblen, both of the Institute for Advanced Study, Princeton, N.J. Dr. Mina Rees, head of the mathematics branch, Office of Naval Research. Col. L. E. Simon, director, Ballistics

Research Laboratories, Aberdeen Proving Ground. J. C. Capt, director, Bureau of the Census. Dr. R. S. Burington, chief mathematician, Bureau of Ordnance, Navy Dept. Dr. Harry Woodburn Chase, chancellor, New York University. Dr. George B. Pegram, dean of graduate school, Columbia University. J. L. Madden, vice-president, Metropolitan Life Insurance Company. Edmund C. Berkeley, chief research consultant, Prudential Insurance Company.

48. Seeber, August 1967; Troy, May 1970.

49. *IBM Business Machines*, 15 March 1948: "IBM Selective Sequence Electronic Calculator Is Dedicated to the Aid of Science," pp. 1–2.

50. Phelps, 1980. H. Kenneth Clark, a member of Eckert's staff, prepared the SSEC demonstration program.

51. *IBM Business Machines*, 15 March 1948.

52. D. R. Hartree, 1949: *Calculating Instruments and Machines* (Urbana: University of Illinois Press), pp. 88–91.

53. W. H. Reid, 21 March 1949: to H. T. Rowe; W. J. Eckert, 8 October 1947: to E. M. Douglas.

54. Among the programmers working under Seeber's direction were John W. Backus, Frank S. Beckman, Edgar F. Codd, Harlan L. Herrick, Joachim Jeenel, Hollis A. Kinslow, William F. McClelland, Donald A. Quarles, Jr., and Elizabeth Stewart. Many additional details about Eckert's department are given in J. F. Brennan, 1971: *The IBM Watson Laboratory at Columbia University: A History* (IBM Corporation).

55. Seeber, August 1967.

56. Phelps, 1980; Seeber, August 1967; Hughes, November 1968.

57. J. W. Mauchly, 1980: "The ENIAC," *A History of Computing in the Twentieth Century*, ed. N. Metropolis, J. Howlett, and G.-C. Rota (New York: Academic Press). The lack of knowledge on the part of the IBM engineers of goings-on at the Moore School is understandable. IBM, even while supplying input and output equipment for the ENIAC, was kept totally in the dark about the project. In Mauchly's words on p. 548, "All they could get from us at the time were carefully framed specifications as to what they should supply." Later the new ideas embodied in the EDVAC and IAS machine designs were promulgated in a comprehensive special Moore School course 8 July to 31 August 1946, sponsored by the Army Ordnance Department and the Office of Naval Research. The principal lecturers were Eckert and Mauchly. Others included von Neumann, Aiken, and engineers from the Moore School, Bell Telephone Laboratories, and RCA. IBM was at first invited to enroll students, but after Watson Laboratory staff members had been nominated the invitation was withdrawn for the reason that IBM had no government computing contract. Bell Telephone Laboratories, General Electric Co., and Reeves Instrument Co. were the only commercial firms represented in the class of two dozen students. Most were from government agencies and the remainder from MIT and two English universities.

58. N. Rochester, November 1980: conversation with C. J. Bashe and J. H. Palmer.

59. D. R. Hartree, 1946: "The ENIAC, an Electronic Computing Machine," *Nature*, pp. 500–506; M. H. Weik, 1961: "The ENIAC Story," *Armament Technology*, pp. 571–575; J. G. Brainerd and T. K. Sharpless, 1948: "The ENIAC," *Electrical Engineering*, pp. 163–172; Goldstine, 1972.

60. J. von Neumann, 30 June 1945: "First Draft of a Report on the EDVAC," Contract No. W-670-ORD-4926 between the United States Army Ordnance Department and

the University of Pennsylvania. Reprinted in N. Stern, 1981: *From ENIAC to UNIVAC* (Bedford, Mass.: Digital Press); Goldstine, 1972.

61. First operation of EDVAC was reported in *Digital Computer Newsletter*, January 1952. Date of first operation of EDSAC is found in M. V. Wilkes, 1975: "Early Computer Developments at Cambridge: The EDSAC," *The Radio and Electronic Engineer*, pp. 332–335. Years of first operation of BINAC (built for Northrop Aircraft Company) and UNIVAC (Census Bureau) are from Stern, 1981, pp. 122–149.

62. Goldstine, 1972; J. H. Pomerene, October 1967: interview by L. M. Saphire. The basic elements of the IAS machine organization were set forth in a paper completed in June 1946 for the Army Ordnance Department: A. W. Burks, H. H. Goldstine, and J. von Neumann, "Preliminary Discussion of the Logical Design of an Electronic Computing Instrument."

63. Palmer, July 1967. The history of the activity between Dayton and Washington during World War II is recorded in E. Tomash and A. A. Cohen, 1979: "The Birth of an ERA," *Annals of the History of Computing*, pp. 83–97.

64. S. S. Snyder, 1980: "Computer Advances Pioneered by Cryptological Organizations," *Annals of the History of Computing*, pp. 60–70.

65. Palmer, July 1967.

66. J. C. McPherson, 28 November 1944: to F. W. Nichol; Anon. (Initials GFD—probably G. F. Daly), October–November 1953: "IBM Development Background—Inventors and Laboratories." Ralph Page, as senior member, acted as manager for the engineers in Poughkeepsie but apparently had no formal title reflecting that responsibility.

67. IBM brochure, 1981: "IBM Yesterday and Today."

68. J. A. Haddad, 30 March 1981: conversation with C. J. Bashe; M. E. Femmer, June 1968: interview by L. M. Saphire.

69. J. C. McPherson, 14 October 1946: to C. A. Kirk. The 603 electronic multiplier was not capable of division. McPherson's reference to "dividing on a larger-capacity basis" was probably made before the decision to omit division from the 603 entirely.

70. Palmer, September 1969.

71. S. W. Dunwell, August 1967: interview by L. M. Saphire.

72. IBM Product Announcements, 19 July 1948: Electronic Calculating Punch, Type 604, Letter 3416; and 29 July 1949: 604—Program Steps, Letter 3556. Also IBM Electric Punched Card Accounting Machines manual, 1948: "Principles of Operation: Electronic Calculating Punch Type 604."

73. U.S. Patent 2,637,763, filed 9 July 1948: R. L. Palmer, "Pluggable Support for Electron Tube and Circuit."

74. J. F. Waymouth, Jr., January 1951: "Deterioration of Oxide-Coated Cathodes under Low Duty-Factor Operation," *Journal of Applied Physics*, pp. 80–86.

75. Haddad, March 1981.

76. J. A. Goetz, 22 March 1981: conversation with C. J. Bashe. John A. Goetz, an engineer with previous experience in design of vacuum tubes, joined IBM in April 1949. He probably spent more time than anyone else in IBM visiting and working with tube manufacturers until the unsatisfactory tube types were replaced with much improved versions.

77. A. L. Samuel, December 1967: interview by L. M. Saphire.

78. Phelps, 1980.

79. W. J. Eckert, August 1946: "Facilities of the Watson Scientific Computing Laboratory," *Proceedings of the Research Forum* (Endicott, N.Y.: IBM).

80. W. J. Eckert, August 1947: "The IBM Department of Pure Science and the Watson Scientific Computing Laboratory," *Educational Research Forum Proceedings* (Endicott, N.Y.: IBM).

81. G. J. Toben, June 1968: interview by L. M. Saphire.

82. G. J. Toben, December 1949: "Transition from Problem to Card Program," *Computation Seminar Proceedings* (Endicott, N.Y.: IBM). The differential analyzer Toben referred to was the mechanical one at the University of California. Toben, June 1968. The two "large-scale digital machines" available for consideration were presumably the ENIAC and the IBM SSEC.

83. G. S. Fenn, 1948: "Programming and Using the Type 603-405 Combination Machine in the Solution of Differential Equations," *Scientific Computation Forum Proceedings* (Endicott, N.Y.: IBM).

84. For storage, the 941 used the mechanical counters of the 602A calculator—a postwar machine, the last of IBM's electromechanical calculators.

85. C. C. Hurd, November 1949: "The IBM Card-Programmed Electronic Calculator," *Scientific Computation Seminar Proceedings* (Endicott, N.Y.: IBM). In attempting to understand the operation of a machine equipped with both plugboards and a program read from cards, one must not imagine that any single description includes all possible combinations of control or allocations of data paths.

Chapter 3

1. T. J. Watson, Sr., 10 February 1948: to J. G. Phillips.

2. G. A. Roberts, 11 March 1948: to J. G. Phillips. Of course, storage capacity and method of programming were precisely the properties of electronic calculators like the IBM 604 that distinguished them from the high-speed computers that were to revolutionize business data processing. (At the Institute of Radio Engineers National Convention in New York on 25 March, J. W. Mauchly's paper described the UNIVAC.) At this time, with Bryce inactive, there was nobody in IBM who could mediate between the instinct of Watson, Sr., and the pragmatism of Roberts.

3. J. C. McPherson, 22 March 1948: "Proposed Selective Sequence Electronic Calculator of Reduced Capacity" (memorandum). For a survey of federal government activities supporting the development of computers and ways to apply them, see M. Rees, 1982: "The Computing Program of the Office of Naval Research, 1946–1953," *Annals of the History of Computing 4*, pp. 102–120.

4. P. J. Cantone, 19, 20 January 1948: to D. Orton; D. Orton, 21 January, 9 February 1948: to P. J. Cantone.

5. J. A. Dollard, 5 April 1948: to D. Orton.

6. *Proceedings — Scientific Computation Forum — 1948* (New York: IBM). The notion of an IBM forum for the exchange of ideas did not originate with Eckert. The department of education had sponsored three before 1948, in 1940, 1946, and 1947. They had been devoted to EAM-aided educational research in general and test-scoring statistical procedures in particular. The last in that series, an "institute" on hospital financial control, was held in Endicott just one week prior to Eckert's more broadly based

scientific forum. Herbert R. J. Grosch, whom Eckert had hired at the Watson Laboratory in 1945, was editor of the 1948 scientific forum proceedings. Four similar meetings, called "Scientific Computation Seminars," followed in the period 1949–1951. The five proceedings volumes, 1948–1951, form a record of the remarkable versatility of punched-card equipment, including the 604 and CPC, in the hands of ingenious scientists and engineers.

7. F. E. Hamilton, 7 May 1948: to J. C. McPherson.

8. O. Kornei, January 1947: "Survey of Magnetic Recording," *Proceedings of a Symposium on Large-Scale Digital Calculating Machinery* (Cambridge: Harvard University Press), pp. 223–237.

9. J. M. Coombs, November 1947: "Storage of Numbers on Magnetic Tape," *Proceedings of the National Electronics Conference, Volume III* (Chicago: National Electronics Conference), pp. 201–209.

10. A. A. Cohen and W. R. Keye, March 1948: "Selective Alteration of Digital Data in a Magnetic Drum Computer Memory" (abstract of a paper presented at the 1948 Institute of Radio Engineers National Convention), *Proceedings of the Institute of Radio Engineers*, p. 379. Engineering Research Associates, Inc. (ERA) was an early computer firm that had its origins in a wartime U.S. Navy cryptologic group. Formed in 1946, it was merged into Remington Rand Inc. in 1952. The ERA 1103, developed at ERA and announced in early 1953, was a large-scale Remington Rand machine for scientific applications, complementing UNIVAC.

11. IBM documents, 15, 16 September 1948: "Magnetic Storage Calculator."

12. J. W. Mauchly, January 1947: "Preparation of Problems for EDVAC-Type Machines," *Proceedings of a Symposium on Large-Scale Digital Calculating Machinery*, pp. 203–207.

13. W. W. McDowell, 15 September 1948: to G. A. Roberts.

14. G. A. Roberts, 1 November 1948: to T. J. Watson, Sr.; E. F. Saber, 7 February 1949: to J. C. McPherson.

15. W. L. Lewis, 21 February 1949: to J. C. McPherson; W. J. Eckert, 24 February 1949: to J. C. McPherson (note).

16. IBM document, revised 24 March 1949: "Magnetic Storage Calculator."

17. J. C. McPherson, 19 April 1949: to W. L. Lewis.

18. C. E. Love, 13 May 1949: to J. C. McPherson; C. E. Love, 11 August 1949: to T. J. Watson, Jr.

19. J. C. McPherson, 26 May 1949: to C. E. Love.

20. G. F. Daly, 23 May 1949: "Engineering Meeting with Mr. T. J. Watson, Jr. and Sales Executives—May 19 to 20, 1949"; T. J. Watson, Jr., 31 May 1949: to J. C. McPherson.

21. J. C. McPherson, 16 August 1949: to C. E. Love; E. S. Hughes, Jr., November 1968: interview by L. M. Saphire; R. A. Rowley, June 1968: interview by L. M. Saphire; J. J. Troy, May 1970: interview by L. M. Saphire; J. B. Tait, 20 May 1981: conversation with J. H. Palmer.

22. Hughes, November 1968; S. W. Dunwell, 29 September 1981: conversation with J. H. Palmer.

23. W. W. McDowell, 9 August 1949: to C. E. Love; C. E. Love, 11 August 1949: to T. J. Watson, Jr.

24. Dunwell, 29 September 1981; J. W. Birkenstock, 11 February 1981: conversation with J. H. Palmer.

25. D. W. Rubidge, 19 August 1949: "Minutes of Calculator Meeting—Conference Room—August 18, 1949."

26. "Agreement—IBM and ERA," 8 March 1950.

27. F. E. Hamilton, 17 November 1949: to J. C. McPherson.

28. T. V. Learson, 23 November 1949: to C. E. Love; J. C. McPherson, 15 December 1949: to W. W. McDowell.

29. Tait, 20 May 1981.

30. W. J. Eckert, 10 May 1948: to J. C. McPherson; C. E. Love, 16 June 1948: to E. C. Strandine.

31. J. Kintas, August 1948: "A Survey of the IBM Project at Beech Aircraft Corporation," *Proceedings—Scientific Computation Forum—1948*, pp. 54–59.

32. W. H. Reid, 31 May 1949: to G. P. Lovell; W. H. Reid, 1 August 1949: to C. E. Love.

33. G. S. Fenn, August 1948: "Programming and Using the Type 603-405 Combination Machine in the Solution of Differential Equations," *Proceedings—Scientific Computation Forum—1948*, pp. 95–98.

34. H. Polacheck, August 1948: "Computation of Shock Wave Refraction on the Selective Sequence Electronic Calculator," *Proceedings—Scientific Computation Forum—1948*, pp. 107–122.

35. C. C. Hurd, 3 January 1979: testimony in U.S. v. IBM, U.S. District Court, Southern District of New York, N.Y., pp. 86324, 86327; C. C. Hurd, 11 October 1972: interview by H. S. Tropp and R. Mapstone (Smithsonian Computer History Project, joint project of the American Federation of Information Processing Societies and the Smithsonian Institution); *IBM Business Machines*, 28 November 1949: "Dr. Hurd Named Director of Applied Science Dept."; C. C. Hurd, 1980: "Computer Development at IBM," in *A History of Computing in the Twentieth Century*, ed. N. Metropolis, J. Howlett, and G.-C. Rota (New York: Academic Press).

36. C. E. Love, 12 September 1949: to J. C. McPherson. The author of the manual was Donald W. Pendery, the third person hired (in January 1949) for the scientific sales program, at the time assigned for training at the Watson Laboratory.

37. C. C. Hurd, 8 November 1949: to C. E. Love.

38. J. C. McPherson, 30 December 1949: to C. M. Mooney; IBM document, 29 January 1950: "Card Programmed Calculators."

39. Hurd, 3 January 1979: p. 86334; C. C. Hurd, 23 September 1982: conversation with E. W. Pugh.

40. S. W. Dunwell, 15 April 1949: to G. A. Roberts.

41. S. W. Dunwell, 22 April 1949: to G. A. Roberts. Dunwell's suggestion was based on a series of brief IBM publications, called "Pointers," which was initiated during the 1930s. Pointers served the exchange, among users of IBM punched-card machines, of new and unusual ideas for using the machines. See *IBM Business Machines*, 20 October 1938: "An Interesting Business."

42. Until users came to form their own organizations for sharing information, the Newsletter was an important communication medium. Newsletter No. 10, in 1955, was the complete proceedings of the Endicott Computation Seminar held in August,

at which seven IBM papers and twenty-four user papers were presented. The last Newsletter was No. 13, published in April 1957.

43. W. W. McDowell, 30 January 1950: to J. C. McPherson; G. A. Roberts, 17 February 1950: to J. C. McPherson; J. C. McPherson, 23 February 1950: to W. W. McDowell; W. W. McDowell, November 1970: interview by L. M. Saphire.

44. IBM document, undated: "Conference on Magnetic Drum Calculators—March 13 & 14, 1950"; IBM document, undated: "Conference on Magnetic Drum Calculators—Appendix"; R. M. Walker, 7 April 7 1950: to J. C. McPherson. A brief appraisal of the consequences of the ERA project, a "system design exercise," is included in E. Tomash and A. A. Cohen, 1979: "The Birth of an ERA: Engineering Research Associates, Inc., 1946-1955," *Annals of the History of Computing 1*, pp. 83-97.

45. A. L. Williams, undated: "Research and Development Engineering Meeting, 10 A.M.—Monday—April 3, 1950, Board Room"; IBM document, undated: "Engineering and Development Meeting, Board Room—World Headquarters, April 3, 1950"; IBM document, undated: "Engineering and Development Meeting, Board Room—World Headquarters, April 3, 1950 (Afternoon)"; T. J. Watson, Jr., 19 January 1983: conversation with C.J. Bashe.

46. *IBM Business Machines*, 25 May 1950: "W. W. McDowell Promoted; Heads Engineering, Research."

47. W. W. McDowell, 17 April 1950: to W. L. Lewis.

48. G. A. Roberts, 19 April 1950: to J. C. McPherson.

49. IBM document, undated: a committee report, written after "several days studying the Magnetic Drum Machine and its applications"; IBM document, 1 May 1950: "Magnetic Drum Calculator."

50. R. M. Bury and C. C. Hurd, 7 July 1950: to C. E. Love.

51. IBM document, 26 April 1950: "Electronic Calculator with Serial Computing on Magnetically Recorded Drum"; IBM document, 27 April 1950: "Drum Calculator Serial Computing."

52. F. E. Hamilton, 12 June 1950: to S. W. Dunwell.

53. IBM documents (2), 1 July 1950: "Electronic Calculator with Serial Computing on Magnetically Recorded Drum."

54. J. P. Eckert, Jr., and J. W. Mauchly, 30 September 1945: "Automatic High Speed Computing—A Progress Report on the EDVAC" (Philadelphia: Moore School of Electrical Engineering, University of Pennsylvania), pp. 2, 6. A report of work under a contract between the U.S. Army Ordnance Department and the University of Pennsylvania.

55. M. V. Wilkes, 1949: "The Design of a Practical High-Speed Computing Machine. The EDSAC," in "A Discussion on Computing Machines" (discussion held 4 March 1948), *Proceedings of the Royal Society of London A 195*, pp. 265-287; M. V. Wilkes, 1968: "Computers Then and Now," *Journal of the Association for Computing Machinery 15*, pp. 1-7.

56. J. H. Wilkinson, 1975: "The Pilot ACE at the National Physical Laboratory," *The Radio and Electronic Engineer 45*, pp. 336-340; A. M. Turing, 1945: "Proposals for Development in the Mathematics Division of an Automatic Computing Engine (ACE)," Report E882 (Executive Committee, National Physical Laboratory), reprinted, with a foreword by D. W. Davies, April 1972: Report Com. Sci. 57 (National Physical Laboratory).

57. W. S. Elliott, September 1949: "The Present Position of Automatic Computing Machine Development in England," *Proceedings of a Second Symposium on Large-Scale Digital Calculating Machinery* (Cambridge: Harvard University Press), pp. 74–80.

58. Bury and Hurd, 7 July 1950.

59. J. V. Williams, Jr., 16 October 1950: "Poughkeepsie Conference on Hamilton Magnetic Drum Calculator, October 2–13, 1950," IBM Technical Report.

60. R. L. Palmer, 16 November 1950: to D. W. Rubidge.

61. C. M. Mooney, 16 November 1950: to T. V. Learson.

62. F. E. Hamilton, 29 November 1950: to E. W. Gardinor.

63. S. W. Dunwell, 18 October 1950: to G. A. Roberts.

64. IBM document, 18 January 1951: "Numeric Electronic Drum Calculator Automatic Programming." The biquinary code was used extensively in a series of Bell Telephone Laboratories relay calculators built for military use during the 1940s. It consists of a two-bit group with weights 0 and 5 and a five-bit group with weights 0, 1, 2, 3, and 4. Each encoding of a decimal digit contains one 1 in the binary group and another in the quinary group. Checking circuits test for one, and only one, 1 in each group, a small elaboration, for the MDC, of the checking logic applied to ten of the bits in the previous, punched-card-oriented, twelve-bit code. The more compact seven-bit code doubled words per track to twenty and halved drum word time (a factor in speed). Despite an increase in the cost of checking and punched-card input-output conversion circuits, savings in other areas resulted in a net reduction in component cost.

65. E. W. Gardinor, 22 May 1951: to W. W. McDowell; S. W. Dunwell, 8 May 1951: to G. A. Roberts.

66. T. V. Learson, 24 May 1951: to E. M. Douglas.

67. W. W. McDowell, 17 July 1951: to A. L. Williams.

68. D. W. Rubidge, 3 August 1951: to G. A. Roberts.

69. Product Development Work Order, Endicott, New York, 18 October 1951: "Drum Calculator"; C. R. Manning, 25 October 1951: to C. M. Mooney.

70. S. W. Dunwell, 12 April 1951: "Meeting on Magnetic Drum Calculator—April 3, 1951"; J. J. Kossuth, 7 September 1951: to F. E. Hamilton.

71. D. W. Rubidge, 23 July 1951: to G. A. Roberts.

72. J. E. Fernekees and L. R. Harper, 26 December 1950: "A Proposal for a Small Drum Calculator," IBM Technical Report; L. R. Harper and J. E. Fernekees, 4 April 1951: "Report on the Progress of the Design and Construction of a Small Drum Calculator," IBM Technical Report.

73. S. W. Dunwell, 5 February 1951: "Specifications for an Electronic Unit for a Calculator-Accounting Machine."

74. D. W. Rubidge, 20 September 1951: to C. M. Mooney.

75. IBM document, undated: "Magnetic Drum Calculator—Hamilton" (a 1951 chronology prepared by the Future Demands department); R. W. Avery, 21 January 1957: "History of Type 650 MDDPM"; F. E. Hamilton and E. S. Hughes, Jr., 25 January 1952: "Operational and Functional Features of MDC Calculator."

76. E. S. Hughes, Jr., 11 December 1950: "Latch Type Ring Circuit," IBM Technical Report. The latch principle, incidentally, was employed in industry-standard integrated transistor circuits more than a decade after the introduction of the 650.

77. J. C. McPherson, 12 November 1952: "Competitive Situation RE Drum Calculators"; J. C. McPherson, 20 November 1952: "Competitive Drum Computers."

78. S. W. Dunwell, 26 September 1952: to G. A. Roberts; S. W. Dunwell, 30 September 1952: "IBM Calculator Program."

79. B. E. Phelps, 7 November 1952: "Notes on MDC as Scientific Computer—Endicott, N.Y.—November 6, 1952." Revolvers were also a fundamental element in the Engineering Research Associates computer design developed for IBM beginning in the summer of 1949. Less than four months after the November 1952 agreement, a U.S. patent on the revolver principle was issued to J. P. Eckert, Jr., and J. W. Mauchly of Remington Rand Inc.

80. S. W. Dunwell, 14 November 1952: "Meeting in Mr. McDowell's Office."

81. B. E. Phelps, undated: "Notes on meeting at Kenyon Laboratory—November 18, 1952."

82. IBM documents, September 1952, October 1952, November 1952: "IBM Development Report—Engineering Laboratories."

Chapter 4

1. H. Lukoff, 1979: *From Dits to Bits* (Portland, Ore.: Robotics Press), pp. 61–63. By March 1947, when the EDVAC project was announced, Edmund C. Berkeley of Prudential Insurance Company had been discussing an "EDVAC" with the Eckert-Mauchly Computer Corporation for some months. N. Stern, 1981: *From ENIAC to UNIVAC* (Bedford, Mass.: Digital Press), pp. 137–139.

2. J. C. McPherson, 28 April 1947: "Electronics Meeting, April 25th."

3. Transcript of a discussion of the SSEC in its application to the life insurance industry held at IBM headquarters, New York, N.Y., 1 March 1948. Edmund C. Berkeley of Prudential Insurance Company (see note 1) was among the actuaries attending.

4. J. W. Mauchly discussed the UNIVAC at the second meeting of the Association for Computing Machinery on 12 December 1947. *Mathematical Tables and Other Aids to Computation III*, April 1948: "News: Association for Computing Machinery," pp. 132–134.

5. The symposia were held 29–31 July 1948 under joint auspices of the Institute for Numerical Analysis and several other societies. "Symposia on Modern Calculating Machinery and Numerical Methods," *Mathematical Tables and Other Aids to Computation III*, January 1949: pp. 381–388.

6. R. Hopkins, 12 August 1948: to L. H. LaMotte; L. H. LaMotte, 25 August 1948: to J. G. Phillips.

7. W. W. McDowell, 14 December 1948: to T. J. Watson, Jr.

8. W. W. McDowell, 17 December 1948: to W. L. Lewis, "Hiring of Electronic Engineers."

9. P. E. Fox, October 1967: interview by L. M. Saphire.

10. E. W. Pugh, 1984: *Memories That Shaped an Industry* (Cambridge: The MIT Press), p. 66. Cathode-ray tubes were prominent also among devices proposed by leading engineers in response to a request by J. C. McPherson (instigated by T. J. Watson, Sr.) for ideas worth pursuing in electronics. J. C. McPherson, 21 November 1946:

to W. W. McDowell; R. L. Palmer, 3 December 1946: to A. R. Noll; B. L. Havens, 6 December 1946: to W. J. Eckert.

11. *Electronics*, September 1947: A. V. Haeff, "A Memory Tube," pp. 80–83.

12. F. C. Williams and T. Kilburn, March 1949: "A Storage System for Use with Binary-Digital Computing Machines," *The Proceedings of the Institution of Electrical Engineers, Part III*, pp. 81–100.

13. Ibid.

14. J. C. Logue, A. E. Brennemann, and A. C. Koelsch, 1953: "Engineering Experience in the Design and Operation of a Large Scale Electrostatic Memory," *Convention Record of the Institute of Radio Engineers 1953 National Convention, Part 7, Electronic Computers*, pp. 21–29.

15. P. E. Fox, 15 April 1981: conversation with C. J. Bashe and J. H. Palmer.

16. P. E. Fox, 18 May 1949: "Cathode-Ray Electrostatic Storage." While it was correct to assume that basic device development was not required, IBM and other users of Williams storage eventually had either to manufacture their own CRTs or to purchase tubes manufactured and tested to their specifications in order to achieve reliable operation at satisfactorily high storage densities.

17. N. Rochester, October 1967: interview by L. M. Saphire; 25 November 1980: conversation with C. J. Bashe and J. H. Palmer.

18. N. Rochester, 20 August 1973: to M. M. Astrahan et al., "Test Assembly." A reminiscence on the Test Assembly, in which Rochester recalled his attitude about the SSEC circa 1949.

19. N. Rochester, 28 January 1949: "The Use of Acoustic Delay Lines in a Calculator Like the 604"; 15 February 1949: "A Calculator Using Acoustic Delay Line Storage"; 17 May 1949: "A Calculator Using Electrostatic Storage and a Stored Program."

20. N. Rochester, 25 November 1980: conversation with C. J. Bashe and J. H. Palmer.

21. W. Buchholz, 12 October 1967: interview by L. M. Saphire; B. E. Phelps, 6 September 1949 to 5 May 1950: daily diaries (magnetic-tape project); N. Rochester, 25 November 1980: conversation with C. J. Bashe and J. H. Palmer.

22. N. Rochester, 28 October 1949: "Plans for the Data Processing Test Assembly."

23. J. P. Eckert, Jr., 1980: "The ENIAC," in *A History of Computing in the Twentieth Century* (New York: Academic Press).

24. M. H. Weik, 1957: *A Second Survey of Domestic Electronic Digital Computing Systems*, Ballistic Research Laboratories Report No. 1010, Department of the Army.

25. H. H. Goldstine, 1972: *The Computer from Pascal to von Neumann* (Princeton: Princeton University Press).

26. Rochester, 28 October 1949.

27. Frizzell and Mussell received assistance from J. V. Williams, Jr., also a former customer engineer, who had participated in developing the 604 calculator. C. E. Frizzell, December 1967: interview by L. M. Saphire; H. A. Mussell, December 1967: interview by L. M. Saphire.

28. L. D. Stevens, 7 December 1949: "Report on Magnetic Drum Circuits." This report states that the design of the drum provided for forty-three tracks, each of 1000-bit capacity; also that "the present eight digit model" used thirty-two tracks to accommodate 1000 eight-digit words, each digit being represented by four bits on separate tracks in BCD code. An additional track stored the signs of numbers,

and two tracks provided gating or control pulses. The remaining eight tracks were reserved for expansion of the word size to ten digits. Basic timing pulses came from a special, permanently magnetized track, not counted among the forty-three, according to J. V. Williams, Jr., 15 November 1949: "Magnetic Drum Memory for the 604." Other details of the drum system are from H. A. Mussell and C. E. Frizzell, 27 December 1949: "Stored Program"; H. A. Mussell, 31 January 1950: "Revised Stored Program"; L. D. Stevens, 12 December 1967: interview by L. M. Saphire.

29. N. Rochester, 13 September 1950: "Tests on the Test Assembly."

30. N. P. Edwards, 24 July 1981: conversation with C. J. Bashe. IBM eventually manufactured its own CRTs in order to achieve the necessary control of quality.

31. The Selectron was a special storage tube 3 inches in diameter and almost eight inches long. It contained an elaborate array of heated cathodes, horizontal and vertical selection bars, and reading and writing plates, with nickel-plated steel eyelets as storage elements. The eyelets, of which there were 256 altogether, were fixed in two rectangular mica sheets, one on each side of the structure. Each eyelet could be selected and, through the proper sequence of applied voltages, made to assume one of two potentials through the effect of secondary emission. Invented by J. Rajchman of the RCA Laboratories and originally planned to store 4096 bits, it had been reduced to 256-bit capacity for improved reliability by the time IBM tested it in the fall of 1949. It was abandoned by IBM, as by the IAS at Princeton, in favor of Williams storage. Engineering Research Associates, Inc., 1950: *High-Speed Computing Devices* (New York: McGraw-Hill), pp. 370–374; Goldstine, 1972: p. 309; J. H. Pomerene, 5 October 1967: interview by L. M. Saphire.

32. B. E. Phelps, 6 September 1949 to 5 May 1950: daily diaries (magnetic tape project).

33. N. Rochester, 22 September 1949: "Magnetic Tape to 604 Connection"; R. P. Crago, 30 December 1949: "Experimental Magnetic Tape Input-Output Device for the 604 Electronic Calculator."

34. N. Rochester, 26 March 1951: "The Integration of Second Order Differential Equations on the Test Assembly."

35. UNIVAC specifications changed somewhat in the course of development. In March 1948, the plan was to represent numeric digits as groups of five bits, which included provision for error detection. Nonnumeric characters would be represented as pairs of numeric digits. J. W. Mauchly, 1948: "The UNIVAC: Abstract of Paper to Be Presented to I.R.E. March 25, 1948." As turned over to the first customer in 1951, the machine handled numeric and nonnumeric characters in a single seven-bit code, again including error detection. J. P. Eckert, Jr., J. R. Weiner, H. F. Welsh, and H. F. Mitchell, 1951: "The UNIVAC System," *Review of Electronic Digital Computers*, Papers and Discussions Presented at the Joint AIEE-IRE Computer Conference, Philadelphia, 10–12 December 1951 (American Institute of Electrical Engineers), pp. 6–16.

36. B. E. Phelps, 19 April 1949: "Notes on Eckert-Mauchly Demonstration."

37. J. C. McPherson, 26 May 1949: to C. E. Love, "Competition from Electronic Calculators."

38. S. W. Dunwell, 8 November 1949: "Electronic Tape Program"; N. Rochester, 18 October 1949: to R. L. Palmer (memorandum attaching incomplete and undated version of Dunwell's requirements, and stating that Dunwell had sent a version of it to G. A. Roberts).

39. N. Rochester, 3 October 1967: interview by L. M. Saphire.

40. N. Rochester and W. Buchholz, 24 March 1950: "Preliminary Outline of Tape Processing Machine."

41. J. A. Goetz, 21 March 1981: conversation with C. J. Bashe. Goetz had an unusually clear recollection of the individuals in Palmer's group and remembered being the twenty-second member to join it when he was hired in April 1949.

42. The emergence of semiconductor crystal diodes with characteristics suiting them for use in vacuum tube circuits had an important influence on the development of computer circuits. They were a product of research conducted during World War II with the objective of developing higher-quality rectifying elements for communications applications such as radar. The theoretical understanding of semiconductor properties thus acquired contributed to the invention of the transistor in 1947.

43. B. E. Phelps, 22 April 1981: conversation with C. J. Bashe.

44. B. E. Phelps, 1 November 1950: "Considerations Involved in Change from Serial to Parallel Tape System"; J. A. Haddad, 19 June 1950: to S. W. Dunwell. During 1950, the emphasis in Product Planning vacillated between lowest possible cost and highest speed achievable at reasonable cost. S. W. Dunwell, 11 April 1950: to R. L. Palmer. It is clear that Phelps and other engineering managers under Palmer were having great difficulty in understanding the relative importance to Product Planning of those two objectives. Phelps, 13 November 1950: to R. L. Palmer; J. A. Haddad, 6 February 1951: to S. W. Dunwell.

45. B. E. Phelps, 27 September 1950: "Meeting at Kenyon Lab on General Aspects of the Tape Program." There is no indication of how the TPM system could have accommodated the increased data rate; the 7000 character per second rate already planned was nearly equal to the machine's internal character rate.

46. *IBM Business Machines*, 16 August 1950: "R. L. Palmer Is Manager, Engineering Laboratory." J. H. Fraser, whose IBM background was in customer engineering and sales, served as manager of the Poughkeepsie laboratory from May 1949 to August 1950.

47. Dunwell, 7 November 1950: to R. L. Palmer.

48. Phelps, 13 November 1950: to R. L. Palmer.

49. C. J. Bashe, 17 November 1950: "An Investigation of Parallel-Bit Transmission in the Tape Processing Machine."

50. J. A. Haddad, 6 February 1951: to S. W. Dunwell.

51. N. Rochester, 17 November 1950: to C. C. Hurd.

52. W. E. Fox and J. B. Greene, 13 September 1951: "Minutes of Meeting to Discuss Future Plans for the Tape Processing System"; W. E. Fox, 19 September 1951: "Proposed TPM Model no. 2 Work Plan and Personnel Estimate"; W. E. Fox, 7 December 1951: to R. L. Palmer, "T.P.M. Week 12-3-51"; W. Buchholz, 20 December 1951: to R. L. Palmer, "Test Program on TPM."

53. B. E. Phelps, 6 June 1951: "Tape Status as of June 1, 1951"; B. E. Phelps, 19 June 1951: to S. W., Dunwell; "Tape Processing Machine, Engineering Model, Manual of Operation," revised September 1952; B. E. Phelps, 18 September 1951: to R. L. Palmer; B. E. Toben, 19 October 1951: to B. E. Phelps, "T.P.M. Tape Drive Specifications."

54. "Tape Processing Machine, Engineering Model, Manual of Operation," revised September 1952.

55. W. E. Mutter, April 1952: "Improved Cathode-Ray Tube for Application in Williams Tube Memory System," *Electrical Engineering*, pp. 352–356.

56. W. E. Mutter, 8 July 1981: conversation with C. J. Bashe.

57. M. M. Astrahan, 7 May 1951: "The Present Status of Electrostatic Memory."

58. J. J. Isole, 22 April 1982: conversation with E. W. Pugh.

59. W. J. Deerhake was responsible for the NORC memory. He and G. F. Bland, who had left Fox's group to work on that machine, discovered the effect described as "mudhole." J. C. Logue, A. E. Brenneman, and A. C. Koelsch, 1953.

60. W. Buchholz, 1 October 1951: "Proposed Arithmetic System for the Tape Processing Machine."

61. W. E. Fox and J. B. Greene, 13 September 1951: "Minutes of Meeting to Discuss Future Plans for the Tape Processing System."

62. S. W. D. (presumably Dunwell), 29 December 1952: "Status of Model Equipment."

63. G. A. Roberts, 2 February 1953: "Report of TPM Survey Team."

64. It seems reasonable to infer from the wording of a memorandum from J. W. Birkenstock, (illegible day) February 1955, to T. J. Watson, Jr., that the use of unimproved TPM specifications in the application studies was part of a Future Demands strategy to impress Engineering with the need for a much better machine: "I am sure that they made a real contribution by pointing out to Engineering the need for . . . a significant improvement over the TPM."

65. Stern, 1981: pp. 146–148.

Chapter 5

1. J. W. Birkenstock, November 1967: interview by L. M. Saphire; J. W. Birkenstock, August 1980: interview by R. H. Stuewer and E. Tomash (oral history program of the Charles Babbage Institute For the History of Information Processing). The contract was for product engineering and manufacturing the air force's K System Bombing Navigation Computer, a mechanical analog device for the B47 designed by the Sperry Gyroscope Company. IBM had built both bombsight and gun turret control devices for the B29 at Endicott during World War II; this new program was assigned to Poughkeepsie. The additional manufacturing space it provoked there was immediately available, upon completion of the program, for application to the fast-growing electronic computer business. Meanwhile Endicott undertook to develop, in part, and manufacture a more technologically advanced bombing and navigation system for the B52. It was the initial undertaking of the organization that evolved into IBM's Federal Systems Division, which has played a major role in the U.S. space program.

2. *IBM Business Machines*, 12 July 1949: "T. J. Watson Jr. Sees Greater IBM"; *Business Week*, 4 March 1950: "Rem Rand Scores."

3. C. C. Hurd, 18 October 1950: to W. L. Lewis.

4. C. C. Hurd, 3 January 1979: testimony in U.S. v. IBM, U.S. District Court, Southern District of New York, N.Y., p. 86339.

5. C. C. Hurd, 11 October 1972: interview by H. S. Tropp and R. Mapstone (Smithsonian Computer History Project, joint project of the American Federation of Information Processing Societies and the Smithsonian Institution); C. C. Hurd, 8 March

1972: *SHARE Meeting for Pioneers*, transcript of discussion at 38th meeting of SHARE led by H. S. Tropp, pp. 44–46; F. J. Gruenberger, October 1968: RAND Corporation memorandum RM-5654-PR, reprinted (with slight adaptations) in F. J. Gruenberger, 1979: "The History of the JOHNNIAC," *Annals of the History of Computing 1*, pp. 49–64.

6. Memorandum, 2 January 1951: to W. W. McDowell, attaching three-page "Tentative Specifications." Report of a committee chaired by R. M. Bury.

7. R. L. Palmer, September 1969: interview by L. M. Saphire.

8. Floating-point arithmetic units were built into some of the relay calculators of the preelectronic era: the Z3 built by German computer pioneer Konrad Zuse (1941), the Bell Telephone Laboratories Model V (1946), and the Harvard Mark II (1948).

9. W. H. Reid, 19 September 1950: to T. J. Watson, Jr.

10. J. C. McPherson, 12 October, 3 November 1950: to Commander, U.S. Naval Ordnance Laboratory.

11. J. W. Birkenstock, 30 November 1950: to T. J. Watson, Jr.

12. J. W. Birkenstock, 15 December 1950: to T. J Watson, Jr.; N. Rochester, 18 October 1955: to R. K. Richards.

13. N. Rochester, October 1967: interview by L. M. Saphire; Hurd, 3 January 1979: pp. 86341–86342, 86356.

14. Birkenstock, November 1967.

15. H. T. Hansford, 23 February 1951: to J. W. Birkenstock.

16. W. W. McDowell, 22 January 1951: to E. M. Douglas.

17. The ultimate project responsibility remained with Palmer. A memorandum from corporate headquarters read, "We are counting on you and your organization to see to it that we do not fail in this endeavor." See W. W. McDowell, 1 February 1951: to R. L. Palmer.

18. A. W. Burks, H. H. Goldstine, and J. von Neumann, 2 September 1947 (second edition): "Preliminary Discussion of the Logical Design of an Electronic Computing Instrument." The report, an expansion of the first edition dated 28 June 1946, is part I, volume I of a series of reports prepared by the Institute for Advanced Study under a contract with the Reasearch and Development Service, U.S. Army Ordnance Department. It is reprinted in *John von Neumann, Collected Works*, ed. A. H. Taub (New York: Macmillan, 1963), volume 5.

19. J. von Neumann, 30 June 1945: "First Draft of a Report on the EDVAC," Moore School of Electrical Engineering, University of Pennsylvania, pp. 14–16. Von Neumann was a consultant to the army's Ballistic Research Laboratory, which administered a contract for EDVAC development between the U.S. Army Ordnance Department and the University of Pennsylvania.

20. Burks et al., 2 September 1947. The authors also pointed out that binary representation promoted simplicity and speed in arithmetic operations: "In binary multiplication, the product of a particular digit of the multiplier by the multiplicand is either the multiplicand or null according as the multiplier digit is 1 or 0. In the decimal system, however, this product has ten possible values between null and nine times the multiplicand, inclusive." Thus binary multiplication is accomplished by adding the multiplicand to an accumulator once for each multiplier digit of 1, the progressive result being shifted one position for each multiplier digit examined.

21. C. C. Hurd, 1981: "Early IBM Computers: Edited Testimony," *Annals of the History of Computing 3*, pp. 163–182.

22. Rochester, October 1967; N. Rochester, 25 November 1980: conversation with J. H. Palmer.

23. P. E. Fox, 8 January 1951: diary entry.

24. N. Rochester, 28 February 1949: to R. L. Palmer.

25. IBM document, 12 February 1951: "Type 60X Electronic Computer, Operator's Reference Manual"; W. Buchholz, 1953: "The System Design of the IBM Type 701 Computer," *Proceedings of the Institute of Radio Engineers 41*, pp. 1262–1275.

26. In the case of the "store address" instructions, the prestore computation in the IAS machine was to be made to happen simultaneously and identically in the two halves of an IAS word. Goldstine and von Neumann struggled with these two instructions, redefining them twice in the first two volumes (April 1947 and April 1948) of "Planning and Coding of Problems for an Electronic Computing Instrument." That three-part paper set forth their work on methods of programming the IAS machine, which, with Burks, they had described in 1946 in "Preliminary Discussion of the Logical Design of an Electronic Computing Instrument."

27. This difference between the Defense Calculator and the IAS machine was earlier illustrated by EDSAC and BINAC, contemporaneous machines that began running in May and midsummer of 1949, respectively. For EDSAC, M. V. Wilkes arrived at the same disposition of the instruction versus number length disparity as did the Defense Calculator designers. BINAC, like the IAS machine, addressed only full-length words (two instructions). Eckert and Mauchly, its builders, maintained that convention in UNIVAC, of which the first model was turned over to the Bureau of the Census in March 1951. They did not, however, multiplex branch instructions; a branch instruction was to be located in the right-hand instruction of a pair; the branch was to the left-hand member of the pair designated.

28. "Type 60X Electronic Computer, Operator's Reference Manual," 12 February 1951.

29. H. D. Ross, Jr., October 1967: interview by L. M. Saphire.

30. IBM document, June 1951: "Defense Calculator, Preliminary Operator's Reference Manual."

31. M. M. Astrahan, June 1968: interview by L. M. Saphire; M. M. Astrahan, 19 February 1951: "Decimal to Binary Conversion and Storage of Instruction or Data Cards," IBM Technical Report.

32. C. C. Hurd, 20 April 1951: "Status of Defense Calculator." See also N. Rochester and M. M. Astrahan, May 1952: "The Logical Organization of the New IBM Scientific Calculator," *Proceedings of the Association for Computing Machinery*, pp. 79–83.

33. Engineering project file, 701 Calculator, Progress Reports section.

34. N. Rochester, 26 March 1951: "The Integration of Second Order Differential Equations on the Test Assembly," IBM Technical Report.

35. C. C. Hurd, 3 April 1951: "Progress Report on Mathematical Planning on Defense Calculator"; Engineering project file, 701 Calculator, Progress Reports section.

36. C. Benton, Jr., 16 March 1951: to E. M. Douglas et al.; T. V. Learson, 29 March 1951: to J. G. Phillips et al.

37. Hurd, 3 April 1951; C. Benton, Jr., 4 April 1951: to E. M. Douglas et al.

38. Hurd, 20 April 1951; P. W. Knaplund, 25 April 1951: "Laplace Equation." This had been chosen as a problem typical of those to which prospective users would apply the machine and illustrates why the electronic computer was an economic development of enormous importance in engineering fields. Each solution of the Laplace equation would provide nuclear reactor engineers with a prediction of temperature distribution in a particular reactor core design and for a particular set of conditions. Thus hundreds of such solutions would be needed during the design process. Yet each solution required that the temperature be calculated at 15,625 physical points in the core, and (because of the "iterative" nature of the solution process) each set of 15,625 calculations had to be repeated 100 times to provide a solution. Each calculation was trivially simple: essentially the finding of the average of six numbers. The calculator could perform these (along with necessary address calculations) at a rate of about 200 per second, but there were 1,562,500 to be done, so that the arithmetic for each solution would require over 2 hours. The amount of data to be stored far exceeded the memory capacity, and so the successive iteration results would have to be kept on magnetic tape; tape reading and writing time would account for over 2 hours. The total solution time was estimated at over 5 hours.

39. H. R. J. Grosch, 23 March 1951: to R. L. Palmer; W. F. McClelland, undated: "Final Activity Report of the Applied Science Mathematical Committee on the 701."

40. G. A. Roberts, 16 April 1951: to T. V. Learson.

41. C. Benton, Jr., 2 May 1951: to J. G. Phillips et al.

42. T. V. Learson, 9 May 1951: to E. M. Douglas.

43. J. W. Forrester, 1948: "Whirlwind and High-Speed Computing," delivered 29 July 1948, at the Symposia on Modern Calculating Machinery and Numerical Methods at the University of California, Los Angeles. The paper was published in Redmond and Smith, 1980: *Project Whirlwind* (Bedford, Mass.: Digital Press).

44. W. W. McDowell, 14 May 1951: to E. M. Douglas.

45. T. V. Learson, 24 May 1951: to E. M. Douglas.

46. IBM document, undated: "IBM-EDPM Type 701, Order Status (5/12/52)." This one-page list from the sales vice-president's files indicates the first order was dated 5 February 1951 and the last 10 January 1952.

47. C. Benton, Jr., 13 June 1951: to J. G. Phillips et al.; T. V. Learson, 1 June 1951: to E. M. Douglas.

48. J. A. Haddad, September 1967: interview by L. M. Saphire; L. D. Stevens, December 1967: interview by L. M. Saphire; Ross, October 1967.

49. J. A. Haddad, 9 July 1951: to J. C. McPherson.

50. IBM document, index page dated 7/17/51: "Defense Calculator Circuit Design Manual"; D. J. Crawford, 1 April 1982: conversation with J. H. Palmer.

51. Ross, October 1967.

52. U.S. Patent 2,754,454, filed 27 May 1952: R. D. McNutt and E. J. Garvey, "Multiple Pluggable Unit."

53. During a series of calls on prospective customers in California in early February, Hurd had visited RAND Corporation, where Johnniac was being designed, and the Institute for Numerical Analysis of the National Bureau of Standards, where SWAC (Standards Western Automatic Computer) was in its initial period of operation. Both machines were, like the Defense Calculator, similar to the IAS machine in design;

both were to be maintained, Hurd was pointedly told, by the engineers who had built them.

54. C. L. Christiansen, 18 March 1982: conversation with J. H. Palmer.

55. Rochester, October 1967.

56. Christiansen, 18 March 1982.

57. Engineering project file, 701 Calculator, Progress Reports section.

58. Crawford, 1 April 1982.

59. H. F. Heath, Jr., 7 November 1951: "Sylvania Diodes—Life Tests," "Diode Humidity Tests," and "Diode Pressure Tests," three brief reports.

60. IBM document, undated: copy of minutes of a meeting on germanium diodes held at Clyde, New York, on 27 March 1951. Surrounding documents indicate the report was written by J. A. Goetz or J. L. Wagner.

61. R. R. Blessing, undated: copy of minutes of a meeting on germanium diodes held in Boston, Mass., on 24 September 1951.

62. D. J. Crawford and H. F. Heath, Jr., undated: "Germanium Diode Testing Program." The report was presented in part at the Annual Convention of the Institute of Radio Engineers, New York, N.Y., on 6 March 1952.

63. Haddad, September 1967.

64. B. L. Havens, 6 December 1946: to W. J. Eckert; U.S. Patent Reissue 23,699, original filed 30 July 1951: B. L. Havens, "Pulse Delay Circuit."

65. B. L. Havens, January 1968: interview by L. M. Saphire.

66. Two additional adder stages (36 and 37) were provided to accommodate overflow digits that might result from arithmetic operations, and two additional accumulator register units received and stored such digits.

67. H. D. Ross, Jr., 1953: "The Arithmetic Element of the IBM Type 701 Computer," *Proceedings of the Institute of Radio Engineers 41*, pp. 1287–1294.

68. C. E. Frizzell, 1953: "Engineering Description of the IBM Type 701 Computer," *Proceedings of the Institute of Radio Engineers 41*, pp. 1275–1287.

69. G. Estrin, September 1952: "A Description of the Electronic Computer at the Institute for Advanced Studies [*sic*]," *Proceedings of the Association for Computing Machinery*, pp. 95–109; J. Bigelow, 1980: "Computer Development at the Institute for Advanced Study," in *A History of Computing in the Twentieth Century*, ed. N. Metropolis, J. Howlett, and G.-C. Rota (New York: Academic Press).

70. U.S. Patent 2,974,866, filed 30 March 1954: J. A. Haddad, R. K. Richards, N. Rochester, and H. D. Ross, Jr., "Electronic Data Processing Machine."

71. T. A. Burke, undated: "Review—Type 701 Electronic Data Processing Machine Program"; Christiansen, 18 March 1982.

72. Stevens, December 1967; Engineering project file, 701 Calculator, Progress Reports Section; W. H. Johnson, 17 April 1952: to G. A. Roberts.

73. Engineering project file, 701 Calculator, Progress Reports section; Burke, "Review—Type 701 Electronic Data Processing Machine Program."

74. Buchholz, 1953; Frizzell, 1953; Ross, Jr., 1953.

75. *New York Times*, 30 April 1952: "Watson Reports IBM Expansion," p. 41.

76. N. Rochester and M. M. Astrahan, May 1952: "The Logical Organization of the New IBM Scientific Calculator," *Proceedings of the Association for Computing Machinery*,

pp. 79–83. The proceedings contain transcripts of papers presented at an ACM meeting 2–3 May at the Mellon Institute in Pittsburgh. The paper was also presented at the Electronic Computer Symposium held the same week at the University of California, Los Angeles.

77. The name no doubt owed its tentative status to its awkwardness. There was difficulty in establishing a suitable label for the array of nearly a dozen separate physical units at the South Road laboratory, although each unit was soon assigned a machine type number in a new 700 series. These began with the 701 Calculator Frame and proceeded in a spaced sequence: 706, 711, . . . , through the 746 Power Unit. This numbering procedure established type categories for the perceived new class of "electronic data processing machines," a term that, abbreviated as EDPM, suggested an advance beyond the familiar "EAM." The latter, itself an abbreviation for "electric accounting machine," was an organizational term that had originated within IBM. It had found favor with customers, many of whom spoke familiarly of their EAM installations and EAM procedures. The establishment of "EDPM" as a comparable generic name for the new line of products was not well served by its use, even tentatively, as a specific name for the Defense Calculator. One result was the ungainly official name, "IBM Electronic Data Processing Machines Type 701 and Associated Equipment," which replaced "Defense Calculator" and "IBM Electronic Data Processing Machine" in mid-1952 and endured throughout 1953. Informal usage quickly filled the vacuum caused by the lack of a short official name, and "the 701" became the commonly accepted designation.

78. L. H. LaMotte, 21 May 1952: "IBM Electronic Data Processing Machine (Defense Calculator)." Of the rental range of $5700, $3100 represented the possibility of omitting from a configuration the two tape units (four tapes) and the drum unit. The remaining $2600 would be applied to an additional electrostatic storage unit. Operation at the planned density of 1024 spots per tube was still in doubt; if only 512 spots could be stored, an installation would need two storage units to achieve a 2048-word memory. Most users, wanting the tapes and drum, hoping for success with the CRT problem, figured the new rental at $11,900 plus $3100, or $15,000.

79. IBM documents, undated: "IBM—EDPM Type 701, Order Status (5/20/52)" and "IBM—EDPM Type 701, Order Status (8/4/52)."

80. Burke, "Review—Type 701 Electronic Data Processing Machine Program"; H. T. Hansford, 28 July 1952: to L. H. LaMotte; L. H. LaMotte, 18 August 1952: to H. T. Hansford.

81. Burke, "Review—Type 701 Electronic Data Processing Machine Program."

82. C. E. Frizzell, December 1967: interview by L. M. Saphire.

83. P. E. Fox, 2 March 1953: to R. L. Palmer.

84. J. C. Logue, A. E. Brennemann, and A. C. Koelsch, March 1953: "Engineering Experience in the Design and Operation of a Large Scale Electrostatic Memory," *Convention Record of the Institute of Radio Engineers, 1953 National Convention, Part 7— Electronic Computers*, pp. 21–29. The paper describes steps taken during 1952 to achieve the higher storage capacity. For more on cathode-ray-tube storage and other engineering problems, see J. S. Haddad, 1983: "701 Recollections," *Annals of the History of Computing* 5, pp. 118–124, in a special issue on the IBM 701.

85. *IBM Record*, April 1953; D. W. Pendery, 25 August 1953: to C. C. Hurd.

86. C. C. Hurd, 1983 (editor's note): "The 701 at the U.S. Weather Bureau," *Annals of the History of Computing* 5, p. 212; J. Smagorinsky, 1983: "The Beginnings of Numerical

Weather Prediction and General Circulation Modeling: Early Recollections," in *Advances in Geophysics, Volume 25, Theory of Climate*, ed. B. Saltzman (New York: Academic Press). The using organizations and installed locations for the nineteen 701 systems are given on a list extracted from the Poughkeepsie plant's manufacturing records in 1974. Airframe companies predominate, reflecting Hurd's 1950 assessment that guided missile development was the most fruitful defense-related field for high-speed computation. The list is included in C. C. Hurd, 1981: "Early IBM Computers: Edited Testimony," *Annals of the History of Computing 3*, pp. 163–182.

87. *Think*, April 1973: G. D. Austrian, "The Machine That Carried Us into the Electronics Business"; B. O. Evans, 2 June 1983: conversation with C. J. Bashe.

88. Forrester, 1948.

89. D. R. Mason, 22 November 1952: to C. C. Hurd.

90. D. R. Mason, 9, 26 January 1953: to C. C. Hurd.

91. D. R. Mason, 18 December 1952: to C. C. Hurd.

92. E. C. Kubie, 16 March 1953: "Optimum Location of Data and Instructions for the MDC Type 650."

93. A. J. Etienne, 20 March 1953: to G. Knight.

94. E. C. Kubie, 9 April 1953: to F. E. Hamilton.

95. E. S. Hughes, Jr., 22 April 1953: to E. J. Garvey.

96. F. E. Hamilton, 5 May 1953: "Proposed Alternative Memory Units for the MDC."

97. J. L. Wagner, 6 December 1946: to J. C. McPherson; J. J. Lentz, 20 February 1948: to J. C. McPherson; J. A. Haddad, 10 August 1949: "Capacitor Storage Means," IBM Techncial Report.

98. A. W. Holt, 1952: "A Very Rapid Access Memory Using Diodes and Capacitors," presented at the March 1952 Institute of Radio Engineers National Convention, abstract in *Proceedings of the Institute of Radio Engineers 40*, p. 231; A. W. Holt, September 1952: "An Experimental Rapid Access Memory Using Diodes and Capacitors," *Proceedings of the Association for Computing Machinery*, pp. 133–141.

99. C. W. Allen, 17 September 1981: conversation with J. H. Palmer.

100. E. S. Hughes, Jr., February 1954: "The IBM Magnetic Drum Calculator Type 650—Engineering and Design Considerations," *Proceedings of the Western Computer Conference*, pp. 140–154.

101. S. W. Dunwell, 2 June 1952: to G. A. Roberts; W. W. Woodbury, 11 June 1954: "The IBM X-795 Experimental Engineering Calculator," IBM Technical Report.

102. IBM document, 1 May 1953: "Progress Report on Intermediate Calculator Survey"; Hamilton, 5 May 1953.

103. IBM document, undated: "Joint Report by Engineering, Applied Science and Product Planning."

104. IBM document, 12 May 1953: "Report by Engineering, Applied Science, and Product Planning, May 12, 1953, on an Intermediate Calculator."

105. Hurd, 11 October 1972.

106. C. C. Hurd, 1980: "Computer Development at IBM," in *A History of Computing in the Twentieth Century*, ed. Metropolis, Howlett, and Rota.

107. IBM document, 11 June 1953: "Ease of Use Comparison—WTW and MDC." Report of a study by R. S. Barton, E. L. Glaser, W. H. Johnson, D. R. Mason, and B. E. Smith.

108. Hurd, 3 January 1979: pp. 86363–86364.

109. J. W. Birkenstock and W. W. McDowell (with provision for signatures of C. C. Hurd and L. H. LaMotte), 24 August 1953: "Magnetic Drum Calculator."

110. Project Report, Magnetic Drum Calculator, 1 March 1954.

111. IBM EDPM Newsletter No. 3, 18 November 1954.

112. S. Rosen, 1969: "Electronic Computers: A Historical Survey," *Computing Surveys 1*, pp. 7–36.

113. A. J. Perlis, December 1954: "Characteristics of Currently Available Small Digital Computers," *Proceedings of the Eastern Joint Computer Conference*, pp. 11–16. "Small," incidentally, was typically applied to computers selling for less than $150,000 to $200,000. It was not clear, however, to what extent input-output equipment was covered in this price. The 650 system, available at the time on rental only, cost $3250 or $3750 per month, depending on memory capacity. In 1956, Burroughs acquired the ElectroData Corporation, developer of the Datatron. Other machines described were: the Miniac of Marchant Research Corporation; the Alwac of Logistics Research, Inc.; the Circle of Hogan Laboratories; the Monrobot of Monroe Calculating Machine Company; and the E101 of Burroughs Corporation.

114. E. H. Dohrmann, 1956: "Data Processing Machine—Business and Industry 'Workhorse'," in *The Punched Card Annual of Machine Accounting and Data Processing, Volume 5*, ed. D. A. Talucci (Detroit: Punched Card Publishing Company); O. M. Scott, 16 May 1955: 650 Application Recap, Letter 4829.

115. W. Buchholz, 15 April 1952: "Common-Trunk Connected Input-Output Components," IBM Technical Report.

116. W. Buchholz, 18 August 1952: "TPM Modifications to Improve File Maintenance and Sorting," IBM Technical Report.

117. F. J. Wesley had been with LaMotte in the Washington Federal office since 1946.

118. G. A. Roberts, 2 February 1953: "Report of TPM Survey Team."

119. M. E. Femmer, June 1968: interview by L. M. Saphire. The tape sorter-collator, for which machine type number 703 had been reserved, was a plugged-program machine using barrier-grid cathode-ray tubes for its memory.

120. W. D. Winger, August 1951–September 1953: IBM Engineering Notebook No. 79806, p. 29, entry for 8 May 1952.

121. F. J. Wesley, 23 July 1953: to L. H. LaMotte.

122. The 702 is described in considerable detail in C. J. Bashe, W. Buchholz, and N. Rochester, 1954: "The IBM 702, an Electronic Data Processing Machine for Business," *Journal of the Association for Computing Machinery 1*, pp. 149–169. Also, C. J. Bashe, P. W. Jackson, H. A. Mussell, and W. D. Winger, 1956: "The Design of the IBM Type 702 System," paper no. 55-719, *American Institute of Electrical Engineers Transactions 74 (Part I, Communication and Electronics)*, pp. 695–704.

123. Society of Actuaries, September 1952: "Report of Committee on New Recording Means and Computing Devices." The report was presented at a special meeting arranged by the society on 25 September 1952 and later published as a book.

124. M. E. Davis, December 1953: "The Use of Electronic Data Processing Systems in the Life Insurance Business," *Proceedings of the Eastern Joint Computer Conference*, pp. 11–18.

125. L. M. Dorn, 1959: "Progress and Problems Regarding Application of a Large Computer in Insurance," *Proceedings of the Sixth Annual High Speed Computer Conference*, Louisiana State University, pp. 131-146; N. Stern, 1981: *From ENIAC to UNIVAC* (Bedford, Mass.: Digital Press), pp. 139, 142. Indeed according to Stern, Prudential agreed to accept UNIVAC only with provision for punched-card output.

126. O. M. Scott, 25 June 1954: 702 EDPM Equipment, Letter 4610.

127. It was discovered by Ernest D. Foss and Richard E. Merwin, working on the laboratory model 702 late in 1955, that random errors then occurring in the CRT memory arose from the use of CRT filament transformers which had been accepted from the vendor in spite of their failure to meet high-voltage "corona" test specifications. These transformers, which operated at more than 2000 volts DC relative to frames and grounding, gave off periodic bursts of discharge due to ionization of the surrounding air, generating sufficient disturbance to cause memory errors. This discovery came too late to be helpful in determining whether the corona effect had been the major source of CRT memory problems in the field; by then, it had been decided to replace all CRT memories with cores. From E. D. Foss, 16 June 1981: conversation with C. J. Bashe.

128. The second 702 went to the Monsanto Chemical Company at its headquarters location in St. Louis, where Tom Watson, Jr., attended its official debut on 12 April 1955. Users of the other twelve systems included the U.S. Navy Aviation Supply Office, General Electric Co. at Hanford, Washington, and Schenectady, N.Y., Commonwealth Edison at Chicago, Bank of America, Chrysler Corp., Prudential Insurance Co., and Ford Motor Co. See L. R. Johnson, 22 April 1976: to J. H. Palmer.

129. *IBM Business Machines*, 15 April 1954: "T. V. Learson named Director of EDPM."

130. IBM Product Announcement, 7 May 1954: Type 704 Electronic Data Processing Machine, Letter 4571; 1 October 1954: Type 701–704 EDPM, Letter 4666.

131. IBM Product Announcement, 1 October 1954: Type 705 Electronic Data Processing System, Letter 4667.

132. J. E. Zollinger, 23 December 1954: to Chief, Bureau of Ordnance; J. C. McPherson, 16 April 1958: to J. J. Kenney, Jr.

133. With four memory cycles for instruction and operand fetches, and result storage, included, the execution time for NORC's three-address floating-point multiply instruction was 72 microseconds.

134. *IBM Business Machines*, 28 December 1956, a special issue on the Williamsburg conference.

135. IBM Product Announcement, 2 January 1957: 709 Electronic Data Processing System, Letter 257-2.

136. U.S. Patent 3,812,475, filed 26 December 1957: C. L. Christiansen, L. E. Kanter, and G. R. Monroe, "Data Synchronizer."

137. IBM Product Announcement, 3 September 1957: 705-III Data Processing System, Letter 257-101.

138. Hurd, 1981.

Chapter 6

1. U.S. Patent 662,619, filed 8 July 1899: V. Poulsen, "Method of Recording and Reproducing Sounds or Signals."

2. *Scientific American*, September 1900: "Poulsen Telegraphone," p. 181.

3. *Scientific American*, 1900.

4. U.S. Patent 662,619, filed 8 July 1899.

5. V. Poulsen, 13 November 1900: "The Telegraphone." (No publication indicated; translation by W. G. Weekly found in IBM Archives, files of A.H. Dickinson.)

6. S. J. Begun, 1937: "Recent Developments in Magnetic Sound Recording," *Journal of the Society of Motion Picture Engineers*, pp. 464–472.

7. W. E. Schrage, June 1935: "Play-Back Recording Method for Broadcasting," *Electronics*, p. 179.

8. *Electronics*, November 1945: "German Magnetic-Tape Recorder," pp. 402–403.

9. U.S. Patent 2,333,463, filed 17 June 1938: J. W. Bryce, "Apparatus for Recording Statistical Records."

10. F. E. Hamilton, 15 April 1953: "Magnetic Storage Device History." Robert E. Lawhead was the technical leader for magnetic-recording projects under Hamilton mentioned in this chapter.

11. Hamilton, 15 April 1953.

12. J. P. Eckert and J. W. Mauchly, 30 September 1945: *Automatic High-Speed Computing: A Progress Report on EDVAC* (University of Pennsylvania), pp. 5, 48.

13. J. C. McPherson, 24 September 1946: to W. J. Eckert, with attached McPherson memorandum of 23 September: "Electronic Calculator"; J. C. McPherson and W. J. Eckert, 12 November 1946: to T. J. Watson.

14. *Philadelphia Inquirer*, 3 March 1947: "New Magic-Brain Computer Does Job 10 Times Faster"; J. C. McPherson, 28 April 1947: "Report of Electronics Meeting Friday, April 25th." The meeting was held in the office of executive vice-president Charles A. Kirk.

15. The same Edmund C. Berkeley became well known as a prolific writer about the nature of computers and their possible uses.

16. McPherson, 28 April 1947.

17. J. C. McPherson, 30 June 1947: to W. W. McDowell.

18. J. C. McPherson, 27 May 1947: to F. E. Hamilton.

19. McPherson, 27 May 1947.

20. McPherson, 30 June 1947.

21. McPherson, 27 May 1947, 30 June, 1947.

22. F. E. Hamilton, R. E. Lawhead, and G. E. Mitchell, December 1948: "Magnetic Storage Research Summary to 2 December 1948"; August 1949: "Magnetic Storage Research Summary, 2 December 1948 to 31 August 1949."

23. Anon., 8 June 1946: "Report of Meeting with Engineers, IBM Laboratory, Endicott, N.Y. Mr. T. J. Watson—Main Speaker."

24. W. W. McDowell, 10 September 1946: to C. A. Kirk.

25. W. W. McDowell, 3 January 1947: to W. L. Lewis.

26. D. W. Rubidge, 8 July 1948: to F. E. Hamilton; attached D. W. R. of same date, "Report on a Preferred Method of Magnetic Tape Sorting."

27. J. C. McPherson, 8 January 1949: to T. J. Watson, Jr., "Magnetic Tape Accounting and Record Keeping"; G. A. Roberts, 16 January 1949: to J. C. McPherson; McPherson, 23 February 1949: to Roberts; McPherson, 1 March 1949: to W. W. McDowell,

"Magnetic Tape Accounting and Record Keeping"; McDowell, 16 March 1949: to McPherson, same subject.

28. G. F. Daly (Initials GFD only), 23 May 1949: "Report on Engineering Meeting with Mr. T. J. Watson, Jr. and Sales Executives—May 19 and 20, 1949." In connection with plans of Metropolitan Life to obtain special equipment, the names Gould and Hillyer Instrument Co. were mentioned as prospective suppliers. Information on UNIVAC contracts is from J. C. McPherson, 26 May 1949: to C. E. Love, "Competition from Electronic Calculators."

29. J. H. Fraser, 19 April 1949: to W. W. McDowell; F. E. Hamilton, 27 April 1949: to W. W. McDowell; McDowell, 2 May 1949: to Fraser; D. W. Rubidge, (undated): "Specifications of Magnetic Tape Recording—Meeting at Endicott, May 31, 1949."

30. W. W. McDowell, 7 June 1949: to J. C. McPherson; attached G. F. Daly report of same date.

31. J. A. Weidenhammer, 9 March 1981: conversation with C. J. Bashe.

32. N. Stern, 1981: *From ENIAC to UNIVAC* (Bedford, Mass.: Digital Press), p. 146.

33. B. E. Phelps, 19 August 1949: "Notes on Eckert-Mauchly Demonstration."

34. H. F. Welsh and H. Lukoff, December 1952: "The Uniservo—Tape Reader and Recorder," *Proceedings of Joint AIEE-IRE-ACM Computer Conference*, J. P. Eckert, Jr., J. R. Weiner, H. F. Welsh, and H. F. Mitchell, 1951: "The UNIVAC System," *Review of Electronic Digital Computers*, Papers and Discussions Presented at the Joint AIEE-IRE Computer Conference, 10–12 December 1951 (American Institute of Electrical Engineers), pp. 6–16.

35. R. M. Bloch, 1949: "The Raytheon Electronic Digital Computer," *Proceedings of a Second Symposium on Large-Scale Digital Calculating Machinery* (Harvard University), pp. 50–64.

36. Phelps, 1983: undocumented conversation with C. J. Bashe.

37. A. S. Hoagland, 1963: *Digital Magnetic Recording* (New York: John Wiley and Sons); R. E. Matick, 1977: *Computer Storage Systems and Technology* (New York: John Wiley and Sons).

38. B. E. Phelps, 3 May 1950: "Present Status of Factors Affecting Net Record Handling Speeds."

39. H. W. Nordyke, Jr., and W. D. Winger, 10 April 1950: "Magnetic Recording Techniques." Nordyke took the lead in experimental magnetic head design. M. E. Femmer was heavily involved in writing circuit and sense amplifier design.

40. J. A. Haddad and H. W. Nordyke, Jr., 5 January 1950: "Factors Affecting Spot Density in Magnetic Tape Recording."

41. L. D. Stevens and H. A. Mussell, 9 February 1950: "Magnetic Tape Reading and Writing Methods"; H. W. Nordyke, Jr., and W. Winger, 10 April 1950: "Magnetic Recording Techniques."

42. Phelps, 3 May 1950.

43. B. E. Phelps, 21 December 1949: daily diary entry; U.S. Patent 2,774,646, filed 31 December 1951: B. E. Phelps, "Magnetic Recording Method."

44. Nordyke and Winger, 10 April 1950; Phelps, 3 May 1950.

45. Phelps, 3 May 1950.

46. Nordyke and Winger, 10 April 1950.

47. B. E. Phelps, 1 November 1950: "Considerations Involved in Change from Serial to Parallel Tape System."

48. Matick, 1977: p. 373.

49. J. A. Weidenhammer, October 1967: interview by L. M. Saphire.

50. W. S. Buslik, June 1970: interview by L. M. Saphire.

51. R. P. Crago and B. E. Phelps, 13 June 1950: "Factors Directly Affecting Tape Units."

52. Nordyke and Winger, 10 April 1950.

53. Weidenhammer, 9 March 1981.

54. C. J. Fitch, January 1957: "Development of the Electrostatic Clutch," *IBM Journal*, pp. 49–56.

55. Weidenhammer, 9 March 1981.

56. Buslik, June 1970.

57. Welsh, and Lukoff, December 1952; Bloch, 1949.

58. Weidenhammer, 9 March 1981. See also U.S. Patent 3,057,569, filed 28 May 1952: J. A. Weidenhammer, "Tape Feed Mechanism."

59. Phelps, 1 November 1950.

60. V. R. Witt, July 1969: interview by L. M. Saphire; 7 April 1982: conversation with C. J. Bashe.

61. J. P. Harris, W. B. Phillips, J. F. Wells, and W. D. Winger, 1981: "Innovations in the Design of Magnetic Tape Subsystems," *IBM Journal of Research and Development*, p. 696.

62. W. S. Buslik, March 1953: "IBM Magnetic Tape Reader and Recorder," *Review of Input and Output Used in Computer Systems, Joint AIEE-IRE-ACM Computer Conference*, pp. 86–90.

63. W. J. Eckert and R. Jones, 1955: *Faster, Faster* (New York: McGraw-Hill), pp. 51–59.

64. B. L. Havens, January 1968: interview by L. M. Saphire.

65. Eckert and Jones, 1955.

66. S. W. Dunwell, 28 March 1950: to R. L. Palmer.

67. U.S. Patent 2,922,231, filed 26 April 1956: V. R. Witt and R. C. Bradford, "Magnetic Transducer."

68. U.S. Patent 3,078,448, filed 15 July 1957: H. A. O'Brien, "Dual-Channel Sensing."

69. S. Rosen, March 1969: "Electronic Computers: A Historical Survey," *Computing Surveys*, pp. 7–36.

70. U.S. Patent 3,007,086, filed 17 April 1959: H. K. Baumeister, "Multi-Position Electromagnetic Actuator."

71. C. L. Christiansen, March 1982: conversation with C. J. Bashe.

72. T. L. Vinson, "area manager" for magnetic-tape devices, had agreed at Palmer's urging to use the new tape unit as a vehicle for introducing transistors into the 700 series. IBM had announced only one fully "transistorized" product—the 608 calculator—prior to the 729 III.

73. Vinson took exception to the Edwards report and made the commitment of 62,500 cps to Palmer.

74. Many details of the 729 III program history are found in C. L. Christiansen, 20 October 1960: memorandum to H. T. Marcy and attached "729 Program Comments"; 20 October 1960: "The 729 III Program—a Review."

75. C. L. Christiansen's successor as manager of the Tractor project was L. H. Blenderman, who had been working in the tape-devices area almost since joining IBM in 1951. He had contributed especially to the design of magnetic heads, starting with those of the company's first tape units.

76. R. W. Hamming, 1950: "Error Detecting and Error Correcting Codes," *Bell System Technical Journal*, pp. 147–160.

77. S. S. Snyder, 1980: "Computer Advances Pioneered by Cryptological Organizations," *Annals of the History of Computing*, pp. 60–70. Essentially a republication of S. S. Snyder, 1977: "Influence of U.S. Cryptological Organizations on the Digital Computer Industry" (National Security Agency).

78. Among those who recommended phase encoding to Weidenhammer were L. H. Thompson and A. Brunschweiger. They had attended a demonstration of the technique by E. Hopner in the IBM laboratory in San Jose, California. A very similar approach, using techniques referred to as "current pulse displacement writing" and "pulse displacement phase detection," was described much earlier in L. D. Stevens and H. A. Mussell, 9 February 1950: "Magnetic Tape Reading and Writing Methods."

79. B. O. Evans, 13 November 1984: to C. J. Bashe.

80. B. O. Evans, 16 May 1960: to G. A. Blaauw et al. (19 addressees), "Attached for your file is a copy of the Fox Hill Report." The report proposed meeting the market needs of the "next few years" by development of "a spectrum of disk-file based systems . . . a sharp departure from the tape processing systems which we have offered in the past." Also, the question was raised by J. A. Haddad and B. L. Havens in an IBM Research and Development Board meeting on 8 September 1960 whether "since a number of people in IBM believe tape is on the way out," there should be a corporate decision on the use of tapes in new machines.

Chapter 7

1. J. C. McPherson and W. J. Eckert, 12 November 1946: to T. J. Watson, Sr. This letter also cites concern over the growing support by the federal government of development efforts in universities and companies.

2. J. C. McPherson, 21 November 1946: to W. W. McDowell, "Electronic Development."

3. P. E. Fox, 18 May 1949: "Cathode-Ray Electrostatic Storage."

4. R. E. Lawhead, 1–2 June 1948: minutes of a "Conference to set up general specifications for, and to decide what type of units should be included in our next large scale Calculator," IBM Watson Laboratory. Lawhead listed the attendees as "Messrs. J. C. McPherson, Dr. Eckert, R. Seeber, Dr. Thomas, R. Walker, J. Lenz, B. Havens, R. L. Palmer, P. Luhn, A. H. Dickinson, E. S. Hughes and R. E. Lawhead." Robert M. Walker, who attended the meeting, was the engineer who worked with Thomas on magnetic-ring storage. The earlier reference to magnetic-ring storage was in J. C. McPherson, 21 November 1946: to W. W. McDowell, "Electronic Development."

5. E. W. Pugh, 1984: *Memories That Shaped an Industry—Decisions Leading to IBM System/ 360* (Cambridge: MIT Press), pp. 87–88. This book is the source of much of the information and perspective found in this chapter.

6. A. Wang and W. D. Woo, 1950: "Static Magnetic Storage and Delay Line," *Journal of Applied Physics 21*, pp. 49–54.

7. A. Wang, 21 May 1982: conversation with E. W. Pugh.

8. M. K. Haynes, September 1967: interview by L. M. Saphire.

9. M. K. Haynes, August 1950: "Magnetic Cores as Elements of Digital Computing Systems" (University of Illinois, Ph.D. dissertation).

10. A. L. Samuel, December 1967: interview by L. M. Saphire.

11. R. L. Palmer, N. Rochester, and A. L. Samuel, 29 September 1949: "A Symposium on Large-Scale Digital Calculating Machinery—A Trip Report"; A. L. Samuel, 12 April 1950: to M. K. Haynes.

12. M. K. Haynes, September 1967: interview by L. M. Saphire.

13. R. G. Counihan, 9 September 1951: "Static Magnetic Volume Storage." Gordon E. Whitney, the first person to join Haynes's group, was also the person who contacted and worked with Rabenda. Richard G. Counihan joined IBM in Haynes's group in July 1951 with a bachelor's degree in electrical engineering from MIT. Two months later he completed an internal report describing all known schemes for organizing magnetic-core storage. He followed this by building some of the systems described in his report, including a 3D array with two-diode matrix select systems, which he called a 5D memory, consistent with the terminology Haynes was then using. See R. G. Counihan, 1 May 1981: conversation with E. W. Pugh.

14. E. J. Rabenda, 9 June 1981: conversation with E. W. Pugh; U.S. Patent 2,750,580, filed 2 January 1953: E. J. Rabenda and G. E. Whitney, "Intermediate Magnetic Core Storage."

15. P. W. Jackson, 7 October 1981: conversation with E. W. Pugh; C. J. Bashe, R. W. Murphy, and H. A. Mussell, 1953: Work Order 2-4087; P. W. Jackson, 31 June 1981: conversation with C. J. Bashe. W.D. Winger and P. W. Jackson had responsibility for I/O on the 702 computer and jointly initiated the card-buffer project to which Bloch was assigned.

16. E. Bloch, 20 September 1981, 14 April 1982: conversations with E. W. Pugh. The perception of Bloch by others reflects the views expressed by his coworkers of that era.

17. The first order of dies for making 60-90 mil cores is documented in a letter from M. K. Haynes, 26 March 1952: to C. L. Snyder, vice-president of General Ceramics. Arndt recalls using 60-90 mil cores supplied to ERA by General Ceramics for experimental work leading to development of the memories used on the ERA 1103 computer. See R. B. Arndt, 6 October, 3 November 1981: conversations with E. W. Pugh. The first 32 × 32 × 17 bit array placed on the MTC at MIT had 60-90 mil cores purchased from General Ceramics.

18. Erich Bloch, October 1968: interview by L. Saphire.

19. P. W. Jackson, 7 October 1981: conversation with E. W. Pugh.

20. M. K. Haynes, 27 February 1961: to J. W. Birkenstock, "Early magnetics work at IBM."

21. J. F. Jacobs, 1983: "SAGE Overview," *Annals of the History of Computing 5*, pp. 323–329.

22. K. C. Redmond and T. M. Smith, 1980: *Project Whirlwind — The History of a Pioneer Computer* (Bedford, Mass.: Digital Press), pp. 176–177.

23. J. W. Forrester, 1983: in "A Perspective on SAGE: Discussion," *Annals of the History of Computing* 5, pp. 375–398.

24. Pugh, 1984: pp. 64–68.

25. Redmond and Smith, 1980: p. 183.

26. J. W. Forrester, 13–14 June 1949: MIT Computation Notebook, No. 47, pp. 15–17 (Bedford, Mass.: MITRE Corporation Archives).

27. J. W. Forrester, 30 June 1949: MIT Computation Notebook, No. 47, p. 27.

28. MIT Servomechanisms Laboratory, 13 October 1950: Project Whirlwind Bi-Weekly Report (M-1112) (Bedford, Mass.: MITRE Corporation Archives).

29. Ferrite materials work at MIT was initiated in A. R. von Hippel's laboratory in 1950. See Pugh, 1984: pp. 73–74, 90.

30. MIT Digital Computer Laboratory, 9 May 1952: Bi-Weekly Report (M-1484) (Bedford, Mass.: MITRE Corporation Archives).

31. Redmond and Smith, 1980: p. 193.

32. J. C. McPherson, 17 July 1952: to J. R. Shipman.

33. J. W. Forrester, 12 May 1953: to A. G. Hill, "Selection of a Company to Work with the Lincoln Laboratory on the Transition System."

34. Pugh, 1984: pp. 94–97. John M. Coombs, the first manager of Project High, had joined IBM in January 1952 from Engineering Research Associates (ERA) a few months before the purchase of ERA by Remington Rand.

35. R. P. Crago, 1983: in "A Perspective on SAGE: Discussion," *Annals of the History of Computing* 5, pp. 375–398.

36. M. M. Astrahan and J. F. Jacobs, 1983: "History of the Design of the SAGE Computer—The AN/FSQ-7," *Annals of the History of Computing* 5, pp. 340–349.

37. J. F. Jacobs, 1983: "SAGE Overview," *Annals of the History of Computing* 5, pp. 323–329.

38. R. P. Crago, 19 December 1978: testimony in U.S. v. IBM, Southern District Court, New York; N. P. Edwards, 1964: SAGE summary chart.

39. Pugh, 1984: p. 95.

40. K. H. Olsen, 8 May 1953: to N. H. Taylor, "A Linear Selection Magnetic Memory Using an Anti-Coincident Current Switch" (Cambridge: MIT Libraries, Magnetic Core Memory Collection, MC-140, of the Institute Archives and Special Collections). This memorandum cites a report by G. E. Whitney, of M. K. Haynes's group at IBM, when listing the advantages of the proposed alternative memory organization.

41. MIT Lincoln Laboratory, 15 June 1953: Digital Computer Quarterly Progress Report; 31 July 1953: Digital Computer Biweekly Report; 15 September 1953: Digital Computer Quarterly Progress Report (Bedford, Mass.: MITRE Corporation Archives).

42. Pugh, 1984: pp. 112–115.

43. J. W. Forrester, 9 April 1954: to J. M. Coombs and R. P. Crago; W. N. Papian and W. M. Wittenberg, 9 April 1954: "Performance Specification for the AN/FSQ-7 Memory Element" (Bedford, Mass.: MITRE Corporation Archives).

44. IBM Duplex Planning Group, 12 July 1954: D. C. Ross, "Memory Element for the AN/FSQ-7 Production System" (Cambridge: MIT Libraries Magnetic Core Memory Collection, MC-140, of the Institute Archives and Special Collections).

45. Astrahan and Jacobs, 1983.

46. The ERA memory had an 8 microsecond cycle versus 6 microseconds for the SAGE memory. It was four times smaller than the SAGE memory, containing only thirty-six planes of 32 × 32 cores each. The cores were the same 50–80 mil size used in SAGE and were also purchased from General Ceramics. Arndt, who managed this effort, recalls that there were never more than ten to fifteen people on the project. See R. B. Arndt, 6 October 1981: conversation with E. W. Pugh. The International Telemeter Corporation ferrite-core memory (MNEMOTRON), with 4096 words of 40 bits each and a 15 microsecond read-write cycle, was shipped in February 1955 for installation by April 1955 on the RAND Johnniac computer. See *Digital Computer Newsletter*, April 1955, p. 125.

47. P. W. Jackson, 7 October 1981: conversation with E. W. Pugh.

48. E. W. Bauer, December 1953–February 1956: Engineering Notebook No. 1373; 6 October 1981: conversation with E. W. Pugh.

49. K. H. Olsen, May 1952: "A Magnetic Matrix Switch and Its Incorporation into a Coincident-Current Memory" (MIT, Master's thesis); 8 May 1953: to N. H. Taylor, "A Linear Selection Magnetic Memory Using an Anti-Coincident Current Switch"; U.S. Patent 2,937,285, filed 31 March 1953: K. H. Olsen, "Saturable Switch." See also J. A. Rajchman, March 1952: "Static Magnetic Matrix Memory and Switching Circuits," presented at the National Convention of the Institute of Radio Engineers; October 1953: "A Myriabit Magnetic-Core Matrix Memory," *Proceedings of the Institute of Radio Engineers*, pp. 1407–1421.

50. U.S. Patent 2,947,977, filed 11 June 1956: Erich Bloch, "Switch Matrix."

51. Bauer, December 1953–February 1956.

52. U.S. Patent 2,881,414, filed 8 July 1954: M. K. Haynes, "Magnetic Memory System." The concept of staggered read was described by Forrester in his notebook even before Haynes began working with magnetic cores, but apparently Forrester did not pursue the idea.

53. U.S. Patent 2,889,540, filed 14 July 1954: E. W. Bauer and M. K. Haynes, "Magnetic Memory System with Disturbance Cancellation." The term *disturb noise* refers to small electrical signals generated on the sense lines by small changes in the magnetization of partially selected cores.

54. Bauer, December 1953 to February 1956; 6 October 1981.

55. P. W. Jackson, 7 October 1981: conversation with E. W. Pugh.

56. The Type 775 record storage unit was announced on 1 October 1954, IBM Letter 4667. On 24 June 1955, IBM Letter 4864, the Type 777 tape-record coordinator was announced with 1024 characters as an intermediate storage device between the IBM 705 computer main memory and up-to-eight Type 727 magnetic-tape units. According to the announcement, "Since the transfer time from memory for 1024 characters is 9.2 milliseconds, the tape unit can be brought up to speed simultaneously and most of the tape starting time of 10 milliseconds will be saved." Also on 24 June 1955, IBM Letter 4863, the Type 760 control and storage unit with a 1000 character magnetic core buffer was announced for use with either the 719 or 730 printers.

57. P. E. Fox, October 1967: interview by L. M. Saphire. Although the barrier-grid tube was not used on IBM's commercial computers, it was used on the File Maintenance Machine, at times called the IBM 703 and later known as the 770 when

contracted to the National Security Agency. The 770 including its barrier-grid memory tube was sufficiently reliable that the agency kept it in service about seven years, resisting IBM's efforts to replace it with newer equipment, according to R. S. Partridge, 4 August 1983: conversation with E. W. Pugh. An early description of the barrier-grid tube is given by A. S. Jensen, J. P. Smith, M. H. Mesner, and L. E. Flory, 1948: "Barrier Grid Storage and Its Operation," *RCA Review 9*, pp. 112–135.

58. T. J. Watson, Jr., 22 April 1954: to Ralph L. Palmer.

59. D. J. Crawford, 14 May 1962: to file, "History of Core Memory Development in IBM During the Period of 1954 to 1956."

60. D. J. Crawford, 14 July 1980: conversation with E. W. Pugh.

61. The three engineers were Edward Bauer, William Lawrence, and Robert Ward.

62. Crawford, 14 May 1962: "History . . . 1954 to 1956."

63. D. J. Crawford, 14 May 1962: to file, "Development of Ferrite Cores for Memory Purposes by IBM."

64. P. K. Spatz, July and August 1954: engineering notebook entries; 1 October 1981: conversation with E. W. Pugh.

65. Crawford, 14 May 1962: "History . . . 1954 to 1956."

66. Peter K. Spatz was assigned in June 1954 to design a ferrite-core memory for the proposed 704 computer. In July he and his group had demonstrated the feasibility of driving long lines of cores using the low-cost switch core matrix drive method. Thus he was able to make a very attractive cost estimate, which he showed to T. V. Learson. This influenced the decision in July to initiate a product program for core memories for the 704 and a similar decision in August for the 705. See Pugh, 1984: pp.137–138.

67. IBM Product Announcement, 7 May 1954: Type 704 Electronic Data Processing Machine, Letter 4571; 1 October 1954: Type 701-704 EDPM-Components, Letter 4666; 1 October 1954: Type 705 Electronic Data Processing Machine, Letter 4667.

68. Crawford, 14 May 1962: "History . . . 1954 to 1956."

69. R. S. Partridge, April 1974: "Storage Specification Cost Sheets."

70. R. E. Merwin, December 1956: "The IBM 705 EDPM Memory System," *Institute of Radio Engineers Transaction on Electronic Computers*, pp. 219–223.

71. W. W. Lawrence, 15 March 1955: "Design and Operation of a Magnetic Matrix Switch Driver for a Large Core Memory," IBM Technical Report.

72. Merwin, December 1956.

73. L. R. Johnson, 15 July 1982: conversation with E. W. Pugh. Johnson, who subsequently joined IBM, was then a new employee with Ford.

74. J. Morissey, 22 July 1982: conversation with E. W. Pugh. Morrissey, who stared work at Los Alamos as a programmer on an IBM 701, moved to the Bank of America in time to watch a ferrite-core memory replace a Williams-tube memory on the IBM 701. He subsequently joined IBM.

75. T. J. Watson, Jr., 18 August 1955: meeting with engineering managers in Poughkeepsie, New York. Among the attendees identified from the transcript were T. J. (Tom) Watson, Jr., president; A. L. (Al) Williams, Executive vice-president; J. J. (Jack) Kenney, vice-president Service; George I. Basile, Product Test; Cuthbert C. Hurd, recently appointed director of EDPM; Ralph L. Palmer, director of engineering; W. F. (Bill) Gerken, of Customer Engineering; O. M. Scott, sales manager; C. L. (Chuck)

Hardway, Learson's staff; J. W. (Jim) Birkenstock; Walter H. Johnson; J. J. (Jim) Troy, director of product design; and C. J. (Charlie) Bashe, of Troy's staff. Apparently the recording was made to help Watson and his staff follow up on any commitments made at the meeting.

76. Crawford, 14 May 1962: "History . . . 1954 to 1956."

77. E. Foss and R. S. Partridge, April 1957: "A 32,000-Word Magnetic-Core Memory," *IBM Journal of Research and Development*, pp. 103–109. Six months after Erich Bloch initiated the Type 738 memory project, Ernest Foss became program manager and Ralph S. Partridge the engineering manager.

78. R. S. Partridge, April 1974: "Storage Specification Cost Sheets."

79. D. J. Crawford, 14 May 1962: "History . . . 1954 to 1956."

80. Pugh, 1984: pp. 162–166.

81. G. Constantine, Jr., 23 July 1981: conversation with E. W. Pugh.

82. R. S. Partridge, 22 July 1981: conversation with E. W. Pugh.

83. Constantine, 23 July 1981.

84. G. Constantine, Jr., and L. B. Stallard, 15 January 1957: "Matrix Switch for a Transistor Driven, High-Speed, Core Memory," Project Silo Technical Memorandum.

85. U.S. Patent 3,126,528, filed 30 June 1958: G. Constantine, Jr., "Magnetic Switching Devices"; U.S. Patent 3,126,533, filed 30 June 1958 (refiled 8 December 1960): G. Constantine, Jr., "Magnetic Switching Device"; G. Constantine, Jr., 1958: "A Load-Sharing Matrix Switch," *IBM Journal of Research and Development 2*, pp. 204–211.

86. E. D. Councill, 24 July 1981: conversation with E. W. Pugh.

87. L. P. Hunter and E. W. Bauer, 1956: "High Speed Coincident-Flux Magnetic Storage Principles," *Journal of Applied Physics 27*, pp. 1257–1261. The fast switching of three-hole cores was first recorded in E. W. Bauer's Engineering Notebook on 6–9 August 1955.

88. E. D. Councill, 25 June 1957: "A Small High-Speed Memory Model," Series 7000 Circuit Memorandum.

89. M. A. Every, 3 June 1981: conversation with C. J. Bashe. Maurice A. Every, who joined IBM in 1952 with a bachelor's degree in power engineering, was put in charge of the three-hole-core memory project toward the end of 1958. Seeing little hope of quick solutions, he arranged to have this memory dropped from the Stretch requirements.

90. W. H. Rhodes, 15 October 1981: conversation with E. W. Pugh; R. M. Whalen, 16 October 1981: conversation with E. W. Pugh. R. M. Whalen, a member of L. A. Russell's Advanced Technology Group, joined Crawford in the visit to Mullard. It was Whalen who built the first two-core-per-bit memories at IBM using circuits provided by Crawford's group. About this time, M. A. Every replaced V. R. Witt as head of Nonmechanical Memory Development, and W. H. Rhodes replaced Every as manager of the high-speed memory for HARVEST.

91. W. H. Rhodes, L. A. Russell, F. E. Sakalay, and R. M. Whalen, 1961: "A 0.7-Microsecond Ferrite Core Memory," *IBM Journal of Research and Development 5*, pp. 174–181.

92. R. M. Whalen, 16 October 1981: conversation with E. W. Pugh.

93. W. H. Rhodes, 15 October 1981: conversation with E. W. Pugh.

94. Rhodes, Russell, Sakalay, and Whalen, 1961: pp. 174–181.

95. Ralph S. Partridge, 22 July 1981: conversation with E. W. Pugh. Partridge, who was designated program manager for the 2 microsecond Type 7302 memory in December 1958, recalls that satisfying the special requirements of the four systems with a minimum of modification to a common memory product was one of his most challenging assignments. On Stretch and Harvest, the memory was configured with 16,384 words of 72 bits per word; on the 7090 with 32,768 words of 36 bits each; and on the 7080 with 160,000 characters of 7 bits each.

96. C. A. Allen, G. W. Bruce, and E. D. Councill, 1961: "A 2.18-Microsecond Megabit Core Storage Unit," *Institute of Radio Engineers Transactions on Electronic Computers 10,* pp. 233–237.

97. R. S. Partridge, April 1974: "Storage Specification Cost Sheets."

98. IBM Product Announcement, 15 January 1962: Type 7094 Data Processing System; 16 May 1963: Type 7094 II Data Processing System; R. S. Partridge, 1975: "IBM Core Memories Shipped."

99. D. J. Crawford, 14 May 1962: to file, "Development of Ferrite Cores for Memory Purposes by IBM."

100. A. H. Eschenfelder, 5 April 1982: conversation with E. W. Pugh; M. C. Andrews, 8 June 1981: conversation with E. W. Pugh.

101. J. M. Brownlow, 27 July 1981: conversation with E. W. Pugh.

102. Pugh, 1984: p. 118.

103. This quotation from Gibson's first technical assignment was supplied by J. B. Little who hired Gibson and who managed the Component Research Department in which the ferrite-core pilot line was established. J. B. Little is introduced in chapter 13.

104. J. W. Gibson, 3 August 1981: conversation with E. W. Pugh.

105. MIT Lincoln Laboratory, 15 September 1954: Digital Computer Quarterly Progress Report (Bedford, Mass.: MITRE Corporation Archives).

106. Pugh, 1984: pp. 150–154.

107. Agreement between IBM and Philips, 1 May 1956.

108. E. W. Pugh, 11 June 1982: to file, "History of CuMn Ferrite Core Process Development and Two Related Patents." E. C. Schuenzel, who joined IBM in July 1954 in Gibson's group, was responsible for the pilot line on which the improved CuMn ferrite-core process was developed. This process was protected by a patent coauthored by Gibson, Schuenzel, and three people from Philips. See U.S. Patent 3,188,290, filed 27 May 1959: A. C. A. M. Bleyenberg, A. J. DeRooy, E. C. Schuenzel, R. W. Dam, and J. W. Gibson, "Method of Manufacturing a Magnetic Core for Use as a Memory Element." The critical two-step cooling process, included as part of this patent, had already been patented by Brownlow. See U.S. Patent 2,987,481, filed 15 October 1956: J. M. Brownlow, "Manganese-Zinc Ferrite Cores."

109. E. C. Schuenzel, 27 February 1959: "Ferrite Cores in IBM 1951 to 1963."

110. H. A. DiMarco, 12 October 1967: "Ferrite Core History." Henry DiMarco, with a bachelor's degree in electrical engineering from Clarkson College in 1950, was responsible for transferring the ferrite-core process from development to the manufacturing organization in which he worked.

111. William J. Walker, a mechanical engineer and the first member of Gibson's group, designed and built IBM's first rotary press for ferrite cores. See J. W. Gibson, 3 August 1981: conversation with E. W. Pugh.

112. *IBM News*, November 1967; L. P. Schab, 9 October 1967: "Press History."

113. D. R. Brown, 11 September 1953: to J. Montgomery of IBM (Bedford, Mass.: MITRE Corporation Archives); D. R. Brown, 20 October 1953: to J. W. Forrester, "Joint MIT-IBM Meeting on Memory-Core Measurement" (Cambridge: MIT Libraries, the Magnetic Core Memory Collection, MC-140, of the Institute Archives and Special Collections).

114. L. Nowakowski, 22 January 1982: conversation with E. W. Pugh.

115. E. W. Pugh, D. L. Critchlow, R. A. Henle, and L. A. Russell, 1981: "Solid State Memory Development in IBM," *IBM Journal of Research and Development* 25, pp. 585–602.

116. U.S. Patent 3,134,163, filed 21 November 1955: H. P. Luhn, "Method for Winding and Assembling Magnetic Cores."

117. L. V. Auletta, H. J. Hallstead, and D. J. Sullivan, 1969: "Ferrite Core Planes and Arrays: IBM's Manufacturing Evolution," *Institute of Electrical and Electronics Engineers Transactions on Magnetics* 5, pp. 764–774.

118. U.S. Patent 2,958,126, filed 4 October 1956: W. P. Shaw and R. W. Link, "Method and Apparatus for Threading Perforated Articles"; W. P. Shaw, 1958: "Wire Inserting Machine Mechanizes Core Plane Assembly," *Automation* 5, pp. 51–54; 2 February 1982: conversation with E. W. Pugh.

119. Pugh, Critchlow, Henle, and Russell, 1981.

120. Watson, Jr., 18 August 1955.

121. Pugh, 1984: pp. 88–89.

122. C. E. McTiernan, 24 November 1959: "License under Forrester Patent No. 2,736,880," summary of meeting between representatives of IBM and Research Corporation on 19 November 1959.

123. C. P. Boberg, 22 May 1961: to H. T. Marcy, "Present Status of Forrester Patent No. 2,736,880." Counts 1, 2, 3, 6, 7, 8, 9, 12, 13, and 14 were awarded to Rajchman, and 4 and 5 were awarded to Forrester.

124. E. Gershuny, 13 May 1982: conversation with E. W. Pugh; C. McTierman, 17 September 1957: to all patent managers.

125. G. R. Williamson, 1 December 1959: to file, "Meeting of Representatives of IBM and Research Corporation to Discuss the Forrester Patent on 11-30-59"; G. R. Williamson, 21 December 1959: to J. W. Birkenstock, "Forrester Avoidance Program."

126. G. R. Williamson, 19 February 1960: to file, "Forrester Patent."

127. Pugh, 1984: pp. 215–218.

128. A. L. Williams, 26 February 1964: to J. R. Killian; MIT and IBM agreement, 26 February 1964.

129. RCA and MIT patent license agreement, 25 March 1964; A. L. Williams, 1 May 1964: to J. A. Stratton.

130. J. F. Hanifin, 9 May 1984: conversation with E. W. Pugh; U.S. v. IBM, 25 January 1956: Final Judgment, Civil Action No. 72-344, U.S. District Court for the Southern District of New York.

131. E. S. Drake, 4 June 1984: conversation with E. W. Pugh; numerical list of U.S. patents issued to IBM and other companies from 1949 to 1978, undated. During the first full year of TDB publication, 292 articles were published; by 1963 the number had increased to 735. Approximately 13 percent of the disclosures submitted during the early 1960s were filed, totaling about 400 patents per year.

132. IBM Corporate Instruction, 29 December 1960; *Business Machines,* January 1961: "The Invention Award Plan."

133. "Progress Report on the EDVAC (Electronic Discrete Variable Computer)," 30 June 1946: University of Pennsylvania, Moore School of Electrical Engineering, Vol. II, pp. 4–22.

134. J. P. Eckert, 9 June 1981: conversation with E. W. Pugh. Eckert says he described his magnetic cell to several people, including R. Snyder at Princeton University and J. W. Forrester at MIT.

Chapter 8

1. W. W. McDowell, 4 January 1950: to J. C. McPherson.

2. J. C. McPherson, 28 March 1950: "IBM Engineering Program."

3. J. D. Hood, 5 October 1951: to W. W. McDowell.

4. *Engineering Laboratory Yearbook,* 1952 (Poughkeepsie: IBM).

5. R. B. Johnson, July 1969: interview by L. M. Saphire. Johnson's date of hire was 15 September 1934.

6. Cooperative Test Service, American Council on Education, October 1936: "Bulletin of Information on the International Test Scoring Machine."

7. G. F. Daly, January 1955: "Historical Record of Card and Machine Development," IBM staff report.

8. IBM Product Planning staff, 9 June 1955: "Analysis of Development of Random Access Systems."

9. R. B. Johnson, 15 December 1957: "Remarks on IBM, San Jose Story."

10. D. W. Kean, 1977: *IBM San Jose: A Quarter Century of Innovation* (San Jose: IBM). This reference contains a great deal of carefully researched detail. Appendix A, p. 103, for example, lists for the first two years all employees and their arrival dates. The Endicott engineers who accompanied Johnson were J. D. Hood and H. F. Martin.

11. Ibid., p. 21.

12. The special representative was Glen E. (Ed) Perkins. According to *IBM Business Machines,* December 1963, he joined IBM in 1925.

13. IBM Product Planning staff, 1955. Also see J. D. Hood, 24 September 1951: to W. W. McDowell, "Automatic Record File System"; S. Brand, 25 May 1953: "Low Speed Random Access Memory System," IBM Technical Report.

14. The broad outlines of a magnetic belt scheme, seemingly simpler than Critchlow's proposal, were discussed months earlier in the Future Demands department at corporate headquarters; see W. H. Johnson, 6 August 1952: to G. A. Roberts, "Review of Requirements for a Large Random Access Memory."

15. L. D. Stevens, December 1957: "Chronological Summary, Evolution of the RAMAC."

16. M. B. Smith, 9 June 1953: to L. H. LaMotte. This memorandum, in summarizing the administrative aspects of IBM's MIFD bid, notes that the Wright Air Development Center, Dayton, Ohio, set up the contract at the recommendation of a study by the Harvard Business School. The contract was won by the Monroe Calculating Machines Company, as noted in J. A. McDonald, 19 August 1953: to L. H. LaMotte.

17. J. A. Weidenhammer, 9 August 1951: "Rabinow Selective Multiple Magnetic Disk Storage Device," IBM Technical Report; J. A. Weidenhammer, 31 August 1951: to D. R. Piatt, "Rabinow Magnetic Disk Storage Device." Weidenhammer (with J. W. Birkenstock and F. E. Hamilton) visited Rabinow in Washington during May 1951 and saw a limited demonstration with a reduced-scale model; his technical report mentions, among many other items, that spinning was being used to distribute and smooth the disk coating mixture of iron powder and synthetic resin. Later in August 1951, when Weidenhammer, J. D. Hood, and others saw a prototype under construction at the F. A. Shepard Laboratories in Summit, New Jersey, Weidenhammer wrote that "actual testing is not to be expected in the near future."

18. J. Rabinow, August 1952: "The Notched-Disk Memory," *Electrical Engineering*, pp. 745–749.

19. Stevens, 1957, identifies the engineer as G. A. Hotham.

20. Ibid.

21. A. J. Critchlow, 2 February 1953: "Proposal for a Rapid Random Access File." Kean, 1977, p. 94, summarizes other parameters of this proposal, among them disk diameter, 16 inches; tracks per inch, 20; tracks per disk side, 82; maximal bits per inch, 200; rotational period, 62.5 milliseconds; and maximal seek time, less than 1 second.

22. Stevens, 1957.

23. IBM Product Planning staff, 1955; Stevens, 1957.

24. R. B. Johnson, 19 May 1977: conversation with C. J. Bashe. Johnson recalled coming to a decision on several matters at the Los Angeles Hundred Percent Club meeting.

25. Stevens, 1957. Assigned to Goddard were W. Gonder, G. Hotham, D. D. Johnson, and J. J. Lynott. Assigned to Haanstra's task force were A. Critchlow, T. Leary, M. Maron, and K. Tremelling. A. E. Ewing, working on magnetic recording, was soon assigned to Haanstra. D. W. Kean continued with a previously assigned task of designing a File-to-Card Machine. E. Quade headed the physics department.

26. W. A. Goddard and G. A. Hotham, 24 November 1953: "Magnetic Disk Random Access File," IBM Technical Report.

27. Kean, 1977: p. 26.

28. D. D. Johnson, 31 August 1953: "An Air Bearing Developed for Magnetic Recording," IBM Technical Report.

29. Stevens, 1957, ascribes the multiplexing idea to J. J. Lynott. For a description of the final actuator, see J. H. Davis and W. E. Dickinson, June 1957: "The Servo Controlled Memory Access in RAMAC," *Automatic Control*, pp. 52–59.

30. Stevens, 1957. Also terminated was the file-to-card machine, a test vehicle described in D. W. Kean and W. A. Goddard, 13 November 1953: "Automatic File-to-Card Machine," IBM Technical Report.

31. IBM press release, 6 May 1955.

32. U.S. Patent No. 2,886,651, filed 8 April 1955: N. A. Vogel, "Air head." In this invention, the bearing's air supply also provided the force that held the head toward the surface, and the head withdrew in the event of air-supply failure. Other advances were described in numerous patents.

33. T. Noyes and W. E. Dickinson, February 1956: "Engineering Design of a Magnetic-Disk Random-Access Memory," *Proceedings of the Western Joint Computer Conference*, pp. 42–44.

34. L. D. Seader, April 1957: "A Self-clocking System for Information Transfer," *IBM Journal of Research and Development*, pp. 181–184. For simplicity and reliability, one clock system (at a nominal 80 kilocycles per second) was used for recording; as a result, for any given track the bit density was inversely proportional to track radius and speed.

35. In 1984, the unit was designated the 16th International Historical Mechanical Engineering Landmark by the American Society of Mechanical Engineers.

36. W. B. Floyd, May 1950: "Electronic Machines for Business Use," *Electronics*, pp. 66–69.

37. L. D. Stevens, 1 November 1983: conversation with C. J. Bashe and L. R. Johnson.

38. H. P. Luhn, 13 March 1953: "Address System for Random Storage," IBM Technical Report. Of primary interest here is the report's first section, said by footnote to have been written on 8 January 1953.

39. R. L. Palmer, 14 December 1951: to a list of engineering managers. For Luhn biographical material, see C. K. Schultz, ed., 1968: *H. P. Luhn: Pioneer of Information Science, Selected Works* (New York: Spartan Books).

40. R. M. Rider, 16 June 1955: "Random Access Systems and Applications," *Proceedings of the Conference on Index Numbers and Applications*, IBM Technical Report, ed. L. H. Haibt and W. W. Peterson, p. 25. The twenty-one-character air force inventory code was noted as a case of exceptional length.

41. W. P. Heising, May 1958: "Methods of File Organization for Efficient Use of IBM RAMAC Files," *Proceedings of the Western Joint Computer Conference*, pp. 194–196. Heising, referring to the basic chaining method, reported the expected number of seeks as $1 + 0.5f$, where f is the fraction of the file space containing records. The expected chain-length proportions for a sample of n random numbers are given exactly by an appropriate binomial probability distribution. These results, which vary slightly with n, converge as n grows large toward those given by the n-independent Poisson probability distribution. The Poisson formula, which is very convenient and provides an excellent approximation for all but small n, served Luhn's purposes in 1953 and Heising's in 1958.

42. A. C. Reynolds, Jr., 30 June 1953: to H. F. Wicklund, "Address Scheme for Random Access Storage."

43. J. W. Haanstra, D. W. Kean, and M. E. Maron, 15 July 1953: "Automatic Addressing for Random Access Storage Units," IBM Technical Report. Luhn's work presumably became known to San Jose personnel in late February 1953, when Stevens and Critchlow visited Wright Field with Luhn.

44. Haanstra did not mention the binary search, even though it had been programmed for the Defense Calculator. See E. F. Codd, 27 April 1951: "Table Look-up: Varying-Interval Table in Electrostatic Storage (Binary Search)," IBM Technical Report.

45. J. W. Haanstra, L. H. Bixby, and M. E. Maron, 2 December 1953: "Manual of Information on the Design of a Magnetic Disk Processing Machine," IBM Technical Report.

46. W. W. McDowell, 17 February 1954: to J. W. Birkenstock.

47. F. J. Wesley, 8 October 1954: to L. H. LaMotte.

48. Kean, 1977; Stevens, December 1957. Teamed with Stevens were J. W. Haanstra, R. Haug, T. G. Leary, M. L. Lesser, J. J. Nolan, and W. W. Woodbury.

49. M. L. Lesser: quoted in Kean, 1977, pp. 38–39.

50. *Digital Computer Newsletter 7*, January 1955.

51. Stevens, 1957.

52. Kean, 1977: p. 45.

53. *Digital Computer Newsletter 8*, October 1956. For a discussion of the machine, see R. P. Daly, February 1956: "Integrated Data Processing with the Univac File Computer," *Proceedings of the Western Joint Computer Conference*, pp. 95–98. Its storage capacity could be tripled with special additional equipment.

54. IBM Product Announcements, 4 September 1956: IBM 305 RAMAC, Letter 256-114 and RAM 650, Letter 256-ll7. G. Smith, 18 October 1956: to Branch Managers, withdraws the word "RAM" (apparently because of a tape-strip development by Potter Instrument Co.).

55. M. L. Lesser and J. W. Haanstra, December 1956: "The RAMAC Data-Processing Machine: System Organization of the IBM 305," *Proceedings of the Eastern Joint Computer Conference*, pp. 139–146; and D. Royse, February 1957: "The IBM 650 RAMAC System Disk Storage Operation," *Proceedings of the Western Joint Computer Conference*, pp. 43–49, provide design rationales. The 350 disk unit in the 305 system was announced with one access mechanism, the 355 disk unit in the 650 system with three. Because of the 650's encoding conventions, 355 capacity was 6 million decimal digits.

56. Two definitions of "track" appeared, it should be noted. Engineers usually confined the term to a disk surface, so that in the 305 context a track contained 500 characters (five sectors). RAMAC product planners, on the other hand, extended the term to both sides of the disk, so that the forked arm, in one seek of a track, reached ten sectors with its two heads.

57. IBM RAMAC 305 Bulletin, 1958 and 1960: "The Chaining Method of Disk Storage Addressing for the RAMAC 305." Also see Manual of Operation, 1957: "305 RAMAC" (IBM Form 22-6264-1).

58. H. P. Luhn, 16 June 1955: "Address System for Random Access Storage," *Proceedings of the Conference on Index Numbers and Methods*, IBM Technical Report.

59. B. E. Phelps, 29 August 1956: to H. P. Luhn.

60. A. I. Dumey, December 1956: "Indexing for Rapid Random Access Memory," *Computers and Automation 5*, pp. 6–9.

61. W. W. Peterson, April 1957: "Addressing for Random-Access Storage," *IBM Journal of Research and Development 1*, pp. 130–146. This paper, which had been completed over six months earlier by an author who was leaving IBM to teach and who knew of Luhn's work as proprietary, reported on computer simulations done in Poughkeepsie to appraise the behavior under various conditions of a randomizing load-and-search scheme referred to as the "open method." The method was especially advantageous for short-lived or rapidly changing tables and files that did not fully occupy available storage. It loaded a record by randomizing to a location and, if that location were occupied, visiting locations consecutively upward (and around to the first location if necessary) until finding an empty location; search for the record compared keys over the same route. Records could be inserted simply by randomizing to a location and then, if necessary, scanning upward for an empty location. Because the average number of locations visited per search had not been reduced to a formula, the empirical study was indeed welcome; for example, since the average rose steeply as storage approached full occupancy, the study gave the user an

empirical basis for trading more storage as a way of reducing search processing. As might be expected, visits per search were higher for the open method than for the chaining method, making the former inadvisable for most applications of disks. The open method was said by Peterson to have been devised in 1954 for symbol-table search during program assembly by A. L. Samuel, G. M. Amdahl, and E. M. Boehm in the Poughkeepsie laboratory. Luhn's work with randomization was not mentioned. Luhn ignored the matter, apparently seeing no graceful way of claiming credit for long-unpublished work.

62. *IBM San Jose News*, July 1957.

63. IBM Sales Manual of Electronic Data Processing Machines, 4 September 1956.

64. IBM 305 RAMAC Bulletins 1 and 2, 1958.

65. *IBM DPD Newstrack*, April 1981.

66. *IBM San Jose News*, 17 June 1959: "Air Force Supply Uses RAMAC."

67. H. K. Baumeister, 10 December 1954: "Floating Magnetic Drum Heads," IBM Technical Report; C. Handen, 1 January 1957: "An Investigation of Air-Lubricated Shoes for High-Density Magnetic Drum Head Applications," IBM Technical Report.

68. J. J. Hagopian was the engineer, as reported by J. M. Harker, D. W. Brede, R. E. Pattison, G. R. Santana, and L. G. Taft, September 1981: "A Quarter Century of Disk File Innovation," *IBM Journal of Research and Development 25*, pp. 677–689.

69. M. C. Shaw and E. F. Macks, 1949: *Analysis and Lubrication of Bearings* (New York: McGraw-Hill), pp. 164–176, speak of a shoe as a stationary plate and a slider as a moving plate, but the literature on disks slowly came to use "slider" for the stationary plate and "surface" for the moving disk.

70. IBM Development Report, 1st Quarter 1955. The project leaders at the outset were C. A. Bergfors and R. M. Hermes.

71. IBM Development Report, 2d Quarter 1956.

72. J. M. Harker, A. S. Hoagland, H. K. St. Clair, and W. A. Goddard, 10 December 1956: "A 50-million Character Random Access Magnetic Disk Memory," IBM Research Report.

73. J. W. Haanstra, 18 April 1956: to S. W. Dunwell, "Stretch RAM." Also see J. M. Harker, A. S. Hoagland, H. K. St. Clair, and W. A. Goddard, 18 December 1956: "Status of Stretch Magnetic Disk Memory," IBM Research Report.

74. Handen, 1957.

75. L. D. Lipschutz, September 1957: "Status Report on SCRAM," IBM Research Report. Also see L. D. Lipshutz, J. P. Harris, O. Kornei, and R. G. Gates, February 1959: "Final Report on SCRAM," IBM Research Report.

76. W. A. Gross, October 1984: "Origins and Early Development of Air-bearing Magnetic Heads for Disk-file Digital Storage Systems," Preprint, *American Society of Mechanical Engineers Lubrication Conference*.

77. W. A. Gross, July 1959: "A Gas Film Lubrication Study, Part I: Some Theoretical Analyses of Slider Bearings," pp. 237–255; W. A. Michael, "Part II: Numerical Solution of the Reynolds Equation for Finite Slider Bearings," pp. 256–259; R. K. Brunner, J. M. Harker, K. E. Haughton, and A. G. Osterlund, "Part III: Experimental Investigation of Pivoted Slider Bearings," pp. 260–274; all in the *IBM Journal of Research and Development 3*.

78. L. H. LaMotte, 29 July 1957: to E. R. Piore.

79. M. M. Gibson, J. W. Haanstra, and T. Noyes, 15 November 1957: "Large Capacity Random Access Memory Study," IBM Technical Report.

80. J. M. Harker, 26 March 1958: "Report on the Test Bed for a High-Speed, High-Capacity Random Access Memory," IBM Technical Report.

81. T. Noyes, 1958: IBM Development Report.

82. D. D. Willard, 1958: IBM Development Report.

83. A. S. Hoagland, July 1958: "Track Density Considerations in Magnetic Recording and the Single Disk File Track Access Servo System," IBM Research Report; Hoagland and C. F. Muehlenweg, October 1958: "Random Access Memory Magnetic Strip File Storage," IBM Research Report; and B. Edwards, March 1959: "Preliminary Investigations of Three Different Magnetic Surfaces," IBM Research Report.

84. A. S. Hoagland, 1961: "A High Track-Density Servo-Access System for Magnetic Recording Disk Storage," *IBM Journal of Research and Development* 5, pp. 287–296.

85. J. M. Harker, H. K. St. Clair, and D. L. Stephenson, 5 June 1958: "Low Cost Data Processing Machines: Preliminary Report."

86. J. M. Harker, 9 February 1959: "Objectives for a Low Cost Random Access File Program," IBM Technical Report.

87. J. M. Harker, August 1960: "Remarks on Air Bearings," IBM RAMP Conference I minutes.

88. A. S. Hoagland, H. A. Mussell, and J. M. Norton, 8 February 1960: "ADF Technical Audit Committee Report." Norton served as committee chairman.

89. Kean, 1977: p. 55.

90. A. F. Shugart, August 1960: "Remarks on Advanced Disk File," IBM RAMP Conference I minutes. For an evaluation of the delivered parallel-disk unit, see B. G. Carlson and E. A. Voorhees, March 1963: "Use of the Disc File on STRETCH," *Disc File Applications, Reports presented at the Nation's First Disc File Symposium*, pp. 17–18, where the authors reported that the unit could record the entire content of the Los Alamos Stretch memory (nearly 100,000 words) in less than a second and that its reliability had been very high.

91. W. L. Slover, March 1963: "Characteristics of the Bryant 4000 Series Disc File," *Disc File Applications, Reports presented at the Nation's First Disc File Symposium*, pp. 29–51. In Section 3.3.6 of "Memory Products," 7 May 1962, STORE Task Group Final Report, IBM technical planners wrote, "In the long term we must consider [the] 1301 no more than equal to Bryant files in competitive systems." However, San Jose soon outdistanced its own 1301.

92. K. E. Haughton and R. K. Brunner, 20 February 1961: "Pivoted Slider Bearings in a Non-ideal Environment," IBM Technical Report.

93. R. J. Cappell, 31 March 1961: "Hydraulic Corrosion Analysis," IBM Technical Report.

94. IBM Product Announcement, 2 June 1961: 1301 Disk Storage. Of the fifty surfaces in a module, only forty were available for data storage. The two outside surfaces were unused, one surface was used for clocking and another for format control, and six surfaces were reserved for field engineering.

95. *IBM San Jose News*, 7 June 1961.

96. R. W. Parker, September 1965: "The SABRE System," Datamation, pp. 49–52.

97. W. A. Stetler, V. G. Spiegel, and R. C. Braen, 15 December 1959: "Vertical Magnetic Drum with Floating Head," IBM Technical Report; *IBM Command Control*

Center News, 15 March 1961; and IBM Product Announcement, 6 December 1962: IBM 7320 Drum Storage.

98. IBM Product Announcement, 23 September 1963: 1302 Disk Storage.

99. *IBM San Jose News*, 9 August 1961.

100. See, for example, H. P. Luhn, 31 August 1959: "Keyword-in-Context Index for Technical Literature (KWIC Index)," IBM Technical Report, which was presented to the American Chemical Society in September 1959 and published in *American Documentation 11*, 1960, pp. 288–295.

101. Kean, 1977: pp. 79–80. Under the name IBM 1360 Photo-Digital Storage System, the first system was delivered on 30 September 1967 to the Lawrence Radiation Laboratory, Livermore, California; see R. M. Furman, 15 May 1968: "IBM 1360 Photo-Digital Storage System," IBM Technical Report. For a technical description of the 1360, see J. D. Kuehler and H. R. Kerby, 1966: "A Photo-Digital Mass Storage System," *Proceedings of the Fall Joint Computer Conference*, pp. 735–742. A simpler system, which stored images on microfilm, was announced as the IBM 1350 Photo Image Retrieval System in May 1966 and soon withdrawn for lack of sufficient acceptance.

102. For a description of the product, see A. F. Shugart and Y. H. Tong, 1966: "IBM 2321 Data Cell Drive," *Proceedings of the Spring Joint Computer Conference*, pp. 335–345. The 2321 proved to be an interim product in the sense that it did not found a continuing product family.

103. N. Statland and J. R. Hillegass, December 1963: "Random Access Storage Devices: An Appraisal," *Datamation*, pp. 34–45. This survey finds Burroughs, Control Data, GE, Honeywell, and RCA offering disk storage; Sperry Univac offering drums; and NCR offering a unit based on magnetic cards.

104. A. F. Shugart, 5 December 1960: to V.R. Witt.

105. J. D. Carothers, R. K. Brunner, J. L. Dawson, M. O. Halfhill, and R .E. Kubec, 1963: "A New High Density Recording System: The IBM 1311 Disk Storage Drive with Interchangeable Disk Packs," *Proceedings of the Fall Joint Computer Conference*, pp. 327–340.

106. IBM Product announcement, 11 October 1962: 1311 Disk Storage Drive.

Chapter 9

1. J. P. Eckert and J. W. Mauchly, 30 September 1945: "Automatic High Speed Computing—A Progress Report on the EDVAC," Moore School of Electrical Engineering, University of Pennsylvania, pp. 39–40, 77. A report of work under a contract between the U.S. Army Ordnance Department and the University of Pennsylvania.

2. A. M. Turing, 1945: "Proposals for Development in the Mathematics Division of an Automatic Computing Engine (ACE)," Report E882 (Executive Committee, National Physical Laboratory). Reprinted, with a foreword by D. W. Davies, April 1972: Report Com. Sci. 57 (National Physical Laboratory), reprint pp. 11–14, 28–32.

3. A. W. Burks, H. H. Goldstine, and J. von Neumann, 2 September 1947 (second edition): "Preliminary Discussion of the Logical Design of an Electronic Computing Instrument," pp. 36–37. The report, an expansion of the first edition dated 28 June 1946, is part I, volume I of a series of reports prepared by the Institute for Advanced

Study under a contract with the Research and Development Service, U.S. Army Ordnance Department. It is reprinted in *John von Neumann, Collected Works*, ed. A. H. Taub (New York: Macmillan, 1963), Volume 5.

4. H. H. Goldstine and J. von Neumann, 16 August 1948: "Planning and Coding of Problems for an Electronic Computing Instrument," pp. 15–23. The report is part II, volume III of a series of reports prepared under a contract between the Research and Development Service, U.S. Army Ordnance Department, and the Institute for Advanced Study.

5. L. H. Thomas, August 1948: "Computation of Statistical Fields for Atoms and Ions," and H. Polachek, August 1948: "Computation of Shock Wave Refraction on the Selective Sequence Electronic Calculator," both in *Proceedings — Scientific Computation Forum — 1948* (New York: IBM), pp. 123–126, 107–122; R. R. Seeber, 11 April 1949: to J. C. McPherson et al.

6. M. V. Wilkes, 1949: "The Design of a Practical High-Speed Computing Machine. The EDSAC," in "A Discussion on Computing Machines" (discussion held 4 March 1948), *Proceedings of the Royal Society of London A 195*, pp. 265–287.

7. M. V. Wilkes, 1975: "Early Computer Developments at Cambridge: The EDSAC," *The Radio and Electronic Engineer 45*, pp. 332–335.

8. D. J. Wheeler, June 1949: "Planning the Use of a Paper Library," *Report of a Conference on High Speed Automatic Calculating-Machines* (Cambridge: University Mathematical Laboratory with the cooperation of the Ministry of Supply), pp. 36–40.

9. D. J. Wheeler, 1950: "Programme Organization and Initial Orders for EDSAC," *Proceedings of the Royal Society of London A 202*, pp. 573–589.

10. Wilkes, 1975.

11. Turing, 1945, p. 12.

12. Wheeler, 1950.

13. M. V. Wilkes, June 1949: Abstract of summary remark in "Discussion of Plans, Projects and General Ideas," *Report of a Conference on High Speed Automatic Calculating-Machines* (Cambridge: University Mathematical Laboratory with the cooperation of the Ministry of Supply), pp. 123–133.

14. M. V. Wilkes, D. J. Wheeler, and S. Gill, 1951: *The Preparation of Programs for an Elevctronic Digital Computer* (Cambridge, Mass.: Addison-Wesley Press).

15. N. Rochester, 2 October 1950: "Assembly of Programs on the Test Assembly," IBM Technical Report.

16. M. Campbell-Kelly, 1980: "Programming the EDSAC: Early Programming Activity at the University of Cambridge," *Annals of the History of Computing 2, pp. 7–36; M. V. Wilkes, 1980: "Early Programming Developments in Cambridge," in A History of Computing in the Twentieth Century*, ed. N. Metropolis, J. Howlett, and G.-C. Rota (New York: Academic Press); W. F. McClelland, 11 May 1982: conversation with J. H. Palmer.

17. Rochester exhibited the Wheeler calling sequence somewhat earlier in a paper on TPM subroutines. See N. Rochester, 27 November 1950: "The Use of Subprograms on the TPM," IBM Technical Report.

18. R. R. Seeber, August 1967: interview by L. M. Saphire.

19. McClelland, 11 May 1982; W. F. McClelland, undated: " 'Split unit' Coding for SSEC," from J. C. McPherson 1949 files.

20. N. Rochester, October 1967: interview by L. M. Saphire; McClelland, 11 May 1982. The word "assembly" was a natural choice to characterize this process; it

endured as the name for a broader class of programming aids. It was used in a statement emanating from England's National Physical Laboratory that described Turing's late 1945 plan, including a subroutine library, for the ACE: "the instructions for a particular problem will be assembled from these prefabricated units." See statement by the Department of Scientific and Industrial Research, published in part in "Calculation and Electronics—Automatic Computator Designed by the N.P.L.," *The Electrician 137*, 8 November 1946, pp. 1279–1280. J. W. Mauchly used it two months later at the January 1947 Harvard symposium: "Here, then, are a number of instructions which were never before assembled into the same problem; so they will not, of course, always be placed at the same point in the memory." He also, however, used the word "compilation" to describe the same process. See J. W. Mauchly, January 1947: "Preparation of Problems for EDVAC-Type Machines," *Proceedings of a Symposium on Large-Scale Digital Calculating Machinery* (Cambridge: Harvard University Press), pp. 203–207.

21. W. F. McClelland, undated: "Notes on Programming Systems and Techniques for the IBM Type 701 Electronic Data Processing Machines." The notes were prepared for a course conducted for customers in the Los Angeles area in March 1953.

22. McClelland, 11 May 1982.

23. N. Rochester, 18 January 1950: "A Program for Sorting," IBM Technical Report.

24. H. H. Goldstine and J. von Neumann, 1 April 1947: "Planning and Coding of Problems for an Electronic Computing Instrument," pp. 4–23. The report is part II, volume I of a series of reports prepared under a contract between the Research and Development Service, U.S. Army Ordnance Department, and the Institute for Advanced Study.

25. W. Buchholz, 13 Feburary 1950: "A Program for Merging Two Files," IBM Technical Report.

26. N. Rochester, 24 October 1950: "Assembly of Programs on the Test Assembly (Revised)," IBM Technical Report.

27. Goldstine and von Neumann chose not to use the explanatory column in the coding examples of volumes II and III of "Planning and Coding of Problems for an Electronic Computing Instrument," in 1947 and 1948, rendering those volumes more difficult to read than volume I.

28. N. Rochester, 31 January 1951: "The Use of Symbolic Addresses in Programming," IBM Technical Report.

29. N. Rochester, 29 April 1951: "Assembly Program No. 1 for the Defense Calculator," IBM Technical Report.

30. J. W. Carr III, December 1951: "Extension of Remarks Made from the Floor," *Review of Electronic Digital Computers, Joint AIEE-IRE Computer Conference* (New York: American Institute of Electrical Engineers), pp. 113–114.

31. M. V. Wilkes, September 1952: "Pure and Applied Programming," *Proceedings of the Association for Computing Machinery*, pp. 121–124; J. W. Carr III, May 1952: "Progress of the Whirlwind Computer towards an Automatic Coding Procedure," *Proceedings of the Association for Computing Machinery*, pp. 237–241.

32. Engineering project file, 701 Calculator, Progress Reports section; N. Rochester, 3 August 1952: "Symbolic Programming," prepared for a customer class in August 1952; N. Rochester, 1953: "Symbolic Programming," *Transactions of the Institute of Radio Engineers Professional Group on Electronic Computers EC-2*, March 1953, pp. 10–15 (correction appears in: vol. EC-2, June 1953, p. 27).

33. IBM document, undated: "Regional Programming," prepared for a customer class in August 1952.

34. Engineering project file, 701 Calculator, Progress Reports section; D. Orton, 25 August 1952: to T. J. Watson, Jr.

35. McClelland, 11 May 1982.

36. I. Ziller, January 1968: interview by L. M. Saphire.

37. W. G. Bouricius, December 1953: "Operating Experience with the Los Alamos 701," *Proceedings of the Eastern Joint Computer Conference*, pp. 45–47; R. B. Lazarus, E. A. Voorhees, M. B. Wells, and W. J. Worlton, May 1978: "Computing at LASL in the 1940s and 1950s," Los Alamos Scientific Laboratory of the University of California Report LA-6943-H.

38. C. L. Baker, 18 February 1953: "Symbolic Coding for Type 701 Calculator," Douglas Aircraft Company, Inc. report.

39. C. C. Hurd, 26 March 1982: unedited transcript of film on FORTRAN history prepared for IBM exhibit at the 1982 National Computer Conference sponsored by the American Federation of Information Processing Societies (Bright Star Films).

40. W. P. Heising, 2 November 1983: conversation with J. H. Palmer; Lazarus et al., May 1978.

41. W. P. Heising, January 1968: interview by L. M. Saphire.

42. Engineering project file, 701 Calculator, Progress Reports section; D. W. Ladd and J. W. Sheldon, September 1952: "The Numerical Solution of a Partial Differential Equation on the IBM Type 701 Electronic Data Processing Machines," *Proceedings of the Association for Computing Machinery*, pp. 115–117; J. W. Sheldon, 1955: "Use of the Statistical Field Approximation in Molecular Physics," *Physical Review 99*, pp. 1291–1301. Solutions to the equation, known as the Thomas-Fermi-Dirac equation, derived in 1930, permitted one to obtain the charge and energy distribution of electrons in certain atomic structures. Except for approximate or limited ones, solutions were not practical before the advent of computers. The 701 program, written by Sheldon with the assistance of two colleagues, took 80 minutes to obtain a solution to the Thomas-Fermi-Dirac equation for a particular configuration of the nitrogen molecule.

43. D. B. MacMillan and R. H. Stark, 1951: " 'Floating Decimal' Calculation on the IBM Card-Programmed Electronic Calculator," *IBM Applied Science Department Technical Newsletter No. 2*, February 1951, pp. 16–26 (published, amended, in *Mathematical Tables and Other Aids to Computation V*, April 1951, pp. 86–92); Heising, 2 November 1983.

44. Ziller, January 1968; Heising, 2 November 1983.

45. C. C. Hurd, 11 October 1972: interview by H. S. Tropp and R. Mapstone (Smithsonian Computer History Project, joint project of the American Federation of Information Processing Societies and the Smithsonian Institution); J. W. Sheldon, 12 October 1951: to C. C. Hurd.

46. Wilkes, Wheeler, and Gill, 1951.

47. R. A. Brooker and D. J. Wheeler, 1953: "Floating Operations on the EDSAC," *Mathematical Tables and Other Aids to Computation VII*, pp. 37–47.

48. Carr, May 1952.

49. Hurd, 26 March 1982; C. C. Hurd, 8 March 1972: in *SHARE Meeting for Pioneers*, discussion conducted by H. S. Tropp at SHARE XXXVIII, San Francisco, California; Bouricius, December 1953.

50. L. H. Amaya, 1983: "The 701 Installation at Lockheed Aircraft," *Annals of the History of Computing 5*, pp. 184–185.

51. *IBM Record*, April 1953: "Staff Conducts Classes, Works Problems"; F. S. Beckman, 29 September 1983: conversation with J. H. Palmer; L. Tatum, 31 October 1952: to L. H. LaMotte.

52. Sheldon, 12 October 1951.

53. J. W. Backus, December 1967: interview by L. M. Saphire.

54. W. G. Bouricius, 15 June 1984: conversation with J. H. Palmer.

55. D. A. Quarles, Jr., 13 June 1984: conversation with J. H. Palmer; J. W. Sheldon, 2 March 1953: to C. C. Hurd and J. C. McPherson.

56. IBM Manual, 1954: "IBM Speedcoding System for the Type 701 Electronic Data Processing Machines" (IBM Form 24-6059-0). Information in the manual is "as of September 10, 1953."

57. J. W. Backus, 1954: "The IBM 701 Speedcoding System," *Journal of the Association for Computing Machinery 1*, pp. 4–6 (the paper was presented at the meeting of the association, 9–11 September 1953); Beckman, 29 September 1983.

58. J. W. Backus and H. L. Herrick, May 1954: "IBM 701 Speedcoding and Other Automatic-Programming Systems," *Symposium on Automatic Programming for Digital Computers* (Washington: Office of Naval Research, Department of the Navy), pp. 106–113.

59. IBM Manual, 1954: "IBM Speedcoding System for the Type 701 Electronic Data Processing Machines" (IBM Form 24-6059-0).

60. F. C. Williams, 1975: "Early Computers at Manchester University," *The Radio and Electronic Engineer 45*, pp. 327–331.

61. T. Kilburn, June 1949: "The Manchester University Digital Computing Machine," *Report of a Conference on High Speed Automatic Calculating-Machines* (Cambridge: University Mathematical Laboratory with the cooperation of the Ministry of Supply), pp. 119–122; N. Rochester, 9 August 1949: "The Logical Organization of Prof. F. C. Williams' Calculator"; *IBM Business Machines*, 22 August 1949: "At Plant 2, Poughkeepsie, N.Y."

62. W. H. Thomas, 13 February 1953: to N. Rochester. The power of index registers to shorten programs is most evident when writing iterative programs for which more than one instruction is to be modified for each execution of a program loop, for example, when adding two vectors in storage to produce and store a third vector.

63. IBM Manual, 1954: "IBM Speedcoding System for the Type 701 Electronic Data Processing Machines" (IBM Form 24-6059-0). Alphabetic abbreviations for the operation codes were written on the coding form and punched on the program cards to make printed program listings more comprehensible.

64. J. C. McPherson, 15 February 1954: "Speedcoding" (memorandum).

65. Backus, December 1967; Heising, January 1968; J. C. Smith, 16 October 1953: "701 Improvement Program"; C. W. Adams, November 1955: "Developments in Programming Research," *Proceedings of the Eastern Joint Computer Conference*, pp. 75–79.

66. Sheldon had headed the Technical Computing Bureau in New York for over three years, during the transition from 604 to CPC to 701. With a strong knowledge of both physics and mathematics and a natural aptitude for developing efficient problem-solving procedures, he was influential in establishing a balanced perception of programming in IBM. His example showed it to be a job to which a broad range

of skills and traits, ranging from intellectual ability to patience, could be applied, one that could be extremely satisfying, and one that was a factor in the developing economic equation that would determine whether a new industry was emerging. In 1955 Sheldon and E. C. Kubie, who had played a crucial role in the late phases of development of the 650, founded Computer Usage Company, a pioneering firm in the business of selling EDP services, including programming.

67. *The IBM Record*, 23 October 1953: "Brown University Applied Mathematics Seminar Members Visit WHQ"; *IBM Business Machines*, 1 March 1955: "Electronic Data Processing Service Is Organized at WHQ" (Field-WHQ News section).

68. D. R. Mason, 1983: "The 701 in the IBM Technical Computing Bureau," *Annals of the History of Computing* 5, pp. 176–177.

69. R. M. Peterson, January 1957: "Automatic Coding at G.E.," *Automatic Coding—Proceedings of the Symposium Held January 24–25, 1957 at the Franklin Institute in Philadelphia* (Philadelphia: The Franklin Institute), pp. 3–16.

70. J. S. Morison, August 1953: "701 Symposium Notes," Douglas Aircraft Company, Inc. report; N. Rochester, 10 September 1953: "A Meeting of 701 Customers in Los Angeles on August 17–18, 1953," IBM Technical Report.

71. J. W. Backus, 1981: "The History of FORTRAN I, II, and III," in *History of Programming Languages*, ed. R. L. Wexelblat (New York: Academic Press).

72. The early UNIVAC compilers copied most subroutines "in line" on the program load tape. A particular subroutine, for example, one that calculated a logarithm, would thus appear on the tape and in the program as often as it was invoked by the programmer's code. The exceptions were subroutines for the four basic operations of floating-point arithmetic, which were perceived to be required for all compiled programs and therefore were loaded into a fixed storage area reserved for them.

73. G. M. Hopper, May 1952: "The Education of a Computer," *Proceedings of the Association for Computing Machinery*, pp. 243–249; G. M. Hopper, 1953: "Compiling Routines," *Computers and Automation* 2, pp. 1–5.

74. D. E. Knuth and L. T. Pardo, 1977: "The Early Development of Programming Languages," in *Encyclopedia of Computer Science and Technology, Volume 7*, ed. J. Belzer, A. G. Holzman, and A. Kent (New York: Marcel Dekker).

75. Mason, 1983.

76. Ziller, January 1968.

77. G. M. Hopper, May 1954: "Automatic Programming—Definitions," *Symposium on Automatic Programming for Digital Computers* (Washington: Office of Naval Research, Department of the Navy), pp. 1–5.

78. Backus and Herrick, May 1954.

79. C. W. Adams and J. H. Laning, Jr., May 1954: "The M.I.T. Systems of Automatic Coding: Comprehensive, Summer Session, and Algebraic," *Symposium on Automatic Programming for Digital Computers* (Washington: Office of Naval Research, Department of the Navy), pp. 40–68. The MIT algebraic system was built by J. H. Laning, Jr., and N. Zierler. Whirlwind did not have floating-point instructions. The system compiled pseudo-floating-point instructions, which were executed interpretively.

80. Backus, 1981.

81. *IBM Business Machines*, 3 May 1954: "EDPM Programming Research Dept. Is Organized" (Field News section).

82. Petersen, January 1957.

83. R. L. Cline, 5 December 1983: conversation with J. H. Palmer; IBM Manual, 1954: "IBM Electronic Data Processing Machines Type 702, Programming Manual, Volume 1" (IBM Form 22-6624-0).

84. *IBM Business Machines*, 15 April 1954: "Special Sales Department is Established for Electronic Data Processing Machines" (Field News section).

85. Cline, 5 December 1983.

86. R. M. Wight, 25 May 1955: to C. A. Sterling, Jr. The 705 orders included conversion of 702 orders that had scheduled delivery dates after 1955.

87. H. B. Ainsley, Jr., 18 May 1955: to T. E. Clemmons.

88. Cline, 5 December 1983; *IBM Business Machines*, 1 March 1955: "Electronic Data Processing Service Is Organized at WHQ" (Field-WHQ News section); *IBM Business Machines*, 15 August 1955: "Marvel on Madison Avenue."

89. Cline, 5 December 1983.

90. E. M. Kerksieck, 10 March 1956: "Report: Applied Programming—1956"; E. M. Kerksieck, 9 January 1957: to C. R. DeCarlo.

91. Bouricius, December 1953. Bouricius left Los Alamos in early 1955 to join the engineering planning function at the IBM Poughkeepsie laboratory; later he established a computing center, equipped initially with a 650 and a 704, to support research and engineering work at the laboratory.

92. F. J. Gruenberger, 1959: "A Short History of Computing in Southern California," *Computing News* 7, 15 March 1959, pp. 23–31 (reprinted in *Annals of the History of Computing* 2, July 1980, pp. 246–250).

93. F. V. Wagner, 16 November 1954: "Los Angeles Cooperative Compiler Project, Policy Committee, Minutes of First Meeting," North American Aviation, Inc. report; W. S. Melahn, 1956: "A Description of a Cooperative Venture in the Production of an Automatic Coding System," *Journal of the Association for Computing Machinery 3*, pp. 266–271; R. G. Selfridge, June 1956: "The PACT Compiler for the 701," *Symposium on Advanced Programming Methods for Digital Computers* (Washington: Office of Naval Research, Department of the Navy), pp. 67–70.

94. F. Jones, June 1956: "SHARE—A Study in the Reduction of Redundant Programming Effort Through the Promotion of Inter-Installation Communication," *Symposium on Advanced Programming Methods for Digital Computers* (Washington: Office of Naval Research, Department of the Navy), pp. 67–70; P. Armer, November 1956: "SHARE," *Proceedings, Second Annual Electronic Business Systems Conference*, pp. 12–17 (reprinted, adapted, in *Annals of the History of Computing 2*, April 1980, pp. 122–129).

95. Beckman, 29 September 1983.

96. F. S. Beckman, 7 March 1955: to D. R. Mason and W. P. Heising; Armer, November 1956.

97. Heising, January 1968; Heising, 2 November 1983.

98. *IBM Applied Science Division Technical Newsletter No. 8*, September 1954.

99. Heising, 2 November 1983.

100. Ibid.; E. F. Shepherd, August 1955: "An Automatic Method of Optimum Programming for the 650 Using the 650," *IBM Applied Science Division Technical Newsletter No. 10*, October 1955.

101. Heising, 2 November 1983.

102. S. Poley and G. E. Mitchell, 15 November 1955: "SOAP, IBM N.Y. Symbolic Optimal Assembly Program, Programmer's Guide."

103. Heising, 2 November 1983.

104. C. R. DeCarlo, 12 September 1956: to EAM Sales Representatives and Applied Science Representatives.

105. R. Mapstone and M. I. Bernstein, 1980: "Meetings in Retrospect," *Annals of the History of Computing 2*, pp. 363–372; J. L. Greenstadt, 8 March 1972: in *SHARE Meeting for Pioneers*, discussion conducted by H. S. Tropp.

106. Heising, 2 November 1983; IBM Announcement, 1 August 1955: Data Processing Center Opening, Letter 4905; Manual of Operation, Preliminary Edition, 1954 revised January 1956: "IBM Electronic Data-Processing Machines Type 704" (IBM Form 24-6661-1).

107. Mapstone and Bernstein, 1980; *Proceedings of the First Meeting of SHARE*, week of 22 August 1955; *Proceedings of the Second Meeting of SHARE*, 12–13 September 1955; *Proceedings of the Third Meeting of SHARE*, 10–11 November 1955; *Proceedings of the Fourth Meeting of SHARE*, 6, 10 February 1956.

108. L. H. LaMotte, 21 February 1956: to T. V. Learson et al.

109. J. C. McPherson, 16 January 1956: to L. H. LaMotte.

110. LaMotte, 21 February 1956.

111. R. Goldfinger, February 1956: "The IBM Type 705 Autocoder," *Proceedings of the Western Joint Computer Conference*, pp. 49–51; E. M. Kerksieck, 1 March 1957: to R. L. Cline.

112. Backus, 1981.

113. J. W. Backus and W. P. Heising, 1964: "FORTRAN," *IEEE Transactions on Electronic Computers EC-13*, pp. 382–385; F. E. Allen, June 1982: "A Technological Review of the FORTRAN I Compiler," *Proceedings of the 1982 National Computer Conference*, pp. 805–809.

114. Backus, 1981.

115. IBM Programmer's Reference Manual, 15 October 1956: "The FORTRAN Automatic Coding System for the IBM 704 EDPM."

116. J. W. Backus, R. J. Beeber, S. Best, R. Goldberg, L. M. Haibt, H. L. Herrick, R. A. Nelson, D. Sayre, P. B. Sheridan, H. Stern, I. Ziller, R. A. Hughes, and R. Nutt, February 1957: "The FORTRAN Automatic Coding System," *Proceedings of the Western Joint Computer Conference*, pp. 188–198. Ten of the authors were IBM employees. The other three joined the FORTRAN project on a loan basis from other organizations: Best from MIT, Hughes from the University of California Radiation Laboratory at Livermore, California, and Nutt from United Aircraft Corporation at East Hartford, Connecticut.

117. Backus, 1981.

118. Ziller, January 1968.

119. Backus, 1981.

120. J. W. Backus, November 1958: "Automatic Programming: Properties and Performance of FORTRAN Systems I and II," *Mechanization of Thought Processes, Proceedings of a Symposium Held at the National Physical Laboratory* (London: Her Majesty's Stationery Office), pp. 231–255.

121. G. F. Ryckman, 1981: Transcript of discussant's remarks at the FORTRAN session of the 1978 ACM SIGPLAN History of Programming Languages Conference, in *History of Programming Languages*, ed. Wexelblat, pp. 66–68.

122. *IBM Business Machines*, 23 January 1957: "SBC—New Initials on the IBM Horizon."

123. *IBM Business Machines*, 27 March 1957: "Manager of Applied Programming Named" (Field-WHQ News section); *IBM Business Machines*, 29 April 1957: "Programming Managers Named in WHQ Applied Science Department" (Field-WHQ News Section).

124. W. P. Heising, 1963: "FORTRAN," *Communications of the Association for Computing Machinery 6*, pp. 85–86.

125. Backus, 1981; G. E. Mitchell, 4 September 1959: "The 704 FORTRAN II Automatic Coding System," IBM Research Report.

126. Heising, 2 November 1983.

127. G. F. Ryckman, 2 November 1955: Letter to SHARE members, in *Proceedings of the Third Meeting of SHARE*, 10–11 November 1955; *Proceedings of the Fourth Meeting of SHARE*, 6, 10 February 1956; T. B. Steel, Jr., May 1964: "Operating Systems," *Datamation*, pp. 26–28; G. F. Ryckman, 1983: "The IBM 701 Computer at the General Motors Research Laboratories," *Annals of the History of Computing 5*, pp. 210–212.

128. C. L. Baker, 22 January 1957: to D. L. Shell with attachment, "Minutes of the First Meeting of the SHARE 709 Committee, 12-14-56," published in *Annals of the History of Computing 4*, July 1982, pp. 280–283.

129. D. L. Shell, April 1957: 709 System Committee report, *Proceedings of the Eighth Meeting of SHARE*, pp. 4–7.

130. E. M. Boehm and T. B. Steel, Jr., 1959: "The SHARE 709 System: Machine Implementation of Symbolic Programming," *Journal of the Association for Computing Machinery 6*, pp. 134–140; I. D. Greenwald and M. Kane, 1959: "The SHARE 709 System: Programming and Modification," *Journal of the Association for Computing Machinery 6*, pp. 128–133.

131. D. L. Shell, 1959: "The SHARE 709 System: A Cooperative Effort," *Journal of the Association for Computing Machinery 6*, pp. 123–127.

132. F. S. Beckman, 17 September 1959: "Lessons in SOS"; F. S. Beckman, 17 October 1983: conversation with J. H. Palmer.

133. V. J. DiGri and R. K. Ridgway, February 1959: "SOS Progress Report to the SHARE 709 Committee," *Proceedings of the Twelfth Meeting of SHARE*, pp. C.9.4–C.9.7.

134. G. H. Mealy, August 1959: "SOS Committee Report," *Minutes and Proceedings of the Thirteenth Meeting of SHARE*, pp. C.14.1–C.14.2

135. A. L. Harmon, February 1960: "704/9/90 Applied Programming," *Minutes and Proceedings of the Fourteenth Meeting of SHARE*, pp. D.9.1–D.9.4.

136. Backus, 1981.

137. Beckman, 17 September 1959.

138. A. S. Noble, Jr., 1963: "Design of an Integrated Programming and Operating System, Part I: System Considerations and the Monitor," *IBM Systems Journal 2*, pp. 152–161; Heising, 2 November 1983; W. P. Heising, 20 January 1984: conversation with J. H. Palmer.

139. S. F. Grisoff, 23 March 1962: "An Introduction to Input/Output Control Systems," IBM Technical Report.

140. Kerksieck, 10 March 1956; E. M. Kerksieck, 18 June 1956: "Proposal for 702/705 Bulletin—Applied Programming Schedule for 1956."

141. E. M. Kerksieck, 1 March 1957: to R. L. Cline.

142. R. L. Cline, November 1958: in meetings of Committee on Systems and Programming, *Proceedings of the Seventh Session—GUIDE*, pp. E-18 to E-20, I-19 to I-21; R. L. Cline, November 1959: in "IBM Presentations" session, *Proceedings of the Ninth Session—GUIDE*, pp. B-1 to B-2.

143. Grisoff, 1962; I. W. L. Jones, April 1964: "Input/Output Control Systems," *Conference on the Impact of Users' Needs on the Design of Data Processing Systems*, organized by the British Computer Society, the British Institution of Radio Engineers, and the Institution of Electrical Engineers, pp. 18–19.

144. J. C. McPherson, 12 July 1956: "Programming Research Meeting—7/12/56" (memorandum).

145. R. W. Bemer, October 1957: in "IBM Report" session, *Proceedings of the Ninth Meeting of SHARE*, pp. 10–11.

146. R. Goldfinger, November 1958: "COMTRAN Status," *Proceedings of the Seventh Session—GUIDE*, pp. B-17 to B-20.

147. H. Kinzler and P. M. Moskowitz, January 1957: "The Procedure Translator— A System of Automatic Programming," *Automatic Coding—Proceedings of the Symposium held January 24–25, 1957, at the Franklin Institute in Philadelphia* (Philadelphia: Franklin Institute), pp. 39–55.

148. C. A. Phillips, undated: "Report from Commitee on Data Systems Languages," presented to Association for Computing Machinery at its 14th National Meeting in Cambridge, Mass., 1 September 1959; J. E. Sammet, 1981: "The Early History of COBOL," in *History of Programming Languages*, ed. Wexelblat; *Datamation*, May–June 1960: "CODASYL's Phillips Writes about COBOL."

149. G. E. Jones, 17 August 1959: to DP salesmen.

150. "Common Business Language Resolution," November 1959: in *Proceedings of the Ninth Session of GUIDE*, p. P-1.

151. A. L. Harmon, February 1960: "704/9/90 Applied Programming," *Minutes and Proceedings of the Fourteenth Meeting of SHARE*, pp. D.9.1–D.9.4.

152. Y. P. Dawkins, 17 June 1960: to DP sales personnel.

153. Y. P. Dawkins, 29 April 1960: to L. E. Clark, W. C. Hume, and R. C. Warren.

154. "Common Business Language" and "General" sessions, May 1960: in *Proceedings of the Tenth Session—GUIDE*, pp. F-12 to F-31, W-2 to W-3.

155. Y. P. Dawkins, 19 September 1960: to branch managers.

156. G. Dillon and A. L. Harmon, June 1961: in "COBOL '61" session, *Proceedings of the Twelfth Session—GUIDE*, pp. Q-1 to Q-6.

157. A. L. Harmon and B. Gordon, May 1960: in "Common Business Language" session, *Proceedings of the Tenth Session—GUIDE, pp. F-12, F-29.*

158. IBM Product Announcement, with attached Sales Manual pages 1401.1-4 (July 1961 revision), 30 June 1961: Applied Programming Systems, Letter 261-47.

159. IBM Product Announcement, with attached Sales Manual page 1620.1 (February 1961), 27 February 1961: IBM 1620 Data Processing System, Letter 261-11.

160. L. H. Haines, 1965: "Serial Compilation and the 1401 FORTRAN Compiler," *IBM Systems Journal 4*, pp. 73–80; F. E. Allen, 1981: "The History of Language Processor Technology in IBM," *IBM Journal of Research and Development 25*, pp. 535–548.

161. Noble, 1963.

162. The sales division's systems engineering function, a new professional discipline combining applied science and other previous technical sales support functions, was established in 1960 at the suggestion of William J. Lawless, to whom Sayre reported. As an employee of the Armed Forces Security Agency, Lawless had attended the Poughkeepsie meeting for 701 customers in August 1952. He was a guest at the 701 introduction at corporate headquarters in April 1953 and joined IBM later that year.

163. D. Sayre, 14 June 1984: conversation with J. H. Palmer.

164. D. Sayre, 26 May 1961: to J. C. McPherson.

165. IBM document, undated: "Action Program," a list and schedule of actions to be taken by IBM divisions following the Programming Conference.

166. *IBM Business Machines*, July 1961: "Milestone: Programmers' Conference."

167. S. Gill, 1958: "Parallel Programming," *The Computer Journal 1*, pp. 2–10.

168. E. F. Codd, E. S. Lowry, E. McDonough, and C. A. Scalzi, 1959: "Multiprogramming STRETCH: Feasibility Considerations," *Communications of the Association for Computing Machinery 2*, pp. 13–17.

169. E. F. Codd, E. S. Lowry, E. McDonough, R. H. Ramey, and C. A. Scalzi, 18 July 1962: "Structure of STRETCH Multiprogramming Supervisory Program," IBM Technical Report.

170. E. F. Codd, E. S. Lowry, E. McDonough, R. H. Ramey, and C. A. Scalzi, 27 February 1962: "STRETCH Experiment in Multiprogramming (Results of Trials)," IBM Technical Report; E. F. Codd, August 1962: "Multiprogramming Stretch: A Report on Trials," *Proceedings of IFIP Congress 62* (Amsterdam: North-Holland), pp. 574–575.

Chapter 10

1. W. H. Brattain, March 1968: "Genesis of the Transistor," *The Physics Teacher*, pp. 109–114.

2. W. Shockley, 1950: *Electrons and Holes in Semiconductors — with Applications to Transistor Electronics* (Princeton: D. von Nostrand), pp. 3–15.

3. C. Weiner, January 1973: "How the Transistor Emerged," IEEE Spectrum, pp. 24–33.

4. J. Bardeen and W. H. Brattain, 15 July 1948: "The Transistor, A Semi-Conductor Triode," *Physics Review 74*, pp. 230–231.

5. R. T. Blakely to J. C. McPherson, 13 July 1948. A copy of *Science News Letter*,10 July 1948: "Vacuum Tube Has Rival," was attached to this brief memorandum.

6. M. L. Wood, 12 November 1980: conversation with C. J. Bashe, J. H. Palmer, and L. R. Johnson.

7. M. L. Wood, 16 October 1984: conversation with E. W. Pugh.

8. Shockley, 1950: pp. 34–36.

9. W. Shockley, July 1949: "The Theory of p-n Junctions in Semiconductors and p-n Junction Transistors," *Bell System Technical Journal 28*, 435–489.

10. The new employee with a Ph.D. from MIT was Geoffrey Knight, Jr., son of a member of the IBM patent department. See H. Fleisher, 1 November 1982: conversation with E. W. Pugh.

11. This speculation for the formation and operation of point-contact transistors later became the standard explanation. See, for example, A. W. Lo, R. O. Endres, J. Zawels, F. D. Waldhauer, C. Cheng, 1955: *Transistor Electronics* (Englewood Cliffs: Prentice-Hall), pp. 29–30.

12. IBM Patent Development Department Report, 12 June 1950: A. H. Dickinson, G. Knight, Jr., R. C. Paulsen, M. L. Wood, C. A. Bergfors, R. I. Roth, and R. T. Blakely, "Transistors." The "livelier surface" of crystals from the 1N48 diodes is described in Knight's section. The automatic test equipment constructed by C. A. Bergfors, who had previously helped build the IBM 603 multiplier, is described in his section of the report.

13. Wood's technician and Watson's chauffeur was Edward Craner, who moved to Poughkeepsie to become a full-time technician when transistor work was transferred there.

14. R. A. Henle, November 1967: interview by L. Saphire.

15. M. L. Wood, 3 May 1951: to W. W. McDowell, "Transistor Research and Development."

16. IBM Patent Development Department Report, 12 June 1950.

17. A. H. Dickinson, 18 May 1950: "Transistors in IBM."

18. A. H. Dickinson, 7 August 1951: to J. C. McPherson, "Semiconductor Research and Development."

19. J. C. McPherson, 5 April 1950: to J. G. Phillips, T. J. Watson, Jr., A. L. Williams, D. L. Bibby, W. L. Lewis, and W. W. McDowell. This memorandum had two attachments: "Memorandum for discussion: IBM Engineering Program," 28 March 1950, and "Conclusions of the Engineering and Development Meeting," 3 April 1950.

20. M. L. Wood, 12 November 1960: conversation with C. J. Bashe, J. H. Palmer, and L. R. Johnson.

21. IBM Patent Development Department Reports, September 1950, 1952, 1953, July 1953–March 1954, and 1954: A. H. Dickinson.

22. L. P. Hunter, 17 December 1982: conversation with E. W. Pugh.

23. A. L. Samuel, 3 July 1951: to W. W. McDowell, "An Expanded Program of Component Research on Transistors and Related Solid-State Devices."

24. R. A. Henle, November 1967: interview by L. Saphire. Henle's master's thesis was titled, "The Transistor in a Trigger Circuit."

25. R. A. Henle, 19 June 1951: "Transistor Adder Circuit," IBM Engineering Report; July 1951: "Transistor Commutator Circuit," IBM Engineering Report; 28 November 1951: "Transistor Binary Coded Decimal Counter," IBM Engineering Report.

26. The "trigger" circuit was the one reported by H. J. Reich and R. L. Ungary, August 1949: *Review of Scientific Instruments 20*, pp. 586–588.

27. R. A. Henle, 10 October 1951: "The Manufacture of Transistors from N-Type Germanium Diodes," IBM Engineering Report.

28. F. Grace, F. Graner, and E. Chapman, 27 February 1952: "The Transistor Laboratory Vacuum Furnace," IBM Engineering Report.

29. A. L. Samuel, 18 September 1951: to J. C. McPherson, "Transistors: extent of outside research and IBM interest."

30. J. C. McPherson, 24 September 1951: to T. J. Watson, Jr., "Transistor Computer."

31. J. C. McPherson, 31 May 1951: to W. W. McDowell, "Transistor Research and Development."

32. R. A. Henle, November 1967: interview by L. M. Saphire. When Henle was assigned to the small accounting machine project, his manager was Harold Fleisher; Carter E. Dorrell worked with him in developing the transistor circuits.

33. Shockley, July 1949; W. Shockley, M. Sparks, and G. K. Teal, 1950: "p-n Junction Transistors," *Physical Review 83*, pp. 151–162.

34. R. N. Hall and W. C. Dunlop, 1950: "P-N Junctions Prepared by Impurity Diffusion," *Physical Review 80*, pp. 467–468.

35. R. N. Hall, November 1952: "Power Rectifiers and Transistors," *Proceedings of the Institute of Radio Engineers*, pp. 1512–1518; J. S. Saby, November 1952: "Fused Impurity P-N-P Junction Transistors," *Proceedings of the Institute of Radio Engineers*, pp. 1358–1360.

36. George D. Bruce may have been the first person to work with junction transistors at IBM. Using his Engineering Notebook No. 1034 during a discussion with E. W. Pugh, 10 November 1982, Bruce verified that he had measured junction devices in December 1952. He had joined IBM as a customer engineer in New York City in June 1950 after getting his bachelor's degree from the University of Pittsburgh. As a subscriber to the *Bell System Technical Journal*, he had become quite interested in transistors and interviewed for a job in development early in 1952. That April he received the desired assignment working on transistors, under D. J. Crawford in Poughkeepsie. He subsequently joined Logue's group and worked on the transistorized 604, following which he worked on the Type 608 calculator.

37. J. C. Logue, A. E. Brennemann, and A. C. Koelsch, March 1953: "Engineering Experience in the Design and Operation of a Large Scale Electrostatic Memory," Institute of Radio Engineers National Convention Record, pp. 21–29; 26 November, 10 December 1984: conversations with E. W. Pugh.

38. J. C. Logue, April 1968: interview by L. Saphire; 30 March 1970: summary of interview.

39. R. A. Henle, 9 December 1982: conversation with E. W. Pugh. Henle used his engineering notebook to verify that he had tried junction transistors in the drum circuit of the small accounting machine in January and that he was in Logue's group by April 1953.

40. G. Bruce, 10 November 1982: conversation with E. W. Pugh.

41. J. C. Logue, April 1968: interview by L. M. Saphire; 30 March 1970: summary of interview.

42. *New York Times*, 8 October 1954: p. 1; IBM Press Release, 8 October 1954.

43. W. Shockley, June 1958: "An Invited Essay on Transistor Business," *Proceedings of the Institute of Radio Engineers*, p. 954. In this article Shockley reports that maximum alpha cutoff frequencies in sec^{-1} were 5×10^7 in 1952, 1.2×10^8 in 1954, 8×10^8 in 1956, and 5×10^9 in 1958.

44. J. C. Logue, 23 January 1984: conversation with E. W. Pugh.

45. G. D. Bruce and J. C. Logue, December 1955: "An Experimental Transistorized Calculator," *Electrical Engineering*, pp. 1044–1048.

46. IBM Product Announcement, 19 August 1955: Type 608 Transistor Calculator, Letter 4924; IBM Brochure, 1955: "The IBM 608 Transistor Calculator"; IBM Sales Manual, 10 November 1955: "Type 608 Transistor Calculator."

47. W. W. McDowell, 2 October 1957: to L. H. LaMotte, J. A. Haddad, H. R. Keith, H. W. Miller, and E. R. Piore, "Solid State Components." Insight into Watson's role in the decision to forbid further use of vacuum tubes in products is provided by several sources, especially B. O. Evans, 13 November 1984: to C. J. Bashe; 29 November 1984: conversation with E. W. Pugh.

48. This policy, for example, was instrumental in the initiation of control store work in Hursley, which led to its use in System/360. See E. W. Pugh, 1984: *Memories That Shaped an Industry* (Cambridge: MIT Press), pp. 199–204.

49. R. F. Rutz and A. W. Berger, May 1955: "A New Transistor with Thyratron-like Characteristics," *Proceedings of the 1955 AIEE-IRE Electronics Components Conference*, Los Angeles, California, pp. 54–56; A. W. Berger and R. F. Rutz, 1955: "A New Transistor with Thyratron Like Characteristics," IBM Technical Publication.

50. R. F. Rutz, 3 December 1982: conversation with E. W. Pugh.

51. R. F. Rutz, 12 February 1953: "A Report on a New Two-Emitter Transistor," IBM Report; July 1955: "A Two-Emitter Transistor with a High Adjustable Alpha," *Proceedings of the Institute of Radio Engineers*, pp. 834–837.

52. R. F. Rutz, 1957: "Two-Collector Transistor for Binary Full Addition," *IBM Journal of Research and Development 1*, pp. 212–222; U.S. Patent 3,047,733, filed 25 May 1955: "Multiple Output Semiconductor Logical Device."

53. Interest in the two-collector transistor was especially stimulated by Bradford Dunham. See, for example, B. Dunham, 1957: "The Multipurpose Bias Device Part I, The Commutator Transistor," *IBM Journal of Research and Development 1*, pp. 117–129; R. F. Rutz, 1957: "Two-Collector Transistor for Binary Full Addition," *IBM Journal of Research and Development 1*, pp. 212–222.

54. Some sense of the controversy over the merit of junction devices versus point-contact devices is provided by A. L. Samuel to H. Fleisher, "Meeting on July 13, 1953," and by H. Fleisher notes of 14 July 1953.

55. R. W. Landauer, 9 October 1980: conversation with C. J. Bashe, J. H. Palmer, and L. R. Johnson.

56. J. C. Logue, 1 September 1954: "Proposal for the Development of High Speed Building Blocks."

57. W. E. Bradley, December 1953: "Part I—Principles of the Surface-Barrier Transistor," pp. 1702–1706; J. W. Tiley and R. A. Williams, December 1953: "Part II—Electrochemical Techniques for Fabrication of Surface-Barrier Transistors," pp. 1706–1708; J. B. Angell and F. P. Keiper, December 1953: "Part III—Circuit Applications of Surface-Barrier Transistors," pp. 1709–1712; R. Kansas, December 1953: "Part IV—On the High-Frequency Performance of Transistors," R. F. Schwarz and J. F. Walsh, December 1953: "Part V—The Properties of Metal to Semiconductor Contacts," pp. 1715–1720; all in *Proceedings of the Institute of Radio Engineers*.

58. Philco First Monthly Progress Report, 15 January–23 February 1955: "Surface-Barrier Transistors for Digital Computers" (H-2034), for MIT-Project Lincoln (Cambridge: MIT Libraries, Magnetic Core Memory Collection, MC-140, of the Institute Archives and Special Collections).

59. R. F. Rutz, 3 December 1982: conversation with E. W. Pugh.

60. The date when Hunter learned of Krömer's work is not known precisely. Hunter believes an English translation was available in November 1954, which he read in January 1955; see L. P. Hunter, 17 December 1982: conversation with E. W. Pugh.

Various reference documents are used to place the date after September 1954 and perhaps as late as April 1955 in R. F. Rutz, 7 December 1982: to E. W. Pugh.

61. H. Krömer, 1954: "Zur Theories des Diffusions- und des Drift-transistors," Parts I, II, and III, *Arch. Elektr. Ubertrag 8*, pp. 223–228, 363–369, and 499–504.

62. R. F. Rutz, December 1954–June 1955: IBM Engineering Notebook No. 1420, pp. 55, 58, 69, 91. The "hook collectors" Rutz was studying permitted junction devices to exhibit the performance characteristics similar to point-contact transistors, and were fabricated with an extra n or p region adjacent to the normal p- or n-type collector region.

63. B. O. Evans, 9 October 1968: interview by L. M. Saphire.

64. L. P. Hunter, 30 March 1955: "Minutes of Interdepartmental Planning Meeting."

65. L. P. Hunter, 17 December 1982: conversation with E. W. Pugh.

66. B. O. Evans, October 1968: interview by L. M. Saphire.

67. R. F. Rutz, 26 April–17 June 1955: IBM Engineering Notebook No. 1420.

68. G. L. Tucker 18 August 1955: to R. E. Swanson, "Recipe for a Transistor Employing Vapor Diffusion"; U.S. Patent 2,810,870, filed 22 November 1955: L. P. Hunter, R. F. Rutz, and G. L. Tucker, "Switching Transistor."

69. In a telephone call by B. N. Slade to H. Krömer at the University of California at Santa Barbara on 21 December 1983, it was learned that a patent application had been filed in Germany but not elsewhere. It probably did not issue and in any event did not tell how to make the proposed structure.

70. Final Hearing, 27 July 1960: Hunter, Rutz and Tucker v. Dacey, Lee and Shockley, Patent Interference No. 89,662; A. J. Riddles, 13 February 1959: to L. P. Hunter, R. F. Rutz, and G. L. Hunter, "Interference 89,662 Involving Switching Transistor Patent 2,810,870."

71. P. K. Spatz, 1 May 1959: "The STRETCH Development Program."

72. H. S. Yourke, 23 November 1982: conversation with E. W. Pugh. During the discussion, Yourke made use of his IBM Engineering Notebook No. 1778, covering the period from August 1955 to January 1958.

73. U.S. Patent No. Re 25,342, filed 31 December 1953: J. C. Logue, "Transistor Circuit with Diode Clamp Shunting Output to Prevent Saturation." This patent originally issued on 3 February 1959 as U.S. Patent 2,872,594, with the title, "Large Signal Transistor Circuits Having Short Fall Times," and came into interference with one filed later by Warnock of Philco (U.S. Patent 2,884,584). A difference between the two structures was that Warnock connected the diode between the collector and base, whereas Logue, whose design was based on point-contact transistors, connected the diode between the collector and ground. Arguing that Logue's structure actually connected the diode between the collector and base via ground, the patent application was refiled in March 1960 with new claims reading on the direct connection between collector and base. The patent reissued in March 1963 with claims dominating the Warnock patent. See Joseph C. Redmond, 12 December 1984: conversation with E. W. Pugh. A review of Logue's patent in 1963 revealed that it covered more than twenty different SMS circuit cards, as well as many circuits planned for SLT used in System/360.

74. R. A. Henle, 9 August 1955: engineering notebook, pp. 109–111; 2 January 1985: conversation with E. W. Pugh.

75. H. S. Yourke, 30 August 1956: IBM Engineering Notebook No. 1778, pp. 50–52.

76. H. S. Yourke, 26 December 1984: conversation with E. W. Pugh.

77. Yourke, 30 August 1956. J. L. Walsh, a coworker in R. Henle's group, witnessed these critical entries on 30 August 1956.

78. U.S. Patent 2,964,652, filed 15 November 1956: H. S. Yourke, "Transistor Switching Circuits"; H. S. Yourke, September 1957: *Institute of Radio Engineers Transactions on Circuit Theory 4*, pp. 236–240.

79. W. C. Seelbach, March 1974: "The Unfolding of a Technology," *Motorola Monitor 12*, asserts: "Hannon S. Yourke reported a new form of logic circuitry, Transistor Current Switching Circuits. The approach clearly was directly opposite to the industry trend towards reduced transistor count. Transistor current switching curcuits, which are now more generally called emitter coupled logic (ECL) and bear striking similarities to differential transistor structures, are relatively high in transistor count. But, relative to the cost-effectiveness of DTL, ECL vis-a-vis the 7030 Stretch program objectives was a performance-effective solution to circuit design problems. Yourke recognized that if logic circuits are to have response times limited primarily by the bandwidth of the transistors and by transit time delay, it is necessary to avoid operation of the transistors in a saturation mode."

80. L. Hellerman, May 1962: "A Computer Application to Reliable Circuit Design," *Institute of Radio Engineers Transactions on Reliability and Quality Control 11*, pp. 9–18. Leo Hellerman joined IBM in 1956. He reported to R. Domenico, who reported to R. E. Henle, when the statistical design work was done. See, for example, L. Hellerman, 6 January 1984: conversation with E. W. Pugh.

81. B. N. Slade, 27 October 1983: conversation with E. W. Pugh. Slade's first manager at IBM was David DeWitt, an important contributor to transistor technology throughout his long career at IBM.

82. Slade, 27 October 1983.

83. E. L. Fritz, 9 March 1984: conversation with E. W. Pugh. This interview is particularly informative because Fritz had personal records to document dates of key events in the development of the automated transistor production line.

84. W. E. Harding, 6 December 1983: conversation with E. W. Pugh.

85. E. L. Fritz, 9 March 1984: conversation with E. W. Pugh.

86. T. J. Leach, 25 March 1960: "Automated Assembly of Alloy-Junction Transistors," *Electronics 25*, pp. 57–61. Thomas J. Leach served as liaison from manufacturing to E. L. Fritz beginning early in 1958 and as leader of the design effort under Fritz beginning in December 1958. See T. J. Leach, 6 March 1984: conversation with E. W. Pugh.

87. W. E. Harding, 1981: "Semiconductor Manufacturing in IBM, 1957 to the Present: A Perspective," *IBM Journal of Research and Development 25*, pp. 647–658.

88. P. N. Whittaker, 23 January 1958: to J. W. Birkenstock et al., "IBM-Texas Instruments Agreement Summary." The agreement was signed and took effect on 23 December 1957.

89. E. L. Fritz, 9 March 1984: conversation with E. W. Pugh; B. N. Slade, 27 October 1983: conversation with E. W. Pugh. The shipment of this equipment to Texas Instruments was recalled by a number of engineers, many of whom opposed giving so much IBM capability to TI. The failure of TI to reduce its prices to IBM, consistent with the cost savings from automated production, contributed to IBM's subsequent decision to establish a Components Division to develop and manufacture its own transistor devices.

90. The project lasted about nine months and reported to M. E. Femmer, associate director of research. The two managers from Research were Gene A. Silvey and Robert E. Swanson. The post-alloy-diffused device was coinvented by R. Schwartz and B. N. Slade. A patent application was filed but a patent never issued due to interference with a patent application by people outside IBM. The process was almost certainly placed into production first at IBM. See B. N. Slade, April 1968: interview by L. M. Saphire.

91. B. N. Slade, 1962: "Device Design Considerations," in *Handbook of Semiconductor Electronics*, 2d edition, ed. L. P. Hunter (New York: McGraw-Hill).

92. A. W. Berger, R. M. Folsom, W. E. Harding, and W. E. Mutter, 31 October 1959: "Diffusion Masking and All Diffused Germanium NPN Mesa Transistors," IRE Electron Devices Conference; B. N. Slade, 1962, "Device Design Considerations," in *Handbook of Semiconductor Electronics*, ed. L. P. Hunter; W. E. Harding, 1983: in "Semiconductor Manufacturing in IBM, 1957 to the Present: A Perspective," *IBM Journal of Research and Development 25*, pp. 647–658.

93. T. J. Leach, 6 March 1984: conversation with E. W. Pugh.

94. IBM Customer Engineering Manual, 1949: "604 Electronic Calculating Punch," (Form 22-8432-1).

95. W. W. Simmons, 10 July 1958: to A. L. Becker et al. Copies of charts presented at the 30 June top-priority meeting were attached. The total number of tube pluggable unit types was represented as 2406.

96. J. C. Logue, 30 March 1970: to L. M. Saphire, "Interview in the IBM Oral History of Computer Technology."

97. *IBM Endicott News*, 30 January 1957: p. 6.

98. U.S. Patent 2,754,454, filed 27 May 1952: R. D. McNutt and E. J. Garvey, "Multiple Pluggable Unit."

99. A. H. Johnson, 12 March 1984: conversation with E. W. Pugh.

100. Edward Wyma and Newton Noell were responsible for the "bird cage" packaging effort. See J. C. Logue, 30 March 1970: to L. M. Saphire, "Interview in the IBM Oral History of Computer Technology."

101. E. J. Garvey, April 1968: interview by L. M. Saphire. Garvey particularly recalls working with A. H. Johnson to define the package before the critical decision was made by Palmer, and he credits Johnson with many of the ideas used in SMS. Johnson also presented the proposal to Palmer.

102. Much of the information concerning PROSERT and SMS was obtained from A. H. Johnson and from documents supplied by him. A copy of slides used for internal presentations soon after the first presentation was given to Ralph Palmer was particularly informative. See A. H. Johnson, 29 August 1958: "The Standard Modular System," IBM Technical Report; U.S. Patent 3,008,113, filed 30 July 1958: A. H. Johnson, "Electrical Interconnecting and Mounting Device for Printed-Circuit Boards"; U.S. Patent 3,077,023, filed 29 June 1959: A. H. Johnson, "Contact Element Forming and Inserting Apparatus and Method Therefor."

103. A. H. Johnson, 12 March 1984: conversation with E. W. Pugh.

104. R. L. Palmer, May 1968: interview by L. M. Saphire.

105. E. J. Garvey, April 1968: interview by L. M. Saphire.

106. P. W. Case, 3 October 1983: conversation with E. W. Pugh; P. W. Case, et al., 1981: "Design Automation in IBM," *IBM Journal of Research and Development 25*, pp. 631–646.

107. R. L. Palmer, 8 February 1958: to J. C. Logue, "SMS Card Responsibility"; R. L. Palmer, May 1968: interview by L. M. Saphire.

108. N. P. Edwards, 23 April 1982: conversation with E. W. Pugh.

109. J. L. Craft, R. A. Henle, E. Shapiro, and R. A. Thorpe, 1 November 1958: "Transistor Feedback Amplifiers," IBM Research Report. This report says the work was completed in April 1956 and was sponsored by the IBM Military Products Division, Owego, N.Y.

110. COMPACT was headed by R. J. Domenico and IMPACT by J. L. Walsh, both reporting to R. A. Henle.

111. J. E. Tilton, 1971: *International Diffusion of Technology: The Case of Semiconductors* (Washington D.C.: Brookings Institution), p. 57.

Chapter 11

1. C. R. DeCarlo, March 1955: "Applications of Data Processors in Production," *Proceedings of the Western Joint Computer Conference*, pp. 61–65.

2. E. Tomash and A. A. Cohen, October 1979: "The Birth of an ERA: Engineering Research Associates, Inc. 1946–1955," *Annals of the History of Computing 1*, pp. 83–97; Sperry Univac's Commemorative Program for the National Computer Conference 1981 Pioneer Day Banquet, 6 May 1981. According to these documents, fourteen UNIVAC I systems were shipped before 1955 by Remington Rand's Philadelphia organization, and its sister operation in St. Paul had shipped about an equal number of computers.

3. T. V. Learson, 1 October 1954: to selected IBM salesmen.

4. *IBM Business Machines*, 15 April 1954: "T. V. Learson named Director of EDPM."

5. *Fortune*, March 1953: "The Year of the Transistor."

6. G. A. Roberts, 15 December 1952: to L. H. LaMotte, "Mr. S. W. Dunwell."

7. S. W. Dunwell, March 1968: interview by L. M. Saphire.

8. T. V. Learson, 23 July 1954: to J. C. McPherson, C. C. Hurd, and B. E. Phelps, "Comparison of the NORC and the 704."

9. B. E. Phelps, 23 July 1954: to T. V. Learson, attaching a preliminary NORC Engineering Survey Committee Report of 22 July 1954 by G. Amdahl, L. Borden, D. J. Crawford, B. E. Phelps, and J. A. Weidenhammer.

10. Learson, 23 July 1954.

11. W. Buchholz, 30 August 1954: "Stored Micro Program," IBM Datatron Memo No. 1.

12. S. W. Dunwell and W. Buchholz, 25 October 1954: "Objectives of the Datatron Program," IBM Datatron Memo No. 0.

13. C. C. Hurd, undated: to file, "Report on Visit of Dr. von Neumann to Poughkeepsie, November 9 and 10, 1954."

14. J. von Neumann, 2 December 1954: "The NORC and Problems in High Speed Computing," *Collected Works of John von Neumann*, volume V, 1963 (New York: Macmillan), pp. 238–247.

15. *IBM Business Machines*, 2 August, 1, 20 October, 1 December 1954, 19 January 1955.

16. S. W. Dunwell, 8 December 1954: to C.C. Hurd.

17. H. S. Beattie, 16 December 1954: to J. C. McPherson with undated attachment entitled "Summary of the Datatron."

18. W. Buchholz, 14 January 1955: "Engineering Meeting on Large Technical Computers." Listed as attendees were G. M. Amdahl, W. Buchholz, M. E. Femmer, P. E. Fox, J. A. Haddad, B. L. Havens, W. W. McDowell, J. C. McPherson, R. L. Palmer, and N. Rochester.

19. Undisclosed was how a small memory of fast registers could reduce references to main memory by a factor of five without unduly limiting the range of applications.

20. C. C. Hurd, 21 January 1955: to file, "High Speed Data Processing Machines."

21. C. C. Hurd, 31 January 1955: to file concerning a 24 January meeting.

22. C. C. Hurd, 31 January 1955: to file concerning a 26 January meeting at UCRL.

23. *Digital Computer Newsletter 7*, April 1955, reported of the ElectroData Corporation that "acceptance tests of three Datatron computers have been completed." ElectroData's usage of "Datatron" seems to have closely followed the demise of the Datatron memos. See W. Buchholz, 17 March 1982: conversation with C. J. Bashe and J. H. Palmer. Buchholz believes that E. S. McCollister left IBM for ElectroData in early 1955, aware that the term "Datatron" was outmoded in Poughkeepsie. Although Buchholz and Dunwell were the main contributors to the thirty-eight Datatron memos, other authors were E. Bloch, L. C. Hubbard, P. W. Jackson, A. S. Lett, W. J. Lawless, H. W. Nordyke, Jr., R. J. Preiss, N. Rochester, A. L. Samuel, and G. Walter. At least one Novacom memorandum authored by Amdahl, Buchholz, Dunwell, and Walter was completed.

24. W. W. McDowell, 21 February 1955: to J. A. Haddad.

25. C. C. Hurd, 28 February 1955: to T. V. Learson.

26. D. A. Bruce (Purchasing Agent, Radiation Laboratory, University of California), 11 March 1955: to C. W. Wiley (Product Planning Department, IBM, Poughkeepsie, New York). Enclosed were "Specifications for New Computer for UCRL, Livermore," 14 March 1955.

27. G. M. Amdahl, C. J. Bashe, R. B. Bevier, W. Buchholz, S. W. Dunwell, B. O. Evans, M. E. Femmer, and C. E. Frizzell, 4 April 1955: "LARC Proposal." See also C. E. Stephens, 12 April 1955, draft of "Specifications for UCRL Computer."

28. T. V. Learson, 12 April 1955: to L. H. LaMotte.

29. J. A. Haddad, 18 April 1955: to file, "Livermore Proposal."

30. C. C. Hurd and W. W. McDowell, 20 April 1955: to University of California Radiation Laboratory, attention D. A. Bruce. R. L. Kocher, 14 April 1955: to C. C. Hurd, noted that UCRL wanted a technical proposal on 19 April and a statement of commercial terms on 21 April.

31. D. A. Bruce, 10 May 1955: to IBM, attention C. C. Hurd.

32. C. C. Hurd, 2 May 1955: to L. H. LaMotte. The "actual availability" of UCRL's 701 for the first three months of 1955 was 84.1, 83.0, and 83.8 percent, according to C. R. DeCarlo, 1 June 1955: to C. C. Hurd.

33. J. Backus, December 1967: interview by L.M. Saphire.

34. J. B. Greene, 25 May 1955: "Engineering R&D Contract—NSA."

35. C. C. Hurd, 28 July 1955: to file, "NSA—Visit of July 28, 1955."

36. J. A. Haddad, 19 August 1955: to T. J. Watson, Jr., "New Capabilities of Magnetic Core Memories." "As a result of intensive effort . . . we have uncovered a new mode

of operation which makes possible significant advances in the speed of magnetic core memories . . . principally through the efforts of Mr. E. A. Brown in our Endicott Laboratory and Dr. L. P. Hunter, Manager of Research of our Poughkeepsie Laboratory . . . many people contributed to the effort involved. In particular, a group of engineers (list appended) unselfishly came back early from vacation in order to crystallize our thinking in time for a presentation to a government agency." In an appendix, Haddad briefly mentioned three-hole cores, as well as core selection by coincidence of magnetic flux, before continuing, "We are now able to consider the design of magnetic core memories which have a total cycle time of 1/2 microseconds as opposed to 6 microseconds with present techniques." The early returnees from vacation were listed as E. W. Bauer, D. J. Crawford, S. W. Dunwell, N. P. Edwards, A. H. Eschenfelder, P. E. Fox, M. K. Haynes, W. W. Lawrence, and W. M. Wittenberg.

37. S. S. Snyder, January 1980: "Computer Advances Pioneered by Cryptologic Organizations," *Annals of the History of Computing 2*, pp. 60–70; and R. L. Palmer, 13 September 1955: to file.

38. C. C. Hurd, 31 August 1955: to L. H. LaMotte. Here Hurd first used "PROJECT STRETCH" in the context of the 10 megacycle machine.

39. C. C. Hurd, 23 August 1955: to L. H. LaMotte, A. L. Williams, and R. L. Palmer.

40. Hurd, 31 August 1955.

41. L. Tatum, 4 October 1955: to J. C. McPherson attaching notes on presentation by J. P. Eckert, Jr., to the Association of Computing Machinery.

42. C. C. Hurd, 15 September 1955: to L. H. LaMotte; C. C. Hurd, 6 October 1955: to L. H. LaMotte.

43. G. M. Amdahl, December 1967: interview by L. M. Saphire. Other factors may have contributed to the resignation, but Amdahl recalled the prospect of being buried in the new organization as the leading one.

44. C. C. Hurd (IBM director, Electronic Data Processing Machines) and B. F. Weigard (IBM assistant controller), 29 February 1956: to W. H. Brummett, Jr. (chief, Contracts and Procurement Branch, Santa Fe Operations Office, P.O. Box 5400, Albuquerque, New Mexico). The letter was accompanied by Appendix A (Scope of Work), Appendix B (Delivery Schedule), and the fifty-four-page technical proposal, "Preliminary Description of Proposed Multiplex 10 Megapulse Automatic Computer," dated 27 February 1956.

45. H. A. Faw, 20 January, 29 February 1956: memoranda for file, "Project Stretch."

46. S. W. Dunwell, 9 March 1956: to C. C. Hurd and others outlining the presentation to LASL planned for 14 March.

47. C. C. Hurd, 30 March 1956: to A. L. Williams.

48. Contract No. AT(29-2)-476 between the AEC and IBM, 20 November 1956.

49. *IBM Poughkeepsie Laboratory Newsletter*, 24 April 1956.

50. J. C. Logue, April 1968: interview by L. M. Saphire.

51. Stretch Memo No. 39, 10 July 1956. This memo consists of papers given on 20 June 1956 at the IBM Engineering Research Conference, Syracuse, New York, by W. Buchholz, S. W. Dunwell, J. E. Griffith, J. C. Logue, L. S. Snyder, and H. K. Wild.

52. W. Buchholz, 31 July 1956: "Memory Word Length," Stretch Memo. No. 40; and W. Buchholz, 19 September 1956: "Memory Word Length and Indexing," Stretch Memo. No. 45. Also see W. Buchholz, January 1981: "Origin of the Word

Byte," *Annals of the History of Computing 3*, p. 72, which explains how "byte" later came to imply eight bits.

53. J. C. McPherson, 17 October 1956: to E. R. Piore.

54. S. W. Dunwell, December 1956: "Design Objectives for the IBM Stretch Computer," *Proceedings of the Eastern Joint Computer Conference*, pp. 20–21. Dunwell did not specify what he meant by "the fastest general purpose computer" in use; presumably he implied the 704.

55. R. A. Henle, December 1956: "High-Speed Transistor Computer Circuit Design," *Proceedings of the Eastern Joint Computer Conference*, pp. 64–66.

56. J. P. Eckert, December 1956: "Univac-Larc, the Next Step in Computer Design," *Proceedings of the Eastern Joint Computer Conference*, pp. 16–20.

57. *IBM Poughkeepsie Laboratory Newsletter*, 29 October 1956: "Plans to Relocate Research Center at Yorktown Outlined," and 31 January 1957: "Computer Group Moves to Product Development."

58. *IBM Poughkeepsie Laboratory Newsletter*, 17 December 1956.

59. H. S. Yourke and E. J. Slobodzinski, February 1957: "Millimicrosecond Transistor Current Switching Techniques," *Proceedings of the Western Joint Computer Conference, pp. 68–72.*

60. In 1957, the Plantation task was divided into two parts: Plantation for Research and Rancho for Product Development.

61. IBM Poughkeepsie Product Development Laboratory Project 7000 File, 1 April 1957.

62. IBM Poughkeepsie Product Development Laboratory Project 7000 File, 28 May 1957.

63. IBM Poughkeepsie Product Development Laboratory special report, 1 June 1957: "Report of the 3-in-1 Committee." The committee members were G. A. Blaauw, F. P. Brooks, and W. Wolensky of Stretch Engineering and E. F. Codd, J. E. Griffith, and D. W. Sweeney of Stretch Product Planning.

64. D. W. Sweeney, May 1968: interview by L. M. Saphire. Soon after the three-in-one study, H. A. Mussell became manager of Basic and R. E. Merwin manager of contract work.

65. W. Buchholz, 3 June 1957: "Fingers or Fists?" IBM Stretch Memo No. 62. In an aside, Buchholz noted that "the idea of transforming data into addresses for the purpose of table look-up . . . was recognized as a basic computer operation by Amdahl, Boehm, and Griffith during the early definition of the 709 in 1955, and it appears in the 709 in the form of 'Convert' instructions. The first written reference appears in Stretch Memo No. 16. Limited application of the scheme to programmed decimal-binary conversion dates back to the 701 project in 1951." See also G. M. Amdahl, E. M. Boehm, and J. E. Griffith, 20 December 1955: "Editing, Part I," Stretch Memo No. 16; and E. M. Boehm and J. E. Griffith, 19 December 1955: "Editing, Part II," Stretch Memo No. 17.

66. IBM Poughkeepsie Product Development Laboratory Project 7000 File, 6 August 1957.

67. P. K. Spatz, 1 May 1959: "The STRETCH Development Program," IBM staff report, p. 19.

68. R. J. Bahnsen and J. F. Dirac, 31 December 1957: "Proposal for a Sigma Lookahead System," IBM Sigma Computer Memo. No. 2. Early discussions in IBM of lookahead principles date back at least to 1955; see Backus, December 1967.

69. W. W. Simmons, 25 November 1957: to L. H. LaMotte and others.

70. IBM Poughkeepsie Product Development Laboratory Project 7000 File, 30 December 1957; IBM Advanced Systems Sales Manual, 15 October 1962; and *IBM Command Control Center News*, 18 January and 23 August 1961.

71. Bahnsen and Dirac, 31 December 1957.

72. J. Cocke and H. G. Kolsky, December 1959: "The Virtual Memory in the Stretch Computer," *Proceedings of the Eastern Joint Computer Conference*, pp. 82–93. ("Virtual memory" attained other meanings later.)

73. IBM Poughkeepsie Product Development Laboratory Project 7000 File, 1 May 1958.

74. Spatz, May 1959: p. 21.

75. P. S. Herwitz and J. H. Pomerene, May 1960: "The Harvest System," *Proceedings of the Western Joint Computer Conference*, pp. 23–32.

76. W. Buchholz, ed., 1962: *Planning a Computer System* (New York: McGraw-Hill). This book is based heavily on studies made during the three-in-one period, as indicated by many of the citations. Among them are G. A. Blaauw, F. P. Brooks, Jr., and W. Buchholz, June 1959: "Processing Data in Bits and Pieces," *Institute of Radio Engineers Transactions on Electronic Computers EC-8*, pp. 118–124; G. A. Blaauw, July 1959: "Indexing and Control-Word Techniques," *IBM Journal of Research and Development 3*, pp. 288–301; W. Buchholz, May 1958: "Selection of an Instruction Language," *Proceedings of the Western Joint Computer Conference*, pp. 128–130; W. Buchholz, December 1959: "Fingers or Fists? (The Choice of Decimal or Binary Representation)," *Communications of the Association for Computing Machinery 2*, pp. 3–11; F. P. Brooks, Jr., December 1957: "A Program-Controlled Program Interruption System," *Proceedings of the Eastern Joint Computer Conference*, pp. 128–132; and Cocke and Kolsky, December 1959.

77. Spatz, May 1959: p. 20.

78. Ibid., p. 21.

79. E. Bloch, October 1968: interview by L. M. Saphire.

80. Spatz, May 1959: p. 22.

81. IBM Poughkeepsie Product Development Laboratory Project 7000 File, 23 January 1958.

82. Spatz, May 1959: p. 26.

83. *IBM Business Machines*, July 1959: "The Story of S-T-R-E-T-C-H."

84. *Electronic News*, 31 August 1959: "Data Topics."

85. E. Bloch, December 1959: "The Engineering Design of the Stretch Computer," *Proceedings of the Eastern Joint Computer Conference*, pp. 48–58.

86. *IBM Poughkeepsie Laboratory Newsletter*, 14 May 1958.

87. J. M. Taylor, 25 March 1971: "Personal Recollections on the Total Engineering Development of the 7090," IBM staff report. One possible reason for Palmer's impatience was Philco's announcement of transistorized computers; see *Digital Computer Newsletter*, January and April 1957.

88. G. R. Monroe, 27 June 1958: to J. W. Haanstra.

89. IBM Product Announcement, 30 December 1958: The IBM 7090 Data Processing System, Letter 258-125.

90. R. B. Bevier, 17 July 1958: to H. A. Mussell, "Transistor Availability."

91. S. W. Dunwell, March 1968: interview by L. M. Saphire.

92. S. W. Dunwell, 26 September 1958: to R. L. Palmer; J. W. Haanstra, 1 October 1958 to G. R. Monroe; G. R. Monroe, 7 October 1958: to J. W. Haanstra; and J. W. Haanstra, 9 October 1958: to S. W. Dunwell, "NPN Drift Transistors."

93. Taylor, 25 March 1971.

94. J. E. Ewing, 21 October 1959: to C. G. Fultz, "7090 Improvements."

95. *IBM Poughkeepsie News*, 16 December 1959: "Milestone Reached as DSD Ships First Two 7090 Systems."

96. IBM Product Announcement, 15 January 1962: "IBM 7094 Data Processing System," Letter 262-9; and IBM Product Announcement, 16 May 1963: "IBM 7094II Data Processing System," Letter 263-39.

97. H. H. Goldstine, W. H. Johnson, H. A. Mussell, H. D. Ross, and J. J. Troy, December 1959: "Stretch Program Technical Review, Section I."

98. A. S. Hoagland, H. A. Mussell, and J. M. Norton, 8 February 1960: "ADF Technical Audit Committee Report."

99. IBM Press Release, 26 April 1960.

100. Contract No. AT(04-3)-352 between the AEC, on behalf of LRL, and IBM, 23 December 1960. The system price, $13,503,700, was reduced to $7,780,000 in Contract Modification No. 1, 15 May 1961.

101. C. R. DeCarlo, 2 February 1961: to W. B. McWhirter.

102. R. L. Kocher, 3 February 1961: to G. E. Jones.

103. W. B. McWhirter, 18 April 1961: to T. J. Watson, Jr., "STRETCH Program"; *Datamation*, June 1961: "The Shrinking of Stretch," p. 17.

104. *IBM Poughkeepsie Laboratory Newsletter*, 12 May 1961: "STRETCH at Los Alamos"; E. Bloch, 15 May 1961: to file, "Summary of STRETCH Acceptance Test in Los Alamos." Stretch delivery was almost a year late. LARC delivery, meanwhile, was about two years late; see H. Lukoff, 1979: *From Dits to Bits: A Personal History of the Electronic Computer* (Portland, Ore.: Robotics Press).

105. H. G. Kolsky, 17 July 1961: "STRETCH Users Group Meeting."

106. IBM Reference Manual, 1960: "7030 Data Processing System" (Form A22-6530). See also chapter 2 of Buchholz, ed., 1962.

107. C. C. Hurd, 20 November 1961: to T. V. Learson.

108. R. L. Palmer, 2 May 1961: "STRETCH." Learson on 24 April asked for Palmer's "observations."

109. R. E. Meagher, 9 May 1961: "Methods of Evaluation and the Stretch System." Also IBM Reference Manual, 1962: "7030 Timing Guide," (Form C22-6719).

110. T. V. Learson, 15 May 1961: to T. J. Watson, Jr.

111. S. W. Dunwell, March 1968: interview by L. M. Saphire.

112. The Kingston-produced 7030s went to (1) Lawrence Radiation Laboratory, (2) Atomic Weapons Research Establishment, England; (3) U.S. Weather Bureau, (4) MITRE Corporation, (5) Dahlgren Naval Proving Ground, (6) IBM, and (7) Commisariat a l'Energie Atomique, France. See R. A. Somerby, 19 November 1965: to P. W. Knaplund; T. R. Horton, 21 February 1962: to W. B. McWhirter; Snyder, January 1980; and R. B. Lazarus, 8 June 1971: to J. Griffith.

113. *IBM Business Machines*, March 1963. Appointed IBM Fellow at the same time as Palmer were J. W. Backus, G. L. Clapper, D. D. Dodge, C. R. Doty, Sr., C. J. Fitch, F. E. Hamilton, and L. H. Thomas.

114. S. W. Dunwell, 8 April 1964: to T. J. Watson, Jr.

115. Buchholz, ed., 1962.

116. T. J. Watson, Jr., 20 April 1964: to S.W. Dunwell.

117. T. J. Watson, Jr., 15 March 1966: Transcription, dated 24 March 1966, of his talk at the Annual Awards Dinner.

Chapter 12

1. IBM report, 1955: "Historical Record of Card and Machine Development (EAM Division)."

2. The punched-card machines used by IBM's customers were available on rental only, until the mid-1950s. Since the machines were owned by IBM, they were referred to as "the inventory," whether in field or factory. The practice of renting exclusively was terminated by a 1956 consent decree arising from the antitrust case of U.S. v. IBM, filed in 1952.

3. The first year in which IBM's gross income from electronic data processing equipment exceeded that from punched-card machines was 1962. C. A. Northrop, testimony in U.S. v. IBM, U.S. District Court, Southern District of New York, defendant's exihibit DX3815.

4. Magnetic-disk storage of adequate capacity, versatility (e.g., removable disk packs), and economy per unit of data to take the place of both punched cards and tape to a significant extent came much later. (See chapter 8.)

5. IBM Development Report, June 1953. (Prepared by IBM headquarters Laboratory Publications Department, quarterly in the early 1950s.)

6. M. Papo, January 1968: interview by L. M. Saphire; J. Ghertman, April 1969: interview by L. M. Saphire.

7. J. Connally, circa 1967: *History of Computing in Europe* (IBM World Trade Corporation).

8. R. W. Avery, 8 December 1954: "Engineering Meeting on Modular Approach to Computer Design."

9. J. A. Haddad, 29 December 1954: to R. L. Palmer.

10. R. W. Avery, 8 February 1955: to H. T. Marcy.

11. M. O. Paley, December 1967: interview by L. M. Saphire.

12. C. W. Allen, 17 September 1981: conversation with J. H. Palmer and C. J. Bashe.

13. M. O. Paley, 15 November 1955: to H. S. Beattie, "Progress Report—MAC Program."

14. Particularly helpful in obtaining approval for a limited announcement of the 608 were G. E. Jones in the office of President T. J. Watson, Jr., and T. V. Learson who had recently become vice-president in charge of sales. R. L. Palmer, January 1968: interview by L. M. Saphire; T. V. Learson, 25 March 1955: "Memorandum of Meeting on March 24."

15. IBM Product Announcement, 4 April 1955: Type 608 Transistor Calculator, Letter 4801; also 26 April 1955: 608 Transistor Calculator (Letter 4817 announcing monthly rental).

16. M. O. Paley, 18 May 1955: to J. C. McPherson with brochure of April 1955, "The MAC Program."

17. R. K. Richards, 6 April 1955: "Modular Accounting Calculator."

18. The committee chairman was R. K. Richards. Other members were C. T. Baker, N. E. Beverly, E. Bloch, W. Buchholz, S. W. Dunwell, G. V. Hawkins, and L. T. Wheelock. From report without typed date or author: "Committee on Extending the MAC Line of Machines," copy from files of W. Buchholz, bearing handwritten initials "W.B." and date "July 20 1955."

19. R. W. Avery et al., 8 August 1957: "IBM Type 660 Data Processing System Specifications"; M. B. Smith, 12 November 1957: to L. H. LaMotte, "Intermediate EDPM."

20. J. T. Ahlin, 15 January 1958: to W. W. Simmons, with 13 January report from Ahlin to Simmons, "660-750 Intermediate Computer Area."

21. B. O. Evans, November 1968: interview by L. M. Saphire.

22. Ibid. The 7070 is referred to here as "the first IBM computer of the solid-state generation" to be announced, because the 608 (announced more than a year earlier) was only a calculator, not a stored-program computer.

23. B. C. Christensen, J. B. Fernbach (USA), J. Ghertman (France), and W. P. Scharr (Germany), 20 July 1955: "Report on World Wide Accounting Machine Program."

24. The French proposal was prepared by Maurice Papo and Eugene Estrems. K. Ganzhorn, February 1968: interview by L. M. Saphire.

25. Christensen, Fernbach, Ghertman and Scharr, 20 July 1955.

26. J. G. Maisonrouge, January 1968: interview by L. M. Saphire.

27. G. V. Hawkins, 5 January 1956: to J. J. Troy. (Incorrectly dated 1955; correction verified by G. V. H. 14 December 1982.) Engineers in the United States assigned to work on WWAM included P. J. de George and R. A. Wadsten, according to Hawkins's memorandum.

28. M. Papo, January 1968: interview by L. M. Saphire.

29. K. Ganzhorn, February 1968: interview by L. M. Saphire.

30. E. Estrems, 20 June 1956: "The IBM World Wide Accounting Machine."

31. R. G. Mork, October 1967: interview by L. M. Saphire.

32. M. Papo, January 1968.

33. T. V. Learson, 23 April 1956: to L. H. LaMotte.

34. R. L. Palmer, 4 February 1957: to L. H. LaMotte.

35. Two additional engineers who participated in the early planning of this machine, which was to become the 1401, were James J. Ingram and Russell A. Rowley. R. G. Mork, 1 July 1981: conversation with C. J. Bashe; J. J. Ingram, 9 November 1982: conversation with C. J. Bashe.

36. F. O. Underwood, June 1968: interview by L. M. Saphire.

37. The TPM used special field-mark characters to separate fields and indicate the signs of numbers. The 702 and 705 used a combination of zone bits on end characters (for numeric fields) and special instructions along with accumulator length (for non-numeric fields). The 305 specified field lengths in the instructions as, incidentally, the Stretch computer did also.

38. F. O. Underwood, June 1968.

39. F. O. Underwood, 12 August 1957: to J. J. Ingram, "Stored-Program Variable Word-Length Core Storage Accounting Machine Proposal."

40. R. L. Palmer, 30 September 1957: to L. H. LaMotte et al.

41. IBM Product Development Laboratories (Data Processing Division) Development Report, Effective 31 December 1958.

42. L. A. Wilson, December 1969, June 1970: interviews by L. M. Saphire.

43. H. T. Ware, 2 October 1957: to W. W. Simmons.

44. W. W. McDowell, 3 October 1957: to L. H. LaMotte.

45. F. O. Underwood, 9 October 1957: to J. J. Ingram, "Accounting Machine, Second Proposal." While the variable-length instruction was an "innovation" as far as Underwood was concerned, the concept was not unknown in the literature. See D. D. McCracken, July 1956: "Word Length in Digital Computers," *Computers and Automation*, pp. 14–15.

46. L. H. LaMotte, 25 November 1957: to A. L. Becker et al., "Top Priority Development Program Meeting"; R. L. Palmer, 5 December 1957: to C. E. Branscomb, "WWAM Card Handling Standardization"; Branscomb, 20 December 1957: to Palmer.

47. B. C. Christensen, 10 October 1957: to L. H. LaMotte.

48. T. J. Watson, Jr., 13 December 1957: to L. H. LaMotte.

49. C. E. Branscomb, March 1968: interview by L. M. Saphire.

50. Endicott had an exploratory electronic accounting machine project at least as early as 1956; it was called the "Transistorized Accounting Machine" (TAM), and the engineer in charge was James J. Ingram. IBM Engineering Laboratories Development Report for Second Quarter 1956. Ingram became manager of accounting machine planning during development of the 1401.

51. The machine eventually announced as the solid-state 7070 had not yet been assigned to Endicott at the time that laboratory was given responsibility for the electronic accounting machine. There is little question, however, that Troy's insistence on computer development in Endicott influenced Palmer's decision to place the 7070 project, as well as the electronic accounting machine, in that laboratory.

52. G. E. Hack, 19 December 1958: "The Application of Complementary Transistor Diode Logic in the IBM 7070."

53. IBM Product Announcement, 5 October 1959: IBM 1401 Data Processing Systems, Letter 259-57.

54. W. H. Dunn, E. J. Grenchus, W. P. Hanf, and W. F. Morgan, 14 May 1958: "Evaluation of SPACE and 310 RAMAC."

55. B. O. Evans, November 1968: interview by L. M. Saphire; J. J. Ingram, 9 November 1982: conversation with C. J. Bashe.

56. C. E. Branscomb, March 1968: interview by L. M. Saphire.

57. B. O. Evans, 1983: "System 360 in Retrospective" (paper submitted to the Center for International Studies at Geneva, Switzerland). Evans recalled that "the 1401 was the Model-T Ford of the computer industry. More than 12,000 were produced as this new business system far exceeded IBM's original estimates." Furthermore, in 1962—the first year in which IBM's gross income from electronic data processing systems exceeded that from electric accounting machines—it was the 1401 system that replaced the 407 accounting machine as the company's most important product.

58. The 608, which was the first digital calculator produced commercially, is not mentioned here because the discussion relates to stored-program computers.

59. Evans, November 1968; Ingram, 9 November 1982.

60. P. J. Cantone et al., 30 January 1959: "Planning Description of the 310 System."

61. J. J. Troy et al., 28 May 1959: "310 RAMAC Design Objectives." The "310" machine, as originally planned, used word-length indicators in its instructions rather than field marks (word marks) stored with the operands.

62. Evans, November 1968; Ingram, 9 November 1982.

63. Ibid.; D. T. Spaulding, 25 October 1983: conversation with C. J. Bashe.

64. Evans, November 1968.

65. E. S. Hughes, November 1968: interview by L. M. Saphire.

66. IBM Product Announcement, 12 September 1960: IBM 1410 Processing System, Letter 260-51; 10 October 1960: Letter 260-62. A second model of the RAMAC, called RAMAC II, had been announced early in 1959, for the 305 system. Retaining the full complement of fifty disks but employing forty tracks per inch, twice the track density of the RAMAC I, it held 10 million characters. The 1405 Models 1 and 2 both used doubled bit density (220 bits per inch), as well as doubled track density, according to: G. Walter, June 1961: "Mechanical Magnetic Storage."

67. IBM Product Development Laboratories (Data Processing Division) Development Report, Effective 31 December 1958; L. A. Wilson, December 1969, June 1970: interviews by L. M. Saphire.

68. L. A. Wilson, December 1969, June 1970.

69. Like the 310, the 11LC, as originally planned, depended on word-length fields in its instructions rather than word marks stored with the data. This feature originated with the 305 RAMAC. K. D. Foulger, 10 May 1983: conversation with C. J. Bashe.

70. The programmers were Barbara L. Wood and Bernard R. Silkowitz.

71. By "1401 instruction set" we mean the assembly language SPS, which, along with appropriate assembly programs, was provided for even the smallest 1401 system at initial delivery.

72. J. H. Palmer, 13 December 1967: to C. E. Branscomb et al.

73. See, for example, L. M. Friedberg, 1967: "RPG: The Coming of Age," *Datamation*, June, pp. 29–31.

74. H. S. Beattie, November 1970: interview by L. M. Saphire.

75. IBM Customer Engineering Manual of Instruction, 1952: "Accounting Machine Type 407."

76. H. S. Beattie, November 1970: interview by L. M. Saphire; H. S. Beattie and J. E. Hickerson, 1 February 1951: "High Speed Printing Mechanisms."

77. J. D. Hood and J. A. Weidenhammer, 17 July 1950: "Discussion of High Speed Printing Mechanisms." Beattie recalled simply that "Rey [Johnson] was a better salesman than I was." H. S. Beattie, November 1970: interview by L. M. Saphire. In view of subsequent events, however, it should be noted that Johnson was not involved in the product design of the high-speed line printer, having contributed only an early model. He was, in fact, later critical of the design approach that was taken. R. B. Johnson, July 1960: interview by L. M. Saphire; F. J. Wesley, 19 December 1952: to L. H. LaMotte, "Serial Parallel High Printing—Wire Type versus Stick Type."

78. W. W. McDowell, 30 December 1952: to E. J. Garvey.

79. J. E. Dayger, 11 September 1974: "History of High-Speed Line Printer Innovations."

80. J. C. McPherson, 31 July 1958: to L. H. LaMotte; P. P. Pappas, 21 January 1957: "Abstract of the Wire Printer Programs at IBM Endicott." Information about changes

in design of the printer were obtained in May 1984 by J. H. Wellburn, from J. F. Schick who followed F. J. Furman as engineering manager of the project in March 1956.

81. J. H. Wellburn, 20 January 1983: conversation with C. J. Bashe.

82. J. E. Brophy, P. Fagg, F. J. Furman, E. E. Plomondon, D. N. Streeter, and J. H. Wellburn, 1 May 1957: "High Speed Printer Study."

83. Wellburn, 20 January 1983.

84. J. E. Dayger, 29 April 1969: to J. J. Troy.

85. Wellburn, 20 January 1983.

86. W. W. McDowell, 2 October 1957: "Solid State Components." IBM Corporate Policy Letter, Research and Engineering No. 2.

87. J. H. Wellburn, 21 June 1957: to R. L. Palmer, "Printer Committee's Report on Intermediate-Speed Printing." According to Wellburn's handwritten notes, this committee began its work on 5 June, and Wellburn gave R. L. Palmer the results verbally on 17 June. Other members were M. E. Baer, J. E. Dayger, F. J. Furman, and E. E. Plomondon.

88. R. E. Paris was the IBM inventor who had conceived of a bar or chain printing mechanism. J. E. Dayger, 9 July 1971: "Recollection of IBM Printing."

89. H. S. Beattie, November 1970.

90. J. E. Dayger, 11 September 1974.

91. Dayger, 11 September 1974; B. J. Greenblott, 1963: "A Development Study of the Print Mechanism on the IBM 1403 Chain Printer," *Trans. AIEE* (Part 1),pp. 500–508.

92. The two models of the Type 1443 printer differed mainly in the size of a pulley that set the speed. The bar printer used for magnetic ink printing was the Type 1445, which was furnished with a special type bar having the character styling used in encoding bank checks.

93. T. Y. Nickel and F. J. Kania, 1981: Printer Technology in IBM, *IBM Journal of Research and Development*, pp. 755–765.

94. Auerbach Corporation, 1962: "Special Report, Optical Character Recognition Devices."

95. F. J. Roehm, 30 September 1965: "History of Character Recognition—MICR and OCR."

96. Roehm, 30 September 1965. This report gives credit primarily to W. E. Mutter for the "lakes and bays" idea, but in combination with other reports it identifies G. L. Shultz, J. R. Johnson, and N. Rochester as contributing to the development of the method. Among the earliest references to character recognition work in Rochester's group are M. M. Astrahan, 17 July 1950, 22 June 1951: Character Recognition Machine Proposals.

97. E. C. Greanias, June 1968: interview by L. M. Saphire.

98. A. J. Bodine, 20 March 1958: "Character Sensing: A Brief Historical Review."

99. The group working on magnetic inks and printing was under the leadership of H. W. Nordyke.

100. Early in 1957, C. W. Allen was made manager of character-recognition development for the bank program in Poughkeepsie, and he was joined by P. Lazarus, A. J. Atrubin, P. H. Howard, and a small group of others who rapidly developed

the necessary theoretical and technological knowledge in MICR. O. Kornei and G. L. Shelton of Research provided design and evaluation of performance for the multigap head. Early contributions to an understanding of the capability of the competitive single-gap system were made by several people under R. B. Johnson in San Jose, including J. L. Masterson and W. E. Dickinson; extensive analysis of the system was done by A. Hamburgen during fall 1957. A. Hamburgen, 19 March 1984: conversation with C. J. Bashe.

101. The OCR technique referred to here was called "moving video" and was due in large part to A. Hamburgen, working with Greanias.

102. Bank Management Commission, American Bankers Association, 1959: *The Common Machine Language for Mechanized Check Handling.*

103. W. S. Rohland, 1962: "Report on Character Recognition for the 1962 R & E Conference."

104. During the development of the 1418 and 1428 optical character readers, W. S. Rohland had assumed the leading technical position in OCR product development.

105. The description of the 1282's logic as "fairly trivial" is from Rohland, 1962. He has also identified it as a simple form of "lakes and bays" logic. W. S. Rohland, 7 March 1984: conversation with C. J. Bashe. Installed and on-order figures are from Roehm, 1965.

106. Rohland, 1962.

107. No mention is made in this account of the problem of character segmentation— that is, determining where one character ends and the next begins. In many applications of character recognition, especially those involving multiple fonts, a variety of printing devices, and little control over the quality of printing, character segmentation is one of the most difficult steps in the recognition process.

108. The autocorrelation method had been investigated and, for a time, favored by L. P. Horwitz and G. L. Shelton, among others in IBM Research. Horwitz, however, pointed early to the method's sensitivity to variations in character size and shape and concluded: "It therefore appears that the mixed font and hand printing problems will require a general form of feature analysis in which local features such as lines, curves and vertices are selected in a noise and distortion insensitive way. It is to the solution of this problem, coupled with the desirability of automatic design, that much of the work in character recognition will be directed in the future." L. P. Horwitz, 26 June 1961: "Some Characteristics of Pattern Recognition Problems," IBM Research Report.

109. Hamburgen, 19 March 1984.

110. B. L. Havens, Lentz, and R. M. Walker were hired from MIT Radiation Laboratory at the same time, in 1945. J. J. Lentz, 20 November 1980: conversation with C. J. Bashe and J. H. Palmer.

111. U.S. Patent 3,517,391, filed 26 October 1953: J. J. Lentz, "Digital Computer."

112. Many of the details herein concerning the "Personal Automatic Calculator" (610) were obtained from the notebooks and recollections of J. H. Palmer.

113. J. J. Lentz, 29 December 1954: "The IBM Personal Automatic Calculator"; IBM Product Announcement, 3 September 1957: IBM 610 Auto-Point Computer, Letter 357-44; J. A. Dowd, May 1958: "The IBM Type 610 Auto-Point Computer," *Proceedings of the Symposium: Small Automatic Computers and Input-Output Equipment—A Report from the Manufacturers*, Los Angeles Chapter, ACM, pp. 77–82.

114. M. H. Weik, December 1955: *A Survey of Domestic Electronic Digital Computing Systems,* U.S. Army Ballistic Research Laboratories Report No. 971, Aberdeen Proving Ground, Maryland; M. H. Weik, 1957: *A Second Survey of Domestic Electronic Digital Computing Systems,* U.S. Army Ballistic Research Laboratories Report No. 1010, Aberdeen Proving Ground, Maryland.

115. H. T. Marcy was manager of the IBM laboratory in Poughkeepsie from July 1957 to December 1961.

116. W. D. Winger, June 1981: conversation with C. J. Bashe.

117. The CADET (announced as the IBM 1620) had very low-cost circuits, of a type called "complementary transistor resistor logic" (CTRL), in which no diodes were used. All logical operations were performed through resistors in combination with transistors. F. M. Mapes, 7 July 1961: "A History of IBM Standard Circuit Families."

118. N. Rochester, 4 November 1949: "A Computer with Memorized Skills." L. A. Wilson, who by mid-1958 had moved to San Jose to work on small machines, is credited with having treated the name of this competitor as an acronym, furnishing the explanatory words "Can't Add—Doesn't Even Try" in reference to CADET's paucity of conventional arithmetic circuitry.

119. IBM Product Announcement, 21 October 1959: IBM 1620 Data Processing System, Letter 259-63.

120. J. Honig and N. Lewis, 10 June 1959: "CADET Computer Evaluation"; M. H. Weik, March 1961: *A Third Survey of Domestic Electronic Digital Computing Systems, U.S. Army Ballistic Research Laboratories Report No. 1115, Aberdeen Proving Ground, Maryland.* This report gives the count of transistors for the 1620 system as 3188, which is less than three-fourths the count given for even the smallest 1401 system.

121. *Computers and Automation,* January 1964: "Monthly Computer Census," p. 37.

122. T. J. Harrison, 17 February 1983: conversation with C. J. Bashe.

123. G. K. Chien, 30 December 1978, 2 January 1979: conversations with C. J. Bashe. Chien was responsible for application and environmental requirements and had a representative at each of the three 1720 field-test sites.

124. T. J. Harrison, B. W. Landeck, and H. K. St. Clair, 1981: "Evolution of Small Real-Time IBM Computer Systems," *IBM Journal of Research and Development,* pp. 441–451.

125. T. J. Harrison, 17 February 1983.

126. IBM Product Announcements, 6 March, 9 August 1961: IBM 1710 Control System, Letters 261-13 and 261-57.

127. Harrison, Landeck, and St. Clair, 1981.

128. C. R. Doty, Sr., July 1964: *Data Communications,* IBM Development Laboratory, Poughkeepsie, N.Y.

129. C. R. Doty, Sr., notes copied by C. J. Bashe from an incomplete autobiographical manuscript on 23 September 1980.

130. Doty, July 1964.

131. F. N. McCabe, 30 March 1948: to G. P. Lovell.

132. W. W. McDowell, 7 July 1950: to P. A. Shackleford; 17 November 1950: to T. V. Learson; W. W. McDowell, 1 August 1952: to L. H. LaMotte and G. A. Roberts, attaching 21 July report from D. R. Piatt to McDowell and 29 July report from J. M. Coombs to R. L. Palmer; E. Bramley, 7 July 1952: "AA Push-Button System Speeds Reservations," *American Aviation,* pp. 24–25.

133. R. B. Smith was mentioned in chapter 9 with regard to the background of the SHARE organization.

134. R. B. Smith, March 1983: conversation with C. J. Bashe.

135. H. P. Luhn, 19 March 1954: to W. W. McDowell and J. W. Birkenstock; P. O. Crawford, 11 June 1954: to W. W. McDowell and J. W. Birkenstock, attaching "A Proposal for the Development of an Integrated Data System for American Airlines," 1 June 1954.

136. L. C. Wood, 29 June 1954: to G. A. Roberts, attaching report "American Airlines Meeting—June 28, 1954—2 P.M." F. J. Wesley of LaMotte's staff suggested in the meeting that a military supply problem (similar to the one that had prompted IBM's original entry into data communications) would be a more promising one in terms of ultimate payoff. Wesley, however, contributed importantly to the project and even more directly to IBM's long-term pursuit of high-capacity direct-access storage devices, by his persuasive memoranda during that same period to LaMotte and others urging support of that system component.

137. J. H. Vincent, P. O. Crawford, and H. P. Luhn, 6 July 1954: to W. W. McDowell.

138. When the SABRE project was moved to SEPD in November 1958, Deerhake remained in Research; P. A. Beeby became engineering manager of SABRE. Transferred from the SAGE program, Beeby was effective in applying SAGE experience to certain important decisions in the SABRE program—such as the decision to use two 7090s in order to provide the necessary central processing capability. R. A. Jensen, April 1968: interview by L. M. Saphire; R. L. West, May 1968: interview by L. M. Saphire. Also in November 1958, R. B. Smith joined SEPD as program manager for SABRE. He was responsible for overall coordination of the project and relations with American Airlines.

139. Many of the details of the history of SABRE, especially in the early years of the project, are from P. O. Crawford, February 1983: conversation with C. J. Bashe.

140. G. Burck and the Editors of *Fortune*, 1965: *The Computer Age* (New York: Harper and Row), pp. 31–34.

141. A description of the kinds of information American Airlines expected to obtain from SABRE is given in W. R. Plugge and M. N. Perry, 1961: "American Airlines' 'SABRE' Electronic Reservations System," *Proceedings of the Western Joint Computer Conference*, pp. 593–601. The accomplishment of these objectives was confirmed in the testimony of American Airlines Vice-President J. J. O'Neill, 1978: in U.S. v. IBM, transcript pp. 76577–76578.

142. R. W. Parker, September 1965: "The SABRE System," *Datamation*, pp. 49–52.

Chapter 13

1. J. H. Gibbon, Jr., 2 January 1947: to Thomas J. Watson; *Time*, 26 September 1949; J. H. Gibbon, Jr., 10 November 1954: to Thomas J. Watson; R. Taylor, 1957: "A Mechanical Heart-Lung Apparatus," *IBM Journal of Research and Development 1*, pp. 330–340.

2. N. W. Burlis, 11 June 1959: to Richard Taylor.

3. W. J. Eckert, August 1946: "Facilities of the Watson Scientific Computing Laboratory," *Proceedings of the Research Forum*, Endicott, New York, pp. 75–80.

4. J. F. Brennan, 1971: *The IBM Watson Laboratory at Columbia University: A History* (Armonk: IBM), pp. 11–13.

5. J. C. McPherson and W. J. Eckert, 12 November 1946: to T. J. Watson, Sr.

6. W. W. McDowell, 17 December 1948: to W. L. Lewis, "Hiring of Electronic Engineers." This memorandum reveals a plan to hire twenty-five electronics engineers during 1949.

7. W. J. Eckert, undated: "The IBM Department of Pure Science." This draft document from Eckert's files appears to have been written about 1947.

8. W. J. Eckert, August 1946: "Facilities of the Watson Scientific Computing Laboratory," *Proceedings of the Research Forum*, Endicott, New York, pp. 75–80.

9. M. C. Gutzwiller, 30 November 1983: conversation with E. W. Pugh.

10. The complete references for these illustrative publications selected from L. H. Thomas's bibliography are as follows: June 1949: "Stability of Solution of Partial Differential Equations," *Proceedings of the Symposium on Theoretical Compressible Flow*; J. Sheldon and L. H. Thomas, 1953: "Use of Large Scale Computing in Physics," *Journal of Applied Physics 24*, pp. 235–242; B. Bakamjian and L. H. Thomas, 1 December 1953: "Relativistic Particle Dynamics II," *Physics Review 92*, pp. 1300–1310.

11. Brennan, 1971: p. 15. Robert M. Walker, who collaborated with Thomas on magnetic ring storage, was also hired at this time at the suggestion of Rabi.

12. Ibid: p. 14.

13. Eckert, undated.

14. Brennan, 1971: pp. 24–25.

15. Ibid.: pp. 17–18. Eric Hankam of the Watson Laboratory staff conducted these lectures.

16. R. W. Landauer, who started his Ph.D. thesis under Brillouin at Harvard, recalls that Brillouin's wife lived in New York City and that a desire to join her was one of many considerations for Brillouin. See also Brennan, 1971: p. 32.

17. H. Fleisher, 1 November 1982: conversation with E. W. Pugh. Palmer asked Harold Fleisher, who was finishing his Ph.D. work at Case Western Reserve, to arrive at IBM before he got his degree so he could help Brillouin prepare notes for his lectures to the engineers in Poughkeepsie. Fleisher therefore joined IBM in February 1950 and completed his thesis while at IBM.

18. W. E. Mutter, 8 July 1981: conversation with C. J. Bashe.

19. T. J. Watson, Jr., 24 July 1951: to W. J. Eckert.

20. P. N. Whittaker, 30 August 1951: to W. J. Eckert, W. W. McDowell, A. R. Noll, and A. L. Samuel.

21. J. C. McPherson, 11 July 1951: "IBM Management Committees—Pure Research"; J. C. McPherson, 27 June 1951: to T. J. Watson, Jr., A. L. Williams, W. J. Eckert, W. W. McDowell, A. R. Noll, and A. L. Samuel. Brennan, 1971: pp. 59–63 lists about forty professionals and twenty technical and administrative people associated with the Watson Laboratory in 1950. About a dozen of these professionals were located at CHQ, programming the SSEC, and a few individuals were already located at the space leased for work on the NORC at 2929 Broadway, according to J. H. Palmer, 21 November 1984: conversation with E. W. Pugh.

22. A. R. Noll, head of patent operations, expressed the view that availability of facilities would determine whether a project was done in a research or an engineering

laboratory. See J. C. McPherson, 14 September 1951: "IBM Management Committees—Pure Research."

23. J. C. McPherson, 28, 29 November 1951: to T. J. Watson, Jr., "Research Program."

24. McPherson, 11 July 1951.

25. Brennan, 1971: p. 32. The building was donated to Columbia because zoning regulations prevented its use for industrial purposes, but IBM paid property taxes even though Columbia University was tax exempt. The laboratory was jointly operated by IBM and Columbia University. See S. H. Koenig, 12 November 1984: conversation with E. W. Pugh.

26. W. J. Eckert, 29 July, 1953: to T. J. Watson, Jr. The other five newly hired Ph.D. scientists mentioned by Eckert were Peter Price, Frederic Holtzberg, Sol Triebwasser, Seymour H. Koenig, and G. Robert Gunther-Mohr. Garwin followed Eckert as director of the Watson Laboratory in 1966, and Koenig served in that capacity from 1967 until the Watson Laboratory at Columbia University was closed in 1970.

27. A. G. Anderson, 2 February 1984: conversation with E. W. Pugh.

28. A. G. Anderson, J. W. Horton, and R. M. Walker, 20 November 1953: "The Spin-Echo Method of Information Storage"; A. G. Anderson, R. L. Garwin, E. L. Hahn, J. W. Horton, G. L. Tucker, and R. M. Walker, 1955: "Spin Echo Serial Storage Memory," *Journal of Applied Physics 12*, pp. 1324–1338.

29. Brennan, 1971: p. 38.

30. One of Anderson's coworkers was Robert M. Walker who had worked with L. H. Thomas on storage rings; another was Donald E. Rosenheim who later played an important role in developing large scale integration of semiconductor circuits. See R. M. Walker, D. E. Rosenheim, P. A. Lewis, and A. G. Anderson, July 1957: "An Experimental 50-Megacycle Arithmetic Unit," *IBM Journal of Research and Development*, pp. 257–278.

31. R. L. Garwin, L. M. Lederman, and M. Weinrich, February 1957: "Observations of the Failure of Conservation of Parity and Charge Conjugation in Meson Decays: the Magnetic Moment of the Free Muon," *Physical Review 105*, pp. 1415–1417.

32. *IBM Business Machines*, 25 February 1957: "Twentieth Century Pioneer."

33. C. S. Wu, E. Ambler, R. W. Hayward, D. D. Hopper, and R. P. Hudson, February 1957: "Experimental Test of Parity Conservation in Beta Decay," *Physical Review 105*, pp. 1413–1415. Excellent background information on the experiments by Wu et al.; Lederman, Garwin, and Weinrich; and a third nearly simultaneous publication by V. Telegdi is provided in *Adventures in Experimental Physics*, 1973; γ Volume, (Princeton: World Science Education), pp. 94–143.

34. G. Bland, 8 January 1981: conversation with E. W. Pugh. The maser was first described by J. P. Gordon, H. J. Zieger, and C. H. Townes, 1954: *Physical Review 95*, p. 482.

35. J. P. Cederholm, G. F. Bland, B. L. Havens, and C. H. Townes, November 1958: "New Experimental Test of Special Relativity," *Physical Review Letters 1*, p. E526; J. P. Cedarholm, 8 February 1984: conversation with E. W. Pugh.

36. N. Rochester, 5, 21 October 1983: conversations with E. W. Pugh.

37. D. R. Young, 2 November 1982, 5 October 1983: conversations with E. W. Pugh.

38. D. R. Young, April 1951: "Temporary Enhancement of Hysteresis in Barium Titanate Samples," *Journal of Applied Physics 22*, pp. 523–524.

39. D. R. Young, 19 October 1951: "Three Dimensional Storage Using Ferroelectric Condensers," IBM Report.

40. It is not clear who first suggested using ferroelectric materials in 2D or 3D storage arrays. It may have been Dudley Buck, but neither D. R. Young nor W. J. Merz, who was an early worker on $BaTiO_3$, could confirm that. See W. J. Merz, 2 November 1983: to E. W. Pugh.

41. Young, 19 October 1951.

42. Lincoln Laboratory, 1 June 1952: Quarterly Progress Report, Division 6 Digital Computer, pp. 6–100. The ferroelectric work was carried out by D. A. Buck in D. R. Brown's group.

43. D. R. Young, 27 March 1952: "Circuits Employing Ferroelectric Condensers," IBM Report. This report says the behavior of the crystals grown at the Bell Laboratories by Joseph P. Remeika was reported by J. R. Anderson at the January 1952 meeting of the American Institute of Electrical Engineers.

44. D. R. Young, 5 October 1983: conversation with E. W. Pugh.

45. R. W. Landauer, 9 October 1980: conversation with C. J. Bashe, J. H. Palmer, L. R. Johnson.

46. R. W. Landauer and J. C. Helland, 1954: "Electronic Structure of Disordered One-Dimensional Chains," *The Journal of Chemical Physics 22*, pp. 1655–1665. The mathematical method devised by Landauer was programmed by Helland. The calculation was proposed to Hunter, Samuel, and others in a memorandum dated 11 November 1952 in response to a request for problems to be run on the new computers. See R. W. Landauer, June 1983: "Personal Comments on the Stone Age of Localization."

47. R. F. Rutz, 3, 6 December 1982: conversations with E. W. Pugh.

48. R. W. Landauer, 27 January 1984: conversation with E. W. Pugh. The intellectual stimulation provided by Landauer has been described to E. W. Pugh by D. R. Young and others.

49. A phenomenological theory for the free energy of barium titanate was developed by A. F. Devonshire, *Philosophical Magazine 40* p. 1040. This theory was extended by W. J. Merz, 1953: *Physical Review 91*, p. 513. Some representative publications of the IBM group are the following: M. E. Drougard, R. W. Landauer, and D. R. Young, 1955: "Dielectric Behavior of Barium Titanate in the Paraelectric State," *Physical Review 98*, pp. 1010–1014; R. W. Landauer, D. R. Young, and M. E. Drougard, 1956: "Polarization Reversal in the Barium Titanate Hysteresis Loop," *Journal of Applied Physics 27*, pp. 752–758; R. W. Landauer, 1957: "Electrostatic Considerations in $BaTiO_3$ Domain Formation during Polarization Reversal," *Journal of Applied Physics 28*, pp. 227–234; E. J. Huibregtse and D. R. Young, 1956: "Triple Hysteresis Loops and the Free-Energy Function in the Vicinity of the 5°C Transistion in $BaTiO_3$," *Physical Review 103*, pp. 1705–1711.

50. An organization chart of the Poughkeepsie Research Center dated August 1956 shows Ralph B. DeLano in charge of Applied Ferroelectric Research and no manager yet assigned to the basic research group. Sol Triebwasser at the Watson Laboratory was studying the properties of other ferroelectric materials. See S. Triebwasser, 17 October 1983: conversation with E. W. Pugh.

51. Young, 5 October 1983.

52. S. P. Keller, 17 October 1983: conversation with E. W. Pugh; 19 July 1982: conversation with C. J. Bashe. The work on infrared stimulable phosphors was started

at Hunter's suggestion by Seymour P. Keller, who had received the Ph.D. degree in chemistry from the University of Chicago in 1951 and joined IBM in Poughkeepsie in September 1953 after taking a postdoctoral year at the University of Wisconsin and a second postdoctoral year at Columbia University. When no device applications were identified, Hunter continued to support basic studies in phosphors, using Keller increasingly as a consultant on other projects and as an interviewer of new applicants.

53. S. Triebwasser, 17 October 1983: conversation with E. W. Pugh. Triebwasser moved to Poughkeepsie from the Watson Laboratory in 1957 to take over the ferroelectric effort when D. R. Young became manager of the cryogenic project.

54. W. Buchholz, 14 January 1955: to G. M. Amdahl et al., "Engineering Meeting on Large Technical Computers at WHQ." This meeting dealt primarily with design objectives for a machine to follow the IBM 704. ERA was rumored to offer an "all-magnetic" machine. Palmer commented that the work on magnetic logic would be resumed under M. K. Haynes in Poughkeepsie.

55. P. K. Spatz, 1 May 1959: "The Stretch Development Program."

56. E. W. Pugh, 1984: *Memories That Shaped an Industry* (Cambridge: MIT Press), pp. 171–172.

57. S. S. Snyder, 1980: "Computer Advances Pioneered by Cryptologic Organizations," *Annals of the History of Computing* 2, pp. 60–70; R. B. Arndt, 3 November 1981: conversation with E. W. Pugh. Of particular interest are five special-purpose machines designed by Seymour Cray for the National Security Agency and delivered between July 1957 and December 1959. These were named Bogart computers (after J. B. Bogart, a well-known editor of the *New York Sun*) because they were intended to serve as "editors" for data streams. The magnetic cores used for logic were made of metallic strips wrapped on ceramic bobbins.

58. B. E. Phelps, 22, 23 April 1981: conversation with C. J. Bashe. Phelps was promoted to manager of component development in September 1953 according to *The IBM Record*, 22 September 1953.

59. L. P. Hunter, 17 December 1982, 5 October 1983: conversations with E. W. Pugh.

60. Estimated expenditures for 1950 of the Engineering Laboratories were to exceed $5 million according to "IBM Engineering Laboratories," an undated report from the files of W. Eckert, probably prepared in 1950. The manpower was listed as 940, of whom 619 was classified as technical. The technical manpower was listed as follows: 209 R&D and 106 production in Endicott, 146 R&D and 92 production in Poughkeepsie, 32 R&D and 21 SSEC at the Watson Laboratory, and 13 in the New York laboratory. Of all the technical personnel, 2 percent had Ph.D.s, 8 percent masters degrees, and 48 percent bachelors degrees. The rest of the manpower data are obtained from Ford, Bacon and Davis, Inc., 22 April 1954: "Report on Organization, Engineering Department, International Business Machines"; Brennan, 1971; D. W. Kean, 1977: *IBM San Jose—A Quarter Century of Innovation* (San Jose: IBM).

61. Poughkeepsie Engineering Newsletter, 28 December 1955. Only 620 persons were accommodated in these buildings in 1984 due to increased space allocated to laboratories and lecture rooms.

62. N. Rochester, 5, 21 October 1983: conversations with E. W. Pugh.

63. R. L. Palmer, 10 October 1967: interview by L. M. Saphire.

64. L. R. Bickford, 19 April 1968: interview by L. M. Saphire.

65. Ford, Bacon, and Davis, Inc., 22 April 1954.

66. *IBM Business Machines*, 1 October 1954, p. 2.

67. Ford, Bacon, and Davis, Inc., 22 April 1954.

68. Much of the background of this meeting is provided by B. O. Evans, 2 June 1983: conversation with C. J. Bashe. Names of attendees have been gleaned from a variety of sources, including G. R. Gunther-Mohr who attended the meeting from the Watson Laboratory. See G. R. Gunther-Mohr, 4 October 1983: conversation with E. W. Pugh.

69. G. L. Tucker, 31 October 1977: interview by Sahid, Dwyer, Schiller, and Bashe for the legal case, U.S. v. IBM.

70. *IBM Poughkeepsie Engineering Newsletter*, 17 January 1956.

71. Ibid., 28 December 1955.

72. R. L. Palmer, July 1967: interview by L. M. Saphire.

73. R. L. Palmer et al., 26 April 1956: tape recording of a meeting held by Palmer in Poughkeepsie with Burke, Collins, Coombs, Evans, Femmer, Fleisher, Hunter, Jewell, Norton, Phelps, Rochester, Weiss, and Woodsum (transcribed and edited by E. W. Pugh on 1 March 1984).

74. G. K. Teal and J. B. Little, 1950: "Growth of Germanium Single Crystals," *Physical Review 78*, p. 647.

75. J. B. Little, 31 July 1981: conversation with E. W. Pugh.

76. J. B. Little, 1 July 1981: conversation with C. J. Bashe and J. H. Palmer.

77. IBM Organization Chart, 9 August 1956: Poughkeepsie Research Center.

78. Others reporting directly to Hunter were B. Dunham (Information Processing Theory), S. P. Keller (Energy Storage Release Research, i.e. phosphors), F. L. Graner (Research Apparatus), W. V. Smith (Microwave Laboratory), J. I. Budnick (Cryogenic Laboratory), and H. Cole (X-ray Laboratory).

79. Two others reporting directly to Palmer were J. M. Norton, manager of exploratory machines and systems, and J. M. Coombs, manager of advanced engineering planning. Under N. Rochester, J. Craft managed the following groups: E. W. Bauer (Multipath Logic), E. Bloch (Core Logic), and O. L. MacSorley (Transistor Circuits). A second department with Rochester acting as second-level manager had M. C. Andrews (Speech Recognition), W. L. Duda (Learning Machines), R. W. Murphy (Programming Research), Rochester, acting (Engineering Psychology), J. P. Roth (Circuit Theory), and J. W. MacDonald (Information Theory). A third department, the Computing Center under W. G. Bouricius, had G. J. Lasher (Math Analysis), J. W. Young (Programming Education), and E. Goldstein (Machine Analysis).

80. Palmer et al., 26 April 1956.

81. Harlow Freitag managed the design automation group within the LSI project.

82. W. W. McDowell, 11 January 1956: to file, with copies to W. J. Eckert, L. P. Hunter, C. C. Hurd, J. C. McPherson, and A. L. Samuel, "Summary of our discussion yesterday with respect to whom we might consider as Director of Research for IBM."

83. *IBM Business Machines*, 28 December 1956: Special Issue on the Williamsburg Conference.

84. Ibid., 22 October 1956. This issue describes the background of Piore and Palmer and their new assignments.

85. T. J. Watson, 19 January 1983: conversation with C. J. Bashe.

86. McDowell, 11 January 1956.

87. IBM Organization Chart, 8 October 1956: Engineering Department.

88. M. C. Andrews, 2 February 1983: conversation with E. W. Pugh.

89. IBM document, May 1957: Committee Reports for Program Research Conference.

90. Andrews, 2 February 1983.

91. *IBM Research Magazine 18*, November–December 1981.

92. A. L. Samuel, December 1967: interview by L. M. Saphire.

93. K. E. Drangeid, 16 May 1980: conversation with E. W. Pugh. When Drangeid joined the Zurich Laboratory in April 1956, he reported to K. Kinberg. The other managers were W. E. Proebster, F. Wiedmer, and H. P. Schlaeppi.

94. A. P. Speiser, 17 February 1984: to E. W. Pugh. Zuse was a German inventor, born in Berlin in 1910, who built a computer (the Z3) for which he applied for a patent in 1941. His early understanding of computer concepts and personal contributions rank him among the pioneers in this field in spite of the fact that his contributions appear to have had very little influence on the mainstream developments. See, for example, P. E. Ceruzzi, 1981: "Early Computers of Konrad Zuse, 1935 to 1945," *Annals of the History of Computing 3*, pp. 241–262.

95. H. P. Schlaeppi, 6 December 1983: conversation with E. W. Pugh.

96. W. E. Proebster, 12 November 1980: conversation with E. W. Pugh. Proebster joined the IBM Zurich laboratory, before a building existed, in February 1956 immediately after receiving the Ph.D. from the Technical University in Munich. He and the other managers initiated projects on improved electronic circuits for computers. J. A. Haddad, one of the first visitors to the laboratory, suggested the ferroresonance project to Proebster.

97. H. P. Schlaeppi is the engineer who started the sampling oscilloscope project. See H. P. Schlaeppi, 6 December 1983: conversation with E. W. Pugh; R. Sugarman, 1957: "Sampling Oscilloscope for Statistically Varying Pulses," *Review of Scientific Instruments 28*, pp. 933–938; H. P. Schlaeppi and H. P. Louis, 1959: "Ein Sampling Oszillograph für 4×10^{-10} sec Zeilauflösung," *Helvetica Physica Acta 32*, pp. 328–331.

98. W. Dietrich and W. E. Proebster, October 1959: "Millimicrosecond Magnetization Reversal in Thin Magnetic Films," *IBM Journal of Research and Development*, pp. 375–376.

99. W. Dietrich, W. E. Proebster, and P. Wolf, April 1960: "Nanosecond Switching in Thin Magnetic Films," *IBM Journal of Research and Development*, pp. 189–196; S. Methfessel, S. Middelhoek, and H. Thomas, 1961: "Partial Rotation in Permalloy Films," *Journal of Applied Physics 32*, pp. 1959–1963.

100. *IBM Research Magazine 18*, November–December 1981.

101. Physicists who studied the properties of magnetic films in the Zurich laboratory included H. Methfessel, S. Middelhoek, C. Schuler, and H. Thomas; the engineers included W. Dietrich, H. P. Louis, H. P. Schlaeppi, and P. Wolf.

102. H. Glättli, 26 November 1956: "Hydraulic Research at Zurich," IBM Research Report; 25 October 1960: "Research on Hydraulic Logic Elements—Slide-Tape Lecture," IBM Research Report.

103. H. H. Gläettli, 1962: "Hydraulic and Pneumatic Switching Elements," International Federation of Information Processing Conference, pp. 632–635.

104. A. G. Anderson, 2 February 1984: conversation with E. W. Pugh.

105. IBM Flash Edition, Field HQ News, 25 March 1959; *IBM Business Machines*, June 1959: pp. 10–11.

106. E. R. Piore, 27 May 1959: to J. J. Bricker.

107. Data on Research manpower in 1959 and projected to 1960 are from L. A. Cookman's files of the 1959 Research Planning Conference.

108. Anderson, 2 February 1984.

109. D. W. Kean, 1977: *IBM San Jose—A Quarter Century of Innovation* (San Jose: IBM), p. 75.

110. Anderson, 2 February 1984.

111. *IBM Research Magazine 18*, November–December 1981.

112. J. P. Roth, 2 November 1983: conversation with E. W. Pugh.

113. *IBM Research Magazine 18*, November–December 1981. The first section of the Mohansic laboratory was ready for occupancy in April 1958 and the second part that August, according to R. J. Elderkin's records, as reviewed by him in 1984.

114. The term "computer science" may have been introduced by Newell, Perlis, and Simon in a letter to *Science* in July 1967. See G. Bell, 1984: *Annals of the History of Computing 6*, pp. 410–413.

115. IBM Research Organization Chart, January 1958.

116. Patents of Hans P. Luhn, undated: a complete list with dates of filing and issuing, prepared by an unknown person.

117. *H. P. Luhn: Pioneer of Information Science—Selected Works*, 1968: ed. Claire K. Schultz (New York: Spartan Books). This book contains discussions by associates of Luhn, reprints of some of his publications, and a listing of patents and publications. Filing dates are not provided. The first chapter, by Claire K. Schultz, provides an excellent overview of Luhn's private and professional life.

118. H. P. Luhn, 1958: "The Automatic Creation of Literature Abstracts," *Journal of Research and Development 2*, pp. 159–165.

119. *Luhn: Pioneer*, p. 8.

120. Ibid., pp. 10–12.

121. IBM Research Order 479-4505, 31 December 1957.

122. The IBM Research Organization Chart of 1 January, 1958 shows the following groups reporting to Rochester: G. L. Shultz, speech recognition; E. T. Klemmer, engineering phychology; J. P. Roth, switching research and mathematics; M. S. Watanabe, information theory; H. B. DeMuth, character recognition; and Rochester (acting), theory of automata. William J. Lawless managed the Machine Organization Department in which James H. Pomerene and others worked on Harvest; and John M. Coombs, the first manager of Project High, headed the Systems Research Department.

123. F. J. Roehm, 30 September 1965: "History of Character Recognition Program MICR and OCR," pp. 18–25.

124. J. P. Roth, 2 November 1983: conversation with E. W. Pugh. The extraction algorithm was first presented by Paul Roth in April 1957 and published in the *Proceedings of an International Symposium on the Theory of Switching*, 1959 (Cambridge: Harvard University Press), pp. 57–73.

125. N. Rochester, 21 October 1983: conversation with E. W. Pugh.

126. H. L. Gelernter, J. R. Hansen, and C. L. Gerberich, about 1960: "A Fortran-Compiled List-Processing Language."

127. H. L. Gelernter and N. Rochester, October 1958: "Intelligent Behavior in Problem-Solving Machines," *IBM Journal of Research and Development*, pp. 336–345; P. C. Gilmore, 19 April 1962: "An Examination of the Geometry Theorem Machine," IBM Research Paper.

128. A. L. Samuel, 1956: "Making a Computer Play Draughts," *Proceedings of the Institute of Electrical and Electronics Engineers 103*, supplement 2, pp. 452–453.

129. *IBM Research News*, 28 August 1959: "A. L. Samuel's Work With Checkers and 704 Featured in Daily Press"; A. L. Samuel, July 1959: "Some Studies in Machine Learning Using the Game of Checkers," *IBM Journal of Research and Development*, pp. 211–229.

130. J. C. Suits, 15 May 1967: to E. W. Pugh, "Research on Research Management." Table 3 in this memorandum lists Research manpower by year end and the number of persons transferred in or out and separated from 1956 to 1966.

131. Data on educational level of Research employees from 1956 to 1962 were obtained from Steve Lonce, of Research Administration, on 1 March 1984.

132. *IBM Research News*, January 1961.

133. H. H. Goldstine, 6 February 1984: conversation with E. W. Pugh. H. H. Goldstine was manager of the Mathematics Department with Math Theory (Goldstine, acting), Experimental Systems Laboratory (H. L. Kurkjian), and Computing Department (E. Goldstein). The four managers in the Math Theory Department were L. P. Horwitz, R. Willoughby, B. Tuckerman, and M. A. Hyman. See IBM Research Organization Charts, 1 July 1958.

134. *IBM Research News*, 28 August 1959.

135. R. E. Gomory, 1958: "Outline of an Algorithm for Integer Solutions to Linear Programs," *Bulletin of the American Mathematical Society 64*, pp. 275–278; A. J. Hoffman, 27 December 1983: conversation with E. W. Pugh.

136. P. C. Gilmore and R. E. Gomory, 1961: "A Linear Programming Approach to the Cutting-Stock Problem," *Operations Research 9*, pp. 849–859; R. E. Gomory and T. C. Hu, 1961: "Multi-Terminal Network Flows," *Journal of the Society for Industrial and Applied Mathematics 9*, pp. 551–570.

137. *IBM Research News*, February 1960.

138. L. Esaki, March 1974: "Long Journey into Tunneling," *Science 183*, pp. 1149–1155.

139. L. L. Chang, 26 March 1984: to E. W. Pugh.

140. P. W. Henderson, August 1984: conversation with E. W. Pugh. Henderson provided a diagram of the building showing the exact sizes of the additions. See also General Building Design Information, 1960: a forty-page document on the T. J. Watson Research Center.

141. IBM document, undated: Facts about the New Research Center, issued about 1960. The actual use of space was such that the building never housed more than 1400 persons.

142. *IBM Research Magazine 18*, November–December 1981: p. 21.

143. P. P. Sorokin, 20 October 1983: conversation with E. W. Pugh.

144. R. W. Landauer, 6 May 1958: "Review of some current expectations concerning the dielectric behavior of ferroelectrics above the Curie Point." This memorandum

was mailed to numerous colleagues. The following year—apparently completely independent of the work at IBM—W. Cochran of Cambridge University developed these ideas more fully in what became known as the "soft mode" theory of ferroelectricity. See W. Cochran, 1959: "Crystal Stability and the Theory of Ferroelectricity," *Physical Review Letters 3*, p. 412; 1960: *Advances in Physics 9*, p. 387. A brief history of the development of the soft mode theory is provided by W. Cochran, 1981: "Soft Modes, a Personal Perspective," in *Ferroelectrics*, (London; New York: Gordon and Breach), pp. 3–8. A briefer unpublished history is provided by R. W. Landauer, 12 January 1976: "Comments on the History of the Soft Mode Concept."

145. R. W. Landauer and L. H. Thomas, 1959: "Width of Electromagnetic Shock Waves in a Nonlinear Dielectric," *Bulletin of the American Physical Society 4*, p. 424.

146. A. L. Schawlow and C. H. Townes, 1958: "Infrared and Optical Masers," *Physical Review 112*, pp. 1940–1949

147. P. P. Sorokin, 1979: "Contributions of IBM to Laser Science—1960 to the Present," *IBM Journal of Research and Development 23*, pp. 476–489. This article is a good survey of technical developments in lasers and provides some historical perspective. The word "laser" was coined by G. Gould in the early 1960s, replacing the older term, "optical maser." Gould also was granted several patent claims for the invention of the laser, but his unpublished work was not available to the scientific community.

148. William V. Smith, who hired Sorokin and Stevenson, is credited by Sorokin and others with initiating the IBM effort to develop the first laser. See P. P. Sorokin, 20 October 1983: conversation with E. W. Pugh.

149. T. H. Maiman, 1960: *Nature 187*, p. 493; 1960: *British Communications in Electronics 7*, p. 674.

150. P. P. Sorokin and M. J. Stevenson, 1960: "Stimulated Infrared Emission from Trivalent Uranium," *Physical Review Letters 5*, p. 557; 1961: "Solid-State Optical Maser Using Divalent Samarium in Calcium Fluoride," *IBM Journal of Research and Development 5*, p. 56. Stevenson left IBM shortly after this work in order to spend full time managing a mutual fund that he had started as a graduate student. Stevenson is now president and chairman of the board of the successor company, Quantum Science Corporation, in New York City.

151. L. F. Johnson and K. Nassau, 1961: *Proceedings of the Institute of Radio Engineers 49*, p. 1704; E. Snitzer, 1961: *Physical Review Letters 7*, p. 510.

152. *IBM Research News*, May 1960: "Machine Translation of a Russian Newspaper."

153. A. D. Booth, June 1957: "Machine Translation of Languages," *Proceedings of the Data Processing and Automatic Computing Machines Conference*. Booth credits himself and Warren Weaver of the Rockefeller Foundation with making this suggestion in 1947. This claim is reasonably supported by subsequent history.

154. A. C. Reynolds 8 December 1952: to H. A. Jurgens, "Mechanical Translation." Reynolds, of the Endicott laboratory, represented IBM at the MIT conference and later participated in discussions of the subject with other IBM people such as W. W. McDowell, C. Hurd, J. W. Sheldon, E. F. Codd, R. J. Nelson, G. W. Petrie, and L. H. Thomas. Yehoshua Bar-Hillel and J. B. Wiesner of MIT were key promoters of the project. See also A. C. Reynolds, 29 December 1952: to E. J. Garvey, "Mechanical Translation Conference at Washington, D.C., December 11, 1952."

155. *IBM Press Release*, 8 January 1954; L. E. Dostert, 14 April 1953: "Proposal for Research and Development in the Field of Mechanical Translation," Georgetown

University, Washington, D.C.; P. Sheridan, January 1955: "Research in Language Translation on the IBM Type 701," Applied Science Division Technical Newsletter.

156. G. W. King joined IBM Research in January 1958 as a consultant to the director of research. He later headed the Experimental Systems Department, which developed the Mark I language translator for the U.S. Air Force. He was associate IBM director for systems and engineering with responsibility for research programs in experimental machines and systems in addition to programs in the engineering sciences prior to his appointment as director of research. King received his Ph.D. in chemistry from MIT in 1935. During the war he served as operations analyst with the Office of Scientific Research and Development and received the Army-Navy Certificate of Appreciation.

157. An article on E. R. Piore's election to vice-president for research and engineering and a discussion of the Mark II Translator appeared in *IBM Business Machines*, July 1960. G. W. King's promotion was carried in the *IBM Research News*, January 1961.

158. E. R. Piore, 28 May 1959: to J. J. Bricker, with enclosure, "Outline of Research Mission."

159. *IBM Business Machines*, July 1960.

160. Allen B. Tucker, Jr., 1984: "A Perspective on Machine Translation: Theory and Practice," *Communications of the ACM 27*, pp. 322–329.

161. E. W. Pugh, 29 October, 4 November 1959: Reports of the first and second meetings held by E. R. Piore to discuss a possible components division.

162. *IBM Business Machines*, August 1961.

163. W. J. Turner, 2 March 1984: conversation with E. W. Pugh.

164. Piore, 28 May 1959.

165. U.S. Patent 2,815,488, filed 28 April 1954: John von Neumann, "Non-linear Capacitance or Inductance Switching, Amplifying, and Memory Organs."

166. E. Goto, 1955: "On the Application of Parametrically Excited Nonlinear Resonators," *The Journal of Electrical Communication Engineers of Japan 38*, pp. 770–775. A brief overview of work on degenerate parametric oscillators for digital circuits is provided in the introduction of a paper by J. W. F. Woo and R. W. Landauer, 1971: "Fluctuations in a Parametrically Excited Subharmonic Oscillator," *IEEE Journal of Quantum Electronics 7*, pp. 435–440.

167. D. A. Buck, April 1956: "The Cryotron—A Superconductive Computer Component," *Proceedings of the Institute of Radio Engineers*, pp. 482–493.

168. C. R. Borders, 7 July 1955: "Report on the Paper Presented by D. A. Buck," Watson Laboratory staff meeting.

169. D. R. Young, 2 November 1982, 5 October 1983: conversations with E. W. Pugh.

170. R. L. Garwin, 31 October 1956: to thirty-three people, "IBM Superconducting Computer Program."

171. J. W. Crowe, October 1957: "Trapped-Flux Superconducting Memory," *IBM Journal of Research and Development*, pp. 295–303; R. L. Garwin, October 1957: "An Analysis of the Operation of a Persistent-Supercurrent Memory Cell," *IBM Journal of Research and Development*, pp. 304–308.

172. D. R. Young, 2 November 1982: conversation with E. W. Pugh.

173. Project Lightning, May 1961: Tenth Quarterly Progress Report and Final Summary.

174. E. W. Pugh, 1981: "The IBM Magnetic Film Memory Development Effort," pp. 153–157.

175. Research was given the status of an IBM division in November 1963.

Chapter 14

1. Final Judgment, 25 January 1956: U.S. v. IBM, U.S. District Court, Southern District of New York.

2. Sperry Univac's Commemorative Program for the National Computer Conference 1981 Pioneer Day Banquet, 6 May 1981. Also see H. Lukoff, 1979: *From Dits to Bits: A Personal History of the Electronic Computer*, (Portland: Robotics Press), pp. 158–162.

3. *IBM Business Machines*, 5 April 1955: "They Are Paid by the 702." *IBM Business Machines*, 1 June 1956: "T. J. Watson, Jr., Named IBM Chief Executive."

4. *IBM Business Machines*, June 1959: "A Letter from the President on Changes."

5. D. T. Spaulding, 25 October 1983: conversation with C. J. Bashe.

6. B. O. Evans, 2 June 1983: conversation with C. J. Bashe.

7. *IBM Business Machines*, June 1959: "Organization Changes . . . What They Mean."

8. B. O. Evans, 1968: interview by L. M. Saphire.

9. The "integrated circuits" referred to were hybrids in which the silicon chip contained a transistor or pair of diodes mounted, along with screened-on conductors and resistors, on a ceramic substrate. Designed in an effort known as Compact, these hybrids were introduced later as Solid Logic Technology (SLT) circuits in System/360.

10. Evans, 1968.

11. J. W. Fairclough, 1983: "Discussion of the SPREAD Report," *Annals of the History of Computing* 5, pp. 27–44.

12. J. C. McPherson, 17 February 1960: to C. R. DeCarlo. See also J. C. McPherson, 30 March 1959: to W. W. McDowell.

13. D. T. Spaulding, September 1968: interview by L. M. Saphire.

14. Evans, 1968.

15. B. O. Evans, 23 March 1961: to W. B. McWhirter.

16. F. P. Brooks, Jr., 1983: "Discussion of the SPREAD Report," *Annals of the History of Computing* 5, pp. 27–44.

17. Evans, 1968.

18. B. O. Evans, 1983: "Introduction to SPREAD Report," *Annals of the History of Computing* 5, pp. 4–5. The SPREAD report is reprinted on pp. 6–26 of the same issue.

19. G. A. Blaauw and F. P. Brooks, Jr., 1964: "Outline of the Logical Structure of System/360," *IBM Systems Journal 3*, pp. 119–135. System/360 was announced with six models, a number soon after reduced to five. Blaauw and Brooks estimated the performance ranges of the six models to be fifty-fold for scientific computation and fifteen-fold for commercial data processing. Subsequent developments broadened these ranges by extending the family to include models above and below the initial set.

20. C. A. Northrop, October 1978: testimony in U.S. v. IBM, U.S. District Court, Southern District of New York.

21. T. J. Watson, Jr., 1963: *A Business and Its Beliefs* (New York: McGraw-Hill), pp. 63–64.

Appendix A

1. A. K. Bhattacharya, 22 January 1982: "The IBM Selective Sequence Electronic Calculator," IBM Research Report; H. K. Clark, 22 November 1948: to J. J. Robbins, "Possible Sequence Modifications on SSEC."

2. E. S. Hughes, Jr., 2 June 1982: responding to C. J. Bashe of 19 May 1982; A. W. Brooke, December 1980: conversation with C. J. Bashe; E. F. Codd, E. S. Lowry, E. S. McDonough, and C. A. Scalzi, 1959: "Multiprogramming Stretch: Feasibility Considerations," *Communication of the Association for Computing Machinery*, Vol. 2, No. 11, pp. 13–17. This paper states, "Local parallelism . . . was present in a very early machine, the IBM Selective Sequence Electronic Calculator, which was capable of working on three neighboring instructions simultaneously."

Appendix B

1. N. Rochester and W. Buchholz, 24 March 1950: "Preliminary Outline of Tape Processing Machine"; "Tape Processing Machine, Engineering Model Manual of Operation," revised September 1952; U.S. Patent 2,245,039, filed 22 March, 1954: N. Rochester, et al., "Electronic Data Processing Machine."

2. G. R. Stibitz, 1980: "Early Computers," in *A History of Computing in the Twentieth Century*, eds. N. Metropolis, J. Howlett, and G.-C. Rota (New York: Academic Press).

Index

Bloch, Richard M., 195
BMEWS (Ballistic Missile Early
  Warning System), 260, 447
Boehm, Elaine M., 649n61, 671n65
Bombing and navigation systems, 130,
  625n1
Boolean algebra, 41, 433
Booth, A. D., 690n153
Bouricius, Willard G., 336, 347–348,
  657n91, 686n79
Branch instruction, 77, 139, 316–317,
  362–363, 451, 627n27
Branscomb, Charles E., 469, 472–473
Brattain, Walter H., 372–373
Brillouin, Leon, 531
Bristol University, 539
Brookhaven National Laboratory, 551
Brooks, Frederick P., Jr., 433, 443, 449,
  578, 580, 582, 671n63
Brown, E. A., 670n36
Brown, Theodore H., 25
Brownlow, James M., 262–264
Bruce, George D., 663n36
Brunschweiger, A., 637n78
Brush Development Company, 76
Bryant Computer Products, 308,
  650n91
Bryce, James Wares
 Aiken contact, 25–26
 chief engineer, 10, 35–36
 invention record, 35–36, 610n3
 joins CTR, 8
 magnetic recording investigations, 189
 Patent Development department, 35,
  373, 377–378
 product contributions, 11, 13, 14, 23,
  27, 30, 31
 relations with laboratory, 35–36,
  610n3
Buchholz, Werner
 Datatron studies, 420, 423–424, 426
 Defense Calculator planning, 142, 158
 joins IBM, 109
 Stretch project, 434, 440, 443, 449,
  456, 457
 Test Assembly planning, 112
 TPM planning, 117, 132
 TPM program, 328
 TPMII (IBM 702) planning, 127–128,
  173, 174–175, 184
Buck, Dudley A., 538, 568
Buffer storage, 90, 175, 177–178, 181,
  185, 236–239, 248–250, 296
Bull Gamma 3 computer, 461, 465

Burks, Arthur W., 319, 627n26
Burroughs Corporation, 475, 483, 490,
  497, 499, 583, 651n103
Bury, Roger M., 626n6
Buslik, Walter S., 203–204, 207
Byte, 435

CADET computer. *See* IBM 1620
  computer
Calculation control switch, 23–24
Calculator vs. computer, 52, 611n11,
  613n40
Calling sequence, 321–322, 323, 324,
  652n17
Cambridge University, 59, 321, 338
Capacitor storage, 167–168
Cape Cod System, 246
Carlson, Bengt G., 446, 454
Carroll, Fred M., 8, 10, 16
Carrying in arithmetic operations,
  37–41, 42, 43, 154
Cathode-ray-tube memories. *See* CRT
  memories
Census Bureau, 5, 174, 574–575,
  615n61, 627n27
CERN (European Organization for
  Nuclear Research), 535
Chaining method of search, 298. *See
  also* Record addressing
Channel. *See* Input-output channel
Character recognition, 495–505, 558
Checking. *See* Error detection and
  correction
Chien, G. K., 680n123
Christiansen, Carl L., 225, 637n75
Chu, Chuan, 271–272
CIA (Central Intelligence Agency), 310
Circuit packaging. *See* SMS; Vacuum
  tube circuits
Clark, H. Kenneth, 614n50
Class selection, 13
Cline, Richard L., 363
COBOL language, 364–365. *See also*
  Compilers, for COBOL
Cocke, John, 433, 442–443, 445, 449,
  581
Codd, Edgar F., 335, 370–371, 614n54,
  671n63
Codes, 76, 82, 86, 95–96, 112, 114,
  170, 173, 593, 620n64
Coincident-current selection, 234–235,
  248–249. *See also* Ferrite-core
  memories; Magnetic-core memories
Collator, 20, 174, 632n119

vice-president for research and
engineering, 422, 543
on WWAM program, 468
Zürich laboratory, 550–552
Machine organization
binary vs. decimal, 136–138, 439–440,
626n20
serial vs. parallel, 59, 132, 136,
435–436
McPherson, John C.
business programming language,
363–364
on computer compatibility, 579
director of engineering, 33
EDPM planning, 423, 424, 435
engineering expansion, 273–274
Future Demands department, 17
on government support in electronics,
525–526
joins IBM, 17
on long-range research, 377
Magnetic Drum Calculator, 73–74,
79–80, 81–82, 86, 88, 89, 99
magnetic-tape project, 102
magnetic-tape studies, 190–194
memory requirements, 231
NORC contract, 133
programming research, 355, 357
pure research management
committee, 531–533
relay calculator and electronic
multiplier, 46
SSEC planning, 47–50
on transistor use, 380–381
Macro instruction, 355, 362, 363, 366
Magnetic-core memories. *See also*
Ferrite-core memories
early metallic cores, 242
first work at IBM, 232
patents on, 267–270
proposal of Eckert and Chu, 271–272
proposal of Forrester, 241–242, 249
proposal of Haynes, 233–234
proposal of Thomas, 232
proposal of Viehe, 267, 269, 271
proposal of Wang, 232–233, 267, 269,
271
Magnetic-disk storage, 280–314. *See
also* IBM auxiliary and file storage
products
access mechanism and actuator, 286,
301, 304, 307. 308, 648n55

advanced disk file, 304–309, 474–477
air-bearing technology, 282–283,
300–303, 307–308, 312
on RAMAC, 287–288, 297, 299
disk sector addressing (*see* Record
addressing)
first described and produced,
287–288
low-cost disk file, 305, 312–313
recording method, 287
removable disk pack, 312–314
on Stretch, 301, 306–307, 650n90
Magnetic-drum auxiliary storage, 125,
134, 141, 157, 281, 288, 297, 310
Magnetic Drum Calculator (MDC),
86–101, 137. *See also* Magnetic
Storage Calculator; IBM 650
computer
Magnetic-drum memories
in 610 Auto-Point computer, 506
in 650 computer, 75–101 passim,
165–167, 169–170, 186
access time, 76, 90–91, 169–170, 172
drum surface treatments, 77, 80, 87
in Test Assembly, 112, 622n28
Magnetic films, 551–552
Magnetic logic, 234, 272, 444, 540–541
Magnetic Storage Calculator, 73–79.
See also Magnetic Drum Calculator;
IBM 650 computer
Magnetic-tape storage, 187–230
on Defense Calculator, 134, 141
in EDVAC plans, 189–190
in Endicott IBM laboratory, 102,
191–194
label records, 362, 363
on NORC, 182, 212
NRZI (non-return-to-zero-IBM)
recording, 200–202
phase encoding, 228
plastic vs. metal, 188, 195–196
in Poughkeepsie IBM laboratory, 109,
194, 195–230
vs. punched cards, 80, 109–110,
190–194
recording methods, 121, 196–202,
228
skew effects, 121–122, 212, 227
Society of Actuaries study, 176–177,
632n123
starting and stopping, 202–210
on Test Assembly and TPM, 111,
113–114, 121–122, 124

About the Authors

Charles J. Bashe joined IBM in 1949, soon after receiving the M.S.E.E. degree from Purdue University. After working on the experimental Tape Processing Machine, he became engineering manager of the Type 702 data processing machine and other development projects in the IBM laboratory at Poughkeepsie, New York. He was subsequently a divisional manager of technical development and a divisional director of input-output device development. In 1980 he was asked to establish IBM's corporate technical history project.

Lyle R. Johnson holds a B.S. and an M.B.A. from the University of Chicago. He served as a radar meteorologist in World War II and was air force project officer for the Remington Rand UNIVAC installed in the Pentagon in 1952. Later, at the Ford Motor Company, he guided preparations for an IBM 702 computer system. At IBM since 1958, his corporate staff positions have included editorship of the *IBM Systems Journal*. He is author of *System Structure in Data, Programs, and Computers* (1970).

John H. Palmer received the A.B. and M.S. degrees at Harvard University, where he did graduate work in Howard Aiken's pioneering computer science curriculum, including programming the Mark I/ASCC. Joining IBM in 1950, he worked on the logical and engineering design of the Type 610 "personal" computer introduced in 1957. Subsequently and throughout the 1960s, he held management positions in IBM groups developing general purpose programs.

Emerson W. Pugh holds the B.S. and Ph.D. degrees from Carnegie-Mellon University, where he was an assistant professor before joining IBM in 1957. He managed the development of the high-performance magnetic-film memory array used in the System/360, Model 95 computer and has held a variety of corporate staff and research management positions, including group director of operational memory and director of Research technical planning. He has served as president of the IEEE Magnetics Society and as editor of the *IEEE Transactions on Magnetics*. Coauthor of *Principles of Electricity and Magnetism* (1960), he is author of the first book in the MIT Press Series in the History of Computing, *Memories That Shaped an Industry* (1984).